ANCIENT PROPHETS AND MODERN PROBLEMS

Bob Hostetler, General Editor

wesleyan
PUBLISHING HOUSE
wphstore.com

CREST BOOKS

Copyright © 2016 by The Salvation Army
Published by Wesleyan Publishing House
Indianapolis, Indiana 46250
Printed in the United States of America
ISBN: 978-1-63257-070-3
ISBN (e-book): 978-1-63257-071-0

Library of Congress Cataloging-in-Publication Data

Brengle, Samuel Logan, 1860-1936.
Ancient prophets and modern problems / Samuel L. Brengle ; Bob Hostetler, general editor.
    pages cm. -- (Samuel L. Brengle's holy life series)
ISBN 978-1-63257-070-3 (pbk.)
1. Christian life. I. Hostetler, Bob, 1958- editor. II. Title.
BV4501.3.B7473 2016
248.4--dc23

                              2015029147

Contents

Preface

Samuel Logan Brengle was an influential author, teacher, and preacher on the doctrine of holiness in the late nineteenth to early twentieth century, serving from 1887–1931 as an active officer (minister) in The Salvation Army. In 1889 while he and his wife, Elizabeth Swift Brengle, were serving as corps officers (pastors) in Boston, Massachusetts, a brick thrown by a street "tough" smashed Brengle's head against a door frame and caused an injury severe enough to require more than nineteen months of convalescence. During that treatment and recuperation period, he began writing articles on holiness for The Salvation Army's publication, *The War Cry*, which were later collected and published as a "little red book" under the title *Helps to Holiness*. That book's success led to eight others over the next forty-five years: *Heart Talks on Holiness, The Way of Holiness, The Soul-Winner's Secret, When the Holy Ghost Is Come, Love-Slaves, Resurrection Life and Power,*

Ancient Prophets and Modern Problems, and *The Guest of the Soul* (published in his retirement in 1934).

By the time of his death in 1936, Commissioner Brengle was an internationally renowned preacher and worldwide ambassador of holiness. His influence continues today, perhaps more than any Salvationist in history besides the founders, William and Catherine Booth.

I hope that the revised and updated editions of his books that comprise the Samuel L. Brengle's Holy Life Series will enhance and enlarge that influence, introduce these writings to new readers, and create fresh interest in those who already know the godly wisdom and life-changing power of these volumes.

While I have taken care to preserve the integrity, impact, and voice of the original writing, I have carefully and prayerfully made changes that I hope will facilitate greater understanding and appreciation of Brengle's words for modern readers. These changes include:

- Revising archaic terms (such as the use of King James English) and updating the language to reflect more contemporary usage (such as occasionally employing more inclusive gender references);
- Shortening and simplifying sentence structure and revising punctuation to conform more closely to contemporary practice;
- Explaining specific references of The Salvation Army that will not be familiar to the general population;
- Updating Scripture references (when possible retaining the King James Version—used exclusively in Brengle's writings—but frequently incorporating modern versions, especially when doing so will aid the reader's comprehension and enjoyment);

- Replacing Roman numerals with Arabic numerals and spelled out Scripture references for the sake of those who are less familiar with the Bible;
- Citing Scripture quotes not referenced in the original and noting the sources for quotes, lines from hymns, etc.;
- Aligning all quoted material to the source (Brengle, who often quoted not only Scripture, but also poetry from memory, often quoted loosely in speaking and writing);
- Adding occasional explanatory phrases or endnotes to identify people or events that might not be familiar to modern readers;
- Revising or replacing some chapter titles, and (in *Ancient Prophets and Modern Problems*) moving one chapter to later in the book; and
- Deleting the prefaces that introduced each book and epigraphs that preceded some chapters.

In the preface to Brengle's first book, Commissioner (later General) Bramwell Booth wrote, "This book is intended to help every reader of its pages into the immediate enjoyment of Bible holiness. Its writer is an officer of The Salvation Army who, having a gracious experience of the things whereof he writes, has been signally used of God, both in life and testimony, to the sanctifying of the Lord's people, as well as in the salvation of sinners. I commend him and what he has here written down to every lover of God and His kingdom here on earth."

In the preface to Brengle's last book, *The Guest of the Soul*, The Salvation Army's third general (and successor to Bramwell Booth) wrote: "These choice contributions . . . will, I am sure, serve to

strengthen the faith of the readers of this book and impress upon them the joyousness of life when the heart has been opened to the Holy Guest of the Soul."

I hope and pray that this updated version of Brengle's writings will further those aims.

—Bob Hostetler

general editor

The Ancient Prophets 1

For about sixty years I have been reading the Bible, and for nearly fifty I have been reading it through regularly, steadily, and consecutively, year after year. When I have finished Revelation, I turn back to Genesis and begin again. Day by day, I read my chapter or chapters with close and prayerful attention and never without blessing. In this way the Book has become very familiar, but not stale. It is always new, fresh, and illuminating, just as bread and water and sunshine and flowers and birds and mountains and seas and starry heavens are always new and fresh and inspiring.

The sweet stories (and there are no stories so sweet as Bible stories), the sordid stories (and there are none more sordid), the nobilities and brutalities, the saintliness and the sin. The chastity of Joseph (see Gen. 39:6–23), and the shameful, cruel rape by Amnon (see 2 Sam. 13); the drunkenness of Noah (see Gen. 9:21–27), and the sobriety of the

Rechabites (see Jer. 35:2–11); the slaughter of innocent birds and beasts for the sins of men and women, and the slaughter of Canaanites for their own sins (see Deut. 20:16–17). The drunkenness and incest of Lot (see Gen. 19:30–38), and the chaste restraint of Boaz (see Ruth 3); the overthrow of Sodom and Gomorrah (see Gen. 19), and the deliverance of Samaria; the cleansing of Naaman's leprosy, and the smiting of Gehazi with the dreaded disease (see 2 Kings 5); the dastardly wickedness of David followed by his deep penitence as expressed in Psalm 51, and the dog-like fidelity and devotion of Uriah rewarded only by the seduction of his wife and his pitiful murder (see 2 Sam. 11). The duplicity and treachery of Absalom (see 2 Sam. 15), and the devoted love of Jonathan (see 1 Sam. 18, 20); the flaming zeal and despondency and trembling and triumphant finish of Elijah (see 1 Kings 17—2 Kings 2), and the horrid doom and death of Ahab (see 1 Kings 22) and painted, powdered Jezebel (see 2 Kings 9:30–37); the afflictions and dialogues of Job, and his deliverance (see the book of Job); the fall of plotting, rapacious Haman, and the exaltation of Mordecai (see Est. 2–7). The single-eyed devotion of Nehemiah outwitting the wiles of relentless foes, and the treacherous brethren; the swift, sure blow that humbled proud, despotic Nebuchadnezzar (see Dan. 4), and the overthrow and death of drunken Belshazzar (see Dan. 5); the storm, fish, gourd, worm, and blistering sun and hot wind with which God gave kindergarten lessons to bigoted, angry Jonah, and His tender mercy to the little children and cattle of Nineveh (see Jon. 4). The jealousies and envies and contentions of the disciples who each desired to be greatest in the kingdom of Jesus as they, in their carnal childishness, pictured what that kingdom would be (see Luke 22:24–30); the love of Thomas who proposed to go to

Jerusalem and die with Jesus, his stubborn refusal to believe in the resurrection of Jesus unless he could put his fingers into the print of the nails and thrust his hand into Jesus' riven side; the kindly, sure way in which Jesus met the distracted, honest, loving doubter (see John 11:16; 20:24–29); the swearing and lying of Peter and his bitter tears of sorrow (see Luke 22:54–62); the penitent plea of the dying thief on the cross (see Luke 23:32–43); the awful fate of false Ananias and Sapphira (see Acts 5:1–11); the stoning of Stephen (see Acts 7); the conversion of Paul (see Acts 9:1–9); the strange apocalyptic mysteries and imageries of Revelation. All these speak to me in a divine voice with comfort, reproof, correction, admonition, and instruction.

Line upon line, precept upon precept—in picture, parable, story, history, biography, drama, tragedy, poetry, song, and prophecy—I hear God in tender entreaty; in patient instruction; in wise rebuke; in faithful warning; in sweetest promise; in sharp, insistent command; in stern judgment and final sentence, making known to us His mind, His heart, His holiness, His wisdom, His love, and His grace. I see God uplifting the oppressed, the fallen, the lowly, and the penitent and setting them on high and casting down from their thrones and seats of pomp and power the proud, the rich, the arrogant, and the mighty.

My daily reading has again brought me into company with the great prophets—Isaiah, Jeremiah, Ezekiel, Hosea, Micah, Malachi, and others. I live again with them in the midst of the throbbing, tumultuous, teeming life of old Jerusalem, Samaria, Egypt, and Babylon. These prophets are old friends of mine. I have lived with them before, and they have blessed me a thousand times. They have kindled in me some of their flaming zeal for righteousness; their scorn of meanness, duplicity, pride, and worldliness; their jealousy for the living God; their fear for those who forget God and live as though He did not exist; their pity for the ignorant, the erring, the penitent; their anxiety for the future of their people; and their courage in denouncing sin and calling men and women back to the old paths of righteousness.

I stand in awe as I note their intrepidity, their forgetfulness of self in denouncing sin and facing the contempt, the scorn, and then the wrath of princes, priests, and kings. Tradition tells us Isaiah was finally thrust into a hollow log and "sawed in half" (Heb. 11:37 NLT). They counted not their lives dear unto themselves. They were "moved by the Holy Spirit" (2 Pet. 1:21 NLT). They yielded themselves up for service, suffering, or sacrifice as His instruments. They were surrendered and selfless, devoted as soldiers unto death, if necessary, that they might save the nation—and if not the nation, then a remnant who clung to the old paths, who would not bow the knee to Baal, who would not yield to the seductions of fashion and the spirit of the times. They were men and women of the age, but they lived and worked mightily for the ages. They were people of the times, and their message was meant for their times, but it had timeless value because they lived in God and worked for God and spoke only as they were "moved by the Holy Spirit." They were not conformers. They could not be used by ambitious or designing people for partisan purposes.

They were diffident by nature. They shrank from the prophetic office. They did not seek it. It was thrust upon them. God called them, and they went forward under divine constraint.

Listen to Jeremiah's story of his call: "The Lord gave me this message: 'I knew you before I formed you in your mother's womb.

Before you were born I set you apart and appointed you as my prophet to the nations'" (Jer. 1:4–5 NLT).

But Jeremiah shrank from the great task and its fearful responsibility and pleaded: "'O Sovereign LORD . . . I can't speak for you! I'm too young!' The LORD replied, 'Don't say, "I'm too young," for you must go wherever I send you and say whatever I tell you. And don't be afraid of the people, for I will be with you and will protect you'" (Jer. 1:6–8 NLT).

But God did not send Jeremiah forth at his own charges and in his own strength. He never sends forth His prophets like that. He equips them. He humbles them until there is no conceit or strength left in them, like Daniel in Babylon and John on Patmos, and they cry out, as Isaiah did, "Woe is me! For I am lost; for I am a man of unclean lips . . . for my eyes have seen the King, the LORD of hosts!" (Isa. 6:5 ESV), and then He empowers them. And as the Lord touched the lips of Isaiah with living fire, so He touched Jeremiah: "Then the LORD reached out and touched my mouth and said, 'Look, I have put my words in your mouth!'" (Jer. 1:9 NLT). That was his equipment for his great and solemn and dangerous office.

Then the vastness of this man's mission was unfolded to him: "Today I appoint you to stand up against nations and kingdoms"—this lad, who never left the little land of his birth except when dragged down to Egypt against his prophetic protest by murderous, fugitive Jews, now set over the nations and over the kingdoms to root out the rank growth of evil, to "tear down, destroy and overthrow" every high and vicious thing that exalts itself against the knowledge of God, and also to "build up and plant" (Jer. 1:10 NLT). Then God told His prophet: "Get up and prepare for action. Go out and tell them everything I tell you to say. Do not be afraid of them, or I will make you look foolish in front of them" (Jer. 1:17 NLT).

It is a fearful thing to shrink in fear from people and thus fall before the frown of God, but that was the alternative set before this young prophet. Speak boldly and feel the strength of the everlasting arms girding you about, or slink away from the face of mere men and women and be confounded by the Almighty!

It was not a joyous, rose-strewn path the prophets trod. It was perilous, lonely, and blood-stained. Along the way they were ambushed by malignant foes and entrenched monopolies of vested interests and confronted by established custom and the unquestioned practice of kings and princes, priests, and people. The prophet was to set himself in opposition to the nation and the nations. Oh, the loneliness of it! The danger! The thankless task! "For see, today I have made you strong like a fortified city that cannot be captured, like an iron pillar or a bronze wall. You will stand against the whole land—the kings, officials, priests, and people of Judah. They will fight you" (Jer. 1:18–19 NLT).

What a spectacle—a lone man, a child, against the world! "They will fight you, but they will fail. For I am with you, and I will take care of you" (Jer. 1:19 NLT).

Ah, I see! He is not alone. Those who are with him are more than all who are against him. "If God be for us, who can be against us?" (Rom. 8:31 KJV). "The angel of the LORD encamps around those who fear him, and delivers them" (Ps. 34:7 ESV). The prophets were solitary and diffident, but they had access to God. The key to secret resources of exhaustless power and wisdom and grace was given to them. They were equipped with God—God the Holy Spirit. He moved them and they spoke, and their message reverberates through all time, judges all people and nations, and illuminates all history.

Many students of prophecy think the prophets have put into our hands a God-given telescope, through which we can peer into the future and foresee the course of all coming history to the utmost bounds of time, and they prepare elaborate charts and write no end of books and make learned mathematical calculations, and often fix dates for the end of all things. But I have never been helped, but rather confused, in thus trying to interpret the great prophets. Their value to me ever since God sanctified me has consisted not in the light they throw upon generations yet unborn, but the light they throw upon my own generation. I want help to interpret my own times. It is precisely because their messages came from God and are timeless that they are so timely. Their prophecies are meant to enable me to understand the present, to recognize my own duty, to interpret the will and ways of God to the people of my own generation, and to guide the steps of the youth of the next generation to fitness for their solemn, unknown tasks. Beyond that, if I see at all, it is but dimly.

There was an element of foretelling in the prophets' messages, but the infinitely greater element was that of *forth telling*, revealing God Himself—His character, His holiness, His everlasting righteousness that is in eternal, deadly antagonism to all unrighteousness and sin, His benevolence and everlasting love that yearns and woos and waits and seeks the erring and the sinful and forgives the penitent soul—the restoring and redeeming God, who is also a God of judgment, "a consuming fire" (Heb. 12:29 NIV). And it is in the light of this revelation of God's character, nature, mind, heart, will, and ways, that I see my duty and interpret the meaning of my own day, and the problems of my own generation, and am in some measure enabled to forecast the future. And this view of the supreme meaning and value of the prophets for our day seems to me to harmonize with Paul's statement of the great purpose of Scripture: "All Scripture is inspired by God," he wrote, and is useful, not for the gratification of curiosity concerning the distant future but "to teach us what is true and to make us realize what is wrong in our lives. It corrects us when we are wrong and teaches us to do what is right. God uses it to prepare and equip his people to do every good work" (2 Tim. 3:16–17 NLT) in this day and generation.

I fell into a nest of spiritualists once, and the timeliest answer I could make to their pretensions I found in the ancient prophecy of Isaiah and in the words of Jesus. Listen to Isaiah replying to the spiritualists of Jerusalem twenty-five hundred years ago: "Someone may say to you, 'Let's ask the mediums and those who consult the spirits of the dead. With their whisperings and mutterings, they will tell us what to do.' But shouldn't people ask God for guidance? Should the living seek guidance from the dead? Look to God's instructions and teachings! People who contradict his word are completely in the dark" (Isa. 8:19–20 NLT).

And this is matched by the words of Jesus in relating the conversation between Abraham in heaven and the rich man in hell. The rich man wanted Lazarus sent to his brothers on earth to warn them to live in such a way that they would not come to him in hell. "But Abraham said, 'If they won't listen to Moses and the prophets, they won't be persuaded even if someone rises from the dead'" (Luke 16:31 NLT).

My soul is often shocked and shamed by the immodest ways some people dress, but I find that Isaiah was confronted by the same lack of modesty in his day. In Isaiah 3:16–23, he gave a description of the fashions of old Jerusalem that reads as though he had just come from Paris, London, or New York.

There was an entrenched liquor traffic in their day, and those faithful prophets, messengers of God, watchful shepherds of souls, flamed in indignation against the drunkard and the bootlegger:

> What sorrow for those who get up early in the morning looking for a drink of alcohol and spend long evenings drinking wine to make themselves flaming drunk. They furnish wine and lovely music at their grand parties—lyre and harp, tambourine and flute—but they never think about the LORD or notice what he is doing. So my people will go into exile far away because they do not know me. . . . The grave is licking its lips in anticipation, opening its mouth wide. The great and the lowly and all the drunken mob will be swallowed up. (Isa. 5:11–14 NLT)

The old prophet Habakkuk wrote of the ancient bootlegger, "What sorrow awaits you who make your neighbors drunk! You force your cup on them so you can gloat over their shameful nakedness" (Hab. 2:15 NLT).

Have we problems? Are we confronted by vice and sin in our city? Is evil triumphant and injustice and wickedness entrenched in high places in the state? We shall find light on every problem in the messages of the prophets, and we shall find help and strength in company with them, for they walked with God and lived and spoke and suffered and died for Him. Listen to Habakkuk's prayer: "I have heard all about you, LORD. I am filled with awe by your amazing works. In this time of our deep need, help us again as you did in years gone by . . . remember your mercy" (Hab. 3:2 NLT). His heart was nearly broken by the sin and injustice and wickedness he saw all around him, and he longed for a revival. And then faith in the almightiness, the goodness, of God, and the final triumph of holiness kindled in him, and he shouted out, "For as the waters fill the sea, the earth will be filled with an awareness of the glory of the LORD" (Hab. 2:14 NLT).

And when the cup of the wickedness of the people was full, and the judgment of God fell upon them, and the desolating scourge of the Assyrian invasion swept over the land and left it wasted and bare, he sang: "Even though the fig trees have no blossoms, and there are no grapes on the vines; even though the olive crop fails, and the fields lie empty and barren; even though the flocks die in the fields, and the cattle barns are empty, yet I will rejoice in the LORD! I will be joyful in the God of my salvation!" (Hab. 3:17–18 NLT).

They lived in a day when light was dim. They had no completed Bible. Jesus had not yet come. The cross had not yet been uplifted with its bleeding, redeeming victim. The bars of the tomb had not yet been broken and the iron doors of death had not swung open that the light of the resurrection might stream through. Pentecost had not yet come. But they believed in the "mighty God, the everlasting Father." They believed Him to be the "Prince of Peace" and that upon His shoulders rested all government, and that "of his government and peace there shall be no end" (Isa. 9:6–7 KJV). They believed that however high sin might vault it would be cast down, it would not finally triumph—that however deeply entrenched and strongly garrisoned injustice and arrogance and pride might be, yet they would be rooted out, pulled down, and trampled in the dust.

But though they flamed like fire heated sevenfold against sin, they had hearts as tender as tiny children, and they wept for sinful and struggling souls, and breathed out promises as gentle as light falling on the eyes of sleeping babes. It was God, the Holy One, in these devoted, yielded prophets that flamed against iniquity, that sobbed and wept over the desolations sin wrought, and that gave promises that still fall into our hearts with heaven's own benediction.

Oh Jeremiah, my brother and friend in this ministry of judgment and mercy, this proclamation of the "goodness and severity of God" (Rom. 11:22 KJV), how I thank you, and thank God for you, as across centuries and millennia you still whisper into my listening ears and my longing heart those sweet words: "The LORD has appeared of old to me, saying: 'Yes, I have loved you with an everlasting love; therefore with lovingkindness I have drawn you'" (Jer. 31:3 NKJV).

I am a lonely man, and yet I am not lonely. With my open Bible, I live with prophets, priests, and kings; I walk and hold communion with apostles, saints, and martyrs, and with Jesus, and my eyes see the King in His beauty and the land that is far off.

Why I Wanted My Wife to Be My Wife

It was my pleasant privilege once to be entertained for several days in the home of some Swedish friends. The family consisted of a husband and wife and three exceptionally bright and lovely children. He was a strong, manly fellow who had made his way to the front rank in his chosen work by sheer force of character, industry, and ability. She was a happy wife who did her own housework, rejoiced in her husband's success, and mothered the children with wise and loving care.

One morning at breakfast, she told me (in the most charming broken English) the one test by which she decided the fate of several suitors, and by which she was assured that in her husband she had at last met her heart's mate with whom she could gladly and unfalteringly link her life for better or worse till death.

During her childhood in her old-fashioned, economical Swedish home, she had to darn stockings and socks, something she disliked very much to do, but which unwittingly was developing in her a selective instinct that was finally to bring her great joy. When she had grown into the radiant beauty of young womanhood and young men began to pay her attention, each appeared as a prospective husband. And to each she applied this test: "Would I be willing to darn his socks?" In each instance, there was a revulsion of feeling that settled the fate of the young man, until she met the one who was to be her husband.

When she applied the test to him, her heart leaped with joy at the prospect. She felt she would gladly spend her life darning his socks, and she longed to begin at once on whole bureau drawers full of them. She did not tell—and possibly she could not tell—what it was in him that made him different from all others. But something in his presence or person unlocked a treasure-store of love and sacrificial devotion in her heart that made her sure that of all men he was the one to whom she could commit herself without doubt or fear. It was what she discovered in herself quite as much as what she found in him that made her certain.

When Abraham Lincoln made his call for volunteers in the War between the States, my youthful father heard and responded to the call. He left his young wife and baby boy and went off to the war, and at the Siege of Vicksburg paid the last full tribute of devotion to his country, while the young widowed mother wept and the little boy looked on with wide-eyed and uncomprehending wonder. He had been an ideal husband and for three years had made Mother supremely happy. Never once did he speak a cross word or show to her other than the most tender and chivalrous devotion. The memory of his love was always with her, and as I grew she would hug me to her heart and tell me how happy my father had made her, and then she would add, as she looked me straight in the eyes, "And someday my boy will make some woman unspeakably happy."

So naturally I came to feel that was part of the mission of my life, one of the objects of my being, to make some woman happy—while to injure a woman, to mar her life and blast her happiness, seemed to me (and still seems) the most supreme cursedness and treason against the most sacred rights and claims of humanity.

From Mother I unconsciously got a high ideal of gentle sweetness and purity, and all womanly virtues that adorn a home and make it a haven of rest and a center of inspiration, courage, and noble ambition. Then one day at school word came to me: "Quick! Come home; Mother is dying!"

When I got home, Mother was dead. The love light had fled from her beautiful eyes, but a smile was on her sweet face. They buried her, but her spirit was with me and the memory of her sweet, womanly character was enshrined deep in my heart. And in all my boyish loves and dreams, it was sweetness and purity rather than flashing beauty and wit that kindled tender emotions within me. My wife must be gentle and sweet and pure of heart. This I gathered unconsciously from my mother.

Following Mother's death, I prepared for college and spent four years in a university in the Midwest. What a bevy of lovely girls surrounded me there! We frolicked and flirted and picnicked and were as frank and open and wholesome in our relations with each other as brothers and sisters, but my heart was lost to none of them. Two of them were as beautiful as any picture John Singer Sargent ever painted, but they were frivolous. One had the most wondrous eyes and the most perfect complexion I ever saw, with masses of lovely hair and a form that would have graced a ducal palace; she was intellectual, also, but it was Lady Clare Vere de Vere[1] transplanted to the Ohio Valley:

> Faultily faultless, icily regular, splendidly null,
> Dead perfection, no more.[2]

Another was very charming, but she lacked depth of character, I thought, and was too petite. Yet another was rich in character, one of the best students I ever knew, and one of the finest of women, but stiff in manner, and there was an irregularity about her features that I regretted (in the callow years of young manhood, very small defects— which may not be defects at all and would probably be unnoticed by older and wiser men—may cause Cupid's darts to miss the mark).

My intellectual awakening was slow, and I do not think those four years quite completed the process, but I was sufficiently awakened to see and feel that my wife must have a range of vision and thought beyond the neighborhood in which we might live, or I could not be happy with her. She must be educated, know books, have some knowledge of the world's best thought, and the culture that only this can give.

I was not myself deeply religious, though I was a member of the church, taught in the Sunday school, sang in the choir, and worked in the college YMCA, but I missed in all those lovely girls a religious conviction and influence which I now see I needed and craved and would have heartily welcomed from any one of them.

Young men may appear careless concerning religious matters, but I am persuaded from a rather wide acquaintance and experience that they do not resent but respond promptly (though maybe jauntily at first or silently for a time) to the gentle spiritual touch of the young woman who has vital spiritual knowledge and is frank and natural and modestly courageous in the expression of her convictions, who appeals to everything that is best in them and shames everything that is false and morally wrong. In these things, young men are often more willing to be led than to take the lead, and here, if they would, young women could often gain a commanding and gracious and lifelong influence over young men, an influence which would be welcomed as guiding, restraining, inspiring, and greatly longed for and needed in the midst of fierce temptations to which young men are subject.

It was while continuing my professional studies at an Eastern university that the conviction possessed me that my wife must not only have sweet womanly virtues and be adorned with refinement and the culture of the schools, but also that she must be genuinely religious—must love God and His law supremely—for without this, I realized, we would fail in the highest fellowship. With this love and loyalty to God abounding, I knew that her love and loyalty to me could not fail.

Indeed, I came not through any experience but through awakened spiritual insight to distrust the permanency of a human love that is not replenished and enriched by the overflow of a divine love, and a loyalty that is not purified and reinforced by the reverential fear and love of God. Where this fear and love abide there can be no failure. "Many waters cannot quench love" (Song 8:7 KJV) that is kindled and fed from this central and exhaustless fire.

But where could I find such a woman? Solomon was a very wise man and had a wide marital experience, and he said, "A prudent wife is from the LORD" (Prov. 19:14 KJV). If she is from the Lord, why not ask Him for her? Why not pray to Him to find her? And this I did.

Marriage is a divine institution, is surrounded by divine sanctions, and should be entered into with a sense of its divine character and responsibilities and blessings, which, abused, can turn into the most fateful of curses. Therefore, God's blessing and guidance should be sought in every step that leads to it.

The year I went east to study, three girls from one of the leading women's colleges of America went abroad to see Europe, and in London, to their utter surprise and joy, they found the Lord in The Salvation Army.

One of them He had chosen for me.

To her heart of sweet womanly graces, and to her culture, He added His grace and spirit. Two years later we met, and I fell in love—I lost my heart. Here she was—the sweet, gracious, cultured woman, filled with God's love, one my head and my heart approved, and for whose dear sake I had denied myself in lonely hours of fierce temptation, though I had not seen her face, and for whom I had prayed and watched and waited.

At an appropriate time, not then being able to see her, I wrote and told her all, and she sent me the sweetest letter—and the bitterest—I ever received. She said she wept at the pain it must give me, and she felt that my love and union with me would put the crown upon her womanhood, but there were obstacles in the way—obstacles she feared were insuperable. She then generously mentioned two others, with either of whom she thought I might be happier than with her. At her invitation I met them, and they were lovely women, but to my mind they were "as water unto wine,"[3] and I pressed my suit in spite of obstacles.

One day she gave me an anonymous little book. I read it with the deepest interest and emotion, not once suspecting who had written it, and when I learned it was her book I loved her none the less.

On another day we were driving among the beautiful hills around her home, and some occasion arose that led her to tell me of a nameless baby, a little child of lawless passions and the night, whose tender life was wasting away through the ignorance and lack of care on the part of its young mother. She coaxed the mother to let her have the baby for a while and took it home and kept it for months, nursing it back to rosy health and dimpled sweetness. And as she talked about that baby I felt that in her heart were the germs of the richest and tenderest mother love, and for this I loved her all the more, for I felt that if I ever had a wife, I wanted one who would not shun but welcome motherhood with great and solemn joy.

On yet another day we stood by the piano in her father's home, when suddenly she turned, slipped out into the hall, and left me. My eyes followed her and my whole heart went out after her.

I did not want to die for her, but to live for her. I wanted to put my arms around her, comfort her, provide for her, protect her, bear her burdens, be her shield, and receive every blow of adversity or sorrow or misfortune that might befall her. I no longer thought of what she might bring or give to me, but only of what I might give to and suffer for her.

And then and there, at last, I had found and entered the pure world of sacrificial love and utter devotion reached by the wife of my Swedish friend—the only world in which I could fulfill my mother's prophecy.

The key that will open a Yale lock was made for the lock, and the woman who can open the inmost treasure-store of a man's heart and can bring forth the refined gold of unselfish love, was made for that man. By this I knew that she, who for twenty-eight wonderful and blessed years was my wife, and became the happy mother of my children, was God's woman for me. And that is why I wanted my wife to be my wife!

NOTES

1. A reference to a poem by Alfred Lord Tennyson about an aristocratic lady who flirted with lower-class men only to reject them once they were interested.

2. Alfred Lord Tennyson, "Maud," pt. 1, section 2, lines 82–83, public domain.

3. Alfred Lord Tennyson, "Locksley Hall," 1835, public domain.

The Cost of Winning Souls **3**

Some years ago a young Salvation Army officer (minister) wrote to her superior saying she meant to resign if she could not get souls saved. But she did not resign.

A pastor who was famous for the revivals that swept his churches and moved the communities where he labored was sent to a big church in New York City. As he walked into a gathering of ministers, he heard them whispering among themselves, "He will find New York different. It is the graveyard of revival reputations." Right there he resolved and publicly declared that there would be a revival in his church or there would be a funeral in his parsonage.

Little faith sees the difficulties and often accepts defeat without a fight. Great faith sees God and fights against all odds and—even if the Enemy apparently triumphs—wins moral and spiritual victory, as did Christ on Calvary and as did the martyrs who perished in flame. What could be more complete to doubting hearts and the eyes of unbelief than the defeat of Christ on the cross or of Thomas Cranmer and Nicholas Ridley in the fire! And yet it was then that their victory over the Enemy was supreme. The Spirit of Jesus is the spirit of conquest.

When Paul—filled with passionate love for Christ, whom he had persecuted, and burning with eager desire to see others experience the great salvation that had reached him—went forth to evangelize the Roman Empire, enemies confronted and hunted him with the same deadly hate and murderous opposition he had once shown to the Jerusalem Christians, while every city he entered reeked with unmentionable vices and reveled in licentious idolatries. He had no completed Bible, no religious press, no missionary organization behind him to ensure his support, and the very name of Christ was unknown, while Caesar was honored as a god.

The wealth, learning, philosophy, political power, religions, vested interests of the world, and the age-long habits, passions, and inflamed appetites of humanity were all opposed to him. Don Quixote's valorous attack on windmills did not appear more absurd than Paul's assault on the sin, corruption, and entrenched evils of the world of his day. And he wielded no other weapon than his personal testimony and the story of a crucified, resurrected Jewish peasant carpenter, whom he heralded as the Son of God and the Savior and Judge of the world, before whom everyone—from the emperor to the lowest slave—must someday appear to be judged for their deeds and be rewarded with eternal bliss or doomed to endless shame and woe. Paul died, but he won souls.

Immeasurable difficulties faced John and Charles Wesley when they and George Whitefield began their careers that reawakened

Christendom. The clergy were (as a class) utterly unspiritual, given over to drinking, horse racing, and fox hunting with the gentry. The educated classes were, in large measure, skeptical and licentious, while the lower classes in the cities were only too often debased and drunken, and found their pleasures in cockfighting and racing dogs on Sundays. But in the midst of these desolate and desperate conditions, the Wesleys started the greatest revival since the apostolic age, and snatched souls by the myriads from the very jaws of hell.

And amid conditions almost, if not equally, as dark and forbidding, the founder of The Salvation Army began and carried on his work that has directly touched and won millions of souls and an even larger number indirectly, quickening the faith and lifting the spiritual level of the whole Christian world, and touching with soul-saving power and life-giving hope great populations in many lands.

But none of these world-embracing, epoch-making revivals began in a large way. Paul usually made an address and gave his testimony in a synagogue—a small meeting-place of the Jews—until he was excluded, and then he went to some home or room that was opened to him. This was followed by house-to-house visitation, often after a day's work at tent-making. The Wesleys began in a similarly humble way, and so did William Booth.

Great revivals among God's people and awakenings among the ungodly never begin in a great way. They begin as oak trees begin. There is nothing startling and spectacular about the beginning of an oak tree. In darkness, in loneliness, an acorn gives up its life. And the oak, at first only a tiny root and a tiny stem of green, is born out of the dissolution and death of the acorn. So revivals are born, so souls are won, and so the kingdom of God comes. Someone no longer trying to save him- or herself or advance his or her own interests dies—dies to self; to the world; to the praise of others; to the ambition for promotion, place, or power—and lives unto Christ, lives to save others, and the awakening comes. Souls are born into the kingdom of God, and they rally round their leader and in turn become soul-winners. Jesus said, "Unless a kernel of wheat falls to the ground and dies, it remains only a single seed. But if it dies, it produces many seeds" (John 12:24 NIV). And so He "endured the cross, despising the shame" (Heb. 12:2 KJV), and died that He might win souls, save men and women, and bring "many sons and daughters to glory" (Heb. 2:10 NIV).

"Anyone who wants to serve me must follow me," said Jesus (John 12:26 NLT). In other words, they must lose their old lives, their old ambitions, their old estimate of values for His sake, His cause, and the souls they would win and for whom He died. "Those who love their life in this world will lose it. Those who care nothing for their life in this world will keep it for eternity" (John 12:25 NLT).

That is the way to become a soul-winner; that is the price that must be paid. The Master could find no easier way, and He can show no easier way to us. It is costly. But shall we wish to win eternal and infinite values cheaply? "For the joy that was set before him [He] endured the cross" (Heb. 12:2 KJV). What joy? The joy of having the Father's approval and of saving souls from eternal death and of "bringing many sons and daughters to glory" (Heb. 2:10 NIV). Shall we hope to share that joy by some cheap service that calls for no uttermost devotion, no whole burnt offering, no final and complete sacrifice? Not otherwise has anyone ever become a soul-winner. We may move upon the surface of people's lives, we may touch their emotions, we may lead them to easy, nonsacrificial religious exercises and activities and think we are saving souls, but we do not really win them until we constrain them to follow us, as we follow Christ, through death—death to sin, death to the flesh and the world—into newness of life unto holiness.

This was Paul's way. "And now I am bound by the Spirit to go to Jerusalem. I don't know what awaits me, except that the Holy Spirit tells me in city after city that jail and suffering lie ahead. But my life is worth nothing to me unless I use it for finishing the work assigned me by the Lord Jesus—the work of telling others the Good News about the wonderful grace of God" (Acts 20:22–24 NLT). It was not easy for Paul. He counted the cost. He paid the price. He turned neither to the right hand nor the left. He marched straight forward.

He was commissioned "to open [people's] eyes, and to turn them from darkness to light, and from the power of Satan unto God, that they may receive forgiveness of sins, and inheritance among them which are sanctified by faith" in Christ (Acts 26:18 KJV). And he added, "I was not disobedient unto the heavenly vision" (Acts 26:19 KJV). "Whatever gain I had, I counted as loss for the sake of Christ. Indeed, I count everything as loss because of the surpassing worth of knowing Christ Jesus my Lord. For his sake I have suffered the loss of all things and count them as rubbish, in order that I may gain Christ" (Phil. 3:7–8 ESV).

It is as we thus count all things as loss and so win Christ that we are empowered to win souls. This is the standard we must set for ourselves, and to which we must woo and draw our younger colleagues by the compulsion of love and faithful teaching and example.

The psalmist David, in his penitential prayer, cried to God for a clean heart and a right spirit, for the joy of salvation, and the enabling of the Holy Spirit. "Then," he said, "I will teach transgressors your ways, and sinners will return to you" (Ps. 51:13 ESV). David felt that if he would effectively teach and convert others his heart must be pure, his spirit must be right. So then the cost of winning souls includes the price that must be paid for a pure heart. I must be clean, my spirit must be right, I must hold back no part of the price, I must bring all the tithes into God's storehouse, if I would be a soul-winner.

"He who is wise wins souls," wrote Solomon (Prov. 11:30 NASB). Then, if I would be a soul-winner, I must pay the price of wisdom. Wisdom cannot be bought with silver and gold. It cannot be passed on like an inheritance from parent to child. It cannot be learned, as we learn mathematics or the sciences, in schools and colleges. It comes only through experience in following Christ.

Knowledge comes, but wisdom lingers, and he bears a laden breast,
Full of sad experience, moving toward the stillness of his rest.[1]

He or she who wants wisdom must not shrink from suffering. "When reviled, we bless; when persecuted, we endure; when slandered, we entreat," wrote Paul (1 Cor. 4:12–13 ESV). Suffering did not daunt him. Abuse and neglect did not embitter him. When his converts were turned against him, he wrote, "I will not be burdensome to you: for I seek not yours but you. . . . And I will very gladly spend and be spent for you; though the more abundantly I love you, the less I be loved. . . . We do all things, dearly beloved, for your edifying" (2 Cor. 12:14–15, 19 KJV).

Anyone with that spirit is full of wisdom, the wisdom of God, "the wisdom that is from above," which is "first pure, then peaceable, gentle, and easy to be intreated, full of mercy and good fruits, without partiality, and without hypocrisy" (James 3:17 KJV). And such people win souls. Their lives, their example, their spirit, their speech are compelling, and they win and knit others to Christ.

The soul-winner must not despise the day of small things. It is better to speak to a small company and win a half-dozen of them to the Savior than to speak to a thousand and have no one saved or sanctified, though they all go away lauding the leader and exclaiming, "Wasn't that grand!"

Some years ago I went to a large city where The Salvation Army owned an auditorium seating nearly a thousand people, and where I thought we had a flourishing corps (church). The officer couple in charge had unusual ability, but had become stale and spiritually lifeless. Where hundreds should have greeted me, fifty tired, listless people were present, twenty of whom were unkempt children. When I rose to lead the singing, there were three songbooks among us, one of which was mine. The officer ran off downstairs to pick up a few more books, and while we waited I was fiercely tempted to walk off the platform and leave the place, telling him I would not spend my strength helping someone with no more spirit and interest than he manifested. Then I looked at the people before me—tired miners, poor and wearied wives, and little, unshepherded children, peering at me with dull, quizzical eyes as though wondering whether I would club them or feed them, give them stones or bread for their hunger—and my heart was swept with a great wave of pity for them, these sheep without a shepherd. So I set myself with full purpose of heart to bless and feed and save them, and in the next six days that big auditorium was crowded and we rejoiced over ninety souls seeking the Savior. True soul-winners count not their lives dear. They give themselves desperately to their task, and there are times when, as Knox prayed, "Give me Scotland, or I die," so they sob and cry, "Give me souls, or I die."

That New York pastor I mentioned earlier had a revival in his church. There was no funeral in the parsonage. Day and night he cried to God for souls. Every afternoon he visited the people in their homes, offices, and shops. He climbed so many stairways that he said if they had been piled one on the other they would have taken him well up toward the moon. For a month or more, he devoted his mornings to study of the Bible and to reading the biographies of soul-winners, books on revivals, revival lectures and sermons, revival songs, and revival stories and anecdotes. He saturated his mind and heart with the very spirit of revivals. He looked into the grave, into hell, into heaven. He studied Calvary. He meditated on eternity. He stirred up his pity and compassion for the people. He cried to God for the Holy Spirit and for power, faith, wisdom, fervor, joy, and love. He woke up in the night and prayed and planned his strategy. He enlisted such members of his church as were spiritual to help him. When he won someone for Christ he enlisted that person as a helper in the fight. And God swept the church with revival fire. Hundreds were won to Christ. Oh, how unfailing is God. However present and ready to help is the Holy Spirit! How surely is Jesus present where men and women gather in His name!

That young Salvation Army officer to whom I referred did not resign. One night, as she closed the meeting, she asked the soldiers (church members) to remain with her for a short while. Then she opened her heart to them. She told them of the letter she had written. She said she could not continue in the work unless she could see souls saved. Many drunkards were in the city. Their homes were being ruined, their wives neglected, and they were hastening to hell because of the drink. She asked her soldiers to remain and spend an hour in prayer with her and for her, and for the salvation of souls, especially of the drunkards of the city. They stayed, and for an hour they prayed. God heard and drew nigh, and Jesus was in their midst.

After the next public meeting, she again requested the soldiers to remain, and again they prayed for an hour or more, and Jesus was there. And after every public meeting for a week or ten days or more, they stayed and prayed, and Jesus was in their midst. And then one night, somewhat to their surprise—strange that we should be surprised at answered prayer—the worst drunkard in the city, with several of his pals, came to the meeting and experienced new life in Christ. Next, his whole family was won, and they all became soldiers. In a brief time twelve drunkards came to faith, and that woman had a blessed revival on her hands. And not only did lost souls enter the kingdom of God but a sincere woman's ministry was saved as well.

We may be sweet singers, eloquent and moving preachers, skillful organizers, masters of crowds, wizards of finance, or popular and commanding leaders; but if we are not soul-winners, if we do not make men and women see the meaning and winsomeness of Jesus, hunger for His righteousness and purity, and bow to Him in full loyalty, then we lack the "one thing . . . needful" (Luke 10:42 KJV). And yet that one thing is within the reach of us all if we live for it, if we put it first, if we shrink not from the cost. We may be, we should be, we shall be at all cost winners of souls!

NOTE

1. Alfred Lord Tennyson, "Locksley Hall," 1835, public domain.

As with Sons 4

The author of the book of Hebrews wrote, "Bear hardship for the sake of discipline. God is treating you like sons and daughters! What child isn't disciplined by his or her father? But if you don't experience discipline, which happens to all children, then you are illegitimate and not real sons and daughters" (Heb. 12:7–8 CEB).

If I turn to the commentaries of Matthew Henry; Adam Clark; Jamieson, Fawcett, and Brown; or others, I would probably find some wise and useful comments about those verses. But life itself will furnish the best and most instructive comment to men or women with open eyes, who observe, meditate, think, and remember the chastenings of their own youth.

For some days, I have been an amused and deeply interested observer of the chastening or discipline of one of my little grandsons who is not yet a year old. He is almost bursting with pep. He simply bubbles over with life. One of his chief joys is to get into his bath. It is perfectly delicious to watch him as he kicks and coos and gurgles and splashes water all over himself and anyone who comes near, blinks when water pops into his eyes, and revels in one of the chief joys of his young life. But how he loathes being undressed and redressed before and after his bath! He kicks and flourishes his arms in impatient protest, cries and objects in all manner of baby ways, while his insistent mother ignores all his objections, not asking what he likes but putting on him such clothes as she thinks best, plumps him into his baby carriage, and wheels the rosy little rogue out onto the porch for his morning nap in the sunshine and soft spring winds.

All this to him is chastening, discipline, and training. It is not severe but gentle and wise, though to him much of it is painful. "For the moment all discipline seems painful rather than pleasant, but later"—let us note this "but later" and give thanks and be humble—"it yields the peaceful fruit of righteousness to those who have been trained by it" (Heb. 12:11 ESV). The child will learn slowly, but surely, through this unwavering process that he must submit to rightful authority and superior wisdom, and that those things that are right and good must come first, not only those things that are pleasant at present. Then someday he will discover that all this painful insistence of his unyielding mother was the expression of wise, thoughtful, sacrificial love.

If his father and mother are wise, their chastening, or discipline, will grow with the growth and unfold with the unfolding of this baby boy. They will probably often find themselves sorely perplexed, their hearts will be searched, and they will discover that their own minds and spirits are being disciplined, chastened, in ways that to them are for the present "painful." But if they are humble and prayerful and patient and trustful, and always put the right and the good first, they will find that while they discipline the child, God in love is training them, and bringing them into intimate, understanding fellowship with Himself in His great and sore travail to save and train a fallen race that wants its own way and prefers pleasure to righteousness. And, if they are wise, they will note that God is just as insistent in disciplining them as they are in disciplining their baby boy, and for the same reason—for their good. "God is treating you like sons and daughters" (Heb. 12:7 CEB).

As the baby gets older, the discipline at times may have to be sterner and more severe. If he will yield to his parents' word, he will be happy. But if he will not be guided by word, then it may be necessary to use the rod. "The rod and reproof give wisdom," wrote Solomon, "but a child left to himself brings shame to his mother" (Prov. 29:15 ESV). I do not know that I can improve upon Solomon; he mentions the rod before reproof, but I would suggest reproof before the rod. Gentle measures should be used first. The Lord pleads with His people. "Do not be like a senseless horse or mule that needs a bit and bridle to keep it under control" (Ps. 32:9 NLT). He has a better, gentler way: "I will instruct you and teach you in the way you should go; I will guide you with My eye" (Ps. 32:8 NKJV). How tender and gracious God is! And how often I have seen a wise mother counsel and guide her child with her eye.

But the child that will not be so guided should be taught by sterner ways. It is not true love that withholds proper discipline from the child. "Those who spare the rod of discipline hate their children. Those who love their children care enough to discipline them" (Prov. 13:24 NLT).

Let us learn from the heavenly Father how to be true fathers and mothers:

- "Discipline your children while there is hope. Otherwise you will ruin their lives" (Prov. 19:18 NLT).
- "Discipline your children, and they will give you peace of mind and will make your heart glad" (Prov. 29:17 NLT).
- "A youngster's heart is filled with foolishness, but physical discipline will drive it far away" (Prov. 22:15 NLT).

The parent who has exercised the kindest, wisest, yet firmest and most unvarying control of the child eventually receives the highest and deepest affection of the child. But firmness must be balanced by justice or the child will be embittered and made into a sullen rebel.

My sweet mother was kind, but she was not invariably firm. After my father's death, she was left alone with me, her tiny boy. All the wellsprings of her deep love and tender affection flowed around me, and often when she should have been firm and unbending, she yielded to melting tenderness, of which I was quick to take advantage. I do not remember it, but she herself told me that I would have been spoiled had she not married again and found in my stepfather a counterpoise to her tenderness. He was firm and unbending, and I stood in awe of him, much to my profit. He had a boy near my own age, and he meted out discipline between us in even measure. But while he was firm with us, I felt in my boy heart that he was not always just. He was hasty. He would fly into a passion. He was not patient and did not always take time to find out all the facts, and at times I was embittered, and might have been spoiled by him as surely as by mother's fondness had their methods not in a measure balanced each other. They both needed a finer, firmer self-control to wisely discipline growing boys.

My sweet, lovely mother needed to firmly control the tenderness of her feelings and the floods of her affection, while my stepfather needed to control the unthinking quickness of his snap judgments and the nervous and passionate haste of his explosive temper. But while he punished us boys sometimes when we did not deserve it, yet he missed us sometimes when we did, so betwixt and between we got about what we deserved, on the whole. I have no quarrel in my memory with his dealings, but only gratitude and affection and a deep wish that in some way after all these scores of years I could repay the debt I owe him.

But it is to my darling mother I owe my deepest debt of love and gratitude. As I grew older, her gentleness and tenderness became the most powerful instrument of discipline to my wayward spirit, just as grace is mightier to break and refashion hard hearts than law, and Mount Calvary more influential for redemption than Mount Sinai. Can eternity blot out the memory and remove the ache in my heart caused by a look she gave me when I was but a lad of thirteen years? My stepfather had been unfair (I felt) in a demand upon me one day, and I flamed inwardly with resentment. When my mother and a lady friend appeared, all my pent-up wrath exploded in hot, angry words about my stepfather. Mother tried to get me to be silent but I was too angry. I blurted out all that was in my heart. I had my say. But that night, as I went to kiss Mother goodnight, as I always did, she gave me a look of grief and pain that has stayed with me for more than half a century. Her loved form has moldered beneath green grass and daisies, the rain has beaten upon her grave, and snows of over half a hundred winters have shrouded it in their mantling whiteness, but the chastening pain that entered my heart from her wounded heart with that look is with me still. To this day, after all these years, I can shut my eyes at any time and see the pained, grieved look in the lovely eyes of my dear mother.

If parents have trained their children so wisely as to hold their deep affection while commanding their highest respect, there will come a time when a look will be weightier than law, and the character of the loved and esteemed parent will exert a greater authority to mold and fashion the child in righteousness than anything the parent can say or do. The commanding authority and chastenings of law must yield to the more penetrating and purifying self-discipline imposed by the recognized faith and hope and love of the parent, and disappointing that parent will bring the deepest and most abiding pain to the child's own heart. This is God's way.

There was a time when Jesus turned and rebuked Peter with sharp, incisive words: "Get behind me, Satan! For you are not setting your mind on the things of God, but on the things of man" (Mark 8:33 ESV). But eventually Jesus' character and spirit had so far mastered Peter that a look sufficed to break his heart. Peter in a panic of fear denied Jesus, cursed and swore, "'Man, I don't know what you are talking about.' And immediately, while he was still speaking, the rooster crowed." And Jesus "turned and looked at Peter." That was all, but it was sufficient. "Peter left the courtyard, weeping bitterly" (Luke 22:60–62 NLT). I think never till his dying day could Peter forget that look. It broke his heart, and "the sacrifices of God are a broken spirit . . . and contrite heart" (Ps. 51:17 ESV).

This is the final triumph of all the chastenings of God's love. Once He has thus broken us He can henceforth guide us with His eye. We shall be happy when we come to look upon the perplexing, painful, and harassing things of life—as well as the plain and pleasant things—as instruments in the hands of our heavenly Father for the chastening, polishing, and perfecting of our character and the widening of our influence.

John Bunyan's enemies offered to release him from prison if he would preach no more, but he replied that he would let moss grow over his eyes before he would make such a promise, so they kept him in that filthy Bedford jail among the vilest criminals for twelve weary years. They thought to stop his ministry, but they only made his ministry age-long and worldwide, for during those years he meditated, dreamed, rejoiced, and wrote his undying book, *The Pilgrim's Progress*. The limitation imposed upon him in prison was God's opportunity to liberate his mental and spiritual powers.

Paul would have been lost and unknown to us in the dimness of antiquity, if it were not for his letters written from prison. Nero put him in chains and shut his body up in a dungeon, and through this limitation God liberated Paul's influence for all time and for the whole human race. It is a law that liberation comes by limitation. We die to live. We are buried to be resurrected. We are chastened to be perfected.

"O the depth of the riches both of the wisdom and knowledge of God! How unsearchable are his judgments, and his ways past finding out!" (Rom. 11:33 KJV).

The Seamless Robe of Jesus 5

Jesus never pitied Himself, nor did He seek the pity of anyone else. One day He asked His disciples, "Who do people say that the Son of Man is?" (Matt. 16:13 NLT).

"John the Baptist," replied one.

"Elijah," said another.

"Jeremiah or one of the prophets," answered a third.

"But who do you say I am?" He asked.

"You are the Messiah, the Son of the living God," replied ever-ready Simon Peter (Matt. 16:16 NLT).

At last their eyes had pierced through the veil of His humanity, the disguise of His lowly village ancestry and His humble occupation as a carpenter, and recognized the King, King Eternal, King of Kings, and Lord of Lords. The splendor of His being, before which seraphim and cherubim, angels and archangels veil their faces, was so accommodated to their poor eyes and minds that their eyes were not blinded and they were not afraid.

"Jesus replied, 'You are blessed, Simon son of John, because my Father in heaven has revealed this to you. You did not learn this from any human being'" (Matt. 16:17 NLT).

The secret was out! The Son of God, the Eternal Word, "full of grace and truth" (John 1:14 KJV), was made flesh and was in the world, dwelling among humankind. But the secret must not go further just yet, so He "sternly warned the disciples not to tell anyone that he was the Messiah" (Matt. 16:20 NLT). It must not be spread abroad. He must draw the veil yet closer about Himself, that only sincere, humble souls might know Him, that the sin of humanity might run its course, and its malignity and utter enmity to God might be revealed in their treatment of Him, the well-beloved, only begotten Son of the Father.

"From then on Jesus began to tell his disciples plainly that it was necessary for him to go to Jerusalem, and that he would suffer many terrible things at the hands of the elders, the leading priests, and the teachers of religious law. He would be killed, but on the third day he would be raised from the dead" (Matt. 16:21 NLT).

Such statements, it should seem, would have dumbfounded the disciples. But not Peter; his poor, dull mind was roused and his tongue loosed, and he took Jesus aside "and began to reprimand him for saying such things. 'Heaven forbid, Lord,' he said. 'This will never happen to you!'" (Matt. 16:22 NLT).

The marginal reading of Peter's wording is, "Pity yourself!" But Jesus did not pity Himself, and He would have none of Peter's pity nor worldly counsel and comfort. He said, "Get away from me, Satan!

You are a dangerous trap to me. You are seeing things merely from a human point of view, not from God's" (Matt. 16:23 NLT).

But while Jesus would not pity Himself, nor even permit Peter to counsel pity, what could be more pathetic, humanly speaking, than the scene at the cross, when He—the most loving and devoted of the sons of men, and the poorest—was stripped of His only suit of clothes, His only earthly possession, and nailed nude to the cross to die, while those who crucified Him divided the poor little bundle of clothes among themselves and cast lots for His seamless robe? His robe without seam, that must not be torn. Think of that careless, cruel soldier stalking about in the robe of Jesus. What a picture!

But while the soldiers, for their own selfish purposes, spared the seamless robe that day, how often has it been torn since then, and that by those who profess to know and love Him.

I like to think of that first society of His people, which we now speak of as the early church, as the seamless robe of Jesus. It enshrined His spiritual presence. He clothed Himself with it as with a garment. Through its members He, the risen Christ, was still seen by human eyes.

He was revealed in its spiritual life. To the wonder-struck multitude on the day of Pentecost, amazed at the glowing, fire-baptized disciples, and inquiring, "What can this mean?" (Acts 2:12 NLT) and the others who, mocking, said, "They're just drunk" (Acts 2:13 NLT)—Peter replied, "God raised Jesus from the dead, and we are all witnesses of this. Now he is exalted to the place of highest honor in heaven, at God's right hand. And the Father, as he had promised, gave him the Holy Spirit to pour out upon us, just as you see and hear today" (Acts 2:32–33 NLT).

The radiant, joy-filled, fearless, conquering life of the early church was the life, the presence of Christ, in its members. "It is no longer I who live, but Christ lives in me," wrote Paul (Gal. 2:20 NLT). And "When Christ who is our life appears, then you also will appear with Him in glory" (Col. 3:4 NKJV).

He was made manifest in the activities of the early church. After healing the lame man at the temple gate called Beautiful, Peter asked the Jerusalem crowd, "People of Israel . . . what is so surprising about this? And why stare at us as though we had made this man walk by our own power or godliness? For it is the God of Abraham, Isaac, and Jacob—the God of all our ancestors—who has brought glory to his servant Jesus by doing this. . . . Through faith in the name of Jesus, this man was healed—and you know how crippled he was before. Faith in Jesus' name has healed him before your very eyes" (Acts 3:12–13, 16 NLT).

What they did, they did by the power of Christ working in and through them, as the branch brings forth fruit by the power of the vine from which comes its life.

But most surely was He seen and known in and by the love His disciples had for one another. "By this all people will know that you are my disciples," said Jesus, "if you have love for one another" (John 13:35 ESV). While they loved they "were of one heart" (Acts 4:32 KJV), and as long as they were of one heart, they were of one mind. Their unity began in the heart, extended to the head, and worked itself out in deeds of loving fellowship and service. Many of them even sold their possessions and had all things in common, so great was their love for the Savior and for each other.

Like the robe of the Master, the infant church was "without seam, woven from the top throughout" (John 19:23 KJV).

The first rip in the seamless robe came when Ananias and his wife, Sapphira, sought credit for a love and generosity of which their wretched hearts were destitute, by pretending to give all when they were holding back part of the price of their sold possession (see Acts 5).

A wider rent was threatened when "the Greek-speaking believers complained about the Hebrew-speaking believers, saying that their widows were being discriminated against in the daily distribution of food" (Acts 6:1 NLT). But this was wisely and promptly arrested by the action of the apostles in appointing "seven men who [were] well respected and [were] full of the Spirit and wisdom" (Acts 6:3 NLT) to look after that business.

The rending of this seamless robe can always be traced back to lack of love. The great heresy of the ages is not manifested so much in false doctrine as in failing love and consequent false living. Faith is lost when love leaks out and living becomes selfish. Heresy begins in the heart, not in the head. The heretic of the early Christian society was the loveless schismatic. "I hear that there are divisions among you," wrote Paul to the Corinthians, "and to some extent I believe it. But, of course, there must be divisions among you so that you who have God's approval will be recognized!" (1 Cor. 11:18–19 NLT).

In the tenth chapter of 1 Corinthians, Paul gave us examples of what befell God's ancient people in the wilderness, and he said, "These things happened to them as examples for us. They were written down to warn us who live at the end of the age" (1 Cor. 10:11 NLT). As we study the history of Israel we see, as types, the things we must do and avoid doing if we would save ourselves and guard the heritage God has given us. Again and again we see the rending or attempted rending of the seamless robe of the ancient people of God. Sometimes it was through envy and jealousy that the rending was attempted. On one occasion Miriam and Aaron would have rent the seamless robe. They spoke against their brother, Moses: "Has the Lord spoken only through Moses? Hasn't he spoken through us, too?" (Num. 12:2 NLT). But the Lord was listening. "The Lord heard them. . . . The Lord was very angry with them" (Num. 12:2, 9 NLT). And Miriam's skin became "as white as snow from leprosy" (Num. 12:10 NLT). Korah and Dathan would also have rent the robe, but again, with sure and swift judgment, God acted as umpire, and Korah and Dathan perished in their presumption (see Num. 16).

Again the rending was attempted by Absalom through unholy ambition. By flattering words and fair promises he sought to steal the hearts of the men of Israel, only to perish in his deceit and pride and have his name handed down through the ages and spit upon as a synonym of unfaithfulness and basest treachery (see 2 Sam. 15).

A fatal rending was finally occasioned by the supercilious pride of those in authority, against which God Himself took up arms. When Solomon's son Rehoboam, turning from the advice of his father's wise old counselors, listened to his young nobles' haughty counsel and declared that his little finger should be thicker than his father's loin, ten tribes forsook him, and ancient Israel was fatally and finally torn asunder and is not yet mended, for to this day the ten tribes are known as the "lost tribes." What the oily duplicity of Absalom failed to accomplish the insolent arrogance of Rehoboam brought to pass. A further rending was caused by the shameless, sinful neglect of those who should have shepherded the sheep. Jeremiah and the lesser prophets wept and lamented and bitterly protested against those who fleece and scatter the sheep instead of feeding and shepherding them, causing the people of God to wander and perish for lack of humble oversight and loving care.

Paul found partiality, favoritism, and a partisan spirit endangering the unity of the seamless robe in Corinth, while at Ephesus he foresaw danger arising from the perversity of those who selfishly sought leadership, and he forewarned them in his farewell address of this danger: "Guard yourselves and God's people. Feed and shepherd God's flock—his church, purchased with his own blood—over which the Holy Spirit has appointed you as elders. I know"—oh, the pity of it!—"that false teachers, like vicious wolves, will come in among you after I leave, not sparing the flock. Even some men from your own group will rise up and distort the truth in order to draw a following" (Acts 20:28–30 NLT), rending the seamless robe to gratify their own lust for leadership.

I think of The Salvation Army as a seamless robe of the Master, beneath whose unrent folds in all lands cluster unnumbered multitudes. Little children, unspoiled as yet, but compassed about with innumerable perils, are there, looking to The Salvation Army for the bread of eternal life whereby their souls shall live, for guidance amid hidden and treacherous snares, and for protection from lurking and watchful foes. Adolescent boys and girls are there, with all their inexplicable moods and trying tempers, their daydreams, their pride and foolishness, their loyalty and rebellions, their ardor and despair, their hopes, their loves, their fun and laziness, their humility, their conceit, their strange insight and hasty judgments, and their sensitiveness and abysmal ignorance—there they are beneath the folds of this seamless robe of the Savior.

Straying girls and wronged women are there. Great sinners, terrible criminals, hopeless outcasts, washed in the blood of the Lamb, are there. Widows and orphans, husbands and wives, bearing burdens of toil and care and anxiety, are there. Aged people, with white hair and feeble steps and dim eyes, are there. The lost and wandering are coming under its worldwide sheltering folds, and for the sake of all these who look trustingly to it for safety and shelter, it must not be torn apart.

For many years, sinister eyes have watched to see it torn in two. Futile attempts have been made by some to rend it, and they have torn off a bit here and there. But the robe still spreads its ample and ever-expanding folds over the nations.

It must not be torn apart, and yet it may be unless we serve the Lord "with all humility of mind" (Acts 20:19 KJV) and in honor prefer others before ourselves, remembering Paul's exhortation to his Philippian brethren: "Complete my joy by being of the same mind, having the same love, being in full accord and of one mind. Do nothing from selfish ambition or conceit, but in humility count others more significant than yourselves" (Phil. 2:2–3 ESV). Let us keep in mind the prayer of Jesus just before the shame and suffering of Pilate's judgment hall and the tragedy of the cross: "I pray that they will all be one, just as you and I are one—as you are in me, Father, and I am in you. And may they be in us so that the world will believe you sent me. . . . I am in them and you are in me. May they experience such perfect unity that the world will know that you sent me and that you love them as much as you love me" (John 17:21, 23 NLT).

May it always be so.

Recent Acts of the Holy Spirit

Someone has said that the Acts of the apostles should have been called the Acts of the Holy Spirit because it is there that the personality, work, and leadership of Him who is the "other Comforter" Jesus promised, are made manifest and shown large. And to show that He still works and leads, and makes men and women as triumphant and glad as in those faraway days of the apostles as in the days of Wesley and the early days of The Salvation Army, I want to pass on portions of two letters I recently received, one from an officer and one from a young soldier, one from the Pacific Coast and the other from the Atlantic seaboard.

The first wrote:

I feel I must write and tell you, knowing you will be interested, that on May 3rd of this year God wonderfully sanctified me.

Though for many years I had claimed the blessing, through the preaching of a wonderful man of God, I was shown that there were still carnal propensities dwelling in my heart. I have felt for some time that there was something wrong with my experience. I was not making the progress along spiritual lines I wanted to make, nor was I seeing the success I wanted to see.

That night I saw it all, and though it took me nearly a week to pray through, on the 3rd of May the work was really accomplished in my heart. What a wonderful peace filled my soul! I never experienced anything like it before. I really received the Holy Ghost that afternoon. He still abides.

As I see my experience now it is like this: About fourteen years ago I claimed the experience and have gone on ever since thinking I had the blessing, but the Devil simply duped me. Though God came to my help when I taught the experience, I was just duped, for I had never really died to sin and really never knew "the old man" to be crucified until the above date.

But now, thank God, there is something more than thinking. The work is done!

When we face our unsatisfactory experience courageously, willing to know the worst about ourselves, and set ourselves to pray before the Lord and to "pray through," the Holy Spirit will surely come and, having come, will abide. But before He can come in to abide, the old sinful nature must be crucified and put off. In closing his letter this brother wrote:

I presume you will remember me as a lieutenant at A_____ when you visited that place thirteen years ago. I remember this incident that occurred at that time. You gave me some letters to put in the post office and stood at the door while I mailed them. I remember distinctly looking at them to see to whom they were addressed. While it was not a sin against God, it was a sin against you and a very great breach of good manners. I want to apologize and ask your pardon.

I do not admit that the brother sinned against me but rather against his own conscience, but this is a fine illustration of the delicacy and tenderness of conscience the Holy Spirit begets, and how courteous and considerate of each other He would make us! And it is because of failure to obey the Spirit in such minor matters that many people are so spiritually coarse and unlovely, or so lean and barren in soul. "The little foxes . . . spoil the vines: for our vines have tender grapes" (Song 2:15 KJV).

The other letter read as follows:

I have been praying for you. As for me, I have entered into a new experience with Jesus. He has lifted me on to a higher plane and showed me things that I never saw before—more light, more love, more peace, more joy, and a better victory.

I have discovered many things about the Devil. It was God's will that I should go through such dark experiences as I wrote you about before. The Lord did not leave me, but He showed me the reality of the Devil and his tricks [see Eph. 6:11]. That certainly was "the slough of lespond," but I came out more than conqueror. Hallelujah!

The Devil surprises me by his perseverance. He is never discouraged. If he can't get the big things, he will try for the small ones. He is putting up a hard fight, but what can he do? The more I fight, the stronger I become and the more I love Jesus. I can't describe to you my experience with Jesus. It is glorious. Hallelujah! He pays me special visits, sometimes in shouting and jumping and the overflowing of the Spirit; and sometimes in calmness with a shower of tears. But, oh, how sweet those tears are! He does not leave me alone, although sometimes I think He does, but I find Him hiding behind that trouble, which He turns into a blessing later.

My heart is flooded with light, love, peace, and joy, and sometimes it is so overflowing that I can't bear it and do not know what to do with myself. Oh, what a change! It began about the time of our correspondence, when you were in C_____, and it is still going higher. The best is yet to come. Hallelujah!

I do not know that I ever saw anyone who had greater darkness and difficulties than this second writer. When I first met him about a year and a half ago, he was full of doubts and questionings and trouble and seemed almost hopelessly in the dark. Again and again he seemed about ready to give up entirely, but with help and encouragement he kept on praying, reading, seeking, and now he has found— and his joy is almost too big for utterance. If people who are not satisfied in their experience would take time to "pray through," they would find their dark tunnels leading out into a large place and into broad day. Jesus still lives and keeps "watch above His own"[1] who hunger to be right. And He pours out the Holy Spirit upon everyone who obeys Him and seeks Him wholeheartedly. But before we can be filled, we must be emptied. Before we can have the "more abundant life," we must die to sin. The old sinful nature must be crucified and put off before Jesus can abide in our hearts and satisfy the hunger of our souls.

Are you satisfied? If not, begin right now and stir up yourself to seek until you have found. Rouse yourself. Find a secret place and pray, and pray again, and yet again, and you shall "pray through" and be satisfied. I know, for I have prayed through. I know, for Jesus has said, "Keep on asking, and you will receive what you ask for. Keep on seeking, and you will find. Keep on knocking, and the door will be opened to you" (Matt. 7:7 NLT). And what Jesus has said is true. What the Lord did for those two writers, He waits and longs to do for you. He is no respecter of persons, and "now is the accepted time" (2 Cor. 6:2 KJV). Say to Him, as Charles Wesley did:

> In vain Thou strugglest to get free,
> I never will unloose my hold!
> Art Thou the Man who died for me?
> The secret of Thy love unfold;
> Wrestling, I will not let Thee go,
> Till I Thy name, Thy nature know.

Yield to me now, for I am weak,

But confident in self-despair;

Speak to my heart, in blessings speak,

Be conquered by my instant prayer;

Speak, or Thou never hence shalt move,

And tell me if Thy name is Love.[2]

And you will soon be crying out as did Wesley:

'Tis Love! 'Tis Love! Thou diedst for me!

I hear Thy whisper in my heart;

The morning breaks, the shadows flee,

Pure, universal love Thou art;

To me, to all, Thy bowels move;

Thy nature and Thy name is Love.[3]

NOTES

1. James Russell Lowell, "The Present Crisis," 1844, public domain.

2. Charles Wesley, "Come, O Thou Traveler Unknown," 1742, public domain.

3. Ibid.

The Traveling Evangelist 7

For many years now, my own work has been the work of a traveling evangelist or campaigner. For five years, long before I met The Salvation Army, I resisted the Lord's call to preach. I wanted to be a lawyer and enter politics. To my youthful mind—foolish, darkened, proud, ambitious—all the supreme prizes of life lay in that direction. I respected preachers, but not their job; it looked small to me, not a man's size. But at last a woe—a solemn, inescapable, eternal woe—faced me if I did not preach, and I surrendered.

Then I discovered that there were prizes, positions, and places of power in the ministry. But the job of the evangelist seemed to me to be beneath the dignity of a full-orbed man. Then one day, when in an agony of desire for purity of heart and the baptism of the Holy Spirit, God graciously sanctified me. The Holy Spirit took possession of my yielded, open heart. Christ was revealed in me, and a great passion for the saving and the sanctifying of others burned within me. About that time, a multimillionaire had built one of the finest churches in my native state, and the congregation through him was looking for a pastor. To my surprise I found that the vice president of my old university had recommended me, and one day I received a call to the pastorate of that church. I was elated. I felt that God Himself had opened a great door of opportunity and usefulness to me.

While still considering this call, I went three hundred miles to a holiness convention to sit under the ministry of some great teachers whose books had blessed me. Then God laid His hand upon me, and I knew that I was not to accept the call to that church! I found that which I had least esteemed, had most despised, was the work to which God called me and for which He had set me apart. I must be an evangelist. I felt ordained to this.

I was young, unknown, and in debt for a part of my education. I had no one to advise me. I was utterly alone and had no assurance that any church would welcome my evangelistic services. But on my knees I talked it over with the Lord as I would with an earthly friend and, by faith, into evangelistic work I plunged. Doors opened, and I saw many souls saved and sanctified. From that work, within ten months, I was led into The Salvation Army, where I found myself in London, blacking boots, scrubbing floors, and selling *War Crys*[1] as a cadet in the International Training School. After receiving my commission, I returned to the USA and commanded (in succession) three corps (churches), two divisions (local regions), and was second-in-command of each of the two principal territories in that country, with headquarters in Chicago and New York.

But "the gifts and calling of God are irrevocable" (Rom. 11:29 ESV), and the inner urge to do an evangelist's work was always with me. A great crisis struck The Salvation Army in America.[2] Our ranks were broken. Our people were full of distress and anxious questionings. Our battle line from the Atlantic to the Pacific, three thousand miles long, was in confusion. I felt, when in my office, a consuming desire to get out on the field; to meet our people face-to-face; to hearten, reassure, cheer, exhort, teach, and lead them, the distraught and sore perplexed, into "the fulness of the blessing of the gospel of Christ" (Rom. 15:29 KJV), and to win souls to the Savior. One day I sought and obtained an audience with the Consul,[3] asked her if I might speak to her about myself and my work, and then told her my convictions. Within three months I was appointed as a National Spiritual Special, and for about thirty years now I have been a traveling evangelist.

It has not been an easy job. It has often been lonely and wearying to the point of exhaustion. It has taxed my mind, challenged my will and utmost devotion, drunk up my spirit, and drained me to the dregs till there seemed to be no virtue left in me. And I have had to slip away into solitude, like my Master, to the mountains, for quiet communion and for the replenishing of exhausted reserves of power and the renewing of all life's forces. It has been a fight but not a defeat. I have not been forsaken. His presence has not failed me. He has assured me that the battle was not mine but His, and He has called on me to trust Him and be not afraid. Again and again I have heard His whisper in my heart, "Have I not commanded you? Be strong and courageous. Do not be frightened, and do not be dismayed, for the LORD your God is with you wherever you go" (Josh. 1:9 ESV), and

"Be steadfast, immovable . . . knowing that in the Lord your labor is not in vain" (1 Cor. 15:58 ESV). Sometimes the whisper has been sweet and full of comfort as the tender, cooing voice of a mother to a weary, distressed child. Sometimes it has been sharp and imperative as the staccato notes of a military command on a field of battle. I have not been mollycoddled. I have never for an instant been permitted to think I was God's pet and that I could expect special favors from Him. He has called me to share His cross and to endure hardness as a good soldier, not pleasing myself, not entangling myself with worldly interests or affairs that did not concern me, but to attend strictly to the work He has given me to do.

And now, out of some thirty years of experience as a traveling evangelist, let me write.

A Salvation Army officer told me the story of a wealthy Parsee from India, a silk exporter with great warehouses in Yokohama. After a flood of flame swept over the doomed city, burning to ashes in five hours sixty-nine thousand houses that in five minutes had been cast to the ground by the heaving earth, the officer and others sought the exporter where he had last been seen. All they could find of him was a small streak of ashes. He had been consumed by the fire.

One month before the fire—and the earthquake it accompanied—the Salvation Army officer who told me the story had visited him in his office asking for a donation to help The Salvation Army in its work for sailors in that city. He listened to the officer's plea, and then replied, "If you can tell me one thing you officers of The Salvation Army do which has not as its ultimate object the winning of people to Christ, then I will give you a liberal donation. But you cannot do it;

you wear uniforms, you march the streets, you carry banners, you beat drums and blow instruments, you conduct meetings, you open shelters and soup kitchens, you build citadels, you conduct training colleges, you run rescue homes, you publish books and papers and solicit money for just one object: to help you win souls to Christ and make them followers of Him. I do not believe in Christ. I do not need your Christ. I am rich, but I will give you nothing." A month later the earth-quake, the all-consuming fire, and the poor little handful of ashes!

The proud, self-complacent Parsee had grasped the central purpose of The Salvation Army. All its officers and workers have (or should have) this supreme object always in full view. But while there is one spirit and one object, there are manifold ministries to express that spirit and secure that object. There are "the apostles, the prophets, the evangelists, the pastors and teachers" (Eph. 4:11 NIV). Some serve tables as did Stephen, Philip, and others, and some give themselves wholly to the ministry of the word and prayer, as did Peter and the other apostles (see Acts 6:1–8). But all have one object to attain—the winning of souls from sin through faith in Christ, and the binding of them in vital union to Christ and making them channels of His saving grace to others.

The evangelist or "campaigner" is the person who, probably more directly than any other, labors to accomplish this great work. Corps officers, divisional commanders, departmental officers, and territo-rial leaders have many executive and administrative duties which do not bear so directly upon the saving of souls as does the work of the traveling evangelist. Their work is vitally essential in preparing the way for and conserving the work of soul-winning, but much that they do bears only indirectly upon the salvation of souls. Campaigners' work, however, is direct, immediate, unchanging. This one thing they do (see Phil. 3:13). The burden of caring for the flock, of collecting and administering finance, erecting buildings, and directing affairs, do not fall upon them as upon others. Their sole burden, their one responsibility, is for the souls of men and women. It is a secret burden, a responsibility which is laid upon them and which they assume in the silence and secret places of their own souls. It is elusive, known and measured only by God and them. It cannot be measured by a yardstick. It cannot be weighed on human scales. It cannot be tabulated in statistics. Campaigners belong to a divine order, just as prophets and apostles. They have a divine calling. Their gift is a divine bestowment, and they are among God's gifts to humanity. "These are the gifts Christ gave to the church: the . . . evangelists" (Eph. 4:11 NLT), whose sole business is the saving of souls, the perfecting of the saints, and the building up of the body of Christ on earth, which is composed of all true Christians.

If we judge the importance of this work in the mind of God by the place Paul assigns them when he mentions the various orders of ministry, then they stand next to the apostles and prophets and before the pastor and teacher.

When we consider this work we will see that this relationship is perfectly logical. The evangelists receive the revelation, the good news of God's love and plan of salvation through faith in Christ, from apostles and prophets, and then by bold and loving presentation of this revelation, this good news, they win souls and turn them over to the pastor to be shepherded, and to the teacher to be instructed in the things of God. Their great work is not the training of souls but the saving of them and, having accomplished this work, they pass on to other fields of labor. They do not erect the building, they provide the material (or, to change the figure, they lay the foundations others build on). They are "fishers of men" (Matt. 4:19 KJV); their business is to catch people. They are reapers of souls on the world's vast harvest fields. That is their one work, and to that they should give themselves with great joy and full and unwearied devotion. They may have other gifts, and if so should not neglect them but cultivate them to the full extent and make them contribute to and support their God-given gift and calling as an evangelist. They should not minimize their calling. They should not vex and discourage themselves by comparing it with that of others, with that of superiors who handle great affairs—as I knew one man to do, much to his own distress and the crippling, in some measure, of his splendid powers.

1. Traveling evangelists should magnify their office. It is true that they are individuals without authority to command and direct others and administer great business, and at times they may be oppressed with a feeling of their own insignificance. But they have spiritual authority, the authority which eternal truth bestows and with which God clothes chosen workers who work and labor in the power of the Holy Spirit. However small they may feel within themselves, they must not minimize their office. Their work is vital. It is God-ordained, and they are walking in the footsteps of the Master who, without any semblance of worldly power or human authority, was the first of their tribe.

Their one weapon is "the sword of the Spirit, which is the word of God" (Eph. 6:17 KJV). Their endowment of power for this work is none less than God the Holy Spirit. The almighty Holy Spirit goes with them to hearten, guide, and give insight, wisdom, courage, boldness in attack, patience in difficulty, and faith and hope in the blackest night. However lonely at times they may feel, they are not alone, "never, no, never alone."[4] They must stir up their faith, recognize the divine Presence, humbly acknowledge their dependence, boldly claim divine help, and draw freely upon the divine resources placed at the disposal of their faith.

It is the special campaigner themselves, and not the details of their campaigns, about which I write. Probably no two people—if left to themselves—would plan an evangelistic campaign exactly alike. Personally, I have never attempted anything spectacular, although I would not discourage this in others. Pageants, spectacular marches and uniforms, striking subjects, special music, all may be most useful to reach the crowd. I have found prayer meetings before a campaign—with personal visitations, announcements, and invitations—most helpful. They stir up interest and a devout, prayerful, expectant spirit that make victory assured.

Campaigners cannot make this initial preparation themselves. Regional and local leaders should do this work in advance of the campaign, and if they do it with heart and soul, and their own hearts are prepared for the visitation of the Spirit, victory is already in sight.

In all my campaigns, it is this preliminary work and this heart preparation for which I have pleaded, and for which I have in secret prayed.

2. Traveling evangelists must spend time and give all diligence to the preparation of their own hearts. If one's own heart is broken, he

or she can then break the hearts of others. If one's own heart is aflame, he or she can kindle a flame in other hearts. A striking program, a brilliant address, or a beautiful song may dazzle the crowd and play on the surface of their emotions, but it is only the passion of the cross that will bring them in contrition and brokenness of heart to the cross. Other things are important, but this preparation of the heart is the one thing without which all other things are empty and vain.

The founder of The Salvation Army, William Booth, always blamed himself if he did not succeed. It is true that other factors are at work for or against the campaign, and the campaigner should not be too quick to assume all the blame of failure. We know there were places where the Master could do no mighty works, because unbelief frustrated Him. And so it may be with us. But usually, if we are warm and tender, joyous and bold, and "full of faith and of the Holy Spirit" (Acts 6:5 ESV), no one will be able to stand before us (see Josh. 1:5). Results rich and enduring will reward our labor.

We must study to show ourselves approved unto God, workers who need not be ashamed (see 2 Tim. 2:15). God is not a hard Master, but He will not—cannot—lightly approve us. We must not presume on His goodwill, but with all watchfulness and diligence so work that He can approve, and that our hearts will not condemn, but will reassure us.

3. Traveling evangelists must exercise their spiritual senses lest, having eyes to see, they see not, and having ears to hear, they hear not (see Ezek. 12:2). They must have eyes that pierce through appearances, that can see the horses and chariots of fire where others see only the arrogant, encircling hosts of Syria. They must have ears to

hear the assuring voice of their Captain and distinguish it from the voices of self-interest, of expediency, and of the fiend who sometimes simulates and is "transformed into an angel of light" (2 Cor. 11:14 KJV). The author of Hebrews spoke approvingly of those "who by reason of use have their senses exercised to discern both good and evil" (Heb. 5:14 KJV). But beyond discernment of good and evil, the campaigner must have eyes to see victory where others see foredoomed defeat. The smallest crowd may have immeasurable possibilities in it. A Luther, Wesley, or William Booth may be looking out through the eyes of some little child or some awkward, shy, or mischievous, adolescent boy. An Elizabeth Fry, Catherine Booth, or Hannah Ouchterlony may spring forth from the chrysalis of some reserved girl who listens with rapt attention. Personally, I seldom speak to a congregation without thinking that I may be directly or indirectly addressing someone who shall yet be a prophet of the Highest, a herald to nations. Possibly I have been somewhat influenced by the results of my first sermon in my first appointment as a young preacher. In that first service, two people—a young man and a young woman—yielded to Christ, and the young man, principal of the public school, preached for me before the end of the year and went later as a missionary to India. Sometimes we reach them indirectly. We get some "nobody" saved and God uses that nobody to reach somebody who becomes great in the Lord's sight. Let us have no hesitancy in permitting our spiritual imagination to reinforce our faith and enkindle our hope and so sustain our courage in the face of massed and mocking foes and threatened defeat.

4. Traveling evangelists must be humble. They must seek nothing for themselves but be willing for others to carry off the so-called

prizes of this life. They are not "lords over God's heritage"; they are shepherds of the sheep, "examples to the flock" (1 Pet. 5:3 KJV). They hold no dominion over the faith of others, but are helpers of their joy (see 2 Cor. 1:24). Like John the Baptist, they are quite willing to decrease, if only Christ increases. Their joy is that of the friend of the Bridegroom (see John 3:29–30). Like Paul they are jealous for others "with the deep concern of God himself," desiring above all things that their "love should be for Christ alone, just as a pure maiden saves her love for one man only, for the one who will be her husband," but also frightened that they will be led away from a "pure and simple devotion to our Lord, just as Eve was deceived by Satan" (2 Cor. 11:2–3 TLB). And like Epaphras, they labor fervently in prayer that their spiritual progeny may stand perfect and complete in all the will of God (see Col. 4:12).

5. Finally, traveling evangelists—coming to an area or church with no power to command but only to preach and pray, to help and inspire, and to seek the lost—should be received as God's messengers, supported by love and prayers and understanding sympathy, and helped in their mission in every possible way, that Christ may be glorified, souls won, little children gathered into the fold, and all brothers and sisters quickened and sanctified.

NOTES

1. The flagship publication of The Salvation Army, published in many different versions around the world.

2. In 1896 Ballington Booth, son of the founders, William and Catherine Booth, resigned as national commander of The Salvation Army in the United States and, taking some personnel and property along with him, started the Volunteers of America.

3. Emma Booth-Tucker, who with her husband Frederick Booth-Tucker, was appointed to succeed Ballington and Maud Booth as national commanders of The Salvation Army in the US.

4. Ludie Carrington Day Pickett, "Never Alone," 1897, public domain.

Must You Be Fed with a Spoon? 8

I am watching with much interest and some personal profit the development of my grandchildren. They are a luxury to my old heart but, like all children, they are somewhat of a problem as well as a joy to their parents. At first, when brought to the table, they were fed with a spoon, but one day the spoon was put into their tiny hands and they were permitted to feed themselves. I was fascinated. The spoon would plunge into the porridge or applesauce and come up at various and sundry angles and start on a wobbling journey to the sweet, wee, wide-open mouth. Sometimes it would hit and sometimes it would miss. If it reached the open mouth, well. Its contents were soon lost in the dark "little red lane" below. But if it missed, or if there were miscalculation as to time and the mouth closed before the spoon arrived, it was awesome. The little mouth closed on air, and another plunge and wobbling effort was made. The bib and plate and platter were often a fearsome sight, and the small face was often battered and buttered in a way that was a joy to behold, but they were learning. It was the only way they could learn. They could not always be fed with a spoon by others. They must feed themselves, and someday they may have to feed others. But their first lesson is to feed themselves.

Of course, their food is all prepared for them by other hands. But the day will come when they will not only have to feed themselves, but they may have to prepare their own food. But before the food can be prepared, it must be found. The farmer must cultivate the soil and raise wheat and corn. The fisherman must catch the fish. The horticulturist must grow the fruit. The herdsmen must raise the cattle and sheep. And it is just possible that in some far-off day these children must not only feed themselves and prepare the food, but also go out and find the food to prepare and eat. Or they may toil for the money with which to buy from those who have labored to produce.

The feeding of men and women is a complex process, which we may live a lifetime without considering, but which is most instructive and humbling to consider.

Can you feed your own soul or must you still be fed? Do you prepare your own soul food or do others prepare it for you? Do you labor for it or do others give it to you?

One Salvation Army divisional commander said, "I will guarantee I can send the worst kind of backslidden officers to a certain corps, and in three months the soldiers will have prayed for them and helped them and loved them and gotten them so blessed that they will be on fire for God and souls."

Those soldiers were no longer spiritual babies who had to be fed with a spoon. No doubt they had vigorous spiritual appetites and enjoyed a meal of "strong meat" (Heb. 5:12 KJV) prepared for them. But they were no longer dependent. They were independent. They were no longer babes in Christ. They had exercised their senses (see Heb. 5:14) and become spiritual men and women, able to feed themselves, able to prepare their own food, and able to work and forage for themselves and find their own food. And not only so, but they were able to feed others. If their officers did not give them suitable soul food, then they fed the officers. If nobody blessed them, then they rose up in their splendid spiritual man- and womanhood and blessed somebody else, and so blessed themselves. Like the widow of Zarephath, who divided her poor little handful of meal and her few spoonsful of oil with Elijah and found the meal and oil unwasting through months of famine (see 1 Kings 17), so they gave of their spiritual food to more needy souls and found themselves enriched from God's unfailing supplies.

I know one of the finest Salvation Army bands in the USA, composed of a splendid group of soldiers, who for years would not have— and for all I know, to this day will not have—as a band member one who did not have the blessing of a clean heart. They said, "We want our band to be not only a combination of musical instruments, but also of harmonious hearts. We want to produce melody from our hearts as from our instruments. We cannot have discord in our band. We must have sweetest harmony." And so, before anyone was admitted as a member of the band, that person must not only give evidence of the ability to play an instrument, but also show the ability to live peaceably, humbly, lovingly, and loyally with others. They were prepared to pray with him or her and lead this person into the blessed experience of holiness, perfect love, purity and power, and then gladly accept him or her as a member of the band. They could feed themselves and others too. And that band became a great spiritual influence in that city and famous for a hundred miles around.

One day Paul came to Corinth and found a man named Aquila and his wife, Priscilla, and he lived and worked with them, because they were tentmakers just as he was. But they later moved to Ephesus, and then one day an eloquent man named Apollos, who was mighty in the Scriptures, fervent in spirit, and speaking and teaching diligently the things of the Lord, came to the city. He was a great orator, teacher, and preacher. But this humble tentmaker and his wife had learned more from Paul than Apollos knew, so they invited him home to dinner with them, "and expounded unto him the way of the Lord more perfectly" (Acts 18:26 KJV).

Aquila and Priscilla had learned to feed themselves and others too—even such a man as Apollos, eloquent, burning with zeal and mighty in the Scriptures. They must have had fullness of love and very gracious ways, and a divine tact to approach a great man like that and lead him into fullness of blessing. Oh, that we were all like that!

One evening I found myself sitting with a fellow Salvation Army officer after a soul-stirring meeting on our way to our lodgings.

"I was at the penitent form [the kneeler for confession]," he said.

"Were you? I missed you and wondered where you were." I had seen him sitting down in the audience while the speaker poured out his heart in a torrent of searching truth upon the crowd. There was a look on his face that puzzled me. I was not sure whether defiance, cynicism, questioning, indifference, or soul hunger was revealed in that look. When the prayer meeting began, every head was bowed, but he sat erect with that puzzling look in his face intensified. People were melting and flowing down to the penitent form, but still he sat erect, open-eyed, apparently unmoved. I knelt to deal with seekers, and when I looked again he was gone, and not until after the meeting did I learn that he had been to the penitent form.

"Yes, I was at the penitent form. An old officer came and asked if he could help me, but I told him, 'No, I want to be left alone.' I was vexed; half angry."

"Angry! What were you angry about?"

"Well, while I listened to the speaker, I wondered, 'Why don't our leaders feed us young fellows? They don't have meetings with us. Why don't they help us?'"

I had up to that time thought of him as a youngster. He belongs to the younger set of officers. I had known him since he was a small lad, and I had always thought of him as a young man, but when he called himself a "young fellow" my mind turned a somersault. I looked at him and asked, "How old are you?"

"Thirty-five."

"And you have been married thirteen years and have a family of children, the oldest of whom is twelve. You are not a young fellow. You are a middle-aged man. And you want your leaders to feed you. But that is not what you need. You need to feed yourself. Your leaders cannot tell you anything you do not know. But do you diligently practice what you know? You don't pray enough. You do not search the Scriptures and feed on the Word of God as you should. 'Man shall not live by bread alone, but by every word . . . of God' [Matt. 4:4 NKJV]. Is not that your trouble? Do you deny yourself as you should? Do you search for soul food in good books? Or do you not spend more time reading the sporting page of the morning and evening papers than you spend over your Bible and books that would enrich your mind and heart? Are you not starving yourself and waiting for someone to come and feed you, when you should be feeding yourself?"

I once knew a man who, when I first met him, was sodden with drink. But within a few days he was saved and sanctified. Shortly after, he became an officer, and then got himself a small but choice library of the most deeply spiritual books. He would sit up till after midnight reading, praying, and meditating on what he read, until in a short time I marveled at him. His mind was all alert, his soul was on fire, and his mental and spiritual equipment was a joy to those who knew him. He labored for spiritual food, and grew in mental and spiritual stature and in favor with God and man. And he was soon able to feed others. Whenever I met him, he wanted to talk about spiritual things. His grasp of doctrine, his knowledge of Scripture and holiness literature, and his intimate acquaintance and communion with God delighted and refreshed me. He was an ordinary country boy, but he became extraordinary by the diligence with which he sought fellowship with God, the eagerness with which he hunted for truth from books and from experienced people, and the loving zeal with which he sought to impart the truth to other souls about him.

Wise old Nehemiah said, "Go your way, eat the fat, and drink the sweet, and send portions unto them for whom nothing is prepared" (Neh. 8:10 KJV).

Learn to feed yourself, and also to share your soul food with yet needier souls, and so you shall know no soul famine, but be "fat and flourishing" (Ps. 92:14 KJV).

First Things First

9

One of the outstanding ironies of history is the utter disregard of ranks and titles in the final judgments human beings pass upon each other. And if this is so of us, how much more must it be so of the judgments of God.

Nero and Marcus Aurelius each sat upon the throne of Rome clothed with absolute power and worshiped as gods, but what a difference! Nero, a monster of iniquity and utter cruelty, execrated of all; Aurelius, a vigorous administrator and benign philosopher, writing meditations which the wise and learned still delight to read and ponder and which after two millennia are a guide to safe and useful living.

Napoleon and Washington were two great statesmen and military leaders. But what a difference! One a ruthless conqueror, building a glittering and evanescent empire on an ocean of blood, dying an exile on a lonely isle with a character for heartless selfishness which sinks lower and lower every year in the estimation of all right-thinking people. The other refusing a crown, but laying the firm foundations of a state destined to be infinitely greater than Napoleon's empire, and dying at last honored by his former foes, with a character above reproach, revered and beloved of all.

Judas and John were two apostles. But what a difference! One was a devil, betraying his Master with a kiss for a paltry handful of silver and making his name a synonym for all infamy and treachery. The other pillowed his head on the Master's bosom and with wide open eyes was permitted to look deep into heaven, behold the great white throne and Him who sat upon it, the worshiping angel hosts, the innumerable multitudes of the redeemed, the glory of the Lamb that was slain, and the face of the everlasting Father, while his name became a synonym for reverence and adoring love.

This summing up and final estimate of these men shows that history cares not an iota for rank or title, but only for the quality of one's deeds and the character of one's mind and heart.

The haughty patricians of Rome doubtless passed by with contemptuous indifference or scorn as the scarred Jewish prisoner, Paul, with sore eyes and wearied feet, went clanking by in chains to the dungeon. But their names have perished, while his name is enshrined in millions of hearts and embalmed in colleges, cathedrals, and cities, and libraries of books are reverently written about his character, his sufferings, and his work.

Who remembers the Lord Bishops of England in Bunyan's day? But what unnumbered Christian hearts have turned with tears of deepest gratitude and tenderest affection and sympathy to the humble, joyous, inspired tinker, who from the filthy, verminous Bedford jail sent forth his immortal story of Pilgrim fleeing from the city of destruction? How many recall Pilgrim as he escaped with hopes and fears and tears and prayers and sighs and songs, pressing on over hills of difficulty, through sloughs of despond, past bewitching bowers of beguiling temptations and giants of despair and castles of doubt, till at last he beheld the delectable mountains, viewed not far away the city of the great King, heard the music of celestial harpers playing on their harps of gold, and, passing through the swelling river, was received with glad welcome on the other shore!

Those whom history acclaims, posterity reveres, and God crowns are those who put first things first, to whom first things have first place in all their thoughts, plans, affections, and activities.

So what shall be first with us? Many hands stretch out toward us, and many voices plead with us for first place. Which shall have the primacy? Which shall have our last thoughts when falling asleep at night and our first thoughts on awaking in the morning?

There are many things that make so subtle and apparently so reasonable an appeal that, if we do not watch and pray and keep in the Spirit, they will usurp first place, and we shall someday wake up and find that we have been bowing down to an idol instead of to the living God.

We may put our work first. Is it not commanded, "Whatever your hand finds to do, do it with your might" (Eccl. 9:10 ESV)? And aren't we exhorted to be "not slothful in business" (Rom. 12:11 KJV)? And are we not assured that "a man who excels in his work . . . will stand before kings" (Prov. 22:29 NKJV)? Is not our work God's work? And can anything equal it in importance? Are we not warned that if we are careless we shall be cursed? If we are slothful, our talent shall be taken from us, given to another, and we ourselves cast out into outer darkness as wicked and slothful servants, where we shall fruitlessly weep and gnash our teeth. Is not our work the building of God's kingdom on earth, the rescue of men and women from sin and its eternal woe? Yes, yes, yes, it is all that, and no words can express the infinity of its importance. But it must not have first place. If it does, we ourselves shall be lost. "On judgment day many will say to me, 'Lord! Lord! We prophesied in your name and cast out demons in your name and performed many miracles in your name.' But I will reply, 'I never knew you'" (Matt. 7:22–23 NLT). Solemn words these, spoken by the Master.

Many years ago, I was billeted with one of the most brilliant and capable staff officers I have known. We had had a great meeting that night and got to bed late and wearied but, according to my custom, I was up early the next morning, seeking God, reading my Bible, and praying. The blessing of the Lord came upon me and I burst into tears. My companion woke up and found me praying, weeping, and rejoicing. He was much moved and confessed to me that he did not often sense that he had found God when he was praying, and explained that he was so busy, so pressed with his work, so absorbed and fascinated with it, that when he prayed his mind wandered to things he should do during the day so he seldom got into real touch and fellowship with God. I earnestly warned him of the danger this meant to his own soul and eventually to his work, the dryness and spiritual barrenness that must come upon him if, through the multiplicity of cares and the pressure of work, God was crowded out or pushed into the background of his life. He admitted the truth of all I said, but he still put his work first. He rose rapidly in rank and important command, then suddenly dropped out of his ministry over some trifling matter and has long been dead. Did his exceptionally bright and promising career end in darkness because he failed to put first things first? I have feared so.

It is possible to so far lose sight of first things that we come at last to do much if not all our work with an eye to our own promotion and future career. We may become embittered toward our leaders and jealous toward our coworkers if we are not promoted as rapidly as others, or if our position does not correspond to what we consider our due. It is a most subtle danger, and through it many a person's splendid spiritual career has come to an end, while he or she yet goes on in a perfunctory performance of official duties, beating time, moving but not progressing, doing no vital and lasting work for God and souls. Of such it could be written, "You have the reputation of being alive, but you are dead" (Rev. 3:1 ESV). I have met people who spent more time repining and complaining and inwardly rebelling about not being promoted than they did in studying and working and fitting themselves for the work that promotion would thrust upon them. "It's not good to seek honors for yourself," wrote Solomon (Prov. 25:27 NLT), but such people quite overlook such texts as that, and while they may attain the desire of their heart, they miss the glory that God gives.

Personally, an awful fear has shaken me at times—the thought that a person may get in this world all the honor and glory that he or she seeks, and find in the next world that there is nothing further coming, like workers who draw an advance on their salary and at the end of the week or month or year have nothing to receive. In the story of the rich man and Lazarus, Abraham said to the rich man, "Son, remember that during your lifetime you had everything you wanted" (Luke 16:25 NLT) and there was nothing due to him in that new world to which his soul had been so suddenly snatched away. He had not put first things first, and he who proudly scorned the poor beggar Lazarus at his gate now found himself an eternal pauper and beggar in hell.

We may gradually put our family first. It has been said that until the age of forty-five we say, "What can I do to advance myself?" After forty-five we say, "What can I do to provide for and advance my children?" However, this may become a deadly snare. Parents' ambition or anxiety may override sober judgment and compromise their devotion to God's cause. "Whoever loves son or daughter more than me is not worthy of me," said Jesus (Matt. 10:37 ESV).

We may put our own culture first. This is not a widespread danger among us, and yet it may become to some a very subtle danger. Study, reading, travel, the cultivation of the mind, and the gratifying of taste may lead to the neglect of God's work and the drying up of the fountains of spiritual power. Personal growth is not to be despised, but rather coveted. The better informed and the wiser and more cultivated we are, provided we are dedicated wholly to God and set on fire with spiritual passion, the more effectually can we glorify God and serve others. It is true that "God chose things the world considers foolish in order to shame those who think they are wise. And he chose things that are powerless to shame those who are powerful. God chose things despised by the world, things counted as nothing at all, and used them to bring to nothing what the world considers important. As a result, no one can ever boast in the presence of God" (1 Cor. 1:27–29 NLT). But

He also chose Moses, educated in all the learning of Egypt, the most cultured man of his age, and Paul, educated at the universities of Tarsus and Jerusalem, for the great work of the ages. Not many such has God chosen, because not often do such cultured individuals choose Christ and the cross. But God can and does use culture, when dedicated wholly to His service, and we should not despise it, but covet it and take every legitimate opportunity to secure it. But woe to those who put it first in their thought and effort. God will laugh at such people, pass them by, and give their crowns to little illiterate nobodies who love, trust, shout, sing, know nothing but Jesus Christ and His crucifixion, and count not their lives dear to themselves, wanting only that they may win the souls for whom the Savior died.

If we would put first things first, we must be ready at any moment to lay aside our books, our music, our studies, our business, and our own pleasure and profit to save souls.

The founder of The Salvation Army, William Booth, on the train in Switzerland, was writing an article when members of his staff called him to look at the Alps towering upward into the blue heavens, gleaming in white, majestic splendor. But his heart and mind were so absorbed with his work and the greater splendors of the Spirit, and of redeeming love, that he would hardly lift his eyes from the work in which he was lost. Again and again I have had to practice this kind of stern self-denial in my world travels if I would keep first things first.

Museums which house the symbols of a nation's history and the products of its genius and labor are a medium of culture. I once spent two weeks within two or three stone-throws of one of Europe's national museums, and passing it on several occasions, longed to run in and spend some time among its strange and ancient treasures. But a mighty work of the Spirit was going on, my time was short, and hungry souls so thronged me, both in and between the meetings, that I had to deny them or deny myself the pleasure and instruction I might have found in that treasure house of science and art and natural wonders. To some it might have made no appeal. To me it did, but it was denied in order that first things might have first place, and any regret for my loss is swallowed up in the joy of my greater gain and the gain of those precious souls to whom I ministered.

This demand that first things shall have first place is not simply a demand of the spiritual life, but of all life, of every profession and activity. The soldier must not entangle him- or herself with the secular affairs of life. The lawyer must make law his or her mistress and give it full devotion. The physician must put the profession of healing before all business or pleasure. The student must deny him- or herself and hold everything secondary to studies. The true lover must forsake all others for the one who is enshrined in his or her heart's best affections.

What, then, shall be first in our thoughts, our affections, our life? What must be placed first is that which, were we to lose it, would mean the loss of all. To lose God is the sum of all loss. If we lose Him, we lose all. If we lose all and still have Him, we shall in Him again find all. "I once thought these things were valuable," wrote Paul, "but now I consider them worthless because of what Christ has done. Yes, everything else is worthless when compared with the infinite value of knowing Christ Jesus my Lord. For his sake I have discarded everything else, counting it all as garbage" (Phil. 3:7–8 NLT). And yet this poor man, persecuted, hated, hunted, stripped of all things, cried out to his brothers in like poverty, "All things are yours: whether Paul, or Apollos, or Cephas, or the world, or life, or death, or things present, or things to come—all are yours. And ye are Christ's, and Christ is God's" (1 Cor. 3:21–23 KJV). "Seek me and live" (Amos 5:4 ESV) is God's everlasting plea to you and me. Uzziah sought God and "as long as he sought the LORD, God made him to prosper. . . . He was marvellously helped, till he was strong. But when he was strong, his heart was lifted up to his destruction: for he transgressed against the LORD his God" (2 Chron. 26:5, 15–16 KJV).

What a grim, revealing glimpse we have in those words, down the long, dim vista of three millennia into the secret of that old king's glory and doom! And "they were written down for our instruction, on whom the end of the ages has come" (1 Cor. 10:11 ESV).

Many years ago I heard the founder of The Salvation Army, in an impassioned plea to his people to wait on God, cry out, "Men are losing God every day, and I should lose Him if out of my busy life I did not take time every day to seek His face." And in a letter quoted by Harold Begbie, he wrote:

> I wish I could have a little more time for *meditation* about *eternal* things. I must not let my soul get dried up with secular affairs—even though they concern the highest earthly interests of my fellows. After all, *soul* matters are of infinite importance and are really most closely concerned with earthly advantages.[1]

If it was so with King Uzziah and with our revered founder, it is so with us! These men, though dead, yet speak to us. And though they came back to us as the rich man who begged Abraham for Lazarus to come back with warning to his brothers, yet they could have no other message, they could not speak otherwise. They have spoken their final word, and to me, at least, it is the word of the Lord.

As the psalmist said, "When You said, 'Seek My face,' my heart said to You, 'Your face, LORD, I will seek'" (Ps. 27:8 NKJV).

Thou, O Christ, art all I want,

More than all in Thee I find.[2]

NOTES

1. Harold Begbie, *The Life of General William Booth: The Founder of The Salvation Army* (London: Macmillan and Company, 1926), 234.

2. Charles Wesley, "Jesus, Lover of My Soul," 1740, public domain.

God Is Faithful

10

A devout woman wrote me a letter from Texas recently and said, "My text for today is, 'He that is faithful in that which is least is faithful also in much; and he that is unjust [unrighteous] in the least is unjust [unrighteous] also in much' (Luke 16:10 KJV)."

What searching words of the Savior are those! They should give us pause. They should set us to searching and judging ourselves. And this searching should enter into all departments of our lives. This judgment should be as before God's eyes, it should be unsparing—far more so than our judgment upon our neighbors. When we judge them, we may do ourselves and them great harm and injustice and bring upon ourselves judgment and condemnation, for we are bidden not to sit in judgment upon others. "Judge not," said Jesus (Matt. 7:1 KJV). "Who are you to judge your neighbor?" wrote James (James 4:12 ESV). But if we candidly and impartially judge ourselves, we may thereby do ourselves and others great good and so escape the judgment of God, for "if we judged ourselves truly"—and so correct ourselves—"we would not be judged," wrote Paul (1 Cor. 11:31 ESV).

So if we would be "faithful in that which is least," what are some of the least things?

Are we faithful in the use of money? Jesus was talking about business and money when He spoke of being "faithful in that which is least." Personally, I have for many years felt that one-tenth of all I had belonged to God. A distinguished Christian leader said to me one day, "You have given yourself to God, why give Him your money?" I confess I was deeply surprised, if not shocked. I ask others to give, and I would feel myself utterly faithless if I did not give freely to my Master's cause and to His poor as I am able.

Are we faithful in the use of our time? Do we gather up the minutes for some useful employment, for prayer, for reading, for visiting? Some people waste much time at night which they should spend in bed, and then they waste much time in bed the next morning when they should be up studying, praying, rejoicing, and attending to the day's duties.

Are we faithful in our speech? Little words are continually slipping out through the portals of our lips. Are they words we would say in Jesus' presence? I was much struck recently as I read Psalm 12, in which God confronted people over their words and they proudly and insolently replied, "Our lips are our own—who can stop us?" (Ps. 12:4 NLT). "The tongue is a small thing," wrote the apostle James (James 3:5 NLT). Are we faithful in its use, or are we careless, thoughtless, foolish, and wicked? For every idle, harmful word we shall have to give an account and we shall be brought into judgment, said the Master (see Matt. 12:36). Oh, how important it is to be faithful in our speech.

Are we faithful in the use of eyes and ears and hands and feet? Are we faithful with ourselves, our hearts, our consciences, our imaginations? Do we live as in God's sight, seeking always to do the things that please Him, so that we have the sweet, silent whisper in our hearts, "My beloved child in whom I am well pleased"?

The apostle John wrote to "the beloved Gaius. . . . Beloved, you do faithfully whatever you do" (3 John 1, 5 NKJV). If you and I do likewise, someday a greater one than John will say to us, "Well done, good and faithful servant. You have been faithful over a little; I will set you over much. Enter into the joy of your master" (Matt. 25:23 ESV).

The Bible and Religious Experience 11

We do not discover God. God reveals Himself to us. God seeks us before we seek God. God reveals His wisdom and power through nature. He reveals His holiness through conscience. He reveals His hatred of sin through His judgments. He reveals His redeeming love through faith. We see God's power in starry heavens, storm-swept seas, rushing rivers, lofty mountains, flaming volcanoes, devastating tornadoes, and in the silent forces irresistibly lifting mighty forests from tiny seeds and holding them aloft in columnar strength and beauty against wind and storm from century to century.

We see the wisdom of God in the marvelous adaptations of nature: the way the eye responds to light and color, the ear to sound, the nose to odors, the tongue to flavors, the skin to heat and cold; how the thumb and fingers set ever so aptly against each other; the processes of the organs of digestion and peristaltic and cardiac action; the varieties of plants and animals; the differences between individuals; and the bond of mother and child.

We see the redeeming love of God in Christ, in His works of pity and mercy, but most clearly in His atoning death on the cross.

But all this manifold unveiling and revelation of Himself God sums up in His Word. He declares Himself in the Scriptures, and therein we see Him as though reflected in a perfect mirror. We read, "The LORD revealed himself to Samuel in Shiloh by the word of the LORD" (1 Sam. 3:21 KJV). He declares His power, His wisdom, His knowledge, His holiness, His righteousness, His mercy, His everlasting love, His redeeming purpose, and His plan in His Word. And this Word is vitally related to all satisfying and assured Christian experience. It floods the Christian with light. It reveals to us God's benevolent and passionately active interest in us. It shows the way and spirit in which to seek God, and the condition of pardon, purity, and power. And when we have met these conditions, the Holy Spirit applies the words of Scripture to our hearts with life-giving energy, so that that text in Proverbs is fulfilled in our experience: "When you walk, their counsel will lead you. When you sleep, they will protect you. When you wake up, they will advise you" (Prov. 6:22 NLT).

Nature only partially reveals God, and the wisest people stumble and falter in trying to interpret God through nature. But in the Word of God we find Him fully and plainly revealed to the obedient and trusting soul.

But even the Scriptures fail to reveal God in all His beauty unless with penitence and faith we have drawn near to Him, been born from above, and been sanctified by the incoming of the Holy Spirit. The Book is in large measure sealed to unspiritual minds.

When Jesus prayed, "Father, bring glory to your name," we read that a voice came from heaven, saying, "I have already brought glory to my name, and I will do so again" (John 12:28 NLT), and people interpreted the voice according to their spiritual condition and relationship. "Some thought it was thunder"—a material interpretation; it had no spiritual significance to them. Others said "an angel had spoken to him"—a spiritualistic interpretation. Only Jesus heard the voice of the everlasting Father. "The voice was for your benefit, not mine," said He (John 12:29–30 NLT).

> Where one heard noise, and one saw flame,
> I only knew He named my name.[1]

One person will read the Old Testament and see nothing but myths; scraps of legendary history; folklore; a record of dreams; bits of biography; exaggerated stories of fights, battles, and wars of semi-savage tribes; and songs of a people slowly emerging from barbarism into civilization.

Another will read it and discover God down among His wayward creatures in their spiritual childhood revealing Himself to them in dreams, visions, judgments, deliverances, special providence, and His Word through His prophets, as they were able to bear the great unveiling, until at last the final and full revelation came in Christ: "In the past God spoke to our ancestors through the prophets at many times and in various ways, but in these last days he has spoken to us by his Son" (Heb. 1:1–2 NIV).

Well may we pray David's prayer (I have prayed it a thousand times): "Open my eyes that I may see wonderful things in your law"

(Ps. 119:18 NIV). And well may we covet the experience of the disciples: "Then he opened their minds to understand the Scriptures" (Luke 24:45 ESV).

It was this that happened to Paul on the road to Damascus (see Acts 9). His spiritual eyes were opened. He saw God in Christ, and the old Scriptures with which he was so familiar took on new meaning, so that he said, "Whatever was written in former days was written for our instruction, that through endurance and through the encouragement of the Scriptures we might have hope" (Rom. 15:4 ESV). When he read the story of the wanderings of his people in the wilderness on their way from Egypt to the land of promise, and how they were overthrown and perished in the wilderness, he recognized God's displeasure and saw a warning example: "Now these things took place as examples for us, that we might not desire evil as they did. . . . They were written down for our instruction, on whom the end of the ages has come" (1 Cor. 10:6, 11 ESV). And to Timothy he wrote, "All Scripture is inspired by God and is useful to teach us what is true and to make us realize what is wrong in our lives. It corrects us when we are wrong and teaches us to do what is right. God uses it to prepare and equip his people to do every good work" (2 Tim. 3:16–17 NLT).

It was this that happened to Martin Luther as on his knees he painfully climbed the stairway in St. Peter's in Rome, and the still small voice sounded in his soul: "The just shall live by faith" (Rom. 1:17 KJV). Scales dropped from the eyes of his soul, God's kindly purpose and way of salvation by faith was seen, and the Scriptures flamed with new and spiritual meaning and became the passionate study of his remaining years.

It was this that happened to Augustine, the brilliant young rhetorician and libertine of Carthage, as—deeply convicted of sin and spiritual impotence—he walked in his garden. He heard a voice in his inner ear that said, "Take and read." And taking up Paul's letter to the Romans he read, "The night is far gone; the day is at hand. So then let us cast off the works of darkness and put on the armor of light. Let us walk properly as in the daytime, not in orgies and drunkenness, not in sexual immorality and sensuality, not in quarreling and jealousy. But put on the Lord Jesus Christ, and make no provision for the flesh, to gratify its desires" (Rom. 13:12–14 ESV). Instantly his inner being flamed with spiritual light. The chains of his fleshly lusts and evil habits fell off, the dungeon doors of his soul flew open, he walked out into the broad day of God's deliverance and salvation, and the Scriptures henceforth were a lamp to his feet (see Ps. 119:105).

The Word of the Lord came in searching experiences and travailings of spirit as God drew near and revealed His will, His name, and His nature to men and women. It came not "from human initiative," wrote Peter. "No, those prophets were moved by the Holy Spirit, and they spoke from God." And he assures us that "because of that experience, we have even greater confidence in the message proclaimed by the prophets. You must pay close attention to what they wrote, for their words are like a lamp shining in a dark place—until the Day dawns, and Christ the Morning Star shines in your hearts" (2 Pet. 1:19–21 NLT).

Ezekiel said, "The word of the LORD came unto me" (Ezek. 3:16 KJV).

Jeremiah wrote, "The word of the LORD came unto me" (Jer. 1:4 KJV).

The book of Genesis says, "Now the LORD had said unto Abraham" (Gen. 12:1 KJV).

And later Jeremiah wrote, "The LORD appeared to us in the past, saying: 'I have loved you with an everlasting love; I have drawn you with unfailing kindness'" (Jer. 31:3 NIV).

The Bible is inspired. There has been much questioning and debate about the nature and extent of biblical inspiration. Some Bible lovers maintain that every word was given by inspiration, while others have argued that the writers chose their own words in which to express the thoughts and revelations welling up within them. But a thoughtful study seems to plainly show that some of the words were given while others were chosen by the writers.

Paul was troubled with a thorn in the flesh, and three times prayed for deliverance from it. Then Jesus spoke to him, and Paul gave us His very words which, translated, read: "My grace is all you need. My power works best in weakness." Those words so assured and satisfied and inspired Paul that he cried out, "So now I am glad to boast about my weaknesses, so that the power of Christ can work through me. That's why I take pleasure in my weaknesses, and in the insults, hardships, persecutions, and troubles that I suffer for Christ. For when I am weak, then I am strong" (2 Cor. 12:9–10 NLT). There is no reason to suppose that those exact words were put into Paul's mouth. It is sufficient to know that the words of Jesus thrilled and cheered and inspired him into glad submission to the will and purpose of God in his affliction, and in his joy and satisfaction his heart overflowed with devotion to his Lord and found verbal expression in these words.

One day the psalmist was so filled with the sense of God's forgiving love and provident care that his whole soul bubbled over in song, and he cried out: "Bless the LORD, O my soul, and all that is within me, bless his holy name! Bless the LORD, O my soul, and forget not all his benefits, who forgives all your iniquity, who heals all your diseases, who redeems your life from the pit, who crowns you with steadfast love and mercy, who satisfies you with good so that your youth is renewed like the eagle's" (Ps. 103:1–5 ESV).

Those words are the words of the writer, but they are written in the glad sense of all God's tender care and goodness and redeeming love, out of a heart that is inspired by the ever-present Holy Spirit to adoring worship and praise. The words are the words of the writer, but the rich experience and deep feelings and adoring wonder from which they flowed are the work and inspiration of the Holy One of Israel.

"I know the Bible is inspired," wrote a great soul-winner, "because it inspires me."[2] And so it does to everyone who, wholly devoted to Christ and simply trusting, is filled with the Spirit. It speaks as the very voice of God. God is in the Word and "the very words . . . are spirit and life" (John 6:63 NLT).

The manner and extent of inspiration may always be a matter of debate, but the fact of inspiration is the joy and strength of every "twice-born" soul.

The Bible is invaluable in personal dealing. "You will always have the poor among you," said the Master (John 12:8 NLT), and we must wisely and adequately minister to their pitiful and crying words. But it is equally probable that the feeble-minded and the weak will be ever with us. And Paul has exhorted and instructed us to comfort and support them and to be patient.

But there is another class, the chronic seekers who, times without number, come to the penitent form, who seem to be tramping forever on an endless treadmill, who are with us and need wise and patient help as much or more than any other class of people. They have been to the penitent form so often that many have lost interest in them and have but little, if any, hope for them. But they are a challenge to our faith, love, pity, patience, spiritual intelligence, and resourcefulness. We must not let them perish in full view, and we must not let them slip away from view and perish in the night. They belong to us. They are our charge, and, if possible, we must win them and lead them into a joyful experience of salvation and perfect love. We need to take ourselves in hand in dealing with them, for possibly their failure is an evidence of our weakness of faith; our lack of burning, compassionate zeal; or of our spiritual and mental ignorance, poverty, and laziness.

We need to do some sober, hard thinking, some real praying, and "stir up the gift of God" within us (2 Tim. 1:6 KJV) if we are to fathom their deep needs and help them. Personally, I fear that in many instances it is the faulty, hasty way they are dealt with in prayer that accounts in part, if not wholly, for their miserable failures. "A curse on anyone who is lax in doing the LORD's work!" wrote Jeremiah (Jer. 48:10 NIV).

A thousand times I have trembled for seekers as I have seen people dealing with them who I have feared needed help themselves. Solomon said, "He who wins souls is wise" (Prov. 11:30 NKJV).

In the old days, when my hearing was more acute, I seldom let anyone leave the penitent form without dealing with the person myself. It was a great tax upon my time and strength, but my heart would not rest in peace until I had done my utmost to lead each one into light and into the sweet and assured rest of faith.

I felt I must make full proof of my ministry, and I measured its acceptance with God, and its harmony with His truth and His principles and Spirit, by its fruits in joyously saved and sanctified souls.

I once conducted meetings in a splendid city in which the territorial headquarters of The Salvation Army for that country is located. In it are many flourishing corps (churches) and service centers which command the respect and high regard of the citizens of both high and low degree.

In two corps in residential sections of that city, I conducted meetings that were well attended and in which people responded promptly to my invitations. Then I went downtown to the corps at the territorial headquarters. There, too, the crowds were large and attentive, but it was next to impossible to get anyone to the penitent form except as a result of the most dogged personal dealing and persuasion. To me this was a sore disappointment, for I always feel that if I preach the truth in love, luminously, pointedly, persuasively, with constant reliance upon the Holy Spirit, the people will promptly yield to my invitations, and if they do not do so, I feel the trouble must be with my spirit or manner of preaching.

I had been to this corps on two different occasions before, and the people seemed much more responsive at that time. I wondered at the present hardness.

After I had preached and poured out my heart upon the people, prayer warriors promptly began to "fish,"[3] but it was only after long effort that they would lead anyone to the penitent form. This continued for several meetings, and I was greatly perplexed. I noticed that those who came did not seem to be broken in spirit. There were no tears, but neither was there any levity. Usually there was a hard, set look on the faces of those who came, which seemed to say, "Well, if I must, I will, but I feel it is useless to come. Nothing will happen." I noted further that as soon as anyone knelt at the penitent form someone would rush to his or her side, enter into conversation, and in a few minutes look up and say that he or she was all right. The seeker then would rise up with the same hard, set expression and take a seat. There was no tear in the eye, no light on the face, nothing that indicated that he or she had met with Jesus and found a great deliverance and peace.

On inquiry I found that most of those who were coming to the penitent form were well-known to the local leaders and had been forward again and again.

Loud music and singing in the prayer meeting may keep up a lively interest, but they sadly interfere with my hearing, so that it is most difficult for me to deal with seekers. I tried to find out how these people at the penitent form were being dealt with, and I discovered that they were usually asked one or two questions, told to obey God and trust, asked if they would do so, and when they said they would they were sent to their seat, as dead and hopeless, apparently, as when they came.

In some instances where their weaknesses and failures were well known they were dealt with in a severe, unsympathetic way that seemed to me anything but helpful, and quite unbecoming from any who felt that they themselves had been hewn from the rock and lifted out of miry clay. Sinners saved by grace must be careful how they deal with fellow sinners, lest, like Moses, they find that they have displeased the Lord.

Finally, a member of that corps came to the penitent form and not only threw himself down on his knees, but fell upon it in a way that seemed to me to indicate hopelessness. I took my Bible and knelt beside him, and I soon found out that he had come there again and again, that his trouble was fleshly sin, that he loathed himself, but that he felt powerless when temptation was upon him. He was eager to break away from his sin, but felt that he was its servant (see John 8:34; Rom. 6:16), its bond slave, and it mocked his struggles and good resolutions to quit it and be free. I felt, I saw, that hitherto he had been led to make resolutions and promises and told to trust in Christ, but that he had never been made to really see Christ as his Lord, his Redeemer, his Savior, who was down with him on his battlefield. I felt I must make him see this, and to this I set myself with prayer and full purpose of heart.

I told him he had been trusting in the strength of his own resolutions, in which there is no strength, and that he would surely fall again unless he found the Lord. We "are kept by the power of God through faith" (1 Pet. 1:5 KJV). Faith is the coupler that links us to God and His power. If the link fails, the power cannot operate in us. We must believe, and keep on believing, if we are to be kept. He saw it. He felt he must have God's power, God's presence, or he would fall again and fall forevermore. When I was assured that he realized this, I then opened my Bible and said to him, "You have made promises to God, now let us see what promises God makes to you." And we read together, "God demonstrates His own love toward us, in that while we were still sinners, Christ died for us" (Rom. 5:8 NKJV); "Where sin abounded, grace did much more abound" (Rom. 5:20 KJV); "Sin shall not have dominion over you, for you are not under law but under grace" (Rom. 6:14 NKJV); and "If we confess our sins, he is faithful and just to forgive us our sins, and to cleanse us from all unrighteousness" (1 John 1:9 KJV).

In these promises, he saw God's love for him in spite of his sin, and his face began to brighten. And, no longer lolling over the penitent form hopeless and seemingly as spineless as a jellyfish, he began to straighten up. It was as though a new backbone were entering into him.

Then I sought to show him how God promises to enter the battle with him against his sins and mocking, gripping habits, and we read, "Fear not, for I am with you" (Isa. 41:10 NKJV).

I asked him, "You have been afraid, haven't you—afraid you would fall? You are afraid now, are you not?"

"Oh, yes!" he replied. "I have been afraid, and I am now afraid."

"But listen: 'Fear not, for I am with you.' This is God's promise to you, my brother. He says, 'I am with you.' Do you not see that you are not alone? He is on the battlefield. He is in the thick of the fight with you. In the darkness of the night, in the glare of the day, when alone or in the throng, He is with you. Do you not see it? Will you, do you, believe it?"

And he began to see.

I kept reading. "'Be not dismayed.' When temptation assails you, when the enemy comes mocking and threatening, you are not alone, my brother. 'Be not dismayed, for I am your God' [Isa. 41:10 NKJV]. He is your God. Call upon Him, trust Him, and laugh at your foe in the name of the Lord, as the stripling David laughed at and defied Goliath. 'I will strengthen you.' Hitherto you have fallen because you were weak, but see, read it, believe it, God says, 'I will strengthen you, Yes, I will help you' [Isa. 41:10 NKJV].

"You wouldn't fall into your shameful sin if some strong, true, trusted friend were by your side, would you? And note, God is with you! And He says He will help you. Away with your fears! "'I will uphold you with My righteous right hand' [Isa. 41:10 NKJV].

"Will you trust him? Will you cast to the winds your fears and henceforth go into every battle believing that God is with you, that almighty strength is pledged to you, that help is at hand, and that you shall be upheld? Will you lift your eyes to the Lord and trust instead of trembling and quailing when the enemies of your soul assail you?"

It was a joy to see my man. He looked; he read. Light burst upon him and beamed in his face. He seemed to be looking into the face of God.

He straightened up. "I see, oh, I see! I will, I do trust him!" And with thanksgiving he arose in the Spirit's power, and through the remainder of that campaign he was radiant. I trust he so remains to this day, and so he does if he obediently, believingly fights with the "sword of the Spirit, which is the word of God" (Eph. 6:17 KJV).

He saw the face of his divine Kinsman-Redeemer and heard the voice of the everlasting Father in the Word, and life and power and joy and peace flowed into him as he believed.

The Bible is the indispensable aid to faith. How do we get acquainted with God? By the work of the Holy Spirit in our minds and hearts as we penitently, obediently believe. But what are we to believe? We are to believe what He has said: "These things have I spoken unto you, that my joy might remain in you, and that your joy might be full," said Jesus (John 15:11 KJV).

"His divine power has granted to us all things that pertain to life and godliness, through the knowledge of him who called us to his own glory and excellence, by which he has granted to us his precious and very great promises, so that through them you may become partakers of the divine nature, having escaped from the corruption that is in the world because of sinful desire" (2 Pet. 1:3–4 ESV).

If we want to be strong, we must live "by every word that comes from the mouth of God" said Jesus (Matt. 4:4 ESV), as the Devil fiercely attacked Him.

"And as he spoke to me," said Daniel, "I was strengthened and said, 'Let my lord speak, for you have strengthened me'" (Dan. 10:19 ESV). And how was he strengthened? By the revelation of God through His Word.

How is a little child quieted, assured, and filled with peace in the night? By the presence and word of father or mother. And so we are assured, and made strong, and "thoroughly equipped for every good work" (2 Tim. 3:17 NIV) through the Scripture that is inspired by God and then brought to our remembrance and applied to our need by the Holy Spirit as we believe. Let us feed our people with the sincere milk of the Word and they will "grow into a full experience of salvation" (1 Pet. 2:2 NLT) and not tremble before the face of any mocking foe, but one person shall chase a thousand and two shall put ten thousand to flight (see Deut. 32:30).

While others debate the inspiration of the Word, let us eat it, drink it, preach it, and live by it, and we shall live in the power of "an endless life" (Heb. 7:16 KJV). It is still, as in the days of Job and the psalmist, "sweeter also than honey and the honeycomb" (Ps. 19:10 KJV) to those who believe and obey it, and more to be desired than "necessary food" (Job 23:12 KJV).

Within that awful volume lies

The mystery of mysteries!

Happiest they of human race

To whom God has granted grace

To read, to fear, to hope, to pray,

To lift the latch and force the way;

And better had they ne'er been born,

Who read to doubt, or read to scorn.[4]

So wrote Sir Walter Scott. And when dying he said to his son-in-law, "Bring me the Book."

"Which one, sir?" asked the son-in-law.

"There is but one," replied the dying man. "Bring me the Bible."[5]

NOTES

1. Robert Browning, *The Poems of Robert Browning*, "Christmas Eve," part 20, lines 52–53 (London: Wordsworth Editions, 1994), 408.

2. Dwight L. Moody, quoted in *The Current* 2, no. 44 (October 18, 1884).

3. A practice of prayerfully discerning and approaching people who seem to be ready to respond to the Holy Spirit's prompting but may need encouragement to do so.

4. Sir Walter Scott, *The Monastery* (Edinburgh: Adam and Charles Black, 1853), 129.

5. Dean F. W. Farrar, *The Church of England Pulpit and Ecclesiastical Review*, vol. 41 (London: Church of England Pulpit Office, 1896), 291.

Whom Do You Trust? 12

An exceptionally bright young woman wrote to me in a recent letter, "I have had experience enough to know that feelings do not count for much, and I do know that deep down in my heart there is a peace and sense of security that were not there when I was at your meetings last week. But I feel that my sense of security and faith are waiting to be tried before I can be quite sure of myself."

In those words are revealed a halting and mixed faith and a subtle temptation of the old Accuser.

Of course, our "faith and sense of security" are always being tried, and we should not ignore but quietly and confidently welcome such trial, for it is by the trial of faith that patience with the long and often stern disciplines of life is wrought in us and our character is perfected. James, in the second verse of his epistle, began with this common experience, saying, "Consider it pure joy, my brothers and sisters, whenever you face trials of many kinds, because you know that the testing of your faith produces perseverance. Let perseverance finish its work so that you may be mature and complete, not lacking anything" (James 1:2–4 NIV).

James got happy over this and exhorted his brothers and sisters to "consider it pure joy" to be tried. Not that the trial itself is pleasant, but the result is glorious. And Peter told us that in the midst of our rejoicing over present salvation through faith, we may be, "for a little while, if need be, grieved by various trials, that the genuineness of [our] faith, being much more precious than gold that perishes, though it is tested by fire, may be found to praise, honor, and glory at the revelation of Jesus Christ" (1 Pet. 1:6–7 NKJV).

So that young woman's feeling that her "faith and sense of security" will be tried is reasonable and normal, but her phrase—"before I can be quite sure of myself"—reveals a halting and mixed faith and the work of the subtle Tempter. He is slyly turning her eyes and her faith from Jesus to herself. "You can't be sure of yourself," he whispers, and almost imperceptibly she looks at self instead of to Jesus.

We are never to be sure of ourselves, but quietly, unwaveringly sure of our Redeemer and Lord. We shall be tried, but we shall not be left alone. As He was with the three young men in Nebuchadnezzar's seven-fold heated furnace, so He will be with us (see Dan. 3:24–25). "I am with you. . . . I am your God. I will strengthen you. . . . I will hold you up" (Isa. 41:10 NLT) is His ringing assurance. "I will never leave you nor forsake you" (Heb. 13:5 ESV). "No temptation has overtaken you that is not common to man. God is faithful, and he will not let you be tempted beyond your ability, but with the temptation he will also provide the way of escape, that you may be able to endure it" (1 Cor. 10:13 ESV).

Our blessed Lord Himself in the days of His flesh "faced all of the same testings we do," so He "understands our weaknesses" (Heb. 4:15 NLT), and is "able to help us" when we are tempted (Heb. 2:18 NLT). And He will help us if—instead of looking to ourselves and trembling in the presence of the mocking Enemy, with his army of fears and doubts—we look courageously and humbly, in the name of Jesus, to our Father who is the Lord God of hosts.

We are to face our fears in His name and rout our Enemy by an appeal to the all-sufficient merits of the blood shed for us, by glad testimony, and by a consecration that welcomes death rather than doubt and denial (see Rev. 12:10–11).

"Our God whom we serve is able to deliver us and he will," said Shadrach, Meshach, and Abednego. "But if not, be it known to you, O king, that we will not serve your gods or worship the golden image that you have set up" (Dan. 3:17–18 ESV). We will burn, but we will not bow. "They loved not their lives unto the death" (Rev. 12:11 KJV). That is consecration, and that is a firm basis for unwavering faith. They were not trusting in themselves, but in the living God, and deliverance came.

It is the Enemy of all souls who tempts us to look forward fearfully to some wholly indefinite trial that may never come, before we can walk in confident peace. Trials may come—they *will* come—but our Lord will be there with abundant grace when they do come if, moment by moment looking unto Him, we go forward in His strength.

It is one of the "wiles of the devil" (Eph. 6:11 KJV) to haunt us with nameless, shadowy fears of tomorrow. It is his way to weaken faith and turn our eyes from our Lord.

They may come, and they may not, but whether they come or not, we are not alone, and we must not fear, though the temptation to fear may be present.

Battle-hardened, mocking Goliath said to David, "Come to me, and I will give your flesh to the birds of the air and to the beasts of the field."

David answered, "You come to me with a sword and with a spear and with a javelin, but I come to you in the name of the LORD of hosts, the God of the armies of Israel, whom you have defied. This day the LORD will deliver you into my hand, and I will strike you down and cut off your head" (1 Sam. 17:44–46 ESV). The Lord was David's shield. He kept the Lord in front of him. "I have set the LORD always before me" (Ps. 16:8 KJV), David wrote long years after, and Goliath could not reach him without first encountering the Lord. And when the Philistine champion drew closer to meet David, the lad ran to meet him and defeated him in the name of the Lord.

That is the way to face fears and spiritual enemies and doubts and temptations. Face them "in the name of the LORD of hosts." Run to meet them, but put no confidence in yourself, only as you are "strong in the Lord, and in the power of his might" (Eph. 6:10 KJV).

Paul knew, as few others, what trouble and danger are. He said, "The Holy Spirit testifies to me in every city that imprisonment and afflictions await me." But, he added, "I do not account my life of any value nor as precious to myself, if only I may finish my course and the ministry that I received from the Lord Jesus" (Acts 20:23–24 ESV).

And again he wrote, "I am sure that neither death nor life, nor angels nor rulers, nor things present nor things to come, nor powers, nor height nor depth, nor anything else in all creation, will be able to separate us from the love of God in Christ Jesus our Lord" (Rom. 8:38–39 ESV). His confidence was wholly in the changeless character and love of his Lord, therefore he trembled in the presence of no one, nor any combination of trials that might overtake him.

A Word to Those Who Are Growing Old

In one of my recent meetings, a dear sister, who has been serving the Lord and walking in the light for many years, confessed with tears that her joy was not what it used to be. In her youth, joy was rapturous, leaping up like springing fountains and singing birds. A verse of Scripture would suddenly stand out with its assuring message and fill her with gladness, and songs in the night welled up from her glad heart, but now she says she often has heaviness of spirit, and the way seems to get harder. And while she feels sure that she is accepted by God, yet she is not enjoying what she once enjoyed.

God forbid that I should offer any false comfort or, through lack of faith, limit His power to fill us with the rapturous joys of youth as we grow older. But is it reasonable for us to suppose that this should be so? In youth as we waited upon the Lord we found our spiritual strength renewed, and we mounted up "with wings as eagles." In middle age,

as we wait upon the Lord, we find our strength renewed and we "run
and [are not] weary." In old age, as we wait upon the Lord, our strength
is renewed, but we must now "walk, and not faint" (Isa. 40:31 KJV).
None of the natural senses are as keen in old age as in youth. The
appetite for food, the joy in society, and the rapturous friendships of
youth do not continue quite the same through the years. And may it not
be so spiritually? It is true that the apostle said while "outwardly we
are wasting away, yet inwardly we are being renewed day by day" (2
Cor. 4:16 NIV). But is not the joy—in some measure, at least—modified
by the sobering experiences of the years? The river that started as a
bubbling, leaping, laughing brook in the mountains, often rushing in
torrents through narrow and precipitous ways, gradually widens and
deepens and flows peacefully and without noise as it nears the sea.
May it not be so in our spiritual life? Is not the river of God's peace
flowing through the hearts of the aged a deeper and richer experience
than the exuberant joys at the beginning of the spiritual life?

The pressing infirmities of the flesh, and the gradual decay of
memory and other powers, may account for some of the apparent loss
of joy in those who are growing old.

The enlarged knowledge of the malignant, massive, stubborn
powers of evil may have a sobering effect upon the mind that, if not
watchfully guarded against and met with quiet, steadfast faith, may
tend to lessen joy.

If our children do not serve God with the ardor we wish, or souls
for whom we pray do not at once experience new life in Christ, or the
work of God that is dear to our hearts languishes, the Devil may tempt
us to doubt or repine, and so our joy is quenched.

What steps can be taken to prevent or arrest the failure of joy?

Older people should still stir up the gift of God that is in them as we stir up a fire that is burning low. Frequent seasons of prayer, along with singing and humming through old songs, with an active exercise of faith, will help to keep the joy bells ringing. I am a rather poor sleeper, and recently in the small hours of the night, before the birds were singing, I found myself wide awake. So, to bless my own soul and control and guide my thoughts without disturbing others, I softly sang, in almost a whisper, "I Need Thee, Oh, I Need Thee," and my heart was strangely warmed and blessed as I sang.

Older people are not wise to spend too much time considering the joys of long ago and comparing them with present emotions. They should live in anticipation of joys yet to come rather than dwell upon joys that are past. God's storehouse is not exhausted. For those who love and follow Jesus, "the best is yet to be."[1] Paul said that he forgot the things that were behind and, looking forward, pressed like an eager racer toward the things that were ahead (see Phil. 3:13–14).

Those who keep looking backward instead of forward are likely to stumble and miss the joys that spring up round about them. It is not good to be comparing the present with the past, but we should each moment seek to exercise full and glad faith in our Lord for the present and the future. He has a portion of joy for us now. But the ineffable glory and blessing and joy are yet to come, when we see Him face-to-face and hear Him say, "Well done; come!"

We must keep our eyes on Jesus, looking unto Him, the Author and the Finisher of our faith (see Heb. 12:2). We must look away from the seen things to unseen, eternal things; to the purpose and covenant of God in Christ, steadfast and sure; to His promises, great and precious, shining like stars forever and assuring us of God's interest in us. We should carefully count up our present mercies and blessings and give thanks for them. It may be better with us than we think. John Fletcher said that he at one time became so eager for what he had not yet received that he failed to rejoice and enjoy the things God had already given him. That is an almost certain way to lose what we have. It is good—indeed, it is a duty—to stretch out for the things ahead, but we must not forget to give God thanks and enjoy the things He gives us now.

In feeble health, we may not be able to realize all we have to be glad about. There may at times be deep and prolonged depression of spirit arising from physical causes. "The body and soul are near neighbors," said the founder of The Salvation Army, William Booth, "and they greatly influence each other." Elijah was physically exhausted when he got under that juniper tree and wanted to die, but God let him sleep, awakened him, gave him a simple meal of bread and water, let him sleep again, awakened and fed him again and let him live in the open, in sunshine and fresh air, and so revived him, gave him a man's work to do, and took him to heaven in a chariot of fire. All God's resources were not exhausted because Elijah was depressed and exhausted. The best was yet to be with Elijah! Simple food, fresh air, sunshine, labor, and rest are still important for old people, if they wish to keep a happy experience.

Finally, older people should still go to the house of God and mingle with God's people. It was in the temple that aged Simeon and Anna the prophetess found the little Lord Jesus. And the psalmist sang, if not from his own experience, then from observation of others and in assured faith, "Those who are planted in the house of the LORD shall flourish in the courts of our God. They shall still bear fruit in old age; they shall be fresh and flourishing, to declare that the LORD is upright" (Ps. 92:13–15 NKJV).

> When darkness seems to veil His face,
> I rest on His unchanging grace . . .
> I dare not trust the sweetest frame
> But wholly lean on Jesus' name.[2]

NOTES

1. Robert Browning, "Rabbi Ben Ezra," *Poems of Robert Browning* (London: Oxford University Press, 1923), 636–638.

2. Edward Mote, "My Hope Is Built on Nothing Less," 1834, public domain.

Answering Atheism 14

A wide knowledge of history tends to sanity, sobriety, and correctness of judgment of people and events, if we have seen God in history. We need such knowledge to give us perspective, to steady us, to save us from sharp judgments, and to insure us against cockiness on one hand and despair on the other. Without this wide, long view, we are like a tiny boat on a tempestuous sea, tossed on the waves, but with it we are more like a great ship that rides serenely over the billows.

To the casual observer the experience of humanity seems tidal—always flowing and ebbing like the tides of the sea—or forever moving in a circle, getting nowhere, evermore coming back from whence it started, like the rivers rising out of and returning to the sea. To such a person the "one far-off divine event, to which the whole creation moves,"[1] the slow but sure workings of Providence, and the unfailing purpose and process of the divine government are hidden.

When I was a child on the wide, bare, unprotected prairies of the American Midwest, black clouds and fierce thunderstorms filled me with anxious fears and vague terror. But as I grew to manhood, I saw them as a part of a vast and ordered whole, and they lost their power to create panic in me.

Once, when sick and prostrated in health, I was thrown into a state of mental and spiritual anxiety, amounting almost to torture, by the nationwide excitement over a great prizefight. I felt our American civilization was only veneered barbarism, and for a time it seemed to me that we were reverting to, and were to be swallowed up by, brutal, sensuous paganism. Then, on my knees praying, I remembered the days when a thousand gladiators fought each other to the death in the Coliseum, or battled and struggled with and were devoured by wild beasts to make a Roman holiday, while the mobs of the city by the hundred thousand, headed by the emperor, senators, philosophers, noble ladies, and all the elite gloated over the cruel, bloody scene. Then in deep reverence, gratitude, and glad trust I gave God thanks, as I saw how far He had led us on—and was still leading—from those ghastly pleasures, those merciless days.

When I was a child, the American Civil War was raging. Soldiers marched and countermarched through our peaceful little valley and village. Armies stormed and thundered across the land. Proud cities were besieged and starved and fell before conquering hosts. Fathers, brothers, and sons were perishing in bloody combat, in fetid swamps and prison camps. Homes were vanishing. Funeral bells were ever tolling. Mothers, sisters, wives, and orphans were ever weeping. The foundations of the social order seemed to be crumbling, and people turned their thoughts to the apocalyptic portions of Scripture, tried to interpret the times by their symbolisms, and turned their eyes to the clouds in expectation of the Savior's bodily appearing, longing for Him to come and work out the salvation which men and women— abasing their pride and yielding to the lordship of Jesus, under the leadership of the sanctifying Spirit—must work out for themselves, or perish. It was years before the light of history enabled me to escape this bald interpretation of apocalyptic symbols and walk in quietness and peace and close attention to daily duty, while a world quaked and trembled in unparalleled hurricanes of war, assured that "the heavens do rule" (Dan. 4:26 KJV), and "a watcher and an holy one" (Dan. 4:23 KJV) in the heavens was interested in our perplexity and sore travail and would guide us through the storm and tempest, purified and chastened, to a haven of peace.

History is repeating itself in spirit among us, and a society—a very militant society—for the propagation of atheism has recently received letters of incorporation from the legislators of New York, and an anti-Bible society has also been incorporated. Its avowed object is "to discredit the Bible," to "make known its human origin, evolutionary formation, and its discreditable history; expose its immoral and barbaric contents; and lay bare its antiscientific, antiliberal, and irrational teachings." Such is its program. It proposes to show that "the Bible is the work of man." It claims that the "falsification by deliberate mistranslation is the sole basis of orthodoxy." It promises that "the inhuman character of the Bible—God—shall be offered in evidence against the Book," and "the Bible patriarchs shall be shown to be a set of unmatched moral monsters." It continues, saying, "The spirit of injustice and intolerance dominate the Bible," "the Sermon on the Mount consists mainly of romantic sentimentalism unrelated to reality," and "the Bible is inimical to civilization. It must and shall be discredited." It urges, "The American Anti-Bible Society has no religious tests for membership, except disbelief in the Bible as divinely inspired. . . . Help us free America from Bible-bondage."

Those are some tidbits from its bulletin or manifesto. The Society for the Propagation of Atheism has already enlisted many young people and students, and societies of "damned souls" (as they dub themselves) are flourishing in many of our schools and colleges. It is all a part of a nationwide, worldwide movement, awash of wide, sweeping waves of atheism gushing forth from the heart of the Russian Revolution, something that all lovers of our Lord and of the Bible will have to face and possibly come into close and desperate grips with in the near future.

If these people were better acquainted with history, they might not be so cocksure of discrediting the Bible and banishing God from His throne. If we are acquainted with history, we shall not be uncertain as to the final issue, but neither will we sit down in a fool's paradise and think we can drive back the waves of mocking, irresponsible, desperate unbelief by witty retort, smart rejoinder, or learned and masterly debate.

How shall we reply to their denial of the divine elements of the Bible? How shall we prove it to be God-inspired? Is it a subject of proof or of faith? How can I be sure of it for myself, and how can I prove it to others? Paul said, "All Scripture is given by inspiration of God" (2 Tim. 3:16 KJV) but that is an assertion, not a proof. It still has to be proved, if it can be.

I had studied the various arguments for the inspiration of the Bible by theologians, and since I had from my infancy onward accepted the Bible as God's Book, they confirmed my unquestioning faith. But there came a time when I needed more than learned arguments to prove it to me. And not until God Himself came to my help was I wholly, invincibly convinced.

That which finally established my faith in the divinity of the Bible was opened eyes, an inner illumination of my own soul which enabled me to behold wondrous things all through its sacred pages. "Open my eyes, that I may see wondrous things from Your law," prayed the psalmist (Ps. 119:18 NKJV). The Book is largely sealed to people with unanointed eyes and self-satisfied or world-satisfied hearts, and from those who turn from the paths of rectitude and "stumble because they are disobedient to the word" (1 Pet. 2:8 NASB).

The pastor of the church of Laodicea became lukewarm as a result of getting rich and increasing in goods until he felt he had need of nothing, but knew not that he was "wretched, and miserable, and poor, and blind, and naked" (Rev. 3:17 KJV).

"I advise you," Jesus said, "to buy from me gold made pure in fire so you can be truly rich. Buy from me white clothes so you can be clothed and so you can cover your shameful nakedness. Buy from me medicine to put on your eyes so you can truly see" (Rev. 3:18 NCV). The Book was sealed to the pastor, and the revelations of the Lord were hidden from him, because of the self-imposed blindness or dimness of his spiritual eyes.

The final blessing Jesus gave His disciples just before He ascended from them was the blessing of this inner illumination of opened eyes.

"Then he opened their minds to understand the Scriptures" (Luke 24:45 NLT).

The sun does not need learned astronomical treatises to prove its existence, nor a manmade candle to enable it to be seen. All it needs is that we should have eyes to see. It is its own evidence. What the sun is in the world of material things, the Bible is in the world of spiritual things. It carries in itself its evidences of inspiration. It is a lamp to the feet and a light to the path of those whose spiritual eyes are open and who will resolutely follow where it leads. Let us notice some of the assertions of the Book and find if they can be proven, not by argument but by life, by experience, for if it does not answer the deep needs of life, the hunger of the soul, the fears, the hopes, the aspirations, and the questionings of the human spirit, the Bible is merely a venerable and curious bit of ancient literature to be read for pleasure or to gratify curiosity.

"People do not live by bread alone," said Jesus, "but by every word that comes from the mouth of God" (Matt. 4:4 NLT). Does the Bible feed the human soul? All the saints and soldiers of Jesus through the ages have been nourished and have lived on the Word of God. "I have esteemed the words of his mouth more than my necessary food," said Job (Job 23:12 KJV). "How sweet your words taste to me; they are sweeter than honey," wrote the psalmist (Ps. 119:103 NLT). "They are more desirable than gold," sang David, "even the finest gold. They are sweeter than honey, even honey dripping from the comb" (Ps. 19:10 NLT). "Your words were found, and I ate them," said Jeremiah, "and your words became to me a joy and the delight of my heart" (Jer. 15:16 ESV).

Does the Bible help men and women to live finer, cleaner, saintly lives? It certainly does. Those who receive the Word of God into their hearts will stop sinning. "I have hidden your word in my heart that I might not sin against you" wrote the psalmist (Ps. 119:11 NIV). "How can a young person stay pure? By obeying your word" (Ps. 119:9 NLT).

Does the Bible offer hope to the soul who has scorned the voice of conscience and turned away from light and goodness and God? It is the only book in the world that does. It, and it alone, tells of a redeeming God, a Savior from sin, and a loving heavenly Father who waits to welcome sinners. "But God showed his great love for us by sending Christ to die for us while we were still sinners" (Rom. 5:8 NLT). "This is a trustworthy saying, and everyone should accept it: 'Christ Jesus came into the world to save sinners'" (1 Tim. 1:15 NLT). "If we confess our sins, he is faithful and just to forgive us our sins, and to cleanse us from all unrighteousness" (1 John 1:9 KJV). Ten thousand times ten thousand sinners saved by faith in the Savior revealed in the Bible will testify to the truth of those words.

Does the Bible offer aid to tempted men and women? Does it comprehend our need? It does as no other book in the world does. It reveals an elder Brother who helps us overcome our temptations. "For because he himself has suffered when tempted, he is able to help those who are being tempted" (Heb. 2:18 ESV). "This High Priest of ours understands our weaknesses, for he faced all of the same testings we do, yet he did not sin" (Heb. 4:15 NLT). "God is faithful, and he will not let you be tempted beyond your ability, but with the temptation he will also provide the way of escape, that you may be able to endure it" (1 Cor. 10:13 ESV).

Does the Bible have any word for the burdened, perplexed, and careworn? It does, sweet words of comprehension and assurance that can be found nowhere else: "Come to me, all who labor and are heavy laden, and I will give you rest" (Matt. 11:28 ESV).

Has the Bible any word for the persecuted, maligned, and oppressed? Listen: "Blessed are those who are persecuted for righteousness' sake, for theirs is the kingdom of heaven. Blessed are you when others revile you and persecute you and utter all kinds of evil against you falsely on my account. Rejoice and be glad, for your reward is great in heaven" (Matt. 5:10–12 ESV).

Has it any word for the oppressed and afflicted? Listen: "He has not ignored or belittled the suffering of the needy. He has not turned his back on them, but has listened to their cries for help" (Ps. 22:24 NLT). "If we suffer we shall also reign with him" (2 Tim. 2:12 KJV). "For our light affliction, which is but for a moment, is working for us a far more exceeding and eternal weight of glory" (2 Cor. 4:17 NKJV).

Has the Bible a word for those whose eyes are dim with tears? "God will wipe away every tear from their eyes" (Rev. 7:17 ESV).

For those who are in pain? "Neither shall there be mourning, nor crying, nor pain anymore" (Rev. 21:4 ESV).

Has it any word about the far future? "What we will be has not yet appeared; but we know that when he appears we shall be like him, because we shall see him as he is" (1 John 3:2 ESV).

How can I prove the inspiration of the Bible?

1. By the way it answers to the human heart. The key that fits an intricate lock was evidently made for that lock. The Bible meets me at every point of my moral and spiritual need. It fits my heart's intricate

needs as the key fits the lock. And I exult to know that the divine hand that fashioned me gives me the Book, and His heart that loves me pours itself with fathomless comforts into my heart through the Book. But I cannot prove to you the truth of the Book any more than I can prove that the sun is shining, that honey is sweet, that the song of the bird is melodious. The inspiration of the Bible is proved by experience, not by logic. "Meditate on it day and night" (Josh. 1:8 ESV), and you shall taste its sweetness, behold its wonders, and hear in its words the whisperings of the everlasting Father to the heart of His child.

2. By the evidence of a redeemed life. How shall I prove to others—to those who question, doubt, and deny—that the Bible is a God-given, God-inspired Book? Shall I go to history, science, or archaeology for proof? Yes, at the proper time and to the right people. But the most convincing proof of the inspiration of the Bible I can offer to an unbeliever is a redeemed life, lived in the power and sweetness of the Spirit; a life that matches the Bible; a life of love, prayer, faith, and devotion; a life of joy and peace and patience and sweet goodwill to all; a life full of good works matching a glad testimony to the saving, sanctifying, keeping power and ever-living presence of the Lord Jesus; a life like that of a Chinese Christian whose neighbors said of him, "There is no difference between him and the Book." He was a living Bible known and read by them all, and they saw and felt its truth in him. He was inbreathed, indwelt of God, and through him they recognized inspiration in the Book. Redeemed lives, drawing light and strength and inspiration from and matching the inspired Book, are the unanswerable proofs of its inspiration.

Sir Wilfred Grenfell of Labrador said that when he was a university student in England he lived with a professor who was a lecturer on the evidences of Christianity. This lecturer was in frequent controversy with skeptics, but never won over any of them. They would meet in public debate, each supported by his friends and followers, who were confirmed in their opinions, but there was no changing of sides and no one became a follower of Jesus. It was heady, a rivalry of wits, a struggle for mastery, an intellectual fisticuffs to no profit. But one day one of the most formidable of these skeptic debaters was stricken with a fatal illness. His friends had no words of comfort and left him to himself. Then a sweet, humble Salvation Army sister stepped in and nursed the dying man. She could not and did not argue with him, but revealed to him a redeemed, Christlike life. Love was in her face, tenderness was in her touch, grace was on her lips, and peace and joy in Jesus radiated from her. Soon, a humble, inspired life did what knowledge and argument had failed to do. He surrendered his life to Jesus Christ and died in the faith.

A skeptic challenged a man of God to debate about religion. "I accept your challenge on this condition," replied the man of God, "that I bring one hundred men with me to testify what faith in Christ has done for them, and you bring one hundred men to testify what atheism has done for them." The challenger withdrew the challenge, and there was no debate.

Meek and lowly, but glad and bold witnesses, who witness by lip and life and shining look, are the strongest argument for the faith they live. The final proof will be given when the risen Jesus appears with crowns and thrones and kingdoms and honor and glory and immortality for those who have believed and loved and followed Him to the end, and opens the dark gates of doom and banishes into "wrath and fury . . . tribulation and distress . . . every human being who does evil" (Rom. 2:8–9 ESV).

NOTE

1. Alfred Lord Tennyson, "In Memoriam," n. d., public domain.

The Lord's Own Prayer 15

One day, at a certain place we are told, the disciples were with Jesus when He was praying, and after He had ceased—I wonder how long He prayed and what was the burden of His prayer?—one of His disciples said to Him, "Lord, teach us to pray, as John also taught his disciples" (Luke 11:1 KJV). He did not say teach us *how* to pray, but teach us to pray. It was not the manner of praying he desired to be taught, but simply to pray. And this Jesus did, both by what He said and even more by what He did, by His example. They often found Him praying, and that taught them to pray as no words or exhortations could teach them. However, Jesus responded to this request and taught them a prayer that, wherever it is known at all, is known as "The Lord's Prayer."

But it is rather the *disciples'* prayer. It is a prayer He gave *them* to use, voicing their needs and their desires.

The *Lord's* Prayer—the prayer Jesus as our Great High Priest addressed to the Father; the prayer in which He poured out the desires of His heart for the Father's glory and His fellowship in that glory and in which He voiced His longings for the disciples then with Him, and for us and for all who would believe in Him; the prayer which no doubt constitutes the substance of His ceaseless and eternal intercession for His disciples of all time and everywhere—is recorded in John 17. That is more appropriately called "The Lord's Prayer."

Jesus had said to Mary at the wedding in Cana, when she told Him of the empty wine vessels, "Woman, what does this have to do with me? My hour has not yet come" (John 2:4 ESV). To His brothers who were skeptical of His claims, and who would hasten Him to Jerusalem, there either to prove or discredit Himself, He said, "My time has not yet come, but your time is always here. . . . You go up to the feast. I am not going up to this feast, for my time has not yet fully come" (John 7:6, 8 ESV). Once the religious authorities were angered at Jesus. John explained that at that point "no one arrested him, because his hour had not yet come" (John 8:20 ESV).

But finally, when Jesus' ceaseless but unhasting ministry was drawing to a close, and He had come up to Jerusalem for the last time, Greek worshipers said to Philip, "Sir, we would see Jesus." When this was told to Jesus, He answered, "The hour is come" (John 12:21, 23 KJV).

Then, with His disciples, He went into the upper room and ate the Passover Feast, ate of the Paschal Lamb, which ever since that dread night when the destroying angel passed over Egypt had pointed in type to Him, the great antitype, God's Lamb, whose blood would cleanse from all sin and shelter from the Destroyer all who believed.

After supper He arose, girded Himself, and washed the disciples' feet, showing them by a kindergarten lesson what, through their dullness and hardness of heart, His words had failed to teach them: that He who would be greatest among them must be, and would gladly be, "servant of all" (Mark 10:44 KJV).

After this object lesson in lowly, loving service, He spoke tender words to them, words of warning, comfort, command, instruction, and encouragement. He unfolded to them the person and mission of the "other Comforter," who would come to them when He was gone. He assured them that while He was going away, He would come again; He would not leave them comfortless or orphans. While absent in body, He would yet be present in Spirit. If they but loved Him and kept His commandment to love one another, they would have with them evermore His manifested presence, His spiritual presence, in their hearts and minds, made possible and real through simple, obedient faith; they would be loved by the Father, and He and the Father would come to make Their abode, Their mansion, with them and in them. His joy would be in them, and their joy would be full. He warned them that the world would hate them because it hated Him, and because they were His friends and not of the world. He told them they would be persecuted and have sorrow, but added, "Your grief will suddenly turn to wonderful joy. . . . Then you will rejoice, and no one can rob you of that joy. . . . Here on earth you will have many trials and sorrows. But take heart, because I have overcome the world" (John 16:20, 22–33 NLT).

They were to be so identified with Him, so "mixed up with Jesus," as a quaint old friend of mine once said, that His union with the Father and the love with which the Father loved Him—His joy, His tribulation, and His triumph and victory—would be theirs. They would share in all that was His. If they loved Him, trusted Him, bore His cross, and shared His sufferings, they would share His glory. If they labored and toiled with Him in tears, they would shout with Him at the ingathering of the sheaves and be jubilant in the harvest home. If they sorrowed with Him, they would also rejoice with Him. He was going to prepare a place for them, and He would come again and receive them that they might be where He was. He would not be in heaven and leave them behind.

It was His farewell address, recorded by John in chapters 13 to 16. It was the final lecture and tender, searching charge to these cadets of His own choice and training, who were soon to be commissioned and sent forth to conquer a hostile world by their testimony and sacrificial devotion and love, and turn it upside down.

He had spoken at length to His humble disciples, and now He lifted His eyes to heaven and spoke to the Father. He prayed, and this He did as naturally and as familiarly as He had spoken to His lowly followers. He said, "Father, the hour has come" (John 17:1 NLT)—the fateful hour for which He had girded Himself and waited, the hour to which without pause and without haste He had pressed forward, the hour to which He had looked from the beginning of His ministry, the hour to which He had looked from of old, from the dawn of time when the morning stars sang together, and the hour to which He had looked from the deeps of timeless eternity. It was the zero hour of the moral world, of the spiritual universe. The zero hour in the great battle for the souls of humanity, the hour when our Kinsman-Redeemer was to "go over the top," go over "alone: for of the people there was none with Him,"[1] go over and die, die for us, die that we might live and never die. It was the hour of His utter humiliation, when all His glory was stripped from Him and laid aside, and He who knew no sin was made sin for us, "numbered with the transgressors . . . wounded for our transgressions . . . bruised for our iniquities," chastened for our peace, and stricken that we might be healed (Isa. 53:12, 5 KJV).

Step-by-step He had descended from infinite heights of glory and honor and power to infinite depths of weakness and reproach and shame. He, the infinitely pure and innocent One, came and united Himself with us as a human being, stood in our place, and took upon Himself our guilt, our sin, our shame, our curse. He was "made a curse for us" (Gal. 3:13 KJV). He was "made . . . sin for us" (2 Cor. 5:21 KJV). He emptied Himself of His divine, eternal majesty and took "the form of a servant, being born in the likeness of men. And being found in human form, he humbled himself by becoming obedient to the point of death, even death on a cross" (Phil. 2:7–8 ESV). This was the hour to which He had looked, to which He had at last come, and for the agony, the loneliness, the shame of which He was then, and had been from the beginning, girding Himself.

But before the dread and awful stroke of this hour fell upon Him, His thoughts turned to His poor, ignorant, weak, imperfect disciples, and with a love that knew no bounds—that forgot self, forgot the shame and agony soon to be poured out upon Him without stint like an ocean flood, even forgot or for a time ignored the glory so soon to follow on His return to the bosom of the Father and the bliss of heaven—He remembered them and prayed for them.

If we wish to know His thought for us, the fullness of blessing He wishes to bestow upon us, the completeness and intimacy of the union into which He wishes to enter with us, and the intimacy of the union and fellowship we are to have with the Father; if we wish to know how His purposes of world conquest are to be accomplished; if we wish to know the high estate, the glory, to which He intends to lift us, we should ponder this prayer, make it a daily study, and cooperate with Him for its fulfillment. He was not then talking to His lowly disciples. He was not commanding and charging them. He was talking to the Father for them, voicing their needs, considering their dangers, pleading their weakness, and with supplications and intercessions seeking for them boundless blessings that would make them kings and priests unto God, lifting them infinitely above the paltry pomp and fading glory of all the kings and governors and mighty ones of earth.

And through them in answer to this prayer are to flow all the streams and rivers of His grace, and be accomplished all the redemptive purposes of His sacrificial life and death here upon earth, and His risen life and resurrection power revealed from heaven. He is the Vine, they are the branches. Through them His beauty is to be made manifest, the beauty of holiness. In them His fruit is to be found, the fruit of the Spirit, the fruit of the life that is eternal, the fruit which is "love, joy, peace, longsuffering, kindness, goodness, faithfulness, gentleness, self-control" and against which "there is no law" (Gal. 5:22–23 NKJV).

The petitions of this prayer are few. He first prays for Himself—that the Father will glorify Him that He in turn may glorify the Father, and that He may again be glorified with the glory that was His with the Father before the world existed. And this petition was heard and considered, and we see the beginning of the abundant answer when the angel strengthened Him during the agony and bloody sweat of the garden, after which, with lamb-like submission and serene, unfailing meekness and patience, He calmly faced the mockery and shame of Herod's soldiers and Pilate's judgment hall, and the deeper and final agony and desertion of the cross.

We see it further answered in His resurrection from the dead, whereby, wrote Paul, He was indubitably "declared to be the Son of God with power, according to the spirit of holiness, by the resurrection from the dead" (Rom. 1:4 KJV). And we see a yet further and fuller answer when on the day of Pentecost the Holy Spirit was outpoured in His name, and His lowly disciples became living flames of love and holiness and power divine. And we see the continuing answer to this petition in every triumph of the gospel, in every penitent soul born into the kingdom, in every child of God sanctified, in every hymn of praise sung, and in every true prayer offered in His name. We see it in the light of His cross shining across centuries and millennia and gradually irradiating the dark places of all life, and the spread of His gospel from that narrow little circle in Jerusalem to all the continents and isles of earth. And as He is glorified, so is the Father.

Then He prayed for His disciples, whom the Father has given and will give to Him—prayed that they may be kept from the evil that is in the world. While He was with them in the world He had kept them. "The LORD God is a sun and a shield" (Ps. 84:11 KJV). He had been their sun. He had lighted their way, and they had walked in His light and had not stumbled out of the way. He was their shield. He had defended them against wily men and yet more wily devils. No enemy had been able to pluck out of His hand any save Judas, who sold himself to the Evil One for a handful of silver.

But now Jesus was leaving them, and they would be exposed to the wiles of the Evil One, who would subtly approach them as an "angel of light" (2 Cor. 11:14 KJV), rush upon and assail them "as a roaring lion" (1 Pet. 5:8 KJV), and make battle against them like an ancient archer with fiery darts of accusation, doubts, fears, and perplexities. And they would be beset by the relentless hostility of the world. The bigotry and hate of others and the proud scorn and fierce persecutions of cruel and idolatrous nations would be poured out upon them. They were as sheep in the midst of wolves. Great and constant would be their danger, measureless would be their need; therefore He prayed, "Holy Father, keep through Your name those whom You have given Me, that they may be one as We are" (John 17:11 NKJV).

He did not pray that they may be caught up out of the world and away from the evil, but that in the midst of it they may be kept through His name. "May the name of the God of Jacob protect you," prayed the psalmist David (Ps. 20:1 ESV). "The name of the LORD is a strong fortress; the godly run to him and are safe," said Solomon (Prov. 18:10 NLT). "Jesus, Jesus, Jesus," moaned and cried a sorely tempted ex-drunkard, and at the name the spell of the temptation was broken and he was kept through that name.

They were His little, defenseless ones, very dear to Him, and He wanted them kept for their own sakes. But they were also His representatives. As the Father had sent Him into the world, so He was now sending them into the world. They went forth in His name, with His word, on His business, and only as they were kept would the purpose of His life and death be fulfilled.

To this end He further prayed, "Sanctify them" (John 17:17 KJV). Set them apart, consecrate them to Yourself and to Your service, seal them and make them holy. Not only "keep them from the evil that is in the world," but also save them from the evil and corruption that is in their own hearts. Make them clean. Refine them as with fire. Purify them until no spot of sin remains upon them, until they are "all glorious within" (Ps. 45:13 KJV). "Sanctify them by Your truth. Your word is truth" (John 17:17 NKJV). Let Your truth search them until they are wholly conformed to Your nature and Your will, until their lives match Your truth and in them the truth lives incarnate and walks the earth.

Not for these alone, however, did He pray, but for all who should through their word believe in Him. His thought was girdling the globe and embracing the ages. Wherever and whenever a penitent, trembling soul believed in Him through their word, that soul came within the desire and purpose of this prayer. He wanted them all to be one, bound up in one bundle of life, one as He and the Father are one, that they might be the habitation of God upon earth, and that the world seeing this might believe in Him. Faith in Him depended on the brotherly love and unity of His disciples. So it did, and so it does to this day. When there is unity, there is faith. Where there is division, there is doubt. Thousands believed and a multitude of priests were obedient to the faith after Pentecost when the disciples were filled with the Holy Spirit and were of one mind and heart. But when this unity of faith and love was lost, the Dark Ages followed, and darkness and unbelief always follow loss of love and unity.

"The glory which You gave Me I have given them, that they may be one just as We are one," said He (John 17:22 NKJV). The religion of Jesus is social. It is inclusive, not exclusive. We can have the glory only as we are united. We must be one in spirit with our brothers and sisters. Let division come, and the glory departs. Let the unity of brotherly love continue, and the glory abides. O, let us beware of the leakage of love, of the loss of the spirit of unity, of the subtlety and snare and death of the spirit of distrust and division.

"I in them, and You in Me; that they may be made perfect in one, and that the world may know that You have sent Me, and have loved them as You have loved Me" (John 17:23 NKJV). In this world the disciples of Jesus are God's home, and that home is to be filled with sweet accord, not discord. He wants us to be "perfect in one" (John 17:23 KJV). Then the world—the poor, proud, foolish, wicked world—shall not only believe, but know that Jesus was sent by the Father, and that the love of the Father is outpoured upon His disciples as it was upon Himself. What responsibility this places upon us to foster the unity of the Spirit, and to beware of the pride and jealousy and envy and suspicion and unholy spirit of lordship that leads to division. Let us be content to wash each other's feet and be ambitious only to be servants of all.

In conclusion He prayed, "Father, I desire that they also whom You gave Me may be with Me where I am, that they may behold My glory which You have given Me; for You loved Me before the foundation of the world" (John 17:24 NKJV). O my soul, you who have wandered in darkness and grubbed in sin and been plucked from the mire shall yet be lifted from the dunghill and seated with Him upon His throne, and shall stand amid the blinding splendor and behold the glory before which angels and archangels, cherubim and seraphim, veil their faces and fall as dead. Toil on, O my soul! If you labor for Him, you will also reap with Him. He is not unrighteous to forget your work and labor of love, and He will not fail to reward abundantly your patience of hope. "Your labor in the Lord is not in vain" (1 Cor. 15:58 NIV). If you are called to suffer with Him, O my soul, count it all joy. Do not repine. Fear not. Faint not. You shall reign with Him. He has so promised. And He will remember. He will not forget His own word upon which He has caused you to hope (see Ps. 119:49).

If you love Him who died for you, who entrusts His honor and His cause to you, prove your love, O my soul, by feeding and watching over His lambs and sheep. Love your brothers and sisters as He has loved you. And as He laid down His life for you so, if necessary, lay down your life for your brothers and sisters, and so shall everyone know that you are His disciple. And "when he sees all that is accomplished by his anguish, he will be satisfied" (Isa. 53:11 NLT).

O what wonder! How amazing!

Jesus, glorious King of Kings,

Deigns to call me His beloved,

Lets me rest beneath His wings!

All for Jesus, resting now beneath His wings.

All for Jesus, all for Jesus,

All my being's ransomed powers;

All my thoughts and words and doings,

All my days and all my hours.

All for Jesus, all my days and all my hours.[2]

And when the days and hours of time are no more, then eternity—eternity with Him, my Redeemer, Lover, Friend, in "the glory that excels" (2 Cor. 3:10 NKJV) and that has no end.

NOTES

1. Adam Clarke, *Matthew to the Acts*, Clarke's Commentary, vol. 5 (New York: Abingdon-Cokesbury, n.d.), 496.

2. Mary D. James, "All for Jesus," 1871, public domain.

The Care of Souls 16

Many years ago I was visiting Riverside, California, for a brief campaign (revival service) and was met at the train by the local Salvation Army captain (pastor) at about ten o'clock in the morning. His face was glowing as he said to me, "We got the worst old drunkard in town saved last night. And I have seen him twice this morning, and he is doing fine." How could the poor "old drunkard" do otherwise, with a captain bubbling over with faith, love, and good cheer, following him up like that? Don't forget, he saw the man twice the next morning. Twice! That is the way newborn babies are cared for, and that is the way to care for newborn souls.

This same captain came east to Pennsylvania and an evangelist visited his corps (church). That evangelist had about fifty people commit to following Christ, and the captain did not lose one but enrolled them all as soldiers (members). On another occasion, he labored until after midnight with a drunkard and then carried him to his lodging place on his back. The proprietor of the lodging house refused to receive him, but the captain carried the chap upstairs to his room, put him to bed, followed him up, and made a fully committed Salvation Army soldier out of him.

On the way home that night, long after midnight, the captain had to cross a great irrigation ditch, and when he came to the bridge he heard a splash and a groan. Rushing forward he found a man's feet sticking up, but his head under the bridge and under the water. He pulled the man out of the water and got the water out of him. The poor fellow—in a fit of discouragement—was trying to commit suicide. But the captain prayed with him, ushered him into the experience of salvation, and the man became an earnest Christian.

That Salvation Army officer is now a lieutenant colonel and a divisional commander and is still passionately seeking and looking after souls.

New followers of Jesus need care just as new babies do. Many years ago I was temporarily put in charge of the Chicago Number 1 Corps (church) for three weeks while awaiting the arrival of the newly appointed officer (minister) in charge. One night I met a man who was fifty years of age. He had been a builder and contractor but had met with reverses, and in his discouragement came to The Salvation Army and yielded to the Lord Jesus Christ. I took special interest in him and gave him a word of cheer and a hearty handshake in every meeting. But one night he failed to come, and I was anxious.

I could not call to see him that night, but I did write him a little note before going to bed and enclosed a little tract. I told him how greatly

I missed him, expressed my hope that he was well, urged him to look to Jesus if he were passing through any temptation, and told him I was praying for him and looked forward to seeing him the following evening. And, sure enough, he was present the next night, and he told me how he had been passing through a fierce temptation the day before and was just about to give up and go back to his old life when my letter with the little tract came with its message of love and faith. "And that," said he, "saved me." He became a soldier and for years was a devoted Christian and worker for the Lord. The little note and tract and a two-cent stamp saved him.

If babies are to live, they must be nursed with tender care. If the flock is to be preserved, the lambs must be shepherded. If the world is to be saved, we must have new followers of Jesus, and they must be guarded with sleepless vigilance and followed with ceaseless and loving care.

An Open Letter to a Young Man Seeking Spiritual Help

17

My Dear Comrade,

Your letter has just now reached me, and I hasten to reply.

You say, "I have sought and found holiness many times, but the longest I have been able to keep it was seven weeks." And then you mention some besetting sin against which you have struggled for five years.

Let me ask: Did you yield to this besetting sin? And then feeling condemned, did you come to the penitent form seeking a clean heart? If so, you have probably made the great mistake so many make of claiming heart purity when what you received was the peace of pardon. If I fall into sin, I must first confess my sin with a penitent heart and trust for pardon through reliance upon the blood of Jesus, and if I do this the peace of pardon will fill my heart. But I must not mistake this for sanctification.

When I am pardoned, I am then called to consecrate my redeemed life to God, and when I wholly consecrate myself to Him who has loved me out of my sins, guilt, and condemnation, I must trust Him to purify my whole being, to sanctify me wholly, and to fill me with the Holy Spirit. And if I believe, He can and will do the wonder work of grace in me. He will make me holy. He will perfect me in love. He will fill me with passion for His glory, so that I sing from my heart:

> Take my love, my Lord, I pour
> At Thy feet, its treasure store;
> Take my life and it shall be
> Ever, only, all for Thee.[1]

And with joy I sing:

> The blood, the blood is all my plea;
> Hallelujah! For it cleanses me.[2]

You speak of keeping the blessing seven weeks. How did you keep the blessing so long? Was it not by walking with the Blesser? If your attention is fixed upon the blessing instead of the Blesser—if you think of holiness as separate from the Holy Spirit—you will lose all. If you fail to recognize, honor, love, trust, and obey the Blesser, you lose the blessing, just as you lose the beauty of the rose when you turn your eyes from the rose, or the sweetness when you take away the honey, or the music when you lose the musician. Why and how did you lose the blessing after seven weeks? Was it not because under stress of temptation you took your eyes off the Blesser? You forgot the sweet, sacred presence of the Blesser and, turning from Him, you yielded to sin, or you doubted, and then the Enemy robbed you of the blessing.

"Watch and pray that you may not enter into temptation" (Matt. 26:41 ESV). When temptation came you should have said, "Get behind me, Satan" (Matt. 16:23 ESV). You should have resisted the Devil and drawn near to God (see James 4:7). The Blesser was there. The Holy Spirit was present. The infinitely loving Redeemer, with all His redemptive power, was with you, but you forgot Him, and so lost the blessing.

You should have turned to Jesus in love and loyalty and trust, and said, "O Lord, I am Yours; keep me! I trust You. I love You. I praise You, and I will not fear my Enemy." If you had done this, you would not have lost the blessing. "Resist the devil, and he will flee from you. Draw nigh to God, and he will draw nigh to you" (James 4:7–8 KJV). That is the way, and I know of no other way of victory. In that way, and that way only, I have been getting victory for nearly half a century, and in that way you can get victory, get it quickly, and get it always.

You are discouraged. You wonder if you can ever gain and keep the victory. You can! The victory is at the door now. The Victor is at the door. Open the door, let Him in, and victory is yours. Drop on your knees now, just now, and tell Him all. Then trust Him, thank Him, praise Him, whether or not you have any great feeling. Just keep on trusting, thanking, praising, and obeying Him, and peace and victory will come.

Keep your eyes on Jesus, and guard yourself against the beginnings of temptation and sin. Keep your mind pure. Fill it with clean thoughts, loving thoughts, and holy affections. Lift your thoughts above fleshly and low things to spiritual levels. Sing songs and make melody in your heart to the Lord.

Deal promptly and sternly with your eyes and your ears. Turn your eyes away from beholding evil and your ears from listening to evil. Make a covenant with your eyes as Job did (see Job 31:1). Stand on guard at eye-gate and ear-gate to see that sin does not get into your heart through those gateways.

Sin does not leap upon us fully armed. It steals in through a look, a swift and silent suggestion, or the imagination. But love and loyalty to Jesus will make you watchful and swift to rise up and cast out the subtle enemy. "Do this and you will live" (Luke 10:28 NLT) and live victoriously.

Often drop on your knees or lift your heart in secret prayer, and do not forget to mingle thanksgiving with your prayers. You do not praise God enough. Begin now. Thank Him now and praise Him, for He is worthy, and you are much behind in this sweet duty.

When you wake up in the morning ask Him for some verse of song to cheer you through the day, and find some verse of Scripture upon which to fix your mind. Finally, seek to pass some of your blessing on to some other soul, as the widow of Zarephath shared her bit of oil and handful of meal with Elijah and found it multiplying through the months of famine (see 1 Kings 17:7–16). So will you find your blessings multiplying as you share them with others.

NOTES

1. Frances R. Havergal, "Take My Life and Let It Be," 1874, public domain.

2. E. F. Miller, "The Blood Is All My Plea," n. d., public domain.

The Mystic Universe in My Backyard

18

I am not sure that I lived so intimately with my darling wife as I have for forty years lived with St. Paul. Far more constantly and intimately than he lived and traveled with his friend Barnabas and his young lieutenants—Silas, Titus, Epaphroditus, and Timothy—he has lived, traveled, slept, and talked with me, only I did the sleeping. I never found him napping. At any hour of the day or night, he was waiting wide awake and ready for me.

A text in John's first epistle and another in his gospel proved to be the open door to my soul, leading into the Holy of Holies, into the experience of cleansing and the spiritual vision and inward revelation of Christ. But I think Paul has been my greatest teacher and mentor, and my most intimate spiritual guide. But one thing I have not found in him—a love of nature. Some of his biographers think he had no such love. He traveled by sea and land, among great mountain passes in Cilicia, through the mountains of Macedonia, over the Balkan hills, over the blue Mediterranean, and among the lovely isles of Greece. But never once does he in any of his epistles mention the wonders of nature, the splendor of sky or sea, the glory and majesty of mountains, the beauty of flowers, or the flight of birds, except in his discussion of the resurrection of the body that springs from the sown seed and the difference in the glory of one star from another.

"There is one glory of the sun, another glory of the moon, and another glory of the stars; for one star differs from another star in glory" (1 Cor. 15:41 NKJV). The fact that there is such glory he admits, but there is nothing to indicate that he was ravished by that glory. Still, we have no right to say that he was not. He was writing epistles to the churches upon infinitely important ethical and spiritual subjects, and there was no occasion for him to enter into rapturous description and comments upon the wonders and beauty of nature. But in my forty years of intimate communion with him I have never once been inspired by him to look for the blinding glories of the passing days and seasons or the pop and splendor of starlit nights.

But not so when I turn to Job, to the psalms of David, to the proverbs and songs of Solomon, and to the sweet talks and parables of Jesus. There we see the sparrows feeding from the heavenly Father's hand, the ravens and the young lions and every creeping thing looking to Him for daily food, the fox fleeing from enemies to its hole, the conies among the rocks, the wild goat among mountain crags, the nesting bird, the busy ant, the swarming bees, the neighing warhorse, the spouting whale, the bridal lilies, the rose of Sharon, the green and smiling meadows, the still waters, the ice, the snow, the hoar frost, the glowing fire, the tempestuous wind and billowing seas, the lowering sky of the morning threatening rain and storm, and the red sky of the evening presaging fair and smiling weather. "The heavens proclaim the glory of God. The skies display his craftsmanship. Day after day they continue to speak; night after night they make him known" (Ps. 19:1–2 NLT). The vast deeps of the heavens are the tabernacle of the sun, which "bursts forth like a radiant bridegroom after his wedding [and] rejoices like a great athlete eager to run the race" (Ps. 19:5 NLT), the race course compasses the whole circle of heaven, and the whole creation in one vast antiphonal choral harmony praises God. So David sang.

But the suggestions, and beauty, and wonder, and mysticism in nature to which Paul has never turned me, but to which Jesus and Job and David and Solomon pointed me, I am now finding in large measure in my tiny backyard. I am discovering a universe in my backyard.

Early one January in the deep, dark, underground, crowded railway of New York, roaring along beneath the great city and plunging beneath the broad and lordly Hudson River, late at night after attending meetings and lecturing cadets, I became chilled. I awoke in the middle of the night to find my head and throat inflamed with a heavy cold. I spent two and a half days in bed under the doctor's care and then crawled out and went to Chicago, where a whirlwind campaign awaited me. I gave myself without stint to those meetings. Once, for the first time I could remember, I feared my chest would fail me as I gasped for breath while speaking. But oh, those meetings! They were times of heaven upon earth. At the last session, which continued from 3 to 7 p.m., the whole place seemed lit up by the reflected glory on the faces in the crowd.

At last, weary and happy, I boarded a train late at night for Texas. The temperature outside was zero, the snow was knee deep, and there was no heat in our car. I sat and shivered in my sweater, winter overcoat, and a big cape, and finally went to bed with my clothes on, still to shiver. When we got to Texas, I was aching in all my bones. For three weeks I fought on, and then the flu claimed me. For the next three weeks I was in bed, and for the next few weeks among pine woods trying to get back my strength.

Presently I came home, but could not walk the length of a city block without panting and gasping for a long breath. My doctor examined me, and then sat down silent and stern, looked at me, and then lectured me: "You have gone to the edge of the abyss. Stop now or you will stop with a crash from which you will find it hard, if not impossible, to recover. If you take my advice, you will stop for six months." He had warned me at other times, but I had not always listened to him—had laughed at him, in fact, and gone my own way. But somehow I felt he was right this time, and I would fail to heed him at a dread risk.

A further exhaustive physical examination revealed an impoverished state of my blood, not pernicious, but sufficiently grave for the doctors to say that I must keep in the sunshine and open air, live largely on green vegetables, and rest.

For nearly thirty years, by day and night, summer and winter, through long hours I had labored for souls and sung and prayed and preached in crowded, steaming, ill-ventilated auditoriums, pleading with listeners and dealing with penitents in an atmosphere so depleted of oxygen and poisoned that every pore of my body, every lung cell and red blood corpuscle cried out for fresh air. And now I have turned to my backyard to get what I need. It has been waiting for me for ten years. I saw no beauty in it that I desired it. But it holds no grudge, welcomes me now, and never hints at my lack of appreciation and my past neglect.

A clump of yellow and blue iris is in one corner. A flowering shrub that has never bloomed for eight years and may be cast out as an unprofitable cumberer of the ground is at one side. A rambler rose bush, now preparing to burst into a blaze of pink flame, and a crabapple tree (which I believe botanists say is a relative of the rose) occupy the center of the yard, and a few square yards of green grass sprawl around iris and shrub and tree.

Just outside the border of my backyard on one side is a big oak tree, and on another side a maple tree, and they cast cool shadows over the grass when the sun is hottest. Some distance away are a few other oak trees. One belongs to a robin and some English sparrows. Another belongs to two young grey squirrels who have bound themselves together by matrimonial ties and only yesterday built a nest for their prospective family in the fork of their tree out of leaves and twigs which they cut with their sharp teeth from tips of the far-reaching branches.

Yesterday one of them slyly visited the tree that belongs to the robin and sparrows. He watched cautiously and climbed quickly. There were some nests up there he hoped to find defenseless. But a sparrow's keen eyes spied him, and she sent out a far-reaching SOS. And from every quarter sparrows came, and then a robin. The *entente* was perfect. And then I heard fierce, shrill war cries and witnessed an aerial battle as thrilling after its kind as any fought over the forts and forests and fields of France. I laughed at the mischievous cunning and daring of the little robber, but I confess my sympathies were all with the allied forces. They chattered and screamed and dashed upon him with sharp beaks and rending little claws. They came from above and all sides, swift and sure, until he turned ignominiously and fled to escape with whole ears and unimpaired eyes. The little grey rascal! It was wilderness epic.

The trees are glorious. They are not so large as their forefathers, but I think of them as the heirs of all the ages. And as I look at their broad-reaching limbs and into their deep-green foliage, they suggest the dark, solemn, whispering, primeval forest that once clothed this continent with its sheen like a great green ocean. Right here the Native Americans, the bear, the deer, the skulking panther roamed only twice as long ago as the lifetime of those now living.

Swift, speeding automobiles and loud, rumbling trucks rush past my backyard, and I hear thundering trains and factory whistles not far away, but here in this wee enclosure, partly in fact and partly in imagination, I am living a wilderness life. An ocean of fresh air, fifty miles deep, washes me in its waves that beat upon all the shores and isles of seas, and the mountains and plains of all continents. And beams of sunshine ninety million miles long unerringly find me with their life-giving rays.

I would like to tell you about the ants and the big, fierce horseflies and the little flowers among the grass, so tiny and so shy as scarcely to be seen, which I have discovered in my backyard. The grass, to the little creatures who live among its spires and tangled masses, is a forest as vast and mysterious as the great forests that have disappeared before the ruthless onslaughts and march of humanity. They live and hunt their prey, and make love, and bring forth their young, and flee their enemies, and live their short little lives among the green aisles and shadows of the grass, and know nothing of the greater world that arches above them, with its strifes and loves and labor and aspiration and sin and shame and redemption.

The astronomers tells us that, so far as they can judge, there are many sidereal universes. The heaven of heavens is full of them. But if that is so, if there are many universes of the infinitely great in the vast abysses of space, then I am sure there are many universes of the infinitely little in my backyard, as dear to God as those composed of flaming stars. And if health and strength can be found in the wilderness of plain or forest, or on mountain or sea, I believe it can be found among the teeming wonders, the mystic universes, and in the ocean of air and sunshine I find in my backyard.

O Lord, I worship amid the wonders of Your creation and give You thanks for a contented mind and the wealthy heritage of my little backyard. Amen.

The Frankness of Jesus 19

Jesus was not a whisperer. No one ever saw Him close to His neighbor's ear, looking stealthily around in case someone should overhear what He was going to say. He stood upright, looked others squarely and kindly in the eye, and spoke what He had to say right out, boldly, frankly, that the whole world might hear. And when He did speak privately to His disciples, He told them to shout it from the housetops. "Truth fears nothing but concealment," says an old proverb, and Jesus spoke only the truth: "To this end was I born, and for this cause came I into the world, that I should bear witness unto the truth" (John 18:37 KJV). He said, "What I tell you in the dark, say in the light, and what you hear whispered, proclaim on the housetops" (Matt. 10:27 ESV). It was against the Mosaic law to spread dangerous doctrines secretly, and the punishment was death (see Deut. 13:6–10). The High Priest and other religious leaders of Jesus' day had a right to inquire into this issue—indeed it was their duty to do so, according to their law, though they had no right to make Jesus convict Himself. However, that was not possible, for He had boldly preached His doctrine before priests and scribes as well as His disciples and the common people, and He answered the high priest: "Everyone knows what I teach. I have preached regularly in the synagogues and the Temple, where the people gather. I have not spoken in secret" (John 18:20 NLT). This refers to Jesus' doctrine, but can it not be given a far wider meaning? Was not His whole life an open book? Was not all His conversation such as could be proclaimed openly to the whole world?

There was nothing dark and hidden about Jesus. He was and is the Light of the World, and He welcomed the light. He entered into no secret cabals and councils. He belonged to no clique or party faction. I really do not believe He would have joined a secret society for two reasons. First, because if there was anything wrong and dark about it, His pure spirit, His guileless soul, would have revolted and denounced and withdrawn from it. And second, because if there was anything good in it, His generous spirit, His loving soul, overflowing with pity and goodwill, would never have been content till the whole world knew about it and had the privilege of sharing in its benefits. A good thing that He could not offer to share with all would have ceased to be a good thing to Jesus.

An astute Frenchman once said to The Salvation Army's founder, "General Booth, you are not an Englishman, you're a citizen of the world. You belong to humanity." And in this the general was like his Master. Jesus belonged to the world. He was the Son of Man, the Son of humanity. No party could claim Him. Thomas Jefferson wrote, "If I could not go to heaven but with a party, I would not go there at all."[1] It was this generous, open, worldwide, selfless spirit of Jesus that made Him so frank in all His speech, so that at the end of His life and His brief but complicated ministry, in which His enemies had sought in every way to provoke and entrap Him, He could say, "I have not spoken in secret" (John 18:20 NLT).

And now He wants us to "follow his steps: Who did no sin, neither was guile found in his mouth: Who, when he was reviled, reviled not again; when he suffered, he threatened not" (1 Pet. 2:21–23 KJV). If we do this we shall not be talebearers, we shall not listen to nor pass on gossip, nor be whisperers. "A whisperer separates close friends," said Solomon (Prov. 16:28 ESV). He also said, "Where there is no whisperer, quarreling ceases" (Prov. 26:20 ESV). And Paul linked "whisperers"—people who go around saying things in secret that they are afraid to say out boldly to everybody—with fornicators, murderers, backbiters, and haters of God (see Rom. 1:29–30). And one of the accursed things he feared for his beloved church in Corinth was "whisperings" (2 Cor. 12:20 KJV).

People who speak in secret what they are afraid to speak openly wrong their own souls, weaken their own character, and corrupt themselves, and those who listen to them are filled with suspicions and dislikes, destroying the beautiful spirit of brotherly love, which is open-faced, frank, generous, and saving in its power. Such whisperings quench the spirit of prayer and cause faith in God and others to languish and possibly die—for faith can live and flourish only in an atmosphere of frankness, kindness, and goodwill.

NOTE

1. Thomas Jefferson, *The Writings of Thomas Jefferson*, vol. 2 (Boston: Gray and Bowen, 1830), 439.

Our Mothers

20

How fitting, how beautiful, that a day should be set aside by the nation and the nations to honor that vast army of delicate soldiers, infinitely greater in numbers than the men who fought in the Great War, that numberless host whose sentinel watch is never done, whose arms are never laid down, whose warfare permits no discharge, and in which there is never an armistice until they fall on the field of battle: the great army of mothers.

We hail them and do them honor. They are a sacrificial host, the great givers and sufferers of the race. We never see a strong man striding forth in his strength for whom some mother has not suffered and given of her strength. We never see a blooming girl with rosy cheeks and laughing eyes and bewitching curls for whom some mother has not given of her own bloom and beauty and youth.

They bleed that we may be blessed. They keep watch that we may take rest and sleep. They suffer and often die that we may live.

Our mothers are our comforters in sorrow and the healers of our hearts when they are hurt. When the little child cries with loneliness in the dark and still night, and sobs and moans and reaches out little hands and arms, it is for Mother. When the child is hurt, he or she runs to Mother and finds balm in her kiss and comfort in the warmth and tenderness of her encircling arms for all fear and grief and healing for every wound.

When the big, foolish, awkward boy has a problem that perplexes, a hunger to satisfy, a shame to confess, or a triumph to announce, he goes to Mother, for she will understand. When the strong man is wearied by the toil and strife of life and his heart is harassed by uncertainties and doubt, he turns to Mother and Mother's God.

And when at last death wrestles with men and women, tightens its icy fingers upon them, and mocks them and claims them for its own as their strength fails, how often their thoughts turn to Mother! When stern old Thomas Carlyle lay dying, he was asked if there was anything he wanted. Turning his face to the wall, the granite of his Scotch heart broke up, and the old man sobbed, "I want ma mither." In the hour of death his heart turned as a little child to his mother.

Here is the might and the responsibility of motherhood. She can hold her children to goodness and God, not by force but by affection, not by the compulsion of command but by the compulsion of high and holy character.

I have been asked how mothers can hold their boys and keep them in paths of rectitude and godliness, and I can only reply to such questioning mothers, "You will help your boys not so much by what you say as by what you are and what you do. Command their respect, their admiration, and their love by loftiness and firmness of character, by patient steadfastness in well doing, by sweetness of spirit, by gentleness and graciousness of speech, and by the power of the Spirit of Christ abiding ungrieved in your cleansed heart, and though they may for a time wander away from you, yet unseen chains still bind them to you, and they will return, drawn back by mysterious cords of love and reverence."

Abraham Lincoln's mother died when he was only eight years old, but at the height of his fame and power he said, "All I am I owe to my angel mother."

I had just passed my fifteenth birthday and was away at school when one day the first telegram I ever received was handed to me. I read, "Come home, come quickly, mother is dying!" When I got home, she was dead. For the next twelve years, I had no home. I went off to school and college, but I received no letters from home. When holiday time came, I saw the other students trooping to the train with laughter, for they were going home, but I stayed behind, for no home awaited me. But my mother's sweet face was ever before me. Her love-lit eyes were ever turned upon me, so it seemed to me, and if ever I was tempted to evil, grief and reproach seemed to fill her eyes, while I could see love and sweet joy beaming in her face and from her eyes when I resisted the temptation. Indeed, her memory and influence were like a presence ever before and around me, and were like a flaming shield between me and youth's temptations. And I have known many a boy whose love and high and tender regard and reverence for his mother were like a pillar of fire and cloud to guide and protect him by day and by night. One boy I know intimately wrote to his mother and told her she was to him as "a piece of God, a dear little piece of God." And every mother should be to her boys and girls as "a piece of God, a dear little piece of God." And so she may be if she loves God with all her heart and seeks in all her words and ways to represent Him to her children.

Some mothers are not worthy of the love and respect of their children. A little orphaned boy was committed to one of our children's homes, and in its sweet and sacred atmosphere he was convicted of sin, but he said, "I can't get saved. When my mother was dying, I spit in her face." Her wickedness had reproduced itself in her little boy, and strangers had to undo the deadly work wrought in his poor little child heart by her sin.

It is religion pure and undefiled that crowns motherhood.

The glory of motherhood is the glory of sacrifice. A little lad noticed that tradesmen presented his mother with a bill for service. So a happy thought wakened within him and he presented a bill:

Mother debtor to Tommy:

Minding the baby	$6
Chopping and bringing in wood	$9
Mailing letters for a week	$10
Going to the shop	$6
TOTAL	$29

He laid it on her plate at the table. Mother looked at it, smiled, and then grew serious. At the next meal, Tommy found a bill at his plate:

Tommy debtor to Mother:

For caring for him through years of infancy	$0
For nursing him through two dangerous illnesses	$0
For getting his meals for him for ten years every day	$0
For washing and mending his clothes	$0
TOTAL	$0

Poor Tommy! When he read it, the long sacrifice and unwearied devotion of his mother dawned upon him, and with tears in his eyes he threw his arms around his mother and begged pardon for his thoughtlessness.

The glory of motherhood is the glory of unfailing patience. The father of John and Charles Wesley said to Susanna, their mother, one day, "Mother, why do you tell Charles the same thing over twenty times?"

She quietly replied, "Because nineteen times won't do."

Oh, the patience of mothers!

The glory of motherhood is the glory of unwavering faith and undying hope. A mother dedicated her baby to God and in prayer felt a conviction and assurance that he would preach the gospel. But instead of giving his heart to God, he fell into sin, and instead of preaching, he became a drunken unbeliever, mouthing infidelity. But the mother still prayed and believed and hoped on. One day she was sent for and told that he was dying of delirium tremens. She went quietly to his home, saying, "He is not dying. He will live and yet preach the gospel." And he did live. And he did preach the gospel—like a living flame of fire. And years later his sweet granddaughter also preached the gospel in The Salvation Army.

The glory of motherhood is the glory of self-forgetful unselfishness. A Salvation Army mother with six sons and daughters in the Army's work lay dying. Her youngest daughter, a cadet (student) in training for ministry, hastened to her side. But the saintly mother said, "Dear, I shall be cared for. I dedicated you, and God has called you to His work. Return to the training school and continue your studies. We shall meet in the morning at home in heaven." The dying mother forgot herself in her love for Christ and her holy ambition for her child.

The glory of motherhood is the glory of love that never fails. Some time ago, I was in a city where a large state prison is located. In my meetings in that city I noticed a sweet-faced, tiny woman with silvery hair and the peace of God in her face. One Sunday we went to the prison for a service with the prisoners and she was there. Her boy—I think he was her only boy—had wandered from home, fallen in with evil people, and was shut in behind the grim prison walls. When the little mother heard the heartbreaking news, all the tender love of her heart for her wayward boy burst into flame, and she left her home in the north and came to this city to live, that she might be near her son. And every Sunday she went to the prison to see him, seeking to win him back to goodness and God.

You can never wear it out, mother love is strong;
It will live through sin and shame, hurt and cruel wrong;
Even though the world revile and your friendships die,
Though your hands be black with sin, she will hear your cry,
Still she'll love you and forgive.[1]

Such is the glory of all true mothers, and for them we give praise to God, and to them we give the tribute of our reverence and tenderest affection.

The bravest battles that were ever fought,
Shall I tell you where and when?
On the map of the world you'll find it not,
'Twas fought by the mothers of men.

Nay, not with cannon or battle shot,
With sword or noble pen.
Nay, not with eloquent word or thought
From mouths of wonderful men;

But deep in a walled-up woman's heart—
A woman that would not yield,
But bravely, silently bore her part;
Lo, there is that battlefield.

No marshalling of troops, no bivouac song,
No banners to gleam and wave;
But oh! these battles they last so long,
From babyhood to the grave.[2]

NOTES

1. Edgar A. Guest, "Mother," 1925, public domain.
2. Joaquin Miller, "Mothers of Men," 1924, public domain.

Jesus Training Paul

21

We learn from the Gospels how Jesus, in the days of His flesh, trained the Twelve. We learn from the Acts and Paul's letters how the risen and glorified Jesus trained Paul. This chapter is a fragmentary study of that training and of some of Paul's struggles, inner conflicts, and fears out of and through which he was trained to triumph by obedient faith.

His experience was not one of ceaseless calm. Storms swept over him. It was not one of perpetual open vision. He was compelled to walk by faith and not by sight. He was sent forth to be a pathfinder, and no pathfinder treads an easy way, whether it is across trackless wastes of sand and sea; through the tangled jungles of a tropical forest; or amid the denser, darker jungles of base, idolatrous superstitions and bloody and licentious rites, or the claims of a cold, self-satisfied, arrogant, petrified priesthood.

Paul was treading a way that no one had trod before him. He had turned his back on all his teachers and all the traditions of his people and was carrying the gospel to the Gentiles, and what he spoke and wrote he learned from no man or woman. A strange, glorious, divine experience had come to him on the road to Damascus and in the street called Straight. But it had to be interpreted, and he found no interpreter. For three years, in the solitude of Arabia and in the silences of the night, he wrestled with his problems and the Lord illumined him, and he began to see new meanings in the ancient Scriptures. They ceased to be a binding, deadening letter and became life and spirit. His mind was liberated as from chains. God ceased to be simply the God of the Jews, a national God. He was the heavenly Father to whom all are dear, and the Lord Jesus Christ was not simply a Messiah for one people, a military conqueror, winning and building up His kingdom by the power of His sword. He was "the desire of all nations" (Hag. 2:7 KJV), bringing spiritual deliverance to all, not with sword and battle and "garments rolled in blood" (Isa. 9:5 KJV), but by the shame and power of the cross, winning His kingdom not by the slaughter of His enemies, but by becoming the Suffering Servant of all.

In Paul's letters, and especially in his letter to the Romans, we find many quotations from the Psalms and the old prophets, and these quotations are portions of the ancient Scriptures into which the Holy Spirit was flashing new meanings to Paul's mind. They became the sheet anchor of his faith when storms swept over his soul and bitter enemies denounced his claims to be an apostle.

One day his call came. The risen Jesus spoke to him and appointed him to be the apostle to the Gentiles. He wanted to stay at home and preach to his own people, but the Lord said, "They will not accept your testimony about me." But Paul argued back, "Lord, they themselves know that in one synagogue after another I imprisoned and beat those who believed in you. And when the blood of Stephen your witness was being shed, I myself was standing by and approving and watching over the garments of those who killed him." Surely, thought Paul, they will—they must—receive my testimony. Little did he yet know the willful stubbornness and fierce bigotry of unbelief. But the call was insistent: "Go, for I will send you far away to the Gentiles" (Acts 22:18–21 ESV). And Paul "was not disobedient to the heavenly vision" (Acts 26:19 ESV).

"I will show him how much he must suffer for the sake of my name," said Jesus to Ananias, when He sent him to the blinded Saul that he might receive his sight and be filled with the Holy Spirit (Acts 9:16 ESV). Little did Paul know what lay before him in the untrodden future. That was graciously hidden from him as it is from you and me.

There is a threefold ministry to which we are called: the ministry of service, the ministry of sacrifice, and the ministry of suffering. Some people seem called and fitted for one and some for another, but Paul was called and chosen to each and all of these ways of ministering the gospel. Great things he suffered. Great sacrifices were demanded of him. Immeasurable toil and great and insistent cares pressed ceaselessly upon him. Body, mind, and soul were each taxed to the limit in his great task. It was not always by some open vision or cheering voice, but often by the things he suffered that his Master taught and fashioned him.

Once in Asia some great trouble befell him, and he wrote, "We were burdened beyond measure, above strength, so that we despaired even of life. Yes, we had the sentence of death in ourselves, that we should not trust in ourselves but in God who raises the dead, who delivered us from so great a death" (2 Cor. 1:8–10 NKJV). In such manner Jesus trained and developed the faith of Paul and taught him to trust only in God. Could He not have taught Paul to trust in some easier way? Possibly, but He chose that way, and it must have been the best way. Paul was strong and self-reliant, and like Jacob at Jabbok, whose thigh was disjointed, he had to be broken to become "as a prince" and have "power with God and with men" (Gen. 32:28 KJV).

In his letter to the Thessalonian church, he exhorted them to "comfort the feebleminded, support the weak, be patient toward all" (1 Thess. 5:14 KJV). How did Paul, with his trained and master mind, learn to be gentle with the feebleminded, "as a nursing mother cherishes her own children" (1 Thess. 2:7 NKJV)? How, with his passionate, aggressive nature, did he come to put his strength at the disposal of the weak? How, with his impetuous and fiery spirit, did he ever become "patient toward all"? Like his Master, who, in the days of His humanity, "learned . . . obedience by the things which he suffered" (Heb. 5:8 KJV), so Paul was trained and so he learned from Jesus in the school of suffering.

We see how latent lightnings in his soul could flash and leap forth like a thunderbolt in his retort to the high priest who had commanded him to be smitten on the mouth: "God will slap you, you corrupt hypocrite! What kind of judge are you to break the law yourself by ordering me struck like that?" (Acts 23:3 NLT). It is true that when rebuked for so speaking to the high priest, he meekly replied, "'I'm sorry, brothers. I didn't realize he was the high priest . . . for the Scriptures say, 'You must not speak evil of any of your rulers'" (Acts 23:5 NLT).

But would Jesus have retorted as Paul did? When He was smitten by an officer because of His perfectly reasonable answer to the high priest, Jesus quietly said, "If I said anything wrong, you must prove it. But if I'm speaking the truth, why are you beating me?" (John 18:23 NLT).

Who am I that I should presume to judge Paul? I dare not judge him. I love him too tenderly. I have lived with him too intimately for over forty years. I am too greatly awed by his sacrificial life, his lofty character, his Christlike spirit, to attempt to pass judgment upon him. But if in that retort he fell below the standard of the Master, how is his spirit to be made meek and lowly as the Master?

"I, Paul, myself entreat you, by the meekness and gentleness of Christ," he wrote the Corinthians (2 Cor. 10:1 ESV). How did he learn this meekness and gentleness of Christ? There is but one way. "Take my yoke upon you, and learn of me," said Jesus, "for I am meek and lowly in heart" (Matt. 11:29 KJV). Paul came to Jesus, took upon himself the yoke of Jesus, received the spirit of Jesus, and submitted wholeheartedly without murmuring and complaint or self-pity to the discipline of Jesus, and so learned his lessons. From the day Jesus met him on the Damascus road, he was no longer persecuting" (see Acts 9:5). He might stand up stoutly against a traducer, but he bowed instantly at the word of Jesus. "The sinful nature [which] is always hostile to God" (Rom. 8:7 NLT) went out of him forever, and he followed Jesus with the passionate ardor of the perfect lover and the docility of the slave of love. Inbred sin is that something within that leads us to selfishly seek our own way instead of God's way, our own pleasure instead of God's pleasure—that exalts itself, that frets and repines or stubbornly resists in the presence of God's will. From all this Paul was set free.

That was the law—the power—of sin and death (see Rom. 8:2), and with that he had painfully and hopelessly struggled until he felt that he was like the ancient Etrurian murderer—who for punishment was chained face-to-face, chin-to-chin, limb-to-limb, to his dead, rotting, putrefying victim—and he cried out, "O wretched man that I am, who shall deliver me from this dead body?" (Rom. 7:24, paraphrase).

But upon meeting Jesus, believing in Jesus, casting himself in self-despair upon Jesus, and yielding to Jesus, Paul exultingly cried out, "There is therefore now no condemnation to those who are in Christ Jesus, who do not walk according to the flesh, but according to the Spirit. For the law of the Spirit of life in Christ Jesus has made me free from the law of sin and death" (Rom. 8:1–2 NKJV). His heart was pure of sin, but purity is not maturity. Purity comes instantly when the surrendered, pardoned soul intelligently and gladly, in simple faith, yields all its redeemed faculties and powers in an utter, unconditional, irreversible dedication to its Lord. But the ripe mellowness, the serene wisdom, the Christlike composure of maturity can only come through manifold experiences as we walk with Jesus in service, sacrifice, and suffering, and learn from Him.

Paul's spirit had to be disciplined, and he had much to learn as well as much to suffer. When Jesus commissioned him, He said, "I have appeared to you for this purpose, to appoint you as a servant and witness to the things in which you have seen me"—the things he had already learned—"and to those in which I will appear to you" (Acts 26:16 ESV). So the teaching and training and maturing of Paul began and continued through the years until at last he could write, "The time of my departure is at hand. I have fought a good fight, I have finished my course, I have kept the faith" (2 Tim. 4:6–7 KJV).

His Lord did not spare him, but He never failed him. And so out of wide experience and intimate knowledge Paul could write letters that were the revelation of the plan, the purpose, the mind, and the character of God in Christ—letters that have come down across two thousand years and are still as sweet and fresh and life-giving as clear waters from everlasting springs, bubbling up in deep, cool valleys, fed by eternal snows from great mountains.

Jesus meant, and Paul felt, that his experiences were not for himself alone. Through him Jesus was teaching the whole church for all time—teaching you and me. When in Paul's sore trials and tribulations his faithful Lord comforted him, he said that it was that he might comfort others with the comfort he had received from God, "For just as we share abundantly in the sufferings of Christ, so also our comfort abounds through Christ. If we are distressed, it is for your comfort and salvation; if we are comforted, it is for your comfort" (2 Cor. 1:5–6 NIV).

We may be sure that when Paul wrote, he wrote out of experience. When he wrote to those he loved at Ephesus, "Put on the full armor of God, so that you can take your stand against the devil's schemes" (Eph. 6:11 NIV), we rest assured that he had firsthand knowledge of those wiles and of the hopelessness of any defense unless we are arrayed in the whole armor of God. When he wrote, "In addition to all this, take up the shield of faith, with which you can extinguish all the flaming arrows of the evil one" (Eph. 6:16 NIV), there surely flashed into his memory some dark and lonely, painful and prolonged period when the Archenemy of his soul plied him with questionings and doubts and fears and forebodings for the future, and accusations for the past, until his harassed soul seemed to him like some soldier on the battlefield who was the target of archers who had dipped their darts in pitch and flame, and against which darts his only defense was his shield, the shield of faith. Those darts would quench their flame in his lifeblood if he did not use this shield, but against it they fell harmless.

In his first letter to the Thessalonians, he reminded them that in spite of the painful and shameful and dangerous treatment he received at Philippi, "We were bold in our God to speak unto you the gospel of God with much contention" (1 Thess. 2:2 KJV). Bold. But listen. In his letter to the Ephesians, written from Rome—where, he said, he was "an ambassador in chains"—he asked for church's prayers that "I may speak boldly, as I ought to speak" (Eph. 6:20 NKJV). Do we not get a hint from this of the temptation from which he suffered, and against which he girded himself and asked the sympathetic help of his brothers and sisters? He was old and worn, bruised and scarred, chained in prison and surrounded by relentless foes, and he was tempted to timidity and cowardice in preaching his gospel. Dear old Paul. Like his Master and ours, he was "tempted in every way, just as we are" (Heb. 4:15 NIV). But he fought on and triumphed. It is no sin to be tempted. It is sinful to yield. Paul did not yield, and so he remained in the school of Christ, and so Christ trained him.

It was out of such manifold experiences that he could write with an assurance that has reassured myriads of tempted, harassed souls, "No temptation has overtaken you that is not common to man. God is faithful, and he will not let you be tempted beyond your ability, but with the temptation he will also provide the way of escape, that you may be able to endure it" (1 Cor. 10:13 ESV).

Paul had mountain peak and paradisiacal experiences, but he also had hours of depression. How could it be otherwise, unless miracles had periodically been wrought for his deliverance?

Jesus would not turn stones into bread to satisfy His own hunger after forty days of fasting. And in training Paul, He did not pet and pamper and so spoil him. Heroes, martyrs, world conquerors, saints, are not made that way. "What are these which are arrayed in white robes? And whence came they?" asked John in Revelation. "These are they which came out of great tribulation, and have washed their robes, and made them white in the blood of the Lamb," was the answer (Rev. 7:13–14 KJV). Paul had great tribulation, and how could he escape the depression of reaction, when bruised from beatings and stonings, smarting and bleeding from cruel whippings, hungry and thirsty, pinched with cold, and exhausted from shipwreck and long and painful journeys? Add to these physical hardships his constant "care of all the churches" (2 Cor. 11:28 KJV), and his anxiety for his poor, persecuted churches in far-off cities. Add further his constant danger from relentless enemies who followed him from city to city. And, finally, add to all these Satan's hellish darts, and we get some conception of the infirmities, reproaches, necessities, persecutions, and distresses in and through which Jesus trained, disciplined, beautified, enriched, perfected, and matured the spirit of Paul, until he gloried and took pleasure in his infirmities, for in these it was revealed to his faith, rather than in his own native strength and powers, the power of Christ rested upon him. He said, "I have learned"—and learning is a process often prolonged and painful—"in whatsoever state I am, therewith to be content. I know both how to be abased, and I know how to abound"—a very difficult lesson, and one very dangerous not to learn. "Every where and in all things I am instructed"—still in the school of Christ—"both to be full and to be hungry, both to abound and to suffer need. I can do all things through Christ which [strengthens] me" (Phil. 4:11–13 KJV).

I see Your school is not an easy one, O Christ, but I would learn from You. Train me; teach me. Do You reply to me as to James and John, "You do not know not what you ask"? Still, O Lord, train me, discipline me, teach me. Do You ask, "Are you able to drink the cup that I am about to drink, and be baptized with the baptism that I am baptized with" (Matt. 20:22 NKJV)? You know, O Lord. I trust Your love and Your wisdom, and into Your hands I commit my spirit. So, teach me and train me that I with Paul may know You and the power of Your resurrection and the fellowship of Your sufferings, that I may comprehend with all the saints what is the breadth, and length, and depth, and height, and know the love of Christ, which surpasses knowledge, that I may be filled with all the fullness of God and thereby show to this generation Your strength, and Your power to everyone that is to come.

A Second Wind

22

When I was a little lad, time went by so slowly and the years seemed so long that I felt I would never be a man. But I was told that the years would not seem so long when I got into my teens. So I waited in hope, and after what seemed a century or two, I reached my teens, and sure enough the years tripped by a bit more quickly. Then I got into my twenties and they sped by yet more swiftly, and I reached my thirties and speedily passed into my forties. And almost before I had time to turn around I found myself in my fifties. About the time I hoped to catch my breath, the wild rush of years carried me into my sixties, and now I'm bracing myself for the plunge into the abyss of retirement!

But is it an abyss? Will it swallow me up, and shall I be lost in its dark and silent depths? Is it not rather a sun-kissed, peaceful slope on the sunset side of life where my often over-tasked body can have a measure of repose, and my spirit, freed in part from the driving claims of spiritual warfare, can have a foretaste of the Sabbath calm of eternity? Well, I shall soon know, for—abyss or sunlit slope—it is just ahead of me. In a very little while I shall find my name in the list of those who are retired. However, I am not distressed in the least about this, but I am thinking about it and laying spiritual anchors to windward against that day.

I know that Jesus said, "Take therefore no thought for the morrow, for the morrow shall take thought for the things of itself" (Matt. 6:34 KJV). But I am sure He did not mean that literally, for if so, we should never buy supplies or set aside money for taxes or a new suit of clothes. What He meant was that we should take no anxious thought. We should not worry and fret about tomorrow.

The best way I know to avoid anxious thought is to take calm, prayerful forethought. So I am taking forethought against the day of my retirement. I am praying for grace and wisdom for that time, and already I am considering what seem to me to be possible dangers and arming my spirit in advance against them. I believe in preparedness. Jesus said, "Be ready all the time" (Matt. 24:44 NLT). So I watch and pray and prepare, that I may not be found wanting. I don't want to lose the dew from my soul. The dew of the morning passes away but there is also the dew of evening—I do not want to miss that.

Sunset is often as glorious as sunrise, and when the sun goes down "the eternal stars shine out."[1] Often the splendor of the night is more wonderful than that of the day. The sun reveals the little things—the flowers and grasses and birds and hills and sea and mountains. But the larger things—the immensities of the heavens with their flashing meteors, their silvery moons, their star-strewn depths sown thick with flaming suns—these are the great things, and they are hidden by the garish light of day but revealed by the kindly darkness of night.

So I suspect the greater glories, the surpassing splendors of the spiritual world, are yet to be revealed to me as the sun of this life begins to sink beneath western hills. "At evening time it shall be light" (Zech. 14:7 KJV). I do not expect to fold my hands and sit in listless idleness or vain repining when I am retired. There will still be abundant work for my head and heart and hands. I shall probably not be so active on the field of ministry, or be going to and fro in the earth on long campaigns as in the past. But I hope to pray more for my comrades who are on the field and in the thick of the fight. There will be plenty of knee work to do, and we have need of knee workers more than ever, for this kaleidoscopic age—electric, restless, and changeful as the wind-swept sea—does not lend itself to prayer, the prayer that gets into close grips with God and the great wants of men and women, and brings down heavenly resources to meet vast earthly needs.

I shall meditate more—at least I hope to—and read and ponder my Bible more, and try to match its wondrous truths with life, the life I still live and must live. And by its light I shall try to interpret the life that surges all around me and manifests itself in the great movements, the triumphs and agonies and birth throes of peoples and nations. Oh, it will be a fascinating study!

I shall find plenty to do. If I can't command a Salvation Army corps or division, or take part in councils, or lead great soul-saving campaigns, I can talk to my grocer and doctor and letter-carrier about Jesus crucified and glorified, and the life that is everlasting. I can wear my (Salvation Army) uniform and go to testify. And I can still take an interest in the children and young people, and maybe out of the books of my experience find some helpful life lessons for them. And in doing this I shall hope to keep my own spirit young and resilient and sympathetic. I don't want to become hard and blind and unsympathetic toward youth, with its pathetic ignorance and conceit, its spiritual dangers, its heart-hunger, its gropings after experiences that satisfy, and its eager haste and its ardent ambitions.

I can write letters to struggling pastors—letters of congratulation for those who are winning victory; letters of sympathy and cheer for those who are being hard pressed by the foe; letters to missionaries in far-off lands; and letters to those who are bereaved, who sit with empty arms and broken hearts in the dark shadows and deep silence beside open graves where I too have sat, whose heartache and deep grief I know, who in vain long "for the touch of a vanished hand, and the sound of a voice that is still."[2]

I can write letters to those who in pain and weariness and possible loneliness are nearing the valley of the shadow of death, where only the Good Shepherd can go with them every step of the way, but where some word of hope and cheer may still reach them from someone who thinks of them in love and ceases not to pray for them.

The thought of retirement does not frighten me, nor cause me to repine, nor kindle resentment in me. Indeed, my long and somewhat heavy and exacting campaigns have left me frequently so weary that my body has cried out, "Here, now, you have driven me long enough; I am out of breath, exhausted, wearied half to death, tired down to the ground. I want you to retire."

But then my spirit has risen up and cried out, "Not a bit of it. Don't think of retirement! I'm not weary. I'm just learning how to fight. I'm getting my second wind. I want to die in the thick of the conflict on the field, at the battle's front, sword in hand, with my boots on."

So there is my problem. Retirement will give my body a breathing spell, but I am studying how to satisfy my spirit and give it worthy employment, with scope to fly and run and walk and not grow weary (see Isa. 40:31). Well, I shall find a way! Paul did, and Bunyan, and blessed and beloved old John on Patmos. Paul was sent to prison, but he talked to his guards and won them to Christ, and before long there were saints in Caesar's household (see Phil. 4:22). And, oh, those prison letters! Why, we would have missed some of the most precious portions of the Bible if Paul had not been forced into retirement through his prison experiences. I am glad he did not sit down and curse his fate and find fault and let his hands hang down and his knees grow feeble, but still strove on and made the years of retirement supplement and complete the labors of his active years.

John found work in his retirement. "Your old men shall dream dreams, your young men shall see visions," said Joel (Joel 2:28 KJV). But John, in his old age, banished to the Isle of Patmos, swept by wintry seas, reversed the order of Joel and saw visions. "I saw, I heard," wrote John. What did he see?

"I saw a great white throne, and him that sat on it" (Rev. 20:11 KJV). "I saw a new heaven and a new earth" (Rev. 21:1 KJV). "I . . . saw the holy city, new Jerusalem, coming down from God out of heaven" (Rev. 21:2 KJV). "I saw the dead, small and great, stand before God" (Rev. 20:12 KJV).

What did he hear?

I heard a loud shout from the throne, saying, "Look, God's home is now among his people! He will live with them, and they will be his people. God himself will be with them. He will wipe every tear from their eyes, and there will be no more death or sorrow or crying or pain. All these things are gone forever. . . .

"All who are victorious will inherit all these blessings, and I will be their God, and they will be my children. But cowards, unbelievers, the corrupt, murderers, the immoral, those who practice witchcraft, idol worshipers, and all liars—their fate is in the fiery lake of burning sulfur. This is the second death." (Rev. 21:3–4, 7–8 NLT)

One day I went through the book of Revelation and noted the things John saw, and the things John heard. And it occurred to me that God is no respecter of persons, but is eternally the same, and if John had visions and heard angelic voices in retirement, may not I? Bunyan the tinker did. In his filthy jail, surrounded by ignorance and vileness, in poverty and distress, oppressed by hard confinement, he caught visions of heaven and hell and delectable mountains and angelic hosts that made his retirement so fruitful as to feed the whole church of God for ages upon ages.

Even poor blind old Samson, sent into dark and bitter retirement through his sin, at last groped his way back to God, wrought havoc among the enemies of the Lord and of His people, and accomplished more in his death than in his life.

So when I am retired I shall not sulk in my tent, nor repine, nor grumble at my lot. Nor shall I seek a secular job to while away my time. For years I resisted God's call to preach. My heart was set on being a lawyer. But against my protest and stubborn resistance was God's insistent call. And since "the gifts and the calling of God are irrevocable" (Rom. 11:29 ESV), and since "God has given me this sacred trust" (1 Cor. 9:17 NLT), I shall carry on and do with my might what my hands find to do, and do so with joy and good cheer. But,

> My soul, be on thy guard,
> Ten thousand foes arise;
> The hosts of sin are pressing hard
> To draw thee from the skies.
>
> Ne'er think the battle won,
> Nor lay thine armor down;
> The fight of faith will not be done
> Till thou obtain the crown.[3]

Oh, my soul,

> Be sober, then, be vigilant; forbear
> To seek or covet aught beyond thy sphere;
> Only be strong to labor, and allow
> Thy Master's will to appoint thee where and how.
> Serve God! And winter's cold, or summer's heat,
> The breezy mountains or the dusty street—

Scene, season, circumstance, alike shall be

His welcome messengers of joy to thee,

His 'kingdom is within thee': rise, and prove

A present earnest of the bliss above![4]

And rejoice, oh my soul,

In the hour of death, after this life's whim,

When the heart beats low, and the eyes grow dim,

And pain has exhausted every limb—

The lover of the Lord shall trust in Him.

When the will has forgotten the lifelong aim,

And the mind can only disgrace its fame,

And man is uncertain of his own name—

The power of the Lord shall fill this frame.

When the last sigh is heard, and the last tear shed,

And the coffin is waiting beside the bed,

And the widow and child forsake the dead—

The angel of the Lord shall lift this head.

For even the purest delight may pall,

And power must fail and the pride must fall,

And the love of the dearest friends grow small—

But the glory of the Lord is all in all.[5]

NOTES

1. Thomas Carlyle, as quoted in Charles Noel Douglas, comp., *Forty Thousand Quotations: Prose and Poetical* (New York: Halcyon House, 1917), 42.

2. Alfred Lord Tennyson, "Break, Break, Break," 1835, public domain.

3. George Heath, "My Soul, Be on Thy Guard," 1781, public domain.

4. T. E. Hankinson, "The Cross Planted upon the Himalaya Mountains," *Poems* (London: Hatchard and Company, 1860), 300–301.

5. Richard Doddridge Blackmore, "At the Last," n. d., public domain.

The Future of
The Salvation Army 23

There are some questions always being asked and never fully answered, for the simple reason that only omniscience knows the answer. And omniscience is not disposed to answer questions which can be solved in some measure by diligent attention to the Spirit and principles revealed in the Bible, and the final answer to which is largely contingent upon our good behavior, our humility, our loyalty to truth and love, our unswerving allegiance to Jesus, and our diligence in keeping His commandments and walking in His footsteps.

I have recently been asked what I think about the future of The Salvation Army.[1] This is an old question, about as old as the Army itself. It was making the rounds when I joined the Army over forty years ago, and someone has been asking it ever since. Both friends and foes of The Salvation Army have asked it. Officers (ministers) and soldiers (church members) lives and whose families have been linked up and entwined with the Army have asked it. And I doubt not that our leaders have pondered over it and given it their profoundest and most anxious thought.

It is a question that those who love God and the souls of men and women can hardly avoid. With some it is a purely academic question. They would like to solve the question for intellectual satisfaction. Others, mere busybodies, would pry into the future, like many who are curious to know all about the affairs of their neighbors, that they may have something about which to gossip. It is not a matter of vital interest to them. Indeed, they are of that large class of people who have no vital interest in anything. They are like the lying woman in Solomon's day who stole another woman's baby, but had so little real interest in the baby that she was willing to have it cut in two rather than to acknowledge her theft and lie.

With others it is a painfully practical question. Their hearts are in The Salvation Army. It is as dear to them as life. They are bound up in the bundle of its life. They have sacrificed every other interest for it. They are given over to it soul and body, and have dedicated not only themselves, but also their children to it. They feel that the highest interests of the kingdom of God upon earth are bound up with the Army, and the coming and establishment of the kingdom are in large measure dependent upon its spiritual life and prosperity.

There are some people who are sure they know the answer. There are optimists who see nothing but the rosiest future for the Army. But there are pessimists who prophesy its imminent disruption and dissolution.

Many years ago, just after a tour that had taken me around the world, an old officer asked me with a quizzical look, "Are you going to leave the Army ship before she sinks?" I assured him that from a rather wide range of intimate observation I saw no signs that the ship was seriously leaking, or likely to sink, but that even if I did, as an officer my business was to stick to the ship and do all in my power to save it, or go down with it and its precious freightage of the souls of men and women and little children. "A hired hand will run when he sees a wolf coming. . . . The good shepherd sacrifices his life for the sheep" (John 10:12, 11 NLT). And the true officer gives his or her life for The Salvation Army and the souls who are in its keeping.

Doubters and timid souls have been prophesying the end of The Salvation Army from its very beginning, but still it lives and prospers. But what will be its future? Will it continue to live and prosper? Or has it fulfilled its mission?

Like a great bridge hung upon two buttresses, so the Army is buttressed upon God and humanity.

Is it God's Army? Did He inspire and gird and guide William Booth when, with his heart aching for sinful souls and his spirit aflame for the glory of God and the honor of Christ, he stepped out on Mile End Waste and began the work that has developed into The Salvation Army? Is God for us, or against us, or indifferent to us? I can sing for myself,

> His love in time past forbids me to think,
> He'll leave me at last in trouble to sink;
> Each sweet Ebenezer I have in review
> Confirms His good pleasure to see me quite through.[2]

But can I be so confident for the Army? His guidance, His overruling providence, His gracious and mighty deliverances in the past are unmistakable. They are on record, known and read by all who care to read. He has overshadowed The Salvation Army with a pillar of cloud and fire as surely as He did ancient Israel. He has gone before and opened the two leaved gates of brass as He did for Cyrus (see Isa. 45:1) and empowered Army officers and soldiers and made them more than conquerors, as He did the apostles and saints of the early church. But do all these wonders of His favor and grace give assurance for the future? Is The Salvation Army sacrosanct? Are we favorites and pets of the Almighty? This leads us to the second point of dependence.

If God is for us, and I fully believe He is, does not that ensure our future? The future of The Salvation Army depends not only upon God—I say it reverently—but also upon you and me and all who have anything to do with the Army. The prophet Azariah cried out, "Hear me, Asa, and all Judah and Benjamin. The LORD is with you while you are with Him. If you seek Him, He will be found by you"—and here is warning for us to heed, for here lurks danger—"but if you forsake Him, He will forsake you" (2 Chron. 15:2 NKJV). And this is a timeless prophecy, eternally true, and not of private interpretation. It is as true today as it was three millennia ago, as true of the Army—of you and of me—as it was of ancient Judah and Benjamin and their king Asa. And it is "written for our admonition, upon whom the ends of the world are come" (1 Cor. 10:11 KJV). Let us search our hearts, order our lives, and be admonished.

Insofar as we have sought God with our whole heart, walked in His ways, and lived and worked in the spirit of our Lord and Master in the past, He has been with us, preserved us, prospered the work of our hands, fulfilled the desires of our hearts, and blessed us in the presence of our enemies. Can we still confidently expect His favor for the future? Yes, but only if we continue to abide in Him and fulfill the conditions that have permitted Him to pour benedictions upon us in the past.

And what are these conditions? I think we shall find them expressed in the closing ministry of Jesus and of Paul. They were expressed by our Lord in those closing days of His ministry when preparing His disciples for His departure and for the days when they must stand alone without His incarnate presence and lay the foundations, build the church, and give it the living example and word that would guide it through the storm and stress of agonizing pagan persecutions, of worldly allurements and seductions, of subtle philosophizings, of pain and poverty, of indifference and scorn, and of the dangers of wealth and power and wide acclaim. And they were expressed through Paul in his later ministry, in his farewell address to the elders of Ephesus at Miletus and in his prison letters to the churches and his young friends and lieutenants, Timothy and Titus.

The warnings, exhortations, example, and the close and intimate instructions of our Lord to His disciples in the closing moments of His ministry, and His High Priestly Prayer recorded in the seventeenth chapter of John, show us the plain path in which we must walk, if the future of The Salvation Army is to be happy and prosperous and its great promise come to ample fulfillment.

And what were the example and teachings of the Master in those fleet, closing days? As He drew near the cross His disciples thought

He was drawing near to a throne and crown, and they were each ambitious and contentious for first place and highest honors. But He told them plainly that He would be rejected and crucified. Then Peter rebuked Him, "Heaven forbid, Lord. . . . This will never happen to you!" (Matt. 16:22 NLT).

But He rebuked Peter and replied, "If any of you wants to be my follower, you must turn from your selfish ways, take up your cross, and follow me" (Matt. 16:24 NLT).

It was not an unusual sight in the Roman Empire to see a line of men following a leader, each bearing a cross on his way to crucifixion. This was the picture He would have them visualize. They were to follow Him, their Leader, each bearing his own cross, not seeking to save his life, but ready to lose it for His sake and for the sake of others. For "all who want to save their lives will lose them. But all who lose their lives because of me will save them" (Luke 9:24 CEB).

So mightily at last did this teaching grip the early disciples and fire their spirits that they actually coveted martyrdom and ran upon death with joy. In this they may have swung to an extreme, but if The Salvation Army of the future is to prosper and win spiritual triumphs, we must follow the Master, not seeking first place or power, but glorying in the cross.

This was Paul's secret. He was the pattern disciple. He had sat at the feet of Jesus and learned of Him until he could write, "What things were gain to me, those I counted loss for Christ" (Phil. 3:7 KJV); "Neither count I my life dear unto myself, so that I might finish my course with joy, and the ministry, which I have received of the Lord Jesus" (Acts 20:24 KJV); "God forbid that I should glory, save in the cross of our Lord Jesus Christ, by whom the world is crucified unto me, and I unto the world" (Gal. 6:14 KJV).

If the future of The Salvation Army is to be spiritually radiant and all-conquering, we must not simply endure the cross, but glory in it. This will arrest the world, disarm hell, and gladden our Lord's heart. We must "by love serve one another" (Gal. 5:13 KJV). We are following Him who "came not to be ministered unto, but to minister, and to give his life a ransom for many" (Mark 10:45 KJV). We, too, must give our lives for others, shrinking from no service, holding ourselves ever ready to wash the feet of the lowliest disciple.

We must still prove our discipleship by our love for one another. It is not enough to wear the uniform, to profess loyalty to Army leaders and principles, to give our goods to feed the poor and our bodies to be burned. We must love one another. We must make this the badge of our discipleship. We must wrestle and pray and hold fast that we do not lose this.

The Salvation Army is so thoroughly organized and disciplined, so wrought into the life of nations, so fortified with valuable properties, and on such a sound financial basis, that it is not likely to perish as an organization. But it will become a spiritually dead thing if love leaks out. Love is the life of the Army. "If we love one another, God lives in us and his love is made complete in us" (1 John 4:12 NIV). But if love leaks out we shall lose our crown; we shall have a name to live and yet be dead. We may still house the homeless, dole out food to the hungry, punctiliously perform our routine work, but the mighty ministry of the Spirit will no longer be our glory. Our musicians will play meticulously and our singing groups will revel in the artistry of song that tickles the ear but leaves the heart cold and hard. Our officers will hobnob with mayors and council members and be greeted in the marketplace, but God will not be among us. We shall still recruit our ranks and supply our training schools with cadets from among our own young people, but we shall cease to be saviors of the lost sheep that have no shepherd.

If the future of The Salvation Army is to still be glorious, we must heed the exhortation, "Let brotherly love continue" (Heb. 13:1 KJV). We must remember that we are all brothers and sisters and be careful that through leakage of love we do not become like the wicked of whom the psalmist wrote, "You sit and speak against your brother; you slander your own mother's son" (Ps. 50:20 ESV), and find our hearts full of strife and bitter envying where the love that suffers long and is kind should reign supreme.

This is that for which Jesus pleaded on that last night before His crucifixion: "My command is this: Love each other as I have loved you. Greater love has no one than this: to lay down one's life for one's friends. You are my friends if you do what I command. . . . This is my command: Love each other" (John 15:12–14, 17 NIV).

This is that for which Paul pleaded and labored: "May the Lord make your love increase and overflow for each other and for everyone else, just as ours does for you. May he strengthen your hearts so that you will be blameless and holy in the presence of our God and Father when our Lord Jesus comes with all his holy ones" (1 Thess. 3:12–13 NIV).

This is that to which Peter exhorted the universal church: "Now that you have purified yourselves by obeying the truth so that you have sincere love for each other, love one another deeply, from the heart. . . . Above all, love each other deeply, because love covers over a multitude of sins" (1 Pet. 1:22; 4:8 NIV).

How else but by fullness of love for one another can we fulfill those supernatural requirements expressed by Paul and Peter? For more than forty years I have pondered and prayed over those two brief and searching words of Paul: "Be devoted to one another in love. Honor one another above yourselves" (Rom. 12:10 NIV). "Do nothing out of selfish ambition or vain conceit. Rather, in humility value others above yourselves" (Phil. 2:3 NIV).

These are lofty spiritual heights scaled only by those in whose pure hearts burns selfless love. This is the lifeblood—the pulsing, eager, satisfying and yet ever unsatisfied, outreaching, world-embracing lifeblood—of The Salvation Army.

Nothing will so certainly ensure the prosperous and happy future of the Army as this spirit, and I am persuaded that nothing other than this can ensure it. Insofar as this spirit rules in our hearts, God can work with us and bless us, and the spiritual triumphs and glory of the Army for the future are assured. But insofar as these graces of the Spirit in us fail, so far will The Salvation Army as a spiritual power in the earth fail. Organization and government are important, vastly important, for the direction and conservation of our activities, but without the lifeblood the organization is a bit of mere mechanism and the government is a pantomime.

Finally, in closing, let me recommend, for prayerful study and meditation, Paul's farewell address to the elders of Ephesus at Miletus, recorded in Acts 20:17–35. Over and over again and again, through more than four decades, I have read and pondered that address, and prayed that the spirit that was in Paul might be in me and in all my comrades, for this is the spirit of Jesus. This is that for which He prayed on that last night of His agony as recorded in the seventeenth chapter of John. And this is that, and that alone, which can and will ensure the victorious and happy future of our worldwide Salvation Army.

NOTES

1. This question was particularly pertinent in the years following the death of The Salvation Army's founder, William Booth, in 1912. *Ancient Prophets and Modern Problems* was first published in 1929, a year of great transition for the organization, which saw the election of Edward Higgins as the Army's third general and the death of the Army's second general (and William Booth's eldest son), Bramwell.

2. John Newton, "Begone Unbelief," 1779, public domain.

Samuel L. Brengle's Holy Life Series

This series comprises the complete works of Samuel L. Brengle, combining all nine of his original books into six volumes, penned by one of the great minds on holiness. Each volume has been lovingly edited for modern readership by popular author (and long-time Brengle devotee) Bob Hostetler. Brengle's authentic voice remains strong, now able to more relevantly engage today's disciples of holiness. These books are must-haves for all who would seriously pursue and understand the depths of holiness in the tradition of John Wesley.

Helps to Holiness
ISBN: 978-1-63257-064-2
eBook: 978-1-63257-065-9

The Heart of Holiness
ISBN: 978-1-63257-066-6
eBook: 978-1-63257-067-3

The Servant's Heart
ISBN: 978-1-63257-068-0
eBook: 978-1-63257-069-7

Ancient Prophets and Modern Problems
ISBN: 978-1-63257-070-3
eBook: 978-1-63257-071-0

Come Holy Guest
ISBN: 978-1-63257-072-7
eBook: 978-1-63257-073-4

Resurrection Life and Power
ISBN: 978-1-63257-074-1
eBook: 978-1-63257-075-8

**Samuel L. Brengle's
Holy Life Series Box Set**
ISBN: 978-1-63257-076-5

SAMUEL L. BRENGLE'S HOLY LIFE SERIES

THE SERVANT'S HEART

Bob Hostetler, General Editor

wesleyan
PUBLISHING HOUSE
wphstore.com

CREST BOOKS

Library of Congress Cataloging-in-Publication Data

Brengle, Samuel Logan, 1860-1936.
   The servant's heart / Samuel L. Brengle ; Bob Hostetler, general editor.
      pages cm. -- (Samuel L. Brengle's holy life series)
   ISBN 978-1-63257-068-0 (pbk.)
   1. Witness bearing (Christianity) 2. Evangelistic work. 3. Christian life. I. Hostetler,
Bob, 1958- editor. II. Title.
   BV4520.B645 2016
   248'.5--dc23
                                        2015026516

This work is a revised combination of the following book from The Salvation Army:
The Soul-Winner's Secret and *Love Slaves*.

Contents

Preface

Samuel Logan Brengle was an influential author, teacher, and preacher
on the doctrine of holiness in the late nineteenth to early twentieth century,
serving from 1887–1931 as an active officer (minister) in The Salvation
Army. In 1889 while he and his wife, Elizabeth Swift Brengle, were
serving as corps officers (pastors) in Boston, Massachusetts, a brick
thrown by a street "tough" smashed Brengle's head against a door frame
and caused an injury severe enough to require more than nineteen
months of convalescence. During that treatment and recuperation
period, he began writing articles on holiness for The Salvation Army's
publication, *The War Cry*, which were later collected and published
as a "little red book" under the title *Helps to Holiness*. That book's
success led to eight others over the next forty-five years: *Heart Talks
on Holiness*, *The Way of Holiness*, *The Soul-Winner's Secret*, *When
the Holy Ghost Is Come*, *Love-Slaves*, *Resurrection Life and Power*,

Ancient Prophets and Modern Problems, and *The Guest of the Soul* (published in his retirement in 1934).

By the time of his death in 1936, Commissioner Brengle was an internationally renowned preacher and worldwide ambassador of holiness. His influence continues today, perhaps more than any Salvationist in history besides the founders, William and Catherine Booth.

I hope that the revised and updated editions of his books that comprise the Samuel L. Brengle's Holy Life Series will enhance and enlarge that influence, introduce these writings to new readers, and create fresh interest in those who already know the godly wisdom and life-changing power of these volumes.

While I have taken care to preserve the integrity, impact, and voice of the original writing, I have carefully and prayerfully made changes that I hope will facilitate greater understanding and appreciation of Brengle's words for modern readers. These changes include:

- Revising archaic terms (such as the use of King James English) and updating the language to reflect more contemporary usage (such as occasionally employing more inclusive gender references);
- Shortening and simplifying sentence structure and revising punctuation to conform more closely to contemporary practice;
- Explaining specific references of The Salvation Army that will not be familiar to the general population;
- Updating Scripture references (when possible retaining the King James Version—used exclusively in Brengle's writings—but frequently incorporating modern versions, especially when doing so will aid the reader's comprehension and enjoyment);

- Replacing Roman numerals with Arabic numerals and spelled out Scripture references for the sake of those who are less familiar with the Bible;
- Citing Scripture quotes not referenced in the original and noting the sources for quotes, lines from hymns, etc.;
- Aligning all quoted material to the source (Brengle, who often quoted not only Scripture, but also poetry from memory, often quoted loosely in speaking and writing);
- Adding occasional explanatory phrases or endnotes to identify people or events that might not be familiar to modern readers;
- Revising or replacing some chapter titles, and (in *Ancient Prophets and Modern Problems*) moving one chapter to later in the book; and
- Deleting the prefaces that introduced each book and epigraphs that preceded some chapters.

In the preface to Brengle's first book, Commissioner (later General) Bramwell Booth wrote, "This book is intended to help every reader of its pages into the immediate enjoyment of Bible holiness. Its writer is an officer of The Salvation Army who, having a gracious experience of the things whereof he writes, has been signally used of God, both in life and testimony, to the sanctifying of the Lord's people, as well as in the salvation of sinners. I commend him and what he has here written down to every lover of God and His kingdom here on earth."

In the preface to Brengle's last book, *The Guest of the Soul*, The Salvation Army's third general (and successor to Bramwell Booth) wrote: "These choice contributions . . . will, I am sure, serve to

strengthen the faith of the readers of this book and impress upon them the joyousness of life when the heart has been opened to the Holy Guest of the Soul."

I hope and pray that this updated version of Brengle's writings will further those aims.

—Bob Hostetler

general editor

PART ONE

The Soul-Winner's Secret

The Personal Experience of the Soul-Winner

Every soul-winner is in the secret of the Lord and has had a definite personal experience of salvation and the baptism of the Holy Spirit, which brings him or her into close fellowship, tender friendship, and sympathy with the Savior. The psalmist prayed, "Purify me from my sins. . . . Remove the stain of my guilt. Create in me a clean heart, O God. Renew a loyal spirit within me. Do not banish me from your presence, and don't take your Holy Spirit from me. Restore to me the joy of your salvation, and make me willing to obey you" (Ps. 51:7, 9–12 NLT).

"Then," said he, "I will teach your ways to rebels, and they will return to you" (Ps. 51:13 NLT). He saw that before he could be a soul-winner, before he could teach others the way of the Lord and lead them to salvation, he must have his own sins blotted out; he must have a clean heart and a right spirit, and he must be a partaker of the Holy Spirit and of God's joy. In short, he must have a definite, constant, joyful experience of God's salvation in his own soul in order to save others. It was no "hope I am saved" experience he wanted, nor was it a conclusion carefully reasoned out and arrived at by logical processes. It was not an experience based upon a strict performance of a set round of duties and attendance upon sacraments, but a mighty transformation and cleansing of his whole spiritual nature and a glorious new creation wrought within him by the Holy Spirit.

This must be a definite experience that tallies with the Word of God. Only this can give that power and assurance which will enable you to lead and win others. You must have knowledge before you can impart knowledge. You must have fire to kindle fire. You must have life to reproduce life. You must know Jesus and be on friendly terms with Him to be able to introduce others to Him. You must be one with Jesus and be "bound up in the bundle of life" (1 Sam. 25:29 KJV) with Him if you would bring others into that life.

Peter had repented under John the Baptist's preaching, had forsaken all to follow Jesus, had waited with prayer and unquenchable desire until he received the baptism of the Holy Spirit and of fire, and had been anointed with power from on high before he became the fearless, mighty preacher who won three thousand souls in a day.

Paul was mightily changed on the road to Damascus, heard Jesus' voice tell him what to do, and was baptized with the Holy Spirit under Ananias's teaching before he became the apostle of quenchless zeal who turned the world upside down.

Luther was definitely transformed and justified by faith on the stairway of St. Peter's in Rome before he became the invincible reformer who could stand before popes and emperors and set captive nations free.

George Fox, John Wesley, Charles Finney, George Whitefield, Jonathan Edwards, William Taylor, James Caughey, Dwight L. Moody, and William Booth all had definite personal experiences that made them apostles of fire, prophets of God, and winners of souls. They did not guess that they had experienced new life in Christ, nor "hope" so, but they knew in Whom they believed (see 2 Tim. 1:12) and knew that they had passed from darkness into light and from the power of Satan to God (see Acts 26:18).

This experience was not spiritual evolution but revolution. No evolutionist ever has been or ever will be a great soul-winner. It is not by growth that we become such, but by revelation. It is not until God bursts through the veil to reveal Himself in our hearts through faith in His dear Son; gives a consciousness of personal acceptance with Him; and sheds abroad His love in the heart, destroying unbelief, burning away sin, consuming selfishness, and filling the soul with the passion that filled the heart of Jesus, that we become soul-winners.

The experience that makes a man or woman a soul-winner is twofold. First, we must know our sins to be forgiven. We must have recognized ourselves to be sinners, out of friendly relations with God, careless of God's claim, heedless of God's feelings, selfishly seeking our own way in spite of divine love and compassion, and heedless of the awful consequences of separating ourselves from God. This must then have led to repentance toward God, by which I mean sorrow for and an utter turning away from sin, followed by a confiding trust in Jesus Christ as our Savior. We must have so believed as to bring a restful consciousness that for Christ's sake our sins have been forgiven and we have been adopted into God's family and made one of His dear children.

This consciousness results from what Paul called the witness of the Spirit (see Rom. 8:16) and enables the soul to cry out in deep filial confidence and affection, "Abba, Father" (Rom. 8:15 NLT).

Second, we must be sanctified. We must know that our heart is cleansed, that pride and self-will and carnal ambition and strife and sensitiveness and suspicion and unbelief and every unholy temper are destroyed by the baptism of the Holy Spirit. We must experience a personal Pentecost and the incoming of a great love for, and loyalty to, Jesus Christ.

It must be a constant experience. People who frequently meet defeat in their own souls will not be largely successful in winning others to Jesus. The very consciousness of defeat makes them uncertain in their exhortation, doubtful and wavering in their testimony, and weak in their faith. This will not be likely to produce conviction and beget faith in their hearers.

Finney, Wesley, Fletcher of Madeley, William Bramwell, Catherine Booth, and scores of others walked with God, as Enoch did, and so walked "in the power of the Spirit" (Luke 4:14 KJV) constantly and were soul-winners all their lives.

It must be a joyful experience. "The joy of the LORD is your strength," said Nehemiah (Neh. 8:10 KJV). "Restore to me the joy of your salvation," prayed David (Ps. 51:12 NLT).

"I feel it my duty to be as happy as the Lord wants me to be," wrote Robert Murray McCheyne, the gifted and deeply spiritual Scottish preacher, who was wonderfully successful in winning souls.

William Caughey, while preaching his sermon entitled "The Striving of the Spirit," cried out, "Oh, my soul is very happy! Bless God! I feel He is with me!"[1] No wonder he won souls.

Whitefield and Bramwell, two of the greatest soul-winners the world ever saw, were at times in almost an ecstasy of joy, especially when preaching. And this was as it should be.

John Bunyan told us how he wrote *The Pilgrim's Progress* in his filthy Bedford dungeon. He said, "So I was led home to prison, and I sat me down and wrote and wrote because joy did make me write."

God wants His people to be full of joy. Jesus said, "These things have I spoken unto you, that my joy might remain in you, and that your joy might be full" (John 15:11 KJV). And again He said, "Ask and you will receive, and your joy will be complete" (John 16:24 NIV). John wrote, "And these things we write to you that your joy may be full" (1 John 1:4 NKJV). "The fruit of the Spirit is . . . joy," wrote Paul (Gal. 5:22 KJV), and again he wrote, "The Kingdom of God is . . . living a life of goodness and peace and joy in the Holy Spirit" (Rom. 14:17 NLT). Joy in the Holy Spirit is an oceanic current that flows unbroken through the holy, believing soul, even when surrounded by seas of trouble and compassed about by infirmities and afflictions and sorrows.

We so often have thought of Jesus as the "man of sorrows" (Isa. 53:3 KJV) as to overlook His fullness of exultant joy.

Joy can and should be cultivated, just as faith or any other fruit of the Spirit is cultivated:

- By appropriating by faith the words that were spoken and written for the express purpose of giving us fullness of joy. "May the God of hope fill you with all joy and peace in believing" (Rom. 15:13 ESV), wrote Paul to the Romans. It is by believing.

- By meditating on these words and holding them in our minds and hearts as we would hold honey in our mouths, until we have gotten all the sweetness out of them.

- By exercise, even as faith or love or patience is exercised. This we do by rejoicing in the Lord and praising God for His goodness and mercy, and shouting when the joy wells up in our souls under the pressure of the Holy Spirit. Many people quench the spirit of joy and praise, and so gradually lose it. But let them repent, confess, pray, and believe, and then begin to praise God again, and He will see to it that they have something to praise Him for. Then their joy will convict others and prove a mighty means of winning souls to Jesus.

Who can estimate the power there must have been in the joy that filled the heart of Peter and surged through the souls and beamed on the faces and flashed from the eyes of the 120 fire-baptized disciples, while he preached that Pentecostal sermon which won three thousand bigoted enemies to the cross of a crucified Christ? O Lord, still "make [Thy] ministers a flame of fire" (Heb. 1:7 KJV) and flood the world with Your mighty joy!

NOTE

1. Brengle may have been mistaken in referencing Caughey's sermon, "The Striving of the Spirit." In a collection of Caughey's sermons containing that sermon, another sermon—"Purification by Faith"— contains the words, "My God is in this place; He is here; I feel Him blessing this poor little heart; my soul is very happy." (James Caughey, "Purification by Faith," *Helps to a Life of Holiness and Usefulness, or Revival Miscellanies* [Boston: J. P. Magee, 1852], 36.)

Obedience 2

"I was not disobedient to the vision from heaven," said Paul (Acts 26:19 NIV), and in that saying he revealed the secret of his wonderful success as a soul-winner. Soul-winners are men and women sent by God, who will receive direct orders that, if affectionately heeded and heartily and courageously obeyed, will surely lead to success. They are preeminently workers together with God (see 2 Cor. 6:1) and soldiers of Jesus Christ, and as such must obey. It is their business to take orders and carry them out.

The Lord said to Jeremiah, "I knew you before I formed you in your mother's womb. Before you were born I set you apart and appointed you as my prophet to the nations" (Jer. 1:5 NLT). And when Jeremiah interrupted and said, "O Sovereign LORD . . . I can't speak for you! I'm too young!" the Lord said to him, "Don't say, 'I'm too young,' for you must go wherever I send you and say whatever I tell you. And don't be afraid of the people, for I will be with you and will protect you. I, the LORD, have spoken! . . . Get up and prepare for action. Go out and tell them everything I tell you to say. Do not be afraid of them, or I will make you look foolish in front of them" (Jer. 1:6–8, 17 NLT).

Soul-winners must get their message from God and speak what and when He commands. They are servants of God, friends of Jesus, prophets of the Most High, ambassadors of heaven to the citizens of this world, and they must speak heaven's words and represent heaven's court and King and not seek their own will, but the will of Him who sent them. "To obey is better than sacrifice" (1 Sam. 15:22 KJV). They must not trim their course to suit others, nor stop to ask what this or that person would do, but must attend strictly to the Lord and steadfastly follow Jesus. Paul told us that Jesus was "obedient unto death" (Phil. 2:8 KJV), and again and again he called himself a servant of Jesus Christ.

This obedience must be prompt. In spite of the appeals and encouragements of Joshua and Caleb, the children of Israel refused to go over into Canaan. But afterward, seeing their sin in refusing to obey promptly, they attempted to go over in spite of the warnings of Moses not now to do so, and met with bitter defeat. Promptness would have saved them forty years of wandering in the wilderness.

Once the soul-winner knows the Master's will, there must be no delay to fulfill it. If you are in doubt, you can take time to assure yourself as to what that will is. God would not have you run before you are sure you are sent, nor go before you have a message, nor falter and possibly fall because of uncertainty. But once you have received your orders and your message, remember that "the king's business require[s] haste" (1 Sam. 21:8 KJV). Strike while the iron is hot. Act and speak when the Spirit moves, and do not dilly-dally like covetous Balaam to see if God will change His mind and His orders.

American admiral George Dewey's matchless victory at Manila (during the Spanish-American War) was won, and the geographical boundaries of the nations changed, by the promptness with which he carried out his orders to destroy the Spanish fleet. I have noticed that if I speak when the Spirit moves me, I can usually introduce the subject of religion and God's claims to any individual or group with happy results. But if I delay, the opportunity slips by, not to return again, or if it does return, it does so with increased difficulties.

This obedience must be exact. Saul lost his kingdom and his life because his obedience was only partial (see 1 Sam. 15). So also did the prophet who warned the wicked King Jeroboam (see 1 Kings 13).

By contrast, Mary told the servants at the marriage in Cana, "Do whatever he tells you" (John 2:5 NLT), and when they obeyed Him, Jesus performed His first miracle. And so He will work miracles today through His chosen people, if they will do whatever He says. Then they will find that it is not themselves but the Spirit who speaks in them, so that they can say with Jesus, "The words I speak are not my own, but my Father who lives in me does his work through me" (John 14:10 NLT). For did not Jesus say, "Ask for anything in my name, and I will do it" (John 14:13 NLT)?

This obedience must be courageous. "Don't be afraid of the people," said the Lord to Jeremiah (Jer. 1:8 NLT). And He said to Ezekiel, "Son of man, do not fear them or their words. Don't be afraid even though their threats surround you like nettles and briers and stinging scorpions. Do not be dismayed by their dark scowls, even though they are rebels. You must give them my messages whether they listen or not!" (Ezek. 2:6–7 NLT).

He was not to say that which would please the people, but that which God gave him to say, and that without fear of consequences, for God would be with him.

"Then Saul admitted to Samuel, 'Yes, I have sinned. I have disobeyed your instructions and the LORD's command, for I was afraid of the people and did what they demanded'" (1 Sam. 15:24 NLT). No wonder God cast him off and gave his crown and kingdom to another! God said, "Don't be afraid, for I am with you. Don't be discouraged, for I am your God. I will strengthen you and help you. I will hold you up with my victorious right hand" (Isa. 41:10 NLT).

Let all soul-winners recognize that they are on picket duty for heaven, and let them throw themselves on heaven's protection and rest in the assurance of their heavenly Father's care and in Jesus' utmost sympathy and support. Let them do their duty courageously, saying with Paul, "I can do everything through Christ, who gives me strength" (Phil. 4:13 NLT).

Again and again I have comforted myself with good King Jehoshaphat's assurance: "Deal courageously and the LORD shall be with the good" (2 Chron. 19:11 KJV). I have encouraged myself with Peter's bold declaration to the enraged and outwitted Sanhedrin: "We must obey God rather than any human authority" (Acts 5:29 NLT). And I have measured myself by Nehemiah's self-forgetful words: "Should someone in my position run from danger? Should someone in my position enter the Temple to save his life? No, I won't do it!" (Neh.

6:11 NLT). And Paul's: "My life is worth nothing to me unless I use it for finishing the work assigned me by the Lord Jesus—the work of telling others the Good News about the wonderful grace of God" (Acts 20:24 NLT). And the three Hebrew children's: "O Nebuchadnezzar, we do not need to defend ourselves before you. If we are thrown into the blazing furnace, the God whom we serve is able to save us. He will rescue us from your power, Your Majesty. But even if he doesn't, we want to make it clear to you, Your Majesty, that we will never serve your gods or worship the gold statue you have set up" (Dan. 3:16–18 NLT). That is the kind of stuff out of which God makes soul-winners.

Do you ask, how can a man or woman get such a spirit of courageous obedience? I answer, by dying—dying to your selfish interests, to the love of praise, to the fear of censure, and to the hope of reward in this world—by a daredevil faith in the reward that God will give in the world to come, by a steadfast looking unto and following of Jesus, and by a constant comparison of time with eternity. I read the other day that it was only dead men who were living preachers.

The obedience must be glad. The command is, "Serve the LORD with gladness" (Ps. 100:2 KJV). "I take joy in doing your will, my God," wrote the psalmist (Ps. 40:8 NLT). There was no grudging about his obedience; it was his joy. It is a love service God wants, and that is always a joy service. "My meat is to do the will of him that sent me," said Jesus (John 4:34 KJV), and Paul declared, "If I do this thing willingly, I have a reward" (1 Cor. 9:17 KJV). It is a glad love service God calls us to, and once we are wholly His and the Comforter abides in us, we shall not find it irksome to obey. And by obedience we shall both save ourselves and others to whom the Lord may send us.

Let me hear Thy voice now speaking,

Let me hear and I'll obey;

While before Thy cross I'm seeking,

O chase my fears away!

O let the light now falling

Reveal my every need,

Now hear me while I'm calling,

O speak, and I will heed!

Let me hear and I will follow

Though the path be strewed with thorns;

It is joy to share Thy sorrow,

Thou makest calm the storm.

Now my heart Thy temple making,

In Thy fullness dwell with me;

Every evil way forsaking,

Thine only I will be.[1]

NOTE

1. Herbert Booth, "Let Me Hear Thy Voice Now Speaking," *The Salvation Army Songbook*, 1913, public domain.

Prayer  3

Prayer is the way of approach to God, and the soul-winner keeps it open by constant use. It is the channel by which all spiritual blessings and power are received, and therefore the life of the soul-winner must be one of ceaseless prayer. "Pray without ceasing," wrote Paul (1 Thess. 5:17 KJV). It is the breath of the soul, and other things being equal, it is the secret of power.

It was written of Jesus, "And it came to pass in those days, that he went out into a mountain to pray, and continued all night in prayer to God" (Luke 6:12 KJV). And this was followed by mighty works.

What an amazing statement is this: "Whatever you ask in prayer, believe that you have received it, and it will be yours" (Mark 11:24 ESV). And this: "If you abide in me, and my words abide in you, ask whatever you wish, and it will be done for you" (John 15:7 ESV). And yet, amazing as these promises are, they stand there in "the Book of Truth" (Dan. 10:21 NLT) as a challenge to every child of God who is passionate about God's glory, longs for the triumph of righteousness, and seeks the salvation of souls.

Soul-winners must pray in secret. They must get alone with God and pour their hearts into the Father's ear with intercessions and pleadings and arguments if they would have success. There is no substitute for much wide awake, expectant, secret waiting upon God for the outpouring of the Holy Spirit, the gift of wisdom, strength, courage, hope, faith, and discernment. If we fail at this point, we will soon fail at every point. Jesus said, "When you pray, go into your room and shut the door and pray to your Father who is in secret. And your Father who sees in secret will reward you" (Matt. 6:6 ESV).

Here, then, is one secret of success: communion and counselings and conversations in the closet with God, who is our Father, and who can and will no more turn away from us when we come in the spirit of an obedient and affectionate child than can the sunlight when we throw open the windows and doors and stand in its beams. I say it reverently. He cannot turn away from us but will surely reward us—and openly, because He said He would, and He cannot lie.

Prayer must be definite. Once, when Jesus was leaving Jericho, blind Bartimaeus sat by the wayside begging, and when he heard Jesus was passing by, he cried out, "Jesus, Son of David, have mercy on me." But that prayer was not definite—it was altogether too general. Jesus knew what Bartimaeus wanted, but He desired Bartimeus to state exactly what he desired, and said to him, "What do you want me to do for you?" Then the blind man prayed a definite prayer—"Rabbi, let me recover my sight"—and the definite prayer then received a definite answer, for Jesus said to him, "Go your way; your faith has made you well," and immediately he received his sight (Mark 10:46–52 ESV).

We should be as definite when we go to God, in asking Him for what we want, as we are when we go to the store. The salesman is prepared to sell us anything and everything in the store, but he in reality sells us nothing until we tell him what we want, and so it is with our heavenly Father.

Our prayers must be bold. Paul said, "Let us come boldly unto the throne of grace, that we may obtain mercy, and find grace to help in time of need" (Heb. 4:16 KJV). Of course, this boldness must be coupled with humility, but the greater the humility, the greater the boldness, if mixed with faith. I have often been amused and amazed at the boldness with which children come to their parents for the things they need and the things they want, and how gladly the loving parents respond to the child's request, especially if the child expresses a genuine need! And Jesus said: "If you, then, though you are evil, know how to give good gifts to your children, how much more will your Father in heaven give good gifts to those who ask him!" (Matt. 7:11 NIV).

The Devil stands mocking and teasing praying souls to drive them from their knees and from their Father's face, but let them rather come boldly in the name of Jesus and wait patiently for the things they desire, and they shall have an abundant reward. It is not our heavenly Father's will to disappoint His trusting children, but rather to give them their utmost desire, "exceeding abundantly" (Eph. 3:20 KJV) above all they ask or think, for His heart is all love toward them. Therefore let us not be timid and wavering, but steadfast and bold as His dear children.

Prayer must be persistent and persevering. Jesus taught this very clearly in His parable of the importunate friend:

Suppose you went to a friend's house at midnight, wanting to borrow three loaves of bread. You say to him, "A friend of mine has just arrived for a visit, and I have nothing for him to eat." And suppose he calls out from his bedroom, "Don't bother me. The door is locked for the night, and my family and I are all in bed. I can't help you." But I tell you this—though he won't do it for friendship's sake, if you keep knocking long enough, he will get up and give you whatever you need because of your shameless persistence. (Luke 11:5–8 NLT)

Then Jesus added, "Keep on asking, and you will receive what you ask for. Keep on seeking, and you will find. Keep on knocking, and the door will be opened to you" (Luke 11:9 NLT). With those words, Jesus meant to teach that we are to hold on in prayer till we get an answer. If the answer is delayed, our own hearts will be searched, the purity of our motives will be proven, and our faith will be purified, tried, developed, and strengthened for future and greater triumph.

Jesus prayed three times that the cup of death in the garden of Gethsemane might pass from Him. It was not death on the cross but death in the garden He feared. And the writer of Hebrews told us that He was heard (see Heb. 5:7). Daniel abstained from all pleasant food for three weeks at one time, and prayed until God appeared to him and said, "Don't be afraid . . . for you are very precious to God. Peace! Be encouraged! Be strong!" (Dan. 10:19 NLT), and added, "I will tell you what is written in the Book of Truth" and then told him all he desired to know (Dan. 10:21 NLT). And Elijah, after his victory over the priests of Baal, sent his servant seven times to look for the cloud that would bring rain, while he bowed his face between his knees and poured out his heart to God in prayer until the cloud appeared. Though the answer may be delayed, it is not God's purpose to deny us without letting us know the reason why.

Prayer must be for the glory of God and according to His will. If we ask things simply to gratify our own desires, God cannot grant them. James said of some, "You ask and do not receive, because you ask wrongly, to spend it on your passions" (James 4:3 ESV). But John said, "This is the confidence that we have toward him, that if we ask anything according to his will he hears us. And if we know that he hears us in whatever we ask, we know that we have the requests that we have asked of him" (1 John 5:14–15 ESV). Jesus said, "If you abide in me, and my words abide in you, ask whatever you wish, and it will be done for you" (John 15:7 ESV).

We are to ask according to the things revealed as His will in His Word and according to the principles laid down in it. Therefore we should study His Word constantly and hide it in our own hearts, and see to it that we hide ourselves in His heart and thus be filled with the truth. We shall then not ask amiss and, being filled with the Spirit, we shall not be denied.

Prayer must be mixed with faith. It must be believing prayer. "Whatever you ask in prayer, believe that you have received it, and it will be yours" (Mark 11:24 ESV). Oh, what a victory I got one morning over the Devil, when he tried to shake my faith and confidence! I laid hold of that promise and wrestled through to the solid rock of believing prayer, and had one of the most glorious soul-saving days in my life! The person whose faith is constantly wavering shall receive nothing from the Lord (see James 1:6–7).

Finally, prayer must be in the name of Jesus. "Whatever you ask in my name, this I will do, that the Father may be glorified in the Son," said Jesus (John 14:13 ESV). "The blood, the blood is all my plea,"[1] and with that plea the vilest sinner may come, while those born of God may approach with unabashed boldness into the presence of their heavenly Father and claim all the resources of heaven in their warfare against sin and in their effort to win souls and build up the kingdom of God.

NOTE

1. F. C. Baker "I Knew That God in His Word Had Spoken," 1885, public domain.

Zeal  4

It is said that Civil War general Philip Sheridan went to battle with all the fury of a madman. He claimed he never went into a battle from which he cared to come back alive unless he returned as a victor. This desperation made him an irresistible inspiration to his own troops and enabled him to hurl them like thunderbolts against his foes. If he became so desperate in killing people, how much more desperate, if possible, should we become in our effort and desire to see them enter into new life!

It was written of Jesus, "Zeal for your house will consume me" (John 2:17 ESV), and so it can be of every great soul-winner.

Not until a person can say with Paul, "My life is worth nothing to me unless I use it for finishing . . . the work of telling others the Good News about the wonderful grace of God" and "I am ready . . . to die . . . for the sake of the Lord Jesus" (Acts 20:24; 21:13 NLT) can he or she hope to be largely used in winning souls. Those who are anxious about their dinner, eager to get to bed at a reasonable hour, concerned about their salary, querulous about their reputation, and afraid of weariness and pain and headache and heartache will not make great soul-winners.

There are various kinds of zeal that should be avoided as deadly evils.

1. Partial zeal, like that of Jehu (see 2 Kings 10:15–31). God set him to destroy the wicked house of Ahab and the worship of Baal, and he did so with fury. "But Jehu did not obey the Law of the LORD, the God of Israel, with all his heart. He refused to turn from the sins that Jeroboam had led Israel to commit" (2 Kings 10:31 NLT). And in due time God had to cut off his dynasty as well.

This kind of zeal is frequently seen in those who violently attack one sort of sin while they themselves secretly indulge in some other sin. Such people are usually not only intolerant of the sin, but also of the sinner, while true zeal makes one infinitely tender and patient toward the sinner, while absolutely uncompromising with the sin.

2. Party zeal like that of the Pharisees and Sadducees. In these days, it takes the form of excessive sectarian and denominational zeal, and makes bigots of people. Zeal for the particular church or organization to which one belongs is right within certain limits. We come to faith through the instrumentality of a certain religious organization and we become children of its household, or we are led into it by the Holy Spirit through a blessed, divine affinity with its members, methods, spirit, and doctrine. In that case, we should be loyal and true to its leaders who are over us in the Lord and who watch for our souls, and follow them as they follow Christ.

We should also be loyal to the principles of the organization so far as they harmonize with the Word of God, and we should by prayer and supplication and ceaselessly zealous work seek to build up this organization in holiness and righteousness. And this we can do with all our might, if we do it in the Holy Spirit, and can be assured that God is well pleased with us. But we must at the same time beware of a party spirit that would despise other work and workers or tear them down that we may rise on their ruins. Such zeal is from beneath and not from above. It is contrary to that love which "does not seek its own" (1 Cor. 13:5 NKJV) and looks out not only for one's own interests but "also for the interests of others" (Phil. 2:4 NKJV). Such party zeal will come back like a boomerang upon our own pates and bring ruin upon ourselves.

"For the love of God is broader than the measure of our mind, and the heart of the Eternal is most wonderfully kind."[1] And true zeal makes us like that.

3. The zeal of ignorance. Paul said of his kinsmen, the Jews: "My heart's desire and prayer to God for them is that they may be saved. For I bear them witness that they have a zeal for God, but not according to knowledge. For, being ignorant of the righteousness of God, and seeking to establish their own, they did not submit to God's righteousness" (Rom. 10:1–3 ESV).

True zeal is from above. Its source is in the mountains of the Lord's holiness and its springing fountains in the deep, cool valleys of humility. It is born of the Holy Spirit and flows from a knowledge of "the truth that is in Jesus" (Eph. 4:21 NIV). This knowledge is twofold.

First, it is the knowledge of the dread condition of the soul without Christ—its slavery to Satan, the inherited depravity of its nature, its bondage to sin, its love of it, its enmity toward God (of which the person may be unaware), its guilt, helplessness, ignorance of the way back to the heavenly Father's house and happiness, and its awful danger, if it neglects the offer of salvation and life in Jesus Christ.

Second, it is the knowledge of the unspeakable gift of God, the possibilities of grace for the vilest sinner, the Father's pitying, yearning love. It is the knowledge of sins forgiven, guilt removed, adoption into the Father's family, illumination, consolation, guidance, and safekeeping. It is the knowledge of depravity destroyed, cleansing through the blood, sanctification by the baptism of the Holy Spirit, salvation from the uttermost to the uttermost, unbroken fellowship with the Father and His Son Jesus Christ through the eternal Spirit, and a life of blessed service and fruit bearing. It is the knowledge of a faith and hope that bear the spirit up over sorrows, trials, losses, pain, and sickness, enabling it at last to cry out in supreme victory and holy triumph, "'O death, where is your victory? O death, where is your sting?' . . . Thanks be to God, who gives us the victory through our Lord Jesus Christ" (1 Cor. 15:55, 57 NASB).

True zeal makes one faithful to Jesus and the souls for whom He died. It led Paul during his three years' appointment at Ephesus "to warn every one night and day with tears" (Acts 20:31 KJV) and to keep back no truth that was profitable for the people, but to show them and teach them "in public and from house to house, testifying both to Jews and to Greeks of repentance toward God and of faith in our Lord Jesus Christ" (Acts 20:20–21 ESV). He was not content simply to get people to accept Jesus as their Savior, but taught them that "this is the secret: Christ lives in you. This gives you assurance of sharing his glory. So we tell others about Christ, warning everyone and teaching everyone with all the wisdom God has given us. We want to present them to God, perfect in their relationship to Christ. That's why I work and struggle so hard, depending on Christ's mighty power that works within me" (Col. 1:27–29 NLT).

Paul was zealous for the perfection in love and loyalty of all his converts, and his zeal led him to seek with all his might to lead them all into this blessed experience. As was Paul, so also was Richard Baxter, who labored indefatigably in spite of lifelong sickness—and at times almost intolerable pain—for the perfection of his people. And so also was John Wesley and George Fox and William and Catherine Booth, and so will be every soul-winner who is full of the zeal of God.

True zeal is sacrificial. Jesus, consumed with zeal for the glory of God in the saving and sanctifying of souls, was led "as a lamb to the slaughter" (Isa. 53:7 KJV). He could say, "I offered my back to those who beat me and my cheeks to those who pulled out my beard" (Isa. 50:6 NLT). He was "despised and rejected of men; a man of sorrows, and acquainted with grief" (Isa. 53:3 KJV). And again, "But he was pierced for our rebellion, crushed for our sins. He was beaten so we could be whole. He was whipped so we could be healed. All of us, like sheep, have strayed away. We have left God's paths to follow our own. Yet the LORD laid on him the sins of us all" (Isa. 53:5–6 NLT).

He poured out His soul unto death for us. He gave His life as a ransom for all. And the gift of His Spirit kindles and sustains this same sacrificial zeal in the hearts of all true soul-winners.

Enlarge, inflame, and fill my heart

With boundless charity divine,

So shall I all strength exert

And love them with a zeal like Thine,

And lead them to Thy open side,

The sheep for whom the Shepherd died.[2]

NOTES

1. Frederick W. Faber, "There's a Wideness in God's Mercy," 1862, public domain.

2. Charles Wesley, "Give Me the Faith Which Can Remove," 1749, public domain.

Spiritual Leadership 5

The soul-winner must have the power of spiritual leadership, and spiritual leadership is a thing of the Holy Spirit, not of birth, rank, title, education, or circumstances.

Joseph was a youthful prisoner in an Egyptian dungeon, but he walked with God and was "a prosperous man" (Gen. 39:2 KJV) because God was with him, and one day he reached his rightful place next to Pharaoh's throne.

Paul was a prisoner under Roman guards on board ship, hastening to Caesar's judgment bar. But one day God's winds made the sea boil, and winds and waves smite the ship, so that the hearts of all the other men on board failed them for fear. Then Paul, by right of spiritual kingship, became the master of all on the ship (see Acts 27).

I knew a Salvation Army lieutenant, a quiet, modest, thoughtful, prayerful, faithful, humble, holy young man of moderate ability. His superiors sat at his feet for spiritual counsel, though the lieutenant knew it not. They hung on his God-wise words, remembered his example, and treasured his spirit. They talked to me about his saintliness and Christlikeness long after he had left them for a flock of his own. They were in charge, but he held spiritual supremacy because he walked with God, and God was with him and in him.

Spiritual leadership is not won by promotion, but by many prayers, tears and confessions of sin, and heart-searchings and humblings before God. It comes by self-surrender; a courageous sacrifice of every idol; a bold, uncompromising, and uncomplaining embrace of the cross; and an eternal, unfaltering looking unto Jesus. It is not gained by seeking great things for ourselves (see Jer. 45:5), but rather by counting those things that once seemed valuable as worthless compared to Christ. Like Paul, I "once thought these things were valuable, but now I consider them worthless because of what Christ has done. Yes, everything else is worthless when compared with the infinite value of knowing Christ Jesus my Lord. For his sake I have discarded everything else, counting it all as garbage, so that I could gain Christ" (Phil. 3:7–8 NLT).

That is a great price, but it must be unflinchingly paid by anyone who would be not merely a nominal but a real spiritual leader, one whose power is recognized and felt in three worlds—heaven, earth, and hell. Moses gained this spiritual leadership among Pharaoh's palace halls and Sinai's solitudes and vastness, when he "refused to be called the son of Pharaoh's daughter; choosing rather to suffer affliction with the people of God, than to enjoy the pleasures of sin for a season; esteeming the reproach of Christ greater riches than the treasures in Egypt" (Heb. 11:24–26 KJV).

Spiritual leaders are not made by human action. Neither conferences, nor synods, nor councils can make them, but only God. Spiritual power is the outcome of spiritual life, and all life—from that of the moss and lichen on the wall to that of the archangel before the throne—is from God. Therefore let those who aspire to this leadership pay the price, and seek the role from God.

Who made Elijah and John the Baptist—hairy, uncouth men of the wilderness and desert—prophets who awed kings and swayed nations? God. Who took Moses from the universities of Egypt and the palaces of Pharaoh and, after drilling him among flocks of sheep in the desert for forty years, made him the meek but unconquerable leader of two million people, and the lawgiver and fountainhead of jurisprudence for all time? God. Who took the baby Samuel and put into his mouth prophetic words to the aged priest, Eli, and made him the spiritual leader of Israel? God. Who took the boy David, trained to feed harmless, patient sheep, put courage into his heart, nerved his arm to fight the lion and the bear and the giant, and gave him skill to lead Israel's armies? And who gave him such skill that the women sang: "Saul has killed his thousands, and David his ten thousands" (1 Sam. 18:7 NLT), while the elders, after Saul's death, came to David, and said, "In the past, when Saul was our king, you were the one who really led the forces of Israel. And the LORD told you, 'You will be the shepherd of my people Israel. You will be Israel's leader'" (2 Sam. 5:2 NLT)? God.

And why did God single out these people and distinguish them, and give them this power above others? Because God was to them the supreme fact. They believed God, sought God, feared and trusted and obeyed God. Read the Psalms and see how God fills the whole heaven of David's thought, desire, and affection, and you will cease to wonder at his leadership. It was based on spiritual life, power, and fellowship with God.

This spiritual leadership, once attained, can be maintained. Witness Moses, Elijah, Paul, Fox, Wesley, Finney, Booth, and ten thousand leaders in humbler spheres who "still bear fruit in old age" and "stay fresh and green" (Ps. 92:14 NIV). They are like a white-haired, old saint of eighty years I once visited who, after I had prayed, burst into prayer also, and said, "O Father, I testify to Thee, and the angels, and these young brothers, that old age is not a time of dotage and second childhood but the springtime of eternal youth."

I hear comparatively young people complaining and expressing fear that when they get old, they will be set aside and superseded by younger people without a tenth of their experience, forgetting that it is not long service and experience that makes spiritual leaders, but vigorous spiritual life, and that if they are set aside, it will be because they have neglected the divine life, the Holy Spirit in them. Nothing can make men and women acceptable leaders, however long their service and varied their experience, if they have lost the spirit of prayer, faith, and fiery-hearted love and the sweet simplicity, trustfulness, and self-sacrifice of their youth, and are now living on past victories, revelations, and blessings. But fresh anointings of the Spirit and present-day experiences will make them acceptable, though their eye be dim, their back bent, and their voice husky with age.

There have been ministers who in their prime fought against the doctrine of holiness and refused the baptism of the Holy Spirit (or who, having received the baptism, neglected and lost it), who filled great pulpits and drew fat salaries but whose influence gradually waned and whose old age was full of complainings and disappointments and bitterness and jealousies, and whose sun went down behind clouds because they neglected God.

But I also know old men and women, full of God, who were persecuted in their prime for Jesus' sake, but who had salt in themselves and kept sweet and delighted themselves in the Lord, whose bow abides in strength (see Gen. 49:24), whose sun shines in fullness of splendor, and who even now fill the world with divine messages that others are eager to hear. Know this, that long service and experience will not save you from becoming obsolete, but God in you will. God is always up to date. And it is God whom people want.

What service had they performed and what experience had Moses, David, Daniel, and Paul when God set them up as leaders? None. But they were in touch with God; they were pliable to His will, teachable, trustful, obedient, courageous, and uncomplaining.

They were full of God. And know this, you who fear the time is coming when your services will no longer be appreciated or wanted and that you will be thrust into a corner, that a man or woman who is full of God cannot be thrust aside. If he is put into a desert place, then all will flock to the desert place, as they did to Jesus and John the Baptist. And if she is thrust into a corner, then the world will stop and bend its ear to her corner to hear the latest message from God. They thrust Paul into prison, but he spoke and wrote words of life and power that burn with the unquenchable fire of the Holy Spirit and are doing more to direct the thought, inspire the faith, and inflame the affections of men and women today than ever before.

The "powers that be" thought they were finished with him when they cut off his head, but after two thousand years his influence goes on increasing.

And so they thought they had silenced Madam Guyon in the Bastille and John Bunyan in Bedford Jail. But who can silence the thunder of God's power or hush His "still, small voice" when He chooses to speak through someone? Their silent prisons become public address systems connected with the skies.

One day, an old man died in one of our large cities. He died long past the age of seventy. He was a minister who, at the age of forty-seven, broke down so utterly in health from overwork that for five years he never read a chapter from a book, not even the Bible. But he held fast his faith in both God and humanity, kept his love all aglow, and at last died full of years and was mourned by hundreds in all parts of the globe who had been saved, sanctified, inspired, and qualified for service by his words and life and the agencies he set in motion for the salvation and sanctification of God's people. And his greatest work was accomplished after he had passed sixty years of age. But while this spiritual power and leadership may be maintained, yet it is a subtle thing that may be lost forever.

When Saul was little in his own sight, he was made king, but when lifted up he became disobedient, and his kingdom was torn from him and given to another. And is it not this we are warned against in the words, "Hold on to what you have, so that no one will take away your crown" (Rev. 3:11 NLT)? The place of Judas among the apostles was given to another (see Acts 1:15–26). The one talent was taken from the "wicked and lazy servant" and given to him who had ten (see Matt. 25:26–28).

I knew a Christian worker who was surrounded by a number of other bright, earnest, teachable, spiritually ambitious young people who looked to him for direction and guidance. He invited them to his home for an evening. While they waited for soul food, coffee and cake were brought out, and when they expected prayer and counsel, the chessboard was produced. The opportunity of the evening slipped away, and the strong bonds that united them in God were relaxed and weakened, if not in one or two cases broken. And, while his official leadership was still recognized, his commanding spiritual leadership was gone, perhaps forever.

"But you, dear friends, must build each other up in your most holy faith, pray in the power of the Holy Spirit, and await the mercy of our Lord Jesus Christ, who will bring you eternal life. In this way, you will keep yourselves safe in God's love" (Jude 20–21 NLT).

Redeeming the Time 6

The soul-winner must value time. Diamonds and gold nuggets are not so precious as minutes. One morning, about five o'clock, John Wesley lost ten minutes through the tardiness of his coachman and mourned for them more than over lost treasure.

Dr. Samuel Johnson tells us, "When [Philipp Melanchthon] made an appointment, he expected not only the hour, but the minute to be fixed, that the day might not run out in the idleness of suspense."[1]

A woman told me that she was sure she got a position as a teacher once by being sharp on time. Another young woman, better fitted for the position, arrived a bit late and remarked, "I thought it wouldn't make any difference if I were a few minutes late." She was politely informed that her services were not wanted, as a teacher had been secured. Eternity is made up of moments, and "lost time is lost eternity."[2]

"Believe me," said William E. Gladstone, "when I tell you that thrift of time will repay you in after life with a usury of profit beyond your most sanguine dreams, and that the waste of it will make you dwindle alike in intellectual and moral stature, beyond your darkest reckonings."[3] And yet thoughtless idlers try to "kill time," and thus destroy their most valuable possession. What is life but a glad, present consciousness of God and self and duty, and a hearty obedience thereto? But those who kill time seek to forget and would be far better dead.

"The future is nothing but a coming present," wrote Jean Paul Richter, "and the present which thou despisest was once a future which thou desiredst."[4] The philosopher Marcus Aurelius wrote, "Every man lives only this present time, which is an indivisible point, and . . . all the rest of his life is either past or it is uncertain."[5]

If you would redeem the time, begin the moment your eyes open in the morning. Let no idle, foolish, hurtful thoughts be harbored for an instant, but begin at once to pray and praise God and meditate on His glories, His goodness, His faithfulness, and His truth, and your heart will soon burn within you and bubble over with joy. Bounce out of your bed at once and get the start of your work and push it, or else it will get the start and push you. For, "If you in the morning throw minutes away, you can't pick them up in the course of the day."[6]

A fellow Salvation Army officer (minister) said to me one day, "There is much in the habit of work. If a man forms the habit, he naturally turns to it. I find it so with myself. I squander less time now than I once did."

The difference between wise and foolish folks, rich and poor, saints and sinners, redeemed and unredeemed, does not usually result so much from different circumstances and the start they had in life, as it does from the difference in their use of time. One used it purposefully, while the other squandered it. One was a miser of minutes, the other was a spendthrift of days and months and years. One was always active, packing into every hour some search for truth, prayer to God, communion with Jesus, service to others, counsel to a saint, and warning or entreaty to wandering souls, while the other was neglecting the opportunity of the present but full of vague dreams for an ever receding, elusive future. The one plods patiently and surely to glory, honor, peace, immortality, and eternal life, as the other drifts dreamily, but certainly, into the regions of "indignation and wrath, tribulation and anguish" (Rom. 2:8–9 KJV) and finally lands in hell.

To redeem time one does not mean feverish hurry, but a prompt, steady, quiet use of the minutes. It was said of John Wesley that he was always in haste, but never in a hurry. "Make haste slowly," is a wise old adage.

To save time the soul-winner will find it profitable to go to bed at a reasonable hour and to get up promptly on waking in the morning. Those who have accomplished anything in the world have usually gone to work early in the day. For example, Albert Barnes wrote sixteen volumes in less than an equal number of years, devoting to them only the hours before breakfast.

If you would save time, keep a Bible, notebook, and pencil always at hand. Never go on to the street or take a journey without at least a New Testament with you, and some other useful book if possible. And don't forget to use them. The gospel of Matthew can be read through in approximately two hours. This may not be the most profitable way to read it, and yet it will pay to read it right through at one sitting so as to see the life of Jesus as a whole, as we would the life of anyone. Paul's first letter to Timothy can be read in aboout twenty minutes, while Jude can be easily read in about three minutes.

Catherine Booth had to snatch time from household duties and the care of small children to prepare her marvelous addresses that stirred England and did so much to make and mold The Salvation Army.

The person who sits about smoking and reading novels or whiling away the minutes idly thrumming on a guitar and reading the daily papers will not succeed at soul-saving work. The soul-winner can redeem time by being "instant in season, out of season" (2 Tim. 4:2 kjv) in dealing with others about the things of God.

John Vassar, an eccentric but marvelously successful soul-winner, once saw two women in the parlor of a Boston hotel. He immediately inquired if they were at peace with God, and kindly and earnestly preached Jesus to them, urging them to make ready for death and judgment by accepting Him as Savior and Lord. A few moments later the husband of one of the women came in and found them in tears. He inquired for the reason.

His wife said, "A strange little man has just been talking to us about religion and urging us to get right with God."

"Well," said the man, "if I had been here I should have told him to go about his business."

"My dear," replied the wife, "if you had been here, you would have thought he *was* about his business."

James Brainerd Taylor met a traveler at a watering trough one day, and during the five minutes their horses were drinking he so preached Jesus to the stranger that the man was saved and afterward became a missionary to Africa. They met no more, and the stranger was ever wondering who the angel of mercy was that pointed him to Jesus. One day in Africa he received a box of books. On opening a small volume of memoirs, he saw the picture of the young man who had been about his Father's business and redeemed the time at that watering trough by preaching Jesus and saving a soul, instead of idly chatting about the weather.

It takes no more time to ask people about their souls than about their health, but it will require more love and prayer and holy tact and soul-wakefulness to do it with profit, and these the soul-winner must have.

With many, much time is lost for want of a system. Things are done haphazardly, duties are performed at random, and after one thing is done time is wasted in deciding what to do next. It is well, then, to have a program for every day or, better still, for every hour.

Of course, in this busy world, with its many surprises and unexpected calls, any program must be flexible and not like cast iron, and in times of emergency the soul-winner must be prepared to cast it to the winds and follow where the Spirit leads, singing with the whole heart:

I would the precious time redeem,
And longer live for this alone
To spend and to be spent for them,
Who have not yet the Savior known,
And turn them to a pardoning God
And quench the brands in Jesus' blood.

My talents, gifts and graces, Lord,
Into Thy blessed hands receive,
And let me live to preach Thy Word,

And let me to Thy glory live;

My every sacred moment spend

In publishing the sinner's Friend.[7]

Finally, if you would redeem the time, keep a conscience void of offense and keep your soul red hot with love for Jesus and this dying world. "Have faith in God" (Mark 11:22 KJV). Expect victory. Nothing will sap your energies, dull your faculties, and take from you all incentive to holy and high effort like doubt and discouragement. It is your duty to expect victory.

Joshua, in a fit of discouragement after his army's defeat at Ai, stopped all efforts, fell flat on his face, and stayed there until God came by and said, "Get up! Why do you lie flat on your face like this? Israel has sinned. They have violated my covenant, which I commanded them to keep. They have taken some of the things reserved for me and put them with their own things. They have stolen and kept it a secret. The Israelites can't stand up to their enemies. . . . I will no longer be with you unless you destroy the things reserved for me that are present among you. Go and make the people holy. Say, 'Get ready for tomorrow by making yourselves holy'" (Josh. 7:10–13 CEB).

God wanted Joshua to be up and doing, and if he could not whip the enemy, then he was to clean out his own camp and not be discouraged. Trust God, and trust others. And where others cannot be trusted, love them and pray for them, and you will surely redeem the time and win souls to God.

NOTES

1. Samuel Johnson, "Selections from Dr. Johnson's Rambler," *The Oxford Miscellany* (Oxford: Clarendon Press, 1907), 39.

2. Max Muller, *A Dictionary of Thoughts*, ed. Tryon Edwards (Detroit: F. B. Dickerson Company, 1908), 446.

3. John Morley, *The Life of William Ewart Gladstone*, vol. 1 (London: Macmillan, 2006), 634.

4. Jean Paul Friedrich Richter, *The Campaner Thal and Other Writings* (Boston: Ticknor and Fields, 1864), n. p.

5. Marcus Aurelius, *The Meditations: Book 3*, The Harvard Classics, vol. 2 (New York: P. F. Collier and Son, 1909), 210.

6. Anna Sewell, *Black Beauty* (New York: HarperCollins, 1998), 190.

7. Charles Wesley, "Give Me the Faith Which Can Remove," 1749, public domain.

The Studies of the Soul-Winner 7

No man or woman need hope to be a permanently successful soul-winner who is not a diligent student of the truth, of the will and ways of God, of souls, and of methods. No one can successfully build a house, write a poem, govern a city, manage a store, or even shoe a horse or make a mousetrap without thoughtful study.

A doctor must think and study—and do so diligently and continuously—in order to understand the delicate human organism, the subtle diseases to which it is subject, and the various remedies by which those diseases are to be cured. A lawyer must be a diligent student if he or she would win cases before judges and juries in the face of self-interest and skillful opponents.

How much more then should the soul-winner study in order to understand the diseases of the soul, the ramifications of evil, the deceitfulness of the human heart, and the application of the great remedy God has provided to meet all the needs of the soul. Or, to change the figure, how must the soul-winner study to win his or her case at the bar of conscience, when the opposing counsel is a deceitful human heart assisted by that old adversary, the Devil, who for six thousand years has been deceiving human souls and leading them down to hell!

Writing to Timothy, Paul said, "Study to shew thyself approved unto God, a workman that needeth not to be ashamed, rightly dividing the word of truth" (2 Tim. 2:15 KJV). He said, "Give attention to reading, to exhortation, to doctrine. Do not neglect the gift that is in you. . . . Meditate on these things; give yourself entirely to them, that your progress may be evident to all" (1 Tim. 4:13–15 NKJV).

Oh, that all who set themselves to be soul-winners might fully recognize the tremendous odds against which they fight and determine by much believing prayer and joyous, diligent study to show themselves to be "approved to God, a workman that need not to be ashamed!" Thank God, none whom God calls need be discouraged or dismayed. Only let them not bury their talents or spend their time in idle dreaming, but let them stir up the gift that is in them and faithfully give a little time each day to those studies that will enlighten the mind and fit them for the work God has called them to, and they shall surely be blessed of God and "thoroughly equipped for every good work" (2 Tim. 3:17 NIV).

The first thing—and the last—to be studied is the Bible. A doctor who knows all about law and art, history and theology, but is unacquainted with medical books, is a failure as a doctor. Likewise, a lawyer who has devoured libraries, traveled the wide world over, and become a walking encyclopedia and dictionary, but is unacquainted with law books, is a failure as a lawyer. So the worker for souls may read ten thousand books, may be able to quote poetry by the mile, may be acquainted with all the facts of science and history, and may even be a profound theologian, but unless that person is a diligent student of the Bible, he or she will not permanently succeed as a soul-winner.

Soul-winners must be full of the thoughts of God. They must eat the Word, digest it, and turn it into spiritual blood, bone, muscle, nerve, and sinew, until they become, as someone has said, "a living Bible, eighteen inches wide by six feet long, bound in human skin."

The evangelist Charles Finney wrote of getting up at four o'clock in the morning and reading his Bible until eight:

I gave myself to a great deal of prayer. After my evening services I would retire as early as I well could; but rose at four o'clock in the morning, because I could sleep no longer, and immediately went to the study and engaged in prayer. And so deeply was my mind exercised, and so absorbed in prayer, that I frequently continued from the time I arose at four o'clock till the gong called to breakfast at eight o'clock. My days were spent, so far as I could get time, in searching the Scriptures. I read nothing else, all that winter, but my Bible; and a great deal of it seemed new to me. Again the Lord took me, as it were, from Genesis to Revelation. He led me to see the connection of things, the promises, the threatenings, the prophecies and their fulfillment; and indeed, the whole Scripture seemed to me all ablaze with light, and not only light, but it seemed as if God's Word was instinct with the very life of God.[1]

This diligent attention to the Word of God is a command. God said to Joshua, "Study this Book of Instruction continually. Meditate on it day and night" (Josh. 1:8 NLT). The object of this earnest study was, "so you will be sure to obey everything written in it." And the result: "Only then will you prosper and succeed in all you do." The blessed life David sang about in Psalm 1 does not come to those who merely refuse to keep company with the ungodly and abstain from their ways, but to those who also "delight in the law of the LORD, meditating on it day and night" (Ps. 1:2 NLT). And the difference between them and the ungodly is the difference between a fruitful tree planted by the river and "worthless chaff, scattered by the wind" (Ps. 1:4 NLT).

Jesus declared the importance of the Word when He told the Devil, "People do not live by bread alone, but by every word that comes from the mouth of God" (Matt. 4:4 NLT).

Catherine Booth read her Bible through a number of times before she was twelve years old. No wonder God made her a "mother of nations." She was full of truth, and she could never open her mouth without saying something that was calculated to expose shams and falsehoods, overthrow the Devil's kingdom of lies, and build up God's kingdom of righteousness and truth in people's hearts.

Whitefield read the Bible through many times on his knees with Matthew Henry's notes. Wesley in his old age called himself "a man of one book."[2] Again and again I have read the Bible through on my knees, and it is ever new and, as David said, "Sweeter also than honey and the honeycomb" (Ps. 19:10 KJV). And like Job I can say, "I have esteemed the words of his mouth more than my necessary food" (Job 23:12 KJV).

It is from this armory that the Christian is to draw weapons with which to fight all hell. It is there that we may study the mind and heart of God, the truth about Jesus Christ, sin and the way of escape from it, and the facts about heaven, hell, a judgment day, and eternity. There we find a law for the lawless, warnings for the careless, promises for the penitent, encouragement for the distressed, balm for the wounded, healing for the sick, and life for the dead. We are to "preach the Word," for it is "useful to teach us what is true and to make us realize what is wrong in our lives. It corrects us when we are wrong and teaches us to do what is right. God uses it to prepare and equip his people to do every good work" (2 Tim. 3:16–17 NLT). And in preaching it, if we preach as they did of old, "in the power of the Holy Spirit sent from heaven" (1 Pet. 1:12 NLT), we will find it "alive and powerful . . . sharper than the sharpest two-edged sword, cutting between soul and spirit, between joint and marrow . . . [exposing] our innermost thoughts and desires" (Heb. 4:12 NLT). I have sometimes read or quoted the Word of God to people, and it fit their case so pat that it smote them like a lightning bolt. "'Does not my word burn like fire?' says the LORD. 'Is it not like a mighty hammer that smashes a rock to pieces?'" (Jer. 23:29 NLT).

But we must not study the Word simply that we may preach it, but that we may live by it, be furnished, strengthened, enlightened, corrected, and made wise by it. It must pass through our own soul and become a part of our own spiritual life before we can preach it with power and apply it effectually to the souls of others. And in order to do this we must be filled with the Holy Spirit. In fact, it is only as we are filled with the Spirit that we will be able to get much benefit from the Word of God or have much love for it.

The Bible is a sealed book to unspiritual people, but when the Comforter comes it is unsealed and its wondrous meaning made clear. I read recently of a lad who could not read receiving the baptism of the Holy Spirit. Then he got his unsaved sister to read the Bible to him and he explained it to her. The Holy Spirit in him enabled him to understand what the Holy Spirit in prophets of old enabled them to write. Only the Holy Spirit can help human hearts and minds to understand His Book.

An old woman loved her Bible very much. A friend who found her reading it frequently gave her a commentary to assist her in getting at its meaning. A few days later, he asked, "How do you like that book I gave you?" She replied, "Oh, that be a very good book, but the Bible do throw a lot of light on that there book."

The Bereans show us the way to read the Bible (see Acts 17:11):

- They received the Word with all readiness.
- They searched the Scriptures. It was not with them just a hasty, careless, thoughtless reading; they searched as prospectors search for gold.
- They did this daily.

Personally, for years I have given the best hour of the day to the Bible, until I want it more than I want my food. It should be read early in the day, before other things crowd in. What is read should be remembered. In eating it is not the amount we eat, but the amount we digest that does us good, and so it is in reading and studying. It is not the amount we read, but what we remember and make our own that does us good.

Besides the Bible, the soul-winner ought to lay out a course of reading, and stick to it, reading a few pages each day. Reading ten pages a day will mean between ten and fifteen books a year, approximately.

Not too much time should be spent reading newspapers. It would probably not be wise to discard them altogether, but better to do that than let them rob you of the time that should be spent in deep study and earnest prayer. I once heard William Booth say, "I have not read a newspaper for ten days."

All useful knowledge may prove valuable to the soul-winner, and we should seek information everywhere. It is well to carry a notebook and constantly make notes.

The soul-winner should study not only books, but also people and methods. John Wesley became a supreme master in practical and experimental theology and a matchless soul-winner largely through his study of people. He examined thousands—men, women, and children—with reference to their religious experience, and especially their experiences of sanctification, until he became acquainted with the human heart and the workings of the Holy Spirit as few have ever done.

I know of no better and surer method of acquainting one's self with the human heart and the way the Holy Spirit works than by this close, personal, private conversation and inquiry about the religious experiences of the Christians around us. This is the scientific method applied to the study of the human heart, the Christian life, and religious experience, and it can be carried on wherever you can find a human being to talk with you. "He who wins souls is wise" (Prov. 11:30 NKJV).

NOTES

1. Charles Finney, *Memoirs of Rev. Charles G. Finney* (New York: A. S. Barnes & Company, 1876), 374.

2. From the preface to Wesley's Standard Sermons, in which he writes, "Let me be *homo unius libri*." *The Works of Wesley*, vol. 1 (Grand Rapids: Francis Asbury Press, 1955), 32.

Physical Health 8 ◀

Soul-winners must take the best care they know how of their bodies, without everlastingly coddling, petting, and pitying themselves. This is our sacred duty. The body is the instrument through which the mind and the soul work in this world. A good body is as essential to the Christian as is a good instrument to the musician or a staunch boat to the strong rower, and should be no more despised and neglected than the hunter's gun or the woodsman's axe. "Don't you realize," said Paul, "that your body is the temple of the Holy Spirit?" (1 Cor. 6:19 NLT). He also said, "If anyone destroys God's temple, God will destroy that person" (1 Cor. 3:17 NCV). As the most skillful musician is dependent upon his or her instrument, so we, in every walk of life, are in a large measure limited by and dependent upon the quality of the body through which our mental and spiritual powers must work.

Most people who have made a mark in the world have had a splendid basis of physical force and power (though there are some striking exceptions). When Moses died on Mount Nebo at 120 years of age, "his eyesight was clear, and he was as strong as ever" (Deut. 34:7 NLT), notwithstanding the fact that for forty years he had the tremendous task of organizing, legislating for, judging, and ruling a great nation of former slaves just delivered from four hundred years of bondage and wandering like sheep in a mountainous wilderness. Paul must have had a robust constitution and fairly good health to have endured the stonings and whippings, imprisonments and shipwrecks, hungerings and thirstings, fights with fierce beasts, and contests with fiercer men, besides the care of all the churches which fell to his lot daily.

John Wesley was a little man, weighing only about 120 pounds, but his health was superb and seems to have been due not so much to natural vigor of constitution—though, doubtless he had that—as to the regular habits and healthful plan of living he adopted. He was one of nineteen children, and his father was a poor clergyman. For several years he had nothing to eat but bread, which may have accounted for his small size, but which he himself said probably laid the foundations of good health he afterward enjoyed. (It must have been whole wheat bread, however, and not the white, starchy stuff of modern bakers.) In after years he always ate sparingly, and only ate a few articles of food at any one meal. He lived much out of doors and preached almost daily (sometimes several times a day) in the open air. At the age of seventy-three he made this remarkable entry in his journal:

I am seventy-three years old, and far abler to preach than I was at three and twenty. What natural means has God used to produce so wonderful an effect?

1) Continual exercise and change of air, by traveling above four thousand miles in a year. [It is well to remember that he did his traveling on horseback and in a buggy through winter's storms and summer's heat.]

2) Constant rising at four.

3) The ability, if ever I want, to sleep immediately.

4) The never losing a night's sleep in my life. [He mentions several all-nights of prayer in his journal, however.]

5) Two violent fevers, and two deep consumptions.

These, it is true, were rough medicines; but they were of admirable service, causing my flesh to come again as the flesh of a little child. May I add lastly, evenness of temper. I feel and grieve; but, by the grace of God, I fret at nothing. But still the help that is done upon earth [God] doeth it Himself; and this He doth in answer to many prayers.[1]

A similar entry was made in his journal in 1782. He said, "I have entered into my eightieth year; but, blessed be God, my time is not 'labor and sorrow.' I find no more pain or bodily infirmity than at five-and-twenty."[2]

And beside the reasons given above he added, "This I still impute, (1) To the power of God, fitting me for what He calls me to do. (2) To my constant preaching, particularly in the morning."[3] The morning sermon was preached at five o'clock in the summer and six o'clock in the winter.

Young people are usually prodigal of their health and strength, and nature will allow them to make large drafts upon these treasures. But nature also keeps strict accounts and will surely require interest and principal in due time. It is a rather remarkable fact that often those who have had poor health in youth so learn to take care of themselves and obey the laws of health and not impose upon their bodies that they outlast and outwork many who started out with a greater physical capital.

Those who desire good health, long life, and a cheerful old age should live simply and regularly. They should seek enough sleep and at the same time be careful not to take too much sleep. Wesley could get along with six hours' sleep at night, though he had the happy faculty of taking naps through the day, even sleeping on horseback. Napoleon frequently got along with three hours' sleep, but General Ulysses S. Grant said that in the midst of his heaviest campaigns he required nine hours. I have heard General William Booth say that he needed eight hours at least. No rule can be laid down to fit every case, however, so that conscientious soul-winners must find out what is best for themselves, make their own rule, and keep it religiously as unto the Lord.

There is a danger of lying in bed too long as well as too short a time. The Duke of Wellington said, "When you find that you want to turn over, you ought to turn out."[4] Lying in bed relaxes the whole system, and if indulged in to excess tends to a general weakening of the system.

Sleep should be taken in a room that is well ventilated in winter as in summer. All good physicians and hygienists insist upon this, and also that one should not sleep in any garment worn during the day.

Benjamin Franklin declared that he had made a great discovery. He discovered that the sun came up in the morning. He thought that it would be a great financial saving to the world if people could only be brought to recognize this fact, and instead of turning night into day by artificial light, should go to bed early and get up with the sun. No doubt there would be many dollars saved and also much nervous energy. We have fallen on evil days, however, and it is not likely we shall ever get back to the habits of our forefathers and go to bed with the birds. Soul-winners, though, ought to conscientiously go to bed as early as possible rather than sitting up and indulging in small talk and late suppers, which if it does not destroy their health will at least greatly injure it and cripple their soul-saving power.

Exercise is also necessary for health. Since the human body, like a chain, is not stronger than its weakest point, a little general systematic exercise is useful to keep every organ of the body in good health and vigor.

On the other hand, those who never relax, however religious they may be, are likely to become morose, irritable, impatient, and a source of anxiety and perplexity to their dearest friends. Or they may become melancholy and full of gloom, and may begin to doubt their call to preach.

There is a legend that when the apostle John was nearly one hundred years of age, he was visited by a man who was anxious to see the "beloved disciple" of the Lord. The man found the old apostle playing with some little children, and he rebuked the aged saint, telling him that it ill-fitted an apostle of the Lord, at his age, to be indulging in childish games. The old man replied, in essence, "A bow that is never unstrung will lose its power; unloose the string and it retains its vigor. So I relieve the tension of my soul by indulging in innocent games with the little ones."

The emotions, sympathies, and every power of mind and soul—along with all the nervous energies of the body—have heavy drafts made upon them in soul-saving work, and the mighty tension of the soul and body at their highest point of efficiency must be entirely relaxed periodically in order to maintain this efficiency. In other words, there must be rest.

I have found that when I get very tired and am least fit to do anything, I then feel an imperative necessity for doing something, and it is then that I must put on the brakes and rest—by sheer force of will, if need be. A friend of mine, who is an unusually successful soul-winner, has a very sensible wife who, when she finds him nervous and worn, insists that he goes to bed for a whole day and vegetates. The next day he finds his nervous force restored and is ready for any amount of hard work.

"Whether you eat or drink," said Paul, "or whatever you do, do it all for the glory of God" (1 Cor. 10:31 NLT). Eating and drinking do not seem to have anything to do with soul-winning, but nevertheless they do. I read recently that three-fourths of the diseases that Americans are afflicted with can be traced to improper eating and drinking. "The fewer the sweetmeats, the sweeter the temper," wrote a wise hygienist. "If you doubt it and have a bad temper, my friend, let me implore you to try it."[5]

Several years ago a friend and I visited Neal Dow, who was sometimes called "the father of prohibition." He was then over ninety years of age and in good health. My friend asked him the secret of his long life and splendid health. The old man replied, "First, I didn't sow any wild oats in my youth; I never used tobacco nor whisky nor stimulants of any kind. Second, I have always gone to bed early, slept well, and gotten up early. Third, I have always taken an active interest in public morals and in the welfare of my fellow men. Fourth, I never eat anything that I have found out by experience hurts me. I am very fond of baked beans, but they do me harm, therefore, I do not eat them." Baked beans may not hurt everybody, but soul-winners who put God's interests and that of other souls before their own pleasure ought to show the good sense of Neal Dow and not eat anything that hurts them, however much they may like it.

I know a minister who was afflicted with gastritis. He wanted some meat for supper; it was on the table in the form of mince pie. He ought to have known, and probably did, that with the kind of stomach he had, mince pie was no diet for him, but he liked it. He ate it, and he nearly died that night. Rich, fatty suppers should not be eaten. Cold bread is preferable to hot bread. It is wise to follow a rule of British prime minister William E. Gladstone: "Give thirty-two bites to every mouthful."[6] That is, give every tooth a taste.

Rev. Daniel Waldo once said, "I am an old man. I have seen nearly a century. Do you want to know how to grow old slowly and happily? Let me tell you. Always eat slowly—masticate well. Go to your food, to your rest, to your occupations smiling. Keep a good nature and a soft temper everywhere."[7]

Dr. J. H. Hanaford, in writing to a public singer who was afflicted with severe congestion and sore throat, said, "I attribute a part of the trouble to using rich pastry, often a prominent cause of catarrh. I suspect in you the too free use of sugar, confectionery, salt, and spices. I am fully convinced that a large percentage of the sore throats, inflamed eyes and nasal passages, and the like, so often attributed to colds, are due to stomach derangement resulting from large quantities of common food, and the too free use of such heating things as sweets, fats and oils, and starches, fine flour being prominent."

Here are some short rules for one who wants good health:

- Don't worry. Paul said, "Don't worry about anything; instead, pray about everything. Tell God what you need, and thank him for all he has done. Then you will experience God's peace, which exceeds anything we can understand" (Phil. 4:6–7 NLT).
- Never despair. Lost hope is a fatal disease. One of the fruit of the Spirit is hope.
- Work heartily, but don't worry yourself to death.
- Court the fresh air day and night.
- Don't overeat. Don't starve. "Let your moderation be known unto all" (Phil. 4:5 KJV).
- Don't forget that "Cleanliness is next to godliness."

Finally, if you have poor health and a broken constitution, don't despair. Richard Baxter, one of the mightiest men of God that ever lived—the Saint Paul and the William Booth of his day—was a lifelong invalid and suffered almost intolerable things. But he praised God for it, for he declared it kept him alive to eternal things, weaned him from the world, and led him constantly to "preach as a dying man to dying men."⁸ David Brainerd, the fragrance of whose holy life, apostolic labors, and self-denial have filled and inspired the church for almost two centuries, died of consumption (tuberculosis) before he was thirty years of age. But few men in health and strength have been so used of God as he was in his weakness.

Personally, I have suffered much from broken health, exhausted nerves, and sleepless nights, and at one time feared that my work was done. But by prayer and care I have been so far restored to health and strength that I can work six days in the week with all my might, sleep like a kitten, and digest my food fairly well. I am full of the joy of the Lord, happy as a lark, and am altogether glad I am alive.

Oh, grant that nothing in my soul
May dwell, but Thy pure love alone;
Oh, may Thy love possess me whole,
My Joy, my Treasure, and my Crown:
Strange loves far from my heart remove;
May every act, word, thought, be love.

Unwearied may I this pursue,
Dauntlessly to the high prize aspire;
Hourly within my soul renew
This holy flame, this heavenly fire;
And day and night be all my care
To guard the sacred treasure there.

In suffering be Thy love my peace,
In weakness, be Thy love my power;
And when the storms of life shall cease,
Jesus, in that important hour,
In death as life be Thou my guide,
And save me, who for me hast died.[9]

NOTES

1. John Wesley, *The Works of the Rev. John Wesley in Ten Volumes*, vol. 3 (New York: J. & J. Harper, 1827), 438–439.

2. John Wesley, *The Works of the Reverend John Wesley, A. M.*, vol. 4 (New York: B. Waugh and T. Mason, 1835), 562.

3. Ibid.

4. Source unknown.

5. Rose Seelye Miller, "Some Thoughts on Economy," *The Rushford Spectator* (Rushford, NY), Thursday, October 3, 1889, 3.

6. Source unknown.

7. Daniel Waldo, quoted in "Hear the Old Man," *The R. I. Schoolmaster*, vol. 4 (Providence: William A. Mowry, 1858), 216.

8. Richard Baxter, *Poetical Fragments* (London: J. Dunton, 1689), 30.

9. Paul Gerhardt, "Jesus, Thy Boundless Love to Me," 1653, public domain.

The Renewing of Power **9**

To do God's work we must have God's power. Jesus said, "Stay here in the city until the Holy Spirit comes and fills you with power from heaven" (Luke 24:49 NLT). And again He said, "You will receive power when the Holy Spirit comes upon you" (Acts 1:8 NLT).

We receive this power when we are sanctified wholly and filled with the Spirit, and we need never lose it. But while the Holy Spirit abides with the believer, there yet seems to be need for frequent renewals of the power He bestows. And, thank God, He has made ample provision to meet this need. "They that wait upon the LORD shall renew their strength," said Isaiah (Isa. 40:31 KJV). "Wait on the LORD; be of good courage, and He shall strengthen your heart," cried David (Ps. 27:14 NKJV).

Years ago Asa Mahan wrote of his old friend, Charles Finney:

The extraordinary power which attended the preaching of President Finney, during the early years of his ministry, was chiefly owing to a special baptism of the Spirit, which he received not long after his conversion. Hence it was that when, through him, "the violated law spake out its thunders," it did seem as if we had in truth "come unto the mount that might be touched, and that burned with fire, and unto blackness, and darkness, and tempest, and the sound of a trumpet, and the voice of words." But when he spoke of Christ, then indeed did his "doctrine drop as the rain, and his speech distil as the dew, as the small rain upon the tender herb, and as the showers upon the mown grass." The reason, also, why he is bringing forth such wondrous "fruit in his old age," is, that while his whole ministry has been under the power of the Spirit, his former baptisms have been renewed with increasing power and frequency during a few years past.[1]

The need for these frequent renewings and anointings does not necessarily arise from faltering faith. Sometimes the soul feels the need of a renewal of its power when confronted by great opposition, danger, and powerful foes. The apostles were filled with the Holy Spirit, and had not only won their great Pentecostal victory but many others as well when suddenly a stubborn wall of opposition arose before them. They were arrested by the rulers, thrown in prison, brought before the high priest, sharply questioned by what power and name they were working their miracles, and then when no ground for punishment could be found, they were threatened and commanded to preach no more in the name of Jesus.

When they were let go, they went to their own people, told them what had happened, and began a sweet, childlike, heaven-storming prayer meeting. They told the Lord the story too, and cried to Him to show forth His power. Then a wonderful thing happened. Pentecost was repeated: "The meeting place shook, and they were all filled with the Holy Spirit. Then they preached the word of God with boldness. . . . The apostles testified powerfully to the resurrection of the Lord Jesus, and God's great blessing was upon them all" (Acts 4:31, 33 NLT). They waited before the Lord and their strength was renewed, their power reinforced from heaven, their past victories put into the shade, and "a large number of priests became obedient to the faith" (Acts 6:7 NIV).

Sometimes the need for this renewal of strength arises after great victories. Victory is usually secured as the result of great spiritual and mental activity—and often physical activity as well. It is only natural that there should be a reaction. The pendulum, if left alone, swings to the other extreme. Depression may follow, the powers of soul and mind relax, joyful emotions subside, and inexperienced soul-winners may at this point get into great perplexity, suffer from fierce temptation, and strain to keep up their accustomed spiritual activity, crying out with David, "Why am I discouraged? Why is my heart so sad?" (Ps. 42:11 NLT). They may fear that their faith is failing.

But what is needed now is not so much anxious wrestling with God as quiet waiting upon God for a renewal of power, saying to the soul, "I will put my hope in God! I will praise him again—my Savior and my God!" (Ps. 42:11 NLT); "My health may fail, and my spirit may grow weak, but God remains the strength of my heart; he is mine forever" (Ps. 73:26 NLT). At such times the strength of the soul is to sit still in quietness and confidence (see Isa. 30:15), assured that God Himself will be its help.

I once heard a wise old evangelist say that while he sat at home after a season of rest, the Spirit of God would come upon him, leading him to earnest prayer and travail for the salvation of others. This was God's way of preparing him for a campaign and for victory, and away he would go for battle and siege, to rescue souls. Never did he fail to win. But after a while there seemed to be an abatement of power, when he would return home for another season of rest and quiet, waiting upon God for the renewal of his strength. And thus he continued till he was over eighty years old, still bringing forth fruit in old age (see Ps. 92:14).

There is sometimes need of a renewal of power owing to weakness and infirmity of the flesh. Paul must have received a great addition of power when, instead of removing his thorn in the flesh, Jesus said to him, "My grace is all you need. My power works best in weakness" (2 Cor. 12:9 NLT). And such was the uplift Paul experienced at that time that ever afterward he took "pleasure in . . . weaknesses, and in the insults, hardships, persecutions, and troubles that I suffer for Christ" (2 Cor. 12:10 NLT), glorying in them, since through them Christ's power rested upon him, and in weakness he was made strong.

Spiritual power is not necessarily dependent upon physical energy, and however much soul-winners may be afflicted with infirmities, there are mighty endowments of power available if they intelligently— and with quiet and persistent faith—seek them from on high.

There will also be times of loneliness and spiritual agony when soul-winners will need to have their spiritual strength renewed—such as Jesus suffered in the garden, or Elijah when he felt that all the prophets were slain and there was none true to God in Israel but himself. When there is widespread barrenness and desolation, when revivals have ceased, when worldliness sweeps in like a flood and there is apparently no vision, when God seems silent, and when the Devil mocks and taunts, a renewal of spiritual strength will be needed—and we may fully expect such a renewal. The angels are all around us, the heavens are bending over us, and Jesus has lost none of His tender interest and sympathy for us in such times. An angel came and strengthened Jesus in His agony, an angel strengthened Elijah for his long and lonely journey, and an angel came to Daniel and said, "O man greatly loved, fear not, peace be with you; be strong and of good courage" (Dan. 10:19 ESV). And not only an angel, but the Lord Himself will surely empower His trusting workers. It was Jesus who cheered Paul in the chief captain's castle (see Acts 23:11) and John on the lonely Isle of Patmos (see Rev. 1:17), and so He still cheers and strengthens His servants and warriors.

These renewals of power are not always necessarily of an extraordinary character. There are sometimes great uplifts of physical strength without any apparent cause, but typically our physical strength will be renewed by rest and the timely eating of proper food. Similarly, there may be times when the Spirit of God falls upon the soul-winner, giving great uplifts and visions and courage. But ordinarily power comes by the use of the simple means of much regular prayer, patient and diligent searching of God's Word, and a daily listening to God's voice. It is renewed like fire, not by the fall of lightning from heaven but by the addition of new fuel, or like physical strength, not by some hypodermic injection of fresh blood but by appropriate food. David called upon his soul to bless God who "satisfies [him] with good things so that [his] youth is renewed like the eagle's" (Ps. 103:5 ESV).

It is by appropriate food, then, that the soul is strengthened. Jesus told us what that food was when He said, "People do not live by bread alone, but by every word that comes from the mouth of God" (Matt. 4:4 NLT). And does not this correspond to Paul's statement that "though our outer self is wasting away, our inner self is being renewed day by day" (2 Cor. 4:16 ESV)? Does it not also align with that passage that says, "The LORD revealed himself unto Samuel in Shiloh by the word of the LORD" (1 Sam. 3:21 KJV)? It is the Lord who renews our strength, but He does it not in some mysterious way but by means of His Word, which we read and meditate upon and appropriate by faith. Through it we see Jesus and come to know our Lord. This will require time and attention on our part, but it will be time well spent.

My own strength is usually renewed by the opening up of some new truth or the powerful application of some promise or portion of the Word of God to my soul, which I am enabled to make my own by a definite and bold act of faith in secret prayer. There is abundant reserve power in God. "The residue of the spirit" (Mal. 2:15 KJV) is with Him. He has not exhausted His resources in the measure of the Spirit of power and holiness which He has given us, and I often comfort and encourage myself with the assurance of James: "He gives us more grace" (James 4:6 NIV). "So let us come boldly to the throne of our gracious God," abide there in communion with God, and "find grace to help us when we need it most" (Heb. 4:16 NLT).

A servant's form He wore,

And in His body bore

Our dreadful curse on Calvary:

He like a victim stood,

And poured His sacred blood,

To set the guilty captive free.

With mercy's mildest grace,

He governs all our race,

In wisdom, righteousness, and love:

Who to Messiah fly

Shall find redemption nigh,

And all His great salvation prove.

Hail, Savior, Prince of Peace!

Thy kingdom shall increase,

Till all the world Thy glory see;

And righteousness abound,

As the great deep profound,

And fill the earth with purity![2]

NOTES

1. Asa Mahan, *The Baptism of the Holy Ghost* (London: Elliot Stock, 1872), 91.

2. Benjamin Rhodes, "My Heart and Voice I Raise," 1787, public domain.

An Undivided Heart

The person who hopes to succeed in the infinite business of saving souls with a divided heart as yet knows nothing in comparison to what he or she ought to know concerning the matter.

I admit that someone may by personal magnetism, power or persuasiveness of speech, and a certain skill in playing upon people's emotions create an excitement that fairly simulates a revival, and yet have a divided heart. But that such a person can bring others to a thorough repentance and renunciation of sin, a hearty embrace of the cross, an affectionate surrender to Jesus as a personal Savior and Master who requires deep humility and meekness and tender love as the marks of His disciples is yet to be proven.

As certainly as like begets like, so certainly will the soul-winner put the mark of his or her own spirit and consecration upon the people

who are influenced. One who is not more than half won to the cause
of our lowly Master will not more than half win others.

Physical scientists manipulate and change dead matter. Journalists
seek principally to amuse or interest people for the passing hour. Lawyers
and politicians simply seek to change and mold opinions. But soul-
winners deal with fundamentals. Their object is not merely to change
opinions and conduct, but to change character. Their goal is to work a
moral revolution in the affections, dispositions, and wills of men and
women—to turn them from temporal things (which they see) to eternal
things (which they do not see), from all vices to virtues, and from utter
selfishness to utter self-sacrifice, and often in spite of all present self-
interest and in the face of the combined opposition of the world, the flesh,
and the Devil. Their purpose is not only to save others from the guilt and
penalty of sin, but also from the pollution and power and love of sin.

Nor do they aim merely to win souls from sin, which is rather a
negative work, but also to usher them into all goodness and love and
holiness through a vital and eternal union with Jesus Christ—like that
of the branch with the vine—a union that gives perpetual vigor,
energy, and fruitfulness in righteousness to all the powers of the soul,
filling it with grace and truth.

This is no little work and can never be the work of a divided heart.
It is like turning Niagara Falls back upon its source or causing the sun
and the moon to stand still on Ajalon. It can be done only by God's
power, and that power is only bestowed upon and only works freely
in and through those whose hearts are perfect toward Him.

Soul-winners, then, must once and for all abandon themselves to the
Lord and to the Lord's work and, having put their hands to the plow,

must not look back, if they would succeed in this mighty business. And, if they continue faithful in this way, they shall conquer though they die.

They must love their Lord and love their work, and stick to it through all difficulties, perplexities, and discouragements, and not be given to change, for there is no discharge in this war.

This is where many fail. They do not have a single eye. They make provision for retreat. They are double-minded, like one officer I knew who dabbled in photography till it divided his life and heart and got him out of the ministry, and another minister of whom I heard the other day who reads another man's sermons to his people while he studies law, saying that when he gets a poor appointment he will fall back on the law and leave the ministry. They forget Paul's words to Timothy: "Soldiers don't get tied up in the affairs of civilian life, for then they cannot please the officer who enlisted them" (2 Tim. 2:4 NLT).

Such people eventually leave the work God called them to do, because (as they say) they have not been treated well, when the fact is, their minds being divided, they ceased to work well. They no longer gave themselves wholly to it, and the people feel a lack of interest and power. Hungering souls that looked for bread received a stone. Poor sinners on the road to hell and possibly on the brink of ruin went away from their cold and heartless services unawakened and unchanged. They lost their grip first on God and then on the crowd, and their superiors—perplexed to know what to do with them and where to place them, since the people no longer want them— are blamed. But blame others as they will, the blame still lies with themselves.

No great work has ever been accomplished without abandonment to it. Michelangelo said his work was his wife and the statues he made were his children. Edison was so wedded to his work that all other things were forgotten and set aside in the pursuit of his marvelous inventions.

Demosthenes, the greatest of ancient orators (if not the greatest of all time), was hissed off the platform at his first appearance. His figure was unprepossessing and his voice weak and harsh, but he determined to be heard. He devoted himself to his studies, shaved one side of his head lest he should be led into society, and practiced elocution day and night. To perfect his enunciation, he filled his mouth half-full of pebbles and practiced while climbing a hill, and to successfully contend against the thunders of the Athenian mob, he went to the seashore and strengthened his voice by practicing it against the thunder of the waves.

Lord Beaconsfield stood for parliament five times and at last won his seat. When he first attempted to speak he was laughed from the floor but he sat down, saying, "You will listen to me yet." And they did, when, as prime minister of England, he arbitrated the destinies of Europe.

A great speaker was asked, "How long did it take you to prepare that address?" He replied, "All my lifetime in general, and fifteen minutes in particular."

When Benjamin Franklin, as a poor boy, opened a printing shop, a prosperous competitor said he would drive him out of town. Franklin showed him a piece of black bread from which he dined and a pail of water from which he drank, and asked if he thought a man who could live on fare like that and work sixteen hours a day could be driven out of town. Who knows the name of that competitor, and who has not heard of Franklin?

If those engaged in secular pursuits are given up to their work and consumed with their purpose, how much more should be the soul-winner, who is fighting for righteousness and holiness, for the kingdom of love upon earth, and rescuing souls from the power of sin and the danger of eternal burnings?

If God has set you to win souls, "make no provision for the flesh, to gratify its desires" (Rom. 13:14 ESV). Burn the bridges behind you. Remember Paul's words to Timothy: "Give your complete attention to these matters. Throw yourself into your tasks so that everyone will see your progress" (1 Tim. 4:15 NLT). Let your eye be single. Make no plan for retreat; allow no thought of it. Like Jesus, set your face steadfastly toward your Jerusalem, your cross, your kingdom, your glory, when—having turned many to righteousness—you shall shine as the stars forever and ever (see Dan. 12:3).

You may be ignorant, your abilities may be limited, you may have a stammering tongue, and you may be utterly lacking in culture, but you can have an undivided, perfect heart toward God and the work He has set you to do. And this is more than all culture and education, all gifts and graces of person and brain. If God has bestowed any of these upon you, see to it that they are sanctified and that your trust is not in them. But if He has denied them to you and yet has called you to His service, do not be dismayed; it is not the perfect head but the perfect heart God blesses. For has He not said, "The eyes of the LORD search the whole earth in order to strengthen those whose hearts are fully committed to him" (2 Chron. 16:9 NLT)?

At this point none need fail. And yet, what an awful thing it is that some will fail, and after having prophesied and cast out devils and done many wondrous works in His name, shall hear Him profess, "I never knew you. Get away from me" (Matt. 7:23 NLT).

> Let nothing now my heart divide,
> Since with Thee I am crucified,
> And live to God in Thee.
> Dead to the world and all its toys,
> Its idle pomps and fading joys.
> Jesus, my glory be.[1]

NOTE

1. Charles Wesley, "Come, Jesus, Lord, with Holy Fire," 1880, public domain.

Finance  11

Soul-winners, to be successful, must not be overanxious about finance, but must laugh at the Devil and all his fears, and count God faithful and trust Him to supply all their needs. They should repeatedly read over the last part of the sixth chapter of Matthew, beginning with verse 19. What could be stronger and more positive than the assurance of Jesus that their needs shall be supplied?

When I was a little fellow, I never worried about where my next pair of shoes or my next meal was to come from. My mother did all that worrying, and I trusted her. Jesus says we are not to be anxious about what we shall eat or what we shall wear: "Isn't life more than food, and your body more than clothing?" (Matt. 6:25 NLT). And if God gives you life, will He not give you meat to sustain life? And if He allows you still to live in your body for a season, will He not give you clothing to protect your body? "Look at the birds. They don't plant or harvest or store food in barns, for your heavenly Father feeds them. And aren't you far more valuable to him than they are? . . . So don't worry about these things, saying, 'What will we eat? What will we drink? What will we wear?' These things dominate the thoughts of unbelievers, but your heavenly Father already knows all your needs" (Matt. 6:26, 31–32 NLT).

Jesus would have me trust my heavenly Father as I did my mother. Then I can be a child again, and all I have to do is to pray and obey and trust the Lord, and have a good time before Him, and He will supply my needs and the needs of my little ones whom He has given me. Yes, that is what He means, for He says, "Seek first the kingdom of God and His righteousness, and all these things shall be added to you" (Matt. 6:33 NKJV).

This freedom from anxiety is the privilege and duty of all soul-winners, from carefree workers who have only to get bread for their own mouths to those who have a large family to feed and clothe, and even those with a thousand-fold financial responsibility like Moses or George Mueller or Hudson Taylor or our Salvation Army leaders.

Faith—simple, unmixed faith in God's promise—can no more exist in the same heart with worry than can fire and water or light and darkness consort together; one extinguishes the other. Faith in the plain, unmistakable promise of God, begotten by the Holy Spirit, so links the soul-winner to Jesus, so yokes and unites him or her in partnership together, that the burden and care is the Lord's, since the cattle on a thousand hills and the silver and the gold are His (see Ps. 50:10; Hag. 2:8). And He would have His children trust Him, walk the waves with Him, never doubt Him, shout the victory through Him, and triumph over all fear and all the power of the Enemy in Him. According to the Word of God this is His will for the soul-winner, and a secret every true soul-winner must and does know.

God does not send soul-winners to a warfare at their own charges, but according to Paul, "shall supply all [their] need according to his riches in glory by Christ Jesus" (Phil. 4:19 KJV).

God's supply depot is abundantly full and runs on time, but the worried and anxious unbeliever wants Him to run ahead of schedule. No, no! He may, in order to test and strengthen faith, not provide the second suit until the first one is ready to be laid aside, and sometimes after supper He may allow you to go to bed not knowing where the breakfast is to come from, but it will come at breakfast time. "Your heavenly Father already knows all your needs" (Matt. 6:32 NLT), so trust Him, as does the sparrow. The wee thing tucks its tiny head under its little wing and sleeps, not knowing where it will find its breakfast, and when the day dawns it chirps its merry note of praise, and God opens His great hand and feeds it. And "you are of more value than many sparrows," said Jesus (Matt. 10:31 ESV). The psalmist said, "The eyes of all look to you in hope; you give them their food as they need it. When you open your hand, you satisfy the hunger and thirst of every living thing" (Ps. 145:15–16 NLT).

Trust Him! He will not fail you. In this, as in all other things, the assurance holds well that "the temptations in your life are no different from what others experience. And God is faithful. He will not allow the temptation to be more than you can stand. When you are tempted, he will show you a way out so that you can endure" (1 Cor. 10:13 NLT). I have proved this in times past, and I may have to prove it again, but "God is faithful" (and the Devil is a liar and always will be).

Finney's clothes got threadbare, but he was so intent on getting souls saved that he didn't notice it until someone came along and measured him for a new suit. I had a similar experience once. God knew when the old suit needed replacing by a new one, and He sent it along on time.

Many people lose their love for souls and their power to win them by allowing covetousness or financial anxiety to crowd childlike trust out of their hearts. The Lord cried to the backslidden, covetous prophets of old, "Who is there even among you that would shut the doors for nought? Neither do ye kindle the fire on mine altar for nought" (Mal. 1:10 KJV). They would do nothing until they knew they would be well paid for it. It was not souls but money they worked for.

Contrast that with Paul's unselfish, disinterested devotion. He said, "I have never coveted anyone's silver or gold or fine clothes. You know that these hands of mine have worked to supply my own needs and even the needs of those who were with me. And I have been a constant example of how you can help those in need by working hard. You should remember the words of the Lord Jesus: 'It is more blessed to give than to receive'" (Acts 20:33–35 NLT).

He also said, "I seek not yours but you" (2 Cor. 12:14 KJV). He even went so far as to say, when they gave him anything, "Not [that] I desire a gift: but I desire fruit that may abound to your account" (Phil. 4:17 KJV). It was not the benefit he derived from receiving so much as the benefit they would derive from giving that rejoiced his heart.

In writing to the Philippians, who had sent him a donation, he revealed a bit of his inner experience. He said, "How I praise the Lord that you are concerned about me again. I know you have always been concerned for me, but you didn't have the chance to help me. Not that I was ever in need, for I have learned how to be content with whatever I have. I know how to live on almost nothing or with everything. I have learned the secret of living in every situation, whether it is with a full stomach or empty, with plenty or little. For I can do everything through Christ, who gives me strength" (Phil. 4:10–13 NLT).

And writing to Timothy, Paul said that a leader in the church must "not love money" (1 Tim. 3:3 NLT), while Peter said we are to "shepherd God's flock . . . because you are happy to serve, not because you want money" (1 Pet. 5:2 NCV).

In all this I do not contend that God would not have soul-winners amply supported and relieved of financial burden and care by the people for whom they give their lives. God says, "Those who work deserve their pay" (Luke 10:7 NLT) and He forbade the muzzling of the ox that trod out the corn (see Deut. 25:4). And by the tithing system, which all Christians ought to adopt, everyone was to assist in the support of the ministry.

But what I do contend is that soul-winners must not be anxious about their bread. They must beware of covetousness. They must seek to save souls, and if those souls do not support the soul-winner as one might wish, must still love them unto death, seek their salvation, and cheerfully and triumphantly trust the God who fed Elijah and rained manna from heaven for forty years to feed a million Israelites to find a way to provide. I maintain against all devils and all unbelief that God will not disappoint, but will satisfy you with the finest of wheat, "more than the richest feast" (Ps. 147:14; 63:5 NLT).

Kings shall fall down before Him,

And gold and incense bring;

All nations shall adore Him,

His praise all people sing;

For Him shall prayer unceasing

And daily vows ascend;

His kingdom still increasing,

A kingdom without end:

O'er every foe victorious,

He on His throne shall rest;

From age to age more glorious,

All blessing and all blessed.

The tide of time shall never

His covenant remove;

His name shall stand forever,

His changeless name of Love.[1]

NOTE

1. James Montgomery, "Hail to the Lord's Anointed," 1821, public domain.

Saving Truth 12

All truth is precious, but not all truth is adapted to secure the immediate salvation and sanctification of souls, any more than all medicine is adapted to cure heart disease or rheumatism. There are certain truths which, preached in the power of the Holy Spirit, are as much adapted to save and sanctify souls as food to satisfy hunger or fire to melt ice. There are other truths, equally biblical, that will no more secure such results than the truths of the multiplication table will comfort a brokenhearted mother while mourning her lost children or the facts of astronomy will quiet a guilty conscience roused from the slumber of sin.

Some time ago I read the amazing and humbling statement that "there were over three thousand churches in two of the leading denominations of this country that did not report a single member added by profession of faith last year." Well may the writer add,

"Think of more than three thousand ministers in two denominations world-renowned for their schools and culture, preaching a whole year, and aided by deacons and Sunday school teachers and Christian parents and church members and prayer meetings and helps and helpers innumerable, and all without one soul added to God's kingdom!"

Why this stupendous failure? It cannot be that truth was not preached and taught in the Sunday schools and prayer meetings. These preachers and teachers and parents were orthodox, cultured, and skilled in biblical lore. No doubt they preached and taught truth from one end of the year to the other, but it was not *the truth*—the truth that saves, the truth that first smites the conscience, lays bare the secrets of the heart, and arouses the slumbering soul until, self-convicted, it feels that everyone it meets is acquainted with its guilt, every wind and every footfall is an accusing voice, and no cover can hide it from God's searching eye. And when conviction has wrought its purpose and penitence is complete, saving truth whispers of forgiveness and peace, and offers mercy and salvation full and free through the bleeding Lamb of God, "before the world's foundation slain."[1] Such truth preached faithfully and constantly in these pulpits and churches— with power and authority, like thunderbolts from the cannon's mouth—might have set the nation ablaze with revival fire.

The fact is, there are different kinds or grades of truth for different classes of people, just as there are different medicines for various diseases and food for different ages and constitutions. Jesus declared this when He said, "There is so much more I want to tell you, but you can't bear it now" (John 16:12 NLT). The soul-winner must recognize this fact, and seek rightly to divide the word of truth (see 2 Tim. 2:15).

The follower of Jesus needs a different kind and application of truth from that needed by those who are far from God, and the sanctified man or woman can receive the strong meat of God's Word, while babes in Christ must be fed on milk (see 1 Cor. 3:1–2; Heb. 5:12, 14).

With skeptics or seekers, the principal appeal should be made to the conscience and the will. They may be moral, and more or less amiable in their family and social relations, and honorable among their business associates. But be sure that under this is secret self-ishness and heart sin—seeking their own way, disobedient to the light, careless to the dying love of Jesus, and in reality if not in pro-fession, enemies of God (see Rom. 8:7). They must be acquainted with these facts, and faithfully and lovingly and firmly warned of their utter ruin if they do not repent. Repentance—deep, thorough, and heartfelt—leading to a confession and an utter, eternal renunci-ation of all sin and a complete amendment of life and a making right (as far as possible) of all past wrong must be presented as the "strait gate" through which they can enter the highway to heaven. We must insist on an immediate and unconditional surrender to all the light God gives, and offer them mercy and tender love through Jesus Christ when they yield.

The motives that lead to repentance are drawn from eternity, and there is a whole armory of truth with which wandering souls can and must be bombarded to bring them to terms. Truth such as the cer-tainty that what they sow they shall reap, that their sins will surely find them out, that death will speedily overtake them, and that if, refusing mercy, they presume on the goodness of God and continue in selfishness and sin, hell shall be their portion forever. Truth that a life of peace and joy here, a happy deathbed, and eternal glory can be offered as the alternative, on condition of obedient faith.

Very much the same kind of truth is necessary for souls that have strayed or turned from the faith, except that the proportions may have to be varied. If they are stubborn, thunder the law at them until they hoist the white flag and sue for mercy. If they are sorrowful but fear it is vain to try again, then they should be encouraged in every possible way to look up and trust; the infinite love and pity of God revealed in Jesus should be pressed upon their attention, and they should be urged to cast themselves upon God's mercy.

If these foundational truths of repentance toward God and faith in our Lord Jesus Christ are faithfully, affectionately, and prayerfully presented, and the wandering or wayward soul grasps and trusts them, that soul will be accepted by the Lord and adopted into His family. They must then be fed upon truths different from those they were fed on before. They will have tender hearts, and so it will be most unwise to thunder the law at them, though they should be fully instructed as to the spirituality of the law, and that it is the law by which God wishes us to order our conduct and for which abundant grace will be given. Nor should they now be asked to surrender—since they did so when they gave their lives to Christ—but should be intelligently instructed as to the nature and extent of the consecration that is expected of them, and should be urged, and wisely and tenderly encouraged, to make this consecration, presenting their bodies as living sacrifices and yielding themselves to God, "as those that are alive from the dead" (Rom. 6:13 KJV).

They should then be instructed as to the fact of inbred sin, which they will soon find stirring within themselves, and the importance and possibility of having this enemy cast out. Holiness should be presented not so much as a stern demand of a holy God but rather as the glorious privilege of the beloved child of God. They should be taught that it is an experience in which "perfect love expels all fear" (1 John 4:18 NLT), a rest of soul in which—as our bones and sinews are covered with skin and thus unseen—the fact of duty, while still remaining in force, is clothed and hidden by love.

Therefore, while the necessity of holiness should be presented, and a gentle and constant pressure brought to bear upon the will, yet the principal effort should be made to remove slavish fear by opening up the understanding, and so drawing out the confidence and affections that the soul—which in conversion bowed at the feet of Jesus as its conqueror—shall now intelligently and rapturously yield to Him as its heavenly Bridegroom. The heart should be moved to fall so desperately in love with Him by the incoming of the Holy Spirit that it shall cry out with David, "I delight to do your will, O my God" (Ps. 40:8 ESV) and with Jesus, "My food is to do the will of him who sent me" (John 4:34 ESV).

If we as soul-winners do not keep a clear, warm, tender experience of full salvation ourselves, there is a danger of driving the people to a legal experience instead of leading them into the experience of "perfect love." A legal experience is one in which we brace up to our duty because the law demands it, in which we are prodded and pushed up to it by the terrors of the law rather than led up to it by the sweet wooings and gentle drawings of love.

When skeptical, seeking, and straying souls are present in a holiness meeting (church service), there will be a strong temptation to address them. But, as the kind of truth they need differs from that needed by Christians, confusion is likely to result if this is done, and an uncertain experience may be engendered in the hearts of those who love God. In such meetings, it will usually be found wisest to go straight for the Christians, to get them sanctified. The Lord has been pleased to give me victory along this line, and I usually find that some souls nonetheless seek salvation in my holiness meetings (church services).

Jesus likens a Christian to a sheep. Our duty, then, in the holiness meeting is not to club them with the law but rather to feed them with the promises and assurances of the gospel, teach them to discern the voice of the Good Shepherd, and remove all fear so that they may gladly follow Him. The staple diet of all saints should be the promises, seasoned with the commandments to give them a healthy relish.

The promises draw us on in the narrow way, and the commandments hedge us in so that we do not lose the way. The promises should be so presented, and the fullness there is in the gospel and in Jesus so brought to view, that the souls of the people will run hard after Him and not need continual beatings to keep them from breaking through the hedge onto the Devil's territory.

To clearly discern and skillfully apply the truth needed by the souls that surround us requires heavenly wisdom, and well did Paul exhort Timothy, "Be a good worker, one who does not need to be ashamed and who correctly explains the word of truth" (2 Tim. 2:15 NLT). But our work will be in vain unless we, in lowliness of mind, sit at the feet of Jesus, seek wisdom from God, and submit ourselves in glad, prayerful faith to the Spirit of truth who can and will guide "into all truth" (John 16:13 KJV).

The Bible, which contains the revealed truth necessary to salvation, will surely puzzle and mystify all who come to it in the big and swelling conceit of worldly wisdom, but it will open its treasure to the plain and humble heart who comes to it full of the Spirit that moved holy men of old to write it.

O Lord, evermore give to Your people leaders and teachers filled with the Spirit and clothed with His wisdom!

> Happy the men to whom 'tis given,
> To dwell within that gate of heaven,
> And in Thy house record Thy praise;
> Whose strength and confidence Thou art,
> Who feel Thee, Savior, in their heart,
> The Way, the Truth, the Life of grace.

> Better a day Thy courts within
> Than thousands in the tents of sin;
> How base the noblest pleasure there!
> How great the weakest child of thine!
> His meanest task is all divine,
> And kings and priests Thy servants are.[2]

NOTES

1. Johann Andreas Rothe, trans. John Wesley, "Now I Have Found the Ground Wherein," 1727, public domain.

2. Charles Wesley, "How Lovely Are Thy Tents, O Lord," 1798, public domain.

Keeping the Flock 13

Soul-winners must give much time, thought, prayer, and effort to the keeping and strengthening of those who come to faith through their efforts. They ought to say with Paul, "It gives us new life to know that you are standing firm in the Lord" (1 Thess. 3:8 NLT). Also like Paul, they should pray earnestly night and day, asking God to supply whatever is lacking in the faith of new Christ-followers (see 1 Thess. 3:10). Paul's ambition was not simply to get people into God's kingdom and united with some local church, but to "present them to God, perfect in their relationship to Christ" (Col. 1:28 NLT).

There is a danger of spending far more effort and care in getting people to the point of commitment than in keeping them after they are there. After a baby is born, it must be intelligently and constantly cared for, or it will very likely die. Soul-winners are not spiritual incubators, but fathers and mothers in the faith, with all the measureless responsibility not only of leading souls to faith in Christ, but also of keeping them after they come to faith.

William Booth once said to a few of us who were traveling with him, "Look well to the fire in your own souls, for the tendency of fire is to go out." And yet a fire will never go out if it is frequently well shaken down and fresh fuel is added. We must look well to the spark of fire kindled in the hearts of new Christians and fan it gently but surely to a flame and help them to care for it, that it may never go out. The saddest thing in all this mighty work of soul-winning is the fact that in so many instances the fire does go out, the light ceases to shine, the salt loses its savor, and souls that were redeemed and washed with the precious blood of Jesus—that have been made "partakers of the Holy Spirit, and have tasted the good word of God and the powers of the age to come" (Heb. 6:4–5 NKJV)—fall away and return to their old sins, like "the dog . . . to his own vomit" and the "sow that was washed to her wallowing in the mire" (2 Pet. 2:22 KJV).

Judas fell from the very face and ministry of Jesus Himself. On another occasion, after one of Christ's searching sermons, we read that "many of his disciples turned away and deserted him" (John 6:66 NLT).

Paul mourned the loss of Demas, who "loved this present world" (2 Tim. 4:10 KJV). He foresaw and foretold the backsliding of some of the Ephesian church leaders (see Acts 20:29–30), and after his mighty victories there, which radiated to all the surrounding nations, he had to write sorrowfully to Timothy, "As you know, everyone from the province of Asia has deserted me—even Phygelus and Hermogenes" (2 Tim. 1:15 NLT). "Things that cause people to trip and fall into sin must happen," Jesus said (Luke 17:1 CEB), and backslidings will follow. But soul-winners must strive mightily against this, until, like Paul, they can appeal to their people and say, "I declare today that I have been faithful. If anyone suffers eternal death, it's not my fault, for I didn't shrink from declaring all that God wants you to know" (Acts 20:26–27 NLT). They must not only win souls, but must also keep them.

They must be visited. Some time ago I visited a Salvation Army corps (church) in California. The officer (pastor) met me at the train, and on the way to my lodgings remarked, "We got one of the worst drunkards in town saved last night, and I have seen him twice this morning and he is doing well." Of course he would do well with such love and care as that! If they cannot be visited at once, drop them a note and enclose a suitable tract.

A businessman of about fifty years of age, together with his wife, came to faith in Christ in one of my meetings. In a subsequent meeting, I missed him, so I wrote him a note telling him I was praying for him. The next night he was present and told how he had been sorely tempted, but that note blessed him and helped him to get the victory. He became a good Salvation Army soldier (member). In all probability, it was that timely little note, written in five minutes and costing only the price of a postage stamp, that kept him from falling.

They should be encouraged to read their Bible daily, together with other good books. When I was in Boston, I went to the Bible Society and got them to donate forty little New Testaments, one of which I would give to each new Christian, after having marked a number of helpful texts and written his or her name on the flyleaf. Years afterward I was visiting a corps when a young man asked me if I remembered him. I did not. He pulled out a little, well-worn Testament, pointed to his name, and asked if I knew that writing. I did.

"You gave me this Testament years ago," he said, "when you were captain in Boston. I have kept it and read it ever since, and am to be enrolled as a soldier tonight."

They must be taught to pray and urged to practice regular and frequent secret prayer, until they know its sweetness and inexpressible necessity and profit. They must be instructed to keep believing, and also made to see the difference between sin and temptation.

They should be patiently encouraged to work for others, especially for their own people. The Bible says, "Andrew went to find his brother, Simon, and . . . brought Simon to meet Jesus" (John 1:41–42 NLT), and new followers of Jesus must do likewise.

They should be patiently, tenderly, firmly led into the experience of sanctification or (as it is otherwise known) perfect love. They must not be allowed to stop at consecration, but must be pressed on into a definite experience of full salvation. It was at this point that Asa Mahan said his friend Charles Finney failed during his early ministry. He was unexcelled in getting people to a complete renunciation of all sin, to making right all past disobedience, and finally to a complete consecration of all to Jesus. He would start them off for the future with vows to obey God at all points, while nothing was said to them about trusting Jesus to cleanse their hearts at once and fill them with the Holy Spirit. Our vows are only ropes of sand until the Holy Spirit has come with consuming fire into our hearts, filling them with perfect love. Mahan wrote:

No individual, I believe, ever disciplined believers so severely, and with such intense and tireless perseverance, on that principle, as my brother Finney, before he learned the way of the Lord more perfectly.

Appalled at the backslidings which followed [his] revivals, his most earnest efforts were put forth to induce among believers permanence in the divine life. In accomplishing this, he knew of but one method—absolute and fixed renunciation of sin, consecration to God, and purpose of obedience. (Not a word about the faith that receives.) During his pastorate in [New York], for example, he held for weeks in succession special meetings of his church for perfecting this work, and never were a class of poor creatures carried through a severer process of discipline than were these. Years after, as their pastor informed me, those believers said they had never recovered from the internal weakness and exhaustion which had resulted from the terrible discipline through which Mr. Finney had carried them.

When he came to Oberlin and entered upon the duties of his professorship, he felt that God had given him a blessed opportunity to realize in perfection his ideal of a ministry for the churches. He had before him a mass of talented and promising theological students, who had implicit confidence in the wisdom of their teacher and with equal sincerity would follow his instructions and admonitions. He accordingly, for months in succession, gathered together those students at stated seasons, instructed them most carefully in regard to the nature of the renunciation of sin, consecration to Christ, and purpose of obedience required of them.

Then, under his teachings and exhortations, they would renew their renunciations, consecrations, and purposes of obedience, with all the intensity and fixedness of resolve of which their natures were capable. The result, in every case, was one and the same—not the new life of joy, and peace, and power that were anticipated, but groaning bondage under the law of sin and death. At the commencement, and during the progress of each meeting, their confessions and renunciations, their solemn consecrations and vows of obedience, were renewed, if possible, with fuller determination than ever before. Each meeting, however, was closed with the same dirge songs: "Look how we grovel here below"; "Where is the blessedness I knew, when first I saw the Lord?"; or "Return, O Holy Dove, Return."

And as they went out, not their songs of joy and gladness were heard, but their groans became more and more terribly audible. "They followed," and followed hard, "after the law of righteousness, but did not attain to the law of righteousness. Wherefore? Because they sought it not by faith, but as it were by the works of the law"; that is, by self-originated efforts and determinations.[1]

Thank God, Finney learned better, and soul-winners should profit by his example. New followers of Jesus Christ must utterly renounce sin, make wrong things right, and consecrate themselves fully to the Lord to obey Him in all things great and small. But they must understand fully that that is only *our* part, and that they must now wait on their heavenly Father and believe for Him to do *His* part, which is to cleanse their hearts and fill them with the Holy Spirit. They must continue in glad, believing, wrestling, never-give-in prayer, till the Comforter comes into their hearts in all His cleansing, sanctifying, and comforting power. They must tarry in Jerusalem till they are endued with power from on high (see Luke 24:49). They must believe God and receive the Holy Spirit, remembering that God is more willing to give the Holy Spirit to them that ask Him than parents are to give good gifts to their children (see Luke 11:13). That is so. I have proved it.

Soul-winners should so organize their work and train their people that they shall have wide-awake, willing workers to assist them in looking after the new believers. It will take patience and tact and prayer to train these workers, but it will abundantly repay all effort. "To every man his work" is the inspired plan (Mark 13:34 KJV).

Moses had such helpers (see Ex. 18:21–26) and Paul depended much on such help (see 2 Tim. 2:2; Titus 1:5). But there must not be too many irons in the fire. Everything must be subordinated to this one end of saving souls and making them into valiant soldiers of Jesus Christ. Paul said, "This one thing I do" (Phil. 3:13 KJV).

Organization must not be overdone, lest the workers become like David in Saul's armor, lest their power be exhausted in routine and they become like a mighty engine that has not sufficient power to run itself. Let the machinery be simple, and the divine, Holy Spirit power be abundant. For this there must be much prayer and patient waiting upon God. The power is His and can be had when persistently, believingly, humbly, and boldly applied for.

To succeed in getting people to work harmoniously together we must be melted or heated by a great common passion, and welded together like two pieces of iron, until there is no longer Greek or Jew, Englishman or Irishman, French or German, American or European, "but Christ is all, and in all" (Col. 3:11 KJV). Love is the only thing that will do this, and love will do it. I heard one of our officers say, "I got saved in a Salvation Army meeting where I could not understand a word spoken. But the love of Jesus was there, and I understood that."

In cold weather, people of all nations will gather around a stove in which there is a fire, and so they will gather around men and women who are full of love. Love "binds us all together in perfect harmony" (Col. 3:14 NLT), according to Paul. It quenches jealousies, destroys envyings, burns up suspicions, begets confidence, and holds people together with bonds stronger than death. Let us have it and have it more abundantly. More love, more love, more love! Without it we are nothing.

We may be gifted in speech and song as are the angels. We may be shrewd and far-seeing and able to accurately forecast the future. We may be encyclopedic in our knowledge. We may have mountain-moving faith. We may be charitably inclined and feed and shelter many poor to the extent of using up all our resources and wearing out our bodies, but if we have not the gentle, holy, humble, longsuffering, self-forgetful, unfailing, unsuspicious, self-sacrificing, generous, lowly love of Jesus, we are nothing. We are as sounding brass and tinkling cymbal (see 1 Cor. 13:1–8).

It was this love that enabled Paul to write, "I will not be burdensome to you: for I seek not yours but you. . . . And I will very gladly spend and be spent for you; though the more abundantly I love you, the less I be loved" (2 Cor. 12:14–15 KJV). And here is another bit of Paul's autobiography that ought to be put on every soul-winner's wall throughout the land, every word of which is freighted with the love that filled his great heart:

> You yourselves know, dear brothers and sisters, that our visit to you was not a failure. You know how badly we had been treated at Philippi just before we came to you and how much we suffered there. Yet our God gave us the courage to declare his Good News to you boldly, in spite of great opposition. So you can see we were not preaching with any deceit or impure motives or trickery.
>
> For we speak as messengers approved by God to be entrusted with the Good News. Our purpose is to please God, not people. He alone examines the motives of our hearts. Never once did we try to win you with flattery, as you well know. And God is our witness that we were not pretending to be your friends just to get your money! As for human praise, we have never sought it from you or anyone else.
>
> As apostles of Christ we certainly had a right to make some demands of you, but instead we were like children among you. Or we were like a mother feeding and caring for her own children. We loved you so much that we shared with you not only God's Good News but our own lives, too.
>
> Don't you remember, dear brothers and sisters, how hard we worked among you? Night and day we toiled to earn a living so that we would not be a burden to any of you as we preached God's Good News to you. You yourselves are our witnesses—

and so is God—that we were devout and honest and faultless toward all of you believers. And you know that we treated each of you as a father treats his own children. We pleaded with you, encouraged you, and urged you to live your lives in a way that God would consider worthy. For he called you to share in his Kingdom and glory. (1 Thess. 2:1–12 NLT)

And again he said, "I kept back nothing that was profitable unto you, but have shewed you and have taught you publicly, and from house to house. . . . I am pure from the blood of all men. For I have not [neglected] to declare unto you all the counsel of God. . . . Therefore watch, and remember, that by the space of three years I ceased not to warn every one night and day with tears" (Acts 20:20, 26–27, 31 KJV).

This is the love that will build up new believers, and nothing else will. We must have love, love, love! We must look for love, pray for love, believe for love. We must exercise love ourselves and inspire all our people to love, and then they will watch over one another, and pray and weep for each other, and bless one another, and be united as one, and the gates of hell cannot prevail against us.

Oh, that we all, as soul-winners, may have melting baptisms of holy love that shall make us like Jesus—patient, gentle, faithful, courageous, tireless, undismayed, and utterly unselfish. Then shall our spiritual children abound and be strong. If we do not have this love, God will give it to us in answer to persistent, believing prayer. He surely will. I do believe.

NOTE

1. Asa Mahan, *Autobiography: Intellectual, Moral, and Spiritual* (London: T. Woolmer, 1882), 246–247.

Saving the Children **14**

Not only did Jesus say, "Let the little children come to me, and do not hinder them" (Mark 10:14 NIV), but He also gave to Peter the positive command, "Feed my lambs" (John 21:15 NLT). In that command, He laid a responsibility upon soul-winners for the children, "for the kingdom of God belongs to such as these" (Mark 10:14 NIV). In no other field and among no other class can soul-winners work with such immediate success and such far-reaching results.

Children are not hard to reach with the gospel, if the soul-winner will merely be simple and use common sense in dealing with them. They are not hardened in sin; their consciences are tender, their hearts open, their minds receptive, their wills pliable, and their faith simple. They are keenly alive to the love of Jesus, the glories of heaven, the terrors of hell, and the omnipresence of God. They learn readily to pray in faith about everything and to cast all their care upon God. No eyes are so keen as theirs to see the Light that enlightens everyone, no hands are so ready to do His bidding, and no feet so ready to run in His ways.

And yet effort must be put forth ceaselessly to win them and keep them after they are won, for the corruption of their own natures, the evil example and teaching of a hostile world, and the wiles of the vigilant and tireless Enemy of all souls will soon blind their eyes and harden their hearts and utterly ruin them, if they are not soon won to Jesus and filled with His love. You may feel yourself unfitted for this task, but if God has called you to be a worker for souls it is your business to fit yourself for it.

The first thing necessary is to believe in the possibility of the conversion of the children. Certainly the plain teachings of Jesus, the examples found in the Bible, and the multitude of examples that anyone with open eyes can see ought to convince the most skeptical person of this possibility.

Almost from Samuel's babyhood the Lord spoke to him and filled his heart and mind with wisdom, so that none of His words fell to the ground (see 1 Sam. 2:26; 3:1–21). God ordained Jeremiah from childhood to be a prophet to the nations, and filled him with His Spirit (see Jer. 1:5–10). If this was possible under the law, how much more gloriously is it possible under the gospel? Catherine Booth experienced salvation when she was a child and William Booth as a mere lad, and all their sons and daughters were but children when they were brought to the Savior.

Jonathan Edwards, in one of his works, tells of a wee girl, not even five years of age, going to and from her bedroom looking most sad and disconsolate. Her mother asked her what was the matter, and the little thing replied, "Mama, when I pray God doesn't come." The mother tried to comfort her, but her little heart was filled with hunger that only the Comforter Himself could satisfy, and she still continued to go disconsolately to her bedroom. But one glad day she ran from her room, leaped into her mother's bosom, threw her arms around her neck, and cried, "O Mama, Mama, when I pray now, God comes!" And up through the years of her childhood and youth and womanhood she lived such a life of Christian humility and grace and truth as was the wonder of all who knew her.[1]

Secondly, since they can be won, you must make up your mind that you will win them. You must put from your mind forever the thought that "anything will do for the children." It will require much prayer, patience, love, tact, and divine wisdom to win them to the Savior and to keep them after they are won. They must have "line upon line . . . precept upon precept" (Isa. 28:13 NKJV). If one teaching of the lesson is not sufficient, then they must be taught it again and again.

"Why do you tell Charles the same thing twenty times over?" asked the father of John and Charles Wesley of their mother. "Because nineteen times won't do," replied the wise and particular mother.

Moses said:

Listen, O Israel! The LORD is our God, the LORD alone. And you must love the LORD your God with all your heart, all your soul, and all your strength. And you must commit yourselves wholeheartedly to these commands that I am giving you today. Repeat them again and again to your children. Talk about them when you are at home and when you are on the road, when you are going to bed and when you are getting up. Tie them to your hands and wear them on your forehead as reminders. Write them on the doorposts of your house and on your gates. (Deut. 6:4–9 NLT)

This was the way the children of the ancient Israelites were to be taught, and this must be the standard soul-winners set for themselves and their people today.

The children should be noticed, and I am increasingly convinced that in every meeting where children are present something should be said that is suitable to them, and the invitation to come to Jesus should include them.

When they do come, they should be dealt with most thoroughly. Their little hearts should be probed, their sins searched out, and thorough repentance required. Their fears must be tenderly removed by showing them the fullness of God's love and the certainty of salvation when they give up sin. Their thoughts should be turned to Jesus and their faith fixed on Him and grounded in His Word. Give them His sure promises, such as, "If we confess our sins to him, he is faithful and just to forgive us our sins and to cleanse us from all wickedness" (1 John 1:9 NLT). Above all, you must be simple and make things very plain for the children. They don't know the meaning of many big words that you understand quite well, so you must take pains to make yourself understood.

The other day I was talking to some children, and I gave them this text: "Remember now your Creator in the days of your youth" (Eccl. 12:1 NKJV). I asked them if they knew what the word *Creator* meant, and none of them knew. Neither did they know what the word *youth* meant. So I had to explain that the text meant that they were to remember and think about God and love Him while they were little boys and girls.

I also gave them the text, "Behold, how good and pleasant it is when brothers dwell in unity!" (Ps. 133:1 ESV). But none of them knew the meaning of the word *unity*. One said that it meant "home," and that was a pretty good guess. But I had to explain that the text meant that it was good and pleasant for little brothers and sisters—and big ones, too—to live together in peace, without quarreling and fighting. They all understood that.

You will have to put on your thinking caps and set your brains to work to make your teaching simple for the children. But love will help you.

Some time ago I heard a youth worker singing lustily to a lot of children: "Get your baggage on the deck and don't forget to get your check . . ."[2]

But he didn't explain that it simply meant that they were to give themselves to Jesus, throw away their sins, and be sure to get His love in their hearts. So when he got through I felt sure that there was nothing but a confused rattle of "baggage, deck, check, quick," in the ears of the children, with no useful or saving idea in their little heads and hearts.

If you pray to God for wisdom and love, He will help you to make the deepest spiritual truths plain to the children. As I simplify my talks God gives me the joy of seeing many young people seeking Him for salvation, and I have occasionally seen some gloriously sanctified.

Some time ago, in one of my meetings, I had a penitent form (the kneeler in front of the church) full of children, with each of whom I dealt personally. I asked one little fellow, "What are you here for, darling?"

"To get saved," said he.

"Get saved from what?" I inquired.

"From my sins."

"And what are your sins?"

"I fight," and then he broke down and cried.

"And what are you here for?" I asked a little girl.

She, too, said she was there to "get saved," and I asked what her sins were. She hesitated a little and then said, "I'm cruel to my sister and brother." And then she broke down and cried.

Another little girl said that she swore, and another said she disobeyed her mother. One little boy confessed that he told lies. Another said he smoked cigarettes, and yet another said he was disobedient to his teacher. And so they told of their sins, broke down and wept, and prayed and asked God to forgive them and make them good. And I believe that most of them entered God's kingdom.

In another meeting a little fellow of ten got sanctified and filled with the Spirit, and had all fear taken out of his heart—where before he had been very timid—because, said he, "Jesus is with me now." In another meeting a little girl, about ten years of age, got sanctified. She lived a holy life for about three years and then died happy, sending me word beforehand that the Lord still sanctified her and was keeping her to the end.

But after we have done all, we must remember that they are only lambs, not sheep. We must not forget that they are growing children, not grown men and women. They are in the formative state, tender and inexperienced, and life and the world are full of interest to them. They have a personality and individuality of their own, and are not always willing to take the simple word of their elders, nor to yield to admonition and instruction, but desire to prove their own powers and to taste and see all things for themselves. Therefore it will be necessary not only to talk much to them about God—and even more so—but also to depend upon the mighty, constant cooperation of the Holy Spirit in securing their salvation and keeping them in the grace of our Lord Jesus Christ.

We must show all diligence in our efforts until, if possible, we can at least say to them as Paul said to Timothy: "You have been taught the holy Scriptures from childhood, and they have given you the wisdom to receive the salvation that comes by trusting in Christ Jesus" (2 Tim. 3:15 NLT).

Blessed Jesus, *save* our children!
Be their Guardian through life's way;
From all evil e'er protect them,
Walk Thou with them, come what may.
In white raiment let us meet them
When earth's shadows flee away.

Blessed Jesus, *lead* our children
Into paths of service sweet;
Up the hill of Calvary climbing,
May they and the sinner meet!
More than conquerors, let us see them
Bring their jewels to Thy feet!

Blessed Jesus, *make* our children

Thine for life and thine for aye!

When death's waters overtake them,

Be their Rock, their Light, their Stay!

Tender Shepherd, let us find them

On Thy breast in realms of day![3]

NOTES

1. Summarized and paraphrased from *The Works of Jonathan Edwards, A.M.* (London: William Ball, 1834), 361–362.

2. Based on the song, "De Gospel Raft," *Minstrel Songs, Old and New* (Boston: Oliver Ditson & Co., 1883). This wording was used in the song "Hideaway" in a 1921 recording by Oscar Ford.

3. Emma Booth-Tucker, "Blessed Jesus, Save Our Children," formerly in *The Salvation Army Songbook*; quoted in Frederick St. George de Lautour Booth-Tucker, *The Consul: A Sketch of Emma Booth Tucker* (London: The Salvation Army Publishing Department, 1904), 99. Emphasis added.

Saving the Children \;\boxed{15}
(Continued)

Rough-and-ready Peter, that old fisherman, thought he was cut out for and best fitted to be a prime minister, secretary of state, or bishop, and it seems had several disputes with the other disciples in which he suggested that perhaps he should be considered the greatest among them (see Mark 9:34, Luke 9:46). How surprised he must have been, then, when he got his commission from Jesus to be a youth worker and received orders to feed the lambs! What a mighty argument he could have made to prove that he was not fitted for work with children! To be sure, he had at least one boy of his own (see 1 Pet. 5:13), and maybe several others, but he was a fisherman, and the care of the children was largely left to his wife. In fact, he had no fitness either by nature or training for that kind of work. All his associations had been with the big, burly men of the sea, and what did he know about talking to children? All his thoughts and desires and ambitions ran in another direction, and was he not too old and set in his ways to change now?

But Jesus, with infinite knowledge, wisdom, and tenderness, looked straight into Peter's eyes and asked him that searching question, "Do you love me more than these?" (John 21:15 NLT). And when in reply to his answer, "Yes, Lord . . . you know I love you," Jesus said, "Feed my lambs," what could Peter say? So Peter was first commissioned to be a worker among the little ones.

"But," you say, "didn't Jesus mean new Christians, when He said, 'My lambs'? And might they not be men and women who had only recently experienced new life in Christ?" True, it is probable that Jesus meant new Christians, but that company includes children. And didn't Jesus say, "for the kingdom of God belongs to such as these" (Mark 10:14 NIV)? So, however we may explain the text, we cannot escape the fact that Peter was commanded to work with and for the children. And if Peter, why not you and I? Are we not commanded to look well to the flock over which the Holy Spirit has made us shepherds (see Acts 20:28)? And was there ever a flock in which there were no lambs? If so, it was a flock doomed to speedy extinction.

Are we not commanded to do with our might what our hands find to do (see Eccl. 9:10)? And do we not find multitudes of little ones un-shepherded, unloved, untaught, and for whose tender little souls no one cares, prays, or weeps before the Lord, and whose little hands are stretched out toward us, saying, "Come, and help us"? Shall we wait until they are old in sin, hardened in wickedness, fixed in unholy habits, and bond slaves of the Devil before we work and plan and pray for them and seek their salvation?

Is it possible that we have a call to the work of saving souls and yet have no commission for the children? No, no, no! To every worker who says to Jesus, "Lord, You know I love You," Jesus says, "Feed my lambs." We may feel that we have no fitness, no tact, no skill, and no gifts for that kind of work, but the commission lays upon us the responsibility to study and think and watch and pray and love and believe and work ourselves into fitness. And by beginning with just such poor, feeble, untrained gifts as we have; by making the most of every opportunity; by being diligent and faithful; by having courage and pluck and good cheer and faith; and by seeking God's blessing day by day, this fitness can surely be attained.

The poor, struggling soul who never dreamed he had any music in his soul or in his fingers until he encountered Jesus at a Salvation Army penitent form, but who sets himself to it and patiently thrums away at a guitar or blows at a cornet for six months or a year until he can play fairly well, can with equal diligence, patience, determination, and attention learn to interest and bless and help the children. But he must put his heart and soul into it.

I read some time ago of a minister who was sure he was called and fitted only to preach big sermons to big folks. But one day he heard a fellow minister talk so instructively and entertainingly to the children that he determined to acquire that gift, and by thought and prayer and practice he, too, became a powerful children's worker.

Go and do likewise.

Do you ask, "How can I become such a worker?"

1. Make up your mind that you ought to do so and that by God's grace you will. Then make it a matter of daily prayer and thought and meditation. Above all, seek help from God.

2. Get all the help you can from others. Study their methods, but don't become a vain imitator of anyone. Be yourself.

3. Study the best books you can find on the subject. There are many bright books that will greatly help you.

4. Try to put yourself in the place of the child, and ask what would interest you. Make things plain and simple. Watch for illustrations and anecdotes that interest children, and which they can understand.

5. Above all, have a heart full of tender love and sympathy for the little ones, and you will be interesting and helpful to them whether you can talk much or not. They will feel your love and respond to it, and so you can point them to Jesus and help them in their first timid steps toward heaven.

> When in the slippery paths of youth
> With heedless steps I ran,
> Thine arm unseen conveyed me safe,
> And led me up to man.

> Through hidden dangers, toils, and deaths,
> It gently cleared my way;
> And through the pleasing snares of vice,
> More to be feared than they.

> When worn with sickness, oft hast Thou
> With health renewed my face;
> And when in sins and sorrows sunk,
> Revived my soul with grace.

Ten thousand thousand precious gifts
My daily thanks employ;
Nor is the last a cheerful heart
That takes those gifts with joy.

Through every period of my life
Thy goodness I'll pursue:
And after death, in distant worlds,
The glorious theme renew.[1]

NOTE

1. Joseph Addison, "When All Thy Mercies, O My God," 1712, public domain.

Recently in my regular Bible reading I came to that tender appeal of King David to his generals as they were going forth to fight with Absalom: "Deal gently for my sake with the young man, even with Absalom" (2 Sam. 18:5 KJV), and my heart was touched with its likeness to Jesus.

Absalom was in rebellion against his father, David the king, had driven his father from his throne, had outraged his father's marital ties, had sacrificed filial affection and trampled upon duty, and was now seeking his father's life. But David knew Absalom only as his wayward boy, loved him still, and commanded his warriors to deal gently with him in the coming battle. He would have the rebellion crushed, but the rebel saved; the sin destroyed, but the sinner rescued.

How like Jesus that is! Is not that the way Jesus feels toward the most desperate, careless sinner? Does not His heart yearn over them with unutterable tenderness? And is not this written for our admonition? Does He not say to us, "Deal gently for My sake"?

The battle went against Absalom that day, and hardhearted, willful, stubborn old Joab slew him deliberately in spite of the king's wish. And so it often is today. Joab's tribe has increased, and while Jesus would have wayward souls dealt with gently, Joab rises up and thrusts them through with reproaches and bitter words and sharp looks, slays them utterly, and Jesus' heart is broken afresh, as David's heart was.

The elder brother in the story of the prodigal son (see Luke 15:11–32), with his ungenerous jealousy and cruel words and hardness of heart, grieved the loving old father as surely as did the prodigal with his riotous living.

There are many reasons we should deal gently.

We should deal gently with people that we may be like Jesus. When Peter denied Jesus and cursed and swore, Jesus loved him still — and turned and gave him a tender look that broke his heart — and Peter went out and wept bitterly. And after the resurrection Jesus did not rebuke and reproach Peter, but tenderly asked him, "Do you love me?" (John 21:15 NLT) and then commissioned him to feed His lambs and sheep.

Should we, then, who at our best are only sinners saved by grace, despise our Lord's example and deal roughly with His sheep that have gone astray? Since He has freely forgiven us our tremendous debt, shall we not forgive our brothers and sisters (see Matt. 18:23–35)?

We should deal gently with them lest we ourselves grieve the Spirit and falter in faith. Paul wrote to the church in Galatia, saying, "Dear brothers and sisters, if another believer is overcome by some sin, you who are godly should gently and humbly help that person back onto the right path. And be careful not to fall into the same temptation yourself" (Gal. 6:1 NLT). I have noticed that when professing Christians act harshly toward those who falter it is usually only a question of time when they themselves fail—in fact, it is pretty certain that they are already losing faith in their hearts. In the very act of killing the rebellious Absalom, Joab himself rebelled against the expressed wish and command of his king, though he did it under the cloak of loyalty.

And so those today who are severe in their dealings with others under the cloak of zeal for righteousness and loyalty to truth are themselves rebelling against the example and spirit of Jesus, and unless they repent, the world shall surely soon witness their fall.

We should deal gently that we might win back wayward souls. Jesus loves them still, seeks them continually, and waits to forgive, cleanse, and restore to them the joy of salvation the moment they return, and we must not hinder, but help. But we shall not do so unless we deal gently. Harsh dealing would not win us, nor will it win them.

Paul wrote to Timothy, "A servant of the Lord must not quarrel but must be kind to everyone, be able to teach, and be patient with difficult people. Gently instruct those who oppose the truth. Perhaps God will change those people's hearts, and they will learn the truth. Then they will come to their senses and escape from the devil's trap. For they have been held captive by him to do whatever he wants" (2 Tim. 2:24–26 NLT).

This gentleness is not inconsistent with great firmness and unswerving loyalty to the truth. In fact, it is only when it is combined with these sturdy virtues that it commends itself to the judgment and conscience of wrongdoers, and is likely to really win them from the error of their ways.

Firmness of manner may unite with great gentleness of spirit. I may be as tender in spirit in warning and commanding my child to beware of the fire as I am in soothing him after he is burned.

While harshness and severity will only harden the wanderer from God on the one hand, a gospel of gush will fill Him with indifference or contempt on the other. The soul-winner, then, must not have the hardness and brittleness of glass or cast iron, nor the malleability of wrought iron or putty, but rather the strength and flexibility of finest steel that will bend but never break, that will yield and yet retain its own form.

It is generally true that holy mothers have more influence with and win more willful boys and girls than do the fathers—not because the mothers are more ready to compromise principle and sacrifice truth, but rather because while unwavering in their fidelity to righteousness, they mingle mercy with judgment and a passion of gentle, unfailing love and most tender solicitude with firmness and loyalty to the claims of God's perfect and holy law.

But how shall one who has not this spirit of perfect gentleness secure it? There is but one way. It is a fruit of the Spirit, and is to be had only at Jesus' feet.

Jesus is like a "Lamb slain" (Rev. 13:8 KJV)—mutely gentle—and yet again He is "the Lion of the tribe of Judah" (Rev. 5:5 KJV)—firm and strong. He combines the strength of the lion with the gentleness of the lamb.

You, then, who would have His Spirit, confess your need. Are you hard, harsh, critical, severe, and unrelenting? Tell Him and ask Him to destroy this carnal mind and give you His mind. And as you ask, believe, for "anything is possible if a person believes" (Mark 9:23 NLT).

To maintain this spirit you must walk in the footsteps of Jesus and feed on His words. Only to those who seek Him day by day with the whole heart, and with joy, is it given to be like Him in these heavenly tempers and dispositions. "Let this mind be in you, which was also in Christ Jesus" (Phil. 2:5 KJV).

What though a thousand hosts engage,
A thousand worlds, my soul to shake?
I have a shield to quell their rage,
And drive the alien armies back;
Portrayed it bears a bleeding Lamb;
I dare believe in Jesus' name.

Me to retrieve from Satan's hands,
Me from this evil world to free,
To purge my sins and loose my bands,
And save from all iniquity,
My Lord and God from heaven came;
I dare believe in Jesus' name.[1]

NOTE

1. Charles Wesley, "Surrounded by a Host of Foes," 1749, public domain.

How to Speak

Thank God for such preachers and such preaching as are spoken of in the Bible, where we read, "At Iconium Paul and Barnabas went as usual into the Jewish synagogue. There they spoke so effectively that a great number of Jews and Greeks believed" (Acts 14:1 NIV)! How did they do it? What was their secret? I think it was threefold.

1. Their manner. They must have won the multitude by the sweetness, grace, persuasiveness, and earnestness of their manner. They certainly did not offend and shock them by coarse, vulgar, uncouth speech, or by a weak and vacillating, light and foolish, or boisterous and domineering manner. They wanted to win souls, and they suited their manner to their purpose.

Solomon said, "Whoever loves a pure heart and gracious speech will have the king as a friend" (Prov. 22:11 NLT). This "gracious speech" is not a thing to be despised. It is rather something to be thought about, prayed over, and cultivated. It was said of Jesus, "Everyone . . . was amazed by the gracious words that came from his lips" (Luke 4:22 NLT). Soldiers said of Him, "We have never heard anyone speak like this" (John 7:46 NLT). Undoubtedly this graciousness was not only in what He said, but also in the way He said it. His manner was authoritative yet gentle, strong yet tender, and dignified yet popular and familiar. You can say to a little child, "Come here, you little rascal," in such a sweet manner as to win his or her confidence and draw him or her to you. You can also say, "Come here, you darling child," in such a rough, coarse way as to fill him or her with fear and drive him or her from you. It is largely a question of manner.

David Garrick, the great actor, was asked why he could move people so mightily by fiction, while preachers, speaking such awful and momentous truths, left them unmoved. He replied, "[They] speak truth as though it were fiction, while I speak fiction as though it were truth."[1] It was a question of manner.

A woman who was so far away from the evangelist George Whitefield that she could not hear what he said was weeping. A bystander asked her why she wept, since she knew not what he said. "Oh," said she, "can't you see the holy wag of his head?" His manner was matchless. Lawyers pleading before judges and juries, and political speakers seeking to win votes cultivate an ingratiating manner. Why, then, should not we who are seeking to win souls to Jesus Christ seek from God the best manner in which to do this?

2. Their matter. I judge that not only was the manner of Paul and Barnabas agreeable and attractive, but their subject matter was interesting and inexpressibly important. They preached the Word. They

reasoned out of the Scriptures. They declared that the prophecies were fulfilled; that Jesus Christ, the Son of God, of whom Moses and the prophets wrote and spoke, had come, was crucified, was buried, but was risen again; and that through obedient faith in Him, men and women might have their sins forgiven, their hearts purified, and their whole being sanctified and filled with God. It was not stale platitudes they preached, or vain babblings about this or that ritual or tradition, or harsh criticisms of authorities and "powers that be," or divers and strange doctrines, but it was "repentance toward God, and faith toward our Lord Jesus Christ" (Acts 20:21 KJV). This was the substance of their message.

It was a joyful message. It was good news. It was a declaration that God was so interested in humanity and "so loved the world that He gave His only begotten Son, that whoever believes in Him should not perish but have everlasting life. For God did not send His Son into the world to condemn the world, but that the world through Him might be saved" (John 3:16–17 NKJV). This war-worn, sorrowful old world needs such a joyful message.

It was an illuminating message. It showed them how to be delivered from sin and made acceptable to God. It also threw a flood of light into the grave and beyond, and "brought life and immortality to light" (2 Tim. 1:10 KJV), proclaiming Jesus as the "first of a great harvest of all who have died" (1 Cor. 15:20 NLT). Their message robbed earth of its loneliness and the tomb of its terrors. It turned the world into a schoolroom and preparation place for the Father's house of many mansions, and made heaven real.

It was a solemn and searching message. It called men and women to remember their sins and repent of them, forsake them, and surrender themselves no longer to the pleasures of ease, but to the service of God. They must take sides. If they would experience salvation, they must follow Christ crucified. Every road leads two ways: If they would put away sin and follow Jesus, He would lead them to heaven, but if they rejected Him they would surely go their own way to damnation, to hell.

3. Their spirit. A speaker's manner may be acceptable and the message true but if his or her spirit is not right, there will not be a "great number" who believe. The cannon may be a masterpiece and the powder and shot perfect, but if there is no fire, the enemy need not fear. The manner may be uncouth and the message fragmentary and faulty, but if the spirit is right—if it is humble and on fire with love—believers will be won.

When Cataline, a Roman citizen, conspired against the state, the matchless Roman orator Cicero delivered a series of orations against him. The people were captivated by the eloquence of Cicero. They went from the Forum praising his oratory, lauding his rhetoric, extolling his gestures, and exalting his graceful management of the folds of his toga.

However, when Philip of Macedon was planning to invade the states of Greece, the Athenian orator Demosthenes delivered a series of orations against him, and the Greeks went from his presence saying, "Let us go and fight Philip!"

Undoubtedly the manner and matter of the two orators were equally above criticism, but they were as far apart as the north and south poles in spirit. One sent the people away talking glibly and prettily about himself, while the other sent them away filled with his spirit and fired with a great impulse to die, if necessary, fighting the invader.

I imagine it was this right spirit, this white heat of soul, this full-orbed heart-purpose that was the principal factor in winning that multitude of believers in Iconium that day. Paul and Barnabas were great believers themselves. They were full of glad, triumphant, hell-defying and hell-defeating faith. They were not harassed by doubt and uncertainty. They did not preach guesses. They knew whom they believed (see 2 Tim. 1:12), because they believed they spoke (see 2 Cor. 4:13), and they so spoke that the faith of a multitude of others was kindled from the fire of theirs.

This faith had also kindled in their hearts a great love. They believed the love of God in giving His Son for them, and their hearts were in turn filled with love for Him. They believed the dying love of the Savior, and their hearts were so constrained with love for Him that they were prepared to die for Him. They believed the love of God for all, until they loved like Him, felt themselves debtors to all, and were ready to be offered as a sacrifice for the salvation of others.

Oh, it was a bright faith and a burning love that set the spirits of those two men on fire! And I think this Christlike spirit molded their manner and made them natural and gentle and strong and true and intense with earnestness, with no simper or whine or affectation of false pathos, no clang of hardness, no sting of bitterness, and no chill of heartless indifference. What school of oratory can touch and train the manner of an actor so that he or she shall for an instant compare with the untrained, shrinking parent who is suddenly fired with a quenchless impulse to plead for the life of his or her child? The best teacher of style in public speech is a heart filled to bursting with love for Jesus, and love, hope, fear, and faith for others. A love that makes a speaker feel that souls must and shall be won from hell and turned to righteousness and heaven and God will surely, in due time, make the manner effective.

And it will also shape and control, if it does not make, the message. It is pitiable to see what flat, insipid, powerless, soulless messages people can manufacture when their faith is feeble and their hearts are cold. But it is marvelous what messages people get whose hearts are afire. Someone asked why the evangelist William Bramwell could say such wonderful things. The reply was, "He lives so near the heart of God and the throne that he gets secret messages and brings them down to us."

Can we not, then, sum up for ourselves the secret of Paul and Barnabas in the words of Solomon: "Guard your heart above all else, for it determines the course of your life" (Prov. 4:23 NLT)?

NOTE

1. Charles Henry Mackintosh, *The All-Sufficiency of Christ*, Miscellaneous Writings of C. H. Mackintosh, vol. 1 (New York: Loizeaux Brothers, 1898), n. p.

After the Meeting 18

A Salvation Army soldier (church member) said to a friend of mine recently, "Our captain [pastor] is good in a meeting; he is a fine talker. He does lay it down to the sinners and the people—sinners and all—like him." But then, after some time, she came back to the subject and said, "Our captain is so light and trifling after the meetings that many are the blessings I get in the meetings and lose afterward through his light talk and jokes and carrying on."

Did the captain wear a mask during the meeting while warning, entreating, and pleading with souls, and take it off after the meeting? Is it possible for someone to be in earnest for the salvation of souls while the meeting is going on and yet become thoughtless and careless as soon as the people are dismissed? Is a soul-winner a mere weather vane blown about with the wind? Or is he or she a person of principle who feels as jealous for the glory of God and as burdened for the salvation of others off the platform as on it? What do you think?

Successful soul-winners used to leave the meetings with serious faces and anxious hearts, and go home to pray and often weep before the Lord if souls were not saved. And I know some like that today. O Lord, revive us again and still pour out on us that Spirit!

It depends on us, each of us for him- or herself, whether or not we will have that Spirit. Others know whether we have it or not. And we are judged, measured, and rewarded, not by what we say on the platform only, but also by what we say and do, and by the spirit we manifest off the platform.

"Be an example to the believers," said the apostle (1 Tim. 4:12 NCV). "Be sober" (1 Pet. 5:8 KJV).

Do not despair if you are given to foolish talking and joking, but seriously set yourself to get the victory over it. The next time you come off the platform in a jesting mood, thank God for showing it to you, then stop and pray for deliverance at once, and He will give it to you. I know a woman who got a lasting victory in that way, one that has been abiding for nearly a score of years.

Do not understand, however, that there should never be any pleasantry in your words or acts. But such should be controlled by the Holy Spirit, that those who got a blessing in the meeting shall not lose it, but rather have it increased after the meeting.

'Tis not the time to rest at ease
When men are dying fast,
And hastening onward to their doom
That's evermore to last.

Then let us work while yet 'tis day,
For night will quickly come,
And then we'll hear the Master say—
"Ye faithful ones, well done!"[1]

NOTE

1. Author unknown, "Upon the River's Brink They Stand," *Salvation Army Songs* (London: The Salvation Army Book Department, 1911), 464.

Dangers the Soul-Winner Must Avoid 19

Sanctification floods the soul with great light and love, and thus subjects the possessor to two great and opposite temptations and dangers.

If we lean to the side of light, we are likely to become critical and faultfinding, impatient with others, too severe in our judgments and requirements of those who may yet be in comparative darkness. And thus, unlike our Lord, we may break the bruised reed that Jesus would not break and quench the smoking wick which Jesus would fan into a flame, and so fail to "faithfully bring forth justice" (Isa. 42:3 ESV). Sanctified people see the way so clearly that they are tempted to think that everyone else should so see it, and that it is only because they *will not* that they *do not*. It will be helpful for us to remember "the quarry from which [we] were dug" (Isa. 51:1 ESV), our own darkness and weakness and slowness (if not obstinacy and waywardness), and to be as merciful and patient in our judgments and criticisms of others as our Lord has been with us. If we do not seek earnestly to do this, we are in awful danger.

On the other hand, if we lean to the side of love, we are likely to be too lenient, too easy (as was Eli with his sons), using soothing ointments when we should wield a sword. Many a work of God has come to naught that might have been saved by a timely, courageous rebuke and faithful dealing.

To keep in the middle of the way—to walk in a blaze of light without becoming critical and harsh and spiritually proud and overbearing, and in fullness of love without being soft and weak and fearful of offending—is the problem every sanctified soul must solve in order to keep the blessing and be increasingly useful.

Not to err on either side will require great humility of mind, courage, firmness, faith, watchfulness, prayer, constant meditation on the work and ways of God, and a patient, trustful waiting on the Lord for the wisdom and leading of the Holy Spirit. Blessed is the one who walks with God in the middle of the way, without falling into the ditch on either side.

On Thee, O God of purity,
I wait for hallowing grace;
None without holiness shall see
The glories of Thy face.

Lead me in all Thy righteous ways,
Nor suffer me to slide,
Point out the path before my face;
My God, be Thou my guide!

All those that put their trust in Thee,

Thy mercy shall proclaim,

And sing with cheerful melody

Their great Redeemer's name.

Protected by Thy guardian grace,

They shall extol Thy power,

Rejoice, give thanks, and shout Thy praise,

And triumph evermore.[1]

NOTE

1. Charles Wesley, "On Thee, O God of Purity," 1743, public domain.

PART TWO

Love Slaves

Love Slaves 1

James, Jude, Peter, and Paul—in an age when labor and service were a badge of inferiority and shame—wrote boldly and proudly as follows: "James, a servant of God and of the Lord Jesus Christ" (James 1:1 NIV); "Jude, a servant of Jesus Christ" (Jude 1 NIV); "Simon Peter, a servant and apostle of Jesus Christ" (2 Pet. 1:1 NIV); "Paul and Timothy, servants of Christ Jesus" (Phil. 1:1 NIV); "Paul, a servant of God" (Titus 1:1 NIV).

That age with its false standards and corrupt glories was doomed and dying, and those early followers of Christ stood on the threshold, ushering in a new era in which service was to become a badge of loyalty and a distinguishing mark of the children of God and the citizens of heaven upon earth. The word *servant* as used by them meant a slave. They counted themselves slaves of God and of Christ.

The word and the relationship seems harsh and forbidding, but not so when we realize its meaning to these apostles. They were love slaves. The bondage that enthralled them was the unbreakable bondage of love.

There was a law among the Hebrews that for sore poverty, debt, or crime, one man might become the servant of another, but he could not be held in servitude beyond a certain period; at the end of six years he must be allowed to go free (see Ex. 21:1–6; Deut. 15:12–17). But if he loved his master and preferred to remain with him as his slave, then the master was to place the man against a door or doorpost and bore a hole through his ear. This was to be the mark that he was his master's servant forever.

It was not the slavery of compulsion and law, but the willing and glad slavery of love. And this was the voluntary attitude of Paul, Jude, Peter, and James. Jesus had won them by love. They had sat at the feet of the great Servant of love, who came not to be served but to serve, to minister to others, and to give His life as a ransom for all (see Matt. 20:28). They had seen Him giving Himself to the poor, the weary, the heavy laden, the vile, the sinful, and the unthankful. They had seen His blessed life outpoured:

> Like the rush of a river,
> Wasting its waters for ever and ever
> Amid burnt sands that reward not the giver.[1]

They had seen Him "wounded for our transgressions . . . bruised for our iniquities" (Isa. 53:5 KJV), chastised for our peace, and stricken that we might be healed, and their hearts had been bowed and broken by His great love. Henceforth they were His bond slaves, no longer free to come and go as they pleased but only as He willed, for the adamantine chains of love held them and the burning passion of love constrained them. Such bondage and service became to them the most perfect liberty. Their only joy was to do those things that were pleasing in His sight. Set at liberty to do this, their freedom was complete, for only they are free who are permitted to do always that which pleases them. Love slaves have no pleasure like that of serving their Master. This is their joy and their very "crown of rejoicing" (1 Thess. 2:19 KJV).

Love slaves are altogether at their Master's service. They are all eyes for their Master. They watch. They are all ears for their Master. They listen. Their minds are willing. Their hands are ready. Their feet are swift. To sit at the Master's feet and look into His loved face, listen to His voice and catch His words, run His errands, do His bidding, share His privations and sorrows, watch at His door, guard His honor, praise His name, defend His person, seek and promote His interests, and, if necessary, die for His dear sake—this is the joy of love slaves, and this they count as perfect freedom.

A fine man was placed on a slave block in an Egyptian slave market. His master was selling him. Men were bidding for him. A passing Englishman stopped, looked, listened, and began to bid. The slave saw him and knew that the Englishman was a world traveler. He thought that if the Englishman bought him, he would be taken from Egypt, far from friends and loved ones, and he would never see them anymore. So he cursed the Englishman, raving and swearing and tugging at his chain that he might reach and crush him. But the Englishman, unmoved, at last outbid all others, and the slave was sold to him.

He paid the price, received the papers that made the slave his property, and then handed them to the man.

"Take these papers; you are free," he said. "I bought you that I might give you your freedom."

The slave looked at his deliverer and his ravings ceased. Tears flooded his eyes, as, falling at the Englishman's feet and embracing his knees, he cried, "O sir, let me be your slave forever. Take me to the ends of the earth. Let me serve you till I die!"

Love had won his heart, and now love constrained him. And he felt there could be no joy like serving such a master.

We see many illustrations of this bondage of love in our daily lives. Surely it is the glory and joy of the true wife. She would rather suffer hardship and poverty in a Kansas sod house, with the husband she loves, than live in a palace surrounded by every luxury with any other.

> And on her lover's arm she leant,
> And round her waist she felt it fold,
> And far across the hills they went
> In that new world which is the old . . .
> And o'er the hills and far away
> Beyond their utmost purple rim,
> Beyond the night, across the day,
> Thro' all the world she followed him.[2]

This bondage of love is, at one and the same time, the slavery and the freedom of the true mother. Offer such a mother gold and honors and pleasure, and she will spurn them all for the sacred joy of serving and sacrificing for her child.

This also is the true freedom and service of the Christian. "My yoke is easy, and my burden is light," said Jesus (Matt. 11:30 KJV). His yoke is the yoke of love, and it is easy. Love makes it easy. His burden is the burden of love, and it is light. Love makes it light.

To the unregenerate soul the yoke looks intolerable, the burden unbearable. But to those who have entered into the secret of the Master, His yoke is the badge of freedom, and His burden gives wings to the soul.

This is holiness. It is wholeness of consecration and devotion. It is singleness of eye. It is perfect love that casts out fear (see 1 John 4:18). Love slaves do not fear the Master, for they joy in the Master's will. The slave of love says, "Not my will, but yours, be done" (Luke 22:42 ESV) and, "Though he slay me, yet will I trust in him" (Job 13:15 KJV). There can be no fear where there is such love.

This is heart purity accomplished by the expulsive power of a new and overmastering affection and purpose. Sin and selfishness are consumed in the hot fires of this great love.

This is religion made easy. This is God's kingdom come, and His will done, on earth as it is in heaven. For what more can the angels do than serve God with this unselfishness and passionate love?

The love slave is gentle and forbearing and kind to all the children of the household and to all the other slaves, for the sake of the Master. Are they not dear and valuable to the Master? Then they are dear and valuable to the love slave for the Master's sake. And such are ready to lay down their lives to serve them even as to serve the Master. Such was Paul's spirit when he wrote, "Even if I am to be poured out as a drink offering upon the sacrificial offering of your faith, I am glad and rejoice with you all" (Phil. 2:17 ESV). And so likewise was it beautiful Queen Esther's spirit when, in uttermost consecration for her people's salvation, she sent word to Mordecai, "I will go to the king, even though it is against the law. And if I perish, I perish" (Est. 4:16 NIV).

Love slaves care nothing for their own lives (see Acts 20:24), because they belong to the Master. They have no other interests than those of the Master, want no other, will have no other. They cannot be bribed by gold or honors. They would rather suffer and starve for the Master than feast at another's table. Like Ruth, they say, "Don't ask me to leave you and turn back. Wherever you go, I will go; wherever you live, I will live. Your people will be my people, and your God will be my God. Wherever you die, I will die, and there I will be buried. May the LORD punish me severely if I allow anything but death to separate us!" (Ruth 1:16–17 NLT).

Do you ask, "How shall I enter into this sweet and gentle and yet all-powerful bondage of love?" I answer, by your own choice and by God's revelation of Himself to your soul. If your love to Him now is a very poor and powerless thing, it is because you do not know Him, you do not draw near enough to see His beauty.

"My God, how beautiful Thou art" is the language of a soul that is learning to know Him. Then comes the realization:

> Thou hast stooped to ask of me,
> The love of my poor heart.[3]

To the people of this world He is not beautiful, for they have not sought to see Him. Let Him show Himself to you that you may fall in love with Him. Paul had seen His glory and been blinded by it. The other apostles had lived with Him and walked at His side. They loved Him because they knew Him so well.

For this reason they could make the great decision. Like Moses they chose "rather to suffer affliction with the people of God, than to enjoy the pleasures of sin for a season; esteeming the reproach of Christ greater riches than the treasures in Egypt" (Heb. 11:25–26 KJV). So you must choose. The choice must be complete, and it must be final. Then as a love slave you must wait upon the Master. If He is silent to you, watch. When He speaks to you, listen. What He says to you, do. His will is recorded in His Word. Search the Scriptures. Meditate therein day and night. Hide His Word in your heart. Be not forgetful. Take time to seek His face. Imagine a slave being too busy to wait on his master, to find out his wishes! Take time, find time, make time to seek the Lord, and He will be found by you. He will reveal Himself to your longing, loving soul, and you shall know the sweet compulsions of the slavery that is love.

> Higher than the highest heavens,
> Deeper than the deepest sea,
> Lord, Thy love at last has conquered;
> Grant me now my spirit's longing
> None of self, and all of Thee![4]

NOTES

1. Rose Terry, "Give! As the Morning That Flows Out of Heaven," *Poems* (Boston: Ticknor and Fields, 1861), n. p.

2. Alfred Lord Tennyson, "The Day-Dream," *The Complete Works of Alfred Tennyson, Poet Laureate* (New York: R. Worthington, 1879), 72–73.

3. Frederick W. Faber, "My God, How Wonderful Thou Art," 1849, public domain.

4. Theodore Monod, "Oh, the Bitter Shame and Sorrow," 1874, public domain.

A Man in Christ   2

"I knew a man in Christ," wrote Paul (2 Cor. 12:2 KJV). Imagine someone writing, "I knew a man in Bonaparte, in Buddha, in Caesar," and we shall see at once how striking, how startling is this expression. We should not only be startled, but also shocked to hear this said of anyone but Christ Jesus. But the Christian consciousness is not offended by hearing of "a man in Christ." It recognizes Christ as the home of the soul, its hiding place and shelter from the storm, its school, its fortress and defense from every foe. He is not simply the Babe of Bethlehem, the Carpenter of Nazareth, the first of the religious teachers of Palestine, and the victim of religious bigotry and Roman power. He is the Prince of Peace, the Mighty God, the Everlasting Father, in whose bosom we nestle and in whose favor we find peace and comfort and salvation.

Do you know any man or woman in Christ? How many people do you know who live in Him and walk in the unbroken fellowship that being "in Christ" must imply? Do you know twenty? Ten?

But let us not judge others. Paul was not doing so. He was very generous in his judgments of his brothers and sisters. He addressed his letters as follows: "Paul, an apostle of Jesus Christ by the will of God, to the saints which are at Ephesus, and to the faithful in Christ Jesus" (Eph. 1:1 KJV). "Paul and Timotheus, the servants of Jesus Christ, to all the saints in Christ Jesus which are at Philippi" (Phil. 1:1 KJV). "Paul, an apostle of Jesus Christ by the will of God . . . to the saints and faithful brethren in Christ which are at Colosse" (Col. 1:1–2).

Paul reckoned his brothers and sisters to be in Christ. But this man whom he knew "in Christ" was not one of them, but Paul himself. He was the man. There was no doubt about him being in Christ. He wrote with complete assurance.

Can you speak with such assurance? Do you know yourself to be in Christ? Or ever to have been in Christ? What a profound fellowship and union!

But listen to Paul further: "I was caught up to the third heaven fourteen years ago. Whether I was in my body or out of my body, I don't know—only God knows. Yes, only God knows whether I was in my body or outside my body. But I do know that I was caught up to paradise and heard things so astounding that they cannot be expressed in words, things no human is allowed to tell" (2 Cor. 12:2–4 NLT).

Did you ever have a moment, or an hour, in which you were lost in fellowship with the Lord, having no thought of time or space, in which experiences were wrought in you, emotions swept through you, purity and love and power and comfort and assurance were imparted to you, that you have never been able fully to explain or express in words, or which, possibly, you have felt to be too sacred to try to tell or describe?

Such was Paul's experience. He was the man to whom the words make reference. And many people who are in Christ—possibly most or all who are in Him—have had some such moment, long or short it may have been, but indescribably sweet, precious above gold or silver, and memorable above any and all other experiences of life.

Oh, how invaluable is such an experience to a soul, especially in a time of fierce temptation! It sweeps away forever the intellectual and moral and spiritual fogs and uncertainties that cloud the mind and heart. It fixes a person's theology. It settles for us the fact that we are living souls, morally and spiritually responsible to God. We feel the breath of eternity in us.

Wrapped in that wondrous fellowship we know there is a heaven, and to lose God, we know, would be hell. Henceforth to us, heaven and hell are realities as assured as light and darkness, as truth and falsehood, as right and wrong. This experience establishes the Godhead of Christ. We know that "Jesus is Lord," not by what we have learned from a teacher, from books and creeds, but by revelation, "by the Holy Spirit" (1 Cor. 12:3 NLT).

If in hours of depression and temptation, the Enemy of our souls should suggest a doubt as to these great truths, we can instantly rout our foe by recalling the intimate revelations of that sacred experience which it is not possible to utter.

There are two experiences mentioned by Paul in 2 Corinthians 12:2–4. One is abiding—the blessed but common everyday experience that is new every morning and fresh every evening, that the dust and toil of the day, and the stillness and slumber of the night, do not break or disturb; it is the very life of the Christian. The other is transitory, the experience of a moment, comparatively.

"In Christ" is the abiding experience. We are to live in Christ. Daily, hourly, momently we are to choose Him as our Master, walk with Him, look to Him, trust Him, obey Him, and draw from Him our strength, wisdom, courage, purity—every gift and grace needed for our soul's life. The supply of all our need is in Him. Our sap, our life, our leaf, and our fruit are from Him. Cut off from Him we wither, we die, but in Him we flourish, we bring forth abundant fruit, we have life forevermore.

"Caught up to paradise" is the transitory experience. It passes in an hour and may, possibly, never in this life be repeated, any more than was the burning bush experience of Moses repeated, or the "still small voice" experience of Elijah, or the Jabbok experience of Jacob, or the transfiguration experience of Jesus.

Those experiences were brief, but their effects, their revelations were for eternity. They were not abiding experiences, but windows opened through which earth glimpsed heaven. The memory of that vision was imperishable, though the vision passed. The veil was withdrawn, and for one awe-filled, rapturous moment, the eyes of the soul saw the face of God and the spirit of a human being had unutterable fellowship with its Father.

People who have had such an experience will be changed, will be different from their former selves, and different from all others who have had no such experience. Henceforth for them "to live is Christ"

(Phil. 1:21 KJV), and the great values of life are not material, financial, social, or political, but moral and spiritual.

One of the poets illustrates this from Lazarus, who was raised to newness of life after four days of death:

> Heaven opened to a soul while yet on earth,
> Earth forced on a soul's use while seeing heaven . . .
> He holds on firmly to some thread of life . . .
> The spiritual life around the earthly life:
> The law of that is known to him as this,
> His heart and brain move there, his feet stay here . . .
> And oft the man's soul springs into his face
> As if he saw again and heard again
> His sage that bade him "Rise," and he did rise . . .
> He knows
> God's secret, while he holds the thread of life.
> He will live, nay, it pleaseth him to live
> So long as God please, and just how God please.[1]

The march of armies and overthrow of empires meant little to that man whose eyes God had opened. He was diligent in his daily business, he loved everybody and everything, and for the rest he trusted God. This is the mark of the man or woman who has seen God, who has been caught up, if only for a brief moment, into that ineffable and paradisiacal fellowship.

Such will be blessed if they are not disobedient to the heavenly vision—if, like Mary, who treasured in her heart the things spoken of her baby, Jesus, they treasure up the sacred revelation given to them in the moment of vision!

We cannot command such moments. They come to us, come unexpectedly, but they never come except to the one who is in Christ, who day by day lives for Christ, seeks His face, meditates on His ways and Word, takes time to commune with Him, wrestles with Him in prayer, seeks to glorify Him by good words and works, and waits and longs for Him more than they who through tedious hours of weary nights wait and long for the morning.

Let no humble, earnest souls be discouraged because they do not constantly live in such rapturous fellowship. Paul did not remain in paradise. It was a brief experience and was followed by a troublesome thorn in the flesh. These glimpses of heaven, these rapt moments of fellowship, are given to confirm faith and fit the soul for the toil and plodding service of the love slaves of Jesus, who fight and labor to help Him in His vast travail to save a world of souls from sin, from the Devil's grip, and from hell.

The common, everyday, abiding experience is a lowly, patient, loving life in Christ. This may be ours unbrokenly, and it should be.

"Anyone who belongs to Christ has become a new person," wrote Paul (2 Cor. 5:17 NLT). That person breathes the atmosphere of heaven while plodding the dusty roads of earth. He or she diffuses peace, promotes joy, kindles love, quiets fear, comforts mourners, and heals the broken heart.

In such a person Christ sees "the travail of his soul" (Isa. 53:11 KJV) and is satisfied. In them the long, stern trial and discipline of Christ's incarnation and the bitter agony of His cross begin to bear their full, ripe fruit, and the Master delights in them, calms them with His love, and rejoices over them with joyful songs (see Zeph. 3:17). In them the earnest expectation of all creation, which awaits the manifestation of the sons and daughters of God (see Rom. 8:19–22), begins to be fulfilled, the long night of earth's shame and sorrow and sin is passing, and the dawning day of the reign of peace and righteousness is breaking.

I knew a father in Christ whose children said, "It is easy to be good when father is around," not because they feared him and must be good, but because goodness flourished in the sunshine of his Christlike presence.

I knew a husband in Christ whose wife said, "He is like David, who returned to bless his household." His presence was a benediction to his home.

I knew a man who had been a hard, brutal drunkard, but was now a blacksmith "in Christ." One day a farmer brought his mare to this blacksmith to have her shod, and with her he brought straps and tackle to strap her up, for she was so fearful or so savage that no one could shoe her otherwise. But the blacksmith "in Christ" said, "Let me get acquainted with her." He walked around her, stroked her gently, and spoke to her kindly and softly, while she rubbed her soft nose against him, smelled his garments, and got acquainted with him. She seemed to make a discovery that this was a new creature—a kind she had never met before, especially in a blacksmith's shop. Everything about him seemed to say to her, "Fear not," and she was not afraid. He lifted her foot and took off a shoe, and from that day forth he shod that mare without strap or tackle, while she stood in perfect quiet and unconcern.

Poor horse! She had waited all her lifetime to see one of the sons of God, and when she saw him she was not afraid.

And the whole earth is waiting for the unveiling, the manifestation, "the revelation of God's sons and daughters" (Rom. 8:19 CEB), waiting for the men and women, boys and girls, who live in Christ and in whom Christ lives. When the world is filled with such people or controlled by them, then—and only then—will strikes and wars, bitter rivalries and insane hatreds, and disgusting and hellish evils cease, and the promise and purpose of Christ's coming be fulfilled.

NOTE

1. Robert Browning, "An Epistle Containing the Strange Medical Experience of Karshish, the Arab Physician," *Poems of Robert Browning* (London: Oxford University Press, 1923), 119–120.

Future Punishment and the Bible

3

Joseph Cook, one of America's soundest and clearest thinkers, said to me a generation ago, "Let the churches banish from their pulpits the preaching of hell for a hundred years, and it will come back again, for the doctrine is in the Bible, and in the nature of things." And in his great lecture, "Final Permanence of Moral Character," he said, "The laws by which we attain supreme bliss are the laws by which we descend to supreme woe. In the ladder up and the ladder down in the universe, the rungs are in the same side-pieces. The self-propagating power of sin and the self-propagating power of holiness are one law. The law of judicial blindness is one with that by which the pure in heart see God."[1]

There is but one law that can save me from "the law of sin and death," and that is "the law of the Spirit of life in Christ Jesus" (Rom. 8:2 KJV). If I refuse to submit to that law, I abide eternally under the law of sin and death and endure eternally its dread penalties.

"Every sinner must be either pardoned or punished," I once heard The Salvation Army's founder say in the midst of an impassioned appeal to people to make their peace with God. They have remained in my memory, always representing a tremendous truth from which we can never get away.

The atonement opens wide the door of pardon, uttermost salvation, and bliss eternal to every penitent soul who will believe in Christ and follow Him, while it sweeps away every excuse from the impenitent heart that will not trust and obey Him. The atonement justifies God in all His ways with sinful men and women.

The holiest beings in the universe can never feel that God is indifferent to sin, when He pardons believing souls, lifts up their drooping heads, and introduces them to the glories and blessedness of heaven, because Christ has died for them. On the other hand, the souls who are lost and banished to outer darkness cannot blame God nor charge Him with indifference to their misery, since Christ, by tasting death for them, flung wide open the gateway of escape. That they definitely refused to enter in will be clear in their memory forever and will leave them without excuse.

We do not often encounter now the old-fashioned universalist, who believed that everyone, whether righteous or wicked, enters into a state of blessedness the moment they die. But others, with errors even more dangerous (because seemingly made agreeable to natural reason and to our inborn sense of justice) have come to weaken people's faith in the tremendous penalties of God's holy law. In fact, there seems to be a widespread and growing tendency to doubt the existence of hell and the endless punishment of the wicked.

A theory often advanced is the annihilation, or extermination, of the wicked. It is said that there is no eternal hell, and that the wicked do not enter into a state of punishment after death but are immediately or eventually blotted out of existence.

Then there is the doctrine of "eternal hope." This asserts that the wicked will be punished after death, possibly for ages, but that in the end they will all be restored to the favor of God and the bliss of the holy. The words of our Lord to the traitor appear to be an unanswerable refutation of this doctrine. If all are to be saved at last, would Jesus have said of Judas, "It would have been better for that man if he had not been born" (Mark 14:21 ESV)? For what are ages of suffering when compared to the blessedness and rapture of those who finally see God's face in peace and enjoy His favor to all eternity?

There is something so awful about the old doctrine of endless punishment, and such a seeming show of fairness about these new doctrines, that the latter appeal very strongly to the human heart and enlist on their behalf all the sympathies and powerful impulses of "the sinful nature [which] is always hostile to God" and which "never did obey God's laws, and . . . never will" (Rom. 8:7 NLT).

In forming our opinions on this subject we should stick to the Bible. All we know about the future state is what God has revealed and left on record in "the law and . . . the testimony" and "if they speak not according to this word, it is because there is no light in them" (Isa. 8:20 KJV). Human reason as well as human experience fails us here, and we can put no confidence in the so-called revelations of spiritualism nor in the dreams of sects who pretend to be able to probe the secrets of eternity. If the Bible does not settle the question for us, it cannot be settled.

The Bible teaches that there is punishment for the wicked after death, and that they are conscious of this punishment. In the record of the rich man and Lazarus, Jesus said, "The rich man also died and was buried, and his soul went to the place of the dead. There, in torment, he saw Abraham in the far distance with Lazarus at his side. The rich man shouted . . . 'Send Lazarus over here to dip the tip of his finger in water and cool my tongue. I am in anguish in these flames'" (Luke 16:22–24 NLT).

Some labor hard to strip this Scripture of its evident meaning and to rob it of its point and power by declaring that it is only a parable. On the contrary, the Savior's statements are given as facts. But even if we admit the account to be a parable, what then? A parable teaches either what is or what may be, and in that case these words lose none of their force but stand out as a bold word picture of the terrible doom of the wicked.

Over and over Jesus spoke of the wicked being cast into "outer darkness," where "there shall be weeping" and "wailing and gnashing of teeth" (Matt. 8:12; 13:42 KJV). Three times in one chapter He spoke of the worm that never dies and the fire that is not quenched (see Mark 9).

Paul said that "indignation and wrath, tribulation and anguish" (Rom. 2:8–9 KJV) shall come upon the wicked. And John said they are in torment (see Rev. 14:10–11).

What can all this mean but conscious punishment? Let those who never before saw the Bible read these words for the first time and they would at once declare that the Bible teaches the conscious suffering of the wicked after death. They might not believe the teaching, but they would never think of denying that such was the Bible's teaching.

The punishment mentioned in the Bible must be felt—it must be conscious—otherwise it is not "torment" and "tribulation and anguish."

The "second death," the death of the soul, must be something other than the destruction of its conscious existence.

Jesus has defined eternal life for us as the knowledge of God: "This is eternal life, that they know you the only true God, and Jesus Christ whom you have sent" (John 17:3 ESV). If then this blessed knowledge constitutes eternal life, what is the death which sin imposes but just the absence of this knowledge, with consequent wretchedness and misery? To lose God, to sink into outer darkness, to lose all fellowship with pure and loving souls, to be an outcast forever—this is "the second death," this is "torment and anguish," this is hell, and this is "the wages of sin" (Rom. 6:23 KJV).

The Bible further teaches that the punishment of the wicked after death will be endless. There are distinguished teachers and preachers who have declared that the Bible does not teach the eternity of sin and punishment. But if we examine for ourselves, we find this teaching as clear as human language can make it. We read: "Whoever blasphemes against the Holy Spirit never has forgiveness, but is guilty of an eternal sin" (Mark 3:29 ESV)—and eternal sin will surely be followed by eternal woe. While sin lasts, misery lasts.

The strongest terms that can be used have been used to teach eternal punishment. When we say a thing will last forever we have put it strongly, but when we duplicate the phrase and say it will last forever and forever, we cannot add to its strength—we have said all that can be said. This is just what the Bible does in speaking of the punishment of the wicked.

The phrase "forever and ever" is the strongest term by which the idea of eternity is expressed in the Bible. It is the phrase used to express the eternal life and glory of the righteous: "And they shall

reign for ever and ever" (Rev. 22:5 KJV). Paul used these words when
he prayed for the continuance of God's glory: "To whom be glory for
ever and ever" (Gal. 1:5 KJV; see also Phil. 4:20; 2 Tim. 4:18; Heb.
13:21). It is also the very phrase used to assert the eternal existence of
God Himself, "the one who lives forever and ever" (Rev. 4:9 NLT).

This phrase, which is used to declare the endless life and glory of
the righteous and the existence of God Himself, is also used to declare
the endless punishment of Satan: "The devil that deceived them was
cast into the lake of fire and brimstone, where the beast and the false
prophet are, and shall be tormented day and night for ever and ever"
(Rev. 20:10 KJV). In Revelation 20:15, we are told that the wicked are
to share the punishment of the Devil himself. And Jesus, in foretelling
the sentence of the wicked at the judgment day, declared, "Then the
King will turn to those on the left and say, 'Away with you, you cursed
ones, into the eternal fire prepared for the devil and his demons'" (Matt.
25:41 NLT), thus showing that the wicked are to share the punishment
of the Devil, which is "for ever and ever."

Did not Jesus mean to teach endless punishment when, three times in
six short verses, He warned His hearers in the most solemn manner to cut
off hands and feet and pluck out eyes rather than to go into hell, "where
their worm does not die and the fire is not quenched" (Mark 9:43–48 ESV)?

Is not endless punishment implied in the parable of the cruel and
unforgiving servant, who, owing an enormous debt with nothing with
which to pay, was delivered to the tormentors till he should pay all that
was due? Does not Jesus mean to teach that the man's debt was beyond
his power to cancel and that, since he proved wickedly unworthy of
mercy and forgiveness, he was buried forever beneath the burden and

torment of his vast debt? And this parable simply pictures the moral and spiritual debt of the sinner—illimitable and ever-increasing, unless, in penitence and obedient faith, he finds release through the blood of Christ before the final sentence of judgment is passed and the prison gates have closed upon him.

We learn from the Jewish historian Josephus that the Jews believed in endless punishment. And when the Son of God came into the world to teach people the truth, He did not deny and combat that belief but spoke fearfully plain words that would confirm and strengthen it.

Well does one writer say, "They who deny that any of the words used of future punishment in Holy Scripture express eternity, would do well to consider whether there is any way in which Almighty God could have expressed it, which they would have accepted as meaning it."[2]

God did not trifle when He inspired those dreadful warnings. Take heed, then, that you do not trifle when you read them, but rather fear and tremble at the Word of the Lord. For just in proportion as you, in the secret of your own heart, doubt the endless punishment of the wicked, in that proportion you will lose the power to resist sin and the desire to save your own soul or those of others around you.

Two powerful motives the Holy Spirit uses to lead men and women to accept the Savior and renounce all sin are the hope of everlasting blessedness and the fear of eternal woe. In the heart of a Christian these motives may, in time, be swallowed up in a higher motive of love and loyalty to God, but they always remain as a framework. No preacher through all the ages has appealed so simply, constantly, powerfully, and with such even balance to these motives as did the Savior. The whole of Matthew 25 is an illustration of His method of appeal.

Eternity furnishes these motives. They balance each other like the two wings of a bird, the two wheels of a carriage—right and left, upper and lower, right and wrong—and this balance is never lost, but evenly held throughout the Bible from the blessing and cursing of Deuteronomy (see 30:19) to the final fixedness of moral character as "filthy" or "holy" in Revelation (22:11 ESV). Deny one of them and your strength against sin is gone. You may live a life most beautiful in its outward morality, but those secret girdings of the will which in the past impelled you to resist sin unto death will weaken, and you will find yourself making secret compromises with sin. You will lose your power to discern the exceeding sinfulness of sin (see Rom. 7:13 KJV). You will be ensnared by Satan masquerading as an angel of light, and someday you will become a servant of sin.

Sinners are not alarmed by the thought that death ends all. They will say, "Let us eat and drink, for tomorrow we die" (1 Cor. 15:32 ESV). It is not death they fear, but that which follows death. Nor do they care for punishment after death if they can only believe it will end sometime; they will still harden themselves in sin and mock God. But preach to them the faithful Word of God until the awful fact of endless punishment, set over against the endless blessedness of God's approval and favor, pierces their guilty consciences and takes possession of their souls, and they will go mournfully all their days until they find Jesus the Savior.

Such has always been the effect of the doctrine when proclaimed in power and pity and love with the fire-touched lips of holy men and women. But let people in their folly imagine themselves wiser and more pitiful and just than God, and so begin to tone down this doctrine, then conviction for sin ceases, the instantaneous and powerful conversion of souls is laughed at, the supernatural element in religion is called fanaticism, the Holy Spirit is forgotten, and the work of God comes to a standstill.

But some object that God is not just to punish souls forever for the sins they commit in the short period of a lifetime. And thus speaking, they think of certain acts of sin such as lying, cheating, swearing, murder, or committing adultery. But it is not for these sins that men and women are sent to hell. God has pardoned multitudes who were guilty of all these sins, and has taken them home to heaven. All who are sent to hell go by the weight and pull of their self-chosen evil and discordant nature and character, because they will not repent and turn from sin to God, but choose to remain filled with unbelief, which begets pride and self-will. Consequently they are out of harmony with—and are antagonistic to—God and all His humble, obedient servants. They will not come to Jesus, that they may be saved from sin and receive a new heart and life. They are dead in trespasses and sins, and they refuse the Life-Giver. Jesus said, "You refuse to come to me that you may have life" (John 5:40 ESV). Again He said, "This is the basis for judgment: The light came into the world, and people loved darkness more than the light" (John 3:19 CEB).

If sinners would come to Christ and receive the gracious, loving life He offers, and allow Him to rule over them, God would not impute their trespasses to them, but would forgive all their iniquities, and their sins would drop off as the autumn leaves from the trees in the field.

But so many will not come. They refuse the Savior. They will not hear His voice. They turn away from His words and remain indifferent to His entreaties. They laugh or mock at His warnings. They walk in disobedience and rebellion. They trample on His holy commandments. They choose darkness instead of light. They prefer sin to holiness, their own way to God's way. They resist the Holy Spirit. They neglect and reject Christ crucified for them—and for this they are punished.

All this stubborn resistance to God's invitations and purposes may be linked to a life of external correctness and even apparent religiousness. Not until all His judgments and warnings, His entreaties and dying love, have failed to lead them to repentance and acceptance of the Savior—and not until they have utterly refused the eternal blessedness of the holy—does God cease to strive with sinners and follow them with tender mercies.

By obstinate persistence in sin, men and women come to hate the thing that God loves and to love the thing that God hates. Thus they become as dead to God's will, to holiness and to His plans for them, as the child destroyed by smallpox or diphtheria is dead to the hopes and plans of his or her mourning father and mother. And as such parents in sorrow put away the pestilence-breeding body of their dead child, so God puts sinners, in their utter spiritual corruption, away from His holy presence "and from the glory of his power" (2 Thess. 1:9 KJV).

How could God more fully show His estimate of sin, together with His love and pity and longing desire to redeem souls, than by dying for sinful men and women?

God in Christ Jesus has done that. But sinners trample on Christ's blood, reject His infinite mercy, resist His infinite love, and so harden themselves; hence they deserve eternal punishment, which will follow sin as surely as night follows day.

Is sin only a mild infirmity that we need not fear and that will yield to gentle reproof? Was the Son of God only playing at being a Savior when He came down and died for us? Or is sin an awful crime against God and all His creatures that can be remitted only by the shedding of blood? Is it a crime for which human souls are responsible, and of which they ought to repent? Is it a crime that tends to perpetuate itself by hardening men and women in evil, and that culminates in eternal guilt when they finally resist the Holy Spirit and totally and forever turn from Jesus the crucified, rejecting Him as their Savior and Lord?

If sin is such a crime—and the Bible teaches that it is—then God, as moral governor of the universe, having provided a perfect way, and having done all He could to persuade everyone to turn from sin, is under obligation, if He meets only with determined resistance, to place sinners under sentence of punishment, to oppose them and put them away forevermore from His holy presence and from the society of holy men and women and angels, where they can no more breed moral and spiritual pestilence nor disturb the moral harmony of God's government and people. And when God does so my conscience takes God's part against my sensibilities, against my own soul, and against a guilty world, and pronounces Him just and holy.

We live in a stern universe where fire will not only bless us, but also burn us; where water will both refresh and drown us; where gravitation will either protect or destroy us. We must not look at things sentimentally. If we love God and serve Him, all things will work for our good. But if we despise or neglect Him, we shall find all things working for our eternal undoing and misery. God does not send people to hell who are fit for heaven. The standard of fitness is made plain in the Bible, and God's tender and pitying love has provided for every sinner pardon for past sins through the death of Jesus, and purity, power, and abundant help for the present and future through the gift of the Holy Spirit, so that there will be excuse for none. If one whom I love commits some terrible crime, violating all the righteous and gracious laws that safeguard society and consequently is cast into prison, my sorrow—if I myself am the right kind of a man—will spring not from the fact that he is in prison but rather from the fact that his character makes him unfit to be out of prison. And if he should go to hell, my sorrow would be due, not to the fact that he was in hell, but rather to the fact that he so neglected and despised infinite love and mercy that he was unfit for heaven. Such a person would possibly be more unhappy in heaven than in hell, just as someone who has terribly inflamed eyes is more unhappy in the light of broad day than in the darkness of midnight.

Finally, for someone to say, "I believe in heaven, but I do not believe in hell," is much the same as saying, "I believe in mountains, but not in valleys; in heights, but not in depths." We cannot have mountains without valleys. We cannot have heights without depths. And we cannot have moral and spiritual heights without the awful possibility of moral and spiritual depths—and the depths are always equal to the heights. The high mountains are set over against the deep seas, and so heaven is set over against hell.

Every road leads two ways. The road that leads from New York to Boston also leads from Boston to New York. A traveler can go either way. So it is with the roadway of life. The soul who chooses the things

God chooses, loves the things God loves, and hates the things God hates, and who, with obedient faith, takes up the cross and follows Jesus, will go to the heights of God's holiness and happiness and heaven. But the man or woman who goes the other way will land in the dark, bottomless abysses of hell. Everyone chooses his or her own way.

Once to every man and nation comes the moment to decide,
In the strife of truth with falsehood, for the good or evil side;
Some great cause, God's new Messiah, offering each the bloom or blight,
Parts the goats upon the left hand, and the sheep upon the right,
And the choice goes by forever "twixt that darkness and that light."[3]

Joseph Cook closed his address entitled "The Certainties of Religion" at the Chicago Parliament of Religions with these words:

I bought a book full of the songs of aggressive, evangelical religion . . . and I found in that little volume words which may be bitter indeed when eaten, but which, when fully assimilated, will be sweet as honey. I summarize my whole scheme of religion in these words, which you may put on my tombstone:

Choose I must, and soon must choose,
Holiness, or heaven lose.
While what heaven loves I hate,
Shut for me is heaven's gate.

Endless sin means endless woe,

Into endless sin I go,

If my soul, from reason rent,

Takes from sin its final bent . . .

As the stream its channel grooves,

And within that channel moves,

So does habit's deepest tide

Groove its bed, and there abide.

Light obeyed increaseth Light;

Light resisted bringeth night.

Who shall give me will to choose,

If the love of Light I lose?

Speed, my soul; this instant yield;

Let the Light its scepter wield.

While thy God prolongeth grace,

Haste thee toward His holy face.[4]

NOTES

1. Joseph Cook, *Rev. Joseph Cook's Monday Lectures on Life and the Soul* (London: Ward, Lock, and Co., 1879), 126.

2. Frank Nutcombe Oxenham, *What Is the Truth as to Everlasting Punishment?* (New York: E. P. Dutton and Company, 1881), 114.

3. James Russell Lowell, "The Present Crisis," n. d., public domain.

4. Joseph Cook, "Strategic Certainties of Comparative Religion," ed. John Henry Barrows, *The World's Parliament of Religions: An Illustrated and Popular Story of the World's First Parliament of Religions*, vol. 1 (Chicago: The Parliament Publishing Company, 1893), 542–543.

I Counted... and I Count

The apostle Paul, in his young and fiery manhood, was on the way to Damascus, "breathing threats and murder against the disciples of the Lord" (Acts 9:1 ESV), when Jesus met him and won his heart, and from that day Paul counted all things loss for Christ. He made an unconditional surrender and found such loveliness and grace in Jesus that he lost his heart to Him and devoted his whole life to the Master. Long years afterward he wrote, "What things were gain to me, those I counted loss for Christ" (Phil. 3:7 KJV).

Youth is the time for the steps that shape all future life. The man or woman who does not make such a consecration in youth is not likely to make it at all. Age is prudent, cautious, and often timid and fearful. Youth is generous and hopeful, courageous, daring, and unentangled. Youth is not held back by prudence and caution. Youth sees visions and is prepared to make sacrifices to realize the vision—

to transform it into something substantial that can be touched, handled, and used.

But by and by, age approaches with its cares and infirmities, weariness and insomnia, and deferred hopes and unfulfilled ambitions. With age comes the temptation to slow down, compromise, draw back, or hold back part of the price (see Acts 5:2).

No doubt Paul was so tempted. But it is also certain that he met the temptation squarely and in the open, for he declared to the Philippians and to the ages, "I counted . . . and I count." He counted the cost in the past, and he continued to count the cost with that same passion and spirit. "I counted . . . [and] I count everything as loss because of the surpassing worth of knowing Christ Jesus my Lord. For his sake I have suffered the loss of all things and count them as rubbish, in order that I may gain Christ and be found in him" (Phil. 3:7–9 ESV). He obeyed the word of Jesus: "Remember what happened to Lot's wife!" (Luke 17:32 NLT). He had put his hand to the plow, and he never looked back.

It was here that wise King Solomon failed. In his youth he had visions, he was humble, he sought the Lord and walked in His way, he obtained promises and prospered. But in his age he went astray, his consecration failed, the vision was dimmed, the glory departed, and great and sad was his fall.

It was at this point that Ananias and Sapphira failed. They had given themselves to the Lord but later they conspired to hold back "part of the price" (Acts 5:2 KJV) and perished in their hypocritical falsehood. It was a withdrawal of this kind on the part of Demas that so hurt Paul's heart when he wrote, "Demas has deserted me because he loves the things of this life" (2 Tim. 4:10 NLT).

It is only a consecration like Paul's—unconditional, complete, and sustained to the end—that will satisfy the human soul, meet the infinite claims of Jesus, and answer the awful needs of a world weltering in pride and lust and covetousness and sin.

People sink to what is low, mean, and devilish, but they can never be satisfied with such things. We may be gratified with base matters, but we can be satisfied only by the highest. As Augustine said, "Thou madest us for Thyself, and our heart is restless, until it repose in Thee."[1]

William Booth, as a boy, might have sold himself to sinful pleasures and enjoyed them to the full, but he would not have been satisfied. He might have engaged in business and built up a fortune and rolled in wealth, but he would not have been satisfied. He might have entered the navy or army and become a great military leader and hero, or he might have plunged into politics and risen to the premiership and guided the destinies of the British Empire, but he would not have been so satisfied as he was in following Jesus to save the lost and "turn them to a pardoning God."[2] He, too, counted all things loss for Christ and continued to so count them to the end of his long and laborious life. It was only by such complete and sustained consecration that he could be satisfied with himself. The human soul demands this; it will not be trifled with nor put off with paltry excuses when we sit alone with our conscience, as someday we surely must.

> I sat alone with my conscience,
> In a place where time had ceased,
> And we talked of my former living

In the land where the years increased.

And I felt I should have to answer

The question it put to me,

And to face the question and answer

Throughout an eternity.

The ghosts of forgotten actions

Came floating before my sight,

And things that I thought were dead things

Were alive with a terrible might.

And the vision of all my past life

Was an awful thing to face,

Alone with my conscience sitting

In that solemnly silent place.[3]

It is only by such uttermost and sustained consecration that we can satisfy the imperious claims of Jesus—claims not of an arbitrary will, but of infinite love. He does not *compel* us to follow Him; He *invites* us to do so, with the understanding that if we choose to follow, we must gird ourselves for lifelong service and uttermost devotion and sacrifice. "There is no discharge in that war" (Eccl. 8:8 KJV). Jesus said, "If any of you wants to be my follower, you must turn from your selfish ways, take up your cross daily, and follow me" (Luke 9:23 NLT). He said:

Don't imagine that I came to bring peace to the earth! I came not to bring peace, but a sword. "I have come to set a man against his father, a daughter against her mother, and a daughter-in-law against her mother-in-law. Your enemies will be right in your own household!" If you love your father or mother more than you love me, you are not worthy of being mine; or if you love your son or daughter more than me, you are not worthy of being mine. If you refuse to take up your cross and follow me, you are not worthy of being mine. If you cling to your life, you will lose it; but if you give up your life for me, you will find it. (Matt. 10:34–39 NLT)

No power compels us to follow Jesus in this way, but we can follow Him no other way. We deceive ourselves if we think we can follow Him in any other spirit than those passages describe.

I may stand at a distance and admire Him, applaud Him, and protest that I am His and that I love Him, but I do not follow Him unless I take up my cross and bear it to the end.

This is His own standard for those who wish to serve Him. There are so-called Christians who think a mere formal recognition of Him while their hearts are set upon money-making or ambitions of their own is sufficient; but He demands soldiers willing to lose all for His cause on earth.

He is a Man of war as well as the Prince of Peace, and no world conqueror ever required of His followers such absolute heart loyalty as Jesus does. And He must require this, for He is the Way—and since there is no other way, we must follow Him or perish (see John 14:6). No one compels another to become an aviator, but once someone chooses to become an aviator, he or she must obey the laws of aviation, or fail.

Jesus is the Truth, and truth is utterly rigorous and imperious in its claims (see John 14:6). We cannot juggle with the truth of the multiplication table. We either follow it or we do not. There is no middle ground. Call it arbitrary if you will, get angry and vex your soul over it if you will, but the multiplication table changes not. It is truth, and you must adjust yourself to it. It cannot bend to you. So Jesus is the Truth—He changes not, and we must adjust ourselves to Him, consecrate ourselves utterly to Him, and abide in Him, or we are none of His.

Jesus is the Life, and life must not be trifled with lest it be lost (see John 14:6). It can be lost, and its loss is irreparable. So we can lose Jesus—and we shall lose Him if we prove unfaithful to Him, if after having put our hand to the plow we turn back.

Finally, it is only by an utter and sustained consecration that we can meet the needs of the world about us. "You are the salt of the earth," said Jesus (Matt. 5:13 NLT). Salt saves from corruption. True Christians alone save society from utter corruption. But if our consecration fails, we lose our savor, our saltiness, and society falls into rottenness.

Who can estimate the harm that is done to Christianity by half-hearted Christians? The world looks on at selfish, ignoble lives spent by those who claim to know Christ, and says, "We see nothing in it. These people are just like us." No one said that of Paul, for they saw always in him a man who felt that Christ was worth leaving the whole world to gain.

"You are the light of the world," said Jesus (Matt. 5:14 NLT). People would stumble and grope in unutterable darkness but for the light of the cross. Womanhood is despised, childhood is neglected, manhood is depraved, terrifying superstitions reign, horrible cruelties abound wherever Jesus is not known and followed. And men and women who, having come to Him and taken up their cross to follow Him, then turn back or fail in their consecration not only sin against God and wrong their own souls; they also commit a crime against humanity, against the children who are growing up and the generations yet unborn.

Soldiers must be faithful unto death, otherwise they will dishonor themselves and betray their country. Far more so must the Christian be true, for we are light-bearers of eternal things, and if that light goes out—if our consecration fails—we will stumble on the dark mountains and at last fall into a bottomless pit of outer darkness, and others will stumble and fall with us.

Paul did not fail. He never swerved in his onward course, never looked back. He rejoiced in his sufferings for Jesus' sake and for the sake of others. And oh, how glad he must have been, how his heart must have exulted at the end, when he cried out, "I have fought a good fight, I have finished my course, I have kept the faith: Henceforth there is laid up for me a crown of righteousness, which the Lord, the righteous judge, shall give me at that day" (2 Tim. 4:7–8 KJV).

Does all this seem hard? Well, that is because I have written about our side only and have said nothing about how the Lord will help and bless and comfort and inwardly strengthen you, if you are wholly His and continue so to the end. He who met Paul on the Damascus road will meet you and give you light. He who stood by Paul in prison and in shipwreck will stand by you. He will show you what He wants you to do and empower you to overcome every difficulty if you will say to Him, "Lord, what do You want me to do?"

And then, at the end of the way there is the crown of life, the unspeakable rapture of His presence and love, the reunion with loved ones gone before, the triumph over every foe, the holy and exalted fellowship with those who have been faithful throughout the ages. It will be worthwhile to see and be associated with all the numberless saints who have overcome, having "washed their robes, and made them white in the blood of the Lamb" (Rev. 7:14 KJV).

But what shame and remorse to be banished with the other crowd—of traitors and cowards, of proud, unclean, selfish, faithless ones! In order to avoid that lot, let us, like Paul, count and continue to count all things as loss for Christ.

NOTES

1. St. Augustine, *The Confessions of St. Augustine*, trans. Edward B. Pusey (New York: Collier Books, 1961), 11.

2. Charles Wesley, "Give Me the Faith Which Can Remove," 1749, public domain.

3. Charles William Stubbs, "I Sat Alone with My Conscience," n. d., public domain.

The Angels' Song of Peace   5

Heavenly beings always put the things of heaven first. Our Lord Jesus always placed the thought of unseen and eternal glory before the trifles of earth.

I have been much impressed with the order of the prayer Jesus gave His disciples. Before teaching them to ask for daily bread or the forgiveness of sins or deliverance from evil or protection in time of temptation, He taught them to pray that the Father's name should be hallowed, that the kingdom of God might come, and that His will might be done on earth as it is in heaven. He put heavenly things first. God was the center of His thought and desire, God's glory His chief concern, and that was what He taught His disciples.

What Jesus taught His disciples He practiced Himself, as we learn from His prayer in John 17. Alone, deserted, on the eve of the denial of Peter and the great betrayal, His thought was for the Father's glory.

He asked that while men put Him to utter shame, the Father would glorify Him, but only that He might in turn glorify the Father.

When the captain of God's host appeared to Joshua, his first and only word was not the outlining of an attack upon the enemy, but this: "Take off your sandals, for the place where you are standing is holy" (Josh. 5:15 NLT). He would impress Joshua with the importance of holy and heavenly things.

And so with the heavenly host which appeared over the plain of Bethlehem. The first note of their song was, "Glory to God in the highest." They put heavenly things first. God was foremost in their thought, then His glory. Afterward they sang, "on earth peace" and "good will toward men" (Luke 2:14 KJV).

The law and the gospel are but the law and the spirit of heaven projecting themselves into this world. They are introduced to men and women for their salvation, for their guidance, and for the direction of their lives, desires, and aspirations. All who seek to keep God's law and who embrace the gospel are introduced into the life and spirit of heaven and become citizens of heaven. As heavenly beings, therefore, they must put heavenly things first; they must live the life of heaven upon earth. In the light of these truths, the Christmas song of the angels, sung over the sleepy little town of Bethlehem, becomes a guide to us in these days. Our chief business is to give glory to God, to put Him first in our lives, to have a divine jealousy for His honor.

This spirit of seeking God's glory first will make us fight sin. We shall hate sin, because it robs God of His own—of His right and His glory in human beings. Those who have this spirit would rather die than commit sin because they love to honor God. God is supreme in their thought. God is first in their love. All their affections embrace God, and their hearts mourn, sob, and break—or wax hot with holy indignation—when they see God dishonored, rejected, and unloved.

This spirit will lead us out to warfare for God. Those who possess it cannot sit still while the Devil has his own way and while God is robbed and wronged. It leads them to go out and plead, exhort, command, and compel others to turn from their evil ways, to give up sin, to yield their hearts to God, and to love and serve Him.

This Spirit also leads us to meditate, to plan, to take counsel with our own hearts, and in every way possible to find out the best means by which we can win others over to God's side, save them from their sins for God's glory, and turn them into warriors for His army.

This spirit makes sacrifice a joy and service a delight. Everything we have is at God's disposal. We give our whole life for the glory of our Lord. We only wish that we had a thousand lives and could live a thousand years to fight God's battles. Oh, blessed are they who are so filled with this spirit of heaven that they put heavenly things first and sing on earth while the angels sing in heaven, "Glory to God in the highest!"

It is only in proportion as this spirit possesses people and takes possession of the earth that the second note of the Christmas song of the angels becomes possible: "Peace on earth and goodwill toward men."

We live in an age when the brotherhood of all is much spoken about, both in exhortation and in literature, but there can be no brotherhood where there is no fatherhood. Brothers and sisters must have a common father, and those who disown or neglect their father have not the spirit that will make it possible to live at peace with, or show good-will toward, each other. We shall have peace on earth and goodwill among people, and we shall have it universally, when everyone recognizes God's fatherhood and gives God the glory which is His due.

Oh, how peacefully men and women live together, and how they love one another when they get right with God! How a true revival settles old grudges and local quarrels and family disputes and other wranglings and strivings! Love to God will beget tender love toward each other—true love, love that is patient, longsuffering, forbearing, unsuspicious, and that leads to just and righteous dealings and to truth and reliability in word and action. These are essential to true peace and goodwill toward all.

The Bible declares that there is a good time coming when we will learn war no more, when we will be ashamed to attack one another in war, when war colleges will be done away with. May that day hasten! But it will hasten only as heavenly things are put first. We may talk about the brutalities of war, about the widows and orphans who mourn their beloved slain, about the soldiers and civilians who are shattered and torn by shot and shell, and about the utter waste of property. But it is only as holy men and women prevail over those who are unholy by winning the world to love God that the glad time foretold by the prophet will be brought about.

Solomon said, "Pride leads to conflict" (Prov. 13:10 NLT). At the heart of every quarrel, in the confusion of every brawl, and in the hate and fury of every war, pride will be found—pride of opinion, of wit or wisdom, of physical strength, of position, of reputation, or of power. Truly humble people never begin strife. They speak softly.

They are willing to make concessions. They are "swift to hear, slow to speak, slow to wrath" (James 1:19 KJV). They "seek peace, and pursue it" (Ps. 34:14 KJV). As far as possible, they "live in peace with everyone" (Rom. 12:18 NLT).

If such people do get mixed up in a contention, they may fight, but it is for the sake of righteous and ordered peace, and not from pride of self. They are peacemakers, not strife-makers. They follow peace with everyone, and they do this because their lives, desires, affections, ambitions, and activities are all guided and ruled by one glad, glorious purpose—the glory of God. That purpose consumes pride. Human pride and pomp look utterly contemptible to the one whose eye is focused on God's glory.

And this desire for God's glory makes them peacemakers. They love their fellows because they are dear to the heart of God. A tender feeling of sympathy, love, and brotherhood steals into their hearts, takes captive all their affections, fills them with love of God's will, banishes hatred, disarms suspicion, and establishes within them God's kingdom of "righteousness and peace and joy in the Holy Spirit" (Rom. 14:17 ESV).

It is this spirit that has made Salvation Army slum officers mightier than police officials in the dark alleys and fetid cellars and garrets of London and New York. It was this that gave William Penn and David Brainerd such heavenly influence with the native tribes of New Jersey and Pennsylvania, and that enabled John Gibson Paton to work such miracles of salvation in the southern islands of the Pacific Ocean.

Unless influenced by this spirit, the nations will go on building battleships, casting great guns, and inventing new technology for the destruction of lives. But let every humble lover of Jesus Christ catch the spirit and sing the Christmas song of the angels, assured that God is on the side of the men and women of peace who love Him, seek His glory, and have hearts which brim over with goodwill.

Our God is "the God of peace" (Rom. 16:20 NLT). Let us wait on Him in fervent prayer and faith for the fulfillment of the angels' song, and put away hate and suspicion and strife forever from our hearts, that, as far as it is up to us, His will may be done on earth as it is done in heaven. He has made the nations of one blood; may they become of one spirit! It is our mission to make them so.

How shall we do this? How can I, a poor, weak, shortsighted, single-handed man, help to fill the world with peace and goodwill?

In the first place, by keeping my own heart with all diligence and letting the peace of God rule in it. To this end, if anyone wrongs me, I must beware of harboring ill will toward him or her and of thinking how I can get even with that person. I must remember how much worse Jesus was treated and how He prayed for His enemies—for the men who were leading Him to death and mocking Him in His agony. I must be filled with His blessed, loving, meek, forgiving spirit. It is no sin to be tempted to be angry and revengeful, but it is a sin if I yield in my heart to this temptation.

I must also be a man of peace in my own family, community, and church. I must seek to soothe instead of irritate the people around me, remembering that "a soft answer turns away wrath, but a harsh word stirs up anger" (Prov. 15:1 ESV).

Most importantly, though I cannot enter into the councils of kings and queens and presidents, and in such high places work for peace among the nations, I can enter into my closet and pray for these leaders with their heavy burdens of care and perplexity and responsibility, asking God to guide and help them to rule the world in peace.

Indeed, we are exhorted to do this. Here is blessed and important knee-work for every humble follower of Jesus, in which he or she may mightily help to prevent war and maintain the peace of the world. Listen to Paul: "I urge you, first of all, to pray for all people. Ask God to help them; intercede on their behalf, and give thanks for them. Pray this way for kings and all who are in authority so that we can live peaceful and quiet lives marked by godliness and dignity" (1 Tim. 2:1–2 NLT).

God does not set us to pray in vain, and if we will pray in love and faith, we can help to establish the peace of the world. Let us exalt our calling to be people of peace, peacemakers, and let us pray with faith and great gladness, and God will hear and give us peace. And "when He gives quietness, who then can make trouble" (Job 34:29 NKJV)?

Misrepresenting God   **6**

I read recently of a speaker who preached on the mercy of God "until it seemed there was nothing in God but mercy." But I fear he misrepresented God. Such misrepresentation is easy, and to people who do not think deeply, and who do not want to take life seriously, it is pleasant. But it is unspeakably dangerous.

If we are to win souls and save our own, we must not distort the picture of God's character that we hold up to view. It is life eternal to know God and Jesus Christ whom He has sent (see John 17:3), but it must be the true and holy God, as He is, and not some false god who conforms to our poor little warped human desires and opinions.

Some religious teachers misrepresent God by making Him utterly savage and cruel. They gloat over unutterably horrid pictures of hell, where they imagine God delighting in the most exquisite tortures of the damned, and thus people are embittered against God until they feel there is no hope of His mercy.

Others misrepresent God by making Him appear as a sort of goody-goody God, who fawns upon sinners with mawkish sympathy and looks upon worldly and trifling people and lukewarm Christians with weak, sentimental pity. Nothing can be further from the truth concerning God. We find God Himself bitterly rebuking those who, living in sin, thought He did not disapprove of their ways. He set before them a list of their sins (see Ps. 50:17–20), and then said, "While you did all this, I remained silent, and you thought I didn't care. But now I will rebuke you, listing all my charges against you. Repent, all of you who forget me, or I will tear you apart, and no one will help you" (Ps. 50:21–22 NLT).

The truth lies between these extremes. There is mercy in God, but it is mingled with severity; there is wrath in God, but it is tempered with mercy.

The great soul-winners from Bible times till now have recognized this. They have held an even balance between the goodness and the severity of God, because that is what the Bible does. And the Bible, of all the innumerable books written, is the only one that gives us an authoritative representation of God.

The book of nature reveals to us the goodness and the severity of God. Fire will not only bake our food and bless us, but it will also burn us. Water will not only quench our thirst and refresh us, but if we trifle with it, it will drown us. If we recognize God's ways of working in nature, and take heed and obey, we shall find nature's laws most kind and helpful. If we neglect or refuse to obey, we shall find them most terrible and destructive. But if we want to know God in all the richness of His character and all the fullness of His self-revelation, we must study the Bible and compare Scripture with Scripture.

The Bible tells us of God's unutterable love leading Him to seek sinners in mercy, but His righteousness requires penitence, faith, separation from evil, and obedience to His will.

Various Bible descriptions show how God holds an even balance between His mercy and His judgments. "Notice how God is both kind and severe," wrote Paul. "He is severe toward those who disobeyed, but kind to you if you continue to trust in his kindness. But"—showing that God's goodness does not destroy His severity, Paul said—"if you stop trusting, you also will be cut off." We must beware! Then he adds a touch of tenderness, making clear how even in His severity God waits to show mercy: "And if the people of Israel turn from their unbelief, they will be grafted in again, for God has the power to graft them back into the tree" (Rom. 11:22–23 NLT).

Again Paul wrote: "For I am not ashamed of this Good News about Christ. It is the power of God at work, saving everyone who believes. . . . This Good News tells us how God makes us right in His sight. This is accomplished from start to finish by faith. As the Scriptures say, 'It is through faith that a righteous person has life'" (Rom. 1:16–17 NLT). And then he adds, "But God shows his anger from heaven against all sinful, wicked people who suppress the truth by their wickedness" (Rom. 1:18 NLT).

And again he wrote:

Don't you see how wonderfully kind, tolerant, and patient God is with you? Does this mean nothing to you? Can't you see that his kindness is intended to turn you from your sin?

But because you are stubborn and refuse to turn from your sin, you are storing up terrible punishment for yourself. For a day of anger is coming, when God's righteous judgment will be revealed. He will judge everyone according to what they have done. He will give eternal life to those who keep on doing good, seeking after the glory and honor and immortality that God offers. But he will pour out his anger and wrath on those who live for themselves, who refuse to obey the truth and instead live lives of wickedness. There will be trouble and calamity for everyone who keeps on doing what is evil. . . . But there will be glory and honor and peace from God for all who do good—for the Jew first and also for the Gentile. For God does not show favoritism. (Rom. 2:4–11 NLT)

The saving mercy of God revealed in the Scriptures is invariably set over against the wrath of God, as the great mountains are set over against the deep seas. The writer to the Hebrews said of Jesus, "He is also able to save to the uttermost those who come to God through Him" (Heb. 7:25 NKJV), while Paul wrote of some upon whom "wrath has come . . . to the uttermost" (1 Thess. 2:16 NKJV).

There is, then, an uttermost salvation for all who "trust and obey" and an uttermost woe for all who go on in selfish unbelief and worldliness and sin. Truly "God is not mocked" (Gal. 6:7 KJV), and He is a God of judgment.

We find Jesus kept this balance when He said that those who hear His sayings and do them are like those who build upon a rock, against which rain and floods and winds cannot prevail, while those who hear and do not obey are like those who build upon sand, which will be swept away by rain and floods and wind (see Matt. 7:24–27). He also said that the wicked shall "go away into everlasting punishment: but the righteous into life eternal" (Matt. 25:46 KJV). He told of the shut door at the marriage, with some on the inside with their Lord and some on the outside, rejected and unknown; of the joy of the Lord into which good and faithful servants enter, and the outer darkness, into which the wicked and slothful are cast; and of the great, fixed gulf which is impassable, with some on the right side in the bosom of comfort and security and peace, and some on the wrong side in the bitter woe of fierce remorse and torment.

We find John the Baptist was faithful to this great truth. He cried out, "Anyone who believes in God's Son has eternal life. Anyone who doesn't obey the Son will never experience eternal life but remains under God's angry judgment" (John 3:36 NLT).

Likewise all through the Old Testament this balance is maintained:

Wash yourselves and be clean! Get your sins out of my sight. Give up your evil ways. Learn to do good. Seek justice. Help the oppressed. Defend the cause of orphans. Fight for the rights of widows. "Come now, let's settle this," says the LORD. "Though your sins are like scarlet, I will make them as white as snow. Though they are red like crimson, I will make them as white as wool. If you will only obey me, you will have plenty to eat. But [and here is the unfailing alternative] if you turn away and refuse to listen, you will be devoured by the sword of your enemies." (Isa. 1:16–20 NLT)

These Bible word pictures show us that no single word—not even the sweet word *mercy*—will sum up the rich and manifold character of God. The Bible says, "God is love" (1 John 4:8 KJV), but it also says, "Our God is a consuming fire" (Heb. 12:29 KJV).

To penitent hearts who trust in Jesus, God will be found to be rich in mercy. But He will defend the moral and spiritual order of His universe by uttermost penalties against those who go on proudly, carelessly, or wickedly in their own ways.

When Dr. Samuel Johnson lay dying, he was much concerned about his soul. A friend said to him, "Sir, you seem to forget the merits of the Redeemer."

"No," replied Dr. Johnson, "I do not forget the merits of the Redeemer, but I remember that He said He would place some on His right hand and some on His left."

Our only hope is in the wounds of Jesus and the shelter of His blood. There, and only there, shall we find mercy, since we have sinned. But there mercy is boundless and free.

Confessing Other People's Sins 7

"Have you eaten from the tree whose fruit I commanded you not to eat?" (Gen. 3:11 NLT), the Lord asked Adam in the garden of Eden. "The man replied, 'It was the woman you gave me who gave me the fruit, and I ate it.' Then the LORD God asked the woman, 'What have you done?' 'The serpent deceived me,' she replied. 'That's why I ate it'" (Gen. 3:12–13 NLT).

They confessed the sins of others and ignored their own, and the curse fell upon them instead of blessing. Nothing more surely makes manifest a person's spiritual blindness and hardness of heart than hiding behind others and confessing their faults instead of his or her own. It is a deadly kind of hypocrisy. It can meet only with God's displeasure.

"People who conceal their sins will not prosper," said Solomon, "but if they confess and turn from them, they will receive mercy" (Prov. 28:13 NLT). There is no more dangerous way of trying to cover one's sins than by blaming others and calling attention to their faults instead of humbly confessing our own.

An incident in the life of King Saul makes this plain:

> One day Samuel said to Saul . . . "This is what the Lord of Heaven's Armies has declared: I have decided to settle accounts with the nation of Amalek. . . . Now go and completely destroy the entire Amalekite nation—men, women, children, babies, cattle, sheep, goats, camels, and donkeys." . . .
>
> [But] Saul and his men spared Agag's life and kept the best of the sheep and goats, the cattle, the fat calves, and the lambs—everything, in fact, that appealed to them. They destroyed only what was worthless or of poor quality.
>
> Then the Lord said to Samuel, "I am sorry that I ever made Saul king, for he has not been loyal to me and has refused to obey my command." . . .
>
> When Samuel finally found him, Saul greeted him cheerfully. "May the Lord bless you," he said. "I have carried out the Lord's command!"
>
> "Then what is all the bleating of sheep and goats and the lowing of cattle I hear?" Samuel demanded.
>
> "It's true that the army spared the best of the sheep, goats, and cattle," Saul admitted. "But they are going to sacrifice them to the Lord your God. We have destroyed everything else." (1 Sam. 15:1–3, 9–11, 13–15 NLT)

Saul tried to cover his own sin by confessing the sins of others. But Samuel answered him, "Because you have rejected the command of the LORD, he has rejected you as king" (1 Sam. 15:23 NLT). So Saul lost his kingdom.

And people still lose their crown of peace and salvation and God's favor by sinning, by disobeying, and by confessing the sins of others instead of their own.

"Confess your sins to each other," wrote James (5:16 NLT). "If we confess our sins to him, he is faithful and just to forgive us our sins and to cleanse us from all wickedness," wrote John (1 John 1:9 NLT).

"I have sinned," cried David (2 Sam. 12:13 NLT). Again, he said, "I recognize my rebellion; it haunts me day and night" (Ps. 51:3 NLT). We can hear the sob of a broken and penitent heart through the open and humble confession. And God put away his sin.

"God, be merciful to me, for I am a sinner," prayed the tax collector, and Jesus said he "returned home justified before God" (Luke 18:13–14 NLT).

"Are you saved?" I asked a woman in one of our prayer meetings.

"No, I am not," she replied with emphasis.

"Were you ever saved?" I asked.

"Yes, I was."

"And what did Jesus do that you turned your back on Him and started for hell?" I questioned.

"A man who called himself a Christian slapped my husband in the face," said she—but she did not tell me the fact (which I learned later) that the man confessed his wrong and apologized.

"Well, that was too bad," I replied. "But you shouldn't have turned your back on Jesus for that. You know they slapped Jesus in the face, they 'smote him with the palms of their hands'" (Matt. 26:67 KJV).

And she opened her eyes wide and looked at me.

"And you know they spat in His face also, and not content with that, they crushed a crown of thorns on His head. But that did not satisfy them, so they bared His back, and tied His hands to His feet, and whipped His poor bare back till it was all cut and torn and bleeding. That was the way the Roman soldiers, under Pilate, scourged Him. And then they smote Him on the head and mocked Him. But not content with that, they then placed a great cross on His shoulders, and it must have pressed heavily upon the poor, wounded back. But He carried it, and there on Calvary they crucified Him. They drove great nails through His hands and feet, and lifting the cross they let it fall heavily into its place. This must have rent and torn His hands and feet very terribly, but He prayed, 'Father, forgive them.' And there He hung in agony and pain, while they robbed Him of His only suit of clothes, gave Him gall and vinegar to drink, and wagged their heads and mocked Him. Then He bowed His head and died. And this He suffered for you, my sister, but you turned your back upon Him because someone ill-treated your husband!"

And as I talked she saw Jesus. The sin of the other man faded from her sight and her own sin grew big before her eyes, until she was in tears. Then, rising, she rushed, sobbing, to the penitent form (the place to kneel for confession) to confess her own sin to the Lord and, I trust, to be restored once more to His favor.

When we get this vision of Jesus, we cease to blame others and look only at our own sin, which we can no longer excuse. We blame ourselves, plead guilty, and confess our wrongdoing with a broken and contrite heart. Then, looking into the pitying face of our suffering Savior, we trust, receive pardon, enter into peace, and become new creatures in Christ Jesus.

This is the vision and faith that begets love for the Savior, that produces obedience in the heart, that saves from all sin, and that gives love and skill to save others also.

Let me beg you to take your eyes off other people and fix them upon yourself and upon Jesus. Then you will "get rid of the log in your own eye . . . [and] you will see well enough to deal with the speck in your friend's eye" (Matt. 7:5 NLT).

And you who have to deal with people who are always confessing other people's sins, let me beg of you to deal with them tenderly, though firmly, lest you forget "the hole of the pit from which *you* were dug" (Isa. 51:1 NKJV, emphasis added) and lest you become severe with your brother or sister for a fault from which you may think yourself delivered, but are not entirely free.

Remember Paul's words: "Brothers and sisters, if another believer is overcome by some sin, you who are godly should gently and humbly help that person back onto the right path. And be careful not to fall into the same temptation yourself" (Gal. 6:1 NLT). I have seen people fall themselves through failing to be gentle with those who have fallen. Remember the words of Jesus: "Learn from me, for I am gentle and humble in heart" (Matt. 11:29 NIV). How hard is that sweet lesson of meekness and lowliness of heart! But that is the first lesson Jesus sets us to learn.

The Dangers of Middle Age 8

We read and hear much about the dangers of youth, and they are very many and often very deadly. But how little do we hear about the dangers of the middle-aged! And yet they, too, are very many and very deadly.

I was reminded vividly of this recently when a man, considerably past fifty years of age, stopped me on the street and sought an interview. After a rather close examination, in which I sought to locate and diagnose his spiritual disease, he told me of his sins and temptations. He had been a follower of Jesus but had fallen. He was becoming more and more entangled in a network of evil and was sinking deeper and deeper in the quicksand of his iniquity—and his sins were sins of the flesh!

The middle-aged are not altogether safe from the awful corruption and blasting sin which lies lurking in the lusts of the flesh. Joseph, when but a young man in Egypt, fully and grandly overcame this danger; he kept himself pure and set an example for the ages. But in middle life David and his son, Solomon, with all their light and wisdom, fell grievously and wallowed in sin and shame, thus bringing reproach upon God's people and God's cause, stirring up the enemies of the Lord to mock and blaspheme, and, doubtless, encouraging others by their example to fall into like sins.

But we do not have to go back to ancient history nor to the ranks of those who make no profession of religion to find how sins of the flesh overthrow middle-aged men and women if they do not watch and pray and walk softly with the Lord. I shall never forget the shock and chill that went through the hearts of American Christians some years ago, when a silver-haired evangelist—the author of a number of books of great spiritual insight and power, and one of the mightiest preachers it has ever been my lot to hear—fell into sin and shame. It was heartbreaking for his influence to be ruined, his good name spoiled, his reputation gone, his family put to shame, God's cause mocked, and for a soul whom he should have shepherded to be dragged to the mouth of hell to gratify his passing pleasure.

And there are a number of others I have known, who had great opportunities of usefulness, whose influence was widespread, and who walked in a broad day of spiritual light but who sank into a dark night of corruption, sin, and shame.

So let not only young men and women but mature ones as well take heed lest they fall. Let them watch for and guard themselves against the beginnings of sin—the unclean thought, the lascivious look, the impure imagination, the unholy desire. Let them hate "even the garment stained by the flesh" (Jude 23 ESV).

Let them beware of selling—for a mess of pottage—their good name, their sphere of usefulness, their place among God's people, the friendships of years, the honor of their children, the happiness of their home, the smile and favor of God, and their hope of heaven. Let them do as the writer to the Hebrews said: "Watch out that no poisonous root of bitterness grows up to trouble you, corrupting many. Make sure that no one is immoral or godless like Esau, who traded his birthright as the firstborn son for a single meal" (Heb. 12:15–16 NLT).

But the more constant spiritual danger of the middle-aged is the loss of the freshness of their early experience, the dew of their spiritual morning, the "devotion of [their] youth," when they were "holy to the LORD" and followed Him "in the wilderness" (Jer. 2:2–3 ESV).

There is nothing in the world so wonderful, beautiful, and delightful as the constant renewal of spiritual youth in the midst of the increasing cares, burdens, infirmities, losses, and disappointments of middle life and old age. And there is nothing so sad as the gradual loss of fervor, simplicity, heart devotion, unfeigned faith, triumphing hope, and glowing love of spiritual youth.

The psalmist called upon his soul to bless the Lord, who satisfied his mouth with good things, so that his youth—his soul's youth—was renewed like the eagle's (see Ps. 103:1–5).

But multitudes, instead of being renewed, fall into decay. They lose the bloom and blessedness of their early experience and become like Ephraim, of whom the prophet said, "Strangers devour his strength, and he knows it not; gray hairs are sprinkled upon him, and he knows it not" (Hos. 7:9 ESV). This loss may steal upon us like a creeping paralysis if we do not watch and pray.

It may come through a widening experience of human weakness and fickleness. We are continually tempted to lean upon human strength and ingenuity rather than upon God and His Word. And when others fail and fall we feel as though the foundations were swept away. At such times the Tempter will whisper, twisting God's Word: "What is the use of your trying to live a holy life? 'There is none who does good, not even one'" (Ps. 14:3 ESV). Then if we do not at once flee to and hide ourselves in Jesus, and lift our eyes to God, and stir up our faith toward Him, a chill of discouragement and doubt and fear will sweep over us; lukewarmness will take the place of the warm, throbbing experience of youth; and a half-skeptical, half-cynical spirit will fill the heart that once overflowed with glad, simple faith and abounding hope. It is this loss that often makes older folks look so coldly upon the return of those who have fallen, and that so unfits them to help and encourage those who are young in the faith.

Nothing filled me with greater admiration for The Salvation Army's founder than his morning-like freshness, his perennial youth, his springing hope, and his unfailing faith in God and humanity—in spite of all the shameful failures and desertions and backslidings which wounded him to the heart and pierced him through with many sorrows. And where he led shall we not follow?

Instead of looking at those who have fallen, why not look at those who have stood? Instead of losing heart and faith because of those who have thrown down the sword and fled from the field, shall we not shout for joy and emulate those who were faithful unto death, who came up out of great tribulation with robes washed in the blood of the Lamb? Why not shout for joy, and triumph with Joseph in his victory rather than sneer and lose faith in God and thus suffer defeat with David in his fall? Why not look at the beloved John and rejoice, rather than at the traitor Judas and despair? Why not consider Jesus, "who endured from sinners such hostility against himself"? If we do, we shall not "grow weary or fainthearted" (Heb. 12:3 ESV).

This loss may come through thronging cares and responsibilities. Youth and old age are largely free from responsibility, which comes pressing hard and insistently upon the middle-aged. There are business cares, family cares, and responsibility for church, city, and state. The wide-open, hungry mouths of the children must be fed; their restless, destructive feet must be shod; their health must be guarded; their tempers and dispositions must be corrected and disciplined; their eager, wayward, unformed minds must be trained and educated; and their souls must be found and saved.

And all these cares, which swarm about like bees, must be met again and again, and often when we are worn and weary and full of pain. No wonder that when Jesus spoke the parable of the sower, He mentioned the cares of life as among the weeds which choke the Word and make it unfruitful (see Luke 8:4–15). But no true follower of Jesus will run away from these cares. There is victory for those who are determined to have victory.

Moses was thronged with the care of a vast, untrained, stiff-necked, hungry multitude in a barren wilderness. But he walked with God, wore a shining face, and—with but one brief loss of patience, for which he duly suffered—he got victory, and God and angels conducted his funeral.

Daniel superintended a huge empire, with 120 provinces, but he found time to pray and give thanks three times a day, and was more than a conqueror.

Paul, in addition to whippings, stonings, imprisonments, shipwrecks, perils, hunger, cold, and nakedness, had pressing upon him
"the care of all the churches" (2 Cor. 11:28 KJV). But he rejoiced and
prayed and gave thanks, and did not murmur, faint, or turn back, and
God made him to triumph.

A distinguished writer has beautifully said:

Comradeship with God is the secret, not only of joy and peace,
but of efficiency. In that comradeship we find rest, not from
our work, but in our work. When Christ says, "Come unto me,
all ye that labour and are heavy laden, and I will give you rest.
Take my yoke upon you, and learn of me" [Matt. 11:28–29
KJV], He does not invite us to lay aside our work. He offers us
rest in our work. The invitation is to those who are laboring and
bearing burdens. The promise is to teach them how so to labor
and how so to bear their burdens so as not to be wearied by
them. It is not a couch which He offers us, but a yoke; and a
yoke is an instrument for the accomplishment of work.

For a yoke is not only an implement of industry; it is a
symbol of comradeship. The yoke binds two together. To take
Christ's yoke upon us is to be yoked to Christ. Work with Me,
says Christ, and your work will be easy; work with Me, and
your burden will be light.[1]

And this comradeship with the Lord Jesus is the secret of victory all
along the way and over every obstacle and every foe. Here—though
you may be tempted and tried, and almost overcome at the noon of

life—in fellowship with Jesus, the flesh loses its subtle power, the charms of the world are discovered to be but painted mockery, the Devil is outwitted, and while life is a warfare it is also a victory.

NOTE

1. Lyman Abbott, *Inspiration for Daily Living: Selections from the Writings of Lyman Abbott* (Boston: The Pilgrim Press, 1919), 329.

Maintaining the Holiness Standard

9

The Salvation Army was born not in a cloister or drawing room but
on a spiritual battlefield—at the penitent form (the place at the altar
for seeking forgiveness). It has been nourished for spiritual conquests
not upon speculative doctrines and fine-spun verbal distinctions but
upon those great doctrines which can be wrought into and worked out
in soul-satisfying experience. Hence, The Salvation Army compels
the attention of all men and women everywhere and appeals to the
universal heart of humanity.

In this it is in harmony with the scientific spirit and practice of
the age, which refuses to be committed to any theory that cannot be
supported by facts.

One of The Salvation Army's central doctrines—and most valued
and precious experiences—is that of heart holiness. The bridge The
Salvation Army throws across the impassable gulf that separates the

sinner from the Savior—who pardons that He may purify, who saves
that He may sanctify—rests upon these two abutments: the forgiveness of sins through simple, penitent, obedient faith in a crucified
Redeemer, and the purifying of the heart and empowering of the soul
through the anointing of the Holy Spirit, given by its risen and
ascended Lord, and received not by works, but by faith.

Remove either of these abutments and the bridge falls. Preserve
them in strength, and a world of lost and despairing sinners can be
confidently invited and urged to come and be gloriously saved.

The first abutment is deep grounded on such assurances as these:
"With you there is forgiveness, so that we can, with reverence, serve
you" (Ps. 130:4 NIV) and, "If we confess our sins, he is faithful and just
to forgive us our sins, and to cleanse us from all unrighteousness" (1
John 1:9 KJV).

The second firmly rests on such Scriptures as these: "God knows
people's hearts, and he confirmed that he accepts Gentiles by giving
them the Holy Spirit, just as he did to us. He made no distinction
between us and them, for he cleansed their hearts through faith" (Acts
15:8–9 NLT) and, "If we are living in the light, as God is in the light,
then we have fellowship with each other, and the blood of Jesus, his
Son, cleanses us from all sin" (1 John 1:7 NLT).

Such is the doctrine passed on to us from the first Christians, and
here are some Scriptures which show how the doctrine was wrought
into triumphant experience in their day:

> Don't you realize that those who do wrong will not inherit the
> Kingdom of God? Don't fool yourselves. Those who indulge in

sexual sin, or who worship idols, or commit adultery, or are male prostitutes, or practice homosexuality, or are thieves, or greedy people, or drunkards, or are abusive, or cheat people—none of these will inherit the Kingdom of God. Some of you were once like that. But you were cleansed; you were made holy; you were made right with God by calling on the name of the Lord Jesus Christ and by the Spirit of our God. (1 Cor. 6:9–11 NLT)

"Once we, too, were foolish and disobedient. We were misled and became slaves to many lusts and pleasures. Our lives were full of evil and envy, and we hated each other. But—when God our Savior revealed his kindness and love, he saved us, not because of the righteous things we had done, but because of his mercy. He washed away our sins, giving us a new birth and new life through the Holy Spirit. He generously poured out the Spirit upon us through Jesus Christ our Savior" (Titus 3:3–6 NLT).

Such was the doctrine of the first Christians, and such was their experience. And to this doctrine and experience The Salvation Army has been committed from the beginning. This has been both its reproach and its glory, and one of the chief secrets of its world-conquering power.

Some years ago, The Salvation Army's founder, William Booth, was in New York, and for nearly a week he stood before the thronging multitudes by night and before his own people by day, pleading for righteousness, for holiness, for God. As he toiled with flaming passion to accomplish his purpose, the great commandment began to unfold to me in fuller, richer meaning than ever before—"You shall love the

Lord your God with all your heart and with all your soul and with all your mind and with all your strength" (Mark 12:30 ESV). As he poured out his heart, I said to myself, "There is a man who loves God with all his heart."

Then, as I considered how his whole life was being poured without stint into God's service, I said, "There is a man who loves God with all his soul."

Again, when I noted how diligently and with what infinite study and pains he labored to make plain the great thoughts of God to the feeblest intellect, to the most darkened and degraded, to the least intelligent of his hearers, I said, "There is a man who loves God with all his mind."

And when I saw him old and worn, snowy white, and burdened with the weight of many years—with the heavy load of a world organization ceaselessly pressing hard upon him, still toiling, praying, singing, exhorting, into the late hours of the night, that Jesus might triumph and sinners be won—when it seemed that he ought to be seeking rest in sleep or retiring from the fight to the quiet and comfort of a pleasant home, yet joyously pressing on, I said, "There is a man who loves God with all his strength."

Afflicted, often wounded and heart-sore, burdened with care, he still seemed to me to fulfill each part of that great fourfold commandment. And that was holiness in action.

And it is this holiness—the doctrine, the experience, the action—that we Salvationists must maintain, or we shall betray our trust, lose our birthright, and cease to be a spiritual power in the earth. We shall have a name to live, and yet be dead; our glory will depart; and we, like Samson shorn of his locks, shall become as weak as others, and the souls with whom we are entrusted will grope in darkness or go elsewhere for soul nourishment and guidance. And while we may still have titles and ranks to bestow upon our children, we shall have no heritage to bequeath them of martyr-like sacrifice, spiritual power, daredevil faith, pure and deep joy, burning love, and holy triumph.

In this matter an immeasurable debt is laid upon us. We owe it to our Lord, who redeemed us by His blood not simply that the penalty of our sins should be remitted and that we should thereby escape the just deserts of our manifold transgressions, but also that we should be sanctified, made holy—that we should become temples of the Holy Spirit and live henceforth not for our own profit or pleasure, but for His glory, as His bondservants and friends, ready for service or sacrifice, and prepared for every good work.

We owe a great debt to the cloud of witnesses—the saintly souls who have gone before us. How shall we meet them without confusion and shame if we neglect or waste the heritage they have left us, which they secured for us with infinite pains, tears, prayers, wearisome toil, and often agony and blood? What a debt we owe to them!

We owe it to our children and our children's children. They look to us for the teaching that will direct them into full salvation. They will narrowly and constantly scan our lives to find in us an example of its fullness and beauty, its richness and power, its simplicity, its humility, its self-denial, its courage, its purity and unfailing constancy and steadfast trust, its goodness and meekness, its long-suffering love, its peace and joy, its patience and hope, and its deep and abiding satisfaction. How careful we should be not to fail or disappoint them!

We must pay this righteous debt. And we will. We must and will maintain our holiness standard in both our teaching and our experience, and in so doing we shall save both ourselves and them that hear us — those entrusted to us. This will be our glory and our joy.

But how shall we do this? It is not a simple or easy task. It may require the courage and devotion of a martyr. It will surely require the vigilance, prayerfulness, wisdom, and faithfulness of a saint.

We must remember that the standard is not man-made, but is revealed from heaven, and that those who experience the fullness of blessing still carry the treasure in earthen vessels. So while we should follow them as they follow Christ, we must not look to them but to Him and to His Word for the perfect and unchangeable standard of holiness.

Those who enter into this experience and abide in it are great students and lovers and seekers of God's Word, and to it they appeal when opponents arise.

Catherine Booth, the cofounder of The Salvation Army, read the Bible through eight times before she was twelve years old. Wesley said of himself, "I am a man of one book." Finney said:

I never pretend to make but one book my study. I read them occasionally, but have little time or inclination to read other books much while I have so much to learn of my Bible. I find it like a deep mine, the more I work it, the richer it grows. We must read that more than any or all other books. We must pause and pray over it, verse by verse, and compare part with part, dwell on it, digest it, and get it into our minds till we feel that the Spirit of God has filled us with the spirit of holiness. . . . I have often been asked by young converts and young men preparing for the ministry what they should read. Read the Bible. I would give the same answer five hundred times, over and above all other things, study the Bible.[1]

A young man in New York plied me with his questionings and debatings recently, but finally he settled down to his Bible and prayer, and God sanctified him and so filled and overwhelmed him with joy that he asked the Lord to stay His hand, for the blessings and glory were more than he could endure. And he wanted to wire me four hundred miles away to tell the story.

Familiarity with what the Bible says, with its doctrines and standards, will avail nothing unless the teaching of the Bible is translated into conduct, into character, into life. It is not enough to know or to approve this, but with our undivided will—our whole being—we must choose to be holy. Without the doctrine, the standard, the teaching, we shall never find the experience. Or, having found it, we shall be likely to lose it. Without the experience we shall neglect the teaching, we shall despise or doubt the doctrine, we shall lower the standard.

When Salvation Army officers (ministers) lose the experience, the holiness meetings (services) languish, and when the holiness meetings languish, the spiritual life of the corps (churches) droops and fails, and all manner of substitutes and expedients are introduced to cover up the ghastly facts of spiritual loss, disease, and death.

If we are to maintain our holiness standard, we must not only know the doctrine and experience in our own hearts, but we must teach it, preach it, and press it upon the people in season and out of season, until, like Paul, we can declare our faithfulness in "warning everyone and teaching everyone with all the wisdom God has given us. We want to present them to God, perfect in their relationship to Christ" (Col. 1:28 NLT).

Personally, I find that the surest way to get souls saved and restored—as well as the only way to get Christians sanctified—is to preach holiness plainly, constantly, and tenderly. Then not only do Christians see their need and privilege, but also sinners lose their self-complacency, discover their desperate condition, perceive the possibilities and joys of a true Christian life, and become inclined to surrender and be saved.

We shall greatly help ourselves and others if we carefully and constantly read and scatter holiness literature. There exists a library of books and papers on this subject that are plain, simple, scriptural, and full of the thrill, passion, and compelling power of life and experience. Let us scatter these books everywhere, but especially among our young people, urging them to read everything that has been published on the subject. Let us sow all lands deep with this literature, for then we shall surely reap a harvest of great richness and prepare the way for the generation which shall come after us.

If we would promote the experience of heart holiness each of us must judge him- or herself faithfully and soberly, but we must be generous and sympathetic in our judgment of others. We must help each other. Sharp, harsh criticism does not tend to promote holiness, and especially so when it is indulged in behind a person's back. Kindly, generous criticism which springs from love and from a desire to help, and which is preceded and followed by heart-searching and prayer that it may be offered and received in a true spirit and manner of brotherly love, will often work wonders in helping a soul. We must not cease testifying to the experience and preaching the doctrine and living the life simply because others fail. We must be faithful witnesses, and we shall someday prove that our labor has not been in vain. The Devil makes war upon this doctrine and experience. Let us resist him, and he will flee.

The world will mock or turn away. Let us overcome the world by our faith. Faithfulness to this truth and experience will sometimes require of us the endurance of hardness as good soldiers of Jesus Christ. Holy men and women do not live always in an ecstasy. Sometimes we pass through agony, and at such times the weakness of the flesh will test our firmness of purpose. But we must be true, and we shall "conquer though we die."[2]

I have known people who, when others have lapsed and failed, have remained clear in experience, definite in testimony, and true and generous in holy living, to become the saving salt and guiding light of their church. I have known pastors jubilant in this experience to leaven and bless a whole community.

We must not be faultfinding, neither must we whine and wail and dolefully lament "the good old days" which we may feel were better than these. But we must kneel down and pray in faith, and rise up and shout and shine and sing, and in the name of the Lord command the sun to stand still in the heavens till we have routed the Enemy and gotten the victory. "Thanks be to God, who always leads us as captives in Christ's triumphal procession and uses us to spread the aroma of the knowledge of him everywhere" (2 Cor. 2:14 NIV). "Not that we think we are qualified to do anything on our own. Our qualification comes from God. He has enabled us to be ministers of his new covenant.

This is a covenant not of written laws, but of the Spirit. The old written covenant ends in death; but under the new covenant, the Spirit gives life" (2 Cor. 3:5–6 NLT).

We must not forget that our sufficiency is of God—that God is interested in this work and waits to be our helper. We must not forget that with all our study and experience and knowledge and effort we shall fail unless—patiently, daily, hourly—we wait upon God in prayer and watchful faithfully for the help and inspiration of the Holy Spirit. It is He who opens our eyes and the eyes of our people to see spiritual things in their true relations. He melts the heart, bends the will, illuminates the mind, subdues pride, sweeps away fear, begets faith, and bestows the blessing. And He makes the testimony, the preaching, and the written word mightily effective.

A Salvation Army officer who had lost the blessing of holiness attended one of my officers' meetings and went away with her heart breaking after God. It was Thursday; she prayed nearly all that night. The next day she spent reading the Bible and *Helps to Holiness*, and crying to God for the blessing. Saturday she went about her duties but with a yearning cry in her heart for the blessing. Sunday morning came, and she was again wrestling with God, when suddenly the great deep of her soul was broken up and she was flooded with light and love and peace and joy. The Holy Spirit had come. She went to the meeting that morning and told her experience. The Spirit fell on her soldiers (members) and they flocked to the penitent form and sought and found. And His presence was an abiding presence with that officer. She went on in the power of the Spirit, from the command of little struggling corps, where she had barely held the work together, to larger and yet larger corps, where she had sweeping victory. If space allowed I could multiply such instances.

Our Lord still baptizes with the Holy Spirit and fire. He has given us a standard of holiness. He has given us a doctrine, and He wants to give us an experience that shall incarnate both standard and doctrine in a heavenly and all-conquering life.

A Chinese man got full salvation and his neighbors said, "There is no difference between him and the Book." That should be said of you and me.

"There is a river whose streams make glad the city of God" (Ps. 46:4 ESV). You and I live on the banks of that river. Let us bathe in its waters, and then we will be like the blessed one who trusts in the Lord, who is as a tree planted by the waters, spreading out its roots by the river, and thriving forevermore (see Jer. 17:7–8).

NOTES

1. Charles Grandison Finney, *Lectures to Professing Christians* (New York: John S. Taylor, 1837), 311.

2. Daniel O. Teasley, "Stand by the Cross," 1907, public domain.

The Terror of the Lord

10

The majesty of God's law can be measured only by the terrors of His judgments. God is rich in mercy, but He is equally terrible in wrath. As high as His mercy is, so deep is His wrath. Mercy and wrath are set over against each other as are the high mountains and deep seas. They match each other as day and night, as winter and summer, right and left, or top and bottom. If we do not accept mercy, we shall surely be overtaken by wrath.

God's law cannot be broken with impunity. "The soul who sins shall die" (Ezek. 18:20 ESV). We can no more avoid the judgment of God's violated law than we can avoid casting a shadow when we stand in the light of the sun or avoid being burned if we thrust our hand in the fire. Judgment follows wrongdoing as night follows day.

This truth should be preached and declared continually and everywhere. It should not be preached harshly (as though we were glad of it) nor thoughtlessly (as though we had learned it as a parrot might learn it) nor lightly (as though it were really of no importance). But it should be preached soberly, earnestly, tearfully, and intelligently, as a solemn, certain, awful fact to be reckoned with in everything we think and say and do.

The terrible judgments of God against the Canaanites were but flashes of His wrath against their terrible sins. People with superfine sensibilities mock at what they consider the barbarous ferocity of God's commands against the inhabitants of Canaan, but let such people read the catalogue of the Canaanites' sins as recorded in Leviticus (see 18:6–25), and they will understand why God's anger waxed so hot. The Canaanites practiced the most shameless and inconceivable wickedness, until, as God said, "Even the land was defiled" (Lev. 18:25 NIV).

"Fools mock at sin," wrote Solomon (Prov. 14:9 NASB), and professedly wise men and women still lead simple souls astray as the serpent beguiled Eve, saying, "You will not surely die" (Gen. 3:4 ESV).

But those who understand the unchangeable holiness of God's character and law tremble and fear before Him at the thought of sin. They know that He is to be feared; "the terror of the Lord" (2 Cor. 5:11 KJV) is before them. And this is not inconsistent with the perfect love that casts out fear (see 1 John 4:18). Rather, it is inseparably joined with that love, and the person who is most fully possessed of that love is the one who fears most—with that reverential fear that leads him or her to depart from sin. For the one who is exalted to the greatest heights of divine love and fellowship in Jesus Christ sees most plainly the awful depths of the divine wrath against sin and the bottomless pit to which souls without Christ are hastening.

This vision and sense of the exceeding sinfulness of sin and of God's wrath against wickedness begets not a panicky, slavish fear that makes a person hide from God, as Adam and Eve hid among the trees of Eden, but a holy, filial fear that leads the soul to come out into the open and run to God to seek shelter in His arms and be washed in the blood of the "Lamb of God who takes away the sin of the world!" (John 1:29 NLT).

Lo! On a narrow neck of land,
'Twixt two unbounded seas I stand;
　　Yet how insensible!
A point of time, a moment's space,
Removes me to that heavenly place,
　　Or shuts me up in hell!

Before me place, in dread array,
The scenes of that tremendous day,
　　When Thou with clouds shalt come
To judge the people at Thy bar;
And tell me, Lord, shall I be there
　　To hear Thee say, "Well done!"

Be this my one great business here,
With holy joy and holy fear,
　　To make my calling sure;
Thine utmost counsel to fulfill,
To suffer all Thy righteous will,
　　And to the end endure.[1]

NOTE

1. Charles Wesley, "Thou God of Glorious Majesty," 1749, public domain.

Holy Covetousness 11

"Covet earnestly the best gifts," wrote Paul to the church at Corinth (1 Cor. 12:31 KJV). Not the highest promotions, not the best positions, but "the best gifts," those gifts God bestows upon the people who earnestly desire them and diligently seek Him.

Nero sat upon the throne of the world. He held the highest position imaginable. But a poor, despised Jew in a dungeon in Rome, whose head Nero cut off like a dog's head, possessed the best gifts. And while Nero's name rots, Paul's name and works are a foundation upon which the righteous build for centuries and millenniums.

There were deacons, archdeacons, and venerable bishops and archbishops in England, some hundreds of years ago, who held high places and power and to whom others bowed low. But a poor, despised tinker in the filthy Bedford jail had earnestly desired and received the best gifts. And while those church dignitaries are forgotten by most, the world knows and loves the saintly tinker, John Bunyan, and is ever being made better and lifted nearer to God by his wise works and words.

You and I should seek these best gifts with all our hearts, and we should be satisfied with nothing short of them. It makes little difference what our position and rank may be; if we have these gifts, we shall have a name and bless the world. But without them, we shall prove to be only sham—painted fire and hollow mockery— and the greater our position and the higher our rank, the greater shams we are, and the greater will be our shame in God's great day of reckoning.

What are these gifts?

There is one that in a sense includes them all—the gift of the Holy Spirit. Have you received the Holy Spirit? Is He dwelling in your heart? Covet Him. Live not a day without His blessed presence in you.

Then there is the gift of wisdom. Covet this. The world is full of foolish men and women who don't know how to save themselves, nor how to promote salvation and peace among their fellow foolish ones who miss the way, who stumble along in darkness and perish in their folly. The world needs wise men and women, people who know when to speak, what to say, and when to be silent—people who know God and His way and walk in it.

God gives wisdom to those who seek Him. "If you need wisdom, ask our generous God, and he will give it to you" (James 1:5 NLT). Nothing will so distinguish you and exalt you among your contemporaries as fullness of wisdom.

There are several marks by which to know this heavenly wisdom. James tells us what they are. He said in James 3:17 that the wisdom that comes from above is:

- "Pure." Those who are truly wise will keep themselves pure. They will flee from all impurity in thought, word, and act. Filthy habits of every kind are broken and put away by this heavenly wisdom.
- "Peace loving." Those who have this gift and wisdom from God do not meddle with strife. They seek peace and run after it (see 1 Pet. 3:11). They are essentially peacemakers. They have learned the secret of the "soft answer" (Prov. 15:1 NKJV) which turns away wrath. They are not quick to take offense.
- "Gentle." Those who live in the spirit of this world may be rough and boorish, but those who are wise from above are gentle and considerate. And this gentleness may exist in the same heart with lion-like strength and determination. Jesus was as a "Lamb slain" (Rev. 13:8 KJV), but He was also "the Lion of the tribe of Judah" (Rev. 5:5 KJV). He was gentle as a mother and at the same time immeasurably strong.
- "Willing to yield." Though they are sinned against seventy times seven in a day, yet those who are heavenly wise stand ready to forgive (see Matt. 18:21–35). Their hearts are exhaustless fountains of goodwill. While, if it be their lot to lead, they "take the responsibility seriously" (Rom. 12:8 NLT) and, if necessary, with vigor, yet they do not count their lives dear to themselves (see Acts 20:24) but are willing to lay down their lives for the good of others (see 1 John 3:16).

- "Full of mercy and the fruit of good deeds." Like their heavenly Father they are "rich in mercy" (Eph. 2:4 KJV).
- "No favoritism." They are not partisans. They rise above party and class prejudice and are lovers of all. They stand for "the fair deal."
- "Always sincere." There is no guile in their hearts, no white lies on their tongues, no double-dealing in their actions. They are square and open and above-board in all their ways and dealings. They live in constant readiness for the judgment day.

Thank God for such wisdom, which He waits to bestow upon all those who covet it and who ask for it in faith. Covet wisdom.

Then there is the gift of faith. Covet faith. In everyone there is, in some measure, the power to believe, but added to this is a gift of faith that God bestows upon those who diligently seek Him. Covet this! Be steady, strong, intelligent believers. Cultivate faith. Stir it up in your hearts as you stir up the fire in your stove. Feed your faith on God's Word.

I once heard a mighty evangelist say that he used to pray and pray for faith, but one day he read, "Faith cometh by hearing, and hearing by the word of God" (Rom. 10:17 KJV). Then he began to study God's Word and hide it in his heart, and his faith began to grow and grow until through faith his works girded the globe. Covet faith.

Again, there is the gift of the spirit of prayer. Everybody can pray, if they will, but how few have the spirit of prayer! How few make a business of prayer and wrestle with God for blessing and power and wisdom! Real prayer is something more than a form of words or a hasty address to God just after breakfast, before worship, or before going to bed at night. It is an intense, intelligent, persistent council with the Lord, in which we wait on Him, reason and argue and plead our cause, listen for His reply, and will not let Him go till He blesses us. But how few pray in this way! Let us covet earnestly and cultivate diligently the spirit of prayer.

We should also covet the spirit of prophecy—that is, the ability to speak to the hearts and minds of others so that they shall see and feel that God is in us and in our words (see 1 Cor. 14:1–3). We may not be able to preach like William Booth, but there is probably not one of us who cannot preach and prophesy far more pungently, powerfully, and persuasively than we do if we earnestly coveted this gift and sought it in fervent prayer, faithful study, and constant and deep meditation. God would help us, and how greatly it would add to our power and usefulness! Let us earnestly covet this gift, asking God to touch our lips with fire and grace. The people wondered at the gracious words of Jesus, so why should we not be such mouthpieces for Him that they shall wonder at our gracious words too!

Solomon said, "Whoever loves a pure heart and gracious speech will have the king as a friend" (Prov. 22:11 NLT). And Paul said, "Let your speech always be gracious" (Col. 4:6 ESV).

But, above all, covet a heart full and flaming and overflowing with love. Pray for love. Stir up what love you have. Exercise love. It is good to take the Bible and, with a concordance, hunt out the word *love* until you know all the Bible says on the subject. And then with a heart full of love, pour it out on the children, the wandering ones, cranky folks, and poor loveless souls, until that wondrous text has its fulfillment in you: "May those who love [God] rise like the sun in all its power!" (Judg. 5:31 NLT). How the frost and snows melt, the frozen earth thaws, the trees burst into bud and leaf, the flowers blossom, the birds sing, and all nature wakes to a revelry of life and joy when the sun rises in all its power!

And we may be so full of love and faith and power and the Holy Spirit that we shall be like that. Then indeed we shall be a blessing. Souls dead in trespasses and sin shall come to life under our loving ministry and message. The weak shall be made strong, the sorrowing shall receive divine comfort, the ignorant shall be taught, and heavenly light shall illumine those that are in darkness. Let us then "covet earnestly the best gifts" (1 Cor. 12:31 KJV).

A Common yet Subtle Sin 12

There is a sin which a priest once declared that no one had ever confessed to him—a sin so deadly that the wrath of God comes upon men and women because of it; a sin so common that probably everybody has at some time been guilty of it; a sin so gross in God's sight as to be classed with sexual immorality, idolatry, murder, and such like; a sin so subtle that those most guilty of it seem to be the most unconscious of it. It is a sin that has led to the ruin of homes, the doom of cities, the downfall of kings, the overthrow of empires, the collapse of civilizations, and the damnation of an apostle of ministers of the gospel and of millions of less conspicuous souls. People in the highest and most sacred positions of trust and who enjoy the most unlimited confidence of others have, under the spell of this sin, wrecked their good names and have brought shame to their families, and misfortune, want, and woe to their associates.

When God gave the Ten Commandments to Moses amid the thunder and lightning of Mount Sinai, one of the ten was against this sin. When Lot lost all he had in the doom of Sodom and Gomorrah, it was primarily because of this sin. When Nadab and Abihu were suddenly consumed by the fierce fires of God's wrath, at the bottom of their transgression was this sin. When Achan and his household were stoned, it was because of this sin. When Eli and his sons lost the priesthood and died miserably, it was at root because of this sin. When Saul lost his kingdom, it was because this sin had subtly undermined his loyalty to God. When Ahab died and the dogs licked his blood, he was meeting the doom of this sin. When David fell from heights of God's tender favor and fellowship, brought shame and confusion upon himself, and incurred God's hot displeasure and lifelong trouble, it was because of this sin. When Elisha's servant, Gehazi, went out from the presence of the prophet smitten with leprosy white as snow, it was because of this sin. When Judas betrayed the Master with a kiss, thus making his name a synonym of everlasting obloquy, and bringing upon himself the death of a dog and a fool, it was because of this sin. When Ananias and Sapphira dropped dead at Peter's feet, they suffered the dread penalty of this sin. When World War I burst forth in 1914, enveloping the earth in its wrathful flame, sweeping away the splendid young manhood of the world in storms of steel and rivers of blood, and engulfing the accumulated wealth of ages in a bottomless pit of destruction, the disaster could be traced to the unrestricted and deadly workings of this awful, secret, silent, pitiless sin.

What is this sin that the priest never heard mentioned in his confessional, this sin that apostles and priests and shepherds and servants have committed, and upon which the swift, fierce lightning of God's wrath has fallen—this sin of which everyone at some time has probably been guilty and yet which is so secret and subtle that those most enthralled by it are most unconscious of it?

When the herdsmen of Lot and Abraham fell into strife, Abraham, the uncle, to whom God had promised all the land, said to the young man, Lot, his nephew, "Let there be no strife between you and me, and between your herdsmen and my herdsmen, for we are kinsmen" (Gen. 13:8 ESV). Then he invited Lot to take any portion of the land that pleased him, and he would be content to take what was left. Lot looked down upon the fertile plains of Jordan and without a thought for his old uncle, to whom he owed all, drove his herds into the lush pastures of the rich plain, near the markets of opulent Sodom and Gomorrah, while the rough and stony hill country was left to Abraham. But God became, more fully than ever, the companion and portion of Abraham, while Lot, through his covetousness, was soon so entangled in the life of Sodom that in the doom of the city he lost all he had, barely escaping with his life, and accompanied only by two weak and willful daughters.

At the bottom of Nadab and Abihu's sacrilegious offering of strange fire before the Lord was their coveting of Aaron's priestly power and authority, and it led to God's swift vindication of Aaron in their awful destruction. When the children of Israel entered the Land of Promise and the walls of Jericho fell before them, Achan saw gold and garments which he coveted and took for himself, regardless of God's commandment, thereby bringing defeat to Israel, death to his fellow soldiers, and terrible doom to himself.

Old Eli's sons, unsatisfied with the rich provision made for the priesthood, coveted that which God had reserved for sacrifice, and against protest took for themselves what was forbidden. They also—despite God's command—coveted the wives and maidens who came to worship at God's altar. When softhearted old Eli heard about their sin, he only feebly reproved them. Consequently, God's wrath swiftly followed, with its doom of death and the loss of the priesthood.

It was Saul's coveting the goodwill of the people rather than the favor of God that led to his disobedience and loss of the kingdom.

Among all Ahab's other reeking iniquities, it was his coveteousness—which led him to destroy Naboth and steal his vineyard—that brought down upon him God's sleepless judgment, till he died in battle and dogs licked up his blood.

David coveted Bathsheba—the wife of another man—and to this day blasphemers sneer and God is reproached, while David escaped the doom that falls on those who are guilty of this sin only by his humble confession, deep repentance, and brokenness of heart. But he could not escape endless shame, sorrow, and trouble.

Gehazi cast longing eyes upon the gold, silver, and rare garments which Naaman pressed upon Elisha the prophet out of gratitude for his cleansing in Jordan, and which Elisha had refused. But, blinded by the glitter of gold and steeped in covetousness, Gehazi had no heart and no understanding for the austere self-denial of the fine old prophet, and he said to himself, "I will chase after him and get something from him" (2 Kings 5:20 NLT). And so he did! Then, to hide his sin, he lied to Elisha. But the old seer's eyes were like seraph's eyes—they saw—and he said to the covetous, lying Gehazi, "'Don't you realize that I was there in spirit when Naaman stepped down from his chariot to meet you? Is this the time to receive money and clothing, olive groves and vineyards, sheep and cattle, and male and female servants? Because you have done this, you and your descendants will suffer from Naaman's leprosy forever.' When Gehazi left the room, he was covered with leprosy; his skin was white as snow" (2 Kings 5:26–27 NLT).

Covetousness ruled Judas's stony, ashen heart, and for thirty pieces of silver he betrayed the Master!

Covetousness possessed the selfish hearts of Ananias and Sapphira. They wanted the praise and honor of utmost sacrifice and generosity while secretly holding on to their gold. And God smote them dead!

As we study the history and biblical examples of this sin of covetousness, we see the deep meaning and truth of Paul's words to Timothy: "People who long to be rich fall into temptation and are trapped by many foolish and harmful desires that plunge them into ruin and destruction. For the love of money is the root of all kinds of evil" (1 Tim. 6:9–10 NLT).

This sin in Lot led to ingratitude toward his uncle and neighborly association with vile sinners. In Nadab and Abihu, it led to envy and jealousy and sacrilege. It led to disobedience in Saul, to sacrilege and licentiousness in Eli's sons, to adultery and murder in David, to brazen robbery in Ahab, to greed and lying in Gehazi, to the betrayal of the innocent Christ with an impudent kiss in Judas, and to bold lying to the Holy Spirit in Ananias and Sapphira. Truly, from its poisonous root has sprung up the deadly, poisonous tree of all evil, and upon it in manifold ways has been outpoured the wrath of God, showing His holy hatred and abhorrence of it.

A close study of the awful ravages of this sin in its workings would show that again and again it has undermined thrones and led to the downfall of empires, and that it has rotted away the strong foundations of chastity and honesty and truth and goodwill in whole peoples, ending in the collapse of civilizations.

Once its workings begin in a human heart there is no end to the ruin and woe it may bring about in that soul, and then in the lives of others. There is no height of honor and holiness from which it may not pull men and women down. There is no depth of pitiless selfishness, lying evasion, brazen effrontery, and self-deception into which it may not plunge them. When proclaiming the Ten Commandments from the flaming mount, God reserved the last to hurl at this sin, not because it was least of all the sins forbidden, but rather because it was a pregnant mother of them all, an instigator and ally of all evil.

Covetousness is a sin that reaches out for people of every age. In some of its forms, it makes its most successful assaults upon those who are well advanced in years. Those in ardent devotion to Christ may successfully resist it in their youth and yet fall before it when their heads are crowned with honors and white with the snows of many winters. The fear of want in old age, the natural desire to provide for children and loved ones, may silently, secretly lead them into the deadly embrace of this serpent-like sin and shipwreck their honor, their faith, their "first love," their simplicity in Christ, their unselfish devotion to the interests of the Lord and the souls of others. Thus it may bring about their final rejection in that day when the secrets of their hearts shall be revealed and their works made manifest by fire.

How may we avoid this deadly, secret, subtle sin? There is but one way—that is, by following Jesus in daily, resolute self-denial, by watchfulness and prayer, by walking in the light as He is in the light, by openness of heart and humility of mind, by utter surrender to the Holy Spirit, by counting all things loss for Christ, by learning and not forgetting that "godliness with contentment is great gain" (1 Tim. 6:6 KJV), by seeking first the kingdom of God and His righteousness, by joyfully trusting and obeying those words of Peter—"Give all your worries and cares to God, for he cares about you" (1 Pet. 5:7 NLT)—and by keeping the heart clean.

"Blessed are the pure in heart: for they shall see God," said Jesus (Matt. 5:8 KJV). "Take care, and be on your guard against all covetousness" (Luke 12:15 ESV).

Sins against Chastity 13

After the preceding chapter appeared as an article in various periodicals in other countries, I received a communication from across the sea, in which a man wrote, "I observe that you make a statement concerning Eli with which I do not altogether agree." The writer said he does not consider Eli's appeal to his sons to be weak, as I stated in the article. Then he compared the sins of the sons of Eli (see 1 Sam. 2:12–17, 22–25) with the sins of Samuel's sons (see 1 Sam. 8:1–3). He argued that the sins of Samuel's sons were more heinous than the sins of Eli's sons, "one of which," he wrote, "was a sin against morality, a natural following out of an instinct for the propagation of the race, and the other a violation of a ceremonial law. But the dealings of Samuel's sons constituted a violation of fundamental righteousness."

Then my correspondent questioned why such terrible judgments fell upon Eli and his sons, while—so far as the record shows—Samuel and his sons escaped. Finally, he asked, "Why this differentiation? Do you consider that it is a more heinous sin to go against forms and ceremonials in connection with religion than it is to deal unrighteously with your neighbor?"

This letter raises the question of the comparative wickedness of sins against womanhood and chastity—a question that is seldom discussed except in private or in scientific or semi-scientific books that are not widely read. If I may, I wish to reply to it publicly, as follows.

First, I have no lawyer's brief for Samuel. He is one of the very few men in the Bible of whom no ill thing is written. He seems to have been acceptable to God from his youth up, and since God has recorded no charge against him I can bring none. "It is before his own master that he stands or falls" (Rom. 14:4 ESV). I can only rejoice with him, as a brother, in his victorious life and walk with God. There is no record as to how Samuel dealt with his miscreant sons, but since he retained God's favor he must have acted in harmony with God's will. I have no doubt, however, that his sons were rewarded according to their works, if not in this world then in the next, even though no mention of it is made in the Bible.

As regards Eli, he seems to have been a kindly old man, but weak in his abhorrence and condemnation of evil, at least in his own sons. God tells us plainly His reasons for dealing as He did with the old man and his vicious sons: "Because his sons are blaspheming God and he hasn't disciplined them" (1 Sam. 3:13 NLT). He knew their evil. As judge and high priest, Eli had the authority and power to stop the evil doings of his sons. And, according to the law of the land (which was the law of God), it was his duty to do so; therefore Eli should have acted. But all he did was offer a feeble reproof. My correspondent objected to my description and wrote, "To me it seems one of the most pathetic and moving appeals that an aged father could make to reprobate sons; he points out to them in moving language the difference between sinning against man and sinning against God."

But Eli was not only a father—he was a ruler, clothed with authority and power. He should therefore have done more than make "a pathetic and moving" appeal. He should have exercised all the authority and power of his great office to put a stop to the vile practices of his reprobate sons. "Whoever loves father or mother more than me is not worthy of me," said Jesus (Matt. 10:37 ESV). "Cursed is he who does the work of the LORD with slackness" (Jer. 48:10 ESV).

Eli might have saved himself, and possibly his boys, if he had acted promptly and vigorously—as he should have—and as a righteous ruler abhorring evil and bent on protecting the sacred rights of society and the reverent worship of God. It is the duty of a ruler to rule diligently (see Rom. 12:8) and impartially, and of a priest to insist on reverence in the service of God. There Eli failed, so the terrible and swift judgment of God cut him and his family down, and the priesthood and judgeship passed to others.

As to the comparative heinousness of the sins of the two sets of men, the sin of Eli's sons was far the worse. Any right-minded individual who considers what it would mean to have the sacred shelter of home invaded and the purity of wife or sister or daughter assailed must admit this. To rob someone of money is bad, but to rob a woman of her virtue is worse. To defraud someone in a court of justice and mete out injustice is vile, but to rob someone of the sanctity of home and the purity of wife or mother or sister or daughter is far viler. To debauch the future mothers of the race, and so to rob unborn children and generations yet to be of the noblest of all rights—the right of pure, sweet, holy, reverent motherhood—seems to me like poisoning the wells and springs from which cities must drink or perish, and hence the darkest of all crimes.

All the moralities and sanctions of religion were despised and cast away, and all the sacred rights of humanity were trampled upon and imperiled by Eli's apostate sons. They were set apart as the heralds and guardians of both religion and morality, yet their actions seem to have been the grossest insult to both God and humankind, and the most flagrant neglect and violation possible of their high and sacred calling.

My correspondent wrote that the offense of Eli's sons was "a natural following out of the instinct for the propagation of the species," as though that were some relief of their crime. But among all nations, and even among savage races, there is a higher instinct that forbids people from following the lower instinct, except lawfully, and among many tribes the punishment was death where this law was violated. Further, it was not the propagation of the species but the gratification of lust that moved these sons of Eli, as it is with all who break the law of chastity. The propagation of the species is the last thing such people desire, the one thing they wish to avoid.

The instinct and power of reproduction is the noblest physical gift God has bestowed upon humanity. It makes us partners with God in the creation of the race, and therefore the prostitution of that noble instinct and power is the vilest and worst of all crimes. It has brought into the world more sorrow, shame, disease, ruin, and woe than probably all other crimes combined.

It is far more dangerous to the morals and ultimate well-being of society (to say nothing of the sin against God) for ministers of religion in exalted positions, such as were Eli's sons, to fall into open, flagrant, unblushing immorality and sacrilege than for a judge to cause justice to miscarry, wicked as that is. We will war against and condemn the unjust judge, but what can we do when the sanctions of religion are destroyed, when the holy fear of God is lost, and when all the foundations of morality are rotted away—when our fathers are slaves of lust and full of corruption, and when the mothers of the race, who are our first and best teachers of righteousness and reverence, have no virtue?[1] "If the foundations be destroyed, what can the righteous do?" asked the psalmist (Ps. 11:3 KJV). The sins of Eli's sons seem to me to be in the forefront of the worst sins and crimes mentioned in the Bible or committed among the human race.

My correspondent asked, "Do you consider that it is a more heinous sin to go against forms and ceremonies in connection with religion than it is to deal unrighteously with your neighbor?" I answer, no! But the sons of Eli were doing far more than going "against forms and ceremonies in connection with religion." They were violating the most sacred rights of their neighbors, as well as robbing God of that reverent service which He claimed and which was His due, and so were bringing the service and worship of God into contempt and undermining all morality at one and the same time.

In all this I am not forgetting nor condoning the wickedness of Samuel's sons, nor do I suspect for an instant that they escaped the due judgments of God. Why there is no record of Him dealing with them we do not know. We do know, however, that the Bible declares the principles of God's moral government, and we may rest assured that in every instance He acts in harmony with those principles, whether or not we have a record of it.

NOTE

1. Brengle was referring to women who voluntarily enter into sexual sin—not those who have been forcibly raped. He would agree that a rape victim has committed no sin to deserve this outrageous act of violence against her.

Whitened Harvest Fields 14

Before fields are ready to harvest, they must be plowed and sowed and tilled. When Jesus said to His disciples, "Lift up your eyes, and see that the fields are white for harvest" (John 4:35 ESV), He looked upon a land plowed by God's faithful judgments, sowed deep with the toils and sacrifices of prophets and teachers from Moses to John the Baptist, and watered with the tears and blood of those who had sealed their testimony with their lives.

When young Adoniram Judson went, as the first American missionary, to Burma (today's Myanmar), he found a land covered with age-long growths of superstition and ignorance. For years he plowed and sowed in hope. He struggled with difficulties of language and spiritual darkness.

After seven years, with as yet no converts, a friend wrote and asked him what the prospects were. He replied, "The prospects are as bright as the promises of God."[1] Already the fields had whitened unto harvest, and shortly after he had written to his friend he was reaping what he had sown—thirty thousand souls were won to Jesus and organized for service.

It is not often that someone sows in tears and reaps in joy as Judson did. The plowers and sowers often toil in hope, and yet must wait for the reapers, who enter the fields and gather in the harvests upon which they themselves have bestowed no labor.

At the present time the world seems to be one vast ripened or ripening harvest field, waiting for earnest and skilled reapers. For many centuries it has been plowed and harrowed by wars and commotions, famine and pestilence, storm and earthquake, and where the plowshare has not reached, the spade of disappointment and sorrow, of bereavement and death, has left no sod unturned. Everywhere the soil has been and is being prepared.

Think of the tears that have been shed for a lost world over the years! So many have wept fountains of tears as they looked at men and women rejecting Jesus! Those tears have fallen like rain. They are a part of the sowing. God remembers them all. He treasures them in His bottle (see Ps. 56:8). Has He not said, "Those who plant in tears will harvest with shouts of joy. They weep as they go to plant their seed, but they sing as they return with the harvest" (Ps. 126:5–6 NLT)?

These tears of faithful workers will not be forgotten by God, and we must not forget them, but reckon with them, for they enter into the preparation of the harvest fields of the world.

Think of the prayers that have been offered over the years—prayers for the salvation of the world, for loved ones, children, and wayward and stumbling souls. Think of the prayers for enemies, for the friends of God and all workers of righteousness, in the secret closet, at the family altar, in the public hall, on the street, in the saloon, in the village, in the bungalow, in the city, in the desert, in the wilderness, in the jungle, on shipboard, and on trains, from lonely little quarters and from dying beds! These prayers ascend to God as incense, and they shall surely return in blessing. He does not forget them, and we must not. They have their part in the preparation of the harvest fields.

Think of the testimonies that have been given—testimonies to the enslaving power of sin and the heartache and dissatisfaction surely following its wildest pleasures; testimonies to the arresting, quickening, convicting power of the Holy Spirit, and to the absolute certainty He produces of a life beyond the grave and of judgment to come. Remember all the testimonies to forgiveness of sins, to the witness of the Spirit, and to the comfort of the Holy Spirit; testimonies to the subtle, lurking, hateful presence and power of inbred sin, and of deliverance and cleansing from all its defilement; testimonies to the incoming of the Holy Spirit and to love made perfect. Recall the continual witness to answered prayers, to divine guidance in times of perplexity, to healing in sickness, to deliverance from temptation, to revelations in times of darkness and loneliness, to fresh infusions of strength and hope in seasons of weakness and distress, to secret girdings for the long march and fierce conflicts of life, to renewals of patience and faith in the midst of backslidings and desolations, and to provision of which the world knows nothing (see John 4:32; Rom. 14:17).

Do not let us forget the great host who have ever proclaimed the spiritual realities of a blessed presence going before as a pillar of cloud and fire to the end of the way, of bending skies, of opening heavens, of songs and shoutings, of playing harps, of waving palms, and of rushing angel wings. And last of all, testimonies in the valley to Jesus, the Good Shepherd, folding His dear ones in the eternal embrace of His infinite love, and to triumph forever over death and hell. Oh, the power of testimonies! They have their part in the preparation of the harvest fields.

Think of the songs of the church, including The Salvation Army! How they have captured and held the attention of the world! The careless sinner and the ripened saint alike are arrested by them. How they soften the heart, recall memories of innocent childhood and of mothers' prayers! How they make one see the infant Jesus in the manger, the wrestling Savior in the garden, the dying Son of God on the cross, the bursting tomb, and the great white throne! They interest, alarm, convict, convert, assure, comfort, correct, inspire, guide, instruct, and illumine. They present the law in its most solemn and searching aspects, they declare the judgments of God, they proclaim the gospel in its most tender and fullest invitations, and they embrace all the vital Bible truths. And think how they are sung from the cradle to the grave! Everywhere they are heard and known, and their sound has gone forth to the ends of the earth. They have reached the hearts of men. Songs have their part—an immense part—in the preparation of the harvest fields.

But when we consider the seed sown by Christian workers and Salvation Army soldiers and officers in the fields of the world, we must add to those tears and prayers and testimonies and songs the vast library of literature filled with burning messages of love, yearning appeals, faithful warnings, thrilling experiences, and patient instructions broadcast over the nations.

And to all this must be added the immeasurable influence of saintly lives in shops and mills, in offices and stores, in mines and kitchens, on battlefields and shipboard—the sacrifices, devotion, faithful, patient service, and loving ministries which may be unheralded, and yet which silently hasten the ripening of the harvest.

Truly, with such seed-sowing the harvest must be great, and already it is whitened and waiting for the reapers. Oh, that the Lord of the harvest may send forth reapers into the whitened fields!

When the harvest is ripe, it must be gathered in haste, or it will be lost forever.

Our harvest is at hand. The children are waiting for us to gather them into the Savior's fold. The great crowds of wandering souls at home and abroad need our faithful ministry speedily. How shall we reach them? Where shall we begin? What shall we do?

We must determine to reach them. There must be mighty ingatherings of the people. To this end there must be mighty outpourings of the Spirit, and for this we must give ourselves fully to God. "The one who reaps draws a wage," said Jesus (John 4:36 NIV). Would you like God for your paymaster?

Then we should give ourselves to Him and do His work. If we do this and wait in faith upon Him, we shall see such Pentecosts and revivals as shall pale all those that have gone before.

If we cannot go ourselves, we may send generous help, that others may be sent. Some time ago I met a plain, humble, little woman at one of our camp meetings (revivals) who supported a missionary in a foreign field, was educating his boy, and at the same time was supporting a poor, friendless, old man in her home city. She did it by baking and selling her pies and cake and bread, and putting the proceeds into God's work. God will surely see that she receives wages.

A comparatively poor man in California, of whom a friend of mine wrote, supports eight foreign missionaries. When asked how he did it, he replied that he lived simply and economically. In other words, he denied himself to help to save the world for whom Jesus died. God will see that he receives wages.

Then we can send books and letters out into the fields to reap for us. A gentleman of whom I heard smoked four cigars a day. He learned that for the price of a cigar he could buy a New Testament, and then and there he resolved to quit smoking and with the money saved to buy and scatter New Testaments, which he has since done at the rate of more than one thousand per year. Some time ago a gentleman living hundreds of miles away was passing through this man's native city. He got off the train and spent the day searching for him to thank him for the salvation he had received through the gift of one of those New Testaments. He, too, shall surely receive wages. A letter of cheer and sympathy sent to a distant, lonely reaper in some faraway field will often hearten the worker and hasten the ingathering of the harvest.

Finally, we can all aid in the reaping of the harvest by watchful diligence and expectant faith in prayer. Did not Jesus command us to pray to the Lord of the harvest to send forth laborers? And shall we not fulfill so simple and yet so urgent a command? Multitudes cannot go to fields of active service; many have but little, if any, money to send; but all can pray and plead His promises till He rains righteousness upon the earth.

I know a man intimately who offered himself for foreign service but was rejected. Then he sought and obtained the fullness of the Spirit and gave himself to prayer and such service as he could offer at home. God heard and answered his prayers and blessed his labors, and today he hears—from the four corners of the earth—of those who have been saved and sanctified and blessed through things he has said and done.

God will be well pleased with those who pray, will bless them, and will visit with grace the ends of the earth in answer to their petitions. And they shall surely receive wages.

O Lord, pour out the spirit of prayer upon Your people, and help us to win the world to You!

NOTE

1. David Shibley, *Great for God: Missionaries Who Changed the World* (Green Forest, AR: New Leaf Press, 2012), 49.

Encouraging One Another 15

Over and over again when Moses was preparing to give up his command to Joshua, he encouraged Joshua and exhorted him to "be strong and courageous" (Deut. 31:6, 7, 23 NLT). And so important was this matter, that when Moses was dead, God Himself spoke to Joshua and said, "Be strong and courageous." And again, "Be strong and very courageous." And a third time, "This is my command—be strong and courageous! Do not be afraid or discouraged. For the LORD your God is with you wherever you go" (Josh. 1:6, 7, 9 NLT).

Centuries after, we hear David chanting his glorious psalm and singing, "Wait patiently for the LORD. Be brave and courageous. Yes, wait patiently for the LORD" (Ps. 27:14 NLT).

Hundreds of years later we hear Jesus saying to His little flock, confronted by a proud, fierce religious hierarchy and a world weltering in sin and darkness, "Fear not, little flock" (Luke 12:32 KJV), and "Take courage" (Matt. 14:27 NLT).

Later still we find Paul, in prison waiting to face the monstrous Nero, writing to Timothy from Rome, and saying, "My son, be strong in the grace that is in Christ Jesus" (2 Tim. 2:1 KJV). And to the Ephesians he wrote, "Be strong in the Lord, and in the power of his might" (Eph. 6:10 KJV).

We get a most impressive lesson from the story of the twelve spies sent by Moses to spy out the land of Canaan. Caleb and Joshua returned with cheery hearts, full of courage, and exhorted the people to go up at once and take the land. But ten of the spies gave an evil report, and the people said, "Our brothers have made our hearts melt" (Deut. 1:28 ESV). So they, disheartened and afraid, turned back into the wilderness and wandered to and fro for forty years, till all of them perished there except Joshua and Caleb and the children who were not responsible for the unbelief and disobedience of the multitude.

Thus we learn from the example of our Lord, of Moses, of David, and of Paul, and from the bad effect of the spies' gloomy report, the importance of encouraging rather than discouraging one another. How shall we do this?

1. By keeping in such close touch and communion with God that our faces shine with inward peace and that the joy in our hearts bubbles out in hearty, happy, helpful testimony, not only in worship gatherings, but wherever we meet a brother or sister.

2. By talking more about our victories than our defeats, by thinking and meditating more upon our triumphs than our trials; by counting our blessings, naming them one by one; and by praising God for

what He has done and what He has promised to do. We should not ignore the dark side of things, but we should not magnify it and refuse to see the silver lining to the cloud that is so dark. God is neither dead nor dying, and He does not forget His people who cry to Him night and day, who wait upon Him and do His will. He can open the Red Sea for His people and drown their enemies in its floods (see Ex. 14). He can make Jericho's walls tumble down before His people who go faithfully about their work and who shout when the time comes (see Josh. 6). He can make the valley of dry bones teem with an army of living men (see Ezek. 37:1–14). Oh, He is a wonderful God, and He is our God! There is nothing too hard for Him (see Jer. 32:17). Therefore, we should trust Him, and encourage others to trust Him and to make their prayer to Him in faith and without ceasing.

3. By dwelling more upon the good than the bad in other people. If we would encourage each other, we should talk more about our brothers and sisters who are always exemplary, generous, hardworking, and faithfully serving than about those who are unfaithful, self-centered, and frivolous. We should think and talk more about leaders who by much prayer and work and diligence are bringing souls into the kingdom of God than about those who are embittered and faltering in their commitment.

4. By trying to comprehend something of the vast responsibilities and burdens that press upon our leaders. What a multitude of perplexities harass their minds and try their patience! Therefore we should not be too quick to criticize but more ready to pray for them and give them credit for being sincere and doing the best they can under the circumstances — probably as well or better than we ourselves

would do if we were in their place. They are helped by encouragement even as we are.

I know a Salvation Army officer who received his target for a special fund-raising effort and, without praying over it or looking to the Lord at all, immediately sat down and wrote to his superior a sharp letter of protest and complaint which discouraged him and made it much harder for him to go happily about his work. I know another old officer in that same area who got his target, which seemed fairly large. He saw his superior, and said, "I think you ought to do me a favor." The poor man's heart began to get heavy but at last he asked, "Well, what is it?" To his amazement and joy, the dear officer replied, "Major, I love The Salvation Army and its work, and I think you ought to increase my target." He encouraged his burdened brother, the major. He is an old officer who goes from one average corps to another, but through all the years and amid all the changes and trials and difficulties, he has kept cheery and trustful and sweet in his soul, and God makes him a blessing.

"They help each other and say to their companions, 'Be strong!'" (Isa. 41:6 NIV). Shall you and I not take that text for a motto? We shall save ourselves as well as others from discouragement if we do.

The influence of one gloomy soul can throw a shadow over a whole family. One person in a church who persistently represents the difficulties of every undertaking can slow down the pace of all. At best, they go forward burdened with that person's weight rather than quickened by his or her example. The glorious work of encouraging others is within the capacity of all. The weakest of us can at least say with loving zeal and earnest testimony, "Come, let us tell of the

LORD's greatness; let us exalt his name together. . . . Taste and see that
the LORD is good. Oh, the joys of those who take refuge in him!" (Ps.
34:3, 8 NLT).

Always he was the dullard, always he
Failed of the quick grasp and the flaming word
That still he longed for. Always other men
Outran him for the prize, till in him stirred
Black presage of defeat, and blacker doubts
Of love and wisdom regnant; and he styled
Himself disciple of the obvious,
Predestined failure, blundering fool and smiled.

But with the smile went heartbreak. Then one day
A little lad crept wailing to his knee,
Clasping a broken toy. "I slipped and fell
And broke it. Make another one for me."
Whereat the answer: "I am but a fool.
I can make nothing." "You can mend it then."
"At least I'll try." And patiently and slow
He wrought until the toy was whole again.

And so he learned his lesson. In the world,
The bustling world that has no time to spare
For its hurt children, all compassionate
He sought, and seeking found them everywhere.
And here he wove again a shattered dream,

And there bound up a bruised and broken soul;
And comrades of the fallen and the faint,
He steadied wavering feet to reach their goal.

Forgotten were his dreams of self and fame;
Forever gone the bitterness of loss;
Nor counted he his futile struggles vain,
Since they had taught him how to share the cross
Of weaker brother wisely; and henceforth
He knew no word but *service*. In it lay
Ambition, work, and guerdon, and he poured
His whole soul in the striving of the day.

And when at last he rested, as Love led,
So now it crowned him. And they came with tears—
Those sorrowing hearts that he had comforted—
Bearing the garnered triumphs of their years:
"Not ours, but His, the glory. Dreams come true,
Temptations conquered, lives made clean again,
All these and we ourselves are work of Him
Whom God had set the task of mending men."[1]

NOTE

1. Eleanor Duncan Wood, "A Mender of Men," *The Altoona Tribune*, May 5, 1913, 8.

How a Nobody Became a Somebody 16

It is one of the shortest, simplest stories ever heard, and yet one of the sweetest and most wonderful, as told by Luke. Jesus had been across the little sea and had cast out a legion of devils from a poor fellow. The devils, by His permission, went into a big herd of swine, and the swine rushed off down a precipice and drowned themselves in the sea. They preferred death to devils. Wise pigs!

The men who fed the pigs fled to the city and told what had been done. Then the people came out to Jesus and found the man out of whom the devils had been cast "sitting at Jesus' feet, fully clothed and perfectly sane." But—and this seems strange—"they were all afraid" (Luke 8:35 NLT). Then the people poured in from all the country and "begged Jesus to go away and leave them alone, for a great wave of fear swept over them" (Luke 8:37 NLT).

Jesus did not insist on His right to stay among them, but gently and quietly withdrew, leaving the newly delivered man to evangelize all that country. When Jesus returned to His own side of the sea, He found the people all waiting for Him, and they "welcomed [Him]" (Luke 8:40 NLT).

In the crowd was the ruler of the synagogue, Jairus, who "fell at Jesus' feet, pleading with him to come home with him. His only daughter, who was about twelve years old, was dying" (Luke 8:41–42 NLT). Jesus went, but as He went, "he was surrounded by the crowds" (Luke 8:42 NLT). It was a crowd bursting with curiosity, wondering what He would do next, and determined not to miss the sight. Jairus was an important person, and that added to the interest.

But in the town was a poor, pale-faced, hollow-cheeked, ill-clad woman, who had been sick with an issue of blood for twelve years. The people, no doubt, had grown very tired of seeing her shambling along week after week to see the doctors, upon whom she had spent all her living in a vain twelve years' search and struggle for health. She was just a "nobody"—everybody was tired of the sight of her— but into the throng she came with her bloodless face and tired eyes and shuffling feet and threadbare, faded clothes. The crowd jostled her, crushed her, trampled upon her feet, and blocked her way, but she had a purpose. She was inspired by a new hope. If she could only reach Jesus and touch the hem of His garment, she was sure her long struggle for health would be ended. And so, dodging, ducking under arms, edging her way through the jam of the great, moving crowd, she at last got close to Him, and, stretching forth a wasted, bony hand, she touched His travel-stained, rough, workman's robe, and something happened! Instantly a thrill of health shot through her, and she was well!

And something happened to Jesus! The crowd had been pressing upon and jostling Him, but He felt that touch and said, "Who touched me?" They all denied, and Peter spoke up, pointing out that many had touched Him. But one timid touch was different from all the rest. Jesus said, "Someone deliberately touched me, for I felt healing power go out from me" (Luke 8:46 NLT).

The nobody had suddenly become "somebody." And somebody she was in very truth from that day forth. "When the woman realized that she could not stay hidden, she began to tremble and fell to her knees in front of him. The whole crowd heard her explain why she had touched him and that she had been immediately healed" (Luke 8:47 NLT).

All eyes were turned upon her now. Jairus, the important ruler, was just one of the crowd. Other people were all "nobodies." No one in all that throng had eyes for anybody else but that shrinking, trembling woman, and Jesus.

And then the sweetest words she ever heard dropped from His dear lips: "'Daughter,' he said to her, 'your faith has made you well. Go in peace'" (Luke 8:48 NLT). And in peace she went.

I venture to think that from that hour she was by far the most interesting woman in that town. The people would talk about her. They would seek her out, and when she walked the street the children would stop their playing, the women their work, and the men their business, to look at her and watch her as far as their eyes could follow her.

She was now "somebody," eclipsing everybody else in that old town. No, not everybody! There was a twelve-year-old girl who was most interesting and much talked about, too—Jairus's daughter. Jesus was on the way to heal her when this woman stopped the procession, and during the delay the little girl died.

Someone came and told Jairus, saying, "Your daughter is dead. There's no use troubling the Teacher now" (Luke 8:49 NLT). But when Jesus heard it, He answered, "Don't be afraid. Just have faith, and she will be healed" (Luke 8:50 NLT). And He went and raised her from the dead.

Now I am sure that while that woman was the most talked about and most interesting woman in the town, that girl was the most interesting child. Those were the two "somebodies" of that whole country round about, and the secret was that they had come into touch with Jesus. Real faith in Jesus, vital union with Him, will always make an interesting somebody out of a dull nobody.

The child couldn't go to Jesus; she was dead. So He went to her. But the woman had to go to Jesus, and this was not easy. The crowd was in the way, and possibly some of them purposely blocked her way. Others may have sneered at her and asked her what was her haste, and what she meant by edging in front of folks who had as much right on the street as she. But she shut her ears, or heard as one who was deaf. She kept her own secrets and pressed on as well as she could until she touched Him. And that touch gave her all her heart's desire and rewarded all her effort.

So, today, people who go to Jesus do not always find it easy. Other people get in the way. Sometimes they stoutly oppose; sometimes they sneer and ridicule. Cares and fears and doubts throng and press around the seeker; darkness of mind and soul obscures the way. But there is nothing else to do except to press on, right on and on. And those who press on and on will find Him, reach Him, touch Him, and get all their hearts' desires and be rewarded above all they ask or think.

It is true! I know it is, for I myself so sought and found Him and was satisfied. And He satisfies me still. He is a wonderful Savior!

Don't underestimate the power of God in you, nor yet what you, by working quietly and steadily with Him, may accomplish. Paul told us not to think too highly of ourselves (see Rom. 12:3). But he said of himself, "I can do all things through him who strengthens me" (Phil. 4:13 ESV). He thought of himself linked to the illimitable strength of Christ, and therefore omnipotent for any work Christ set him to do.

The future before you is big with opportunities and possibilities. Open doors on every hand invite you to enter and do service for the Master and for others, and the strength that worked in Paul works in you, if you do not hinder it by selfishness and unbelief.

No one can tell how much the future spread of God's kingdom may depend on you. "See how great a forest a little fire kindles!" (James 3:5 NKJV). Keep the fire of love and faith and sweet hopefulness burning in your heart, and you may start a blaze that will someday sweep the country or the world. Whoever you are—whether you are a respected leader or the newest follower of Jesus on earth—upon you the glory of the Lord may so shine that through you a great quickening may come to your corps, church, workplace, neighborhood, or home that will make the future so bright that the past will pale before it.

Would you like to be that man or woman? Then seek the Lord, daily, constantly, with your whole heart. Seek Him through His Word. Seek Him in secret prayer in the night watches and in the noonday. Seek Him in glad obedience. Seek Him in childlike faith. Seek nothing for yourself. "Do you seek great things for yourself? Seek them not" (Jer. 45:5 ESV) is the word of the Lord to you if you want Him to work mightily in you.

If honor comes, thank God, lay it at the torn feet of Jesus, and forget it, lest it ruin you. "Love . . . is not puffed up" (1 Cor. 13:4 NKJV). If honor comes not—if you seem to be forgotten in the distributions of rewards and honors and promotions—still thank God and go on. Seek the honor which comes from God alone, the honor of walking in the footsteps of Jesus, of loving, serving, sacrificing, suffering for others, and you shall have your reward. You surely shall, and it will be great, exceeding abundantly above all you ask or think. The crowning joy is yet to come. The final and all-sufficient and unfading rewards will be given by the Master's own hand. Don't worry if some lesser reward eludes you, lest through your fretting you lose the honor that comes from God alone and miss the crown Christ keeps in store for you. Beware of fretting over rewards and promotions and honors given by mere mortals! It is a snare set for you by the Enemy of your soul. Take your eyes off other people and see Jesus only. If others are good and spiritual and devoted to the Lord, emulate them, follow them as they follow Christ; but if they are faulty, don't worry about them (see Ps. 37:1–5), but pray for them and remember the word of Jesus to Peter: "What is that to you? You follow me!" (John 21:22 ESV).

Be filled with the spirit of Jonathan and his armor bearer. They went up alone and routed the Philistines. They were jealous for the glory of God and the overthrow of His impudent and insolent foes and were willing to jeopardize their lives to defeat God's enemies (see 1 Sam. 14).

Be filled with the spirit of Paul, who wrote, "Whatever gain I had, I counted as loss for the sake of Christ" (Phil. 3:7 ESV) and, "My life is worth nothing to me" (Acts 20:24 NLT) and, "I will very gladly spend and be spent for you; though the more abundantly I love you, the less I be loved" (2 Cor. 12:15 KJV).

May this spirit of Paul abound in you! This is holiness. This is heaven begun. This is the Spirit of Jesus still abiding in men and women.

Don't forget that "you He made alive, who were dead in trespasses and sins" (Eph. 2:1 NKJV). And don't forget "that few of you were wise in the world's eyes or powerful or wealthy when God called you. Instead"—note well—"God chose things the world considers foolish in order to shame those who think they are wise. And he chose things that are powerless to shame those who are powerful. God chose [What a chooser is God!] things despised by the world, things counted as nothing at all, and used them to bring to nothing what the world considers important. As a result, no one can ever boast in the presence of God. [But] God has united you with Christ Jesus" (1 Cor. 1:26–30 NLT).

My Testimony

Today (June 1, 1919), I am fifty-nine years old, and there is not a cloud in my spiritual heaven. My mouth is full of laughter and my heart is full of joy. I feel so sorry for folks who don't like to grow old, who are trying all the time to hide the fact that they are growing old and who are ashamed to tell how old they are. I revel in my years. They enrich me. If God should say to me, "I will let you begin over again, and you may have your youth back once more," I would say, "O dear Lord, if you do not mind, I prefer to go on growing old!"

I would not exchange the peace of mind, the abiding rest of soul, the measure of wisdom I have gained from the sweet and bitter and perplexing experiences of life, and the confirmed faith I now have in the moral order of the universe and in the unfailing mercies and love of God, for all the bright but uncertain hopes and tumultuous joys of youth. Indeed, I would not!

These are the best years of my life—the sweetest, the freest from
anxious care and fear. The way grows brighter, the birds sing sweeter,
the winds blow softer, the sun shines more radiantly than ever before.
I suppose my outward man is perishing, but my inward man is being
joyously renewed day by day.

Victor Hugo supposedly said, "For half a century I have been writing my thoughts in prose, verse, history, philosophy, drama, romance,
tradition, satire, ode, songs. I have tried all. But I feel that I have not
said the thousandth part of what is in me." And he said, "Winter is on
my head [but] eternal spring is in my heart."[1] Truly, that is the way I
feel these days.

One of the prayers of my heart as I grow older is that of David: "Now
that I am old and gray, do not abandon me, O God. Let me proclaim
your power to this new generation, your mighty miracles to all who
come after me" (Ps. 71:18 NLT).

David was jealous for the glory of God and for the highest well-
being of his own generation and every generation that was to follow.
And he prayed no selfish prayer, but poured out his heart to God that
he might so live and speak and write that God's glory and goodness
and power might be made known to the people of his own time and
to all who should come after him. And how wonderfully God heard
and answered his prayer! Oh, that God would grant me a like grace!

If the eye of any friend falls upon this testimony, let me beseech
you to unite with me and for me in this prayer of David, which I make
my own.

This past year has been wonderful. Since the first of January, considerably over three thousand souls have knelt at the penitent form in

my meetings, seeking pardon and purity. Seldom have I seen such manifestations of God's presence and power as during these months. I rejoice in God my Savior, and my soul magnifies the Lord (see Luke 1:46–47).

I wish I knew more of the secret of growing old gladly and could better tell it to others. But some lessons that I have learned, or partially learned, I here pass on: Have faith in God—in His providence, His superintending care, and His unfailing love. Accept the bitter with the sweet and rejoice in both. The bitter may be better for us than the sweet. Don't grow impatient and fretful. If you fall into many trials, count it all joy, knowing that the trial of your faith produces patience; "let patience have her perfect work, that you may be perfect and entire, wanting nothing" (James 1:4 KJV).

What a high state of grace that is—to be "perfect and entire, wanting nothing"! And yet it is to be attained through the joyful acceptance of annoying trials and petty vexations, as a part of God's discipline (see James 1:2–7).

Keep a heart full of love toward everybody. Learn to be patient with folks who try your patience. If you can't love them naturally and easily, then love them with compassion and pity. But love them, pray for them, and don't carry around hard thoughts and feelings toward them.

Here is a tender little poem by Whittier, our Quaker poet:

> My heart was heavy, for its trust had been
> Abused, its kindness answered with foul wrong;
> So, turning gloomily from my fellow men,
> One summer Sabbath day I strolled among
> The green mounds of the village burial place,

Where, pondering how all human love and hate

Find one sad level; and how, soon or late,

Wronged and wrong-doer, each with meekened face,

And cold hands folded over a still heart,

Pass the green threshold of our common grave,

Whither all footsteps tend, whence none depart,

Awed for myself and pitying my race,

Our common sorrow, like a mighty wave,

Swept all my pride away, and, trembling I forgave![2]

Don't waste time and fritter away faith by living in the past, by mourning over the failures of yesterday and the long ago. Commit them to God and look upward and onward. "Forgetting those things which are behind," said Paul, "and reaching forth unto those things which are before, I press toward the mark for the prize of the high calling of God in Christ Jesus" (Phil. 3:13–14 KJV).

Someone has said that there are two things we should never worry over and two days about which we should never be anxious. First, we should not worry over the things that we can help, but set to work diligently to help them. Second, we should not worry over the things that we cannot help, but commit them to God and go on with the duties close at hand. Again, we should not be anxious about yesterday; our anxieties will not mend its failures nor restore its losses. Second, we should not be anxious about tomorrow. We cannot borrow its grace. Why, then, should we borrow its care?

Give good heed to failing bodily strength. The Salvation Army's founder, William Booth, once said that the body and soul, being very near neighbors, have a great influence upon each other. We must remember that our bodies are to be treated like our beast, and Solomon said, "Whoever is righteous has regard for the life of his beast" (Prov. 12:10 ESV). When we were young, we could stay up all night, eat ice cream, nuts, and cake at midnight, and go about our work the next day, not much the worse, so far as we could judge, for the shameful mistreatment of our bodies. But woe unto men and women who, growing old, think they can treat their bodies so!

We must remember that our bodies are the temple of the Holy Spirit. Hence, while they need sufficient nourishing food and restful sleep, they must in no sense be pampered, and all nervous excesses must be strictly avoided or the body will react upon the mind and the spirit and weakness and impatience and gloom will cloud the soul. And then, instead of ripening into mellow sweetness with age, the soul will turn bitter and sour—and what can be more pitiful than an embittered and soured old soul?

But oh, the joy of living a life of sobriety, faith, quietness and confidence, of meekness, service, and love, and of "growing in every way more and more like Christ, who is the head of his body, the church" (Eph. 4:15 NLT). Such a life is never old, but eternally renewing itself, eternally youthful, like a springing, sparkling fountain that is fed by unfailing waters that flow down from the heights of the everlasting hills. "I take refuge in you, LORD. . . . How great is the goodness that you've reserved for those who honor you, that you commit to those who take refuge in you—in the sight of everyone!" (Ps. 31:1, 19 CEB).

Grow old along with me!

The best is yet to be,

The last of life, for which the first was made:

Our times are in His hand

Who saith, "A whole I planned,

Youth shows but half; trust God: see all, nor be afraid" . . .

Then, welcome each rebuff

That turns earth's smoothness rough,

Each sting that bids nor sit nor stand but go!

Be our joys three-parts pain!

Strive, and hold cheap the strain;

Learn, nor account the pang; dare, never grudge the throe! . . .

He fixed thee mid this dance

Of plastic circumstance,

This present, thou, forsooth, wouldst fain arrest;

Machinery just meant

To give thy soul its bent,

Try thee and turn thee forth, sufficiently impressed . . .

The future I may face now I have proved the past.[3]

NOTES

1. M. Houssaye, "When Victor Hugo Is a Hundred Years Old," *The Pennsylvania School Journal* 60, no. 2 (August 1911): 63–64. The text is from an imagined conversation between Hugo and four atheists.

2. John Greenleaf Whittier, "My Heart Was Heavy," eds. Eliakim Littell and Robert S. Littell, *Littell's Living Age* 129, no. 1662 (April 15, 1876): 130.

3. Robert Browning, "Rabbi Ben Ezra," *Poems of Robert Browning* (London: Oxford University Press, 1923), 636–638.

Samuel L. Brengle's Holy Life Series

This series comprises the complete works of Samuel L. Brengle, combining all nine of his original books into six volumes, penned by one of the great minds on holiness. Each volume has been lovingly edited for modern readership by popular author (and long-time Brengle devotee) Bob Hostetler. Brengle's authentic voice remains strong, now able to more relevantly engage today's disciples of holiness. These books are must-haves for all who would seriously pursue and understand the depths of holiness in the tradition of John Wesley.

Helps to Holiness
ISBN: 978-1-63257-064-2
eBook: 978-1-63257-065-9

The Heart of Holiness
ISBN: 978-1-63257-066-6
eBook: 978-1-63257-067-3

The Servant's Heart
ISBN: 978-1-63257-068-0
eBook: 978-1-63257-069-7

Ancient Prophets and Modern Problems
ISBN: 978-1-63257-070-3
eBook: 978-1-63257-071-0

Come Holy Guest
ISBN: 978-1-63257-072-7
eBook: 978-1-63257-073-4

Resurrection Life and Power
ISBN: 978-1-63257-074-1
eBook: 978-1-63257-075-8

**Samuel L. Brengle's
Holy Life Series Box Set**
ISBN: 978-1-63257-076-5

SAMUEL L. BRENGLE'S HOLY LIFE SERIES

RESURRECTION LIFE
AND POWER

Bob Hostetler, General Editor

wesleyan
PUBLISHING HOUSE
wphstore.com

CREST BOOKS

Copyright © 2016 by The Salvation Army
Published by Wesleyan Publishing House
Indianapolis, Indiana 46250
Printed in the United States of America
ISBN: 978-1-63257-074-1
ISBN (e-book): 978-1-63257-075-8

Library of Congress Cataloging-in-Publication Data

Brengle, Samuel Logan, 1860-1936.
  Resurrection life and power / Samuel L. Brengle ; Bob Hostetler, general editor.
    pages cm. -- (Samuel L. Brengle's holy life series)
  Originally published: London : Salvationist Pub. and Supplies, 1953.
  ISBN 978-1-63257-074-1 (pbk.)
  1. Resurrection. 2. Christian life. I. Hostetler, Bob, 1958- editor. II. Title.
  BT873.B74 2016
  232'.5--dc23

                                    2015035642

Scripture quotations marked (NLT) are taken from the Holy Bible, New Living Translation, copyright © 1996, 2004, 2007, 2013 by Tyndale House Foundation. Used by permission of Tyndale House Publishers, Inc., Carol Stream, Illinois 60188. All rights reserved.

Scripture quotations marked (KJV) are taken from the HOLY BIBLE, KING JAMES VERSION.

Scripture quotations marked (ESV) are from The Holy Bible, English Standard Version® (ESV®), copyright © 2001 by Crossway, a publishing ministry of Good News Publishers. Used by permission. All rights reserved.

Scripture quotations marked (NIV) are taken from the Holy Bible, New International Version®, NIV ®. Copyright © 1973, 1978, 1984, 2011 by Biblica, Inc. Used by permission of Zondervan. All rights reserved worldwide. www.zondervan.com. The "NIV" and "New International Version" are trademarks registered in the United States Patent and Trademark Office by Biblica, Inc.

Scripture quotations marked (CEV) are taken from the *Contemporary English Version* © 1991, 1992, 1995 by American Bible Society. Used by Permission.

Scripture quotations marked (NKJV) are taken from the New King James Version. Copyright © 1982 by Thomas Nelson, Inc. Used by permission. All rights reserved.

Contents

Preface

Samuel Logan Brengle was an influential author, teacher, and preacher
on the doctrine of holiness in the late nineteenth to early twentieth century,
serving from 1887–1931 as an active officer (minister) in The Salvation
Army. In 1889 while he and his wife, Elizabeth Swift Brengle, were
serving as corps officers (pastors) in Boston, Massachusetts, a brick
thrown by a street "tough" smashed Brengle's head against a door frame
and caused an injury severe enough to require more than nineteen
months of convalescence. During that treatment and recuperation
period, he began writing articles on holiness for The Salvation Army's
publication, *The War Cry*, which were later collected and published
as a "little red book" under the title *Helps to Holiness*. That book's
success led to eight others over the next forty-five years: *Heart Talks
on Holiness*, *The Way of Holiness*, *The Soul-Winner's Secret*, *When
the Holy Ghost Is Come*, *Love-Slaves*, *Resurrection Life and Power*,

Ancient Prophets and Modern Problems, and *The Guest of the Soul* (published in his retirement in 1934).

By the time of his death in 1936, Commissioner Brengle was an internationally renowned preacher and worldwide ambassador of holiness. His influence continues today, perhaps more than any Salvationist in history besides the founders, William and Catherine Booth.

I hope that the revised and updated editions of his books that comprise the Samuel L. Brengle's Holy Life Series will enhance and enlarge that influence, introduce these writings to new readers, and create fresh interest in those who already know the godly wisdom and life-changing power of these volumes.

While I have taken care to preserve the integrity, impact, and voice of the original writing, I have carefully and prayerfully made changes that I hope will facilitate greater understanding and appreciation of Brengle's words for modern readers. These changes include:

- Revising archaic terms (such as the use of King James English) and updating the language to reflect more contemporary usage (such as occasionally employing more inclusive gender references);
- Shortening and simplifying sentence structure and revising punctuation to conform more closely to contemporary practice;
- Explaining specific references of The Salvation Army that will not be familiar to the general population;
- Updating Scripture references (when possible retaining the King James Version—used exclusively in Brengle's writings—but frequently incorporating modern versions, especially when doing so will aid the reader's comprehension and enjoyment);

- Replacing Roman numerals with Arabic numerals and spelled out Scripture references for the sake of those who are less familiar with the Bible;

- Citing Scripture quotes not referenced in the original and noting the sources for quotes, lines from hymns, etc.;

- Aligning all quoted material to the source (Brengle, who often quoted not only Scripture, but also poetry from memory, often quoted loosely in speaking and writing);

- Adding occasional explanatory phrases or endnotes to identify people or events that might not be familiar to modern readers;

- Revising or replacing some chapter titles, and (in *Ancient Prophets and Modern Problems*) moving one chapter to later in the book; and

- Deleting the prefaces that introduced each book and epigraphs that preceded some chapters.

In the preface to Brengle's first book, Commissioner (later General) Bramwell Booth wrote, "This book is intended to help every reader of its pages into the immediate enjoyment of Bible holiness. Its writer is an officer of The Salvation Army who, having a gracious experience of the things whereof he writes, has been signally used of God, both in life and testimony, to the sanctifying of the Lord's people, as well as in the salvation of sinners. I commend him and what he has here written down to every lover of God and His kingdom here on earth."

In the preface to Brengle's last book, *The Guest of the Soul*, The Salvation Army's third general (and successor to Bramwell Booth) wrote: "These choice contributions . . . will, I am sure, serve to

strengthen the faith of the readers of this book and impress upon them the joyousness of life when the heart has been opened to the Holy Guest of the Soul."

I hope and pray that this updated version of Brengle's writings will further those aims.

—Bob Hostetler

general editor

Resurrection Power 1

With the death of Christ, the hopes of His disciples also died. When the tortured, crucified Jesus gave His last expiring cry on the cross, the disciples' faith suffered a total eclipse. Three years before, with bounding joy and swelling hopes, they had left all to follow Him. They had heard His matchless words. They had seen His wondrous works. They had felt His spirit of infinite compassion and tenderness, of absolute justice, of righteousness, and of holiness, and they were sure that He was their King. They expected at any time to see Him take the reins of the government, assert His authority and power, cast out Pilate and his hated Roman garrison, ascend the throne of David, and restore their fathers' kingdom to greater splendor than that of Solomon's time. So sure were they of this that they wrangled among themselves as to which of them should be the greatest in this ideal kingdom.

Jesus told them plainly that they misunderstood His spirit and mission—that He would be despised, rejected, and killed, but that He would rise again. But they did not understand this. They did not believe it. Peter boldly contradicted Jesus and said this should not be, until Jesus had to rebuke him sharply, saying, "Get away from me, Satan! You are a dangerous trap to me. You are seeing things merely from a human point of view, not from God's" (Matt. 16:23 NLT).

Later they came up to the Passover at Jerusalem and were met by immense throngs of people casting their garments and palm branches before Him, and crying out, "Hosanna to the Son of David! Blessed is he who comes in the name of the Lord! Hosanna in the highest!" (Matt. 21:9 ESV).

How these lowly followers must have exulted in that hour! Now Jesus would ascend the throne. Now He would be a king. Now they would share in His glory, and all of their old neighbors would stare and gape in amazement and envious wonder. But the tide turned. The fickle multitude that had so royally welcomed Him one day were crying out, "Crucify Him," the next, and instead of ascending a throne He was hung upon a cross. He had a crown upon His head, but it was of thorns. A man was on His right hand, and another on His left, but they were crucified thieves. He was coming into His kingdom, but it was by the narrow gate of death and the hard way of the tomb. He had talked of His kingdom and glory, but what did this shameful death mean? How could they understand Him? Well, they did not understand, and when He died, their hopes died, too. However, they assisted at His burial, and then, disappointed and disillusioned, they went their way.

They forgot that He had said that He would rise again. Strange that they would forget such a startling statement. But they did forget, or else they might not have become so hopeless. But the fulfillment of God's promises does not depend on our feeble memory of those promises. Jesus rose as He had said. He laid down His life, and He took it up again. The grave could not hold the Prince of life. He broke its bars. He scattered its darkness. He conquered its terrors. He robbed it of its victory. "O death, where is your victory? O death, where is your sting?" (1 Cor. 15:55 NLT).

The disheartened disciples saw Him. They looked again into His eyes of infinite comprehension and compassion. They listened again to His voice that stirred all the deeps of memory, called forth all the holiest affections, and aroused all the old awe, wonder, and enthusiasm. "By many infallible proofs" (Acts 1:3 KJV) He made them to know that it was He, the very same Jesus whom they had loved and for whom they had forsaken all—the Christ of God; the patient Teacher; the dear Friend; the faithful Reprover; the bold, uncompromising, unfaltering Leader; the deathless Lover; the crucified and dead but now living Redeemer and Savior; their Daysman; their Kinsman; God's Lamb that takes away the sin of the world. On that fateful Good Friday when Jesus died, the bewildered disciples found all their hopes turned to ashes, but on Easter morning the ashes burst into quenchless flame, for Jesus was risen! And many years afterward, Peter—with overflowing gratitude and joy—wrote, "Blessed be the God and Father of our Lord Jesus Christ! According to his great mercy, he has caused us to be born again to a living hope through the resurrection of Jesus Christ from the dead" (1 Pet. 1:3 ESV).

The resurrection was God's complete attestation and vindication of Jesus as the Christ of God, His well-beloved Son in whom He was well pleased. At Jesus' baptism, the Holy Spirit, in the form of a dove, had descended upon Him, and a voice from heaven had declared, "This is my beloved Son, with whom I am well pleased" (Matt. 3:17 ESV). But later, even John the Baptist began to doubt and sent messengers to Jesus to ask, "Are you the Messiah we've been expecting, or should we keep looking for someone else?" (Matt. 11:3 NLT). But the resurrection was God's complete answer to every question, and it swept away forever every ground of doubt. As Paul declared (in a complex but wonderful sentence), the lowly, suffering, crucified Jesus was "declared to be the Son of God in power according to the Spirit of holiness by his resurrection from the dead" (Rom. 1:4 ESV).

Jesus Christ was the revelation of God. In Him the Father was unveiled. The Father's heart of love, pity, sympathetic understanding, and infinite yearning—more tender and unfailing than that of a mother—was made known in Jesus. In Him, too, was seen the Father's hatred of sin, His holiness, His spotless purity, His exact and unswerving justice, and His detestation of all unrighteousness.

Jesus came into the world to reveal the Father and to do the Father's will. He also came to save lost humanity, to save us from our sins and from ourselves—from our bad nature, our corruption, our bent toward evil, our pride, our lust, and our hearts' deceitfulness. He came to bring us back to God, into reunion with God, in our affections, sympathies, will, and nature. He came to make us holy, happy, dutiful, unafraid children of the Father once more. And the resurrection was the final stone in the everlasting foundation on which this work was to be built.

We are saved by faith. Faith links us to God. As we trust Him, He can work in us and do for us. But when we doubt, we frustrate His good will toward us and prevent His love from accomplishing all His kindly purposes for us. We must trust Him or He cannot save us. Jesus was constantly endeavoring to establish faith in His disciples' hearts. He wrought His miracles and uttered His wonderful sayings that they might believe, and yet they continued to fall back into doubt. Tired and weary, He fell asleep one evening in their little boat. A storm swept down upon them and, in a panic, they awakened Him and said, "Teacher, don't you care that we're going to drown?" (Mark 4:38 NLT). He arose, stilled the storm, and quietly asked, "Why are you afraid? Do you still have no faith?" (Mark 4:40 NLT). Again and again He had to ask them why they doubted.

Just before His crucifixion Jesus told them plainly that He had come from the Father and that He was going back to the Father. With a glimpse of fleeting insight and in a burst of enthusiasm they exclaimed, "At last you are speaking plainly and not figuratively. Now we understand. . . . From this we believe that you came from God" (John 16:29–30 NLT). But Jesus knew them better than they knew themselves. He knew that the foundation He was building for their faith and hope was not yet complete. He knew how weak and uncertain their faith was, and He quietly replied, "Do you finally believe? But the time is coming—indeed it's here now—when you will be scattered, each one going his own way, leaving me alone. Yet I am not alone because the Father is with me" (John 16:31–32 NLT).

And true, they left Him alone. They fled away, and He died alone. The foundation of their faith was not fully laid by His life, miracles,

and words, but it was made complete by His resurrection from the
dead. Now they could and would and did believe with a

> Faith that will not shrink,
> Though pressed by every foe;
> That will not tremble on the brink
> Of any earthly woe.[1]

Now they had a foundation for faith on which they could build
God's city, and on which they could stand unshaken and exultant,
"when earth's foundations melt away."[2]

All they needed now was the baptism of Jesus, the baptism with
the Holy Spirit and fire, which would purify their hearts and empower
them "with inner strength through his Spirit" (Eph. 3:16 NLT), that
Christ might live in their hearts by faith. This, after patient waiting and
fervent prayer, they received on the day of Pentecost.

Through the faith perfected in them by Jesus' resurrection, they
were led to wait for and receive His baptism with the Holy Spirit, and
Christ was revealed in their hearts.

With the sure knowledge they now had, and with Christ's Spirit in
them, they had faith to face a frowning world and turn it upside down.
They could now go forth and overthrow every empire of evil and top-
ple every throne founded on injustice and upheld by the pomp of mere
earthly pride and power. With them came the almighty Holy Spirit. All
power in heaven and earth belonged to their Master, and they were His
ministers, His ambassadors. He was behind them, with them, and in
them, and His Spirit went before them. They spoke and worked by

His authority, and all His infinite resources of power, love, patience, and long-suffering were at the disposal of their faith. They could ask for what was needed to accomplish the superhuman task He had given them, and it would be given to them. They were insufficient of themselves for their work, but their sufficiency was of God. They were to know the power of His resurrection and be made partakers of that power. The power that had raised their Master from the dead was the same power that worked in them. Oh, the wonder of it! It inspired them. It thrilled them. It made them unafraid and unconquerable in the face of all the massed and mocking forces of sin and hell.

They looked into the eyes of their foes without quailing. They faced whippings, stonings, and imprisonments without faltering. If they suffered for the cause and name of their dear Master, they counted it a joy. When they were imprisoned, they sang psalms in the night, and the jailer became a Christian. They rejoiced in tribulation. They gloried in affliction and distress. They smiled at death, for they knew it had no sting for them. They shouted over the grave, for it was already spoiled and robbed of its victory. They posted over land and sea to tell all the world the wondrous story of the resurrection. And everywhere they went, the heavenly power went with them, and hoary superstitions and the haunting fears of sin's dark night began to vanish away.

Henceforth, for them to live was Christ, and to die was gain (see Phil. 1:21). He was the Vine, they were the branches, and as the branch receives life and power from the vine, so their life and power were from Christ. And as the vine produces fruit through the branches, so the fruit of Christ's life and Spirit was formed in them.

In Him was sacrificial, deathless love, and this love was reproduced in them. Oh, how they loved! They loved their enemies. They
prayed for their persecutors. When Stephen was stoned to death, he
prayed, "Lord, don't charge them with this sin!" (Acts 7:60 NLT). And
Paul, when the love of some of his brothers failed, wrote, "I will
gladly spend myself and all I have for you, even though it seems that
the more I love you, the less you love me" (2 Cor. 12:15 NLT).

Joy, the very joy of Jesus, was perfected in them. He bequeathed
His joy to them (see John 15:11). When He died, He was so poor He
had little to leave them but His joy. But what a treasure!

With that joy, He also left them His peace. "Peace I leave with
you" (John 14:27 KJV). It was the resurrection peace, the peace of an
assured and endless life over which death has no power. Storms might
rage around them, but that deep central peace flowed on undisturbed,
for it flowed into them from the Father, through their union with the
resurrected Jesus.

Patience was perfected in them. Eternity was in their hearts. They
were no longer creatures of time, and they could well afford to wait
and bear long with the poor slaves of sin around them, as their dear
Savior did. Oh, how patient He had been with them! And for His sake
and by His indwelling Spirit they, too, became patient.

The gentleness, goodness, faith, and meekness of their Lord were
also reproduced in them and made manifest in word and deed. It was
Christ living His life in them.

Can this resurrection life and power be yours and mine? Yes, it is
for all. It is for every living branch, great or small, that is in the true
Vine. Do you believe that He rose from the dead? Do you believe that

He is the living Christ and not simply a dead Jew in a Jerusalem grave? And do you with joy confess this with your mouth? Then this resurrection life and power and undying hope is yours, if you will receive it. "If you openly declare that Jesus is Lord and believe in your heart that God raised him from the dead, you will be saved" (Rom. 10:9 NLT), and in that salvation are all the vast powers and deathless hopes and overflowing joys of His resurrection life, to be drawn upon by faith, as those with an account draw money from their bank to meet their need. And now according to our faith it will be unto us.

> No human or angelic mind
> Had ever dreamed the Son of God
> On Calvary's cruel cross should die
> To save us by His precious blood.
> He died for rebels; now He lives
> And reigns for us in glory bright;
> His precious blood in peace He pleads
> For us, the newborn sons of light.[3]

All is ours, since we are Christ's and Christ is God's.

NOTES

1. William Hiley Bathurst, "Oh, for a Faith That Will Not Shrink," 1831, public domain.

2. Johann A. Rothe, "Now I Have Found the Ground Wherein," trans. John Wesley, 1754, public domain.

3. Author unknown, "When Christ the Lord at God's Command," *Salvation Army Songs,* comp. William Booth (London: The Salvation Army Book Department, 1911), 568.

Evidences and Practical Lessons

After John the Baptist died, his amazed and sorrowful disciples buried him then went and told Jesus, and from that time we hear no more of them. They ceased to be a distinct company of men. The power that united them failed in John's death, and they fell apart and were soon lost in the crowd.

When Jesus died and was buried, we find the same disintegrating forces at work among His disciples. Amazed, disappointed, and heartbroken, they said, "We had hoped that he was the one to redeem Israel" (Luke 24:21 ESV), and they started for their homes.

But a wonderful thing happened. Jesus' scattering, discomfited disciples were rallied by the strange story that His grave was empty, that an angel had been seen sitting in the vacant tomb, that a vision of angels had said He was alive, and that Jesus Himself had appeared to certain of their company. From that hour we find the power that bound

them together strengthening until some fifty days later, on the day of
Pentecost, by the descent of the Holy Spirit upon them, they are
welded into a divine oneness such as was never known before, and
Jesus' prayer—that they might be one, even as He and the Father are
one—was answered.

How different are the graves of John and Jesus! That of John is
still shrouded in darkness, but that of Jesus is aflame with light. It is
the first rift in the surrounding gloom through which we look up into
the face of angels, see the future world, and get foregleams of the full
glory yet to be revealed.

In the presence of Jesus' resurrection, all other miracles pale like the
stars before the rising sun. It is the crowning evidence that He is the
Son of God, and that "as the Father has life in Himself, so He has
granted the Son to have life in Himself" (John 5:26 NKJV), with power
to destroy death and give eternal life to those who believe in His name.

The strife is o'er, the battle done;
The victory of life is won;
The song of triumph has begun.[1]

But how do we know that He rose again?

1. We know it by the testimony of those who saw Him: the women,
Peter, the two on the road to Emmaus, the other disciples, and then
some five hundred to whom He showed Himself. And, finally, Paul,
like a baby whose birth was long overdue (see 1 Cor. 15:8).

Again and again, under varying circumstances and before increasing
numbers of unimpeachable witnesses, Jesus showed Himself, until

the last vestige of doubt that their Lord had risen vanished from the disciples' minds. And this became the foundational fact upon which they took their stand and preached that He was the Son of God— preached with such power that their very enemies were won over by the thousands and a great company of the priests who had consented to and demanded Jesus' death were obedient to the faith (see Acts 6:7). They testified to it, preached it, wrote about it, gloried in it, triumphed over all their fears, and faced martyrdom, joyously dying in that faith.

2. We know it by the fact that the disciples—though they were poor and unlearned, despised and hated, and at first were bewildered and confounded by their Master's death—were not scattered and lost as John's disciples were, but were joined together in a far stronger and more vital and joyous union after the death of Jesus than when He was with them in the flesh.

3. We know it by the church that dates back to within fifty days of the death of Jesus, and was built upon the faith that He arose from the dead. Such an institution as the Christian church could not have been built upon a falsehood.

4. But the most vital evidence of Jesus' resurrection—that which brings the most complete satisfaction to the heart that comes into possession of it and confirms all other evidence—is that which is given to us individually with the baptism of the Holy Spirit.

When my friend in New York sails for Liverpool, how do I know that he has arrived safely? I know it by the cablegram or letter he sends back to me. How do I know that Jesus is not dead, but living, not buried still in Joseph's rocky tomb, but risen and ascended to the right hand of the Father where all power in heaven and earth is His?

I know it by the Holy Spirit whom He has sent to me, that fills my whole soul with light and love, and makes me know my risen Lord better than I knew my mother. This is the crowning evidence, which He gives to those who obey Him.

The other evidences are historical and general and are to be sifted, considered, and weighed as is the evidence of any other historical fact. The evidence given in the baptism of the Holy Spirit is personal and living, confirming the faith of him or her who receives it. The former may satisfy the head; this satisfies the heart.

The external historical evidences are for the natural being. The inward spiritual evidence is for the spiritual being. The first are given once and for all, are never repeated, and cannot be added to nor subtracted from. The latter is repeated as often as God can find a hungry, obedient heart that will be satisfied with nothing short of knowing Jesus and being filled with His Spirit. It is God's new, ever-recurring, ever-living and eternal answer to the soul that from the heart sings, "Thee to know is all my cry."[2]

He has given this evidence to me. Some precious lessons lie on the surface of the Scriptures, but others must be dug for as for silver and gold. Some are learned in the school of obedience and others in the school of affliction. Some are revealed to us by a great burst of light like the sun shining through rifts in thick clouds, and some dawn upon us and unfold so gradually that we can hardly tell when we came into possession of them. So it is with the lessons we learn from Jesus' resurrection.

The first and plainest lesson we learn is that of immortality. In the presence of the risen Jesus, we can confidently say death does not end all. There is life beyond the grave. The tomb, for those who love Him, is merely the narrow portal out of the prison-house of the body into the liberty and light and love of the Father's home.

Our loved ones die, but we do not mourn like those who have no hope. They have outstripped us in the race. They have reached home ahead of us and are watching and waiting for us. Their trials are past. Their warfare is accomplished. All tears are wiped from their eyes. They are absent from the body but are present with the Lord (see 2 Cor. 5:8). They are with Jesus, and they see His face (see Rev. 12:4). By and by, in a very little while, if we are faithful unto death, we shall meet them again and shall know each other there and be forever with the Lord (see 1 Thess. 4:17).

But there is a deeper lesson than this for us to learn—one that is nearer home and more needful to us in this present life. The apostles labored constantly to make people see and know that the soul, while yet in the body, may enter into the resurrection power of Jesus and rise and walk with Him in newness of life (see Rom. 6:4).

As Jesus after His resurrection was freed from the limitations of the fleshly body, so in Him we can now be free from the limitations of the fleshly spirit—the carnal mind. We can die to sin and be altogether spiritual and holy, and we can live the life of heaven here upon earth, filled with a constant sense of God's favor, having power always to overcome sin and to do the will of God on earth as it is done in heaven.

Paul said we are reconciled to God by Jesus' death, but we are saved by His life (see Rom. 5:10). As we see Him dying for us, our enmity is conquered by His love. We surrender ourselves to Him, and we feel and know that He freely pardons the past. But as we try to live for Him, we find that we are weak and carnal, and again and again we fail until we see that only His life, His Spirit in us, can save and keep us. Then, opening our hearts to Him that He may live in us, we find ourselves saved by His life, cleansed from sin, sanctified wholly, and kept by His power.

As Mary's ointment filled the whole house with perfume after the alabaster box was broken, so the resurrection life and power of the crucified Jesus waits to fill all hearts that will receive Him.

> Lo, a new creation dawning!
> Lo, I rise to life divine!
> In my soul an Easter morning;
> I am Christ's and Christ is mine.[3]

A brilliant young minister came to one of my holiness meetings and wanted to talk with me. When I saw him, he opened his heart and told me what an awful struggle he was having with fleshly temptations, so much so that he would walk the streets almost in agony. He had been reconciled to God by the death of Jesus, but he had not yet learned that he could be saved to the uttermost by His life. But after having the way of holiness explained to him, he yielded himself to Jesus and received Him by faith into his heart. He found himself filled with resurrection power and saved to the uttermost.

Some weeks later he wrote me: "I have burned the last bridge behind me, and am all under the blood. Oh, what weeks these have been since I saw you, such as I never believed could be realized this side of heaven."

Then he continued to relate how his wife got the blessing. A revival broke out in his church, and nearly all the leading members got sanctified, while many wandering souls entered God's kingdom. The fire continued to burn in his heart, the life of Jesus still saved him, and a year later he wrote me that he had had a second revival in his church, with scores of people flocking to the Lord for salvation, while his own soul was "dwelling in Beulah land."[4]

Many years have now passed since I first met him, but the fire still burns in his heart. For years he has been president of a university, where he leads hundreds of young men and women into the fullness of blessing, and teaches and trains them for wise and valiant service. And everywhere and always he testifies how he, a young, struggling, ambitious preacher, found Christ in all fullness at a Salvation Army penitent form (the place where people kneel in the church to pray) with an old drunken "bum" kneeling on one side and a woman of the streets on the other. The glory and power of God accompany his testimony and his ministry.

He received the very same life and Spirit that the disciples had received in the upper room on the day of Pentecost, and it is for you, too. Jesus is not dead, but living. Is He living in your heart? Are you a partaker of His resurrection power? Do you, in Him, have victory over all sin and all devils?

> What profits it that He is risen,
> If dead in sins thou yet dost lie?
> If yet thou cleavest to thy prison,
> What profit that He dwells on high?

What profit that He loosed and broke

All bonds, if ye in league remain

With earth? Who weareth Satan's yoke

Shall call Him Master but in vain.[5]

His life and power is your portion. Rise up in glad faith before Him and claim it now.

NOTES

1. Anonymous hymn, possibly from the twelfth century; translated into English by Francis Pott.

2. Elizabeth MacKenzie, "From My Soul Break Every Fetter," 1887, public domain.

3. Attributed to Francis Bottome, "Precious Jesus, O to Love Thee," 1873, public domain.

4. Charles A. Miles, "Dwelling in Beulah Land," 1911, public domain.

5. Attributed to J. G. Wolff, "Who Follows Christ Whate'er Betide," trans. Catherine Winkworth, 1855, public domain.

Is Death a Mystery? 3

A man who had been blind from his birth said he thought the sun must look like the sound of a bass drum. We smile wisely at this, forgetting that we probably miss the mark quite as far in matters more important, because we approach them with the wrong faculty.

The beauties of a landscape and the glories of the vaulted heavens are not made known to us through the sense of hearing. The harmony of a song is not made known to us by the sense of sight. If we would know the flavor of some fruit, we must not seek to discover it by the sense of touch or sight or smell, but by taste.

We cannot dispose of a question of conscience by an exercise of memory or solve a problem in mathematics by the conscience. Everything we can know is revealed to us through some corresponding sense or faculty, and every other sense and faculty must stand back in utter helplessness while this revelation is made.

Is death a mystery? To every faculty and sense but one it is an awful and unfathomable mystery. We look into the coffin where our precious dead lies and peer into the yawning grave with our poor little reason and understanding, and it is like looking out of our lighted rooms into the impenetrable blackness of a dark and stormy night. It is all heartbreaking amazement, desolation, and mystery. Our understanding is helpless and dumb in the presence of a problem it was not made to solve, and our stricken hearts break under a burden of sorrow that reason cannot lift.

But are we left without any sense or faculty that can lift this burden, soothe this sorrow, or solve this mystery? No, thank God, no! Faith is the faculty with which we must approach this problem, and to faith there is no mystery in death.

To our sainted dead, the coffin is not a narrow and locked prison, but an easy couch of sleep. The grave is not a bottomless abyss, but an open door through which the dear one has passed into the presence of the King, into the unveiled vision of Jesus and the unbroken joys and fellowships of the saints made perfect—a door of escape from the limitations, tears, toils, temptations, and tortures of time into the ageless blessedness of eternity where "God shall wipe away all tears from their eyes; and there shall be no more death, neither sorrow, nor crying, neither shall there be any more pain" (Rev. 21:4 KJV). To faith death simply means that the appointed task in this world's harvest field is done and the dear one has gone home. The day's lessons have been learned, and the Father has come to take His child home from school. Or, some evil was coming from which God in His wisdom saw fit to snatch His loved one (see Isa. 57:1–2).

Faith accepts death as God's appointment. This is a fact to be believed, not to be reasoned over. And if we simply believe it, the sting of death is drawn. But may we not ask why? May we not seek to understand? Yes, but we must do it with great caution, as a blind man feels his way along crowded streets and unknown thoroughfares. And we must do it under the constant leadership of faith, if we do not wish every step to be one of peril and possibly of ruin.

Philosophy may enable us to endure the agony following the death of our loved ones, but only faith nourished and made strong by constant feeding upon the promises and examples of God's Word can enable us to triumph in that hour.

A woman, recently bereft of her mother who was all that she had left of her family and dear ones, wrote that she read and reread the fifteenth chapter of 1 Corinthians, and to that word of God she anchored her faith. And through that word, God comforted her with great comfort. The pain may pierce like a sword and ache like a carbuncle. The sorrow may be inexpressibly bitter and the desolation unutterable, but faith finds its firm footing on God's Word. It grasps the promises and fixes its eyes upon His unchangeable character of wisdom and love, and emerges from the flood and storm chastened, but strengthened—still sorrowing, but triumphant and serene. And we shall be wise if, while still surrounded by our loved ones, we fill our minds and hearts with those precious truths God has revealed, so that when the storm overtakes us, as it someday surely will, we shall be prepared.

Comforted  4

In one of my meetings some time ago, I saw a sight to make all heaven rejoice. Two strong men stood embracing each other and, with faces aglow, sang with all their might, "Hallelujah! 'Tis done! I believe on the Son,"[1] while the others who were there praised the Lord with great joy.

I had seen the marvelous illumination of the Pan-American Exposition and World's Fair, but the illumination on the faces of those two men put that to shame. A light never seen on sea or land, the solar light of heaven, lit up their eyes and beamed from their countenances, and they looked to be carefree—two of the gladdest men in the world. Their joy was clean and pure, unutterable and without alloy.

Who were they? Were they carefree in the blush and glory of life's morning, untouched as yet by its sorrow and unsmitten in its strife and conflict, with all its full pleasures, triumphs, and prizes before them? Were they yet to prove the sweet, pure joys of wedded life and home, and listen for the first time to the prattle of their children and the music of her voice who was to be all their own, who was to be their very other self?

Some months ago one of those men left his home early in the morning and, returning within a few hours, found it—with his wife and children—burned to ashes. He had drunk sorrow's bitterest cup to the dregs and had been swept by desolation's fiercest storms. The other was a precious soul who had stepped onto the ship at Liverpool a few weeks before to return to his darling wife and seven young children, only to be met on landing by the awful word that she was dead and they were motherless.

They were not young men anymore, nor were they old. They were too old to begin life over again with the bounding enthusiasm and confident hopes of youth, and too young to lie down and die. Life's morning was past, and the fierce heat of a noonday sun had smitten them.

What, then, was the secret of their joy? Where was the hiding place of their triumph? The one, to drown his sorrows, had plunged into dissipation and sought to soothe his heartache with drink, only to find that he had forsaken the fountain of living waters and hewed out for himself cisterns—broken cisterns—that could hold no water (see Jer. 2:13). But that night he had returned to the Savior. After a struggle, he had found Jesus, found "peace in believing" (Rom. 15:13 KJV) and "joy in the Holy Spirit" (Rom. 14:17 NLT). And there he and his friend stood embracing each other, rejoicing, comforted, with their broken hearts healed by the touch of the pierced hands, triumphant over all the crushing sorrows of earth and all the malice and rage of hell.

Oh, that men and women would bring their crushed and aching hearts to Jesus, for in Him they would find peace and healing and heart's ease.

I have seen His face in blessing
When my eyes were dimmed with tears;
I have felt His hand caressing
When my heart was torn by fears.
When the shadows gathered o'er me,
And the gloom fell deep as night,
In the darkness, just before me,
There were tokens of His light.

I have stepped in waves of sorrow
Till my soul was covered o'er;
I have dreaded oft the morrow
And the path which lay before.
But when sinking in my sadness,
I have felt His helping hand,
And ere day dawn came to His gladness
With the courage to withstand.

I was wandering, and He found me,
Brought me from the verge of hell;
I was bruised, and He bound me,
Sick was I, He made me well.
I was wounded, and He healed me

When a-wearied of the strife;

I was erring, and He sealed me,

Dead, His Spirit gave me life.

By His life's blood He has claimed me

As a jewel in His sight;

As His own child He has named me,

Brought me forth to walk in light.

So I'm fighting till He calls me,

Walking in the path He trod;

And I care not what befalls me

Living in the life of God.[2]

Are you storm-tossed and troubled and heartbroken? If so, look to the Lord Jesus. He is the great Consoler. He is the Healer of broken hearts. He has the balm for every wound. Has it not been said of His people, "In all their affliction he was afflicted" (Isa. 63:9 KJV)? Does not the mother suffer in her child's suffering? So likewise does He in "our light affliction, which is but for a moment" work out for us "a far more exceeding and eternal weight of glory; while we look not at the things which are seen, but at the things which are not seen: for the things which are seen"—these sufferings and sorrows—"are temporal; but the things which are not seen"—the truths and consolations of the Lord—"are eternal" (2 Cor. 4:17–18 KJV).

We also read, "If we suffer, we shall also reign with him" (2 Tim. 2:12 KJV) and "we suffer with him, that we may be also glorified together" (Rom. 8:17 KJV). The victory of those two men with which this chapter opened was but a foretaste of the blessed time to which all God's children are hastening, when He "shall wipe away all tears from their eyes; and there shall be no more death, neither sorrow, nor crying, neither shall there be any more pain: for the former things are passed away" (Rev. 21:4 KJV).

Come, ye disconsolate, where'er ye languish,
Come to the mercy seat, fervently kneel;
Here bring your wounded hearts, here tell your anguish;
Earth has no sorrow that heaven cannot heal.

Here dwells the Father; love's waters are streaming,
Forth from the throne of God, plenteous and pure;
Come to His temple for mercy redeeming;
Earth has no sorrow that He cannot cure.

Here waits the Savior, gentle and loving,
Ready to meet us, His grace to reveal;
On Him cast the burden, trustfully coming;
Earth has no sorrow that heaven cannot heal.

Here speaks the Comforter, Light of the straying,
Hope of the penitent, Advocate sure,
Joy of the desolate, tenderly saying,
"Earth has no sorrow My grace cannot cure."[3]

NOTES

1. Philip P. Bliss, "Hallelujah! 'Tis Done," 1874, public domain.

2. William John McAlnan, "I Have Seen His Face in Blessing," 1894, public domain.

3. Thomas Moore, "Come, Ye Disconsolate," 1816, public domain.

Meditations on the Resurrection

SUNDAY

The great preacher John Jasper, of Richmond, Virginia, during a funeral sermon looked down as though peering into the yawning grave of the whole earth and cried out, "Grave! Grave! Oh Grave! Where is your victory? I hear you've got a mighty banner down there and terrorize everyone who comes along this way. Bring out your armies and furl your banners of victory. Show me your hand and let them see what you can do." Then he made the dramatic reply, in the voice of the grave, "Ain't got no victory now; *had* victory, but King Jesus passed through this country and tore my banners down. He says His people shan't be troubled any more forever; and He tells me to open the gates and let them pass on their way to glory."

A young man who had just lost his young wife after ten months of married bliss wrote me the other day: "Oh, hallelujah! My heart aches, but it also leaps with joy to think that my Louise is in heaven with Jesus!"

That is the message of Easter. The grave has no victory (see 1 Cor. 15:55). It does not hold our treasures. To be absent from the body is to be present with the Lord, and to those who love the Lord, death is merely the narrow gateway into that life without tears or pain or fear of parting.

MONDAY

Hope looks upward and onward with glad expectancy and is unknown except among Christians. The godless world is hopeless. Hundreds of millions in China look back and down, worshiping their ancestors. Hundreds of millions of Hindus long to be lost in vague unconsciousness because active life to them is full of terrors. But since Jesus was resurrected, the Christian is jubilant with hope. The grave has no terrors for us, for we know we will never lie down in it—it only receives our cast-off bodies. We will live because our Lord lives. We will never die, but will someday simply move out of the tenement of our perishing bodies and be forever with the Lord. Our friends who died in the Lord are not dead, but living, robed in splendor, throned in light, washed from every stain, and freed from every throb of pain. Blessed be God for the streams of light pouring forth from the open and empty grave of Jesus, flooding the future with joyous hope—hope that lights up the face with radiance and "does not put us to shame" (Rom. 5:5 ESV).

Be strong, my soul!

Thy loved ones go

Within the veil. God's thine, e'en so.

Be strong!

Be strong, my soul!

Death looms in view.

Lo, here thy God! He'll bear thee through.

Be strong![1]

TUESDAY

The sorrowful women had returned from Jesus' grave with an unbelievable story. It was empty, and two men in shining garments had told them He was not there, but was risen. The women told the dazed disciples, but to them it was an idle tale. Their hearts were still numb from the scenes of the crucifixion and the awful shock of His death, and they could not believe. But soon the glorious fact of His resurrection burst upon them—was forced upon them—and they immediately set all Jerusalem in an uproar, began to turn the world upside down (see Acts 17:6), and the world began to roll "out of the darkness into his wonderful light" (1 Pet. 2:9 NLT).

But there are still those to whom this glad story is just an idle tale. I knew a mother who lived near a church where this fact was constantly witnessed to, but to her it was an idle tale, and for years—with a face of unutterable sadness—she went weekly to her little boy's grave, refusing to be comforted. She might as well have lived before the resurrection, for it gave her no comfort. She believed not.

Is it so with you? Do not refuse to be comforted. He is risen, and our dead who die in the Lord are not in the grave, but with Him in paradise.

WEDNESDAY

"I am not ashamed of the gospel of Christ," wrote Paul (Rom. 1:16 KJV). And well might he so write, for it is the very fullness and perfection of good news, not only in word but in act, not only in promise but in fulfillment, not alone in prophecy but in realization.

The words and performance of Jesus match each other exactly and make the completed gospel. He never spoke of death as we do. He called it sleep: "The girl isn't dead; she's only asleep" (Matt. 9:24 NLT) and, "Our friend Lazarus has fallen asleep" (John 11:11 NLT). And by His word He awakened them from the sleep that we call death.

"I am the . . . life," He declared. "Everyone who lives in me and believes in me will never ever die" (John 11:25–26 NLT). And when they thought He was dead, and sought Him in the grave among the dead, He suddenly appeared before them in imperishable life. This is the completed gospel which, believed, is the power of God unto salvation.

It thrilled the dying ancient world with new life and hope. It pierced the awful darkness and gloom with heavenly light. Slaves heard it, believed, and rose up free men and women in Christ Jesus. Bigoted Pharisees and proud philosophers heard it and became humble followers of Jesus. The vilest drunkards, prostitutes, thieves, and murderers heard it with joy and became saints. It was the power of God unto their salvation, and it has lost none of its power.

THURSDAY

"He is not here," declared the two angels to the sorrowful women who came to the grave on that first Easter morning (Luke 24:6 KJV). And indeed He had not been there except to claim again the bruised and torn body that had been laid there. He had been in paradise with the blessed thief who trusted Him and whom He saved on the cross. His body was but His temple. "Destroy this temple, and in three days I will raise it up," He said. "But when Jesus said 'this temple,' he meant his own body" (John 2:19, 21 NLT). We must not confuse the temple with the worshiper within the temple. The temple may decay and fall into ruin, but the worshiper still lives on in other scenes. Our precious dead are not in the dark, damp graves; they are in mansions of light and love, at home with the Lord if they died in Him. It can be said of every one of them as it was of Jesus, "He is not here." It is only their bodily temples that we lay in the grave.

FRIDAY

"Can the dead live again?" asked Job (Job 14:14 NLT). But what of those who never die? "Everyone who lives in me and believes in me will never ever die," said Jesus to sorrowing Martha (John 11:26 NLT).

That which we call death—the separation of the soul from the body—was never so called by Jesus and Paul. They called it sleep. They reserved the dreaded word *death* for that more awful state— the separation of the soul from God. Eternal life is more than eternal existence; it is eternal blessedness in union with God.

And that wonderful experience can begin here and now for all who with penitent faith lay hold on Christ, and what we call death cannot destroy that blessedness. It only frees it from earthly limitations. The bird in the cage lives in the atmosphere. When the cage is opened and the bird flies forth, it still lives in the atmosphere, but without limitations. Our body is our cage. We live and move and have our being in God while in the body, but when we escape from it and leave it empty, we still live in God. To trust and love and obey God is to live in Him. Not to believe in Him—to disobey Him and be out of sympathy with Him—that is to die, indeed, and to be fixed in that state forever is eternal death.

O my soul, when you love and trust and obey, you have the life that is everlasting. Death cannot touch you. And when people say, "He is dead," you shall be reveling in fullness of life.

SATURDAY

Yesterday I read a fine article and exhortation by a brother who urges us to get ready because eternity is coming. Eternity is not coming. Eternity is here. We are enwrapped by it. It arches over us as do the heavens above us. It enfolds us as does the atmosphere about us. We call that little period in which we live in our bodies "time," and when we lay off the body, we say we shall enter into "eternity." It is as though the deep-sea diver should say, "If I should now get out of my diving suit, I should be in the ocean." He is in the ocean now, only its power to effect him is limited by the suit. If he got out of his suit, the ocean would swallow him up. So eternity will swallow us up and work our everlasting undoing unless we learn to live the eternal life while in the body. John Wesley said that the one who lives a truly religious life is now living in eternity.

We are now becoming what we shall ever be—lovers of God and the things of God, or haters of God and the things of God. We are now learning the sweet and heavenly art of loving, trusting, and obeying God, fitting ourselves to live in eternity. Or else by unbelief, disobedience, and selfishness, we are forming ourselves into vessels of wrath and dishonor, and hastening to endless darkness, loneliness, and woe. Where will you spend the rest of eternity?

NOTE

1. Anonymous, *The Lutheran Witness* 18, no. 4 (July 21, 1899): 1.

What Is Fundamental? 6

Recently two leading Christian denominations met in annual assembly, and these conventions flamed with doctrinal discussion and dissension, while newspapers—always eager for such reports—scattered (and are still scattering) the fire. There has probably been no period of greater doctrinal unrest since the days of Luther and Calvin and Knox than at the present time. No article of faith is too sacred to be questioned, no doctrine is too precious to be hurled into the seven-times-heated furnace of debate and tried in the hot fires of public discussion.

But no devoted, believing heart need faint. It is not the first time that a trial of truth has been made by such fire. The Son of God knows all about the furnace, and He keeps watch over His own. He still walks in the midst of the fire as He did in old Babylon (see Dan. 3), protecting that which is true, so that there shall not be even the smell of fire upon it. And it is ever so that "truth, crushed to earth, shall rise again."[1]

If there is any chaff mixed with the wheat of sound doctrine, it is well that the winnowing should blow it away. But the wheat must be saved, or men and women will grope in spiritual uncertainty and perish of soul-hunger.

The truth can be known and not simply guessed at. Jesus said to some who had believed in Him, "You are truly my disciples if you remain faithful to my teachings. *And you will know the truth*" (John 8:31–32 NLT, emphasis added).

Some doctrines can be verified in soul-satisfying experiences. When we, brokenhearted on account of our sin, look to Jesus, seeking forgiveness, and the burden rolls away, we know it. When we pass from the death of sin into the life of holiness, we know it. When the Holy Spirit reveals Christ within us, we know it. When the Bible suddenly flames with light, revealing all the hidden things of our secret life, the deep needs of our soul, and all God's ample provisions of grace, we know it. When Jesus (whom we despised) suddenly becomes to us altogether lovely, and the will of God (which was to us a galling yoke) now becomes our delight, we know it.

"We *know* that we have passed from death unto life" (1 John 3:14 KJV, emphasis added). "Anyone who loves is a child of God and *knows* God" (1 John 4:7 NLT, emphasis added). "By this we *know* that we abide in him and he in us, because he has given us of his Spirit" (1 John 4:13 ESV, emphasis added). "We *know* that God's children do not make a practice of sinning. . . . We *know* that we are children of God and that the world around us is under the control of the evil one. And we *know* that the Son of God has come, and he has given us understanding so that we can *know* the true God. And now we live in fellowship with the true God because we live in fellowship with his Son, Jesus Christ" (1 John 5:18–20 NLT, emphasis added). "When I am raised to life again, you will *know* that I am in my Father, and you are in me, and I am in you" (John 14:20 NLT, emphasis added). "And we have received God's Spirit (not the world's spirit), so we can *know* the wonderful things God has freely given us" (1 Cor. 2:12 NLT, emphasis added).

Thank God there are some certainties that are not settled by debate but by tasting and seeing that the Lord is good (see Ps. 34:8).

Some newspapers are full of the wordy attacks and counterattacks of so-called "fundamentalists" and "modernists." But I reckon that those great doctrines that can be verified in conscious experience are the fundamentals of the Christian faith. We must begin with those. We must be born again to see the kingdom of God and the things of the kingdom. Some things are learned not by debate and much study but by doing: "Anyone who wants to do the will of God will know whether my teaching is from God or is merely my own" (John 7:17 NLT).

One day something marvelous and transforming happened to Paul. He said, "It pleased God . . . to reveal his Son in me" (Gal. 1:15–16 KJV). And Paul did not consider this experience something peculiar to himself, for he wrote to his Corinthian brothers and sisters, and said, "Surely you know that Jesus Christ is among you; if not, you have failed the test of genuine faith" (2 Cor. 13:5 NLT).

Paul and Luke were dear and intimate friends, but I do not think, after the wonder of this spiritual revelation of Christ in him, Paul ever spent any time splitting hairs and arguing with Luke about the biological reasonableness of his story of the virgin birth of Jesus, so far did the spiritual wonder of his experience of Christ formed within him excel the natural wonder of the virgin's experience.

Some time ago a venerable archdeacon of the Episcopal church, sixty years of age, came to see me about his soul. He was brought up a Wesleyan, and he knew a great number of Wesley's hymns by heart. For years he had preached in the Methodist church before uniting with the Episcopal church. He is probably as well versed in theology as I, or better. He believes the truths I believe and is grounded in sound doctrine, but he was restless and uncertain and afraid. He had no peace. But as we prayed, and he looked unto Jesus, peace came to his heart, and some days later I received from him a letter telling of his joy. "Yesterday and today are days of heaven upon earth," he wrote. "I am possessed by a holy stillness, a blessed quietness. I am becalmed in Christ. Praise God!"

He wrote further, "I seem to grow by leaps and bounds in the things of God. I can really see His hand in every hour and every event since that blessed hour with you. I am looking up, trusting, resting, enswathed in His presence!" He had found that which is fundamental.

God does not hand us a hymnbook and a volume of systematic theology and say, "Believe them and you will be saved." He offers us His Son, and says, "Believe in the Lord Jesus and you will be saved" (Acts 16:31 NLT). It is not an elaborate and orderly system of truths but "the truth," not a book of doctrines but a Person God offers us, and to whom He points us for salvation. "To all who believed him and accepted him, he gave the right to become children of God" (John 1:12 NLT).

It is not the acceptance of certain doctrines that saves the soul and gives it peace and purity and power, but a penitent and childlike faith in a divine Savior and loving loyalty to Him. And those who thus yield themselves up to Christ will have a revelation of Christ in their own souls. God will be unveiled to their understanding, and they will come to know that best and noblest of all knowledge, the knowledge of God and of Jesus Christ, which is life eternal. And then they will discover that they are not the first and only people to whom God has revealed Himself. They will find recorded God's revealings and unveilings of Himself through many ages to other penitent, trusting, loyally obedient, and chosen souls.

The Bible gives this record and becomes to them a living book. It interprets their own experiences to them, while their experiences with God help them to understand the Bible. They will further discover that wise and devout people—men and women of faith and prayer, students of the Bible and of religious experience—have gradually formulated and written down the things revealed in the Bible and in the experience of those who have come to know and walk with God. And these things are the doctrines, the articles of faith, the theology of those who believe them.

There is a sense in which all thoughtful, studious, prayerful Christians become their own theologians, working out under the leading of the Holy Spirit their own theology and discovering what they believe to be the true doctrines of the Bible. They may accept the teachings or doctrines of their parents and spiritual leaders, and hold them intellectually, but their theology is really limited to those articles of faith which vitalize their lives, guide and inspire their conduct, mold their spirits, comfort and guard their hearts, purify their natures, and kindle their hope for the future. It may be meager and quite inadequate to express and comprehend all that God has revealed in His Word to humanity, but it is all they have really made their very own. It will be a vast help to them, therefore, to find out what other devout people have discovered in the Word of God and have believed. It will enlarge, strengthen, confirm, and establish their faith and make it more intelligently their own. It will do them good, immeasurable good, to study and know the doctrines of the Bible and of their church. It will make them wiser, more steadfast and efficient, more full-orbed and luminous Christians.

The whole people of God for thousands of years have been laboring to grasp and make clear the teachings of God's Word, and the creeds of Christendom sum up the faith of the masterminds and devout spirits of the ages.

The importance and need of sound doctrine was never greater than now. Doctrinal preaching has very largely fallen into disuse. Family religion is neglected, and children grow up not knowing the faith of their fathers and mothers. People's minds are in a state of flux. Bold and blatant attacks are made upon the most sacred beliefs of God's people. Some declare conversion and regeneration to be the results of auto-suggestion.

Christ, according to some modern teaching, was a good man, but only a man—a psychologist who practiced hypnotism and so worked what were called miracles. Politically, according to the views of some, He was well to the left and, if He were living today, would lead a political and social revolution. He was not the Son of God, they assert, but the son of Joseph; not "the Lamb of God who takes away the sin of the world" (John 1:29 NLT) but a martyr to ideas that were in advance of His age but now well-known to every student of sociology and psychology.

The Bible has been described as a unique compilation of the folklore, scraps of history, myths, stories, songs, and religious literature of a Semitic tribe slowly emerging out of slavery and barbarism into civil and moral order and spiritual consciousness, but not a record of God's self-revealing. Such are some of the interpretations of the things so sacred and dear to our hearts which we and our children have heard.

Into this chilly, weltering sea of doctrinal confusion, evasion, and denial, let us boldly pour the warm stream of doctrinal assurance and certainty. Amid this Babel of anxious questionings and paralyzing doubts and bold denials, let us sound forth our proclamation of restful, assured, and well-reasoned faith.

The world needs a revival of faith in the truths and doctrines we have unwaveringly held from the beginning, which have nourished and comforted our souls and the souls of our fathers and mothers, firing them with quenchless zeal, making them more than conquerors on the hardest spiritual battlefields and fruitful in the most barren spiritual desert lands of earth. These doctrines find their sweetest and purest expression in our hymns and songs, their confirmation and incarnation in our holy and victorious lives, and their final affirmation and vindication on triumphant deathbeds.

These doctrines can be preached, and we ought to preach them. Doctrinal preaching need not be prosaic and dry as dust. It can be made thrillingly interesting by the use of illustrations, instructing and enlarging the understanding, kindling the affections, chastening the emotions, and purifying the heart. And it may be that one of the greatest services we can yet render to this and coming generations is to arrest the doctrinal drift of the times with a robust and reasonable faith, based on Scripture and confirmed by signs and wonders performed by the Holy Spirit in transformed lives.

NOTE

1. William Cullen Bryant, *Yale Book of American Verse*, ed. Thomas R. Lounsbury (New Haven: Yale University Press, 1912), 12.

The Miracle of Sustained Faith in Christ

I have a half brother who is an agnostic. After the death of our mother, when I was but a lad in my early teens and he was a little child of nine, we were separated. His father (my stepfather) took him south into the mountains of Arkansas, and later this boy went far west to the sounding shores of the Pacific while I went to the Atlantic seaboard. But we were not more widely separated in space than we became in faith. He is a man of the strictest integrity, clean living, high minded, honorable, and faithful in his friendships, and on several occasions he has been elected to positions of trust by his fellow citizens. But he is not a Christian.

I love him with a great and tender love. I have prayed with him and for him. Once he knelt at the penitent form in one of my meetings, and with all earnestness I have talked and written to him, but he remains an agnostic.

Recently he sent me an article clipped from a newspaper concerning an old clergyman in New York who, after fifty years, declared his unbelief in Christ and the Bible. My half brother seems to think that the apostasy of this old preacher is an argument against faith in Christ and the authority of the Bible.

But what is it that keeps faith in Jesus Christ alive century after century? People have been declaring their unbelief for ages. Ministers of the gospel have fallen from faith again and again. One of Jesus' own disciples betrayed Him, and the eleven remaining ones forsook Him in His hour of shame and death—yet people still believe in Him and prove their faith by transformed lives of utter self-sacrifice and lifelong devotion. What is the secret of this persistent faith? Is it in learned and subtle arguments? Is it what people have written in books that have kept this faith alive for two millennia? No, it is not these. It is not even the Bible records alone that constantly renew this faith.

There is but one thing that can account for it, and that is the ever-recurring revelation of Christ by the Spirit in penitent, obedient, believing souls. The ever-loving Christ coming to and abiding in hearts prepared and willing to receive Him keeps faith in Christ alive. We do not build our faith upon and sacrifice our lives for things people do not know or only half believe. In a court of law there may be a thousand people present who do not know anything about the case being tried, and no one cares to hear what they have to say; everyone is interested in what actual witnesses—who *do* have knowledge of the case—have to say.

Was Christ divine? Is He Lord? I do not know it only by what other people have said or written. Paul declared a great fact and principle when he wrote to the Corinthians, "No one can say Jesus is Lord, except by the Holy Spirit" (1 Cor. 12:3 NLT). This knowledge comes by revelation to each soul who will receive it. The Bible declares it, but until I get an experience that matches the Bible as a key fits a lock, I do not know it. I read the Bible for years. I taught it. I studied theology. I had books on the evidence for Christianity, and they seemed convincing to me, but I did not find the final and all-convincing evidence upon which I can anchor my soul in every storm and in the blackest night in those books; I found it in a personal revelation of Jesus Christ in my own heart. There was a glad sweet day when Christ revealed Himself within me. I could no more doubt this than I could doubt my own existence. My heart was filled with rapture. My soul was bathed in love. My eyes overflowed with tears of gratitude for His great love for me, and I sorrowed with a godly sorrow that I should ever have doubted or sinned against Him.

From that day, I was a transformed man. Worldly ambitions were swept away. Fleshly passions and tempers were mastered and subdued. Selfishness was lost in love, and if I had a thousand lives, each one would have been devoted to His service. And since that day I have been constantly witnessing this same transformation in other lives. I find my experience and the Bible constantly answering each other. They match each other as the key fits the lock. And it is this that keeps alive my faith in Christ. The Bible is the textbook showing how I may obtain this experience. When I obtain this experience, it confirms my faith in the Bible, while the Bible interprets my experience to me.

I remember kneeling in prayer with others for a young lady who was seeking the Savior as her Sanctifier. While we were praying, she suddenly burst into tears and exclaimed in a kind of rapture, "Oh Jesus!" and when she arose it was with a transfigured face. The light of heaven was upon her. Tears were in her eyes and there were rainbows in the tears. She had looked to Him and her face was radiant. She was beautiful. She was young and strong and well. All the full tides of youthful life were pulsing through her. But within six months, she was prepared to leave home and native land—and lover and friend—for Africa. She lived and labored and loved the people in the heart of the Congo country until one day her Lord said to her, "It is enough, come up higher," and she went to heaven by way of Africa. She said Christ had been revealed to her and within her.

I knew a man nearly forty years of age—educated, thoughtful, earnest—but without the knowledge of Christ in his heart. He took much offense at my testimony and for a year resisted me. Then, meeting another with a similar testimony, he came to me with great frankness and said, "In the mouths of two witnesses this thing is established. How can I get this revelation for myself?" I explained as fully as I could, and I told him to seek God with all his heart in obedient faith. One night he came to me and asked me to go with him to a meeting. I was not a Salvationist at the time, but I suggested going to The Salvation Army. When we arrived at the hall, everyone else was on the street conducting an open-air meeting.

We took a front seat, and soon I heard him whispering to himself. Turning, I found him with his elbow on the seat behind him, his face in his hand, and an upward look that was transfigured. He was whispering to himself, "Blessed Jesus, blessed Jesus!" I rejoiced, for I was sure the great revelation had come, and in my heart I prayed for him.

It is now nearly forty years since then, but I remember that prayer. It was one of the simplest prayers I ever prayed: "Oh Lord, bless him so that he will never get over it in this world or the world to come!" After the meeting began and the opportunity was given for testimonies, he stood and said, "No one can conceive what God has been doing in my soul this last half hour. Jesus Christ has come to my heart and revealed Himself within me." On the way home that night, he praised God almost every step of the way. The next night he came to my room and was still praising God. Everyone who knew him remarked at the transformation that had taken place in his life, in his looks, and in his words. He said that Christ was revealed to him and within him.

I knew an old man who had been an alcoholic for fifty-two years. Born of alcoholic parents, he began to drink when he was a little child. He was nursed at his alcoholic mother's breast and cradled in his alcoholic parents' home. At seven years of age, he was found drunk in a saloon, and he continued to drink for decades. He went to prison for crimes committed while under the influence of strong drink. He had an eye punched out in a drunken brawl and a leg and several ribs broken in fights. He grew up in vice and ignorance, never learning to read until after he found Christ.

One Fourth of July, at the age of fifty-nine, he came in from the mountains to a little town in California to drink and fight and have what he called "a good time." After visiting a saloon or two, he came to the railway station and saw a Salvation Army officer couple (ministers), in full uniform, waiting for the train. He thought he would have some sport and, eyeing them up and down and noting their uniforms, he questioned, "And w-w-what b-b-baseball t-t-team d-d-do you b-b-belong to?" They told him they were Salvationists, and they said that he ought to give his heart to God. But the man replied, "God wouldn't have anything to do with me. I'm a drunkard. I'm a prison bird. I'm on the road to hell."

But they spoke kindly to him, telling him that he need not go to hell, that God loved him, Jesus had died to save him, and that he could be a good man and go to heaven if he would repent and believe. They did not call him names. They did not point out to him what he already knew— that he was a disgrace to himself and society. They said to him, "Brother, you can be saved, and you can be saved here and now." They got the poor, wretched fellow down on his knees, and when he arose a great transformation had begun. Christ was coming into that dark heart. From that day forward, he drank no more. He gave up tobacco and amended all his ways, and for fifteen years lived an earnest Christian life and then died rejoicing in God. He said Christ had revealed Himself to him and in him.

This revelation was Paul's secret. Proud, gifted, highly educated, he hated Christ. He persecuted the Christians. He condemned them to death. But one day he said, "It pleased God . . . to reveal his Son in me" (Gal. 1:15–16 KJV). From that day he was a transformed man and henceforth gladly endured whippings; stonings and imprisonments; hunger and cold; weariness and pain; and innumerable perils on land and sea, in the country, and among enemies and false brothers. At last in prison, in sight of the executioner's block, when his head was to be cut off, he wrote triumphantly, "I have kept the faith" (2 Tim. 4:7 KJV). "We are more than conquerors through him that loved us" (Rom. 8:37 KJV).

This was the secret of Augustine, the brilliant but licentious young rhetorician of Carthage and Milan. The whole tide of his life was turned from sin to holiness, from impurity to purity, from deeds of darkness to light, and he said that Christ was revealed to him and in him.

Lord Tennyson was one day walking with a friend who asked him what he thought of Christ. The poet-philosopher and profound thinker was silent for a while. Then, stooping, he plucked a little flower and, holding it before him for a moment, said in his deep voice, "What the sun in heaven is to this little flower, that Jesus Christ is to my soul."

> I found Him not in world or sun,
> Or eagle's wing, or insect's eye;
> Nor thro' the questions men may try,
> The petty cobwebs we have spun:
>
> If e'er when faith had fall'n asleep,
> I heard a voice, "Believe no more,"
> And heard an ever-breaking shore
> That tumbled in the Godless deep,
>
> A warmth within the breast would melt
> The freezing reason's colder part,
> And like a man in wrath the heart
> Stood up and answer'd, "I have felt."
>
> No, like a child in doubt and fear:
> But that blind clamour made me wise;
> Then was I as a child that cries,
> But crying, knows his father near;

And what I am beheld again

What is, and no man understands;

And out of darkness came the hands

That reach thro' nature, moulding men.[1]

So wrote Tennyson in "In Memoriam." And in his poem "The Two Voices," he finds doubt over-mastered by what he calls "that heat of inward evidence."[2]

William E. Gladstone (whom many reckon to have been the greatest of all English statesmen) was a devout and humble Christian. In reply to a question about his Christian belief, he wrote, "All I think, all I hope, all I write, all I live for, is based upon the divinity of Jesus Christ, the central joy of my poor, wayward life."[3] On another occasion, he said, "If asked what is the remedy for the deepest sorrows of the human heart—what a man should chiefly look to in his progress through life as the power that is to sustain him under trials and enable him manfully to confront his afflictions—I must point him to something which, in a well-known hymn is called, 'The old, old story,' told of in an old, old book, and taught with an old, old teaching, which is the greatest and best gift ever given to mankind."[4]

If only one soul in the whole world has this revelation of Christ within, then faith in Christ is not dead and cannot die. But while there are millions who do not believe and who imagine that their unbelief will gradually cover the earth as the waters of the deluge once covered it in olden days, yet there are other millions whose hearts are full of praise, worship, and utter devotion to the dear Son of God who died for them. And this devotion—this tender, patient love, this constant faith—does not spring from what they have read in books, but is something that has come down from His heart to theirs through the eternal Spirit, when with penitential tears they have renounced sin and yielded their hearts to Him in simple, obedient trust as Savior and Lord. Then, to their awed, adoring, wondering souls He has revealed Himself within. And henceforth they believe with "that heat of inward evidence" to which nothing can be added until in the world to come they see Him face-to-face.

The Bible tells us how each of us may get this revelation for ourselves, and millions upon millions testify that—humbly and faithfully following these directions—they have received the great revelation. Let doubters doubt, let deniers deny, but all who will may prove it so—and this I have done. And all who will may prove it for themselves. I cannot prove to you that an article of food is sweet or sour; you must taste and see for yourself. So the psalmist says, "Taste and see that the LORD is good" (Ps. 34:8 KJV).

Faith in Christ is more than intellectual assent. It is a vital, throbbing, transforming moral assent that carries the soul into experiential fellowship and union with Christ. "Anyone who wants to do the will of God will know whether my teaching is from God or is merely my own," Jesus said (John 7:17 NLT). And again, He said, "If you love me, obey my commandments. And I will ask the Father, and he will give you another Advocate. . . . [And] you will know that I am in my Father, and you are in me, and I am in you" (John 14:15–16, 20 NLT).

My half brother—and every uncertain man or woman—can *know* when he is prepared to *do* His will and *obey* His commandments. There is a simple way to test whether a wire is dead or alive. Touch it. So there is a simple way to prove whether or not Jesus Christ is Lord. Do what He bids. Keep His commandments, "and his commandments are not burdensome" (1 John 5:3 NLT).

NOTES

1. Alfred Lord Tennyson, "In Memoriam," 1849, public domain.

2. Alfred Lord Tennyson, "The Two Voices," 1842, public domain.

3. William Gladstone, quoted in *The Literary World*, no. 29 (May 28, 1898): 169.

4. William E. Gladstone, quoted in *Bible Society Record*, no. 35 (1890): 11.

Paul's Secret: Alive in Christ 8

Among the grimmest words in the Bible are those of the risen Jesus to John on Patmos: "Write this letter to the angel [shall we say pastor?] of the church in Sardis. This is the message. . . . I know all the things you do, and that you have a reputation for being alive—but you are dead" (Rev. 3:1 NLT).

A dead shepherd of the sheep. A dead watchman of the city. A dead teacher of the unlearned. A dead nurse of little children. A dead physician of souls. A dead ambassador of heaven. *Dead!* Moving about, but dead. Occupying an important place, and so excluding any other who might fulfill its functions, but dead. Having the reputation of being alive, but dead. What could be sadder? What could be so ghastly?

But in contrast to this spiritually dead preacher was Paul. He was alive, all alive—throbbing, pulsing, overflowing with life—full of life divine, eternal. The most conspicuous among all Paul's wonderful traits was his robust, abounding spiritual life.

"This is eternal life," said Jesus, "that they may know You, the only true God, and Jesus Christ whom You have sent" (John 17:3 NKJV). If this is life, and life eternal, then Paul had it. The psalmist wrote of the wicked, "God is not in all his thoughts" (Ps. 10:4 KJV); but God was in all of Paul's thoughts. Paul knew God. "God, whose I am, and whom I serve," he said on the deck of a doomed ship (Acts 27:23 KJV). Paul knew Jesus Christ whom God had sent. Christ filled the whole heaven of Paul's soul. Eleven times he mentions Christ by name in the first chapter of Ephesians, and about every verse enshrines his Lord.

That is the great wonder of Paul's letters: they enshrine and enthrone Christ. Cut out the name of Jesus and His titles and the pronouns referring to Him, and you would so mutilate every chapter and nearly every verse in Paul's letters as to make them wholly unintelligible. Christ was his meat and Christ was his drink. He lived by Christ. He lived for Christ. He lived in Christ, and Christ lived in him. He lived Christ. Listen: "My old self has been crucified with Christ. It is no longer I who live, but Christ lives in me. So I live in this earthly body by trusting in the Son of God, who loved me and gave himself for me" (Gal. 2:20 NLT). And again he wrote, "For to me to live is Christ" (Phil. 1:21 KJV). How heartily—with what spirit and understanding—Paul would have sung some of our songs. How I would love to hear him and his companions sing:

My heart is fixed, eternal God,

Fixed on Thee, fixed on Thee;

And my unchanging choice is made,

Christ for me, Christ for me;

He is my prophet, priest, and king,

Who did for me salvation bring,

And while I've breath I mean to sing,

Christ for me, Christ for me.[1]

With what full and deep-toned fervor, with what exultant joy and
star-like eyes and shining faces they would sing:

Christ is my meat, Christ is my drink,

My medicine and health,

My peace, my strength, my joy, my crown,

My glory and my wealth.

Christ is my father and my friend,

My brother and my love;

My head, my hope, my counselor,

My advocate above.

My Christ, He is the Heaven of heavens,

My Christ what shall I call?

My Christ is first, my Christ is last,

My Christ is all in all.[2]

Paul was no pillar saint, no Simon Stylites, no cloistered mystic sitting in rapt ecstasies or singing himself away to everlasting bliss in emotional spiritual songs. His heart was in heaven, his affections were there, but his feet resolutely trod the rough roads of earth and his hands grappled with its rough work. All the while his head planned campaigns for the conquest of earth's enthroned evils and cruelties and tyrannies, and for the healing of its foul diseases and festering sores. But in all his travels he had one single thought—to carry Christ to the people sitting in darkness and in the shadow of death. And in all his labors he had but one purpose—to make Christ known. In all his plans for spiritual conquest he had only one aim—to enthrone Christ in the faith and affections of others. He knew Jesus, and he knew that only Jesus could dispel the darkness in which the people sat and remove their fear of death by bringing them the life that is eternal. He knew that Jesus is the Friend and Brother of the toiler and that He can make all labor sweet. He knew that only Christ can overthrow entrenched evils and heal the deadly disease of sin by enthroning His Spirit in the human heart.

Let us note some of the evidence of life eternal in Paul, and so learn how more accurately to engage our own spiritual lives and how to nourish them. Nothing can be more important to us than this, whether as individuals or leaders, or more vital to the cause we serve and represent.

This life was manifest in Paul's spiritual appetites, just as all life is made manifest in its appetites. Paul hungered and thirsted after God. Hunger and thirst are two appetites that are inseparable from life—all life. When we cease to hunger and thirst, we are either sick or dead.

The more robust the life, the finer and firmer the health, the keener the appetite and more imperious the hunger and thirst will be.

Paul's hunger and thirst for God were insatiable. He drank and drank again, and yet he still was dry. He could have said with the psalmist, "As the deer longs for streams of water, so I long for you, O God. I thirst for God, the living God" (Ps. 42:1–2 NLT). Or he could have sung with Charles Wesley:

> I thirst for a life-giving God,
> A God that on Calvary died;
> A fountain of water and blood,
> Which gushed from Immanuel's side!
> I gasp for the stream of Thy love,
> The spirit of rapture unknown,
> And then to redrink it above,
> Eternally fresh from the throne.[3]

He was always reaching out after God, counting the dearest things as loss and rubbish that he might know Christ and win Him. Like a strong, determined runner, he pressed "toward the mark for the prize of the high calling of God in Christ Jesus" (Phil. 3:14 KJV).

This life was manifest in Paul's spiritual sensitivity. Not only was Paul's spiritual appetite keen, but all his spiritual senses were alive and wide awake. The soul has some senses that correspond to the senses of the body. Isaiah complained of those who had eyes to see but saw not, and ears to hear but heard not (see Isa. 6:9; 42:20). Jesus said repeatedly, "He who has ears to hear, let him hear!" (Matt. 11:15 NKJV). And when

He found the hearts of His disciples hardened by unbelief, He reproached them: "You have eyes—can't you see? You have ears—can't you hear?" (Mark 8:18 NLT). And the writer to the Hebrews mentions "those who by reason of use have their senses exercised to discern both good and evil" (Heb. 5:14 KJV).

It is this openness of spiritual senses that makes and characterizes spiritual leaders. Spiritual leaders are those who live in the Spirit, who dwell in such constant and intimate closeness with God that they and their Lord commune with each other, giving and receiving messages. They have such confidence in the report of their spiritual senses that when God gives them a vision, they are not disobedient to it. When God speaks, they rise up and follow. They know their Shepherd's voice, and that voice leads them on. Jesus said, "My sheep hear my voice, and I know them, and they follow me . . . [and] a stranger will they not follow, but will flee from him: for they know not the voice of strangers" (John 10:5, 27 KJV).

The modern physiologist who is sure that there is a sufficient material explanation for all the phenomena of mind and spirit, conscience and will—as well as of matter—would say it was no divine voice, but only the explosion of some overwrought brain cell or the erratic or unexplored activity of one of the endocrine glands. The devotee of the new psychology would have some other so-called scientific explanation that would exclude God. But the follower of Jesus can say with Paul, "I know whom I have believed" (2 Tim. 1:12 KJV) and assert that it is the voice of the Good Shepherd who goes before His sheep, while the sweetness and strength of their lives, and the glory and triumph of their martyrdoms, prove the truth of their confident assertion:

Where one heard noise, and one saw flame,

I only knew He named my name.[4]

It was the divine messages she heard and obeyed, and the spiritual visions he saw and followed, that made William and Catherine Booth the founders of The Salvation Army. It was the word sounding in the depths of his soul, "The just shall live by faith" (Rom. 1:17 KJV), that liberated Martin Luther. It was the word of the Lord in his own heart that sent Livingstone to what was then referred to as "darkest Africa," and the vision of its awful darkness, shot through by the light of the cross, held him there through long and painful years, until on his knees he died praying for its redemption. It is the vision and the voice that has called men and women from mines and mills and farms and schools into Salvation Army ministry, and sent them to the four corners of the earth to be saviors of the lost. And it is the vision and the voice still appealing to the seeing eye, the listening ear, and the understanding heart that can qualify and sustain us as spiritual leaders.

Paul's spiritual senses were not dead or dull, but alive, alert, and in constant use. His spiritual ears were open; he heard voices and received divine messages. His spiritual eyes were open; he saw heavenly visions and was not disobedient. His spiritual sensibilities were alive; he had intense feelings.

His spiritual ears were open. "The Sovereign LORD has spoken to me, and I have listened," wrote Isaiah. "Morning by morning he wakens me and opens my understanding to his will" (Isa. 50:4–5 NLT). And so Paul's ears were awakened. He had ears to hear, and he heard. Christ spoke to him in the great crises of his life and ministry, and his life and ministry were almost a continual crisis. A voice was always speaking in night visions or whispering in seasons of communion to reassure and guide him. On his way to Damascus, blinded by a sudden and great light from heaven, he heard a voice saying, "'Saul! Saul! why are you persecuting Me? . . . I am Jesus, whom you are persecuting. It is hard for you to kick against the goads'" (Acts 9:4–5 NKJV). And in his defense before King Agrippa, Paul told us more that was then said to him:

> Now get to your feet! For I have appeared to you to appoint you as my servant and witness. Tell people that you have seen me, and tell them what I will show you in the future. And I will rescue you from both your own people and the Gentiles. Yes, I am sending you to the Gentiles to open their eyes, so they may turn from darkness to light and from the power of Satan to God. Then they will receive forgiveness for their sins and be given a place among God's people, who are set apart by faith in me. (Acts 26:16–18 NLT)

That was Paul's call to the ministry, his mighty ordination by the laying on of the pierced hands. What could quench the zeal of a man in whose soul was sounding such a message? And that was merely the beginning of messages from Jesus to Paul.

One night in Corinth, as Paul was beset by sleepless enemies and possibly battling with doubts and fears, the Lord appeared and spoke to him in a vision: "Don't be afraid! Speak out! Don't be silent! For I am with you, and no one will attack and harm you, for many people in this city belong to me" (Acts 18:9–10 NLT).

In his farewell address to the Ephesian elders at Miletus, Paul said, "And now I am bound by the Spirit to go to Jerusalem. I don't know what awaits me, except that the Holy Spirit tells me in city after city that jail and suffering lie ahead" (Acts 20:22–23 NLT). What a message! But it did not dampen Paul's ardor. His Lord, who had died for his sins, was marking out his way and going on before, and Paul followed without a whimper of self-pity or complaint or a moment's hesitation. He was very eager to go to Rome and preach the gospel there in the very center of the world's pride and pomp and power, but in Jerusalem he was arrested and held in prison for two years while enemies plotted against him. All his plans and hopes seemed finally and hopelessly blasted. But one night, as he lay in prison, the Lord stood by him and said, "Be encouraged, Paul. Just as you have been a witness to me here in Jerusalem, you must preach the Good News in Rome as well" (Acts 23:11 NLT).

And soon he was on his way to Rome with all passage money paid by the government, for he went as a prisoner and in chains. But to Rome he was going, and before Caesar he was to bear testimony to his Lord and plant saints in Caesar's household. But Paul was not only "bound in the bundle of life with the LORD" (1 Sam. 25:29 KJV), he was also bound in the common bundle of life with all of humanity, and he was not immune from any woe, disaster, sorrow, or sore amazement that might befall them. He was not the pet of Providence. His Lord did not shield him from hard blows, but comforted and strengthened him to bear them not only with patience, but also with joy.

He was on his way to Rome, but one day he and his fellow travelers found themselves caught in the grip of the sailor's dread, the tempestuous wind called Euroclydon. And for many weary nights and days they were tempest tossed, until one night all hope that they might be saved was taken away. What then were Paul's thoughts? Did doubts assail him? Did he wonder and question the revelation that he should go to Rome? He was a man with a nature like ours; he had the same temptations and was assailed by the same spiritual enemies. We can only guess what his thoughts were and the spiritual bewilderment and distress he may have been in as he lay wide awake that night when hope was taken away. But then the angel of God stood by him, saying, "Don't be afraid, Paul, for you will surely stand trial before Caesar! What's more, God in his goodness has granted safety to everyone sailing with you" (Acts 27:24 NLT). Paul believed, and was so assured that by his own cheerful countenance he lifted the hearts and hopes of the two hundred and seventy-six hopeless men on board and practically took command of the ship.

Tennyson might have had Paul in mind when he wrote, "Well roars the storm to those that hear a deeper voice across the storm."[5] One day Paul was praying for the third time for deliverance from a tormenting bodily affliction, "a thorn in the flesh," when he heard the voice of his Lord whispering, "My grace is sufficient for you, for my power is made perfect in weakness" (2 Cor. 12:9 ESV). In other words, "No, Paul, I will not remove the thorn, but I will give you grace to endure, to conquer in spite of it; and when people see you radiant and triumphant in your weakness, then they will confess the divinity in your life and give glory to Me." And Paul was so content with his Master's will, so eager to bring glory to Jesus, that he blessed that thorn and cried out, "Therefore I will boast all the more gladly of my weaknesses, so that the power of Christ may rest upon me. For the sake of Christ, then, I am content with weaknesses, insults, hardships, persecutions, and calamities. For when I am weak, then I am strong" (2 Cor. 12:9–10 ESV).

On another day he was praying and communing with his Lord, when suddenly he found himself caught up into some ineffable fellowship. He says it was the third heaven, where he heard words not lawful, not possible, to utter. Paul was alive in Christ. He had ears to hear and he heard. He had eyes to see and he saw.

The divine life was manifested through his activities. He worked harder than all others (see 2 Cor. 11:23). From city to city, continent to continent, on land and on sea, he went, carrying the message of a crucified, risen, coming Savior. The only rest he got was in prison, and there he won his guards and jailer to Christ. There he wrote some of the letters that comprise one-third of the New Testament and have blessed the world for two millennia—and will bless until time shall be no more.

The divine life in Paul was manifested in his quick sensibilities. When he saw injustice and wrong, he flamed with moral indignation. When he saw souls going down to doom, or Christians falling away from Christ, he wept. When he saw them turning to Christ, he exulted and rejoiced. For three years in Ephesus, he earned his own living by working at his trade of tent-making, and then by day and night as he had opportunity he visited from house to house and warned people with tears (see Acts 20:31). He wept with those who wept and rejoiced with those who rejoiced. With new followers of Jesus, he was gentle as a nurse with a little child, and he so loved them that he said he would gladly give his own life for them.

The divine life in him was manifested by its power. He stirred up bitter opposition, so bitter that his enemies were continually seeking to kill him, and once when they thought they had succeeded, they dragged him out and threw him on the city's garbage pile. But this life in him also kindled flaming, sacrificial love. No one was ever more deeply and tenderly loved than Paul. The Galatians would have plucked out their eyes and given them to him. Priscilla and Aquila offered their own necks for him.

The divine life in him brought dead souls to life. Onesimus, a runaway slave who had probably seen and heard Paul in his master's house, found the apostle in a Roman prison, became a follower of Jesus, and was sent back to his master. The church in Corinth was founded by Paul and its members — among whom were those who had been sexually immoral, idolaters, adulterers, homosexuals, thieves, greedy, drunkards, revilers, swindlers, a cross-section of the age — were his converts. Dead souls came to life when Paul touched them. Jesus said, "Have faith in me, and you will have life-giving water flowing from deep inside you" (John 7:38 CEV). Such rivers flowed from Paul, like the holy river seen by Ezekiel, healing, life-giving: "Life will flourish wherever this water flows" (Ezek. 47:9 NLT).

Finally, the divine life in Paul was manifested in his triumph over circumstances. They threw him into prison, and the jailer became a follower of Jesus. They stoned him and threw him on a pile of city refuse, giving him up for dead; but by and by, with a deep sigh, a gasp, and a struggle, he arose and went back to the city to comfort the disciples, and then passed on to other scenes of labor and suffering. Three times the Romans beat him with rods. Five times the religious authorities stripped his back bare and beat him with thirty-nine stripes—all the law would allow. Three times he suffered shipwreck. For a night and a day he clung to a spar of a wrecked ship while the wild waters raged and threatened to engulf him. He was hungry and cold, naked and thirsty, while salt waters billowed around him. His own countrymen slandered him. False brothers betrayed him. Robbers in the Macedonian hills and the Cilician mountains made his journeys dangerous. His life was so constantly endangered that he said, "I die daily" (1 Cor. 15:31 KJV). But his face was calm and radiant. He was not embittered or daunted. He was full of courage and deep and quiet peace which often leaped up into exultant joy. He gloried in his tribulations. I ask him, "Paul, Paul, how did you endure it all? What, oh what, is your secret? Tell me." And he replies, "I was less than the least of all saints. I was not worthy to be called an apostle. I was a 'blasphemer, persecutor, and insolent opponent' of the faith [1 Tim. 1:13 ESV], but I obtained mercy. The grace of our Lord was exceedingly abundant with faith and love. I am the chief of sinners. 'But God had mercy on me so that Christ Jesus could use me as a prime example of his great patience with even the worst sinners. Then others will realize that they, too, can believe in him and receive eternal life' [1 Tim. 1:16 NLT]. Christ died for me, and now the love of Christ constrains me, and I rejoice in my sufferings, as I participate in the continuing sufferings of Christ for His body, the church. My whole secret is this: 'My old self has been crucified with Christ. It is no longer I who live, but Christ lives in me. So I live in this earthly body by trusting in the Son of God, who loved me and gave himself for me' [Gal. 2:20 NLT]."

What a life! What an age-long, worldwide influence! He may tower immeasurably above us, but we have his secret. We can share the life that was his and exert some of that heavenly influence, if we are not dead while having a reputation for being alive.

NOTES

1. Richard Jukes, "My Heart Is Fixed, Eternal God," 1862, public domain.

2. John Mason, "I've Found the Pearl of Greatest Price," 1683, public domain.

3. Charles Wesley, "What Now Is My Object and Aim?" 1761, public domain.

4. Robert Browning, "Christmas Eve," 1850, public domain.

5. Alfred Lord Tennyson, "In Memoriam," 1849, public domain.

The Detachment of the Resurrection Life

9

The Chicago Post, a secular newspaper, in discussing a popular novel, refers to "the cry for light" by the book's hero, and says,

> The authentic note of the human soul rings poignantly in that cry. It is both incitement and appeal. Can that cry be answered? Yes, but not by weak compromise [and] not by abandoning the high demands of the cross for the pliant policy of "everything goes well, and everything is all right!" That sort of religion for a time may get glad hands, but it will never make glad hearts. Yes, there is light, and those who have seen its radiance must make it their task to remove the obscuring screens and let it shine, "The light of the knowledge of the glory of God in the face of Jesus Christ," as Paul calls it. That is the light of the world.[1]

The glory of God is seen in the face of Jesus Christ, and the knowledge of that glory alone can enlighten the world, dispelling its darkness, conquering its slavish fears, destroying its subtle sins and giant evils, and turning it once more into the Eden that was lost through disobedience.

This is our great task—so to live and love and labor as to unveil the face of Jesus Christ, and to let the world see the glory of God—the glory of His sacrificial love, atoning blood, sympathy, care, mercy, justice, and truth. And this we can only do as we keep ourselves disentangled from the world, as was our Master.

No one ever mingled with sinners more freely than did Jesus, and yet we read that He was "holy, blameless, pure, set apart from sinners" (Heb. 7:26 NIV). He was in the world, but not of it. He was brother to everyone, but He "didn't trust them, because he knew all about people. No one needed to tell him about human nature, for he knew what was in each person's heart" (John 2:24–25 NLT). He mingled and ate and walked and talked with them—not declining their invitation but accepting their hospitality—yet kept Himself separate from them and so drew them after Him and upward with Him. He walked with them and yet went before them. He came down to them and yet was above them. He loved them, yearned over them, and longed for their friendship and fellowship, and yet He would not compromise with them.

The Pharisees and rulers were frankly perplexed and puzzled by Him, because He seemed to be unconscious of—or to ignore—all the generally accepted moral and social distinctions, and moved freely among all classes of the people regardless of their reputed character. If a Pharisee invited Him to dinner, He went to dinner with a Pharisee.

If a tax collector gave Him an invitation, He accepted the invitation of the tax collector. If a fallen woman washed His feet with her tears and wiped them with the flowing tresses of her hair, He did not rebuke her or shrink from her touch but gently defended her from her critics and declared her sins forgiven.

Jesus commended the Samaritan whom the Jews despised. He heeded the cry and healed the daughter of the Syrophoenician woman who was only a Gentile dog in the eyes of His countrymen. He was a brother to all. He was the universal friend "without partiality, and without hypocrisy" (James 3:17 KJV). And He maintained this all-embracing wideness of sympathy and this freedom of action by His detachments. He belonged to no party. He committed Himself to no one. Since He belonged to no restricted, oath-bound brotherhood, He could be everybody's brother. Since He belonged to no party, He looked upon all parties without prejudice, and with utter impartiality He could judge righteously. Only so He could draw all men and women to Him and save them. And only so can His disciples to whom He has committed that great and unfinished work can save them also.

The Devil, by subtle appeal, sought to entangle Jesus, but the Master chose the hard and slow but sure way of the cross and returned from the wilderness temptations "in the power of the Spirit" (Luke 4:14 KJV). And always the Spirit accompanies with power those—and only those—who, keeping themselves disentangled, follow Him wholly.

How insistent and subtle was the temptation to entangle Joseph in the social life and fleshly lusts of Egypt! But he kept himself separate, and through the shame and pain, and the hardship of prison, he rose to supreme power and leadership because God prospered him. How fearlessly and marvelously Daniel and his three friends cut their way through the meshes of the nets of Babylon that would have snared them, and stood free and more than conquerors amid the dangerous intrigues and jealousies and idolatries of the great city, until the king was convinced and constrained to declare their God to be the living God, who alone can deliver and whose kingdom can never be destroyed but shall abide world without end, steadfast forever.

"And darkness covered the deep waters," we read in the first chapter of Genesis. "Then God said, 'Let there be light,' and there was light. And God saw that the light was good. Then he separated the light from the darkness" (Gen. 1:2–4 NLT). In this we have not only the statement of a great cosmic fact, but also a parable of the divine division between spiritual light and darkness—between those who are born of God and those who are still in their sins. The unregenerate world is in darkness. We ourselves "at one time . . . were darkness," wrote Paul. We walked in darkness, and the darkness blinded our eyes. "But now [we] are light in the Lord," he wrote (Eph. 5:8 ESV). But now we are "all children of the light and of the day; we don't belong to darkness and night" (1 Thess. 5:5 NLT). We have been called "out of the darkness into his wonderful light" (1 Pet. 2:9 NLT), and we are bidden to live as children of the light.

But as it was said of Jesus, so it is today: "The light shines in the darkness, and the darkness did not comprehend it" (John 1:5 NKJV). Unregenerate men and women cannot understand our aloofness. They are mystified by the austerity of God's people. They "are surprised that you do not join them in their reckless, wild living" (1 Pet. 4:4 NIV), that we are not prepared to join with them in their feasts.

The world offers its friendship to the saints, but on its own terms. The Devil promised Jesus the kingdoms of the world if He would fall down and worship Satan. And so we are promised ease and success, riches, popularity, and dominion, but only on terms of the world for its own ends. Wherever the children of God have been seduced by the world's glitter and flattery, and accepted its offers and entered into alliance with it, spiritual decay has begun, quick discernment of the Spirit and sensitivity of conscience has been lost, the spiritual appetite for prayer, Bible reading, and soul-winning has become dulled and sickly, and spiritual vision has blurred.

The Bible is full of examples illustrating this fact, and the history of the church from the days when church and state were wedded together by Constantine is replete with examples of such decadence. But every great spiritual movement—the Reformation, the rise of Puritanism, the Quakers, Methodism, and The Salvation Army among them, as well as every local revival—has been accompanied by a call for people who would be saved and purified and empowered by the Spirit to come out and be separate. Self-denial and cross-bearing are wholly inconsistent with worldly alliances and entanglements.

"How can light live with darkness?" asked Paul. "Come out from among unbelievers, and separate yourselves from them, says the LORD" (2 Cor. 6:14, 17 NLT). We must hold fast to that principle and steadfastly maintain that practice if we wish to retain spiritual power.

We must keep ourselves separate and disentangled for the sake of our freedom of action. We are soldiers, and true soldiers do not entangle themselves in business or social or political alliances, and they especially hold themselves aloof from embarrassing associations with the people with whom they are at war. We are ambassadors of Jesus Christ and of heaven, and however friendly ambassadors may be with the nation they represent, they must not for an instant allow themselves any association, however innocent it may appear, that may in any measure curtail their freedom of action in the interests of their own country.

We are kings and priests of God, like Nehemiah. We have a great work to do and all sorts of schemes, intrigues, and stratagems will be used to entangle us. Advisors will try to become controllers. Rich people will give us money on condition that they can have a veto on our freedom in the use of it. Political parties and fraternal organizations will be our friends but will insist on having a voice in our decisions.

We must maintain our freedom that our judgment may be unclouded and impartial. In Christ Jesus, Paul wrote, "there is not Greek and Jew, circumcised and uncircumcised, barbarian, Scythian, slave, free; but Christ is all, and in all" (Col. 3:11 ESV). If he were writing today I think he would say, "There is neither English nor Irish, German nor French, American nor Japanese, African nor Asian, Catholic nor Protestant, Muslim nor Jew, but Christ is all and in all." Jesus tasted death for everyone. "The arms of love that compass me would all the world embrace."[2] If we would walk in our Savior's footsteps, we must enter into no association and allow ourselves to become possessed of no party spirit that would cloud our judgment of any group and narrow the breadth of our sympathy or chill the ardor of our love for all humanity.

It was at this point that the ancient Jews—and especially the Pharisees—failed. They were God's chosen people. Through them the great revelation of God, of His character, mind, and will came. They were separated from all the peoples of the earth by divine command. But they forgot or failed to comprehend that this was for the purpose of so protecting them from degrading influences and of illuminating and instructing them that they might become a channel through which God could bless all the families of the earth. They failed to grasp the purpose of their separation.

God's thought was to protect and liberate them from enslaving idolatries, degrading superstitions, debasing lusts and orgies of passion, injustice, and pride and pomp and vaulting ambitions. But they fell into a pit of spiritual pride and became utterly narrow and bigoted, trusting in themselves that they were righteous and despising others. Through them God wanted to reveal and pour out the ocean of His redeeming love upon the whole world. But they failed Him. And so may we, if we do not keep ourselves—like our Master—"holy, blameless, pure, set apart from sinners" (Heb. 7:26 NIV), and at the same time keep our hearts full of "the wisdom from above [that] is first pure, then peaceable, gentle, open to reason, full of mercy and good fruits, impartial and sincere," sowing in peace the fruits of righteousness (James 3:17–18 ESV).

NOTES

1. Quoted in Howard Agnew Johnston, *Scientific Christian Thinking* (New York: George H. Doran Company, 1922), 224.

2. Charles Wesley, "Jesus! The Name High over All," 1749, public domain.

Redeeming the Time 10

What! So soon? Another year? Every January, it seems impossible that another year could have passed so swiftly. And yet the start of a new year assures me that once more the earth has run its wondrous race through lanes of light and vast voids of space and deep abysses of the night, amid the silent pomp and splendor of star-strewn heavens, completing another of its ceaseless cycles around the sun, ending another year.

Shortly thereafter, on January 9 each year, the passage of time also brings me to the anniversary of that glad hour when God sanctified my soul. I never cease to wonder at His loving-kindness and mercy when that day comes. "Let all that I am praise the LORD; with my whole heart, I will praise his holy name. Let all that I am praise the LORD; may I never forget the good things he does for me. He forgives all my sins and heals all my diseases. He redeems me from death and crowns me with love and tender mercies. He fills my life with good things. My youth is renewed like the eagle's!" (Ps. 103:1–5 NLT).

When I was a little boy on the sun-bathed prairies of southern Illinois, a year seemed interminable. It moved forward on leaden feet, but now the years pass me like the flash of sunlit bubbles on wind-tossed waves, as though they must hasten and lose themselves in that eternity when time shall be no more. And yet what an unspeakable gift of God is a year! Who can compute its value or estimate its worth? We give and receive our little gifts and rejoice, but how paltry they are compared to God's gift of a year of days!

He has given me one more year, and I praise Him. It has been a good year. He has crowded it with mercies. He has crowned it with blessings. He has kept me from sin. He has not permitted me to fall. He has not let my Enemy triumph over me. He has directed my paths and ordered my steps. He has given success to my labors. He has kept my heart and mind in peace, and in loving-kindness has opened to me the gates of another year, through which I enter with trust, and yet with trembling. I do not fear that I shall fall—though I know I must watch and pray lest I fall—but I trust unfalteringly that my watchful Keeper, my Good Shepherd, who has guarded me with such sleepless care through these many years, will hold me up.

I rejoice with the psalmist, who sang, "My help comes from the LORD, who made heaven and earth! He will not let you stumble; the one who watches over you will not slumber. . . . The LORD keeps you from all harm and watches over your life. The LORD keeps watch over you as you come and go, both now and forever" (Ps. 121:2–3, 7–8 NLT).

And yet I tremble at the solemn responsibility laid upon me in the gift of another year of days, lest I fill them up not as full of prayer and praise and useful service as I should. Paul wrote of "redeeming the time" (Eph. 5:16 KJV) or, rather, as the Greek text has it, "buying up the time, because the days are evil."

It is so easy to kill time—to let it slip through one's fingers like sands of the seashore, or to fritter it away doing some good thing, or *better* thing, instead of the *best* thing. One of the snares of this age is its exceeding busyness—and it is a snare set especially to trap the servants of God and ministers of the gospel. It makes us too busy to wait patiently on God in secret prayer, too busy to quietly read the Bible for personal soul food, too busy for meditation—and yet "blessed" people are those who "delight in the law of the LORD, meditating on it day and night" (Ps. 1:2 NLT). It makes us too busy to speak to others about their souls and lead them to the Savior, too busy to give time to self-examination and solemn, secret worship and adoration of the Lord. It makes us so busy about the Lord's work that God Himself is forgotten, or only dimly remembered, and crowded into the corner and background of our thoughts, affections, time, and work.

Oh, Lord, pluck our feet out of this net! Let us not fall into this pit dug for us by the Enemy of our souls! And yet how easy it is to redeem the time if we just rouse ourselves into spiritual wakefulness and set ourselves with quiet, steady purpose of heart to do so. "Let us not sleep, as others do," wrote Paul, "but let us keep awake and be sober" (1 Thess. 5:6 ESV).

A big policeman sat in front of me on the streetcar. He had just come in out of biting wind and bitter cold. As I rose to leave the car,

I laid my hand on his shoulder and said, "God bless you today!" He glanced up with surprise but with a look of gratitude, as though I had given him a cup of cold water on a hot and dusty day. And as I pressed my way out of the car, my own heart was refreshed. With one word, I had bought up that moment and redeemed so much time.

A poorly clad man stood irresolutely in the wintry wind on a busy street corner. As I passed him, I tapped him on the shoulder and said, "God bless you!" And as I looked back I saw his plain face light up as though a burst of sunlight had fallen upon it.

I sat at dinner in the home of a stranger, with three men and their wives. With a little watchfulness and without any effort, the conversation was turned to spiritual things, after which we prayed. Later one of the women remarked to one of the others, "I felt as though we were talking to God." And so we were—to God and about God and His gracious ways and work in the soul—and our hearts burned within us. So the time that might have been lost in profitless small talk was redeemed—bought up—and given to the Master.

I sat in the train, and taking my Bible I began to read. A vibrant voice from the other side of the car inquired, "You have something good there, haven't you?" I looked up into the clear eyes of a gray, but vigorous, strong-faced man. "Yes," I replied, "the Bible." And for hundreds of miles we rode and talked together about the things of God—the things that make for our eternal peace and welfare. I found him to be the lieutenant of one of the mightiest living financiers, burdened with great responsibilities and apparently glad to have someone to talk to him about the riches that shall not perish when the heavens have rolled together as a scroll and fled away, and the earth—with all therein—is burned up.

An elevator operator, once employed at our headquarters, used to redeem the time, and he won over sixty souls to Jesus among those he carried up and down in his elevator.

I asked a lady, who was rejoicing in the Lord, when she became a follower of Jesus. She asked me if I did not remember speaking to her on the streetcar about her soul, some months before. I did not remember. "Well," said she, "that set me thinking, and I found no rest till I found Jesus and knew I was born again."

I went to a Christian home one night. As I was being shown to my bedroom, I leaned over the stairway and asked my host if he was enjoying the blessing of a clean heart indwelt by the Holy Spirit. The next day at the dinner table I asked him again, and he promptly replied, "Yes. Your question last night made me see my need, and this morning in the office of my store, alone with God, I sought and found the blessing."

Many years ago in Nashua, New Hampshire, I asked permission of a lady in whose home I was being hosted to mark a text in her Bible. Years later we met in California, and she reminded me of it. She said, "An unbeliever came to our home after you left and was railing against God and religion. My Bible was lying open on the center table. He took it up. His eyes fell on that marked text, and it smote his heart and conscience. He fell under deep conviction and became a follower of Jesus as a result of that reading."

It is enough to make one weep and shout for joy to see how unfailingly God works with those who constantly and unselfishly and in faith work for Him.

"Be prepared, whether the time is favorable or not," wrote Paul to Timothy (2 Tim. 4:2 NLT). It is not always some great, conspicuous public effort that brings forth the most fruit to God's glory, but often the wayside word. It was not amid the thronging multitude of Jerusalem in the courts of the temple that Jesus started His greatest revival, but on the curb of a wayside well where He found a fallen woman and told her of the Living Water. Her heart was won, and she went to the city and kindled faith in the hearts of the people, until they came out in throngs to see and hear Jesus and the whole city was revived.

If we watch and pray, if we give heed to the movings of the Spirit within us, we shall find ourselves redeeming the time in the most unexpected and yet most effective ways. For it is the word that is unexpected, the word that seems "out of season" (2 Tim. 4:2 KJV), arresting the attention of the hearers and catching them off guard, that enables us to enter into the strong city of Mansoul before the gates can be shut to capture it for the Master. I have especially found, again and again, that a word spoken to a child will bring forth precious fruit. But thereon hangs a number of sweet stories I must write about at some other time.

Bless God for the year just closed, and bless God for the new, clean, inviting year stretching out before me! I welcome it! I throw my arms wide open to embrace it! It will have sunny days and cloudy days, but each will be the day the Lord has made. And my soul exults to run its race and fight its battle and score its triumphs in these coming days, for I expect triumph over every foe, victory over all enemies of my soul, and good success in all my labors this coming year.

He has said, "My presence will go with you, and I will give you rest" (Ex. 33:14 ESV). He has said, "Be sure of this: I am with you always, even to the end of the age" (Matt. 28:20 NLT). I believe, so how can I fail to be victorious? Why should I not exult and be glad? Why should I not be strong in the Lord and in the power of His might? What more can He say than all He has said to encourage my faith? Why should I not believe? I *will* believe, I do believe and, believing, I have peace—perfect peace—and so go forth in full confidence of victory every day.

I invite you to join me in a covenant of faith to live this year with and for God, redeeming the time!

> I would the precious time redeem,
> And longer live for this alone,
> To spend and to be spent for them
> Who have not yet my Savior known;
> Fully on these my mission prove,
> And only breathe, to breathe Thy love.

> My talents, gifts, and graces, Lord,
> Into Thy blessed hands receive;
> And let me live to preach Thy Word,
> And let me to Thy glory live;
> My every sacred moment spend
> In publishing the sinner's Friend.

> Enlarge, inflame, and fill my heart
> With boundless charity divine,
> So shall I all strength exert,
> And love them with a zeal like Thine,

And lead them to Thy open side,

The sheep for whom the Shepherd died.[1]

NOTE

1. Charles Wesley, "Give Me the Faith Which Can Remove," 1749, public domain.

Go for Souls—and Remember Your Allies 11

A troupe of theatrical people filled (with the exception of another gentleman and myself) the sleeper car in which I was to cross New Mexico on a recent journey. The girls of the theatrical troupe were pretty, painted little things, with penciled eyebrows and lashes, and bizarre dresses. And, of course, they were friendly with all the men of the party—yet not in a bold way to arouse suspicion that they were bad. They were just frivolous and void of all apparent seriousness.

My heart was a bit heavy and cast down when I looked at them and listened to their empty chatter. There was nothing in common between us, it seemed to me, but I found my heart going out with pity and sympathy toward the young things who seemed so pathetic in their spiritual poverty and ignorance of all the high and true and lasting values of life.

When the porter began to make up the berth for the night, one of the older girls, waiting, sat on the arm of one of the seats of my berth.

I removed my coat from the seat and begged her to sit down. She hesitated—possibly she felt the lack of common interest as much as I, for she saw me in full Salvation Army uniform—but then sat with me. For a few moments we sat opposite each other in silence while she watched in rather a grave way what appeared to be a furious flirtation going on across the aisle.

I wanted to speak to her but hardly knew how to begin. At last, however, I made some commonplace remark about the weird desert through which we were passing—the indescribably wild, bare mountains flooded and glorified by the transfiguring light of the setting sun which rimmed the desert in—and soon we were in conversation. I asked her about her work, and she told me of the long hours they spent in play and rehearsal—from ten to twelve hours every day—a matinee in the afternoon, and play again from 7:30 to 11:30 p.m., never getting to bed before 1 a.m. I noticed that beneath the camouflage of paint and powder and wild profusion of golden hair she looked tired and, I thought, a bit world-weary and disappointed. I asked her if she didn't miss home life, and she told me she had a good home in Chicago, but that she got restless after spending two or three weeks there and then must go on the road again.

I told her that I understood, that I was sure that this restlessness would grow and become more and more consuming, and that I knew of just one cure—that of which old St. Augustine wrote: "Thou, O God, hast made us for Thyself, and we are restless till we rest in Thee."[1] I told her that our souls were too great to be satisfied with anything less than God Himself, and that He is the rightful home and great Friend of the soul. I told her that when I was a little orphan boy, through the death of my father, it was not the four walls of the house where Mother and I lived that made my home, but Mother herself. She was the home of my little child-soul. But by and by she, too, died, and then my soul found its true rest and rightful home in God, in fellowship and union and sweet and tender friendship with Him.

I told her of Jesus and His great love and sacrifice for us all, and she listened—oh, so quietly and intently—and then she arose and gave me her hand in an eager and warm clasp. Then, looking deep into my eyes, thanked me with an earnestness that made me forget the paint and powder—for her soul was looking directly at mine—and then she was gone. But an indescribable sweetness filled my heart. I felt Jesus' presence, as when He was upon earth, still seeking the lost to save them. And then I realized, it seemed as never before, how He was the Friend of sinners, how He loved them and longed for them. And that night He gave me a fresh baptism of love for the lost and wayward, the straying, and the befooled souls who are trying to find satisfaction without Him.

At three o'clock in the morning, in the stillness and darkness, that weary troupe of players slipped out of the train so silently that I did not hear them go, and I may never see them again. But my soul has been sweetened by the chance meeting with them. The quiet talk with the girl who is beginning to be disillusioned and to feel the vanity of all things without Christ, left a blessing in my soul that will abide, and in the strength of that I shall go for many days.

William Booth, The Salvation Army's founder, called us to "Go for souls!" Souls! They are all about us. We move among them and through the pulsing, throbbing midst of them like a great ocean. They beat around us like the waves of the sea. They are ever with us. We cannot get away from them unless we flee to the wilderness, and even there they will come to us. And if we, like our Lord, are the friends of sinners we shall not find them hard to approach. The difficulty is in ourselves rather than in them. We ourselves may be stiff and formal, hesitant, shy, and uncertain just what to say and how to begin. But I find that if I lift my heart to God in secret prayer for wisdom and words and love, the way opens and I can talk with almost anyone.

On that same sleeper car I talked to the porter, and he seemed most grateful that I should have thought enough of him to inquire about his soul. I found he was a Christian, and we had fellowship together.

People everywhere have open hearts to you, and it will be a rare thing for anyone to snub your coming in love, with a shining face and a warm heart full of real compassion and sympathy. Indeed, do they not expect you to speak to them? Let us not disappoint them. Let us deal with them boldly, kindly, tenderly, and faithfully, and Jesus will be with us and our hearts will surely burn with the sweetness of His presence and favor. He will be pleased with us as He sees us about His business, seeking the souls for whom He died.

There are difficulties in the way of reaching souls today. There is the drift away from organized religion. People do not care to go to religious services. The church is no longer attractive to masses of people. They much prefer to go shopping on Sundays or spend their evenings in the movie theaters. But we must not magnify this difficulty. In Paul's day the masses of people went to pagan temples and theaters. In Wesley's day they went hunting and to cockfights. And when William Booth began his work in London they thronged the streets and flooded the saloons. But those men of God compelled their attention, and so must we.

Yes, there is a decay of the sense of sin and the reverent fear of God among people today. But this is due to a failure to hear the whole counsel of God proclaimed by fire-touched lips and hearts aflame with the sense of God's claims and the danger of neglect. Let us get a fresh sense of sin's deadly character and the everlasting darkness and desolation into which it plunges human souls, and let us feel afresh "the terror of the Lord" (2 Cor. 5:11 KJV). Let us recall that apart from Christ He is a consuming fire (see Heb. 12:29), and we shall awaken hearts to a sense of sin and that reverent fear of God which is "the beginning of wisdom" (Prov. 9:10 KJV) and which leads men and women to "depart from evil" (Job 28:28 KJV).

Personally, I always carry with me in my heart the knowledge that God is love, and in my conscience the sense that "our God is a consuming fire" (Heb. 12:29 KJV). That knowledge casts out slavish fear, and that sense creates reverent fear, destroys trifling with sacred truths and duties, and makes me walk softly, lest I fall and become a castaway. Oh, that we may be so filled with the Spirit that we may arouse wholesome fear in the hearts of men and women, shake them out of their complacency, and make them realize how deeply they have grieved and offended God, how constantly and heartlessly they have sinned against infinite love and holiness, and how deadly is their peril unless they make haste to repent and find shelter in the wounds of Christ. But while we face difficulties in doing this, we also have allies.

The human heart is our ally. It is sinful and corrupt, but it was made for God, and is sad and restless and constantly subject to vexation, disappointments, and vague longings and fears until it finds God. And when we once succeed in interpreting to people this trouble in themselves, we have gone a long way to win them. This interpretation is made not only by what we say, but also by what we are—by the radiance and rest, peace and joy, earnestness and purity of our lives—and by the looks on our faces which reflect the blessedness that is resident in our hearts.

Human weakness is our ally. Human beings are weak and dependent— they must have help or perish. From the cradle to the grave, from birth to death, they are dependent upon others and upon God's unfailing fullness. Houses are built for them, clothes are made for them, food is produced for them, books are written for them, teachers are provided for them, laws are enacted to protect them, police are hired to defend them, highways and railroads and ships all around the world serve them and make possible the supply of their daily needs, the gospel is preached to save them—and behind it all is the heavenly Father pouring sunshine and rain upon them, without which they would perish. They come into the world as helpless babies, with a gasp and a cry, and they go out of the world just as helpless, with a gasp and a sigh. If we can make them feel this helpless dependence we have gone a long way toward winning them.

The human conscience is our ally. In every human heart, conscience sits in judgment upon a person's own acts, choices, and character. In the clamor and riot of passion, pleasure, and business, its voice may not be heard or heeded, but if we can silence the clamor by a song, a testimony, a word of God, till the still small voice of conscience is heard, we will have gone a long way. Conscience is God's ally and ours in every human heart.

Good Christian people are our allies. They may not come to our church to help us there, but they are helping to dispel the darkness that envelops those who are still lost in their sins. God hears their prayers, and they—maybe all unconsciously—are our helpers. We are not alone; there are seven thousand who have not bowed the knee to Baal (see 1 Kings 19:18). And we never know when they may so drive back the Enemy at their point in the far-flung battle line that it will make him an easy conquest in our particular sector. We are not alone in our warfare.

Deaths, funerals, and open graves are our allies. Through these, like landscapes lighted on dark nights by lightning flashes, men and women glimpse eternity, and its solemnities compass them round. God speaks and they must hear. Let us appeal to the realities of eternity and press them home with earnestness upon the attention of our hearers, and we shall go a long way toward winning them.

God the Holy Spirit is our ally. He is before and behind and all about us. He is ever whispering to people's hearts, striving with their wills, quickening their consciences, keeping alive the memory of their sins. Let us cooperate with Him, and work in glad and bold confidence, since He is our Helper. He will bring Calvary's scenes before us, if we wait on Him, and He will help us to make others see Jesus. He will help us to pray, believe, and win souls.

NOTE

1. St. Augustine, quoted in Rufus M. Jones, *Fundamental Ends of Life* (Whitefish, MT: Kessinger, 2003), 115.

A timid little woman went "fishing"[1] in a prayer meeting one night and spoke to two young men about their souls, urging them to give their hearts to God. They were really interested but managed to appear unconcerned and amused. It was her first attempt at this practice and her faith failed. Instead of kindly and earnestly sticking to them, she went back to her seat and wept, feeling that she had done more harm than good. But God was not discouraged. He did not leave those young men.

That night in bed one of them woke up and found the other weeping. "What's the matter, Tom?"

"Oh, I feel I'm on the road to hell. That woman spoke to us kindly and we laughed in her face. I'm not fit to live. I wish I were saved."

"I wish I were, too, Tom."

They got out of bed and prayed until they found peace with God. The Holy Spirit was far more interested in those boys than that little woman was, and He was working with her. But she did not believe and so she got no comfort. But God's strength was made perfect in her weakness. He did not fail her because her faith failed. He remained true, though she doubted.

It is this faithfulness of God—His unchangeable goodness and love—that should make us strong and steady in faith. God's character is the ground of our faith and hope. His faithfulness is like the great mountains that stand unchanged through the storms of a thousand years. People who live among the mountains or by the ocean do not expect to wake up some morning and find the mountains vanished or the sea dried up. They may be hidden for a time by fog and cloud but the wise people still reckon that they are there.

Let us be wise concerning God. We should not be doubtful and fearful and downcast, but glad and radiant with the peace, joy, and strength that are born of faith in God, in His gracious, holy, changeless character.

For three years, Jesus was training a few stupid men to believe, so that they might reveal God to the world and turn it upside down. But they were slow to learn, and again and again He said, "O you of little faith" (Matt. 8:26 ESV); "Have you still no faith" (Mark 4:40 ESV); and "If you have faith" (Matt. 17:20 ESV).

His heart was hurt by their distrust. But oh, how glad He was when He found someone who believed, who trusted Him against all contrary appearances. One day a Gentile woman came to Him and cried to Him to cast out a demon from her daughter. "But Jesus gave her no reply, not even a word" (Matt. 15:23 NLT). His disciples were ashamed to have such a woman following and crying after Him along the streets, and urged Him to send her away. Then He said to them in her hearing, "I was sent only to help God's lost sheep—the people of Israel" (Matt. 15:24 NLT).

What hope was there for her after that? She was a Gentile and a woman. But she drew near and "worshiped him, pleading again, 'Lord, help me!'" Then for the first time He spoke to her: "It isn't right to take food from the children and throw it to the dogs" (Matt. 15:25–26 NLT).

What a trial of faith! But Jesus is not always easy with us. His fondness for us is not foolish. He does not hesitate to try us, and happy are we if our faith does not fail. There shall be a big reward.

This woman's faith did not fail. It rose above every difficulty. It triumphed over every objection. The scorn of the disciples and the seeming indifference of the Master merely increased the doggedness of her faith. She cried out, "That's true, Lord, but even dogs are allowed to eat the scraps that fall beneath their masters' table" (Matt. 15:27 NLT). She would take the dog's place. She would not doubt. She did not faint, but persisted in prayer.

At last Jesus had found one who really believed, and how glad He was. His great, yearning love was met by great faith, and His heart was satisfied. He answered, "Dear woman . . . your faith is great. Your request is granted" (Matt. 15:28 NLT). It was as though the Lord had said to her, "Help yourself. My treasure house is open to you. Take what you want." Faith had won. She could have all her heart's desire. "And her daughter was instantly healed" (Matt. 15:28 NLT).

True faith is the most wonderful thing in the world. With it a handful of ignorant Jewish fishermen and tax collectors turned the world upside down. It makes beggars act like kings, for they know they are children of the King. Though they are so poor that they don't know where they will get their next crust, and have no place to lay their heads, yet they sing, "I'm the child of a King. . . . A tent or a cottage, why should I care? They're building a palace for me over there."[2]

"Hasn't God chosen the poor in this world to be rich in faith?" wrote James (James 2:5 NLT).

Faith makes the sorrowful to rejoice. I saw a devoted young wife and mother, whose young husband had suddenly died, smile through her tears as she believed God. Her face was a benediction; it was like the rising of the sun on a cloudless morn. "As sorrowful, yet always rejoicing," wrote Paul (2 Cor. 6:10 ESV).

Faith lightens the load of the heavy-laden. Paul fairly reveled in this fact. He wrote to his friends and fellow Christians in Philippi, "I can do everything through Christ, who gives me strength" (Phil. 4:13 NLT).

What could have enabled William Booth to go on through the years of obscurity and scorn, opposition and poverty, and to have borne his immeasurable burden of care and responsibility, but faith in God? I have sometimes thought he must have had some inward spiritual secret that bore him up and on. But I am persuaded that his secret was the old secret of the saints and warriors of the Lord from Abraham until now. He "believed God" (Gal. 3:6 KJV). He counted on God, even when God, like the mountains, was hidden by clouds. And as he believed, he found that God was there.

Faith empowers one to do the impossible. Peter walked on the sea while he believed, and not until he doubted did the waves open their hungry mouths to swallow him up.

I know a young fellow who seemed to have no gifts or skill for winning souls, but through faith and faithful work he has become one of the most skillful soul-winners I know.

Faith may see difficulties, but it does not magnify them; it minimizes them. It takes no account of them. It rises above them. It has vision. It sees God. It looks at His power and love and resources, and casts itself on Him, and through Him it triumphs.

> Faith, mighty faith, the promise sees,
> And looks to that alone;
> Laughs at impossibilities,
> And cries: It shall be done![3]

Faith may be sore tempted, but it does not yield to discouragement. When we yield to discouragement, we at that moment cease to believe. We let our troubles get between us and God and shut Him out. They appear to be bigger than God, or at least bigger than any interest He has in us.

Doubt puts us behind our difficulties. The difficulties, then, hide God from us, and so we get discouraged. Faith puts us in front of our difficulties, on the Godward side of them, and in quietness and confidence we face them, assured that God is with us and will in His own way and time deliver us. It was so with Daniel and his three friends in Babylon, and it has been so with God's people from then until now.

Finally, faith obeys. It does not sit in dreamy idleness but works as it has opportunity. The disciples had toiled all night in fishing and caught nothing. Jesus, standing on the shore in the dawn, said to them,

"Go out where it is deeper, and let down your nets." Peter answered, "If you say so, I'll let the nets down again" (Luke 5:4–5 NLT). And he got such a multitude of fish as to break his net. He beckoned his partners, and they came and filled their little ships to the point of sinking. Peter was fairly embarrassed by the abundant fruit of his obedient faith. But real faith obeys where there is no sign.

Adoniram Judson, the first American missionary to Burma, which today is officially known as Myanmar, labored for seven years without anyone coming to faith in Christ. A friend wrote, asking him what the prospects were. He replied, "The prospects are as bright as the promises of God."[4] The promises are like the stars; the darker the night, the brighter they shine. Shortly after, Judson's faith was rewarded with thirty thousand new followers of Jesus. It is a wonderful thing to truly believe God, to keep a listening ear for His word, and a heart and hand ready to obey. Have faith in God.

NOTES

1. A practice of prayerfully discerning and approaching people who seem to be ready to respond to the Holy Spirit's prompting but may need encouragement to do so.

2. Harriet E. Buell, "A Child of the King," 1877, public domain.

3. Charles Wesley, "Father of Jesus Christ, My Lord," 1742, public domain.

4. David Shibley, *Great for God: Missionaries Who Changed the World* (Green Forest, AR: New Leaf Press, 2012), 49.

Red-Hot Religion 13

One of the unsolved problems of science is to produce a physical light that is cold. The problem we face is to produce a spiritual light that is hot—and that is none other than the old-time religion. Jesus said of His forerunner, John the Baptist, "He was a burning and a shining light" (John 5:35 KJV). He shone until Jerusalem and Judea and all the regions around Jordan were startled and awakened by the light, and went out to see and to hear. And he burned into their hard, cold hearts until multitudes confessed their sins. King Herod himself and his adulterous wife were so scorched by the heat of the burning herald of righteousness that Herod shut John up in prison, and at the request of his dancing stepdaughter, urged on by his wicked wife, had John's head cut off to escape the burning, as though the loss of his head could quench the fire that shone and burned in John's heart and life.

Solomon said, "Wisdom lights up a person's face" (Eccl. 8:1 NLT). And the psalmist said, "Those who look to [the Lord] for help will be radiant with joy" (Ps. 34:5 NLT).

We read that when Moses came down from the mount where he had met with God, "the Israelites could not gaze at Moses' face because of its glory" (2 Cor. 3:7 ESV; see also Ex. 34:29–35). And we also read of Stephen, "Everyone in the high council stared at Stephen, because his face became as bright as an angel's" (Acts 6:15 NLT).

Some time ago a Chicago multimillionaire spoke at a Salvation Army meeting, and among other things said that the one thing that always most impressed him as he looked upon a company of Salvationists was the light in their faces. (May that light never go out!) This light is produced by that heavenly wisdom that comes from the knowledge of God through faith in Jesus, and by the peace of a good conscience and love to all.

But those who most mightily move men and women to righteousness are not only shining, but also burning lights. John burned his way into the dulled consciences of the people of his day and stirred all Judea and Galilee. Stephen burned into the guilty souls of priests and rulers until their wrath knew no bounds, and they cast him out and sent him to heaven in a shower of stones. The apostles burned their way into idolatrous cities and into a pagan civilization reeking with unmentionable lusts and unspeakable cruelties (see Rom. 1:22–32) until the world was transformed.

William and Catherine Booth, the founders of The Salvation Army, shone and burned their way through immeasurable obstacles of vice, ignorance, indifference, ridicule, contempt, and stubborn opposition.

And multitudes of lesser men and women have won their way and triumphed by the same burning. I know a Salvation Army officer who burns his way to victory in every corps (church) he commands. He is an ordinary-looking man, with slender gifts, but he has the fire. He burns.

What is this fire? It is love. It is faith. It is hope. It is passion, purpose, and determination. It is utter devotion. It is a divine discontent with formality, ceremonialism, lukewarmness, indifference, sham, noise, parade, and spiritual death. It is singleness of eye and a consecration unto death. It is God the Holy Spirit burning in and through a humble, holy, faithful heart. It is the spirit that inspired young Queen Esther to go to the king and plead for her people, saying, "If I perish, I perish" (Est. 4:16 KJV).

It is the spirit that inspired Jonathan and his armor-bearer to go up singlehanded against the mocking Philistines and rout their army. It is that which inspired David to run out to meet the insolent giant and put to flight the proud foe. It is the spirit that emboldened Daniel to face the lions' den and his three friends the sevenfold-heated furnace rather than be false to God and conscience and the old-time religion of their fathers. It is the spirit that led Peter and his friends to defy the threatening rulers and go to prison and glory in whippings and sufferings for Jesus' sake. It is the spirit that led Paul and Silas to boldly preach Christ to unruly mobs and religious bigots, to rejoice in stonings and stripes, and to sing psalms in a noisome midnight dungeon until the jailer himself became a follower of Christ. It even led them to work until saints were found in the household of that half-demon Caesar Nero—he who murdered his own mother and stamped his wife and unborn child to death. He set Rome ablaze and fiddled while the city burned, then charged the Christians with the burning and had them covered with pitch and set on fire, lighting the parks and streets with flaming saints, even possibly those of his own household!

It is the spirit that inspired John Knox to cry out to God, "Give me Scotland or I die," and that led Luther—in the face of almost certain death—to say to his friends, "I will go to Worms, though there be as many devils in the city as there are tiles on the roofs of the houses."

This burning is the spirit that led young men and women of a Salvation Army corps to come to the officers repeatedly and ask for the keys to the hall so they might spend half the night in prayer, until their corps blazed with revival and growth. It is the spirit that inspired an officer in a desperately hard ministry setting—in a city full of indifference and opposition—to have an all-night of prayer every week with two or three kindred souls who shared his burden, until God moved the whole city, the mayor became his friend and protector, the city officials and pastors attended his Sunday afternoon meetings in the city hall, and the people gave him money for a new building and instruments for a big band, while the platform was filled with those who caught the flame from their leader.

How can we get the fire? Not by feasting, but by fasting. Not by playing, but by praying. Not by sleeping and slothfulness, but by watching and by diligently seeking God and the souls that wander from Him. Not by reading newspapers and devouring the comics and sporting news, but by searching the Scriptures.

Red-hot men and women are those who have become acquainted with God. They have waited for Him obediently in the way of His commandments. They have not only repented of sin and turned toward

Him, but they have also longed and watched for Him more eagerly than shipwrecked sailors watch for the morning. They have hungered and thirsted for Him, and they have found Him. And when they have found Him they have burst into flame. Holy fire kindles in every soul that lives with Him.

I recently visited a town where a schoolboy's cap was thrown up and lodged on an electric wire. A friendly boy climbed the pole and, reaching for the cap, was struck dead by the electric current. So fire of holiness and love flashes through one who touches God, slaying the old life, leaving a new creation in place of the old nature—new desires, new passions and tempers, new hopes and affections, new ambitions and visions. But while the man or woman becomes new, the religion is old—old as Pentecost and Calvary; old as thundering, smoking, flaming Sinai and the burning bush that Moses saw; old as Abraham and Enoch and Abel.

Red-hot men and women are people of faith. They believe God, and they burn because they believe. They "believe that God exists and that he rewards those who sincerely seek him" (Heb. 11:6 NLT), and therefore they seek Him diligently day-by-day and He rewards them by sweet assurances and intimations of His love and favor. They seek His face that they may behold His beauty and catch its reflection (see Ps. 27:4). They seek His will that they may do it (see Matt. 7:21). They listen for His voice that they may open the door of their hearts to Him and entertain Him as their Guest (see Rev. 3:20) and, hearing, follow where He leads (see John 10:3–5, 16). They seek His commandments, promises, and precepts, that they may live by every word that proceeds out of the mouth of God (see Matt. 4:4).

Red-hot men and women have seasons of solitude for secret prayer. They get alone with God as Jesus did in His all-nights of prayer, as John did in the wilderness, as Moses did on Sinai, and as Elijah did on Horeb. There, in deep meditation and fellowship with Him, they see how small and transient is the world with its prizes and pomp. They count it all as garbage compared to Christ, that they may know Him. They are people of prayer, praying in secret, and also seeking out kindred spirits to pray with them.

Red-hot men and women love God. They love His people, His house, His service. They love righteousness and holiness, and they hate sin and every evil way. They turn away their ears from that which they should not hear. They stand on guard at the gateway of eye and ear and every sense, lest sin get into their hearts through unguarded ways.

These red-hot men and women are self-sacrificing and self-denying. They do not entangle themselves with the affairs of this life any more than does the good soldier who goes forth to war. They do not mix with the people of the world except to do them good and, if possible, win them to Christ. They guard the fire in their hearts as their sole possession on earth and their passport to heaven.

Oh, let us be burning and shining lights, and then great shall be our reward, great shall be our peace and joy, good success shall surely accompany all our labors, and the Savior's words, "Well done," shall greet us as we are welcomed through the gates of pearl into heaven, our eternal home.

The Disappointed Angels 14

Angels excel in strength and are very wise, no doubt, but they do not know everything. And I have been wondering if those sweet angels who sang so joyously at Jesus' birth have not been greatly disappointed. Did they not expect the world to receive Him as King and gladly submit at once to His gentle, righteous reign of peace and goodwill? I think they probably did. But if so, how great must be their amazement and disappointment as the ages roll by and the exceeding sinfulness of sin is more and more revealed, the fierce malignity of the Devil is made more and more manifest, and the unreasonable and wicked unbelief of humanity becomes more and more apparent.

How reasonable it was for them to expect that the whole world would bow and worship before Jesus, and crown Him Lord of all! And when His gracious words fell from His pure lips, and His kindly miracles of healing the sick and feeding the hungry and raising the dead were performed, how high must have been their hopes that now His own would receive Him! And yet the more He displayed the glory of His grace, His tender sympathy, His pitying love, His divine power, the more malignant became the devils, the more hard and bitter became the hearts of men and women, the more cruel their hate, the more sullen and obstinate their unbelief, and the more determined their opposition.

Jesus' Sermon on the Mount, recorded in Matthew 5–8, if heeded and followed by everyone, would immediately solve all the moral problems that perplex society and banish all the moral ills that separate and afflict humanity. It is a simple, easily understood, perfect rule of conduct for all and, if adopted and obeyed, would at once give us a perfect moral society. If that sermon were heeded, our jails and prisons could be turned into warehouses, locks on doors and windows could be removed and the keys thrown away, bank vaults could be left open, armies could be sent back to useful labor, warships could be turned into commercial freighters, guns could be beaten into plowshares, police could throw away their weapons, and lawyers could become kindly advisors to the ignorant and bereaved in the proper settlement of affairs.

There would then be no more saloons, brothels, gambling dens, and dance halls. Slavery of any kind would cease to exist, for everyone would treat others as they would want to be treated. There would be no more stealing, murder, slander, gossip, quarreling, hate, envy, jealousy, lying, or hypocrisy, and moral wrong would vanish from the face of the earth overnight. All bewildering religious and educational systems could be simplified. All the ponderous parliaments and legislatures could be replaced by a few good, wise people. Nearly all the multitudinous laws enacted by those legislative bodies could be swept away and forgotten if everyone would resolve to humble themselves and take the Sermon on the Mount as their rule of life and conduct. Poverty and disease and ignorance would gradually—and probably very rapidly—be overcome. Love, brotherly kindness, compassion and tender goodwill, sympathy and helpfulness would fill the earth with peace, contentment, and innocent and pure joys.

Will such a time ever come? Not until people accept Jesus as Teacher, Lawgiver, Savior, and Lord. Will this ever happen? It happens every day! More men and women love, serve, honor, and own Jesus as Teacher, Savior, and Lord today than ever before.

Not all will accept Him. But He will conquer, not by some spectacular display of glory and power that will blind and overpower people, but by the sweet reasonableness of His doctrine and the infinitude of His love and patience. He will conquer by His truth and by His Spirit in the hearts of those who accept Him as Teacher, Savior, and Lord. He will conquer by His cross.

A stretcher-bearer was gathering up the wounded in battle. He passed a badly wounded enemy soldier who spat at him. A private who saw this said to the stretcher-bearer, "Leave that fellow to me. I'll soon make him spit no more, the dog!" But the stretcher-bearer replied, "No, let him alone until I come back. Then I'll get even with him!" When he returned, the wounded enemy insulted him again, but instead of knocking him on the head, the stretcher-bearer lifted him up tenderly and bore him away to the doctor's care. That is the spirit of the cross, and by that—and that alone—the world will be conquered by Christ.

His kingdom is a moral and spiritual kingdom, and is to be won and established by love, by moral and spiritual weapons, and by an appeal with only moral and spiritual motives. It is a kingdom of love and cannot be established by force or spectacular display.

I sympathize very tenderly with those whose hearts are heavy because of the slow progress of His conquest, and I understand how many, discouraged by the apparent hopelessness of winning the world by the preaching and living out of the gospel, look and long for His second advent in power and glory as the only means left for the overthrow of His enemies and the conquest of the world. But, personally, I look for no such spectacular victory.

Only through the blood of His cross will He "reconcile all things unto himself" (Col. 1:20 KJV). "This includes you who were once far away from God. You were his enemies, separated from him by your evil thoughts and actions. Yet now he has reconciled you to himself through the death of Christ in his physical body. As a result, he has brought you into his own presence, and you are holy and blameless as you stand before him without a single fault" (Col. 1:21–22 NLT).

Not otherwise will He ever win men and women to Himself. He had no other way that I can discover. He will conquer, but only by the cross. He will come in power and great glory some wondrous day, but not to change people's hearts, which can be done only by His cross. He will come to judge. He forever forswore the spectacular way when He refused to cast Himself from the pinnacle of the temple at Satan's bidding and chose the lowly, painful way of loving sacrifice.

If God interfered to prevent sin by some flaming spectacle of power and glory, this would ignore and destroy the freedom of the human will and render all human goodness an impossibility. If God forces us into goodness, we become good machines, not good people. God is too wise and too loving to do this. What, then, does God do to overcome our sin? God leaves the freedom of our will untouched. He presents to our will, at great cost to Himself, the most powerful motives, leading us to *choose* to be good. We can become good only by the exercise of our own free will. By these motives, shining everywhere on earth (but most resplendently in the incarnate Son and by His Spirit), He woos the free heart and waits in love.

Oh, what a lover is God! How He woos and how He waits. Angels and humans may be disappointed and cry out with the souls of those whom John saw in his vision on Patmos, "O Sovereign Lord, holy and true, how long before you judge the people who belong to this world and avenge our blood for what they have done to us?" (Rev. 6:10 NLT).

The weary ages may roll by in sin and sorrow, in toil and travail and agony and blood, because people will not listen and submit to Jesus, but God woos and waits in love, and wins—and will win, by the cross—such as are willing.

There in the Sermon on the Mount is God's ideal for a perfect society. No nation has yet adopted it—not even the church which, professing to be composed of those who accept Jesus as Savior and Lord, attempts to bring its members into full harmony with that blessed rule of life and conduct. And yet it is to this that nations, communities, families, and individuals must come, before the sins and sorrows and sufferings of humanity can be brought to an end and the angels' Christmas anthem of "Glory to God in the highest, and on earth peace, good will toward men" (Luke 2:14 KJV) be translated into fact.

There is God's plan. There is God's remedy for all the woes and wars and fears and bewilderments of humanity. If Jesus should come in person to teach and govern us, He would have nothing more to say than what He has said. He would have no other law to enact, no other plan to offer. He would still bid men and women to come to Him and learn to be meek and lowly in heart, to be sorry for sin, to repent, to mourn for their evil actions, to be merciful, to be hungry for righteousness, to be pure in heart, to be peacemakers, to be loving, to be forbearing, to be doing always to others as they would have others do to them, to be serving God with good will from the heart, and not to be seen of others.

Will human society ever be won to the standard set by Jesus? Listen to Isaiah: "He will not falter or lose heart until justice prevails throughout the earth" (Isa. 42:4 NLT). He has set Himself to this great task and He will prevail, but it will be only so fast as individual men and women are won to Him. Everyone who follows Jesus and becomes sanctified, and goes around with peace and love and good-will and faith in his or her heart, becomes a light in the world and hastens the day of Jesus' triumph. Everyone who refuses to yield to Him, everyone who yields and then loses faith, everyone who lives a mixed life, adds to the gloom, delays the progress of His truth, and only hinders the coming of His triumph and prolongs the disappointment of the angels.

Let us bring to Him our best gifts as the wise men did on that first Christmas Day and reward His tender, wooing love and long patience by dedicating ourselves afresh to Him and to the great purpose for which He died on the cross, the fulfillment of which He still patiently waits and intercedes for, and which those disappointed angels must be waiting and longing for with unutterable amazement and wonder because of the slowness of men and women to believe and obey.

> Jesus shall reign where'er the sun
> Does His successive journeys run;
> His kingdom stretch from shore to shore,
> Till moons shall wax and wane no more.[1]

NOTE

1. Isaac Watts, "Jesus Shall Reign," 1719, public domain.

Greatly Beloved **15**

It was very early—too early—in the morning, when I awoke from a sleep that was not altogether refreshing, and felt dull, restless, and depressed. But I remembered God, turned to Him, and cried for help and strength, when instantly as a voiceless whisper in my heart came the words of the angel to Daniel: "O man greatly beloved, fear not! Peace be to you; be strong, yes, be strong!" (Dan. 10:19 NKJV).

Peace—great peace—and strength, sufficient strength, abounding strength for my drooping spirit, were in those sweet, strong words. But my adversary, the Devil, was present to rob me of their riches.

Those words were spoken to Daniel, a great saint and prophet and governor of an empire. Dare I—how dare I—take them as spoken to me? Then I remembered that "no prophecy of the scripture is of any private interpretation" (2 Pet. 1:20 KJV), or "self-solving," but is for all who believe and obey. That thought helped me somewhat. For "all

Scripture is inspired by God and is useful to teach us what is true and to make us realize what is wrong in our lives. It corrects us when we are wrong and teaches us to do what is right. God uses it to prepare and equip his people to do every good work" (2 Tim. 3:16–17 NLT). And "such things were written in the Scriptures long ago to teach us. And the Scriptures give us hope and encouragement as we wait patiently for God's promises to be fulfilled" (Rom. 15:4 NLT). So I began to dare to apply the words to myself and get comfort from them.

But Daniel was called "beloved" by the angel. Now I felt I could understand how God could love Daniel, for he seems—of all historic characters—one of the most lovable and love-worthy. But was I beloved, lovable, or love-worthy? I dared not make any such claim. But then I remembered Jesus' words: "For God so loved the world that He gave His only begotten Son, that whoever believes in Him should not perish but have everlasting life" (John 3:16 NKJV), and Paul's words, "But God showed his great love for us by sending Christ to die for us while we were still sinners" (Rom. 5:8 NLT). And surely, whether lovable or unlovable, worthy or unworthy, it made no difference, for I was caught in the boundless sweep of those great assurances and promises. I, too, with Daniel, was "beloved," and I began to feel comforted as I appropriated the measureless riches of the angel's words and compared them with other Scriptures.

But Daniel was "greatly beloved." I might be loved, but was I, too, "*greatly* beloved"? That word, *greatly*, seemed too much. There was such a wealth of tenderness and condescension on the part of God in it that I hesitated before it. But then I remembered Paul's words to the Ephesians who were common folks just like me: "God is so rich in mercy, and he loved us so much, that even though we were dead because of our sins, he gave us life when he raised Christ from the dead" (Eph. 2:4–5 NLT), and I saw that God's great love extended to me—even to me—and so I was "greatly beloved"! And in the presence and embrace of such love, how could I fear? Fear and depression were cast out, and peace surged into my soul.

But the angel said to Daniel, "Be strong, yes, be strong!" (Dan. 10:19 NKJV). And I did not feel strong in that early morning hour. But I remembered that three times in a few verses in the first chapter of Joshua, God had said to Joshua, "Be strong and courageous. . . . Be strong and very courageous. . . . This is my command—be strong and courageous! Do not be afraid or discouraged. For the LORD your God is with you wherever you go" (Josh. 1:6–7, 9 NLT).

But those words were spoken to Joshua, a great warrior and general who God commissioned for special and great work. Could I draw comfort from them as though they were spoken to me? Well, I did. Faith must dare. What daring faith the Syro-Phoenician woman had (see Matt. 15:22–28). We can receive only as we believe. Doubt dams and diverts the river of God's grace; it freezes the flow of His benefits and mercies, and the soul dies of thirst and starves in the presence of plenty like the unbelieving nobleman of Samaria (see 2 Kings 7).

But Paul wrote to Timothy, "Be strong through the grace [the favor] that God gives you in Christ Jesus" (2 Tim. 2:1 NLT). But that, too, was for a specific individual, one who was called to a special work. Dare I apply it to myself? Yes, I dared.

Again, Paul wrote a general letter to the Ephesians, who were everyday, common people, just like myself, and said, "Be strong in the

Lord and in his mighty power" (Eph. 6:10 NLT). And as I considered these texts, I saw and felt that God wished, expected, and commanded me to be strong. And since His commands are always accompanied by enabling power, I felt that it was my precious, blood-bought privilege, as well as duty, to be strong in spirit, giving glory to God.

And peace and fearlessness and strength came into me as I entered with Daniel into that treasure-house of God's love—courage, peace, and strength. I just felt at home, where I could help myself to all the love and courage and peace and power I wanted. It was just as though my Lord said, "Oh man, greatly beloved, help yourself, take what you want. Let it be to you as you will."

An old friend of mine used to startle and amuse and challenge me by crying out, "All heaven is free plunder to faith." And in this early morning experience I began to feel that it was truly so. And now that I was in the treasure-house, I continued to examine, and I found Paul praying for the Ephesians that "according to the riches of [the Father's] glory he may grant [them] to be strengthened with power through his Spirit in [their] inner being, so that Christ may dwell in [their] hearts through faith" (Eph. 3:16–17 ESV). And that was just what I felt God was doing for me. I felt no longer dull and depressed but all alive toward God and others, and ready for service or suffering or sacrifice.

And then I read that this was all performed, not by some new, strange power I had not known before, but "according to the power at work within us" (Eph. 3:20 ESV)—the power that convicted me and brought me to Jesus and pardoned my sins and led me into the Holy of Holies, into the blessing of a clean heart and a life hidden with Christ in God.

What is that power? The same power that worked in Jesus when God "raised him from the dead, and set him at his own right hand in the heavenly places, far above all principality, and power, and might, and dominion, and every name that is named, not only in this world, but also in that which is to come" (Eph. 1:20–21 KJV). Matchless, exhaustless power! And this power was working in me!

Further, I read where Paul prayed for the Colossians, that they might be "strengthened with all might, according to his glorious power, unto all patience and longsuffering with joyfulness" (Col. 1:11 KJV). And I saw that this strengthening was for spiritual ends, to make me like my Lord—patient, longsuffering, and joyful (see Rom. 15:13; Neh. 8:10).

Finally, I remembered an experience when I was far away in the Mississippi Valley, a thousand miles from my home. I was weary, heartsick, homesick (as homesick as I would ever permit myself to be), exhausted, and lonely. I longed for the quiet and rest and comfort of home, the fellowship of my wife, and the arms of the children about my neck. In this state of weariness, loneliness, and temptation, I went to the Lord in prayer, somewhat in the spirit of repining and whining, and it seemed to me as though the Lord spoke to me just a bit sharply through His words to Joshua: "Have I not commanded you? Be strong and courageous" (Josh. 1:9 ESV).

It sounded in my heart like the sharp, quick command of an officer ordering a charge on the enemy. I braced up and replied, "I will. I will, Lord, be strong and courageous." Strength and courage possessed me, and I went to my meeting feeling as though I could run through a troop and leap over a wall (see Ps. 18:29), that I could chase a thousand, and that if I could find another fellow of the same mind and heart, we could put ten thousand to flight (see Deut. 32:30).

God loves us, each of us, however unworthy we may feel ourselves to be—loves us with a great and quenchless love, as the sun shines with a great warmth and splendor of light for each and every living thing, from humans to the vilest reptile and tiniest and most insignificant insect and mite. Let us receive and rejoice in His love with believing hearts.

And it is His will that we should have peace—unbroken and full—like a noble and exhaustless river; that we should be without fear that weakens and torments; and that we should be strong—strong in faith, strong in spirit, "strong in the Lord and in his mighty power" (Eph. 6:10 NLT), and strong through the glory and comfort of an indwelling God.

And yet we may miss it all by neglect. And we shall, if we do not esteem and cultivate His friendship—if we do not diligently seek His face day-by-day and believe. "Be careful then, dear brothers and sisters. Make sure that your own hearts are not evil and unbelieving, turning you away from the living God. You must warn each other every day, while it is still 'today,' so that none of you will be deceived by sin and hardened against God. . . . Remember what it says: 'Today when you hear his voice, don't harden your hearts'" (Heb. 3:12–13, 15 NLT).

To slightly adapt a well-worn verse:

> Lord, in Thy love and Thy power make me strong
> That all may know that to Thee I belong;
> When I am tempted, let this be my song,
> Victory for me, victory for me![1]

And what shall we offer in return for such great love, for such boundless benefits and tender mercies? Listen:

> I knelt in tears at the feet of Christ,
> In the hush of the twilight dim,
> And all that I was, or hoped or sought,
> Surrendered unto Him.
> Crowned, not crucified—my heart shall know
> No King but Christ, who loveth me so.[2]

NOTES

1. Herbert Booth, "Cleansing for Me," 1886, public domain.

2. Florence E. Johnson, "Crown or Crucify," in Meade MacGuire, *The Life of Victory* (Takoma Park, MD: Review and Herald Publishing Association, 1924), 4.

The Blessing Regained 16

A letter from a Salvation Army officer in another country reached me with an anguished cry for spiritual help. She told how, "definitely sanctified and led by the Holy Spirit in every detail," she "entered Army work as a girl of seventeen, full of zeal and ambition for the kingdom." But she came into contact with some people to whom she looked for spiritual counsel and help who were, to her mind, "scarcely saved." Through looking too much at the unfaithfulness of others, her own zeal lessened and she ceased to do as much as formerly. Instead of having continued victory, she has had defeat ever since.

For six years, she said, she has been struggling to carry on her work and to win souls while in an unsanctified state. What a dry, hard, unsatisfying struggle! She said she has often tried to live a holy life, but has not succeeded even for one day. She closed her letter with the cry, "Oh, if I only knew someone who has really reclaimed that blessing for which my soul yearns!"

How we long for a human touch—for a brother or sister who has passed over the sorrowful way we tread and can speak with the comfort of intimate knowledge to our hearts, one who understands and sympathizes and can help without condemning us. And such a One we find in Jesus. He took upon Himself our nature. He bore our sins. He is touched with the feeling of our infirmities. He was tempted in every way as we are, that He might meet this cry of our hearts, this deep human need of ours for a human touch, an understanding and unfailing sympathy. In Him we behold the condescension of God to the fathomless needs and bitterest cries of our smitten, broken hearts. And why does this sister need to cry, "Oh, if I only knew someone who has really reclaimed that blessing for which my soul yearns," since she can go to Him? It only shows the subtlety and obstinacy of doubt and fear, until I think I hear the Master pleading once again in tender rebuke, "O you of little faith, why did you doubt?" (Matt. 14:31 NKJV).

When people lose the experience of full salvation, they will never get it again if they spend their time in continual examination of their feelings and in vain regrets over lost emotions. The look must be forward not backward, outward not inward, and upward not downward. They must look to Jesus, not to other people, nor to the desolate heart that has lost His presence and joy. Attention must be given to the volitions, not to the emotions. Jesus said, "Anyone who chooses to do the will of God will find out whether my teaching comes from God or whether I speak on my own" (John 7:17 NIV). He did not say "feel." We must give our whole attention to willing and doing, not feeling.

Comfortable feelings will follow right willing and doing if we have faith. If we have faith—ah, there's the rub!

It is hard to get people to believe once they have lost the blessing. Yet God bends over them in infinite and everlasting love as eager and willing to restore the blessing as He was to give it at the beginning. "He restores my soul," cried the psalmist (Ps. 23:3 ESV). "I will restore to you the years that the swarming locust has eaten, the hopper, the destroyer, and the cutter. . . . You shall eat in plenty and be satisfied, and praise the name of the LORD your God, who has dealt wondrously with you. And my people shall never again be put to shame" (Joel 2:25–26 ESV).

God never denies a penitent, seeking, trusting soul. He will restore the wanderer (see Jer. 3:12, 14, 22) and do exceeding abundantly more than all that person asks or thinks (see Eph. 3:20), if he or she will seek wholeheartedly in simple faith and obedience.

The shepherd is eager to bring back the lost sheep. The faithful physician is glad to restore the patient to health, even if the illness was brought on by the patient's own carelessness or wrongdoing. The captain will spare no pains to rescue a drowning sailor, though it was through his or her own folly that the sailor was swept overboard. The loving father watches and waits long with an aching heart for the return of the prodigal child. And God is like the shepherd and physician and captain and father. God will not be mocked, and we trifle with Him at our peril. But:

> The love of God is broader
> Than the measure of man's mind:
> And the heart of the Eternal
> Is most wonderfully kind.[1]

God will surely give the blessing once more to this sister and any like her—and quickly—if they will cease to dishonor Him by doubting His love. How the Devil has been deceiving and mocking her, and how a heart of unbelief has given the Devil his opportunity!

"Oh, if I only knew someone who has really reclaimed that blessing for which my soul yearns," she wrote, as though God's Word, God's unchangeable character, God's boundless love revealed in Christ Jesus, were not sufficient ground for faith. But I quite understand this weakness and trembling and bitterness of doubt, for I have passed through it with tears of anguish, which were my meat by day and by night—and I know that the lost blessing may be found once more!

John Wesley used to say that most people lost the blessing two or three times before they learned how to keep it. Many years ago, during one of my campaigns in Sweden, a Salvation Army officer (minister) who had lost the blessing wrote me a letter in which she told me how she had attended one of my meetings hoping to get the lost blessing once more. I cannot quote her exact words, but I have never forgotten the substance of her letter. She said she sat through the meeting and listened with unutterable longing, but when the invitation was given to come and pray at the penitent form (the place at the altar for seeking forgiveness), she hesitated, shrank back, and did not come. She left the meeting with an added sense of loss and condemnation. She prayed in agony all the way home and tossed on her bed that night in prayer.

The next day she was sick in bed but spent the day praying, reading her Bible and my little book *Helps to Holiness*. The next day she was able to get up but went about her work with a great cry in her heart for the blessing, but no light came. On Sunday morning she arose with a breaking heart, wondering how she could face the services of the day. Long before the meeting started, she got alone with God and poured out her heart to Him, when suddenly the blessing streamed into her soul and she was flooded with light and love and peace. She went to the meeting and told her experience, and that morning the penitent form was crowded with seekers. She said they laughed and cried and told how they had longed for the blessing, and that day they had great victory.

Two years later I was going through Stockholm from Finland, and the commissioner (Salvation Army regional leader) spoke to me about that woman. He said that for a long time she had no power, but from that glad Sunday morning she had been a victorious soul, radiant with love and joy, winning souls everywhere, quickening dead corps (churches) into life and liberty, and turning barren wastes into veritable gardens of the Lord, until he felt that in time she would be capable of leading the largest ministry in Sweden.

In Australia, a Salvation Army officer told me that for ten years she had not had the blessing and that her soul was drying up. She was going about her duty in a mechanical way, with no joy or assurance in her heart, and she felt she never could get back the lost blessing. I assured her that God was not more willing to pour sunshine upon her than He was willing to shine in her heart once more if she would trust and obey. After some questioning I found that she had been bitterly criticizing a superior under whom she had worked some time before. I pointed out that this was a violation of the Lord's commands. I told her she must write him a letter, tell him his faults (if she thought best), and ask his forgiveness for having talked to others about him. She said she could not, for she knew just the spirit in which he would receive such a letter. But I assured her it made no difference how he received it—her duty was to write it, and without writing it she could not have God's favor. She shook her head and went away.

On Sunday morning, the last day of our stay in that city, she came to me and said, "I feel as though I have been in hell all night!" I replied, "You have not been in hell; you have only been in the vestibule of hell. But if you do not submit to God and do as I tell you—write that letter and let God have His way with you—you will be in hell someday, and maybe sooner than you think!" I felt confident that she was facing a crisis; that the Holy Spirit was making, possibly, a final appeal to her; and that her eternal destiny would be determined by her decision.

That night we had a great meeting. Thirty souls were at the penitent form. She sat halfway down the hall, a picture of despair. I went to her and urged her to settle it, and she came forward at once. I can see her still, down there on the other side of the world, a struggling, seeking soul. At last she promised God she would write that letter and peace began to nestle in her heart.

The next morning she came to me with a radiant face and said, "Oh, God has come back to my heart! He has been with me all night! I feel as though I have been in heaven!" Later she wrote several letters to me, saying that she had never known such depths of peace and sweetness of soul as the Lord had now given her. Then a heavy, unexpected trial came that taxed her faith to the utmost—but the Comforter was in her heart, and He did not fail her. Her faith held firm while the storm swept over her, and she was all the stronger for the trial.

I could easily cite many more examples of people who had lost the blessing who came seeking and finding once more in my meetings, and their letters to me have pulsed with joy as they related their experiences.

If you have lost the blessing, you may have it again. God waits to bless you if, with penitent heart and full consecration, you will now believe. Do it now, for Jesus has not changed in His love for you. His blood has not lost its efficacy. Only believe!

But you may be someone who is "blind, forgetting that they have been cleansed from their old sins" (2 Pet. 1:9 NLT). Such a case is pitiable indeed. But God can quicken a dead soul to life again. Jesus is the Resurrection and the Life, and the deadest, driest, most helpless soul who looks to Him will live and flourish and rejoice once more.

NOTE

1. Frederick W. Faber, "There's a Wideness in God's Mercy," 1854, public domain.

Hold Fast 17

In times of peril, when great ships are tossed on mountainous waves and plunged into deep and treacherous troughs of stormy seas, we must stand alert and responsive, ready for every duty we have learned in untroubled days.

This war-worn world has plunged into such a raging sea as it has never known before, and mighty nations are tossed like storm-beaten ships on its wild waves.[1] People's hearts are troubled. Their minds are perplexed. Their faith is tried in sevenfold-heated fires. Their patience is taxed to the uttermost while the accumulated wealth of the world is thrown with wild haste into the bottomless pit of war and the youth of the world is being swept away in storms of steel and torrents of blood. The eyes of courageous men and weeping women are strained and wearied, trying to peer through the darkness to discover a rift in the black clouds of war.

It is a perilous time! The old order changes, yielding place to the new. And we are sweeping into an era the character of which no one can forecast, yet which we hope will be more glorious than any former time.

But if this better time is yet to be, it must come not from a triumph of big guns, powerful navies, and conquering armies, but from the progress and triumph of the Spirit of Jesus into human hearts.

It is righteousness that exalts a nation (see Prov. 14:34) and the Spirit of Christ that promotes peace on earth and good will toward all. Ten righteous souls could have saved Sodom, but for lack of them the city was destroyed. Righteous men and women—people of justice, loving-kindness, goodwill, and purity—are more surely the bulwarks of nations than battleships and trained armies.

I honor the police officers and soldiers who maintain law and order, who uphold the rights of people to life and liberty and the lawful pursuits of happiness. But how immeasurably increased would be their task if God's ministers and heralds of the gospel were to cease saving souls and training them in truth and righteousness! Charles Spurgeon is reported to have said, "Take the Salvation Army out of London and you will have to increase its police force by seven thousand."[2]

No one is doing—or can do—a greater work for any country than saving men and women from sin and making them just and true and holy. In view of this, we must hold fast to the principles and spirit we have learned in calm and untroubled days. We serve our country and all humanity by doing so. An evil person—full of falsity, wrath, hasty speech, and uncontrolled passion and appetite—is a menace to any country, especially so at such a time as this, and we can find no higher service than that of saving people from all sin and getting them baptized with the Holy Spirit and the fire of truth and love.

We must hold fast to our faith—faith in God, faith in His care, faith in His superintending providence, and faith in His pity and love despite all contrary appearances. We must hold fast to our faith in His unalterable purpose to establish righteousness in the earth, with punishment for the guilty, correction and discipline and trial for good men and women, and in the end abundant and everlasting reward for those who diligently seek Him.

In times of trial, distress, and perplexity, faith must be fought for. A weak and flabby will and nerveless purpose will let faith slip. It is a priceless treasure that must be held fast. It was this deathless grasp of faith—or grasp of God by faith—that sustained the saints and soldiers of God in ages past. It was at a time when everything was swept away by invading armies and famine was stalking through the land, that Habakkuk cried out: "Even though the fig trees have no blossoms, and there are no grapes on the vines; even though the olive crop fails, and the fields lie empty and barren; even though the flocks die in the fields, and the cattle barns are empty, yet I will rejoice in the LORD! I will be joyful in the God of my salvation!" (Hab. 3:17–18 NLT).

He believed God. He held fast in the darkest hour when all the foundations on which people of the world build their hopes were ruthlessly swept away.

O for a faith that will not shrink

Though pressed by every foe,

That will not tremble on the brink

Of any earthly woe![3]

We must hold fast brotherly love and Christlike compassion. Christ's loving-kindness did not fail. When they spat on His face, crowned Him with thorns, scourged and bruised and ripped and mocked Him in His agony, He prayed for them and pitied them in their blind rage and spiritual darkness and ignorance. Oh, to be like Him! To fail is to disappoint Him at the point of battle where He has placed us. It is to defeat His far-reaching plans, and this we must not—we will not—do.

There is no time for hate, O wasteful friend:

Put hate away until the ages end.

Have you an ancient wound? Forget the wrong.

Out in my West, a forest loud with song

Towers high and green over a field of snow,

Over a glacier buried far below.[4]

We must hold fast to prayer and patient communion with God. During the war of the American Revolution, Bishop Francis Asbury, that wonderful and saintly Methodist, gave part of each hour of the day to prayer, and so—keeping his heart like a watered garden—was a true spiritual shepherd of the people. Our strength and comfort will come only from God through unbroken fellowship with Him. This can be maintained and nourished only by much prayer. When your heart is aching and breaking and darkness surrounds you, pray. Remember God and pray.

We must hold fast to the Bible. It throws floods of light upon our pathway and our duty in just such times as these. The Minor Prophets have furnished much food for my soul of late. No war-swept country of Europe suffers more than did the land of those ancient saints and seers of God, but through all the woe and desolation, the word of the Lord was their counselor and comfort, and they have a living message for us today.

In the Bible we discover both the judgments and the tender mercies, the goodness and the severity of God (see Rom. 11:22). There we find the great truths that will nourish our faith, fortify and sustain our souls, and rightly guide our conversation and conduct in dark and troubled days. Fed on these words of God, we walk with inner strength and assurance and are able to possess our souls in patience while the world reels through the storm into a bright and better day.

We must hold fast to our hope. In a time of great trouble and deep depression, the psalmist cried out: "Why am I discouraged? Why is my heart so sad? I will put my hope in God! I will praise him again— my Savior and my God!" (Ps. 42:11 NLT).

To the saints at Rome, in Caesar's household, to those who stood in constant danger of the martyr's death in all hideous forms, Paul wrote, "I pray that God, the source of hope, will fill you completely with joy and peace because you trust in him. Then you will overflow with confident hope through the power of the Holy Spirit" (Rom. 15:13 NLT). God will not fail, and we must hope on through storm and stress until the dawn of a perfect day.

We must hold fast to golden silence and sobriety of speech. Our speech should be gracious, thoughtful, healing, and helpful. "Be quick to listen, slow to speak, and slow to get angry," wrote James. "Human anger does not produce the righteousness God desires" (James 1:19–20 NLT).

Upright men and women cannot do other than to condemn wrong once they see it. They cannot be morally sound and condone injustice and evil. But if this condemnation is to effect righteousness, it must not be explosive but ordered and sustained. Then, like the tidal forces of nature, it is irresistible, and it works out "the righteousness God desires."

Finally, we must hold fast to our God-appointed task of winning souls to God's kingdom. That is a warfare from which there is no discharge, and if it is unfalteringly and faithfully waged, it will populate heaven with redeemed and happy souls and rob hell of its prey.

> Pour out thy love like the rush of a river,
> Wasting its waters for ever and ever,
> Through the burnt sands that reward not the giver;
> Silent or songful thou nearest the sea.
> Scatter thy life as the summer showers pouring.
> What if no bird through the pearl rain is soaring?
> What if no blossom looks upward adoring?
> Look to the life that was lavished for thee.[5]

Let us hold fast that which we have, that no one can take our crown.

NOTES

1. This meditation was written during World War I.

2. Original source unknown.

3. William H. Bathurst, "O for a Faith That Will Not Shrink," 1831, public domain.

4. Edwin Markham, "The Hidden Glacier," in *The Shoes of Happiness, and Other Poems* (Garden City, NY: Doubleday, 1922), 100.

5. Rose Terry, "Give! As the Morning That Flows Out of Heaven," in *Poems* (Boston: Ticknor and Fields, 1861), n. p.

What about My Future? 18

The question, "What about my future?" agitates many Christians' hearts and minds and is often anxiously asked. It is a question I have asked myself, and one which frequently gave me much concern, especially in times of weakness and weariness of body and depression of mind and spirit, until by prolonged and careful study of God's Word on the subject—and much meditation and prayer—faith triumphed over doubts and fears.

This question troubles us most when:

- We are weary and worn by overwork or sickness.
- We marry and children come—and sweet little mouths clamor to be fed, helpless little bodies have to be clothed, unfolding and eager little minds need to be educated, and the precious health of darling loved ones must be considered.

- Age creeps on at a fast pace. When we pick up our Bible some morning and find the words glimmering before us and running together, and no rubbing of the eyes or change of light will help us read with ease, and the physician we consult says, "You have reached the age where you must use glasses." When we can no longer bound up stairs or run uphill without breathing hard and painfully fast. When our digestion weakens and we must be careful about our diet. When our voice no longer rings with the full resonance of youth and sleep fails just a little in restoring all the springs of our body and mind. When gray hairs begin to show among the black or brown. When we want the younger crowd to count us as one of themselves but instead they stop their loud laughter and assume an air of decorous respect when we appear, in deference to our age. When we wake up to the fact that we are not young anymore, but that age is overtaking us—then this specter of the future sits down before us and demands our attention and persistently asks again and again, "What provision are you making for me?"

Now, what shall we answer to this question? Thank God, it can be answered. He Himself has answered it, and we can laugh at it and be glad and joyous and triumphant—if we will.

The first answer is close at hand and is good, though of itself it does not always fully satisfy us. It is this: There may not be any future before us. Death may be at our door, ready even now to strike us down! We may not live to see tomorrow, so why be troubled about it and fill today with the cares of tomorrow that may not be? Jesus Himself said,

"Don't worry about tomorrow, for tomorrow will bring its own worries" (Matt. 6:34 NLT).

> Why shouldst thou fill today with sorrow
> About tomorrow,
> My heart?
> One watches all with care most true;
> Doubt not that He will thee too
> Thy part.[1]

But suppose tomorrow does come with many others. What then about my future? I answer: Have faith in God. In the strongest, plainest possible language He has spoken to our fainting, fearful hearts and assured us of His unfailing care. And the only reason we do not have perfect peace regarding the future is because we do not have perfect faith in Him right now. Someone has said that if we could have foreseen the dangers attending our birth and the first years of our utterly helpless infancy we would have faced birth with far more fear than we now face death. But the Lord put it into the hearts of some to love and pity and care for us when we were helpless, crying, whining infants, and He will cause someone to love and pity and care for us in old age if we walk in His ways and keep a glad trust in Him. "Give your burdens to the LORD, and he will take care of you. He will not permit the godly to slip and fall" (Ps. 55:22 NLT). He bids us to consider the lilies, the grass, and the sparrows for whom He cares, and He assures us that He will far more surely care for us.

Who feareth hath forsaken
The heavenly Father's side;
What He hath undertaken
He surely will provide.

The very birds reprove thee
With all their happy song;
The very flowers teach thee
That fretting is a wrong.

"Cheer up," the sparrow chirpeth;
"Thy Father feedeth me;
Think how much He careth,
Oh, lonely child, for thee!"

"Fear not," the flowers whisper;
"Since thus He hath arrayed
The buttercup and daisy,
How canst thou be afraid?"[2]

The Hebrews were assured of God's care: "Be satisfied with what you have. For God has said, 'I will never fail you. I will never abandon you.' So we can say with confidence, 'The LORD is my helper, so I will have no fear. What can mere people do to me?'" (Heb. 13:5–6 NLT).

If God allows me to occupy my body, will He not see that I have food to feed it and garments to clothe it? He said He would (see Matt. 6:25–34). And shall I not stoutly trust Him and laugh at fear and be glad? By His grace, I will. Nothing is more likely to disjoint our relationship with God and precipitate trouble upon us than a faithless anxiety about the future and our loved ones.

The children of Israel had seen God's mighty works and unfailing faithfulness in bringing them out of Egypt through the Red Sea and the wilderness and up to Kadesh-Barnea, but they would not trust themselves in His hands to go over into Canaan! They said, "Why is the Lord taking us to this country only to have us die in battle? Our wives and our little ones will be carried off as plunder! Wouldn't it be better for us to return to Egypt?" (Num. 14:3 NLT). And this fearfulness proved their undoing, for while their children escaped, they all perished in the wilderness, except for Caleb and Joshua, who believed God. Job said, "What I always feared has happened to me, and what I dreaded has come true" (Job 3:25 NLT). And so it always does.

Two Salvationists—a husband and wife—felt called into ministry as officers. But they said, "No, we must educate our children," and refused. Then they lost their faith and left the Army. After some time, when their daughter was about fourteen years of age, beautiful as a picture, she went to The Salvation Army, surrendered her life to Jesus Christ, and wanted to join the ranks. But her parents said, "No, the Army will give you no social opportunities." Then the girl herself lost faith, and at sixteen—betrayed and soon to become a mother—was threatening to take her own life to hide her shame. They feared to obey God lest their children should lose educational and social opportunities. But in their disobedience and unbelief, their fears came upon them.

Do your present duty faithfully and joyfully. If we begin to be anxious about the future, it saps our joy, robs us of our trust in God, and blinds our eyes to those things we should now do to make our future safe. Our very anxiety about the future may help to produce conditions that will favor our fears and bring them in overwhelming power upon us.

Some years ago, two or three officers at a Salvation Army divisional headquarters became suspicious about their future in the Army, and they lost their joy and power. The miserable spiritual gangrene spread to the corps officers (pastors), and they lost their joy and gladness and sweet, simple trust in straining their poor eyes to look into the future that God had hidden from them and for which He commanded them to trust Him without an anxious thought. Since the officers had lost the joy and power, the poor, starved soldiers (church members) lost heart and interest. Subsequently, the light and glory fled from the worship gatherings, the public lost interest and ceased to come, the finances shrank, and the whole work languished, withered, and almost died. Those poor, foolish, fearful doubters could not see that their anxiety about the future was producing the conditions that would bring all their fears upon them like an avalanche. Not until others who were full of faith, joy, and the Holy Spirit rejoiced and prayed and shouted and rallied the doubting ones did the work recover from the blighting effect of their fear and unbelief.

The soul who doubts and fears and murmurs is walking right into the jaws of trouble. But for the one who keeps glad in God, rejoices, prays, and trusts in the teeth of hell, the path grows "brighter until the full light of day" (Prov. 4:18 NLT). God has pledged Himself to stand by such a person.

NOTES

1. Paul Fleming, in *The Optimist's Good Night*, comp. Florence Hobart Perin (Boston: Little, Brown, and Company, 1912), 231.

2. Mark Guy Pearce, *Christ's Cure for Care* (London: Hodder & Stoughton, 1902), 80.

Temptation 19

As the storm and whirlwind that twist the roots and toughen the fibers of an oak also help in its growth and development, so temptation is a part of our lot as moral beings in this state of probation. As occasional struggle with furious hurricanes and wild waves is a part of the sailor's discipline, and bloody battles and fierce danger are a portion of the soldier's lot, and difficult and hard lessons enter into the training of a student, so we are on trial. Our moral character is being fashioned and tested, and one of the most important factors in the formation of right character is temptation. An unchaste woman tempted Joseph, and he began the ascent to sublime heights of holy character and influence by resisting and overcoming the temptation.

Moses, doubtless, was tempted to remain in the selfish enjoyment of the luxury and learning and pomp and power of Pharaoh's court. But he resisted and overcame, "choosing rather to suffer affliction with the people of God, than to enjoy the pleasures of sin for a season; esteeming the reproach of Christ greater riches than the treasures in Egypt" (Heb. 11:25–26 KJV). And he became the world's outstanding lawgiver.

Daniel was tempted by the wine from Nebuchadnezzar's table, and peculiar strength was added to the temptation by the fact that he was a captive slave boy, far from home and in the king's palace, being trained for special duties in the king's service. But he "resolved that he would not defile himself with the king's food, or with the wine that he drank" (Dan. 1:8 ESV). And he received at last the highest honors the king could bestow.

Those temptations were part of their discipline and were turning points in those men's lives. They were God-permitted opportunities. Weak men would probably have yielded to the temptations and gone down in a night of moral blackness and ruin, but they overcame and—walking out into an eternal day of moral beauty and grandeur—became friends of God with holy characters that shine with undimmed splendor through the centuries. Temptation solicited them to evil, to sensual indulgence, to selfish pleasure, to personal safety, and to worldly glory. But they refused and chose the way of righteousness, self-denial, shame, reproach, and the cross. They feared, loved, trusted, and obeyed God, and God blessed them, walked with them, taught them, comforted them, and strengthened them until He could pile the cares, perplexities, and mountain-like responsibilities of empires upon them without them failing Him or murmuring at the burden.

And we, in turn, and according to our strength and duties, must be tempted. We cannot evade it, but—thank God—we, as they, can overcome it and rise by means of our fellowship with Jesus and holy men and women of all time. The Bible is teeming with encouragements to tempted souls.

We are assured that "the temptations in [our lives] are no different from what others experience" (1 Cor. 10:13 NLT). Others have gone this way before us triumphant, and so may we. Even while we are struggling with temptation, we may rest assured that others are fighting the same devil, battling with the same kind of trial. We are not alone. A great company of secret ones whom God knows is passing through the same fire with us, and if we are true we shall meet and know them by and by. No matter how strange and awful they may seem to us, our temptations are common to all humanity.

We are assured that "God is faithful. He will not allow the temptation to be more than you can stand. When you are tempted, he will show you a way out so that you can endure" (1 Cor. 10:13 NLT). God measures the full force of every trial and temptation, and will not allow it to exceed our strength, if we will promptly look to Him and seek His help. God allowed Satan to go only so far with Job (see Job 1:12; 2:6). And when we trust Him, He says to our temptations (as He does to the sea), "This far and no farther will you come" (Job 38:11 NLT).

We are assured that Jesus is able to sympathize with our weaknesses, "for he faced all of the same testings we do, yet he did not sin" (Heb. 4:15 NLT). And "since he himself has gone through suffering and testing, he is able to help us when we are being tested" (Heb. 2:18 NLT).

Again, we are told, "God blesses those who patiently endure testing and temptation. Afterward they will receive the crown of life that

God has promised to those who love him" (James 1:12 NLT), and we cannot have the crown of life under any other condition. How can the oak have the crown of life, strength, and lordly beauty, unless it withstands the storm? How can the soldier have the crown of victory if he or she gives up the battle and runs away from the fight?

What are we to do since we know we will be tried by temptation? The instruction of Jesus to His disciples was, "Keep watch and pray, so that you will not give in to temptation" (Matt. 26:41 NLT). Many temptations can be avoided by watchfulness and prayer. If we run carelessly into temptation, we may find it more difficult to get out than we supposed, and we may find ourselves ruined or subjected to lifelong sorrow, shame, weakness, suffering, and conflict as a result of our folly. If David had watched and prayed, as he should have, he would not have brought such shame and reproach to the cause of God as he did. If Peter had watched and prayed instead of sleeping while Jesus was agonizing in the garden, he probably would not have denied his Lord, nor cursed and sworn as he did.

If temptation comes upon us which we cannot escape, however much we may watch and pray, then we are to do like Roosevelt's Rough Riders in the thunder of battle: rush forward with a shout and fight to a finish. James said, "Dear brothers and sisters, when troubles of any kind come your way, consider it an opportunity for great joy. For you know that when your faith is tested, your endurance has a chance to grow" (James 1:2–3 NLT). Face each temptation as it comes. Fight it out.

It is well for us to consider that eternal life and heaven hang on the issue, and we must overcome or perish. We need not perish, for we are invited to "come boldly to the throne of our gracious God. There we will receive his mercy, and we will find grace to help us when we need it most" (Heb. 4:16 NLT). All of heaven is on our side. Our heavenly Father is pledged to give us more grace. Jesus is all compassion and pitying love. He cannot forget His forty days and nights of temptation in the wilderness and His agony in the garden, and "he knows how weak we are; he remembers we are only dust" (Ps. 103:14 NLT). He will surely give us grace to help in time of need. We are not to come timidly and fearfully, but boldly. If my child is in danger, I don't want him to be afraid to come to me for help. I want him to come promptly, boldly, even if it is due to his own fault that he is endangered. I am his father and he is my child and he has a right to come. And so God would have us come to Him with all confidence, and He will not fail us, but will with the temptation also make a way to escape, that we may be able to bear it.

When the Comforter Is Come

One cold, wintry day, the great, warmhearted preacher Henry Ward Beecher was walking down an almost deserted street when he found a little child crying bitterly. He picked up the child in his strong arms and folded the child on his broad breast. When the child ceased sobbing, he asked, "What is the matter, little one?"

The child replied, "Nuffin' is the matter since you comed!"

So it is with the troubled soul when the Comforter comes to abide. He dries our tears, banishes our sorrow, assures our hearts, and gives perfect peace. He is ever coming to men and women, but He finds them so preoccupied with their own affairs that He cannot abide with them. The floods of worldliness, pleasure, passion, and business so overflow them that, like Noah's dove when sent out from the ark (see Gen. 8:8–9), He can find no place to rest. But when He finds a troubled soul whose pleasures have dried up, whose passion is stilled, whose business is secondary to the needs of the spirit, and who hungers and thirsts for God, then He can find a resting place. Then He will abide. This coming of the Comforter is a holy event, a solemn act. It must be preceded by an intelligent and sincere covenant between the soul and God. It is a marriage of the soul to the Redeemer and is not a trial marriage. No true marriage is rushed into carelessly. It is carefully considered. It is based on complete separation and consecration, the most serious pledges and vows. So, if the Comforter is to come to abide, to be with and in us evermore, we must come out and be separate for Him, consecrate ourselves fully and forever to Jesus, and covenant to be the Lord's "for better, for worse," and trust Him. The soul that is thus truly and solemnly dedicated to Him becomes His, and He will come to that soul to abide forever, to be a shield and an "exceeding great reward" (Gen. 15:1 KJV). What happens when He comes?

There is rest in the heart, and that rest is reflected in the face. Those who really have the blessing have peaceful faces. The eyes take on new brightness and luster. Notice how those who have the blessing look you straight in the eye. Their look is direct and penetrating. They seem to see right through you. I have sometimes felt, when holy people have been looking at me, as though the eyes of Jesus were turned upon me. Often such a look will convict the sinning and unsanctified person of his or her need and lead that person to cry for pardon and purity.

The evangelist Charles Finney went into a factory once, and some of the girls began to laugh. He looked at them until one or two burst into tears, and they had to stop the machinery and have a prayer meeting. A great revival followed.

There is certainty and confidence in the heart, and this is felt in the testimony. The testimony may not be very noisy, but it will have power, because there is no note of uncertainty and doubt in it. There is a ring of faith and knowledge and assurance that carries conviction to those who hear. The Comforter is behind it. The fire of His blessed presence is felt and this leads to unusual results. People take notice of what is said. They are no longer indifferent. A division takes place. Some will be glad and some will—strange to say—be mad. It was so on the day of Pentecost. A multitude believed and became followers of Jesus, but some were filled with mocking and rage.

Such testimony makes people feel the sweetness of the Spirit, the reality of sin, the possibility of righteousness, and the certainty of a coming judgment. The simplest Holy Spirit testimony has something of this power in it. Reality is in it, eternity is in it, God is in it, and so it has power.

In New Zealand, a seventeen-year-old girl got the blessing of holiness in one of my meetings. Her brother had laughed and made fun of her religion, but now she had the Comforter abiding with her to help her. Peace and love and power were in her heart, and a few days afterward, her brother came to her. "Say, Sis," he said, "I want to have a few words with you." He led her to another room and shut the door. Then, bursting into tears, he said, "I've been watching you these few days and I want to get saved. Won't you pray for me?" She was glad, and prayed with him, and he was gloriously saved. The last I heard of him he had been used in the salvation of six of the clerks in the bank where he worked. He said he was going to try to win them all for the service of God.

A great love for God and loyalty to Jesus Christ fill the heart when the Comforter comes. He glorifies Jesus and testifies of Jesus (see John 15:26; 16:14). And now, for very love of Jesus, service becomes natural and increasingly easy, and the soul is prepared for sacrifice and suffering. Love flows like a river when the Comforter comes. But the Devil is not dead, and so there may be fierce and strange temptations at times. But just as the boat on the stormy sea could not go down with Jesus on board, so the soul cannot be defeated with the Comforter abiding within. "I pray that God, the source of hope, will fill you completely with joy and peace because you trust in him. Then you will overflow with confident hope through the power of the Holy Spirit" (Rom. 15:13 NLT).

> I know Thee, Savior, who Thou art,
> Jesus, the feeble sinner's friend;
> Nor wilt Thou with the night depart,
> But stay and love me to the end:
> Thy mercies never shall remove;
> Thy nature and Thy name is Love.[1]

NOTE

1. Charles Wesley, "Come, O Thou Traveler Unknown," 1742, public domain.

The Whisperer 21

A dear brother wrote, "There is such a need of solid work down this way, and I somehow do not seem able to rise to the demands. I do feel, however, that Jesus saves me, and I enjoy victory. But I do not seem to enjoy the blessing as I should. I am sure I strive with all my heart to live close to God, and there never was a time when I felt His presence more, but there is something in the way. Please pray for me!"

What can be the trouble? Having nothing from which to judge but that brief paragraph, I strongly suspect that the "something in the way" is a bit of subtle unbelief that leads him to hesitate to testify definitely to the blessing of holiness. The Enemy whispers, "You do not feel as you ought to feel; there is something in the way," but he does not recognize the Devil with his sly suggestions, and so instead of fighting the good fight of faith and resisting the Devil, steadfast in the faith, our brother has unwittingly agreed with the Devil that "something is in the way," and that something is a tiny root of practical unbelief, which frustrates God's grace.

Revelation 12:10 says, "The accuser of our brothers and sisters has been thrown down to earth—the one who accuses them before our God day and night" (NLT). How was he thrown down? Note the answer in verse 11:

- They "defeated him by the blood of the Lamb" (NLT)—that is, they believed, they trusted the efficacy of the precious blood;
- And "by their testimony" (NLT)—that is, honoring the blood by believing, they further honored it by daring to testify in the face of a mocking and accusing Devil that the blood cleanses from all sin (see 1 John 1:7);
- And "they did not love their lives so much that they were afraid to die" (Rev. 12:11 NLT)—that is, they made a complete, uttermost consecration of their lives to Him who shed His blood for them and were prepared to die for their testimony.

These three conditions, firmly and fully met, will lead one into the enjoyment of the blessing and, maintained, will make the blessing permanent. This is where many fail.

I had a great fight and gained a great victory at that point more than thirty years ago. Early in the morning, before most people wake up, the Devil whispered to me, "You don't feel as you did; you know you don't." And while I listened to him, I did not feel as I had; my joy was quenched. "If you had the blessing you would feel different," whispered the fiend. And all that day I was followed by that mocking, sinister Whisperer, and all day long I resisted and kept throwing myself upon the promise, "Whoever comes to me I will never cast out" (John 6:37 ESV). I read my Bible, prayed, and held fast my faith in the teeth of the Enemy, but no light came, no deliverance burst upon me. About all I could do was to stand with my back to the wall and fight. But that I did.

That night I went to a holiness meeting, and when I got there the Tempter whispered, "Don't testify to the blessing here; you know what a fight you have had all this day, and you will tell a lie if you testify to it." Finally, in a desperation of faith, I said, "I will testify to it! I have given myself wholly to the Lord. I have not consciously withdrawn myself out of His hands. I can do no more than trust Him. I can, I will, I do trust the blood to cleanse me now." So I arose and testified as straight and clear as I could to a present and full salvation and, oh, what a victory I got! The Whisperer fled. The mocking, teasing voice was hushed. And then I saw that we overcome him by the blood of the Lamb and by the word of our testimony when we are wholly the Lord's.

The Devil fights against definite testimony and stirs up vague, subtle doubts in our hearts to hush our testimony, "For with the heart one believes and is justified, and with the mouth one confesses and is saved" (Rom. 10:10 ESV). And thus is the Enemy overcome.

We should testify joyfully to the Lord that the blood cleanses. We should testify boldly, defiantly to the Devil that the blood cleanses. We should testify quietly to our own hearts that the precious blood cleanses. We should testify humbly to husband, wife, friend, and family that the blood cleanses. We should testify in private and public, in each other's homes and in large gatherings that the blood of Jesus, the Lamb slain from the foundation of the world (see Rev. 13:8), cleanses from all sin.

If we will give our Lord honor and glory by our humble but definite testimony, He will give us the witness of the Spirit and help us to understand and outwit our old Enemy and accuser, the Devil, who is the whisperer.

How to Keep Sweet ▰ 22 ▰

"Do tell me how to keep cool!" I implored of the secretary as I walked into a New York office on a recent, roasting, steaming hot day.

"I wish someone would tell me how to keep sweet!" she replied, with a pathetic look on her anxious face.

Strange to say, the Scriptures never tell us to keep sweet, but the Savior bid us, "Have the qualities of salt among yourselves," and then added what may stand for sweetness: "And live in peace with each other" (Mark 9:50 NLT). And Paul wrote, "Let your conversation be gracious and attractive" (Col. 4:6 NLT). Possibly the word *gracious* in this text stands for the sweetness so longed for by that secretary, but the saving power of salt was uppermost in Paul's mind.

Nevertheless, her longing to be kept sweet was a heavenly desire, no doubt placed in her by the Holy Spirit. And God was, and is, waiting to fulfill that desire. Unfortunately, too many are quite content to be sour, grouchy, ill-tempered, impatient, angry, hasty, and hurtful in speech and temper.

Some people seem naturally sweet-tempered. They are seldom disturbed. They abound in good health, good temper, and goodwill. But without God's help this natural sweetness will not last. Only the conscious and constant indwelling of the Holy Spirit can keep secretaries on hot days in busy offices, tired mothers with crying children in cramped rooms, and burdened executives with anxieties and vexations always sweet to the very end, always Christlike, always firm without stubbornness, always calm without indifference, always meek without weakness, always yielding without cowardice, and always cheery without levity or neglect of responsibility.

"Let the peace that comes from Christ rule in your hearts," wrote Paul (Col. 3:15 NLT). He does not seem to think it a difficult matter for peace always to pervade us. All we have to do is *let it*. It is at hand. We do not have to ascend into heaven to get sunshine; it pours itself in boundless floods all about us. All we need to do is open wide our doors and windows and let it in. So with this peace of God.

Paul wrote, "Let the word of Christ dwell in you richly, teaching and admonishing one another in all wisdom, singing psalms and hymns and spiritual songs, with thankfulness in your hearts to God" (Col. 3:16 ESV). What a cheerful verse that is! Some people turn as naturally and instantly to the Word of God for instruction, guidance, comfort, and courage as the magnetic needle turns to the pole. They find the Word in their hearts and mouths (see Deut. 30:14; Rom. 10:8). When they go, it leads them. When they sleep, it keeps them. When they awake, it talks with them (see Prov. 6:22). But this Word is not to be kept locked up in the heart. It is to bubble forth in springs of refreshment for others. It must be used to admonish, cheer, correct, and inspire others. It must not be a stagnant pool, but a flowing, sparkling stream, if it is to be kept sweet. And as it sweetens others, it will surely sweeten us.

Paul also wrote, "Let this mind be in you, which was also in Christ Jesus" (Phil. 2:5 KJV). Jesus sought nothing for Himself. He gave all. He was among His contemporaries as one who serves. He came not to be served, but to serve, and to give His life as a ransom for many (see Matt. 20:28). Where service is voluntary and glad, it sweetens all life. Where it is forced by necessity and done reluctantly, grudgingly, with inward discontent and fretting of spirit, it robs the soul of joy and becomes nothing other than slavery. All who would keep sweet must deliberately choose the lowly mind of the Master and rejoice in all they put their hand to do. Doing all work as unto the Lord, as though it were done for Him, will surely sweeten all work. And this can be done. It is the very ideal of the Bible. We are not to work and serve as people-pleasers but "as bondservants of Christ, doing the will of God from the heart, rendering service with a good will as to the Lord and not to man" (Eph. 6:6–7 ESV).

"Let your speech always be gracious, seasoned with salt" (Col. 4:6 ESV). No one can keep sweet who gives way to unloving speech, to fretful, complaining talk, to angry words, or to idle, critical gossip. As James wrote, "And so blessing and cursing come pouring out of the same mouth. Surely, my brothers and sisters, this is not right! Does a spring of water bubble out with both fresh water and bitter water?" (James 3:10–11 NLT). Opening the mouth in speech is like opening the draft of your fire. Shut off the draft and the fire dies down. So shut off evil speech if you would keep sweet.

Finally, "Let brotherly love continue" (Heb. 13:1 ESV). The love of God is the great sweetener of all life. The heart that loves unfailingly will be a fountain of sweet waters from which healing streams will flow. Such a heart blesses its possessor and all who are around. It is both a fountain and a fire. If the fires of love are fed with fresh fuel every day from God's Word, if they are blown upon by the breath of prayer and praise, if the drafts are kept open by testimony and service to others, they will never go out but will burn on and on until they are caught up and commingled with the eternal fires of love that burn in the hearts of and enlighten forever the angelic hosts of heaven and the very heart of God Himself. Oh, how they love in heaven! Let us emulate them upon earth, and I am sure we shall know the secret of keeping sweet. The only good thing in life is love, and every drop of sweetness comes from this.

My heart was restless, weary, sad, and sore,
And longed and listened for some heaven-sent token:
And, like a child that knows not why it cried,
'Mid God's full promises it moaned, "Unsatisfied!"
Yet there it stands. O love surpassing thought,
So bright, so grand, so clear, so true, so glorious;
Love infinite, love tender, love unsought,
Love changeless, love rejoicing, love victorious!
And this great love for us in boundless store:
God's everlasting love! What would we more?[1]

NOTE

1. Frances Ridley Havergal, "Everlasting Love," in *Compensation and Other Devotional Poems* (New York: Anson D. F. Randolph & Company, 1881), 97.

When the Word of God Comes 23

Human beings cannot by searching find out God, but God can and does reveal Himself to them. In spite of the doubts and denials of agnostics and skeptics, God can and does make Himself known to His creatures. He does communicate with them. He opens their ears. He speaks to their hearts. He tells them His secrets. He shows them things to come. He reveals to them His will.

"Now the word of the LORD came to Jonah" (Jon. 1:1 ESV). Happy man! Men and women of force and spirit like to be brought into confidential relations with their rulers, to be entrusted with responsibility and sent on high missions. And here is an unknown, undistinguished soul singled out from the crowd by the Lord God Almighty and made an ambassador of heaven. What dignity and honor!

Mighty transformations are wrought by the coming of the word of the Lord to human hearts! They can never be the same as before. It will either exalt them to the place of partners and coworkers with God and give them a seat with Jesus on His throne, or it will banish them from His presence and doom them to hell. If obedient to the word, they will be saved, empowered, and brought into closest fellowship with God, into confidential relations with Him, and they will be transformed into the likeness of His Son. But if disobedient, they will shrivel as Judas did, and in the end be lost.

It is an awesome thing for the word of the Lord to come to a man or woman. It means that person's hour has come. It means facing the opportunity and purpose for which we were born. Our destiny for eternity turns on the way we receive that word and the use we make of it.

"A still small voice" (1 Kings 19:12 KJV) speaks out of the silence of eternity into our heart, and we know that it is the word of the Lord that has come to us. And from that hour, if we hush and listen and humble ourselves to obey this voice, we will cease to be of the common herd and become heirs of God and workers with Him.

The word of the Lord came to Noah, and he hearkened and stepped out from the ranks of the men of his generation, built the ark, and became the heir of the world. The word of the Lord came to Abraham, and he believed and obeyed, left his kindred and fatherland, and went forth, not knowing where he was going. He became "the father of the faithful," and in him all the families of the earth are blessed. The word of the Lord came to Moses while he was feeding sheep on the wild, barren mountains, and he went forth with his shepherd's rod to humble Pharaoh, deliver Israel, and become the world's lawgiver.

The word of the Lord came to Saul of Tarsus, the bigoted and murderous persecutor. And, humbling himself as a little child, he became the herald of the cross to all, the flaming evangelist, the worldwide, tireless missionary, the profound, tender teacher, the masterly organizer, the love slave of Jesus, and the triumphant martyr, the apostle Paul. The word of the Lord came to Luther, one of the numberless unknown monks, and he arose a free man. And with stroke upon stroke he broke the shackles of superstition and ecclesiastical tyranny until nations were set free. The word of the Lord came to John Wesley, and he heard and went forth to nearly threescore years and ten of tireless toil. His patient, loving, unwavering, self-sacrificing service set the world on fire with love, as it had not been since the days of Peter and Paul, and turned back the tide of infidelity and heathenism that was rolling over and swallowing up Christendom.

The word of the Lord came to William Booth when he was a boy of fifteen, and The Salvation Army—with its thousands of workers in dens and pubs and slums, in the bustling city and the dreary wilderness, under the midnight sun of Norway and the tropical sun of India and Sri Lanka, in London and Paris, in Berlin and New York, and in the far reaches of Africa and Alaska—was born. The word of the Lord came to multiplied thousands of humble, unknown men and women in kitchens and laundries, in mills and mines and markets, in stores and factories and offices, on shipboard and on farms, and made them mighty in simple faith and burning love and Christlike unselfishness to confound the wisdom and cast down the strength of this world, and to establish the kingdom of heaven on earth.

The word of the Lord comes not with thunder crashes that startle the world, but in still whispers to the heart of the one to whom it is addressed. The world hears no sound, but soon knows to whom God has spoken—knows by the love-lit eye, the shining face, the elastic step, the ringing voice, the positive, courageous message, the humble, patient devotion to duty, if the word is gladly received. Or it knows by the darkening countenance, the downcast, averted, or defiant eye, and the shrinking form that drops back to the rear seats or flees to far and dark corners if the word of the Lord is not gladly received. When the word of the Lord comes to a person, it means honor and dignity and joy. But it also may mean sorrow and trial and long and sore discipline, which, if willingly embraced, will mean final and eternal and inexpressible honor, dignity, and joy.

It must have thrilled Elijah's heart with joy when the Lord came to him. But how his faith must have been tried as the Devil whispered to him each day and night, "What if the ravens do not come?" And when the brook from which he drank began to dry up; and when he—a strong man—was made dependent upon a poor, desolate widow; and when her only child died and he was reproached for its death, it must have been a fierce trial of faith, a sore discipline of patience and hope! Yet, after Elijah's struggle and long warfare, the heavenly chariot swung so low that he stepped in and was swept to heaven in a whirlwind of fire without tasting death.

It is a joyous thing to hear God's word, and through it to become a man or woman with a mission, even though to flesh and blood it proves a grievous thing. It is the only way to true peace and highest usefulness here, and to endless glory and unfailing joy hereafter. It means toil and labor and conflict, but if our faith does not fail, it means final and eternal victory, too. Paul cried out—after his sore trials, his stupendous labors, his multitudinous conflicts and sorrows, and in sight of the executioner's ax—"I have fought a good fight, I have finished my course, I have kept the faith: henceforth there is laid up for me a crown of righteousness, which the Lord, the righteous judge, shall give me at that day" (2 Tim. 4:7–8 KJV).

Jesus still asks us, "Can you drink the cup I drink or be baptized with the baptism I am baptized with?" (Mark 10:38 NIV). For it is through that gateway of trial and suffering that we enter into the realms of blessedness, from which we shall go out no more, but will reign with Him forever. "If we suffer, we shall also reign with him" (2 Tim. 2:12 KJV). "We share in his sufferings in order that we may also share in his glory" (Rom. 8:17 NIV).

It is ever by the word of the Lord that God reveals Himself to His people. Happy will you be if you have an ear to hear, a heart to understand, and the will to obey the word of the Lord which comes to you and bids you rise and be a soul-winner. You, too, may know God's secret.

The Unpardonable Sin 24

A woman who was a complete stranger to me came to me in great distress, thinking that she had committed the unpardonable sin. She had, under stress of great temptation, broken a vow to the Lord. Later, with many tears and deep penitence, she confessed to Him and believed that He had forgiven her, but felt that the Holy Spirit had left her. She thought she knew the moment when He left and, with much detail, told me all the mental and spiritual exercises and agonies through which she had passed. Fortunately, I had had a similar experience many years before, in which I thought I was lost, and for weeks I walked in an agony of mental and spiritual suffering that is hard, if not impossible, to describe. Then one morning, in the twinkling of an eye, God lifted me out of that pit as a brother read these words to me: "No thoughts which cause us disquiet and agitation come from God who is Prince of Peace; they are, rather, temptations of the Enemy [or from

self-love or from the good opinion we hold ourselves], and therefore
we must reject them and take no notice of them."[1]

With lightning-like rapidity my mind took in the significance of
those words and I was free. I saw that I had no good opinion of myself.
All self-conceit had been burned out of me by the revelation of my
corrupt heart and of my utter dependence upon Another for salvation
and holiness of heart. I had no self-love, but rather self-loathing, for
I saw how hateful had been the pride and sin of my heart. Then I saw
that these disquieting thoughts were not from God, for He is the Prince
of Peace. Therefore, they must be of the Devil, and instantly it was as
though an octopus loosened its long arms from about my mind and
fled away. My soul nestled down into the arms of the Prince of Peace
and peace—an ocean of peace—washed over my tired mind and heart
and bore me up on its broad bosom, and since then peace has been the
heritage of my faith.

What was my trouble? What was the trouble with the woman who
came to me for advice? Just this: We were in such spiritual confusion
that we had taken our eyes off Jesus.

The Son is the Mediator. It is His blood that atones for sin. He is
our surety. It is in His name that we must ask for pardon and purity
and power and every grace and gift. It is as though a banker gave us
his bankbook and said, "Draw on me for all that you need."

The office of the Holy Spirit is to illuminate mind and heart, and to
make us see and feel the great love of the Father in the gift of His
Son—and the love of the Son in giving His life for us: "The Spirit . . .
will testify all about me" (John 15:26 NLT); "He will bring me glory
by telling you whatever he receives from me" (John 16:14 NLT);

"When the Spirit of truth comes, he will guide you into all truth. He will not speak on his own but will tell you what he has heard" (John 16:13 NLT).

The Holy Spirit is like a great searchlight, which throws its rays in a flood upon some noble object. We are not to focus upon the blinding light, but upon the object revealed by the light. So we are not to turn our eyes upon the Spirit, but on the Son, upon whom the Spirit pours His glorious light. "We do this by keeping our eyes on Jesus, the champion who initiates and perfects our faith" (Heb. 12:2 NLT). We must not turn our eyes from Jesus. He is our hope. He is the Rock of ages, cleft for us.

The Spirit also throws His light upon the Scriptures, and in them—under that glorious illumination—we find that which we are to believe concerning God and His love for us revealed in the Son. The Scriptures are the food of faith. I have never yet talked with one who thought he or she had committed the unpardonable sin—and I have talked with many—who was not continually telling me of feelings. They were starving and destroying faith by dependence upon feelings instead of nurturing it on the assurance and promises of God's Word.

They say, "I felt the Spirit leave me." The Word says, "I will never fail you. I will never abandon you" (Heb. 13:5 NLT).

They say, "I feel God has forgotten me." The Word says, "Never! Can a mother forget her nursing child? Can she feel no love for the child she has borne? But even if that were possible, I would not forget you! See, I have written your name on the palms of my hands" (Isa. 49:15–16 NLT).

They say, "I feel God has cast me off forever." The Word says, "I have chosen you and will not throw you away" (Isa. 41:9 NLT).

They say, "I feel God will not answer me." The Word says, "Call to me and I will answer you" (Jer. 33:3 ESV) and, "The same Lord . . . gives generously to all who call on him. For 'Everyone who calls on the name of the LORD will be saved'" (Rom. 10:12–13 NLT).

They say, "But I feel if I come to Him, He will not receive me." The Word says, "Come to me . . . and I will give you rest" (Matt. 11:28 NLT) and, "Whoever comes to me I will never drive away" (John 6:37 NIV).

They continually examine the pulse of their feelings instead of committing themselves into the care of the Great Physician and letting Him handle their case. They look at some past failure by day and night instead of looking to Jesus, who waits to save. They weep and cry for mercy, but they won't take it when it is extended to them. They cast away hope, while He whispers, "Hope in God" (Ps. 43:5 NLT), "for God chose to save us through our Lord Jesus Christ, not to pour out his anger on us. Christ died for us so that, whether we are dead or alive when he returns, we can live with him forever" (1 Thess. 5:9–10 NLT).

They continually say, "I felt," "I feel," while He says, "Believe"— "Believe in the Lord Jesus and you will be saved" (Acts 16:31 NLT). They want salvation by feeling before they take it by faith. They have lost sight of the Father and the Son and are seeking deliverance where it can never be found.

Such people feel or imagine that they have committed the unpardonable sin—the sin against the Holy Spirit—but they have done no such thing. The sin they are committing is the sin of unbelief, because they do not believe in Jesus; they turn their eyes away from Him and seek salvation in some other name. And "there is salvation in no one else! God has given no other name under heaven by which we must be saved" (Acts 4:12 NLT)—not even the name of the blessed Holy Spirit.

All the people I have ever met who thought they had committed the unpardonable sin were full of contrition. They wept and prayed and condemned themselves, and had love for the Savior, only they refused to believe that His mercies were still offered to them. The vast ocean of His love had become a burning desert to them. It had dried up. His compassions had clean failed forever. But it was not so with those men of whom Jesus spoke when He mentioned the unpardonable sin (see Matt. 12:32). They were not anxious. They shed no tears. No fears that they had committed an unpardonable sin filled their breasts. They refused to believe the credentials of Jesus, the mighty signs and wonders He worked, the wondrous creative and recreative miracles He performed—such as opening eyes that had been blind from birth, healing lepers with a word, raising the dead, stilling stormy seas by His command, and multiplying a little boy's lunch of loaves and fishes until they fed thousands.

I say they refused to believe these acts He performed in love before their eyes to enable them to believe, to justify them in believing that He, a humble carpenter from Nazareth, was indeed the Son of God. To believe His mighty claim to be the Son of God meant that they must humble themselves, confess their sins, put away their evil actions, sacrifice their pride, and follow Him; and this they would not do. They hardened their hearts and declared that the miracles He worked in the power of the Spirit were performed not by the Holy Spirit but by Beelzebub, the prince of devils.

This was the sin against the Holy Spirit, and the reason it was unpardonable was because it hardened the heart against those evidences and gifts and tender graces which alone could produce repentance and faith, and without which there can be no pardon. I have never seen anyone whom I could truly say had committed such a sin. And I have always been able to say to those weeping, anxious, penitent souls who mourned because they thought they had sinned the unpardonable sin, that I was fully convinced that they had not committed it. I could say this with the deepest conviction and the fullest confidence.

Those who had committed that sin had no sorrow, shed no tears, felt no anxious fear. They and their kind planned the destruction of Jesus, and not only of Jesus but also of Lazarus, whom He had raised from the dead, because the raising of Lazarus led simple, honest souls to believe on Jesus. They hired false witnesses to testify against Jesus, and when Pilate would have let Him go they appealed to Pilate's fears of his master, the emperor of Rome, and said, "If you release this man, you are no 'friend of Caesar'" (John 19:12 NLT). They cried out, "Crucify him! Crucify him! . . . Kill him, and release Barabbas to us!" (Luke 23:18, 21 NLT). And Barabbas was a murderer.

And when the Roman soldiers had crucified Jesus, they "shouted abuse, shaking their heads in mockery. . . . The leading priests, the teachers of religious law, and the elders also mocked Jesus. 'He saved others,' they scoffed, 'but he can't save himself!'" (Matt. 27:39, 41–42 NLT).

So He meekly bowed His head and died, while they mocked and refused to believe. There was sin, ripe and full and unpardonable, because it had carried those who were committing it beyond the power of tears and penitence and sorrow for sin. And such is the sin against the Holy Spirit, which "will never be forgiven, either in this world or in the world to come" (Matt. 12:32 NLT).

No one whose heart is broken with sorrow for his or her sins, and who is willing to come to Jesus and trust His atoning love, has committed that sin or any sin that is its equivalent.

Look to Jesus. Turn your eyes from yourself, your feelings, and your failures, and fix them on Jesus. Behold the Holy Spirit pointing you to Jesus, and hear the Spirit whispering, "Behold, the Lamb of God, who takes away the sin of the world" (John 1:29 ESV).

Look to Jesus. He is our hope. He is our peace, and if you believe in Him you shall "not perish but have eternal life. God sent his Son into the world not to judge the world, but to save the world through him" (John 3:16–17 NLT).

NOTE

1. St. Francis de Sales, *Letters of Spiritual Direction*, trans. Péronne Marie Thibert (New York: Paulist Press, 1988), 120.

Speaking with Tongues and the Everlasting Sign

When God sent Moses to free His people from Egyptian bondage and usher in the dispensation of the law at Sinai, He confirmed the message of His servant with signs and plagues and a great deliverance. And so, when the new dispensation of His Son was inaugurated, we read that "God confirmed the message by giving signs and wonders and various miracles and gifts of the Holy Spirit whenever he chose" (Heb. 2:4 NLT).

Among these signs and gifts of the Holy Spirit was "the ability to speak in unknown languages" (1 Cor. 12:10 NLT), mentioned in the Acts of the apostles and in Paul's first letter to the Corinthians. The bare mention of this gift is found in Acts, but in the church at Corinth it seems to have been one of a number of burning questions that required Paul's attention. And so, besides mentioning it in one chapter, he devoted another long chapter to a discussion of its relative value and its regulation.

The Corinthian church, while apparently vigorous and gifted, was not spiritually healthy. There were contentions among them (see 1 Cor. 1:11), arising from their divided preference for certain leaders (see 1 Cor. 1:12; 3:1–7). In at least one instance, there was practiced the most shameful licentiousness (see 1 Cor. 5:1–13). They went to court against each other before unbelievers (see 1 Cor. 6:1–8) and were unsound in their views of marriage (see 1 Cor. 7). Some of the men were gluttonous and others drunken (see 1 Cor. 11:21), while others of them seem to have been afflicted with conceit and spiritual pride (see 1 Cor. 14:36–37).

Paul fairly confronted all these conditions and wrote a letter full of homely, practical, and spiritual instruction to enlighten their understanding and correct their glaring faults.

In chapter 12, he mentioned nine gifts of the Spirit, seven of which were mentioned before "the ability to speak in unknown languages" (1 Cor. 12:10 NLT). And yet these Corinthians attached so much importance to the gift of tongues that Paul devoted one of the longest passages to showing how comparatively unimportant it is and how much better it would be for them to seek other gifts that were far more useful. Indeed, he said, "As for tongues, they will cease" (1 Cor. 13:8 ESV).

From a study of chapter 14, we learn:

1. That those who speak in unknown tongues speak not to other humans but to God (see 1 Cor. 14:2), and that they should not speak in church but keep silent, unless someone interprets (see 1 Cor. 14:28).

2. That while speaking in an unknown tongue may edify the one who speaks, it does not edify those who hear (see 1 Cor. 14:4), and it

leaves the speaker's own understanding untouched, by which it would seem to be a sort of ecstasy which can do no permanent good.

3. That instead of making sounds which are unintelligible both to ourselves and others, we should most earnestly desire to sing, pray, and speak with the understanding (see 1 Cor. 14:9, 15, 19). The apostle is here, as always, intensely practical and full of common sense, for he exalted that which is useful above that which is spectacular and exhorts the Corinthians to seek the gift of prophecy which will intelligently bless people, rather than the gift of tongues which may make them stare and wonder and go away unblessed, as he hinted that their preference for tongues was an evidence of childishness and infantile understanding, which prefers the gaudy toy to that which is highly useful (see 1 Cor. 14:20).

4. That Paul considered prophecy to be more valuable than speaking in unknown tongues (see 1 Cor. 14:19). Prophecy here does not mean foretelling future events but "forthtelling," out of corresponding experience, the saving and glorious truth of the gospel of Christ in a message that will edify, correct, and comfort (see 1 Cor. 14:3).

5. That the gift of tongues is not a sign to believers that they have the Holy Spirit but to unbelievers (see 1 Cor. 14:22), and it will be no sign to them if there is no interpreter. On the contrary, they will consider the speaker to be insane (see 1 Cor. 14:23).

6. That speaking in an unknown tongue hinders united worship and communion of spirit (see 1 Cor. 14:16–17). For people cannot say "amen" to what they do not understand, nor be blessed by a babble of meaningless sounds. Indeed, it may even do harm and work damage by leading the hearers to mock at what to them seems like the cackle of hysteria or the ravings of them that are insane (see 1 Cor. 14:23).

7. Finally, that the apostle did not become vexed and impatient with those who in ecstasy of joy or devotion and spiritual rapture speak an unintelligible language. "Don't forbid speaking in tongues," he wrote (1 Cor. 14:39 NLT). But we must not forget that he forbade them to speak in public unless there was an interpreter.

Paul's heart was full of the love of which he wrote in chapter 13, and he wanted that love to abound in the Corinthians' hearts. Love will make those who do not speak in tongues patient with those who do, so that they will not forbid them to speak. And love will make those who speak in tongues exercise their gifts in private before the Lord, for their own edification, instead of in public when there is no interpreter, to avoid offense and confusion.

In case there were any who thought that by keeping silent they grieved the Holy Spirit, Paul added, "People who prophesy are in control of their spirit and can take turns. For God is not a God of disorder but of peace, as in all the meetings of God's holy people" (1 Cor. 14:32–33 NLT).

As a wise and devout commentator has written, "This means, not that the divine Spirit should be overruled, but that the disorder of the human spirit, under divine influence, should be steadied and ruled by the rational faculty, in accord with the principles of order and becomingness."[1]

So here let none claim that they are obliged by the powerful and uncontrollable impulses of the Spirit to overbear reason, order, or decency. And that such claims of being moved by the divine Spirit to disorder are false is clear from the solemn fact that "God is not a God of disorder" (1 Cor. 14:33 NLT).

Where confusion or disorder occur, it is due to the uncontrolled human spirit and is a violation of God's will as expressed in His Word.

As floods of water flowing into a canal can accomplish a useful purpose only so long as the banks are sufficiently high and unbroken to hold the water, so the Holy Spirit coming into a person can only fulfill His gracious purposes so long as that person's spirit is firm and under strong and intelligent discipline and control. And it is for the guidance of such discipline and control that the apostle wrote this long passage on the gifts of prophecy and tongues.

These gifts, the apostle assures us, shall not continue. "As for prophecies, they will pass away; as for tongues, they will cease" (1 Cor. 13:8 ESV). In the minds of many, the special significance of this chapter is a thing of the past, and it is without application to us today. But this is not true. The gift of tongues may or may not have ceased, but the great principles of the chapter abide for our guidance. And we are only safe from the delusions of the Devil and of our own spirits as we carefully follow its plain principles and instructions. Running through it all is the heavenly love that seeks to edify rather than to amaze and mystify, which knits hearts together in divine unity and fellowship instead of driving them asunder by disorder and confusion.

NOTE

1. Daniel Denison Whedon, *Commentary on the New Testament, Intended for Popular Use*, vol. 4 (New York: Phillips & Hunt, 1875), 110.

The Fleeing Prophet 26

Men and women who do things for God and who have God on their side usually, in the beginning, find their way rough, hedged in, and difficult. "It is good for people to submit at an early age to the yoke of his discipline," wrote Jeremiah (Lam. 3:27 NLT), and this is their lot and their portion. Their hearts are encouraged and their spirits supported not by favorable circumstances and applauding crowds and smiling heavens, but by a stern sense of duty; a secret, silent whisper of faith and hope; and a hidden fire of love which "laughs at impossibilities and cries: 'It shall be done!'"[1] With Queen Esther they say, "If I perish, I perish" (Est. 4:16 KJV), and follow where God leads. With Job, they say, "Though he slay me, yet will I trust in him" (Job 13:15 KJV).

It was doubtless so with Noah through those long years of waiting and working, while the faith was being fashioned and tried which made him heir of the world. It certainly was so with Joseph, through those years of slavery and imprisonment before he was lifted up to Pharaoh's side and made ruler of Egypt and set to teach his senators wisdom. It was so with Moses during those forty years in Pharaoh's palace as the reputed son of Pharaoh's daughter, in which he mastered the wisdom and learning of Egypt, and those other forty years when his masterful spirit was chastened among the mountains and in the desert, feeding sheep. It was so with David and Daniel and Paul. It was so with William Booth. They struggled on against ridicule, reproach, and persecution, when to human vision it seemed that God Himself, if not against them, was indifferent to them. They were possessed of the spirit of John Milton, who—poor, old, and blind—wrote:

I argue not
Against heaven's hand or will, nor bate a jot
Of heart or hope; but still bear up and steer
Right onward.[2]

They knew the secret of the psalmist, who wrote: "You have tested us, O God; you have purified us like silver. You captured us in your net and laid the burden of slavery on our backs. Then you put a leader over us. We went through fire and flood, but you brought us to a place of great abundance" (Ps. 66:10–12 NLT). In due time, when He had tried and proved them, the universe saw that God was on their side.

They did not consult with their convenience or their fears, but only with their sense of duty and their heart of faith and love. Thus they were unmoved amid the storm and trial, and prospered. They did not observe the winds before sowing, nor regard the clouds before reaping.

In the morning they sowed and in the evening withheld not their hand (see Eccl. 11:6). Like Joseph, they would not commit sin to escape persecution. Nor would they turn aside a hair's breadth from the path they had marked out for themselves to avoid chains and dungeons. Nor would they shut themselves up in some quiet temple to save their lives. They did not judge the righteousness of their cause by outward appearance, nor compute the possibilities of success by favoring circumstances and applauding multitudes. They were kindred spirits to the one who

> Through the heat of conflict, keeps the law
> In calmness made, and sees what he foresaw.[3]

But how different are men or women who are running away from duty and God! Circumstances seem to favor them. The south wind blows softly and, in spite of the warnings of wisdom and goodwill, they sail away to storm-swept seas to wreck and ruin.

We read of Jonah, "He found a ship" (Jon. 1:3 NLT). "How lucky!" he must have thought. "What good fortune! My stars favor me! So far all is well!"

Oh, the wayward souls who find ships waiting for them and, forgetting God, duty, faith, and the souls who lean upon them, take counsel with their seeming good fortune, hug themselves with complacency, and blithely set sail for Tarshish!

Absalom found Ahithophel and the men of Israel ready to flock to his standard when he raised it in revolt against King David, his father. He "found a ship." Judas found the high priest and his party ready to pay hard, cold cash for the betrayal of Jesus. He "found a ship." These are terrible examples. But we often find men and women illustrating in their lives the same principle.

A Salvation Army officer (pastor) left his post, reviled his former leaders and old colleagues, and found a rich man ready to provide him a home and job with a big salary, which he at once accepted. "He found a ship." Another ran away from his post and at the first place he visited, he found that they wanted a cook, and since he was a cook, he felt highly favored and was delighted. "He found a ship." But storms soon overtook both of those ships, and most interesting and instructive was the sequel.

Run away from the duty to which God in infinite wisdom and fore-knowledge calls you, the path which He in boundless love marks out for you, and the Devil will surely arrange to have a ship ready to carry you down to Tarshish. But he cannot ensure you against a storm, and he would not if he could. Storms certainly await you, however softly the south wind may blow.

You remember what happened to Jonah. You know the end of Absalom and Judas. Not that I would for an instant compare you with them, but the smallest disobedience is a step toward the steep and awful decline that leads to doom.

My officer friends, like multitudes of others whom I could mention, were soon overtaken by storms of unrest and disappointment and were swallowed and lay in the belly of trouble, shame, and sorrow, until the Lord in mercy delivered them and they found their way back to the port they had deserted and went, humbly and wisely, on their belated way to their appointed Nineveh.

NOTES

1. Charles Wesley, "Father of Jesus Christ, My Lord," 1742, public domain.

2. John Milton, "To the Same," lines 6–9, 1655, public domain.

3. William Wordsworth, "Character of the Happy Warrior," 1806, public domain.

Songs as Aids to Devotion 27

I recommend the hymns of the church—and in particular *The Salvation Army Songbook*—for devotional reading. Like the Psalms, these songs were written to be sung, and it is through singing that we get the most help and inspiration from them. But, like the Psalms, they may also be read with immeasurable blessing and profit.

They scale the heights and delve the depths of Christian experience. In them the sweetest, choicest saints and Christian warriors of many centuries and countries tell us of their struggles, hopes, fears, heart-searchings, defeats, recoveries, victories, triumphs, and divine revelations and discoveries. They will not give up their sweetness and strength to those who read carelessly and in haste; but to those who, unhasting, read with thought and prayer they open a treasure house of spiritual instruction, comfort, guidance, inspiration, and encouragement. They provide a fat feast of the best things with the finest and most gracious spirits this world has ever known.

The overworked mother or father, the common laborer, the mechanic or clerk or teenager who becomes familiar not alone with the tunes and words of a few songs but who knows them well and has grasped the experiential meaning of the songs will have become almost a master in practical and experiential theology. Such a person will be better equipped to explain the mysteries of redemption and to deal with seeking souls than nine-tenths of all the theological students graduated from seminaries and universities.

And while these songs enlighten, enrich, and enlarge the mind, they more particularly kindle devotion in the heart and make us feel the reality and pull of eternal things when they are read with thought and prayer. It is more for this that I myself read them, for it is this keen and alert sense of the things of the Spirit and of eternity that will keep our devotion alive and warm and tender.

It is this devotional spirit—the spirit of love, faith, sacrifice, and spiritual worship—that is at the same time most important and most difficult for us to maintain. Without it, we perish. "Would that you were either cold or hot!" said the Master to the church at Laodicea. "So, because you are lukewarm, and neither hot nor cold, I will spit you out of my mouth" (Rev. 3:15–16 ESV). They either lost or never had the spirit of devotion, and so a dreadful condemnation and doom awaited them. And such will await us if we become lukewarm.

But how shall we keep up this grace, this tenderness, this devotion of spirit? Never have there been so many helps, and never were there so many hindrances as now. The helps are on every hand, but the hindrances are omnipresent, too. I wake up in the morning and the patient, silent, watchful, wooing Holy Spirit is brooding over me, waiting to help me praise God and worship and pray with my waking breath. The Bible and *The Salvation Army Songbook* are there to guide my thoughts and my utterances, and when I kneel and open them, it is as though I were in a blessed prayer and praise meeting with Moses, Joshua, Samuel, Job, David, Isaiah, Daniel, Jonah, Jeremiah, Matthew, Luke, John, Paul, Peter, Martin Luther, Charles Wesley, William Booth, Emma Booth-Tucker, Isaac Watts, Reginald Heber, John Lawley, and such kindred spirits, and the fire of love ought to kindle and burn in my heart, and my soul ought to soar and shout and sing for joy.

But maybe the sun is up; business presses; the express train—like time and tide—waits for no one; and the morning paper is at the door with its welter of world news and gossip, its tales of murder and robbery, divorce and war, baseball and stock markets, diplomacy, funny and utterly foolish pictures, and—unlike the Holy Spirit and the Bible and songbook—these are noisy, loud, and insistent. It is one of the easiest things gradually to yield to and be finally overcome by them, until the heart that was once hot with love and zeal has become lukewarm and the tongue that was once a flame of fire is now a spiritual icicle. The reading of the songbook, with set purpose to drink in the spirit of the songs and to get blessed, will help one to escape this subtle and deadly temptation.

We can never more be cold toward Jesus or think mean and little thoughts of Him if we drink in and live in the spirit of these songs.

See from His head, His hands, His feet,

Sorrow and love flow mingled down!

Did e'er such love and sorrow meet,

Or thorns compose so rich a crown?

Were the whole realm of nature mine,

That were a present far too small;

Love so amazing, so divine,

Demands my soul, my life, my all.[1]

In these songs we find inbred sin and corruption—in all its subtle workings—exposed, and the way of heart purity and holiness made plain. We find Christian experience in all its phases illustrated. We see how the saints have struggled with our problems, our sins and weaknesses, our uncertainties and heart deceitfulness, our perplexities and temptations. We find that we are not traveling through an unbroken wilderness but over a highway made plain by unnumbered saints who have traveled its rough ways and full lengths and beaten them smooth on their knees. We find warnings, instructions, and encouragements all the way from the penitent form to the banks of the river and the gates of pearl.

Here we learn how others have fought sin, unbelief, and devils and overcome; how they stirred up the gift of God within them, believed and overcame in spite of hell; how they prayed and wept, shouted, sang, and fought their way through, triumphing over every foe; and how they encouraged their troubled and perplexed hearts with God's promises and past blessings and sat down at His table and fed on fat things in the very presence of their enemies. Oh, if you want to be spiritually robust and filled with holy laughter, feed your mind and heart on the songbook. Here you will get glimpses of the bitter remorse and woes of hell and be keyed up to resist sin and try to snatch souls from the yawning pit. And here you will get visions of the rest, sweetness, and sinless bliss of heaven, of the jubilant throngs of the redeemed, and of the white-robed, radiant armies of the saints who have overcome and are now crowned and bathed in light in the unveiled presence of their Lord.

Many years ago I began to read hymns just for blessing my own soul. And later, while lying helpless in the hospital, not knowing but that my end was nigh, and informed that my wife, the darling of my heart, was given up to die, I turned to the sections labeled "Heaven" and "Comfort and Guidance," where I found a whole armory of tried weapons, and with them and my Bible I fought crowded devils and thronging fears and got victory.

One day at a camp meeting I sat alone under great trees with a Salvation Army colonel (later a commissioner) who had just lost his wife. He quoted Charles Wesley's "Wrestling Jacob":

> Come, O thou Traveler unknown,
> Whom still I hold, but cannot see!
> My company before is gone,
> And I am left alone with Thee;
> With Thee all night I mean to stay
> And wrestle till the break of day.[2]

And as in deep and quiet tones he spoke the words of that noble hymn, the power and value of our songs as devotional helps (when spoken or read, apart from singing) burst upon me as never before. Another time, I was in Australia, sitting amid the flickering lights of a slowly dying fire one night, when an old saint quaintly quoted one of our songs, one verse of which has been like a sheet anchor to my soul ever since:

> His love in time past forbids me to think
> He'll leave me at last in trouble to sink;
> Each sweet Ebenezer I have in review,
> Confirms His good pleasure to help me quite through.[3]

Let me exhort you to sing "psalms and hymns and spiritual songs among yourselves, and [make] music in your hearts" (Eph. 5:19 NLT). Keep hymns and spiritual songs by your bedside with your Bible and carry them with you on the train to read. They will enrich your faith, invigorate your hope, and keep warm and tender your love.

NOTES

1. Isaac Watts, "When I Survey the Wondrous Cross," 1707, public domain.

2 Charles Wesley, "Come, O Thou Traveler Unknown," 1742, public domain.

3. John Newton, "Begone, Unbelief," 1779, public domain.

An Accident 28

From infancy my life has been punctuated by tragic losses, surprises, and pains. I do not remember my devout father. He made the soldier's supreme sacrifice during the American Civil War when I was a little child, and my earliest recollections are of a bereaved and weeping mother, sighing, sad-faced, and heartbroken.

In my adolescence, when a young fellow most needs his mother, I was away from home at school when I received my first telegram. It read: "Come home. Come quickly. Mother is dying." When I reached home my mother, in whose heart I had lived—who had taught me to pray and had planted deep in my young heart the reverent fear of God—lay with folded hands and infinite serenity and peace on her loved face, dead. For the next twelve years, I had no home.

At the beginning of my Salvation Army ministry, a Boston rough hurled a brick at my head and felled me with a blow that laid me up for eighteen months and gave me a shock from which I have not wholly recovered in thirty-five years.

In the midst of my Army ministry, I was stricken with an agonizingly painful and dangerous sickness in a far-off land, where I lay at death's door among strangers for weary weeks, returning home at last almost helpless, a mere shadow of a man. Some years later, lying in a hospital with a great surgical wound that threatened my life, word was brought to me that my sweet wife, the darling of my life, was dying. And now at sixty-four years old, I find myself battered and broken from an automobile accident.

I do not argue, though in fact it may be so, that these are the best things that could have befallen me. But I do testify that by God's grace, by His wise and infinitely loving—if mysterious—overruling, they have all worked together for my good, for the enrichment of my soul and, I trust, of my ministry. They have worked in me to humble my proud and wayward nature. They have thrown me back on God. They have made me think. They have led me to deep searchings of heart in lonely and still hours of the night and to patient and prolonged searching of the Bible and of history to find out God's ways with humanity. They have been rigorous and unsparing but also unfailing, compelling teachers of fortitude, patience, sympathy, and understanding. They have taught me the solidarity of humanity, have revealed the brotherhood of all, and have drawn out my heart in sympathetic understanding of others. For danger, loss, and suffering draw us together and make us conscious that we are drawn up in one bundle of life together for prosperity or woe, while joys and pleasures and abundance separate people into rival groups, contending for mastery and selfish interests, forgetful and indifferent to the welfare of others. Let earthquake, famine, pestilence, fire, or flood devastate a city or a country, and how instantly the hearts of people flow together in self-forgetful, sacrificial helpfulness and sympathy!

It is worthwhile occasionally to meet with some tragic trouble just to discover this fact or to have it confirmed anew, and especially to discover what a glorious company is the secret order of the sons and daughters of God—and what instant and intimate fellowship we have in the church and The Salvation Army when some big hurt comes.

I was not yet on my proper cot, and the surgeon was still examining my injuries, when anxious brothers and sisters came to inquire about our safety. And I was hardly through breakfast the next morning when two fellow officers, who had traveled all night from Chicago, walked into my room with others, looking like angels. And angels—God's messengers of love—they were.

Another colleague, without my knowledge, had spoken for a trained nurse, and when she was not properly forthcoming, got her quickly and installed her over me with the sweetest but firmest admonition that I was to obey her and that I must at once stop talking and relax. "For," said she, "you are more deeply shocked than you imagine."

This I soon found to be true. The wild excitement of the accident, in spite of the hard blows, seemed to fling me upward on the crest of a great wave. But I soon found myself in the deep trough of a troubled sea of physical depression and pain. I shall not soon forget what a long and painful journey it was as I laboriously turned over in bed from my right side to my left and back again, and how—to relieve the strained muscles of my neck—I moved my head by pulling the hair on my forehead.

Not only did colleagues, friends, and citizens—including the mayor of the city who made three visits to me—begin to pour in, but also messages by cable, wire, and letter flooded me. And nearly everyone asked how it happened.

Well, of course, it was all "the fault of the other fellow." My colleagues and I had been conducting spiritual campaigns in the area for five weeks, and between four hundred and five hundred souls had sought pardon and purity. The presence and power of the Holy Spirit were manifest in every place. We were driving to Grand Rapids, Michigan, for our final week and were full of quiet and joyful anticipation of a time of unusual blessing.

We lunched at Muskegon and then continued in the car that had brought us from Manistee. We had forty-eight miles of finely paved road ahead of us when about four miles out in the country we found ourselves with a perfectly clear right-of-way one instant, but the next instant perfectly blocked. A reckless or unfortunate driver in a big sedan collided with the stationary car on the other side of the road, skidded across our path, and struck us broadside like the shock of doom. It was as sudden, unexpected, inescapable, and about as irresistible as a thunderbolt. Our lighter car crumpled up, turned over twice, and piled itself on top of us. The engine was on my chest, and my companion was pinned across my hips. My left elbow was pressed so deeply over my heart that I feared I would lose my breath. My right side was caved in, my shin was nearly crushed, and a blood vessel burst just below my knee, while I was bruised from head to foot. The women were lying under the wreck behind and crying feebly for help. The engine poured oil into my eye, ear, and over my uniform, until I was soaked to the skin. My stomach was dispossessed of my noon lunch and such remains of breakfast as it had not otherwise disposed of, while the clouds poured down rain.

We were soon rescued by passing automobiles. An ambulance came and took away three of our wounded and two from the other car, while I, dazed and aching, stalked around in the rain picking up mangled suitcases and wondering how I was to get to Grand Rapids.

At last a gentleman kindly suggested that it might be well for me to go back to Muskegon and be examined for injuries, and since our car was wrecked and my driver gone, I consented and was soon glad the trip to the hospital was only four miles instead of forty-four to Grand Rapids. The least jolt of the car hurt my side. Great was my surprise to hear the extent of my injuries and the time I would have to stay in the hospital. And great was my sorrow at missing my week of meetings. But I confess I felt a secret but abiding joy welling up within me that I should have been chosen as one among others to have such an awesome if painful experience. For I felt deep inward assurance that this, too, could and would be made to work for my good, for the greater glory of my Master, and possibly for the admonition and strengthening of the faith of some of my coworkers.

When I have said this to some friends they have eyed me quizzically for a moment, as though they thought my head had received a greater shock than at first suspected and that I had not fully recovered from it. They have turned their eyes away and remarked with something like a sigh, "Well, it may be so, if you can look at it in that way." But that is the only way I can look at it and get comfort and strength to bear it with patience and joy, or harmonize it with what I know of

God's character and will and ways with us, as revealed in the Bible where it shows the afflictions He permitted to fall upon His saints and soldiers of old.

Messages came in from near and far, telling of anxious fears, tender sympathy, ardent prayers, and sweet affection. And in many of these messages were such questions as, "Why this?" "Why did it befall you whose hands were so full of useful work? Why did it not fall upon someone who was doing nothing, or who had nothing to do?" "Was it devil, man, or God that precipitated this upon you?"

Such questions are natural, but are they asked in wisdom? Is there a sure, cut-and-dried answer? But all morally earnest and thoughtful persons meeting with such an accident will find in the secrets of their own hearts some answer or answers.

One will find it in some moral or spiritual need or danger, discovering that he or she had begun to drift, to neglect prayer, to become too much absorbed with the things of this life. Paul said he himself was in danger of undue exaltation through the abundance of the revelations given him; therefore God let him be humbled by Satan's thorn.

Another may find his or her answer in a new and needed line of service, in comforting and strengthening other afflicted ones, or in revealing Christ's sufficiency for suffering, as well as service or sacrifice. Sometimes we must wait patiently and watch for an answer, the very silence and uncertainty speaking to us, as Jesus to Peter, "You don't understand now what I am doing, but someday you will" (John 13:7 NLT). God may have infinitely bigger purposes than any we imagine. "I looked for a dewdrop, and found an abyss," wrote one man as he considered the infinite sweep of the plans and purposes of God.[1]

Personally, I was much comforted by the thought that "all things work together for good to them that love God" (Rom. 8:28 KJV), and that this was an opportunity to prove to myself and possibly reveal in some measure to others the all-sufficiency of His grace for suffering as well as for service. It is easy to preach in full and robust health about "grace as fathomless as the sea . . . grace, enough for me."[2] But the test comes in proving and practicing it in danger, broken health, poverty, loneliness, neglect, and sore trial.

> The toad beneath the harrow knows
> Exactly where each tooth-point goes.
> The butterfly upon the road
> Preaches contentment to that toad.[3]

The rub will come to that butterfly when it, too, gets under the harrow. Can it preach contentment then?

Truly, I would not like to go through life without some hard blows when so many of my fellow humans must suffer them, and when my Master was a "man of sorrows, and acquainted with grief" (Isa. 53:3 KJV), wounded and bruised. If I am to understand Him and my fellow humans, I must share in the common experience of life. If I am to have wide knowledge of His power and willingness to help and sustain, I must have wide experiences that call for His help. A manifold testimony with power demands a firsthand knowledge of manifold mercies. The value of testimony depends upon the degree and certainty of knowledge.

Lost? I have known that, but He found me. Guilty? Condemned? Undone? I have known that, and He forgave me. Unclean? I have known the impurity of my own heart, but He cleansed me. Weak? Powerless? I have known that, but He baptized me with the Holy Spirit, and power came into me. Poor? I have known dire poverty and have been without a dollar, but He clothed and fed me. He said He would, and He did. Lonely? I have wandered with aching heart through the dark labyrinthine dungeons of loneliness, and I found Him there and was no longer lonely. Perplexed? Bewildered? I have been at my wit's end, but He was not at His wit's end. He lightened my way. Fearful? Afraid? I have known nights of torturing fear, and then He has drawn close and said, "It is I; be not afraid" (Matt. 14:27 KJV), then all my fears have fled away, and I wondered at the fullness of my peace and calm. Sickness? Danger? I have lain hard up against the gates of death, looking for them to open. But He has the keys of death. And He did not open, and I came back and am here instead of over there—here, singing, "My soul, be on thy guard,"[4] instead of over there singing the song of Moses and the Lamb (see Rev. 15:3) with the multitude which no one can number. Pain? Agony? I have been wracked and tortured until it seemed I could bear no more. And then I remembered His pain and agony for me on Golgotha, and my spirit bowed in adoration and rose up in exultation that I should be permitted to know something of His physical agony, and then I welcomed pain with a shout of solemn, triumphant joy. My pain seemed to fade away, and I forgot it in the fullness of my peace, joy, and fellowship with Him. God has not promised us freedom from affliction, but He has assured us that "our light affliction, which is but for a moment, is working for us" (2 Cor. 4:17 NKJV). What servants are our afflictions!

He does not make pets of His people, and especially of those whom He woos and wings into close fellowship with Himself and fits and crowns for great and higher service. His greatest servants have often been the greatest sufferers. They have gathered up in themselves and endured all the pains and woes, sorrows and agonies, fierce and cruel martyrdoms of humanity, and so have been able to minister to all its vast and pitiful needs and comfort its voiceless sorrow.

God has no interest in developing a race of mollycoddles. He could work miracles every day, saving children from stubbing their toes and bumping their noses, from tumbling downstairs, from burns when they disobey Mother and touch fire, from being crushed when they run recklessly in front of motor cars, from getting stomachaches when they eat green apples, or from the bitter lot of poverty and neglect when Father ruins himself and his fortune by gambling and drink or when a wicked mother forsakes them and runs off with a new lover. But God does not see fit to work such miracles, and since He does not do it for little children, I see no reason why we should question and vex our hearts and minds because He does not do it for us who are grown up.

Indeed, I think I can see some plausible reasons why He should not do so. We should be more certainly and hopelessly spoiled by such unfailing divine interposition than children spoiled by fond and foolishly indulgent parents. We need discipline, training, forethought, watchfulness, courage, self-restraint, steadfastness, patience, sympathy, faith, forbearance, a proper sense of our own limitations, dependence, and other virtues that unfold our personality and enrich and ennoble character. And God uses these sharp, hard instruments of danger, buffeting, sore and unexpected and inescapable trials and hurts, to develop these virtues in us and, often, through us in others. He means us no harm. He assures us that "all things work together for good to them that love God" (Rom. 8:28 KJV). Then He leaves us free to believe and prove it and be at peace, or to doubt it, repine, rebel, and suffer needless woes of heart and mind piled on top of every affliction that may overtake us. Let us stir up our faith and sing:

> Since all that I meet shall work for my good,
> The bitter is sweet, the medicine is food.
> Though painful at present, wilt cease before long,
> And then, O! how pleasant, the conqueror's song![5]

When in Honolulu some years ago, I was given a tour of a great sugar mill. There were acres of bewildering machinery working in every direction. There were great iron fingers that grasped the cane, lifting it from the plantation cars and dropping it onto an endless belt that carried it into the merciless grip of great steel rollers that crushed all the sweet juice from the cane and poured its flood into boiling vats. There were fiery furnaces, hissing steam, cogs and wheels and belts, and lifts and plunging chutes defying description, but all working to turn out one hundred pounds of sugar every thirty seconds, so that little boys and girls in New York, London, and country crossroads might have lollipops, soldiers on weary marches might have milk chocolate, sweet June brides might have frosted wedding cakes, kindly old grandmothers might have sugar in their afternoon tea or coffee, and that the whole family might enjoy its Christmas pudding.

So, bewildering as life may seem—with its commingling of joy and sorrow, health and sickness, pleasure and agony, pain and loss, life and death—it is nevertheless all working for the good of those who love God, and preparing us all for the painless, tearless life that shall endless be.

> Behind, a Presence did move
> And grasp me by the hair;
> And a voice in mastery asked, as I strove,
> "Guess now who holds thee." "Death," I said, and there
> The silver answer rang out, "Not Death, but Love."[6]

It is Love who holds us.

NOTES

1. An apparent reference to Robert Browning, "Saul," 1855, public domain. The poem contains the lines, "Each faculty tasked to perceive him, has gained an abyss, where a dewdrop was asked."

2. Edwin O. Excell, "Grace, Enough for Me," 1905, public domain.

3. Rudyard Kipling, "The Enlightenments of Pagett, M. P.," 1919, public domain.

4. George Heath, "My Soul, Be on Thy Guard," 1781, public domain.

5. John Newton, "Begone, Unbelief," 1779, public domain.

6. Edmund Clarence Stedman, ed., *A Victorian Anthology, 1837–1895* (Cambridge: Riverside Press, 1895), accessed September 3, 2015, www.bartleby.com/246/.

Samuel L. Brengle's Holy Life Series

This series comprises the complete works of Samuel L. Brengle, combining all nine of his original books into six volumes, penned by one of the great minds on holiness. Each volume has been lovingly edited for modern readership by popular author (and long-time Brengle devotee) Bob Hostetler. Brengle's authentic voice remains strong, now able to more relevantly engage today's disciples of holiness. These books are must-haves for all who would seriously pursue and understand the depths of holiness in the tradition of John Wesley.

Helps to Holiness
ISBN: 978-1-63257-064-2
eBook: 978-1-63257-065-9

The Heart of Holiness
ISBN: 978-1-63257-066-6
eBook: 978-1-63257-067-3

The Servant's Heart
ISBN: 978-1-63257-068-0
eBook: 978-1-63257-069-7

Ancient Prophets and Modern Problems
ISBN: 978-1-63257-070-3
eBook: 978-1-63257-071-0

Come Holy Guest
ISBN: 978-1-63257-072-7
eBook: 978-1-63257-073-4

Resurrection Life and Power
ISBN: 978-1-63257-074-1
eBook: 978-1-63257-075-8

**Samuel L. Brengle's
Holy Life Series Box Set**
ISBN: 978-1-63257-076-5

SAMUEL L. BRENGLE'S HOLY LIFE SERIES

COME HOLY GUEST

Bob Hostetler, General Editor

wesleyan
PUBLISHING HOUSE
wphstore.com

CREST BOOKS

Copyright © 2016 by The Salvation Army
Published by Wesleyan Publishing House
Indianapolis, Indiana 46250
Printed in the United States of America
ISBN: 978-1-63257-072-7
ISBN (e-book): 978-1-63257-073-4

Library of Congress Cataloging-in-Publication Data

Brengle, Samuel Logan, 1860-1936.
  Come holy guest / Bob Hostetler, general editor.
     pages cm. -- (Samuel L. Brengle's holy life series)
  "This work is a revised combination of the following books: Guest of the Soul
and When the Holy Ghost Is Come."
  ISBN 978-1-63257-072-7 (pbk.)
  1. Holy Spirit. 2. Christianity. I. Hostetler, Bob, 1958- editor. II. Brengle, Samuel
Logan, 1860-1936. Guest of the soul. III. Brengle, Samuel Logan, 1860-1936.
When the Holy Ghost is come. IV. Title.
  BT121.3.B68 2016
  231'.3--dc23
                                    2015030476

This work is a revised combination of the following books from The Salvation
Army: *Guest of the Soul* and *When the Holy Ghost Is Come*.

Contents

Preface

Samuel Logan Brengle was an influential author, teacher, and preacher
on the doctrine of holiness in the late nineteenth to early twentieth century,
serving from 1887–1931 as an active officer (minister) in The Salvation
Army. In 1889 while he and his wife, Elizabeth Swift Brengle, were
serving as corps officers (pastors) in Boston, Massachusetts, a brick
thrown by a street "tough" smashed Brengle's head against a door frame
and caused an injury severe enough to require more than nineteen
months of convalescence. During that treatment and recuperation
period, he began writing articles on holiness for The Salvation Army's
publication, *The War Cry*, which were later collected and published
as a "little red book" under the title *Helps to Holiness*. That book's
success led to eight others over the next forty-five years: *Heart Talks
on Holiness*, *The Way of Holiness*, *The Soul-Winner's Secret*, *When
the Holy Ghost Is Come*, *Love-Slaves*, *Resurrection Life and Power*,

Ancient Prophets and Modern Problems, and *The Guest of the Soul*
(published in his retirement in 1934).

By the time of his death in 1936, Commissioner Brengle was an internationally renowned preacher and worldwide ambassador of holiness.
His influence continues today, perhaps more than any Salvationist in
history besides the founders, William and Catherine Booth.

I hope that the revised and updated editions of his books that
comprise the Samuel L. Brengle's Holy Life Series will enhance and
enlarge that influence, introduce these writings to new readers, and
create fresh interest in those who already know the godly wisdom and
life-changing power of these volumes.

While I have taken care to preserve the integrity, impact, and voice
of the original writing, I have carefully and prayerfully made changes
that I hope will facilitate greater understanding and appreciation of
Brengle's words for modern readers. These changes include:

- Revising archaic terms (such as the use of King James English) and
  updating the language to reflect more contemporary usage (such as
  occasionally employing more inclusive gender references);
- Shortening and simplifying sentence structure and revising
  punctuation to conform more closely to contemporary practice;
- Explaining specific references of The Salvation Army that will
  not be familiar to the general population;
- Updating Scripture references (when possible retaining the King
  James Version—used exclusively in Brengle's writings—but frequently incorporating modern versions, especially when doing
  so will aid the reader's comprehension and enjoyment);

- Replacing Roman numerals with Arabic numerals and spelled out Scripture references for the sake of those who are less familiar with the Bible;
- Citing Scripture quotes not referenced in the original and noting the sources for quotes, lines from hymns, etc.;
- Aligning all quoted material to the source (Brengle, who often quoted not only Scripture, but also poetry from memory, often quoted loosely in speaking and writing);
- Adding occasional explanatory phrases or endnotes to identify people or events that might not be familiar to modern readers;
- Revising or replacing some chapter titles, and (in *Ancient Prophets and Modern Problems*) moving one chapter to later in the book; and
- Deleting the prefaces that introduced each book and epigraphs that preceded some chapters.

In the preface to Brengle's first book, Commissioner (later General) Bramwell Booth wrote, "This book is intended to help every reader of its pages into the immediate enjoyment of Bible holiness. Its writer is an officer of The Salvation Army who, having a gracious experience of the things whereof he writes, has been signally used of God, both in life and testimony, to the sanctifying of the Lord's people, as well as in the salvation of sinners. I commend him and what he has here written down to every lover of God and His kingdom here on earth."

In the preface to Brengle's last book, *The Guest of the Soul*, The Salvation Army's third general (and successor to Bramwell Booth) wrote: "These choice contributions . . . will, I am sure, serve to

strengthen the faith of the readers of this book and impress upon them the joyousness of life when the heart has been opened to the Holy Guest of the Soul."

I hope and pray that this updated version of Brengle's writings will further those aims.

—Bob Hostetler

general editor

PART ONE

Guest of the Soul

The Atonement 1

It was once my joyful privilege to spend five months in intensive and fruitful evangelistic work in Norway in early 1907. Two movements were attracting wide attention in the country. In Oslo, then known as Christiana, what is popularly known as the "tongues movement" was arousing unusual interest—as indeed it was throughout Norway and in other parts of Northern Europe. It was claimed that the apostolic gifts of the Spirit were restored to the church, and many were seeking the baptism of the Holy Spirit with special emphasis placed upon the gift of tongues as the one necessary and invariable sign of the baptism.

At the same time, in Bergen, the second city of the kingdom, the so-called "new theology" had been accepted and preached with eloquence and zeal by one of the most popular and influential state clergymen in the city.[1] Other pastors flew to the faith's defense with learned arguments, which left the man or woman on the street in much perplexity and uncertainty. Since I was to visit Bergen, the local Salvation Army officer (minister), Adjutant Theodor Westergaard,[2] wrote and begged me to speak on the subject, promising to secure the finest hall in the city (the one in which the controversy had begun and been carried on) and to gather a representative audience to hear me.

I have never considered myself so much an advocate as a witness, and I did not wish to begin a few days' revival campaign by getting mixed up in a controversy of which I knew so little, and with a gentleman of whom I knew nothing. However, I wrote the adjutant that, if he wished to advertise me to speak on the atonement from the standpoint of an evangelist and a witness, he might do so. I was then visiting the cities on the south and west coasts of Norway, conducting two, three, and four meetings a day, traveling (poor sailor that I am) on little, comfortless coastal steamers, with no books but my Bible and songbook and no one with whom I could talk over the subject. With almost every waking hour filled with work, and wearied by long and exacting meetings, I could make only a few notes on an envelope I carried in my pocket. But I prayed, meditated, communed with God, sought His inspiration and guidance, thought my way through my subject, and trusted for divine help.

The following is the substance of my address that evening in Bergen, clothed in the language used as nearly as I was able to recall after some weeks in which I was still engaged in exacting labors.[3] It is in no sense an exhaustive study of the atonement. I was in a strange city on the eve of only a few days of evangelistic labors for the salvation and sanctification of souls. The object of the address was not so much to answer critics and to satisfy the demand of scholarship as to reach the hearts of plain men and women with the importance, need, and nature of God's great gift of love and sacrifice in His Son for the redemption of humanity.

I had just one hour and had to speak through an interpreter, who took up half my time. There was no opportunity for elaborate reasoning or to discuss various theories of the atonement. I was able to give only a simple presentation of truth that would win people to Christ and reconcile them to God. During the following eight days' meetings, more than six hundred men, women, and children publicly sought pardon and purity.

No other subject the human mind can consider is so vitally important, so humbling, and yet so ennobling in its effect as the atonement—the work and act of our Lord Jesus Christ in suffering and dying for human souls that He might save them from sin.

It is a subject which leads to the profoundest questions and often to the most perplexing and distressing doubts which cannot be ended by argument nor settled by human learning and skillful reasoning, but only by faith in the records found in the Bible and worked out in experience. Nevertheless, arguments and illustrations may in some measure help our faith and guide our minds to a right understanding of a matter which is either of infinite importance or else of no importance at all.

SIN: WHAT IT IS

Right in the forefront of the discussion we are face-to-face with the great problem of sin. If there is no sin, no evil estrangement from God, then there is no need of an atonement, of a divine sacrifice to save us.

What is sin? Is it only a mild infirmity due to immaturity, which will be outgrown and corrected by age, like many of the faults and ignorances of children? Or is it a malignantly wrong attitude of the will and affections that will never correct itself? Is it a moral disease like measles and whooping cough that we need not seriously fear, and to which we may indeed safely expose our children? Or is it like a hopeless leprosy or cancer, for which there is no known cure?

I once stepped off the train at home and was met with the announcement that my boy had the measles. I was not alarmed, and he soon recovered. But later I visited a leper hospital, and, oh, the horror of it! There were hopeless invalids with their eyes eaten out and their hands and feet eaten away by the awful disease, looking longingly for death to come and give them release. There was no human cure for them.

If sin is something that corresponds not to measles but to leprosy, I can understand how God, if He loves us and is truly interested in us, might make some great sacrifice, some divine interposition to save us. And it is this sacrifice, this interposition, which constitutes the atonement.

But is sin like leprosy—an awful moral corruption, a malignant attitude of the will and the affections, a corruption of the moral nature that corresponds to leprosy? The Bible says it is. But do the Bible and human history and human experience agree?

In our sheltered Christian homes, and under the protection of laws framed in the light of twenty Christian centuries, we are apt to forget or entirely overlook the malignant character of sin. People brought up in homes where the Bible is read and hymns are sung—where the

Ten Commandments are upheld, where a blessing is asked upon the food, and prayers are offered morning and evening—have little conception of the willful devilry into which men and women sink, and they are liable to be led by their own respectability into a false conception of sin.

SIN: AN ACT

What is sin? God says, "Thou shalt not kill" (Ex. 20:13 KJV). Is it sin to kill? An intelligent woman accidentally poisoned a baby in her home. Was it sin? No one who knew her considered it so. It was an awful mistake, and not a sin, for her will and affections were not malignant, and she was one of the chief mourners at the funeral of the baby.

A little five-year-old child was the firstborn pet and darling of the parents, but then another little one was born into the household, and some foolish women—wickedly foolish women—came into that home and said to the little five-year-old, "You are not Mama's baby and darling now. Mama has another baby that she loves." Jealousy was kindled in that little heart, and one day the child went to its mother with blood on its little hands and said, "Now I am Mama's baby, and now Mama will love her darling." Mama flew to the infant, only to find its head battered in with a hammer by the little five-year-old. That was sin—baby sin, but still sin!

Bear with me while we take a glimpse into the dark depths of what God sees—at what grieves and provokes Him, at some symptoms and manifestations of this hateful thing called sin, which stirred His heart of infinite love and pity and holiness to make such sacrifice to save sinners.

At the height of Rome's power and civilization, the emperor murdered his mother, stamped the life out of his wife and unborn child, and lighted the streets of the city with Christians, whom he had covered with pitch and set on fire. That is sin—sin full-grown. That is not spiritual measles. It is moral and spiritual leprosy.

When I was in Switzerland, I was told of a man and woman who threw their newborn child, born out of wedlock, to the pigs. That was sin! Why are we shocked at the bare recital of such a story? It was a common thing at the height of Greek and Roman civilization to expose children to beasts, and they were expected to destroy the weak baby.

Do you say we have outgrown this? Why has not China outgrown it? A lady missionary from China told me that she asked a Chinese mother whether she had ever killed one of her girl babies. The woman replied, "Yes, several of them." And when the missionary asked how she could find it in her heart to do such a brutal thing, the woman laughed. It is still common in China. One of our Salvation Army officers rescued a deserted baby left to be devoured by dogs. It is not that we have outgrown China, but we have been lifted out of that terrible darkness and brutality by pierced hands. It is the light of the cross shining upon us that has made the approval of such deeds impossible among us.

SIN: A STATE OF HEART

But sin is not merely an act. It is a state of the heart as well. A professing Christian said to me, "There is pride in my heart, and I get angry." And I tried to draw a word picture which would show her the sin of pride and anger.

Here is Jesus in Pilate's judgment hall. They have spat in His face, crowned Him with thorns, stripped Him, tied His hands to His feet, and beaten His bare back till it is bruised and bleeding. They have placed the cross upon His shoulders and, pale and worn with the bitter agony, with the spittle on His face and the blood on His brow, He struggles up the hill under the heavy load.

You come behind Him, and you say, "I am His follower. I am a Christian. I love Him." He is the very essence of lowliness and humility, but you come strutting behind Him in pride—proud of the feather in your hat, the bloom on your cheek, your money in the bank, your home that is better than other people have, your good name, or some gift that lifts you above others. You are proud of these things, and you look down with a certain superciliousness and condescension on others, consider yourself just a little bit better than they, and hold yourself aloof from them, while professing to follow this lowly Cross-Bearer. You have a right to be grateful to Him for those gifts that have lifted you above others but no right to be proud, and your pride is an abomination and sin before Him, a spiritual leprosy which only God can heal.

But He has reached the top of the hill. Hard, rough soldiers have thrown Him down upon the cross, driven the nails through His hands and feet, and, lifting the cross, have set it in its socket with a terrible thud, adding agony to the suffering Victim. And they mock Him, rob Him of His only suit of clothes, and cast dice for His seamless robe. And He prays, "Father, forgive them; for they know not what they do!"

And you stand at the foot of the cross, a professing Christian, His follower. And some man or woman approaches you, and you frown and step aside, for you are angry with that one. In the presence of that compassionate and forgiving Sufferer on the cross, I say that your anger is a sin, which cannot be washed out with rose water. It is moral leprosy. It is a malignant thing, which cannot be washed out with a few tears, but must be purged with blood, the blood of God's dear Son.

SIN: A CRIME AGAINST GOD

But sin is also a crime against God. If I murder a man, I sin against him, his poor wife, and his helpless children. But they do not punish me; the state punishes me. I have sinned against the state and the whole community. I have broken its laws. I have made a breach in the safeguards that secure the people from crime and danger, and that breach can be closed only by my punishment.

Looking at it in this light, we can rise to the vision of sin as a blow against God and His righteous government and the safeguards He has placed around His moral creation. David stole the wife of Uriah the Hittite and secured Uriah's murder but, when self-convicted by the prophet Nathan's story, he saw that he had sinned against God and cried out, "Against you, and you alone, have I sinned; I have done what is evil in your sight" (Ps. 51:4 NLT).

Hundreds of years before, Joseph had been tempted to commit a similar sin. He resisted and overcame the temptation, saying, "How then can I do this great wickedness, and sin against God?" (Gen. 39:9 KJV).

How could those men say that this sin, which in such a peculiar sense is a sin against another human being, was sin against God? Listen! Do you remember Jesus' parable describing the final judgment?

Then the King will say to those on his right, "Come, you who are blessed by my Father, inherit the Kingdom prepared for you from the creation of the world. For I was hungry, and you fed me. I was thirsty, and you gave me a drink. I was a stranger, and you invited me into your home. I was naked, and you gave me clothing. I was sick, and you cared for me. I was in prison, and you visited me."

Then these righteous ones will reply, "Lord, when did we ever see you hungry and feed you? Or thirsty and give you something to drink? Or a stranger and show you hospitality? Or naked and give you clothing? When did we ever see you sick or in prison and visit you?"

And the King will say, "I tell you the truth, when you did it to one of the least of these my brothers and sisters, you were doing it to me!"

Then the King will turn to those on the left and say, "Away with you, you cursed ones, into the eternal fire prepared for the devil and his demons. For I was hungry, and you didn't feed me. I was thirsty, and you didn't give me a drink. I was a stranger, and you didn't invite me into your home. I was naked, and you didn't give me clothing. I was sick and in prison, and you didn't visit me."

Then they will reply, "Lord, when did we ever see you hungry or thirsty or a stranger or naked or sick or in prison, and not help you?"

And he will answer, "I tell you the truth, when you refused to help the least of these my brothers and sisters, you were refusing to help me."

And they will go away into eternal punishment, but the righteous will go into eternal life. (Matt. 25:34–46 NLT)

And what meaning has the parable but this: that the King so identifies Himself with every needy and suffering subject in His vast domain that neglect of or a blow against that subject is counted by the King as a sin against Himself? It is God's law that is broken. It is God's authority that is defied. It is God's holiness and justice that are despised. When a man or woman sins, it is against God.

Indeed, sin is nothing less than lawlessness—a huge selfishness— that amounts to moral and spiritual anarchy. We sinners would pull God off His throne and kill Him if we could. I was not a bad boy as people count badness, but I can remember how, in my childish pride and vaulting ambition, I wondered why I should be a creature subordinated to God and subject to His righteous and unfailing judgments, and I disliked Him and wished I could pull Him off His throne and seat myself upon it, so that I might be responsible to no one but myself. And does not Jesus teach in His parable of the householder that this is the character of sin?

Now listen to another story. A certain landowner planted a vineyard, built a wall around it, dug a pit for pressing out the grape juice, and built a lookout tower. Then he leased the vineyard to tenant farmers and moved to another country. At the time of the grape harvest, he sent his servants to collect his share of the crop. But the farmers grabbed his servants, beat one, killed one, and stoned another. So the landowner sent a larger group of his servants to collect for him, but the results were the same.

Finally, the owner sent his son, thinking, "Surely they will respect my son."

But when the tenant farmers saw his son coming, they said to one another, "Here comes the heir to this estate. Come on, let's kill him and get the estate for ourselves!" So they grabbed him, dragged him out of the vineyard, and murdered him. (Matt. 21:33–39 NLT)

What does Jesus teach here but that sin is a state of heart rebellion that, carried to its final issues, would rob and kill God Himself if that were possible? We sinners want to have our own way and gratify our own desires and pleasures, regardless of the glory of God and the highest good of others. In reality, we want to be a law unto ourselves. We want to be our own God.

Sin can fawn and appear innocent and fair to behold, but it is utterly false and cruel. There are men and women, possibly in your neighborhood, who would not hesitate an instant to rob you, if they could, of your last penny and leave you a homeless beggar. They would not hesitate a moment to debauch your innocent boy, your lovely daughter, your sweet sister, and sink them to the lowest depths of infamy, and then glory in their shame. How little do we know the awful depths and darkness of sin—the corruption, iniquities, wickednesses, vile affections, lusts, and vaulting ambitions into which sin leads men and women! And what will God do with a hateful thing like this? What attitude must God take toward sin?

SIN: A CONCERN OF GOD

1. God cannot be ignorant of sin.

2. God cannot be indifferent to sin. It cannot be said of Him, as it was of Gallio, that He "cared for none of those things" (Acts 18:17 KJV).

3. God cannot approve sin, for then He would be the chief of sinners.

4. God must be utterly and totally antagonistic to sin, and He must do so with all the strength of His great moral being.

He must hate and condemn sin. Frederick W. Robertson, the great preacher, when he heard of a so-called gentleman plotting the ruin of a beautiful, innocent girl, ground his teeth and clenched his fists in hot indignation. If a righteous man feels that way in the presence of sin, how must a holy God feel? If God does not hate sin, He is not holy. If He does not condemn sin, He is not righteous. If He is not prepared to punish sin, He is not just. But God is holy, righteous, and just. His great heart demands—and His holiness calls for—the utter condemnation of sin. But while God is holy and hates sin with a perfect hatred, yet God is love, and while His holiness demands the punishment and utter destruction of sin, His great heart of love calls for the salvation of the sinner.

SIN: A PROBLEM FOR GOD

How shall God accomplish this double and seemingly contradictory demand of His holy and loving heart? How shall God's love and holiness harmonize to secure mercy for the sinner and judgment against the sin? How can God be just and yet justify the ungodly? How can God look upon sin and justify an ungodly man or woman and yet be a holy God? If a judge on the bench is careless in dealing with criminals or a magistrate winks at crime, they are dangerous people. The judge or magistrate who does not watch over the interests of society and deal hardly and severely with wrongdoing is a dangerous character. And is it not exactly the same with God? How shall God deal with this matter of sin? How shall His great heart of love secure its end—the salvation of the soul—and His great heart of holiness secure its end—the condemnation of sin? How shall God justify the ungodly and yet Himself be just?

Here is a problem for God: Fools mock at sin, but God does not. Foolish men and women think it is a very simple problem, this matter of the forgiveness of sins. But it is the profoundest problem in the moral universe, one which no other religion save the Christian faith has been able to solve—and in its solution lie our hope and our peace.

Suppose a man commits many crimes—and adds to them rebellion and murder—and is cast into prison. His friends appeal to the ruler to forgive him, and they think it an easy and a simple thing for him to do. But can the ruler do it? He has the authority, but can he do it and be just and safeguard his people? There are many things he must consider:

1. Would it not harm the man himself to pardon him, if he were not truly repentant?

2. Would it not encourage evil men and women in wickedness, and that possibly in far distant parts of the ruler's dominion?

3. Would it not endanger society and dismay good people by sweeping away the safeguards of law and order and by ignoring, if not destroying, the distinction between well-doing and wrongdoing?

God is confronted with a problem like this. How do we know, when we talk lightly about God's mercy, what other worlds are looking on to see how God will deal with sin in this world? Children watch to see how the wrongdoer will be treated, and nothing will encourage them more quickly to walk in evil ways than to see the wrongdoer smiled and fawned upon.

Parents who have several children know how very careful they must be in dealing with a wrongdoer. Their hearts may feel very tender toward the little one who has done wrong, and their hearts may be breaking with desire to save him or her from punishment. But that child's future and highest good must be placed first, and the other children must not be allowed to think it a light thing to do wrong. There are two ways of ruining children—the way of the harsh father and the way of the indulgent mother. Too much indulgence and too great severity alike will ruin the children. Blessed are the children whose parents know how to keep an even balance between their desire for their children's pleasure and happiness and the necessity of being firm and unbending in the presence of wrongdoing.

To hold an even balance between goodness and severity is divine. "Behold therefore the goodness and severity of God," said Paul (Rom. 11:22 KJV). God is faced with the same kind of problem as we are. How can He at the same time be merciful and just and yet secure the well-being of all His vast dominions? If God pardons sinners before they are penitent, He will only do them harm.

SIN: HOW CAN GOD FORGIVE IT?

How then can God forgive sin and be just?

1. He must secure a true spirit of repentance in the sinful soul or the person whom He forgives will only be hardened in sin.

2. He must make all wrongdoers to know that they cannot sin with impunity in His vast empire.

3. He must safeguard all other moral beings. He must make them feel the holiness of the law and the righteousness of His judgments, until they cry out, "Just and true are your ways, O King of the nations. . . . Yes, O Lord God, the Almighty, your judgments are true and just" (Rev. 15:3; 16:7 NLT).

How can He do this? I think we can make it plain by a simple illustration. Our own relations with one another—parents with children and rulers with their subjects—reflect in some measure the relations of God with us and the problems with which God is confronted in that relationship.

A great teacher who was also a student of human nature once had under his care a boy who was a ringleader in wrongdoing. The boy had been punished before, but broke the rules again and again most flagrantly. One day he committed a more than usually grave offence and was called up for punishment. The punishment was to be two or three sharp raps with a cane on his open palm.

The boy had been punished before, but seemed to enjoy breaking the rules of the school and causing trouble. The teacher knew that he could not allow this to continue. But he was greatly perplexed. He did not want to cast the boy out of the school. He loved the boy and longed to bless and save him, but how could he make him see and understand? How could he let the child go free and at the same time make the other children feel that it was not a slight thing to break the rules of the school?

He stood there with an aching heart in the presence of the defiant boy, when all at once a happy inspiration came to him. He said something like this to the boy: "I don't wish to punish you, but when law is broken somebody must suffer. It is always so, not only in school but out of school as well. So instead of punishing you today, you shall punish me. I will suffer for you."

The boy looked at him and grew crimson. "Give me the punishment," continued the teacher. The boy looked as if he were in a bath of fire. His heart began to melt under a manifestation of love such as he had never witnessed or heard of before. The teacher stretched forth his open hand and said, "Strike!" After long hesitation the poor little fellow nerved himself and struck one blow. And then his proud, rebellious heart broke. He burst into penitential tears, and from that day he became a new creature.

The teacher never had any more trouble with that boy, while the other children felt that it was not a light thing to break the rules of the school. The teacher had found a way to justify a disobedient child and yet make wrongdoing look hateful in the eyes of every other child. He himself suffered, "the just for the unjust" (1 Pet. 3:18 KJV).

An ancient king passed a law against a certain grave crime. The punishment was to be the loss of both eyes. The first criminal discovered was the king's own son. And now what would the king do? How could he save his son and uphold the law throughout his dominion, and compel his subjects to revere him and admire his justice? How could justice and mercy be wedded? The king had said that two eyes must be put out. Could they not be the eyes of a slave? If so, his subjects might fear, but not revere, the king. They would despise him, and the son would go on in his shameless career.

This is what the king did. He put out one of his son's eyes and put out one of his own eyes, and the people could only exclaim, "The king is merciful, and the king is just." He had found a way to save his son and at the same time to uphold the law.

THE ATONEMENT: GOD'S GRACIOUS SOLUTION

Will God act so? Will God suffer to save the sinner? Is there any other way by which God can justify the sinful human soul and yet Himself be just? Is there any other way by which God can display His hatred of sin and His pitying love of the sinner? Is there any other way by which God can break the sinner's proud and unbelieving heart and melt it into penitence and contrition? Is there any other way by which God can retain the respect and confidence of unfallen angels when He pardons sinners and treats them as though they had not sinned? Will God suffer for me? Will He take my place and in His love and pity die in my stead to save me from my sin and its dire consequences?

The Bible says that God will suffer, and that God has suffered. This is the atonement: God's act of condescension and mercy, which bridges the gulf between sinful humans and the holy God; between a wicked, fallen creature and an offended Creator; between a willful and defiant child and a wounded, grieved, and loving Father.

JESUS CHRIST: WHO IS HE?

But when and where did God suffer for me? On Calvary!

But was that dying man on Calvary God? He was the God-man, the Son of God, God the Son (see John 1:1–14; 1 Tim. 3:16).

How can we know God, and where can we find Him? The heaven of heavens cannot contain Him. We cannot see Him. We cannot by searching find Him, but He has focused Himself, as it were, in Jesus Christ. He has humbled Himself to our flesh and blood and stooped to take our nature upon Himself (see Phil. 2:5–8; Heb. 2:14, 16).

The Bible says, "In the beginning was the Word, and the Word was with God, and the Word was God. . . . The Word was made flesh, and dwelt among us . . . full of grace and truth" (John 1:1, 14 KJV). The Bible says He was God.

The apostle Paul told early church leaders, "Shepherd the church of God which He purchased with His own blood" (Acts 20:28 NKJV). So that Sufferer hanging there was God, suffering for us—God, the blessed Son. Wonder of wonders! Think of Him pouring out His life, an innocent Sufferer for sinful men and women, for you and me! "God was in Christ, reconciling the world to himself" (2 Cor. 5:19 NLT), and "in all their suffering he also suffered" (Isa. 63:9 NLT).

The Father's heart of love was pierced with pain by the thorns that pierced the head of the Son. The Father's heart was hurt with the nails that pierced the hands and feet of the Son. The Father's heart was thrust through with anguish at the guilt and sins of men and women when they thrust the spear into the heart of Jesus. The Father suffered with and in the blessed Son.

The whole Trinity is involved in the atoning work of Jesus Christ on Calvary. The Father "so loved the world, that he gave his only begotten Son" (John 3:16 KJV). "God made Christ, who never sinned, to be the offering for our sin, so that we could be made right with God through Christ" (2 Cor. 5:21 NLT). And it was "through the eternal Spirit" that Christ "offered himself without spot to God" (Heb. 9:14 KJV) in our place and on our behalf. Truly did Paul say, "Great is the mystery of godliness: God was manifested in the flesh" (1 Tim. 3:16 NKJV).

The Bible says that Jesus is God. Jesus said so; John said so; Paul said so. The church in all its creeds says so. The wisest Christian teachers say so. The saints and martyrs, who have perished by flame and wild beast's fang, say so. The great soul-winners say so. The humble penitents, rejoicing in the assurance of sins forgiven, say so. And with commingling tears and smiles and heaven-lit faces, they cry out with Thomas, "My LORD and my God!" (John 20:28 KJV).

But the testimonies of the Bible and the creeds and the martyrs and the saints and the soul-winners and the rejoicing penitents do not make me to know that Jesus is Lord, and I may still doubt. How shall I know? May I know? Someone who was born blind may hear a thousand testimonies to the beauties of the starry heavens and the glories of sunrise and sunset and yet doubt them all. It is all hearsay. Is there any way to destroy the doubts forever? Only one, and that is to bestow sight. Then that person will doubt no more. He or she knows and sees firsthand.

An astronomer writes a booklet announcing the discovery of a new star. I may read the booklet and yet may doubt. What shall I do? Throw the booklet away and sit down and write a bigger book than that, to prove that there is no such star and that the astronomer is star-mad or a liar? No, instead let me turn my telescope to that point in the heavens where the new star was reportedly found and find a star mirrored in my telescope! But what if I am mistaken? Then let another, or two, or a thousand people in different parts of the earth turn their telescopes to that point in the heavens. And if they, too, unanimously say, "There is a star," how can I doubt any longer?

JESUS: THE INWARD REVELATION

How can we know that Jesus is Lord? Paul said, "No one can say Jesus is Lord, except by the Holy Spirit" (1 Cor. 12:3 NLT). The Holy Spirit must reveal Him to each heart before doubts about His person can be destroyed. The Bible is the book on divine astronomy that tells when and where to discover Him, "the Bright and Morning Star" (Rev. 22:16 NKJV). It does not reveal Him any more than the book on astronomy reveals the stars. It is only a record of self-revelation, and it tells us how to secure a revelation of Him to our own hearts.

Let us, then, carefully read the instructions in the Bible, the textbook on this heavenly astronomy. Let us look with the eye of faith through the telescope of God's Word, and by true repentance and obedient faith put our souls into that attitude which will enable Him to reveal Himself to us. Let us do what He tells us to do without murmuring and complaining, and then, as myriad others before us have done, we shall find Him formed within our hearts, "the hope of glory" (Col. 1:27 KJV). Our doubts will vanish; our sins will be forgiven; our guilt will be put away. We shall be born again, born of the Spirit. We shall have our eyes anointed with spiritual salve and have our hearts made pure to see God and discover who Jesus is. Then the atonement, made by the shedding of His blood, will no longer be an offense to our imperfect reason and a stone of stumbling to our unbelief; it will be the supreme evidence of God's wisdom and love to our wondering and adoring hearts.

It was this inward and spiritual revelation of Christ that gave Paul such assurance and power. He said, "I know whom I have believed" (2 Tim. 1:12 KJV); "It pleased God . . . to reveal his Son in me" (Gal. 1:15–16 KJV); and "It is no longer I who live, but Christ lives in me" (Gal. 2:20 NLT).

Oh, the joy and infinite peace and satisfaction contained in this spiritual manifestation of Jesus to the heart! It is a fulfillment of those wonderful words of Jesus: "I will come to you. . . . In that day you will know that I am in my Father, and you in me, and I in you. . . . I will . . . manifest myself to [you]" (John 14:18, 20–21 ESV).

I sat beside a student when Christ was manifested to him and saw his face shining almost like the face of an angel. I heard him whisper, "Blessed Jesus! Blessed Jesus!" Later I heard him saying over and over again and again, "Glory be to Jesus! Glory be to Jesus!"

I knelt beside a young lady in prayer, when all at once she burst into tears and cried out in joy, "O Jesus!" He had come, and she knew Him as Lord. Six months later she said, "I'm going to Africa," and with Christ in her heart she went joyfully as a missionary to darkest Africa, where she lived and labored and loved, until one day He said, "It is enough, come up higher," and she went to heaven by way of Africa.

A great businessman found Jesus and with radiant face and deepest reverence said, "I was so mixed up with Jesus that for several days I hardly knew whether it was Jesus or I."

A timid little boy, who was afraid to be left alone in the dark, had the great inward revelation and said quietly and joyfully, "I'm not afraid now, for Jesus is with me."

JESUS: THE GREAT UNVEILING

Who, then, is Jesus Christ? Listen to Isaiah: "For a child is born to us, a son is given to us. The government will rest on his shoulders. And he will be called: Wonderful Counselor, Mighty God, Everlasting Father, Prince of Peace. His government and its peace will never end" (Isa. 9:6–7 NLT).

We look into the Bethlehem manger, and we see only a Child, a little Son, and we are indifferent, though wise men and angels welcome and worship Him with reverent awe and wonder. But little by little, overcome by the insurrection of our passions and tempers and led captive by sin, finding no help in ourselves and proving that "all human help is useless" (Ps. 60:11; 108:12 NLT), we look again and see that He is our help and that "the government will rest on his shoulders" (Isa. 9:6 NLT). And repenting with brokenness of heart and believing in Him, we find pardon and victory and peace as we look. And when the impurity of our nature is more fully revealed, we find instant cleansing in His blood and sanctification full and free in His baptism with the Holy Spirit, and we cry out, "Wonderful!"

Or we are filled with perplexity. Life is a labyrinth, the universe is a riddle, and we walk in a maze. We are at our wits' end. Sages and philosophers cannot answer our anxious questions about the mystery of life; none can solve the problems of triumphant evil and thwarted goodness, of pain and sorrow and loss and death. And again we look and discover that in Him "are hid all the treasures of wisdom and knowledge" (Col. 2:3 KJV). He answers our questions. He resolves our riddles. We rest in Him as our Counselor.

Or we are oppressed with our utter littleness and weakness. We feel as helpless as an insect in the presence of the giant forces of the material universe. We are powerless to resist the vast world movements, the strikes, the conspiracies, the wars, and the political and social upheavals. And in our horror and despair we look again, and see Him in the earthquake and tempest, "towering o'er the wrecks of time,"[4] stilling the storm, raising the dead, calming the fierce and wild passions of humanity, and slowly but surely enlightening and molding the nations. And we cry out, "Mighty God!"

Or we are bereft and lonely and heart-sore. We cry like an orphaned child in the night. There is none to help, and no one understands. Then He draws nigh with infinite comprehension of our heartache and weariness and pain, and with fathomless consolations He folds us in the embrace of His love. We pillow our heads and our hearts on His bosom, nestle close, and whisper, "Everlasting Father, Prince of Peace!"

JESUS: THE ETERNITY OF OUR LORD

Again, we strain our eyes, peering into the future, wondering what its issues will be and what it holds for us and ours. Our loved ones and friends die and pass out of our sight. Life weakens, its full tides ebb, the sun is setting, the night is falling, and we stand by a silent, shoreless sea where we look in vain for a returning sail and upon which we must launch alone. And we cling to life and shrink back with fear. And then He comes walking on the waters and says, "Don't be afraid. I am here!" (John 6:20 NLT). And we are comforted with a great assurance that nothing shall separate us from His love, that He is Lord of life and death, of time and eternity, and that "His government and its peace will never end" (Isa. 9:6–7 NLT).

This is Jesus. We saw Him first as a little babe, a helpless child, on the bosom of a virgin mother, in a stable among the cattle. But oh, how He has grown as we have looked! He "inhabits eternity" (Isa. 57:15 ESV). "The heaven and heaven of heavens cannot contain [Him]" (1 Kings 8:27 KJV). But He stooped to our lowly condition and humbled Himself, suffered and died for us, and made atonement for our sins.

And "how shall we escape, if we neglect so great salvation?" (Heb. 2:3 KJV).

Oh, the bitter shame and sorrow,

That a time could ever be

When I let the Savior's pity

Plead in vain, and proudly answered:

"All of self and none of Thee!"

Yet He found me; I beheld Him

Bleeding on the cursed tree,

Heard Him pray, "Forgive them, Father,"

And my wistful heart said faintly:

"Some of self and some of Thee!"

Day by day His tender mercy,

Healing, helping, full and free,

Sweet and strong, and, ah! So patient,

Brought me lower, while I whispered:

"Less of self and more of Thee!"

Higher than the highest heavens,

Deeper than the deepest sea,

Lord, Thy love at last has conquered,

Grant me now my spirit's longing—

"None of self and all of Thee!"[5]

I once heard General William Booth, founder of The Salvation Army, while in the midst of an impassioned appeal for people to repent and make their peace with God, cry out, "Every sinner must be either pardoned or punished." And ever since, those words have remained in my memory as the expression of a tremendous truth from which there is no escape.

As I have written elsewhere:

The atonement opens wide the door of pardon, uttermost salvation, and bliss eternal to every penitent soul who will believe on Christ and follow Him, while it sweeps away every excuse from the impenitent heart that will not trust and obey Him.

The atonement justifies God in all His ways with sinful men and women.

The holiest beings in the universe can never feel that God is indifferent to sin, when He pardons believing souls, lifts up their drooping heads, and introduces them to the glories and blessedness of heaven, because Christ has died for them. On the other hand, the souls who are lost and banished to outer darkness cannot blame God nor charge Him with indifference to their misery, since Christ, by tasting death for them, flung wide open the gateway of escape. That they definitely refused to enter in will be clear in their memory forever and will leave them without excuse.[6]

"Judas went to his own place," the Bible says (Acts 1:25, paraphrase). Now, I ask again, "How shall we escape, if we neglect so great salvation?" (Heb. 2:3 KJV).

Was it for me, for me He died?
And shall I still reject His plea?
Mercy refuse with foolish pride,
The while His heart still yearns for me?
Shall I my cup of guilt thus fill?
While Jesus pleads and loves me still?
Dear Savior, I can ne'er repay
The debt of love I owe!
Here, Lord, I give myself away,
'Tis all that I can do.[7]

NOTES

1. The Church of Norway was at this time an officially recognized, state-funded church of Lutheran background.

2. Theodor Westergaard later became colonel in The Salvation Army.

3. For a detailed description of the meeting, which proved historic, see Clarence W. Hall, *Samuel L. Brengle: Portrait of a Prophet* (New York: The Salvation Army, 1933), 172–181.

4. John Bowring, "In the Cross of Christ I Glory," 1825, public domain.

5. Theodore Monod, "None of Self and All of Thee," 1875, public domain.

6. Samuel L. Brengle, *Love Slaves* (New York: The Salvation Army, 1923), ch. 3.

7. Source unknown.

The Blessedness of the Pentecostal Experience 2

Pentecost was the first great event in the history of Christianity after the ascension of Jesus. It was the fulfillment of Joel's prophecy and Jesus' promise. Joel, hundreds of years before, had prophesied: "Then, after doing all those things, I will pour out my Spirit upon all people. Your sons and daughters will prophesy. Your old men will dream dreams, and your young men will see visions. In those days I will pour out my Spirit even on servants—men and women alike" (Joel 2:28–29 NLT).

And Jesus Himself had promised that if He went away He would send another Comforter or Helper, who would be with them evermore: "Once when he was eating with them, he commanded them, 'Do not leave Jerusalem until the Father sends you the gift he promised, as I told you before. John baptized with water, but in just a few days you will be baptized with the Holy Spirit'" (Acts 1:4–5 NLT).

On the day of Pentecost came the ample fulfillment. They were all filled with the Holy Spirit. That was the final and all-sufficient evidence that Jesus had not been swallowed up and lost in the cloud that had received Him out of their sight but that He had gone home to heaven, that He was upon His throne, and that in His exaltation and exultation He had not forgotten them. They were still in His thoughts and in His love. He was still depending upon them and equipping them with power to carry on His work and fulfill His purpose.

They were exultant. Their joy overflowed. They shined and they shouted. Their hearts caught fire. Their minds kindled into flame. Their tongues were unloosed. They must testify. They trooped downstairs from the upper room and out into the street. This was no mere drawing-room blessing they had received. It was too big, glorious, and good to be confined. They must tell it abroad.

The city of Jerusalem was full of strangers from all parts of the world who had come to the great feast, and to these strangers in their own language the glorious news was told. The populous city was stirred, there was a rush together of the curious multitude, and they were confounded and amazed. They marveled, as each heard the apostles speak in his or her own language. In their amazement and doubt they exclaimed, "What can this mean?" (Acts 2:12 NLT). And well they might. It meant that God had come to tabernacle in the hearts of men and women, and that all heaven was enlisted in a campaign for the salvation of the world, a campaign that would not cease till the earth was "filled with the knowledge of the glory of the LORD, as the waters cover the sea" (Hab. 2:14 KJV).

But some mocked and said, "They're just drunk" (Acts 2:13 NLT). And so they were—drunk with holy joy, gladness, love, quenchless hope, and life eternal.

Peter said, "What you see was predicted long ago by the prophet Joel" (Acts 2:16 NLT), and so it was. The other Comforter had come, and the great days of the church were inaugurated with a mighty revival, in the first meeting of which three thousand people experienced new life through faith in Christ. And every revival from then until now—whether local, in some little church or Salvation Army hall or mission station, or worldwide in its sweep like the Wesleyan revival or that led by William Booth—has flowed from the presence and activities of the Holy Spirit as He has been received in trusting hearts and honored in faith and service.

All lovers of Jesus should in these days seek fresh renewings and a greater fullness of the Holy Spirit. We should study what the Bible says about Him as a person. He is not a mere influence, passing over us like a wind or warming us like a fire. He is a person, seeking entrance into our hearts that He may comfort us, instruct us, empower us, guide us, give us heavenly wisdom, and fit us for holy and triumphant service.

If we will seek His presence and yield ourselves to Him in secret prayer, He will make the Bible a new book to us. He will make Jesus precious to us. He will make God the Father ever real to us. We shall not walk in darkness, but shall have the light of life. We shall not be weak in the presence of duty or temptation, but "strong in the Lord and in his mighty power" (Eph. 6:10 NLT). We shall be "ready for every good work" (Titus 3:1 ESV).

I suggest to all my readers that by way of preparation they prayer-fully and carefully study what Jesus said of the Holy Spirit, "the Com-forter," in John 14–16, and the Acts of the apostles, which in many respects might be called the Acts of the Holy Spirit, be read and reread again and again, and pondered in faith and prayer.

God has greater things for us and all His people than the world has ever yet seen, if we only believe in the Lord Jesus Christ and permit the Spirit to lead us.

The Bible says, "As many as are led by the Spirit of God, they are the sons of God. . . . And if children, then heirs; heirs of God, and joint-heirs with Christ" (Rom. 8:14, 17 KJV). And heirs can draw on the estate for all those things needed for their well-being and the full development and use of their powers.

The blessing of the Spirit is not given to everybody. Jesus spoke of Him as one "whom the world cannot receive, because it neither sees him nor knows him" (John 14:17 ESV). Jesus did not say, "may not receive," but "cannot receive." He is given only to those who can receive, to those who see and know. A person who has eyes closed to the light, a heart turned from true knowledge, cannot receive. And yet such people are responsible for their own deprivation because their blindness is due to their own action. Such people cannot receive the Holy Spirit because they have turned away from the Savior and the truth that alone could fit them to receive Him.

The Holy Spirit is given only to those who, accepting Christ and following Him, are prepared to receive. The Pentecostal baptism is for an inner circle. It is a family affair. It is for the children who have become sons and daughters of God through penitent, obedient faith.

It is part of their heritage. It is the portion of that immeasurable inheritance in Christ that is bestowed upon them while upon earth. What the measure of that full inheritance will be in the heavenly world no tongue can tell and no heart can conceive. Pentecost is the foretaste. It is that which, received and properly, wisely, diligently used, will fit us for the final and full reward, but which, rejected or neglected, will leave us eternal paupers among those who weep and gnash their teeth in outer darkness.

This Pentecostal blessing is for our comfort while we are away from home and the unveiled presence of the Father. "I will not leave you comfortless," said Jesus, "I will come to you" (John 14:18 KJV). The coming of the Comforter is also the coming of Jesus in the Spirit. Where the Spirit is, there Jesus is. When He is come, we are no longer orphans, lonely and bereft. Though unseen, He is present with us, and our hearts are strangely warmed and comforted. To some of us, this world would be desolate and lonely beyond words if it were not for the presence of the Comforter.

The Pentecostal blessing is for our instruction in the things of God. The Holy Spirit is the great, secret, silent, inward Teacher, speaking to the ears of the soul, whispering in the silences of the night, instructing in the hours of prayer and communion. As Jesus said, "But the Helper, the Holy Spirit, whom the Father will send in my name, he will teach you all things and bring to your remembrance all that I have said to you" (John 14:26 ESV). We are dull and ignorant, making no assured progress in the school of Christ, until the Comforter is come. When He comes, He arouses and quickens our dull minds. He opens wide the closed eyes and the sealed ears of the soul, and we see and hear things that were hidden from us. He brings our inner life into harmony with the mind of God as revealed in the Bible, and its spiritual meaning begins to open up to our understanding. He quickens our memory, and we now can remember the Word of the Lord. We can go home from a meeting and tell what we have heard when the Comforter is in our hearts.

The Pentecostal blessing is for our guidance. There is one way that is everlasting. "Lead me along the path of everlasting life," prayed the psalmist (Ps. 139:24 NLT). There is one—and only one—road that leads home. Heaven is at the end of that way. There are many attractive and alluring byways, but only the one true way, and we need the Comforter to guide us in that way (see John 16:13) and teach us the truth about God, Jesus, salvation and holiness, sin and its consequences, the shed blood that saves from sin, the way of faith and the life of obedience, and the will of God and the joy set before us. It is the way of the cross, of duty, of lowly, humble, faithful service. It is the way of love, truth, justice, and all right and holy living. It is the way of patient well-being, forbearance and kindness, and the spirit that forgives and gives and asks no reward but the grace to give more fully, love more tenderly, believe more firmly, serve more wisely, hope more joyfully, and never to fail.

The Pentecostal blessing is for power. Jesus said, "You will receive power when the Holy Spirit comes upon you" (Acts 1:8 NLT). We are naturally weak. We fall before temptation. We faint with hopelessness, discouragement, or fear in the presence of difficulty or danger. We flame with hasty temper or passion under provocation. We are puffed up with false views of our own ability or importance, or we are cast down by a feeling of our own impotence. But when the Comforter comes, He strengthens us inwardly. He humbles us with a true view of our weakness, our ignorance, our foolishness, and our insufficiency, and then lifts us up with the revelation of God's sufficiency and eagerness to reinforce us at every point of our spiritual need. As Paul wrote, "I fall to my knees and pray to the Father . . . that from his glorious, unlimited resources he will empower you with inner strength through his Spirit" (Eph. 3:14, 16 NLT).

We should watch and pray and trustfully wait—daily, hourly, and moment-by-moment—for that inner strengthening by the Spirit, that we may be strong to work, fight, resist, serve, sacrifice, suffer, dare, bear up, press on joyfully, and not grow weary or fainthearted.

Before Pentecost Peter was ignorant of himself. So conceited was he that he rebuked Jesus for saying that He was to die on a cross, so sure of himself that he boasted that he would die with Jesus, and yet so inwardly weak that when a servant girl pointed him out as one of the disciples, he cursed and swore that he did not know Jesus. But when a few days later the Holy Spirit had come and strengthened Peter inwardly, he boldly preached Christ Jesus to the multitudes in Jerusalem. And when he and John were beaten and threatened and thrown into prison, they gloried that they were counted worthy to suffer and bear shame for Jesus. They were comforted, instructed, guided, and made inwardly strong to do and dare and bear and suffer—by the Pentecostal baptism.

"Sanctification through the Holy Spirit is for power for service!" so many people say. And so it is. It does reinforce and empower the soul. Those who are given over to the Spirit are "endued with power from on high" (Luke 24:49 KJV) and have a spiritual energy and effectiveness that are not of this world. Their lives and their words take on

a strange new influence and power which come from the active cooperation of an unseen guest, a holy and divine presence abiding in love
within them, and this fits them for the service of their Lord.

But service is not the whole purpose of our beings. What we are is
more important than what we do. Goodness is better than greatness. We
may do much and earn a great name and still end in hell. But the person who loves God and others, though unknown beyond a small circle,
is on the way to heaven, and is well-known there. There are those who
are first who shall be last, and those who are last who shall be first.

The Pentecostal blessing is for daily life. The baptism of the Holy
Spirit brings us into union with Christ and into loving fellowship with
the heavenly Father, to fit us snugly into God's great, complex scheme
of life and equip us for such service or sacrifice as falls to our lot. The
busy housewife, the burdened mother, the toiler in mine or factory or
farm or train or ship, the clerk at his or her desk, the merchant prince,
the bootblack and the prime minister, the king and the president, the
schoolboy and girl—all need the Pentecostal blessing for daily life
and duty, as much as any minister or missionary, if they are to live
worthy lives that shall glorify God and do their work in a spirit well
pleasing to Him. We each and all need the blessing of Pentecost, not
simply for service, but for holy, worthy living, for the perfecting and
completing of character from which will flow influences that are often
more effective than the busy activity we call service.

A hardheaded businessman saw a poor widow woman with her
brood of fatherless children going to the house of God Sunday after
Sunday, and one day it convicted him of his sin and neglect and turned
him in repentance and faith to the Savior. Her "patience in well-doing"

(Rom. 2:7 ESV)—which is a fruit of the Spirit—was more effective than any word she could have spoken.

A lawyer came to his wife's pastor and asked to be received as a member of the church. The pastor was glad, for he had preached sermons to reach this man. So he asked, somewhat shamefacedly, which of his sermons had brought him to decision.

"Well, pastor," replied the lawyer, "to tell the truth, it was not one of your sermons. A few Sundays ago I was leaving the church and found old Auntie Blank haltingly trying to get down the icy steps, and I took her arm and helped her. Then she turned her radiant face up to mine, and asked, 'Do you love my Jesus?' It cut to my heart. I saw her peace and overflowing love and joy, in spite of her poverty and rheumatism, and it convicted me of my sin and led me to Christ."

The fruit of the Spirit, manifest in life and look and everyday, unpremeditated speech, often works more silently, deeply, and effectively than our preaching, and only the Pentecostal blessing can produce this fruit to perfection in our lives.

Many years ago I was campaigning in a little city in Minnesota just at the time of the annual meeting of the Methodist Conference. The town was full of Methodist preachers, many of whom attended our Salvation Army open-air meetings, and some of whom came to our hall. Some of them invited me to their testimony meeting on Sunday morning, just before the bishop's great sermon, to give my testimony, which I did. After speaking for some time, I was going to sit down, but they begged me to speak on, so I continued. Then the presiding elder, host of the conference, came in. Seeing me in the pulpit, he peremptorily ordered me to sit down. The preachers protested, while my peace flowed like a river. I assured him I would be through in a moment, and I hurried out to my meeting.

Several of the preachers said, "We have not believed in the blessing, but that Salvationist has it, else instead of smiling and keeping calm and full of peace, he would have taken offense at that presiding elder." They came to our little hall, and in the holiness meeting came to the mercy seat for the blessing. One of them received the fiery, cleansing, humbling baptism and became a witness to the blessing and a flaming evangelist throughout that region.

It was not my preaching, but the fruit of the Spirit that won him. And it was not of me. I am not by nature calm and peaceful. Quite the contrary. It was supernatural. My proud heart had been humbled to receive the Comforter, and graciously and in love He had come. It was He in my heart who kept me peaceful and calm, and to Him be the glory. "Those who love your instructions [and in whom the Comforter abides] have great peace and do not stumble" (Ps. 119:165 NLT). The Pentecostal blessing is given to cleanse and empower the soul and produce such heavenly fruit in earth's harsh climate.

"The Holy Spirit produces this kind of fruit in our lives: love, joy, peace, patience, kindness, goodness, faithfulness, gentleness, and self-control" (Gal. 5:22–23 NLT). And Christians in whom this fruit—full, rich, and ripe—is found have received this Pentecostal blessing and, in spite of infirmities and human frailties and limitations, are reproducing the life of Jesus upon earth. And out of them, most often unconsciously, flow influence and power that are like "rivers of living water" (John 7:38 ESV) in desert lands. In them Christ is magnified (see Phil. 1:20) and the Father is glorified (see John 15:8).

The Guest of the Soul 3

A friend of mine said recently, "I like the term, 'Holy Ghost,' for the word *ghost* in the old Saxon was the same as the word for *guest*." Whether that is so or not, it may certainly be said that the Holy Ghost is the Holy Guest. He has come into the world and visits every heart, seeking admittance as a guest. He may come *to* the soul unbidden, but He will not come *in* unbidden. He may be unwelcome. He may be refused admission and turned away. But He comes. He is in the world like Noah's dove, looking for an abiding place. He comes as a guest, but as an abiding one if received. He forces Himself upon no one. He waits for the open door and the invitation.

He comes gently. He comes in love. He comes on a mission of infinite goodwill, of mercy and peace and helpfulness and joy. He is the Advocate of the Father and of the Son to us humans. He represents and executes the redemptive plans and purposes of the triune God. As my old teacher, Daniel Steele, wrote, "He is the Executive of the Godhead."

When the Holy Spirit comes into a human heart, He convicts of sin. We cease to be self-complacent when He comes. Self-righteousness is seen to be a sheet too short to cover us; our moral and spiritual nakedness is exposed. Our pride is rebuked, and we are ashamed. Our self-conceit vanishes, and we are abashed. Our eyes are opened, and we see how self-deceived we have been—how un-Christlike in our tempers, how corrupt in our desires, how selfish in our ambitions, how puffed up in our vanity, how slow to believe, how quick to excuse ourselves and justify our own ways, how far from God we have wandered, how unfit for heaven we have become.

He thus reveals us to ourselves in love that He may save us, as a wise and good physician shows us our disease in order to get our consent to be cured. But His supreme work of conviction is to convince us how hopelessly we miss the mark because we do not believe and trust in Christ from the heart. This is the sin we do not recognize as sin until He convinces us of it: "The world's sin is that it refuses to believe in me" (John 16:9 NLT).

The Holy Spirit also convicts of righteousness. We no longer justify ourselves and condemn God. Our mouths are stopped. We see that God is true and righteous altogether, and in the presence of His holiness and righteousness, all our righteousness is seen to be as filthy rags. We can only cry, as did the leper, "Lord, if you will, you can make me clean" (Luke 5:12 ESV). And then we see that Christ Jesus was "pierced for our rebellion, crushed for our sins. He was beaten so we could be whole. He was whipped so we could be healed" (Isa. 53:5

NLT), that "He personally carried our sins in his body on the cross so that we can be dead to sin and live for what is right" (1 Pet. 2:24 NLT), that He "suffered for sins, the just for the unjust" (1 Pet. 3:18 KJV), that "God made Christ, who never sinned, to be the offering for our sin, so that we could be made right with God through Christ" (2 Cor. 5:21 NLT), that we might be able joyfully to sing:

> O Love, Thou bottomless abyss,
> My sins are swallowed up in Thee,
> Covered is my unrighteousness,
> Nor spot of guilt remains on me,
> While Jesus' blood, through earth and skies,
> Mercy, free, boundless mercy, cries.[1]

The Holy Spirit convicts of judgment, both now—accompanying our every act, word, thought, intent, and motive, as our shadow accompanies our body—and to come—exact, final, irrevocable, from which there is no escape and no appeal. He convicts of judgment unto life if we are found in Christ, approved of God—life full, complete, eternal and overflowing with bliss, bliss ineffable. And He convicts of judgment unto banishment if we are found out of Christ, disapproved of God—banishment unto outer darkness, banishment eternal, judgment unto woe immeasurable, banishment into shame unutterable, the harvest of our pride, the reaping of our sin. The seed may be small, but the harvest great. From little seeds mighty trees and vast harvests do grow.

When the Holy Ghost becomes the Holy Guest, He opens the eyes of our understanding to understand the Scriptures. Without His aid, the

Bible is just literature, and some of it is dry and hopelessly uninteresting and incomprehensible literature. But when He removes the scales from our eyes and illuminates its pages, it becomes most precious, a new and living Book, in which God speaks to us in love, in promise, in precept, in types, in symbols, in warning, in rebuke, in entreaty, and always in love to save. It reveals God. It comforts, rebukes, inspires, convicts, converts, and rejoices the heart. It is "sharper than the sharpest two-edged sword," exposing "our innermost thoughts and desires" (Heb. 4:12 NLT).

When the Holy Ghost becomes the Holy Guest in the yielded welcoming heart, He dwells there un-grieved and with delight. "As the bridegroom rejoices over the bride" (Isa. 62:5 ESV), so He rejoices over that soul, while the soul has sweet, ennobling, purifying fellowship and communion with the Lord. He illuminates that soul. He purifies it, sanctifies it, empowers it, instructs it, comforts it, protects it, adjusts it to all circumstances and crosses, and fits it for effective service, patient suffering, and willing sacrifice.

Some time ago my dear friend of many years, Commissioner Charles Sowton, who has since gone to heaven, was passing through New York with his devoted wife. He had only recently settled into his appointment in Australia, a country he enjoyed, where he felt at home, and whose people he had come to admire and love, when orders came to farewell and proceed to England to a new appointment.

To go from sunny Australia to foggy London in midwinter was not pleasant. To leave a field and work and people he loved for work where all would be new and strange was not what he expected or would have chosen. But he told me that the text, "Even Christ didn't live to please himself" (Rom. 15:3 NLT), kept whispering in his heart, and so with perfect and glad resignation, and in great peace, he and Mrs. Sowton were on their way to their new home and tasks.

As he told me this, his face was as serene as a summer's evening, and my own heart sensed the divine calm that possessed him and was refreshed and blessed. It was the indwelling Holy Guest who whispered those words to his heart and fitted him without murmuring into this providence of God. And He who made him so ready for service and so peaceful in sacrifice.

When the Holy Guest abides within, the soul does not shun the way of the cross, nor seek great things for itself. It is as content to serve in lowly as in lofty ways, in obscure and hidden places as in open and conspicuous places where applause waits. To wash a poor disciple's feet is as great a joy as to command an army, to follow as to lead, to serve as to rule—when the Holy Guest abides within the soul. Then the soul does not contend for or grasp and hold fast to place and power. It glories rather in fulfilling Paul's exhortation, "Let this mind be in you, which was also in Christ Jesus" (Phil. 2:5 KJV), and it studies Paul's description and illustration of that mind: "Though he was God, he did not think of equality with God as something to cling to. Instead, he gave up his divine privileges; he took the humble position of a slave and was born as a human being. When he appeared in human form, he humbled himself in obedience to God and died a criminal's death on a cross" (Phil. 2:6–8 NLT).

And having thus glimpsed the mind, the character of Christ, the soul yields itself eagerly to the Holy Guest to be conformed to that mind. That is its ambition, its whole desire, its joy and exceeding great reward. To do the will of the Master, to please Him, to win souls for Him, to serve and suffer and sacrifice for and with Him is its great business. But to be like Him, to live in His favor, to fellowship and be in friendship with Him is its life, its great and solemn joy.

When a guest comes into my home—a guest who is high-minded, wise, large of soul, pure of heart, generous in impulse—that person imparts to me something of his or her own nobility. Mean things look meaner, low things sink lower, base things seem baser by comparison, and what is true, honest, just, pure, and lovely (see Phil. 4:8) are the things upon which I would think and about which I would converse. These and these only are the worthwhile things in such a guest's ennobling presence. But if this is so when a mere man or woman, however upright and holy, comes in, how much more when God the Holy Spirit comes in!

Some people lay great stress upon the second coming of Christ as an incentive to fine and holy living, and I would not minimize this. But Jesus said, "When I am raised to life again"—when the Comforter has come in as the Holy Guest—"you will know that I am in my Father, and you are in me, and I am in you" (John 14:20 NLT). In other words, when the Holy Guest abides within, the Father and the Son are there too. And what finer, more searching and sanctifying incentive to holy living can one have than this indwelling presence of Father, Son, and Holy Ghost as Guest of the Soul?

Finally, the great work of this Holy Guest is to exalt Jesus, to glorify Him who humbled Himself unto the shameful and agonizing death of the cross, to make us see Him in all His beauty, to knit our hearts to Him in faith and love and loyalty, to conform us to His image, and to fit us for His work.

The Holy Ghost as Guest within us does not concentrate our attention upon His own person and work, but upon Jesus and His work and sacrifice for us. He does not glorify Himself. He whispers continually of Christ and His example. He points us to Jesus. He would have us "consider the Apostle and High Priest of our profession, Christ Jesus, who was faithful" (Heb. 3:1–2 KJV). He would have us "consider him who endured from sinners such hostility against himself, so that you may not grow weary or fainthearted" (Heb. 12:3 ESV) and feel our cross too heavy to bear. "Even Christ didn't live to please himself" (Rom. 15:3 NLT), He whispered to my friend, who heard the sweet whisper and was content to follow and be as the Master.

When I joined The Salvation Army after having been a Methodist pastor, I was assigned to black the boots of other cadets in the training college. I was tempted to feel it was a dangerous waste of my time, for which my Lord might hold me to account as He did the man who buried his talent instead of investing it. Then the Holy Guest whispered to me of Jesus and pointed me to Him washing the weary and soiled feet of His lowly disciples. And as I saw Jesus, I was content. Any service for Him and His lowly ones, instead of abasing, exalted me.

What we need evermore in every place, at all times, in prosperity and adversity, in health and sickness, in joy and sorrow, in sunshine and shadow, in wealth or grinding poverty, in comfort and distress, in the fellowship and love of friends and in desolation and loneliness, in victory and defeat, in liberty or in prison, in deliverance or temptation, in life and in death—what we need and shall ever need is to see Jesus, and, seeing Him, to walk in His footsteps, "'Who committed no sin, nor was deceit found in His mouth'; who, when He was reviled, did not revile in return; when He suffered, He did not threaten, but committed Himself to Him who judges righteously" (1 Pet. 2:22–23 NKJV).

And this the Holy Guest delights to help us to do as we "watch and pray" (Matt. 26:41 KJV), as we trust and obey. To those who obey Jesus—and only to them—is this Holy Guest given (see Acts 5:32). And when He is given, it is that He may abide as Comforter, Counselor, Helper, and Friend.

NOTE

1. Johann A. Rothe, "Now I Have Found the Ground Wherein," 1727, public domain.

The Trial of Faith Wrought into Experience 4

The world owes an immeasurable debt to Christianity for its treasures of music and song. Jesus sang (see Matt. 26:30). Oh, to have heard Him! And Paul, especially in his letters to the Ephesians and Colossians, exhorts the Christians there to "sing psalms and hymns and spiritual songs to God with thankful hearts," "making music to the Lord in your hearts" (Col. 3:16; Eph. 5:19 NLT). They were to sing to be heard not only by other people, but also by the Lord Himself.

Every great revival of religion results in a revival of singing and of the composition of both music and song. The Franciscan revival in the thirteenth century was marked by exultant singing. And so it was in the days of Luther, the Wesleys, William Booth, and Moody. And so it will always be.

The joys, faith, hopes, and aspirations; the deepest desires; the love and utter devotion; and the sweet trust of the Christian find noblest and freest expression in music and song. And yet it is probable that in no way do people more frequently and yet unconsciously deceive themselves (and actually lie to each other and to God) than in the public singing of songs and hymns.

Languidly, lustily, thoughtlessly in song they profess a faith they do not possess, a love and devotion their whole life falsifies, a joy their lack of radiance on the face and of light in the eye contradicts. They sing, "Oh, how I love Jesus!" while their hearts are far from Him, with no intention of doing the things that please Him. Or while they are restless and defeated, they sing:

> I've wondrous peace through trusting,
> A well of joy within;
> This rest is everlasting,
> My days fresh triumphs bring.[1]

While they live selfishly and spend much of their time in murmuring and complaining instead of praise, they sing:

> Take my life, and let it be
> Consecrated, Lord, to Thee;
> Take my moments and my days,
> Let them flow in ceaseless praise.[2]

It is a solemn thing to stand before God and sing such songs. We should think. A hush should be upon our spirits for we are standing upon holy ground where mysteries are all about us, enshrouding us, while the Angel of the Lord looks upon us through pillar of cloud and fire, and devils leer and lurk to entrap and overthrow us.

Nearly fifty years ago, at The Salvation Army's training school at Clapton, we cadets were singing:

> My will be swallowed up in Thee;
> Light in Thy light still may I see
> In Thine unclouded face.
> Called the full strength of trust to prove.[3]

And there my heart cried out, "Yes, Lord, let me prove the full strength of trust!" And then I was hushed into deep questioning and prayer, for a whisper deep within me asked, "Can you, will you, endure the tests, the trials, that alone can prove the full strength of trust? A feather's weight may test the strength of an infant or an invalid, but heavier and yet heavier weights alone can test the full strength of a man. Will you bear patiently, without murmuring or complaining or fainting, the trials I permit to come upon you, which alone can prove the full strength of your trust and train it for larger service and yet greater trials?"

My humbled heart dared not say, "I can," but only, "By Thy grace I will." And then we continued to sing:

> My will be swallowed up in Thee . . .
> Let all my quickened heart be love,
> My spotless life be praise.[4]

And my whole soul consented to any trial which the Lord in His wisdom and love might permit to come upon me. I willed to be wholly the Lord's, to endure, to "bear up and steer right onward"[5] in the face of every tempest that might blow, every whelming sea that might threaten to engulf me, every huge Goliath who might mock and vow to destroy me. I was not jubilant; my soul was awed into silence, but also into strong confidence and a deep rest of quiet faith.

I felt sure from that hour that if I was to be a saint or soldier of Christ, a winner of souls, and a conqueror on life's battlefields, then I was not to be a pampered pet of the Lord—that I must not expect favors, that my path was not to be strewn with roses, that acclaiming multitudes were not to cheer and crown me, that I must walk by faith, not sight, that I must be faithful and hold fast that which God had given me, that I must still pray when heaven seemed shut and God not listening, that I must rejoice in tribulation and glorify my Lord in the fire, that I must keep hot when others grew cold, stand alone when others ran away, look to no human being for my example but seek always to be an example to all. I knew that I must stand on instant guard against the lure of the world, the insurgence and insistence of the flesh, and the wiles of the Devil, that I must not become sarcastic, cynical, suspicious, or supercilious, but have the love that "thinks no evil . . . bears all things, believes all things, hopes all things, endures all things . . . [and] never fails" (1 Cor. 13:5–8 NKJV), that I must not be seduced by flattery, nor frightened by frowns. I felt that, while esteeming others better than myself (see Phil. 2:3) and in honor preferring others before myself (see Rom. 12:10), and while I was not to be wise in my own conceits (see Rom. 12:16), yet I was in no sense to permit my own personality to be submerged in the mass; that

I must be myself, stand on my own feet, fulfill my own task, bear my own responsibility, answer at last for my own soul, and, when the judgment books are opened, stand or fall by my own record.

That moment when we sang those words was to me most solemn and sacred and not to be forgotten. There God set His seal upon my consenting soul for service, for suffering, for sacrifice. From that moment, life became a thrilling adventure in fellowship with God, in friendship and companionship with Jesus. Everything that has come into my life from that moment has, in some way, by God's sanctifying touch and unfailing grace, enriched me. It may have impoverished me on one side, but it has added to my spiritual wealth on the other, as Jacob's withered thigh, Joseph's slavery and imprisonment, Moses' enforced banishment from Pharaoh's court, and Paul's thorn and shipwrecks and stonings and imprisonments enriched them.

Pain has come to me, but in it I have always found some secret pleasure and compensation. Sorrow and bereavement have thrown me back upon God and deepened and purified my joy in Him. Agony—physical and mental—has led to some unexpected triumphs of grace and faith, and some enlargement of sympathy and power to understand and bless others. Loss and gain, loneliness and love, light and darkness, trials and things hard or impossible to understand—everything has brought its own blessing as my soul has bowed to and accepted the yoke of Jesus and refused to murmur or complain but rather to receive the daily providences of life as God's training school for faith, patience, steadfastness, and love.

Paul was right—and my soul utters a deep "amen"—when he wrote, "And we know that God causes everything to work together for the good

of those who love God and are called according to his purpose for them"
(Rom. 8:28 NLT). Listen to Paul's record of some of the "everything"
which worked together for his good. He had been ridiculed and treated
with scorn by his enemies as an apostle and minister, and he replied:

> Are they servants of Christ? I know I sound like a madman, but
> I have served him far more! I have worked harder, been put in
> prison more often, been whipped times without number, and
> faced death again and again. Five different times the Jewish
> leaders gave me thirty-nine lashes. Three times I was beaten
> with rods. Once I was stoned. Three times I was shipwrecked.
> Once I spent a whole night and a day adrift at sea. I have trav-
> eled on many long journeys. I have faced danger from rivers
> and from robbers. I have faced danger from my own people, the
> Jews, as well as from the Gentiles. I have faced danger in the
> cities, in the deserts, and on the seas. And I have faced danger
> from men who claim to be believers but are not. I have worked
> hard and long, enduring many sleepless nights. I have been hun-
> gry and thirsty and have often gone without food. I have shivered
> in the cold, without enough clothing to keep me warm.
>
> Then, besides all this, I have the daily burden of my concern
> for all the churches. (2 Cor. 11:23–28 NLT)

What a list, and it is not complete! A study of his Corinthian letters
reveals much more of his mental and spiritual trials and conflicts
which meant unmeasured suffering to his sensitive soul, so chaste in
its purity, so keenly alive to all the finest and loftiest views of life,

and so hungry for human as well as divine love and fellowship. This was a man who gloried in his tribulations, because they worked in him patience, experience, and hope (see Rom. 5:3–4), and he declared that in all things he was more than conqueror (see Rom. 8:37). Indeed, he called those things a "light affliction, which is but for a moment" (2 Cor. 4:17 KJV).

He looked at them in the light of eternity, and they were so swallowed up in that vastness, that infinitude, that he said they were "but for a moment." And then he added that such afflictions are actually "working for us"—our slave, working out for us—"a far more exceeding and eternal weight of glory, while we do not look at the things which are seen, but at the things which are not seen. For the things which are seen are temporary [fleeting, soon to pass away and be forgotten], but the things which are not seen are eternal" (2 Cor. 4:17–18 NKJV).

Paul said, "We know"—his uncertainties, doubts, fears, questionings, had all vanished, being swallowed up in knowledge—"that God causes everything to work together for the good of those who love God" (Rom. 8:28 NLT).

But how did he know? How had Paul reached such happy assurance? He knew by faith. He believed God, and light on dark problems streamed into his soul through faith.

He knew by joyful union with the risen Christ, who had conquered death and the grave. This union was so real that Christ's victory was his victory also.

He knew in part by experience. Paul had suffered much, and by experience he had found all things in the past working for his good, enriching his spiritual life through the abounding grace of his Lord.

And this gave him assurance for "everything" and for all the future. Nothing could really harm him while he was in the divine will, in the eternal order, while he was a branch in the living Vine, a member of Christ's body (see Rom. 12:5; 1 Cor. 12:20–27).

Listen to him: "Can anything ever separate us from Christ's love? Does it mean he no longer loves us if we have trouble or calamity, or are persecuted, or hungry, or destitute, or in danger, or threatened with death? . . . No, despite all these things, overwhelming victory is ours through Christ, who loved us" (Rom. 8:35, 37 NLT).

Hear Paul again: "We can rejoice, too, when we run into problems and trials, for we know that they help us develop endurance. And endurance develops strength of character, and character strengthens our confident hope of salvation. And this hope will not lead to disappointment. For we know how dearly God loves us, because he has given us the Holy Spirit to fill our hearts with his love" (Rom. 5:3–5 NLT).

Hear him yet once more: "And I am convinced that nothing can ever separate us from God's love. Neither death nor life, neither angels nor demons, neither our fears for today nor our worries about tomorrow—not even the powers of hell can separate us from God's love. No power in the sky above or in the earth below—indeed, nothing in all creation will ever be able to separate us from the love of God that is revealed in Christ Jesus our Lord" (Rom. 8:38–39 NLT).

Any and everything, present and future, which produced patience, experience of God's love, and hope in Him, Paul was sure was working for his good, and he welcomed it with rejoicing, for it came bearing gifts of spiritual riches. That is how he knew. We may believe what is revealed in the Bible about this and enter into peace, great peace, but we come to know, as Paul did, by putting God and life to the test—by experience.

I happened to be present when a young wife and mother was weeping bitter tears of anguish. An older wife and mother, with a face like the morning, full of heaven's own peace, who had herself wept bitter tears of anguish, put her arms around the younger woman and in tender and wise words of perfect assurance comforted her. And as I noted the gentleness, wisdom, calmness, and moral strength of the elder woman, I thought, "Ah, her trials that were so painful worked for her good. They left her enlarged in heart, enriched in experience and knowledge, sweetened in character, wise in sympathy, calm in storm, perfect in peace, and with a spirit at home and at rest in God while yet in the body."

And I looked forward with joy in the hope that the younger woman, believing in Jesus, patiently submitting to chastening and trials as opportunities for the exercise and the discipline of faith, would enter into an experience of God's love and faithfulness that would leave her spirit forever strengthened, sweetened, enriched, and fitted to comfort and strengthen others. And so, after years, it proved to be.

Our true good in this and all worlds is spiritual. And trials, afflictions, losses, and sorrows, borne with patience and courage and in faith, will surely develop in us spiritual graces and "the peaceful fruit of righteousness" (Heb. 12:11 ESV) which are never found in those whose sky is never overcast, whose voyage over life's sea is never troubled by storm and hurricane, whose soldiering is only on dress parade and never in deadly battle, or who, facing storm or battle, flee away and so escape it.

Holiness of heart does not ensure us against painful things that try our faith, but it does prepare us for the trial, while the patient endurance of trial reveals the reality of our faith, the purity and integrity of our hearts, and the grace and faithfulness of our Lord.

When Abraham was tried in the offering up of Isaac, the angel of the Lord said, "Now I know that you truly fear God. You have not withheld from me even your son, your only son" (Gen. 22:12 NLT). And again and again the most obstinate opponents of Christianity have been conquered by the patient endurance and the radiant joy of suffering Christians. It was so not only in the days of far-off persecutions—in Rome, when Christians were thrown to the wild beasts, roasted over slow fires, tortured in every conceivable way—but also in our own day and in the history of The Salvation Army that the blood of the martyrs and the patience and triumphant joy of the saints have won the hardest skeptics to Jesus.

Paul looked upon his sufferings as a part of the sufferings of Christ, as though Christ's sufferings did not end upon the cross but were completed in the sufferings of His disciples. Paul wrote, "I am glad when I suffer for you in my body, for I am participating in the sufferings of Christ that continue for his body, the church" (Col. 1:24 NLT).

Happy are we if we can receive all suffering in that spirit, whether it is suffering of body, mind, or soul. It will then work for our good and through us for the good of others, whether or not we can understand how it is to do so.

It will purge us of vanity. It will deepen us in humility, enlarge us in sympathy, and make us more fruitful in the graces of the Spirit.

How bitter that cup
No tongue can conceive,
Which He drank quite up

That sinners might live.

His way was much rougher

And darker than mine:

Did Christ, my Lord, suffer,

And shall I repine?

Since all that I meet

Shall work for my good,

The bitter is sweet,

The medicine is food;

Though painful at present,

'Twill cease before long,

And then, oh, how pleasant

The conqueror's song![6]

NOTES

1. John Lawley, "Come, with Me Visit Calvary," 1905, public domain.

2. Frances Ridley Havergal, "Take My Life and Let It Be," 1874, public domain.

3. Charles Wesley, "Come, Holy Ghost, All-Quickening Fire," 1739, public domain.

4. Ibid.

5. John Milton, "To the Same," 1655, public domain.

6. John Newton, "Begone, Unbelief! My Savior Is Near," 1779, public domain.

A Perfect-Hearted People 5

God is looking for people whose hearts are perfect toward Him—
a perfected-hearted people; so there is a kind of perfection required of
His people by God.

A friend asked me some time ago whether I believed in and taught
perfection. I replied that that depended upon what he meant by the
term *perfection*.

If he meant absolute perfection, I did not. Nor did I believe in the
possession by humans of angelic perfection, nor yet in their realizing
such perfection as Adam must have originally possessed.

God alone is absolutely perfect in all His attributes, and to such
perfection we can never hope to attain. There is also a perfection
possessed by the angels, which we shall never have in this world.
Adam also had certain perfections of body and mind which are out of
our reach.

There is, however, a perfection which we are given to understand God requires in us. It is a perfection not of head but of heart—not of knowledge but of goodness, humility, love, and faith. Such a perfection God desires us to have, and such a perfection we may have. In saying this, I cannot be accused of being a crank or a fanatic, for I am proclaiming only the plain, simple truth as it is revealed in God's Word, and we ought to desire to rise up to all the privileges God has conferred upon us.

"Be perfect, even as your Father in heaven is perfect," said Jesus (Matt. 5:48 NLT). What sort of perfection is this that we are to possess? God is a Spirit; we are simply men and women. And further, "No one has ever seen God" (John 1:18 NLT). How then are we to know what that perfection is which He requires of us—a perfection which it is possible for men and women to manifest? In this, Jesus is our pattern. It is true that "no one has ever seen God. But the unique One, who is himself God, is near to the Father's heart. He has revealed God to us" (John 1:18 NLT). That is, Jesus manifested the Father's nature and perfections in a human life that we can see and understand.

This perfection of heart, of purity, and of goodness, was seen in Jesus in several particulars, and in these we are to follow His example.

We are to be perfectly submitted to God. We are to come to the place where we no longer fight against God's will, where we do not complain or talk back or resist, but yield in perfect submission to all His will.

In the terrible burning of the ferry *The General Slocum* in New York Harbor in 1904, almost all the mothers and children of one church lost their lives. The next Sunday the bereaved fathers and husbands came to the church, and the pastor—who had lost his whole family—rose and said, "The LORD gave, and the LORD has taken away; blessed be the name of the LORD" (Job 1:21 ESV). Those men were perfectly submissive to God in their hearts, and they did not fight against God's providences nor fail God in the hour of their suffering and trial.

It is possible to be submitted to God in this way. We may not understand God's providences, but we can say "amen" to them from our hearts.

Like Jesus, we may perfectly trust God. We may possess a confidence in God that holds out in ways we do not understand, like the confidence a very little child has in a parent, that will trust mother or father with all the heart.

Job was rich, prosperous, and happy. Then trouble came. He was afflicted. He lost his children. He lost his property, and his herds were carried off by marauders. What did Job do? He did not complain and blame God, but said, "The LORD gave, and the LORD has taken away; blessed be the name of the LORD" (Job 1:21 ESV). And when his faithless wife advised him to curse God and die, Job defended God's way and said, "'You speak as one of the foolish women would speak. Shall we receive good from God, and shall we not receive evil?' In all this Job did not sin with his lips" (Job 2:10 ESV).

Then his friends tried to shake his confidence, and Job—afflicted, full of pain, poor, and bereaved of his children—seemed to be forsaken by God. But he looked up from his ash heap and exclaimed, "Though he slay me, yet will I trust in him" (Job 13:15 KJV).

It is always so with the perfect-hearted man or woman. I want my friends to trust me, and if they failed to do so when I was out of their sight it would break my heart. So God wants us to trust Him where we cannot see Him.

Paul and Silas, on one of their missionary journeys, were arrested and placed in one of those loathsome Roman prisons—in the inmost, wet, slimy, foul dungeon—with the wounds on their backs from the scourging they had just received gaping wide and with their feet in the stocks. But they did not worry and complain and determine to go home when they were released. They sang and praised the Lord.

That is the kind of spirit God wants His people to possess: a spirit that will rejoice with a perfect trust in Him under adversity.

God desires His people to be perfect in love, to love Him perfectly. We are not expected to love God with the heart of an archangel, for we are only poor humble souls with limited power to love, but God does expect us to love with all our hearts—with all our power to love.

The little child is to love with all his or her power. And as our powers develop and grow, our love is to develop and grow apace with our power to love. But we are always to love with all the heart.

There must be perfect loyalty. Love is not an emotion, a happy feeling. It is not something on the surface. It is a deep principle, revealing itself in perfect loyalty to God.

What constitutes a perfect husband or wife, or son or daughter? Imagine a big, ignorant young man who could not shine in a social situation. He is hardworking, rough, uncultured, and awkward, and in the eyes of the world is a most imperfect man. But he has a dear old mother whom he loves. He works to give her his meager wages at the end of the week. He carries up the coal to heat her rooms. And when his day's work is done he comes home to cheer his old mother with his presence. He does all he can to make her latter days comfortable and happy. He is a very imperfect man, but his mother would tell you with pride, "He is my perfect son." What makes him a perfect son? Perfect loyalty to his old mother.

So our heart may be perfect if it beats in perfect loyalty to God— wholly yielded up to fulfill all His purposes. We may be very imperfect as a man or woman, and our imperfections may be apparent to everyone. We may blunder and make many mistakes. We may be ignorant and uncultured. Yet God looks down and counts us a perfect-hearted person. When God sees a heart perfect in loyalty to Him, He overlooks many mistakes and blunders of the head.

God also requires of us perfect obedience. Our performance may not always be perfect, but our spirit may be perfect.

God's eyes are in all parts of the earth, seeking for men and women with hearts perfect toward Him in submission, trust, love, and obedience. And when He finds such a heart, He reveals Himself to that person and shows Himself on behalf of him or her.

Now let me ask you, what kind of heart do you have? Have you submitted to Him? Have you consecrated yourself wholly to Him? Have you put all your powers at His disposal? Have you let Him have all His way with you? How anger and pride and selfishness and uncleanness must grieve Him! The perfect-hearted person has put all these things away.

How can I put away these things that seem to be a part of my very being? How can I change the color of my eyes or add a cubit to my stature? I cannot! Work as I will, I shall always fail to change my moral nature. But God can. It is His work.

If we go down before Him in complete humility and say, "Lord, I am willing to have my heart changed. Though it may mean that I shall be despised and hated and persecuted, I will take up my cross; I will crucify myself. I am willing that my selfishness and pride and hate and uncleanness shall be taken from me, and that You shall reign in me and create in me a clean heart, perfect in its love, submission, loyalty, trust, and obedience"—if we will say that to Him, He will answer our prayer today, now, this moment, if we will but believe.

A Thirteenth-Century Salvationist   6

Most of the Ten Commandments can be made into laws of the land by legislative enactment, but not so the Sermon on the Mount. It is not only a sin to murder and steal; it is also a crime, a breach of law. But no statesman has ever yet passed a law compelling people to be poor in spirit, meek, merciful, pure of heart, loving to enemies, and glad when lied about and persecuted. Human beings may be restrained by the strong hand of the law from stealing or committing murder, but they can be constrained to be meek and lowly in heart, to bless them who curse them, to pray for them who despitefully use them, and to love those who hate them only by grace.

"The law was given by Moses, but grace and truth came by Jesus Christ" (John 1:17 KJV). He was "full of grace and truth" (John 1:14 KJV). When His heart broke on Calvary it was like the breaking of Mary's alabaster box of ointment. And when He poured out the Holy Spirit at

Pentecost, rivers of grace and truth began to stream forth to every land, to all people.

The nature religions and philosophies of the Gentile world and the religion of the scribes and Pharisees, sunk into legal forms and ceremonies, were powerless to give peace to troubled consciences, strength to slaves of vice and corruption, or life to souls that were dead in sin. But that is just what the grace of God in Christ did. It met and fitted men and women's moral and spiritual needs as light meets the eye, as the skin fits the hand.

What happened when Paul went to luxurious, licentious Corinth and preached Christ to the reveling populace? Fornicators, idolaters, adulterers, homosexuals, thieves, covetous people, drunkards, and revelers became saints. Their eyes were opened, their darkness vanished, their chains fell off, and they received "beauty for ashes, the oil of joy for mourning, the garment of praise for the spirit of heaviness" (Isa. 61:3 KJV). Christ made them free. They loved each other. They lived in close association with each other, but they did not shut themselves away from their non-Christian neighbors. They went everywhere declaring the good news of redeeming love and uttermost salvation in Christ.

But not all who named the name of Christ departed from iniquity. Heresies crept in. Persecutions arose. The awful corruptions and subtle philosophies of the heathen world undermined the morals, weakened the courage, and dimmed or destroyed the faith of many. The whole social and political order of the ancient world began to crumble. The Roman Empire fell before the assaults of northern barbarians, and the Dark Ages supervened. The secret of salvation and sanctification by faith, which made Paul's converts in Corinth victorious over the proud and putrid world in which they lived, the flesh which had enslaved them, and the Devil who had deceived them, was largely, if not wholly, lost.

Earnest souls, sick of sin, weary of strife, and ignorant of the way of victorious faith in an indwelling Christ, fled to the desert and wilderness to escape temptation. Many of them became hermits, living solitary lives on pillars in the desert and in dens and caves of the earth, while others formed monastic communities of monks and nuns. They harked back to the grim austerity and asceticism of Elijah and John the Baptist, and lost the sweet reasonableness and holy naturalness of Jesus. In the solitude of desert dens and the darkness of wilderness caves and on the tops of lonely pillars they kept painful vigil and fought bitter battles with devils. With prolonged fastings and flagellations they struggled to overcome the unsanctified passions of the flesh.

There were saints among these seekers, who found God and kept sacred learning and faith alive. It was the hermit St. Jerome who translated the Scriptures into the common language, giving us the version known as the Vulgate. It was the monk Thomas à Kempis who wrote *The Imitation of Christ*. Some of the sweetest and most stirring hymns of Christendom leaped forth from glad and loving hearts in monasteries of the Dark Ages. Those ages were dark, but not wholly dark.

As the iron empire of Rome, corroded and rusted by luxury and utterly corrupt vices, began to crumble and fall before the fierce, barbaric hordes of the north, feudalism sprang up and the great mass of people became serfs who tilled the fields and fought the wars of petty lords who lived in castles overlooking the towns and villages that dotted the plains. Towns and cities, torn and reddened by internal factional strife, made war on each other. The baron made war on his enemy, the rich abbot, and endowed and adorned his castle and church with spoils of his petty warfare. The clergy were generally greedy and corrupt. Poverty, illiteracy, filth, and disease were universal. Brigands infested the forests and mountains, and pitiful, loathsome lepers begged for alms along the highways.

At the end of a thousand years of such dimness and darkness, when a new dawn was breaking (which he was greatly to hasten), St. Francis of Assisi appeared. He was the son of a prosperous Italian cloth merchant and a gentle and devout French lady who probably sprang from the nobility. A beautiful, courteous lad, with flashing eyes and equally flashing spirit, who sang the songs of the troubadours in his mother's native tongue and delighted in the sports and revelry and daredevil doings of the youth of the town—such was Francis Bernadone. Little did he seem to have in him the stuff of a saint who would transform the Christendom of his day and hold the wondering and affectionate gaze of seven centuries. His father was a tradesman, but he was rich and freehanded with his dashing and attractive son.

The boy was lavish with money and courteous and lively in spirit, which made him the friend and companion of the young nobility who dwelt in castles. War broke out between Assisi and the city of Perugia, so Francis, burning with the pride of youth and the fires of patriotism, went forth with the young noblemen and their bands of serfs to fight the enemy. But the battle went against the Assisians, and a company of the leaders—including Francis—were captured and spent a year in prison.

The youthful aristocrats, deprived of liberty, languished. But Francis, whom they kept among them, never lost his spirit, but cheered his companions with his kindness, his gaiety, and his songs. He laughed and sang and made merry, and possibly partly in jest but more in earnest, through some strange youthful premonition, he assured them that he would one day be a great prince, with his name on the lips of all. Little did he or they suspect what kind of a prince he would be, or the nature of the acclaim with which people would greet him.

Months of sickness followed his imprisonment. He began to think on the things that are eternal, the things of the spirit. Recovered from his illness, he went forth again on a fine steed, in glittering armor, to war. But, for some rather obscure reason, he returned and fell into strange meditative moods. His companions suspected that it was an affair of the heart and asked him if he was dreaming of a lady love. He admitted that he was—a fairer love than they had ever imagined: Lady Poverty! He was thinking of giving up all for Christ.

One day while Francis was serving a customer in his father's shop, a beggar came in and asked for alms in the name of God. Francis, busy with his customer, sent him away empty-handed, but afterward said to himself, "If he had asked in the name of some nobleman, how promptly and generously I should have responded. But he asked in the name of the Lord, and I sent him away with nothing!" Leaving the shop, he ran after the beggar and lavished money upon him, and from that day he was the unfailing friend of beggars and all the poor.

Lepers were peculiarly repulsive to him, and he stood in a kind of fear of them. One day when riding, he met a leper, and a fear he would not have felt on a field of battle gripped him. He rode past the poor creature and then, ashamed of himself, won a greater victory than ever was won by armed warriors on a field of blood. He wheeled his horse around and returned, and leaping down, he kissed the leper and gave him all the money he had with him. Joy filled his heart, and ever after he was the friend, the benefactor, and the frequent nurse and companion of lepers.

He was a creature of generous, self-sacrificing impulse. But once he yielded to the impulse it became a lifelong principle, and he served it with the unfailing devotion of a lover to his mistress. However, like little Samuel, he "did not yet know the LORD, neither was the word of the LORD yet revealed unto him" (1 Sam. 3:7 KJV). But one day he was praying before the altar in a poor, half-ruined little church: "Great and glorious God, and Thou, Lord Jesus, I pray, shed abroad Thy light in the darkness of my mind. Be found of me, O Lord, so in all things I may act only in accordance with Thy holy will." His eyes were upon a crucifix as he prayed, and it seemed to him that the Savior's eyes met his. The place suddenly became a holy place, and he was in the presence of the Lord and Savior as was Moses when he drew near the burning bush on Horeb.

The sacred Victim seemed alive, and as a Voice spoke to Moses from the bush, so a wondrous, sweet, ineffable Voice seemed to speak from the crucifix to the longing soul of Francis, bidding him to repair the church that was falling into decay and ruin. From that day he was assured that Christ knew him, heard him, loved him, and wanted his service. He could say, "I am my beloved's, and my beloved is mine" (Song 6:3 KJV).

Francis was essentially a man of action rather than of contemplation, so instead of retiring to a hermit's lodge in the desert or a monastery on some hilltop, he sallied forth at once to repair the little church of St. Damien in which he had been praying and had heard the Voice. He begged stones and carried them himself, repairing the church with his own hands. And when that was completed he repaired yet another church. It had not yet dawned upon him that the Voice was calling him to repair, not the four walls of a church made with hands, but the spiritual church with its living stones not built with hands.

His proud and disappointed father fell upon him, beat him, and imprisoned him in his home. But during the absence of his father, his mother released him and he returned to the church, where he lived with the priest, wearing—instead of his rich clothing—a hair shirt and a rough brown robe tied around him with a rope, which was later to become the uniform of the myriad brothers of the Franciscan order. He worked or begged for his bread and in Assisi was looked upon as a madman. His father and brother cursed him when they saw him.

He publicly renounced all right to his patrimony and adopted utter poverty as one of the rules of his life. He made poverty one of the rules—indeed, the most distinctive rule of the order he founded. And later, when the bishop of Assisi gently reproved him and argued that he should not go to such an extreme, he silenced the bishop, who had trouble with his own riches, by shrewdly replying, "If we own property we must have laws and arms to defend them, and this will destroy love out of our hearts."

In a short time—as with a true Salvationist, or any true Christian— the sincerity, sweetness, joy, and devotion of his life began to disarm criticism, win approval, and cause heart searchings in many of his fellow townspeople.

His first convert was a wealthy man called Bernardo, who had been impressed by Francis's joyous, simple life. He invited Francis to spend the night with him and only simulated sleep that he might watch the young man. When Francis thought he was asleep, he knelt by his bedside and spent most of the night in prayer. The next morning Bernardo, who became one of the most noted and devout of the brothers, decided to sell all, give to the poor, and cast in his lot with Francis.

A third, named Pietro, joined them, and the three went to church where, after praying and examining the Scriptures, they adopted as the rule of their new life the words of Jesus: "If you want to be perfect, go and sell all your possessions and give the money to the poor, and you will have treasure in heaven. Then come, follow me" (Matt. 19:21 NLT).

Jesus called together his twelve disciples and gave them power and authority to cast out all demons and to heal all diseases. Then he sent them out to tell everyone about the Kingdom of God and to heal the sick. "Take nothing for your journey," he instructed them. "Don't take a walking stick, a traveler's bag, food, money, or even a change of clothes. Wherever you go, stay in the same house until you leave town. And if a town refuses to welcome you, shake its dust from your feet as you leave to show that you have abandoned those people to their fate."

So they began their circuit of the villages, preaching the Good News and healing the sick. (Luke 9:1–6 NLT)

The literal strictness with which Francis and his early disciples followed and enforced the rule of utter poverty gave them great freedom from care, great freedom of movement, and much joy. But later, this led to much strife and division in the order, the beginnings of which in his lifetime saddened the last days of the saint.

The pope sanctioned Francis's rule and granted him and the members of the order the right to preach. Like the early disciples, they went everywhere testifying, singing, preaching, laboring with their hands for food, and, when unable to get work, not hesitating to ask from door to door for bread.

At first they were scorned and often beaten, but they gloried in tribulation. "My brothers, commit yourselves to God with all your cares and He will care for you," said Francis, and they went with joy, strictly observing his instructions:

Let us consider that God in His goodness has called us not merely for our own salvation, but also for that of many men, that we may go through all the world exhorting men, more by our example than by our words, to repent of their sins and keep the commandments. Be not fearful because we appear little and ignorant. Have faith in God, that His Spirit will speak in and by you.

You will find men, full of faith, gentleness, and goodness, who will receive you and your words with joy; but you will find others, and in great numbers, faithless, proud, blasphemers, who will speak evil of you, resisting you and your words. Be resolute, then, to endure everything with patience and humility.

Have no fear, for very soon many noble and learned men will come to you; they will be with you preaching to kings and

princes and to a multitude of people. Many will be converted to
the Lord all over the world, who will multiply and increase His
family.[1]

How like William Booth, the founder of The Salvation Army, that
sounds!

And what he preached, Francis practiced to the end. He died pre-
maturely, surrounded by his first followers, exhausted, blind, and, at
his own request, stripped except for a hair shirt and laid upon the bare
ground. His rule, his order, and his life and example were a stern and
mighty rebuke to the wealth, greed, and laziness of the priests and the
monks. But he exhorted his brothers not to judge others, not to condemn or be severe, but to honor them, give them all due respect and
pray for them, remembering some whom they might think to be members of the Devil would yet become members of Christ.

Within a brief time, five thousand friars in brown robes were going
everywhere with their glad songs, their burning exhortations, their
simple testimony and sacrificial lives, and all who met them met with
a spiritual adventure not to be forgotten. In Spain, some of them fell
upon martyrdom. They went to Germany, France, and to far Scandi-
navia, where they built the great cathedral of Upsala. Francis himself
went to the Holy Land with the crusaders, and at the risk of his life,
boldly entered the camp of the Saracens with two of his brothers and
sought to convert the Saracen leader and his host. In this he failed,
but he made a deep impression on the followers of Mohammed.

Once he was called to preach before the pope and the College of
Cardinals. He carefully prepared his sermon, but when he attempted

to deliver it he became confused, frankly confessed his confusion, forgot his prepared address, threw himself upon the Lord, and spoke from his heart as moved by the Spirit—spoke with such love and fire that he burned into all hearts and melted his august audience to many tears. Long before Hus and Luther appeared, thundering against the abuses of the church, Francis wrought a great reformation by love, simplicity, and self-sacrifice. He was a kindred spirit of George Fox and John Wesley and William Booth, and would have gloried in their fellowship.

After seven centuries, his words are still as sweet as honey, as searching as fire, as penetrating and revealing as light. One winter's day, bitterly cold, he was journeying with a Brother Leo, when he said:

> May it please God that the Brothers Minor [the "Little Brothers," the name he adopted for the Franciscan order] all over the world may give a great example of holiness and edification. But not in this is the perfect joy. If the Little Brothers gave sight to the blind, healed the sick, cast out demons, gave hearing to the deaf, or even raised the four-days' dead—not in this is the perfect joy.
>
> If a Brother Minor knew all languages, all science, and all Scripture, if he could prophesy and reveal not only future things, but even the secret of consciences and of souls—not in this consists the perfect joy.
>
> If he could speak the language of angels; if he knew the courses of the stars and the virtues of plants; if all the treasures

of earth were revealed to him, and he knew the qualities of birds, fishes, and all animals, of men, trees, rocks, roots, and waters—not in these is the perfect joy.

"Father, in God's name, I pray you," exclaimed Leo, "Tell me in what consists the perfect joy."

"When we arrive at Santa Maria degli Angeli, soaked with rain, frozen with cold, covered with mud, dying of hunger," said Francis, "and we knock, and the porter comes in a rage, saying 'Who are you?' and we answer, 'We are two of your brethren,' and he says, 'You lie; you are two lewd fellows who go up and down corrupting the world and stealing the alms of the poor. Go away!' and he does not open to us, but leaves us outside in the snow and rain, frozen, starved, all night—then, if thus maltreated and turned away we patiently endure all without murmuring against him; if we think with humility and charity that this porter really knows us truly and that God makes him speak thus to us, in this is the perfect joy. Above all the graces and all the gifts which the Holy Spirit gives to His friends is the grace to conquer one's self, and willingly to suffer pain, outrages, disgrace, and evil treatment for the love of Christ."[2]

This sounds like echoes from the Sermon on the Mount and the epistles and testimonies of Paul. It is a commentary upon Paul's psalm of love in the thirteenth chapter of 1 Corinthians, and on his testimony: "I take pleasure in infirmities, in reproaches, in necessities, in persecutions, in distresses for Christ's sake" (2 Cor. 12:10 KJV).

It is a commentary on the words of Jesus—"Life is not measured by how much you own" (Luke 12:15 NLT)—and on those other, often forgotten and neglected words: "Blessed are you when others revile you and persecute you and utter all kinds of evil against you falsely on my account. Rejoice and be glad, for your reward is great in heaven, for so they persecuted the prophets who were before you" (Matt. 5:11–12 ESV).

Francis had found the secret of joy, power, purity, and of that enduring influence which still stirs and draws out the hearts of people of faith, simplicity, and steadfastness. Across the centuries, he speaks to us in a wooing, compelling message that humbles us at the feet of Jesus in contrition and adoring wonder and love.

He found hidden reservoirs of power in union with Christ; in following Christ; in counting all things loss for Christ; in meekly sharing the labors, the travail, the passion, and the cross of Christ. Thus his life became creative instead of acquisitive. He became a builder, a fighter, a creator. He found his joy, his fadeless glory, his undying influence, not in possessing things, not in attaining rank and title and worldly pomp and power, but in building the spiritual house, the kingdom of God—in fighting the battles of the Lord against the hosts of sin and hate and selfishness.

This creative life he found in the way of sacrifice and service. He found his life by losing it. He laid down his life and found it again, found it multiplied a thousand fold, found it being reproduced in myriads of others.

And this I conceive to be the supreme lesson of the life of Francis for us today. For it remains eternally true, it is a law of the Spirit, it is the everlasting word of Jesus, that "whoever finds his life will lose it, and whoever loses his life for my sake will find it" (Matt. 10:39 ESV).

O Lord, help me; help Your people everywhere; help the greedy, grasping, stricken world to learn what these words of the Master mean and to put them to the test with the deathless, sacrificial ardor of the simple, selfless saint of Assisi!

> I knew that Christ had given me birth
> To brother all the souls of earth,
> And every bird and every beast
> Should share the crumbs broke at the feast.[3]

NOTES

1. Source unknown.

2. Possibly drawn from an account in *Life of St. Francis of Assisi* by Paul Sabatier (New York: Charles Scribner's Sons, 1917), 138–139.

3. John Masefield, "The Everlasting Mercy," 1917, public domain.

Looking Backward and Forward 7

Seventy years are less than a pinpoint in the vastness of God's eternity, but they are a long, long time in the life of a man. When I was a child, a man of seventy seemed to me to be as old as the hills. I stood in awe of him. No words could express how venerable he was. When I looked up to him it was like looking up to the snowy, sun-crowned, storm-swept heights of great mountains.

And now, having lived threescore years and ten,[1] I feel as one who has scaled a mighty mountain, done an exploit, or won a war. What toil it has involved! What dangers have been met and overcome! What dull routine, what thrilling adventure! What love, what joy and sorrow, what defeats and victories, what hopes and fears! What visions and dreams yet to be fulfilled! And the river not far away, yet to be crossed. "My soul, be on thy guard!"[2] I remember and marvel.

Yet I feel I am but a child. At times I feel as frisky as a boy and I have stoutly to repress myself to keep from behaving frivolously. And I hear my friend, brother, mentor, and companion of half a century, Paul, saying, "Older men are to be sober-minded, dignified, self-controlled" (Titus 2:2 ESV). Then again I feel as old as I am. The leaden weight of seventy years presses heavily upon me.

I look back and it seems like centuries since I was a carefree little lad. Then some vivid memory will leap up within me, and the seventy years seem like a tale of yesterday and I am again a "wee little boy with the tousled head"[3] playing around the flower-embowered cottage in the tiny village by the little Blue River where I was born.

The average age of man is much less than seventy years, so I am a leftover from a departed generation. But while the snows of seventy winters are on my head, the sunshine of seventy summers is in my heart. The fading, falling leaves of seventy autumns solemnize my soul, but the resurrection life up-springing in flower and tree; the returning songbirds; the laughing, leaping brooks and swelling rivers; and the sweet, soft winds of seventy springtimes gladden me.

A history of the world during these seventy years would show such an advance socially, politically, educationally, economically, scientifically, and morally as has not been seen during any previous thousand years of recorded history. People without a background of knowledge of history may dispute this, but as desperate as the moral, social, and economic conditions of great masses are today, those who know the story of the ages will not dispute it.

Women no longer have to be mistresses and playthings of prime ministers and kings to influence the political destinies of nations. They now sit as men's equal in parliament and senate, proclaim from pulpit and platform the gospel of God's holiness and redeeming love, and are mistress of their own fortune and person.

Childhood is protected by law. Human trafficking, while still carried on, is outlawed by civilized nations. Human slavery and serfdom have been swept away among all but the least advanced peoples. Africa has been opened to the light of civilization and the gospel, and its open sores are being healed. The cannibal islands have been evangelized, and shipwrecked sailors and missionaries are safe on their shore.

When I was a child, it took weeks to communicate with Europe and months to reach Asia. Today, King George speaks words of welcome in London to the peace envoys of nations, and the whole world listens in. We in America hear his royal voice five hours before he spoke, according to our clocks! Admiral Byrd at the South Pole speaks, and we hear him over twelve thousand miles of land and sea before his voice could reach his companion one hundred feet away! Time and space are conquered, and the whole world has become one vast whispering gallery since I was a child.

Diseases which had scourged humankind from time immemorial are now being banished from the earth. War, as the policy of nations, is renounced and denounced. Open diplomacy is an accomplished fact.

Wealth is now looked upon as a trust for humanity. Instead of fitting out pirate ships and ravaging the coasts of China as would have been done long ago, Mr. Rockefeller gives millions to establish one of the most beautiful and up-to-date hospitals and medical schools in the world in Beijing, and untold millions are cabled across the ocean to feed the starving peoples.

When I consider the vanishing darkness, the toppling thrones, the crumbling empires, the fallen crowns, the outlawed tyrannies, the mastery of nature's secrets, the harnessing of the earth's exhaustless energies, the penetration of all lands with the story and light of the gospel, which I have witnessed in my day, I can't help but feel that I was born at the beginning of the end of the Dark Ages.

But while the light increases and widens, the darkness still does not comprehend it. And while God's "truth is marching on,"[4] "evil people and impostors . . . flourish" (2 Tim. 3:13 NLT), become more and more self-conscious and class-conscious, and organize and mass themselves to fight against God and His Christ and His saints and soldiers more subtly and determinedly than at any time since the days of the Roman persecutions and the Spanish Inquisition—and this may result in:

> Vast eddies in the flood
> Of onward time . . .
> And throned races may degrade.[5]

This makes me wish for the strength of youth that I might share in the battles yet to be. But that is denied me. I must go on, like Tennyson's ships, "to the haven under the hill."[6] But I go on serene in unshaken confidence that the flood, in spite of all eddies, flows onward not backward, that the light will evermore increase, and that any triumph of "evil people and impostors" will be short.

Many of God's children are longing for Jesus to come in person, visibly to lead His hosts to victory. But ever since that wonderful morning forty-five years ago when He baptized me with the Holy Spirit and fire, purifying my heart and revealing Himself within me, I have felt that He meant to win His triumphs through dead men and women—dead to sin, to the world, to its prizes and praises, and all alive to Him, filled with His Spirit, indwelt by His presence, burning with His love, glad with His joy, enduring with His patience, thrilled with His hope, daring with His self-renunciation and courage, being consumed with His zeal, all-conquering with His faith, rejoicing in "the fellowship of his sufferings," and gladly made "conformable unto his death" (Phil. 3:10 KJV). I expect the true Vine to show forth all its strength, its beauty, and its fruitfulness through the branches.

I do not expect the love of the Father; the eternal intercession of the risen and enthroned Son; the wise and loving and ceaseless ministry of conviction, conversion, regeneration, and sanctification of the Holy Spirit; and the prayers, preaching, sacrifice, and holy living of the soldiers of Jesus and saints of God to fail. Jesus is even now leading on His hosts to victory.

I cannot always—if ever—comprehend His great strategy. My small sector of the vast battlefield may be covered with smoke and thick darkness. The mocking foe may be pressing hard, friends may fear and falter and flee, and the Enemy may apparently triumph as he did when Jesus died and when the martyrs perished in sheets of flame, by the sword and headman's axe, mauled by the lion's paw, crunched by the tiger's tooth, and slain by the serpent's fang. But the Enemy's triumph always has been and always will be short, for Jesus is leading on and up, ever on, ever up, never backward, never downward, always forward, ever toward the rising sun. Revivals, resurrection life and power, are resident in our religion. A dead church may, when we least expect, flame with revival fire, for Jesus, though unseen, is on the battlefield, and He is leading on. "I am with you always, even to the end of the age" (Matt. 28:20 NLT).

In the lonely and still night, while others sleep, He stirs some longing soul to sighs and tears and strong crying and wrestling prayer. He kindles utter, deathless devotion in that soul, a consuming jealousy for God's glory, for the salvation of others, for the coming of the kingdom of God. And in that lonely and still night and out of that travail, that agony of spirit mingled with solemn joy, a revival is born. "The Kingdom of God can't be detected by visible signs" (Luke 17:20 NLT). There may be no blast of trumpets, no thunder of drums, no flaunting of flags. The revival is born in the heart of some lonely, longing, wrestling, believing, importunate man or woman who will give God no rest, who will not let Him go until He blesses. Bright-eyed, golden-haired, rosy-cheeked dolls can be made by machinery and turned out to order, but living babies are born of sore travail and death agony. So revivals may be simulated, trumped up, made to order, but that is not how revivals begotten by the Holy Spirit come.

Three local leaders of The Salvation Army were concerned about the spiritual life of their corps (church). Souls were not being saved. They agreed to spend time in prayer. Saturday night they did not go home. Sunday they were not in the meetings. No one knew where they were. Sunday night there was a great "break" among the people in attendance. Many souls were at the penitent form (place at the altar for seeking forgiveness). Many tears were shed. All hearts seemed moved and softened. About ten o'clock at night, with tears streaming down their faces, these three leaders came from under the platform where they had spent Saturday night and all day Sunday in prayer. That was the secret of the great meeting.

Seventy years have passed over my head, fifty-seven of which I have spent in the service of my Lord, and forty-three with The Salvation Army. And the experience and observation of these years confirm me in my conviction that revivals are born, not made, and that God waits to be gracious and aid and answer prayer.

I experienced new life in Christ one Christmas Eve at the age of thirteen, and I have never looked back, though I sidestepped and faltered a bit at times in my early years. Immediately I joined the church, yielded loyally to its discipline, kept its rules, and though I didn't have the blessing of a clean heart I felt keenly that I must not prove false or do anything that would bring reproach upon the church or the cause of Christ. When I was fifteen years old, my mother slipped away to be with the Lord, and I became homeless for the next twelve years, with no one to counsel me, but this loyalty to the rules of the church safeguarded me.

For five years, I taught a Sunday school class, and at the age of twenty-three, I became a pastor, with four preaching places on my circuit, in three of which we had blazing revivals. Although I wasn't yet sanctified, I preached all the truth I knew with all my might, and believed what I preached with all my heart, and God blessed me, for He has always blessed and always will bless such preaching.

When He gloriously sanctified me, my knowledge and keen perception of truth were greatly enlarged and quickened, and my preaching became far more searching and effective. And now for forty-seven years God has been giving me revivals with many souls. This has been the glad and consuming ambition of my life. Place, promotion, power, and popularity have meant nothing to me compared with the smile of God and the winning of souls to Him. And this has enabled me to give myself wholly and effectively to my job without thought of what my job would give to me, and I shout "amen" to my Lord's word, "It is more blessed to give than to receive" (Acts 20:35 KJV).

Many kind and generous things have been said to me and about me, but the greatest compliment ever paid to me was by General William Booth, when, on two different occasions, he said to me, "Brengle, you are equal to your job," a job to which he appointed me, and in which he took special interest.[7] Since I knew his tongue was not that of an oily flatterer, and that he was not carrying flowers around for promiscuous presentation, I rejoiced, for one of my great desires was to gladden his heart, so often wounded, to put my full strength so far as possible under his vast burden, and to ease his anxieties where some others failed him.

The greatest compliment ever paid to my work was by Commissioner James Hay, following my seven months' campaign in Australia. He wrote the chief of staff,[8] saying that the campaign not only brought showers of blessing, but opened up spiritual springs. Showers are transient in effect, but springs flow on forever.

My father-in-law lived to be nearly ninety, and he said, "As men grow old they become either sweet or sour." He ripened sweetly and became more and more gracious in his old age. I want to be like that.

Let me grow lovely, growing old,

So many fine things do;

Laces, and ivory, and gold,

And silks need not be new;

And there is healing in old trees;

Old streets a glamour hold;

Why may not I, as well as these,

Grow lovely, growing old?[9]

Some painful and a few bitter things may have happened to me during these forty-three years I have been in The Salvation Army, but really I cannot recall them. I refuse to harbor such memories, so they fade away. Why should I pour bitter poison into the sweet wells of my joy, from which I must continue to drink if I would really live? I won't do it. Paul is my patron saint, and he has told me what to do: "Whatsoever things are true . . . honest . . . just . . . pure . . . lovely . . . of good report; if there be any virtue, and if there be any praise, think on these things" (Phil. 4:8 KJV). That I will, Paul.

At the same time, I do not want to indulge in saccharine sentimentality, for I remember that Jesus did not say, "You are the sugar of the earth" but "You are the salt of the earth" (Matt. 5:13 NLT). I must not lose my saltiness. But too much salt is dangerous, so I must beware. Nor must I ever forget, as our evangelist Paul bid me, to "patiently correct, rebuke, and encourage . . . people with good teaching. For a time is coming when people will no longer listen to sound and wholesome teaching. They will follow their own desires and will look for teachers who will tell them whatever their itching ears want to hear. They will reject the truth and chase after myths" (2 Tim. 4:2–4 NLT).

And though retired I must still "keep [my] head in all situations, endure hardship, do the work of an evangelist, discharge all the duties of [my] ministry" (2 Tim. 4:5 NIV). For the solemn day of accounting is yet to come—coming surely, swiftly—when I must render an account of my stewardship, when the final commendations or condemnations shall be spoken, when the great prizes and rewards will be given, and the awful deprivations and dooms will be announced.

Apostles though they were, Peter and Paul never lost their awe of that day. Nor must I, for Jesus said: "On judgment day many will say to me, 'Lord! Lord! We prophesied in your name and cast out demons in your name and performed many miracles in your name.' But I will reply, 'I never knew you. Get away from me, you who break God's laws'" (Matt. 7:22–23 NLT).

Remembering these words, I gird my armor closer, grip my sword, and—watching, praying, marching straight ahead—I sing:

My soul, be on thy guard!
Ten thousand foes arise;
The hosts of hell are pressing hard
To draw thee from the skies.

Ne'er think the battle won,
Nor lay thine armour down:
The fight of faith will not be done
Till thou obtain the crown![10]

It is a fight of faith, and faith is nourished by the Word of the Lord, to which I return daily for my portion and am not denied.

NOTES

1. Brengle attained his seventieth birthday in 1930.

2. George Heath, "My Soul, Be on Thy Guard," 1781, public domain.

3. Walter H. Brown, "O Little Mother of Mine," *The Labor Digest* 5, no. 1 (January 1912): 30.

4. Julia Ward Howe, "The Battle Hymn of the Republic," 1861, public domain.

5. Alfred Lord Tennyson, "In Memoriam," 1849, public domain.

6. Alfred Lord Tennyson, "Break, Break, Break," 1835, public domain.

7. The job here referred to is that of international evangelist for The Salvation Army.

8. The chief of staff is the second-in-command of the international Salvation Army.

9. Karle Wilson Baker, "Let Me Grow Lovely," 1923, public domain.

10. Heath, "My Soul, Be on Thy Guard."

When I was a cadet in The Salvation Army's international training college forty-seven years ago, we had on the staff a young officer who had been a wild, reckless sinner. He had experienced new life in Christ only a short while when war broke out in Egypt and, being a military reservist, he was sent to the front. He had no Bible, and he could remember just one promise: "My grace is sufficient for you" (2 Cor. 12:9 NKJV).

In every temptation that assailed, every danger, every hour of spiritual loneliness, it was through this text that he looked up to God and claimed heavenly resources for his earthly needs. And he was not disappointed. His needs were met. God never failed him.

What a happy man to have such a promise! And yet how poor he was! He was like a beleaguered army with only one line of communication open, like a city with only one aqueduct for water or one dynamo for light, like a room with only one window or a house with just one door, like a car with one cylinder or a man with only one lung. There was only one star in his sky.

I remember how poor I felt him to be. He was not a juicy soul. He was not radiant. His face did not shine. It lacked solar light. I rejoiced that he was spiritually alive, but it was such an impoverished life! He was like a diver in the deep sea whose supply of oxygen came down through a pipeline, instead of being like a man on top of the world with all the winds blowing upon him, all the stars twinkling and dancing above him, all the glory of the cloudless days irradiating him.

When I am asked for my favorite Bible verse, I smile. It is not one text more than another, but *a whole Bible* that blesses, assures, warns, corrects, and comforts me. A hundred promises whisper to me. I never know when one of the promises—perhaps one that I have not met for days or even months—may suddenly stand before me, beckon me, speak to me tenderly, comfortingly, authoritatively, austerely, as though God were speaking to me face-to-face.

The ancient heroes of the cross obtained promises by faith. You can buy a Bible for a few dollars, and if you have not the money to buy, a Bible Society will give you one. And the Bible teems with promises. They are on almost every page. But your eyes will not see them, your mind will not grasp them, your heart will receive no strength and consolation from them, if you do not have faith. The person who goes through the Bible without faith is like those who walked over the diamond fields of Africa all unconscious of the immeasurable wealth beneath their feet.

When I say that I smile at being asked for my favorite promise and reply that it is the whole Bible which blesses me, I do not mean that there is no one promise that looms large to me, but rather that there are so many that bless me and meet my daily needs that I am like a man with a home full of sweet children, every one of whom is so dear to him that he cannot tell which he loves most and which is most needful for his happiness. My spiritual needs are manifold, and there seems to be a promise just suited to my every need, that matches my need as a Yale key matches a Yale lock, as a glove fits the hand, as light answers to my eye and music to my ear, as the flavor of delicious food matches my sense of taste, and as the attar of roses answers my sense of smell, as the love of one's beloved and the faithfulness of one's friend answer the hunger of the heart.

For three or four years, I had known that someday I would have to come to close grips with myself and get the blessing of a clean heart if I was ever to see God in peace and have the power of the Holy Spirit in my life. At last I began to seek in earnest, and for three or four weeks I had become more and more hungry for the blessing. There were two things confronting me that I felt I could not do, but self had to be crucified. The way of faith was hidden from me because I hesitated to approach it by the way of wholehearted obedience.

But God was faithful. He did not leave me, but deepened conviction until I was in an agony. At last, at about nine o'clock on Friday morning, January 9, 1885, I could hold out no longer. My heart broke within me, and I yielded. Then instantly was whispered in my heart this text: "If we confess our sins, he is faithful and just to forgive us our sins, and to cleanse us from all unrighteousness" (1 John 1:9 KJV). The last part of the text was a revelation to me: "to cleanse us from all unrighteousness" — *all* unrighteousness.

I dropped my head in my hands and said, "Father, I believe that," and instantly peace passing all understanding flooded my soul, and I knew that I was clean. "The law of the Spirit of life in Christ Jesus" had "made me free from the law of sin and death" (Rom. 8:2 KJV). Two days later I preached on the blessing and testified to it. But I trembled lest I might lose it. Then the Lord spoke to me in the words of Jesus to Martha, mourning over her dead brother, Lazarus: "I am the resurrection and the life. Anyone who believes in me will live, even after dying. Everyone who lives in me and believes in me will never ever die" (John 11:25–26 NLT).

Again I believed, and in that moment Christ was revealed in me as surely as He was revealed to Paul on the road to Damascus. I melted into tears and loved my Lord as I never dreamed one could love. Since then I have again and again cried out with Paul, "My old self has been crucified with Christ. It is no longer I who live, but Christ lives in me. So I live in this earthly body by trusting in the Son of God, who loved me and gave himself for me" (Gal. 2:20 NLT). And again and again I have said with Paul, "I once thought these things were valuable, but now I consider them worthless because of what Christ has done. Yes, everything else is worthless when compared with the infinite value of knowing Christ Jesus my Lord" (Phil. 3:7–8 NLT).

When again I feared lest I might fall, these two texts reassured me: "Don't be afraid, for I am with you. Don't be discouraged, for I am your God. I will strengthen you and help you. I will hold you up with my victorious right hand" (Isa. 41:10 NLT) and, "Now all glory to God, who is able to keep you from falling away and will bring you with great joy into his glorious presence without a single fault" (Jude 24 NLT).

Then I was tempted with the thought that, when I got old, the light would fade and the fire in my soul would go out. But these texts came with comforting assurance and power to my heart: "I will be your God throughout your lifetime—until your hair is white with age. I made you, and I will care for you. I will carry you along and save you" (Isa. 46:4 NLT) and, "The righteous . . . are planted in the house of the LORD; they flourish in the courts of our God. They still bear fruit in old age; they are ever full of sap and green" (Ps. 92:12–14 ESV).

I saw that I must not fear or be dismayed in the presence of any trouble or difficulty, but must quietly trust in the Lord. And I must not drift about as so many do, but remain "planted in the house of the LORD."

When I have gone to distant battlefields in far-off lands, among strangers, this promise has put comfort and strength into me: "My presence will go with you, and I will give you rest" (Ex. 33:14 ESV). And when I have felt any insufficiency I have been reassured with this promise: "Who makes a person's mouth? Who decides whether people speak or do not speak, hear or do not hear, see or do not see? Is it not I, the LORD? Now go! I will be with you as you speak, and I will instruct you in what to say" (Ex. 4:11–12 NLT).

These are only a few of a multitude of precious promises and words of the Lord which came to me years ago and which are ever whispering in my mind and heart, challenging my faith, my love, my utter devotion.

They are the joy and rejoicing of my heart, a heritage from the Lord, a lamp to my feet, a light to my path, a sword with which to thrust through the accusations and doubts and fears with which Satan is ever ready to assail me.

PART TWO

When the Holy Ghost Is Come

Who Is He?

On that last eventful evening in the upper room, just after the Passover Feast, Jesus spoke to His disciples about His departure. He commanded them to love one another. He told them not to be troubled in heart, but to hold fast their faith in Him. He assured them that though He was to die and leave them, He was going to the Father's many-mansioned house to prepare a place for them.

But already they were troubled, for what could this death and departure mean but the destruction of all their hopes, of all their cherished plans? Jesus had drawn them away from their fishing boats, their places of custom and daily employment, and inspired them with high personal and patriotic ambitions. He encouraged them to believe that He was the Seed of David, the promised Messiah, and they hoped that He would cast out Pilate and his hated Roman garrison, restore the kingdom to Israel, and sit on David's throne, a King, reigning in righteousness and undisputed power and majesty forever. And then, were they not to be His ministers of state and chief men in His kingdom?

He was their Leader, directing their labors. He was their Teacher, instructing their ignorance, solving their doubts and all their puzzling problems. He was their Defense, stilling the stormy sea and answering for them when questioned by wise and wily enemies.

They were poor and unlearned and weak. In Him was all their help, and what would they do—what could they do—without Him? They were without social standing, financial prestige, learning or intellectual equipment, political or military power. He was their all, and without Him they were as helpless as little children, as defenseless as lambs in the midst of wolves. How could their poor hearts be otherwise than troubled?

But then He gave them a strange, wonderful, and reassuring promise. He said, "If you love me, obey my commandments. And I will ask the Father, and he will give you another Advocate, who will never leave you" (John 14:15–16 NLT). I am going away, He said, but another shall come, who will fill My place. He shall not go away, but abide with you forever, and He "shall be in you" (John 14:17 KJV). And later He added, "It is expedient for you"—that is, better for you—"that I go away: for if I go not away, the Comforter will not come" (John 16:7 KJV).

Who is this other One—this Comforter? He must be some august Divine Person, and not a mere influence or impersonal force, for how else could He take and fill the place of Jesus? How else could it be said that it was better to have Him than to have Jesus remaining in the flesh? He must be strong and wise, and tender and true, to take the place of the Blessed One who was to die and depart. Who is He?

John, writing in the Greek language, called Him *Paraclete*, but we in English call Him "Comforter." But *Paraclete* means more—much more—than *Comforter*. It means "one called in to help: an advocate, a helper." The same word is used of Jesus in 1 John 2:1: "We have an advocate"—a Paraclete, a Helper—"with the Father, Jesus Christ the righteous" (KJV). Just as Jesus had gone to be the disciples' Advocate, their Helper, in the heavens, so this other Paraclete was to be their Advocate, their Helper, on earth. He would be their Comforter when comfort was needed, but He would be more. He would also be their Teacher, Guide, and Strengthener, as Jesus had been. At every point of need He would be there as an ever-present, all-wise, and almighty Helper. He would meet their need with His sufficiency, their weakness with His strength, their foolishness with His wisdom, their ignorance with His knowledge, and their blindness and shortsightedness with His perfect, all-embracing vision. What a Comforter! Why should they be troubled?

They were weak, but He would strengthen them with might in their inner beings (see Eph. 3:16). They were to give the world the words of Jesus and teach all nations (see Matt. 28:19–20), and He would teach them all things and bring to their remembrance all Jesus had said to them (see John 14:26).

They were to guide new believers in the right way, and He was to guide them into all truth (see John 16:13). They were to attack hoary systems of evil and inbred and actively entrenched sin in every human heart, but He was to go before them, preparing the way for conquest by convincing the world of sin, of righteousness, and of judgment (see John 16:8). They were to bear heavy burdens and face superhuman tasks, but He was to give them power (see Acts 1:8). Indeed, He was to be a Comforter, Strengthener, and Helper.

Jesus had been external to them. They often missed Him. Sometimes He was asleep when they felt they sorely needed Him. Sometimes He was on the mountains while they were in the valley vainly trying to cast out stubborn devils or wearily toiling on the tumultuous, wind-tossed sea. Sometimes He was surrounded by vast crowds, and He entered into high disputes with the doctors of the law, and they had to wait until He was alone to seek explanations of His teachings. But they were never to lose this other Helper in the crowd nor be separated for an instant from Him, for no human being, nor untoward circumstance, nor physical necessity, could ever come between Him and them, for, as Jesus said, He "shall be in you" (John 14:17 KJV).

From the words used to declare the sayings, the doings, the offices, and the works of the Comforter, the Holy Spirit, we are forced to conclude that He is a Divine Person. Out of the multitude of Scriptures that could be quoted, note this passage, which (as nearly as is possible with human language) reveals to us His personality: "Now there were in the church at Antioch prophets and teachers, Barnabas, Simeon who was called Niger, Lucius of Cyrene, Manaen a lifelong friend of Herod the tetrarch, and Saul. While they were worshiping the Lord and fasting, the Holy Spirit said, 'Set apart for me Barnabas and Saul for the work to which I have called them.' Then after fasting and praying they laid their hands on them and sent them off. So, being sent out by the Holy Spirit, they went down to Seleucia" (Acts 13:1–4 ESV).

Further on we read that they were "forbidden by the Holy Spirit to speak the word in Asia," and when they would have gone into Bithynia, the Spirit "did not allow them" (Acts 16:6–7 ESV).

Later, when the messengers of Cornelius, the Roman centurion, were seeking Peter, "the Holy Spirit said to him, 'Three men have come looking for you. Get up, go downstairs, and go with them without hesitation. Don't worry, for I have sent them'" (Acts 10:19–20 NLT).

These are just a few of the passages of Scripture that might be quoted to establish the fact of His personality—His power to think, will, act, and speak. And if His personality is not made plain in these Scriptures, then it is impossible for human language to make it so.

Indeed, I am persuaded that if an intelligent person who had never seen the Bible should for the first time read the four gospels and the Acts of the apostles, he or she would say that the personality of the Holy Spirit is as clearly revealed in Acts as is the personality of Jesus Christ in the Gospels. In truth, the Acts of the apostles are in a large measure the acts of the Holy Spirit, and the disciples were not more certainly under the immediate direction of Jesus during the three years of His earthly ministry than they were under the direct leadership of the Spirit after Pentecost.

But there are those who admit His personality yet (in their loyalty to the divine unity) deny the Trinity, and maintain that the Holy Spirit is only the Father manifesting Himself as Spirit, without any distinction in personality. But this view cannot be harmonized with certain Scriptures. While the Bible and reason plainly declare that there is but one God, the Scriptures just as clearly reveal that there are three persons in the Godhead: Father, Son, and Holy Spirit.

The form of Paul's benediction to the Corinthians proves the doctrine: "May the grace of the Lord Jesus Christ, the love of God, and the fellowship of the Holy Spirit be with you all" (2 Cor. 13:14 NLT). Again, it is taught in the promise of Jesus, already quoted, "I will ask the Father, and he will give you another Advocate, who will never leave you" (John 14:15–16 NLT). Here the three persons of the Godhead are clearly revealed. The Son prays, the Father answers, and the Spirit comes.

The Holy Spirit is "another Comforter," a second Comforter succeeding the first (who was Jesus), and both were given by the Father.

Do you say, "I cannot understand it"? Neither do I. Who *can* understand it? God does not expect us to understand it. Nor would He have us puzzle our heads and trouble our hearts in attempting to understand it or harmonize it with our knowledge of arithmetic. It is only the fact that is revealed; *how* there can be three persons in one Godhead is not revealed.

The how is a mystery, and is not a matter of faith at all. But the fact is a matter of revelation, and therefore a matter of faith. I myself am a mysterious trinity of body, mind, and spirit. The fact I believe, but the how is not a thing to believe. It is at this point that many puzzle and perplex themselves needlessly.

In the ordinary affairs of life, we grasp facts and hold them fast without puzzling ourselves over the "how" of things. Who can explain how food sustains life, how light reveals material objects, or how sound conveys ideas to our minds? It is the fact we know and believe, but the "how" we pass by as a mystery unrevealed. What God has revealed, we believe. We cannot understand how Jesus turned water into wine, how He multiplied a few loaves and fishes and fed thousands, how He stilled the stormy sea, how He opened blind eyes, how He healed lepers, and how He raised the dead by a word. But the facts we believe. Wireless telegraphic messages are sent over the vast wastes of ocean. That is a fact, and we believe it. But how they go we do not know. That is not something to believe.

An old servant of God has pointed out that it is the *fact* of the Trinity—and not the *manner* of it—which God has revealed and made a subject for our faith.

But while the Scriptures reveal to us the fact of the personality of the Holy Spirit, and it is a subject for our faith, to those in whom He dwells this fact may become a matter of sacred knowledge, of blessed experience.

How else can we account for the positive and assured way in which the apostles and other disciples spoke of the Holy Spirit on and after the day of Pentecost, if they did not know Him? Immediately after the fiery baptism, with its blessed filling, Peter stood before the people and said, "[This] was predicted long ago by the prophet Joel: 'In the last days,' God says, 'I will pour out my Spirit upon all people'" (Acts 2:16–17 NLT). Then he exhorted the people and assured them that if they would meet certain simple conditions they would "receive the gift of the Holy Spirit" (Acts 2:38 NLT). He said to Ananias, "Why has Satan filled your heart to lie to the Holy Spirit?" (Acts 5:3 ESV). He declared to the high priest and council that he and his fellow apostles were witnesses of the resurrection of Jesus, and added, "And so is the Holy Spirit, who is given by God to those who obey him" (Acts 5:32 NLT). Without any apology, explanation, "think so," or "hope so," they spoke of being "filled," not simply with some new, strange experience or emotion, but "with the Holy Spirit" (Acts 9:17 NLT). Certainly they must have known Him. And if they knew Him, may we not know Him also?

Paul said, "And we have received God's Spirit (not the world's spirit), so we can know the wonderful things God has freely given us. When we tell you these things, we do not use words that come from human wisdom. Instead, we speak words given to us by the Spirit, using the Spirit's words to explain spiritual truths" (1 Cor. 2:12–13 NLT). And if we know the words, may we not know the Teacher of the words?

John Wesley wrote:

> The knowledge of the Three-One God is interwoven with all true Christian faith; with all vital religion.
>
> I do not say that every real Christian can say with the Marquis de Renty, "I bear about with me continually an experimental verity, and a plenitude of the presence of the ever blessed Trinity." I apprehend that this is not the experience of "babes," but rather "fathers in Christ."
>
> But I know not how anyone can be a Christian believer, till he "hath [as St. John speaks] the witness in himself"; till "the Spirit of God witnesses with his spirit, that he is a child of God"; that is, in effect, till God the Holy Ghost witnesses that God the Father has accepted him through the merits of God the Son. . . .
>
> Not that every Christian believer *adverts* to this; perhaps, at first, not one in twenty: but if you ask any of them a few questions, you will easily find it is implied in what he believes.[1]

I shall never forget my joy, mingled with awe and wonder, when this dawned upon my consciousness. For several weeks I had been searching the Scriptures, ransacking my heart, humbling my soul, and crying to God almost day and night for a pure heart and the baptism with the Holy Spirit, when one glad, sweet day—it was January 9, 1885—this text suddenly opened to my understanding: "If we confess our sins, he is faithful and just to forgive us our sins, and to cleanse us from all unrighteousness" (1 John 1:9 KJV). And I was enabled to believe without any doubt that the precious blood cleansed my heart, even mine, from all sin. Shortly after that, while reading these words of Jesus to Martha—"I am the resurrection and the life. Anyone who believes in me will live, even after dying. Everyone who lives in me and believes in me will never ever die" (John 11:25–26 NLT)—instantly my heart was melted like wax before fire. Jesus Christ was revealed to my spiritual consciousness, revealed in me, and my soul was filled with unutterable love. I walked in a heaven of love. Then one day, with amazement, I said to a friend, "This is the perfect love about which the apostle John wrote, but it is beyond all I dreamed of. In it is personality. His love thinks, wills, talks with me, corrects me, instructs and teaches me." And then I knew that God the Holy Spirit was in this love, and that this love was God, for "God is love" (1 John 4:8 KJV).

Oh, the rapture mingled with reverential, holy fear—for it is a rapturous, yet divinely fearful thing—to be indwelt by the Holy Spirit, to be a temple of the living God! Great heights are always opposite great depths, and from the heights of this blessed experience many have plunged into the dark depths of fanaticism. But we must not draw back from the experience through fear. All danger will be avoided by meekness and lowliness of heart; by humble, faithful service; by esteeming others better than ourselves and in honor preferring them before ourselves; by keeping an open, teachable spirit—in a word, by looking steadily unto Jesus, to whom the Holy Spirit continually points us. For He would not have us fix our attention exclusively upon Himself and His work in us, but also upon the Crucified One and His work for us, that we may walk in the steps of Him whose blood purchases our pardon and makes and keeps us clean.

Great Paraclete! To Thee we cry:
O highest gift of God most high!
O fount of life! O fire of love!
And sweet anointing from above!

Our senses touch with light and fire;
Our hearts with tender love inspire;
And with endurance from on high
The weakness of our flesh supply.

Far back our Enemy repel,
And let Thy peace within us dwell;
So may we, having Thee for Guide,
Turn from each hurtful thing aside.

Oh, may Thy grace on us bestow

The Father and the Son to know,

And evermore to hold confessed

Thyself of each the Spirit blest.[2]

NOTES

1. John Wesley, *The Works of the Reverend John Wesley, A. M.*, vol. 2 (New York: J. Emory and B. Waugh, 1831), 24.

2. Rabanus Maurus, "Veni Creator Spiritus," trans. Robert Bridges, n. d., public domain.

Preparing His House 2

Jesus said, "I assure you, no one can enter the Kingdom of God without being born of water and the Spirit. Humans can reproduce only human life, but the Holy Spirit gives birth to spiritual life" (John 3:5–6 NLT). And Paul wrote to the Romans, "Those who do not have the Spirit of Christ living in them do not belong to him at all" (Rom. 8:9 NLT).

So it must be that all children of God, all true followers of Jesus, have the Holy Spirit in some gracious manner and measure, or else they would not be children of God, for only those "who are led by the Spirit of God are children of God" (Rom. 8:14 NLT).

It is the Holy Spirit who convicts us of sin, who makes us feel how good and righteous, just and patient God is—and how guilty we are, how unfit for heaven, and how near to hell. It is the Holy Spirit who leads us to true repentance and confession and amendment of life.

And when our repentance is complete and our surrender is unconditional, it is He who reasons with us, calms our fears, soothes our troubled hearts, banishes our darkness, and enables us to look to Jesus and believe in Him for the forgiveness of all our sins and the salvation of our souls. And when we yield and trust, and are accepted by the Lord and saved by grace, it is He who assures us of the Father's favor and notifies us that we are now His. "For his Spirit joins with our spirit to affirm that we are God's children" (Rom. 8:16 NLT). He is "the Spirit of adoption by whom we cry out, 'Abba, Father'" (Rom. 8:15 NKJV).

> And His that gentle voice we hear,
> Soft as the breath of even;
> That checks each thought, that calms each fear,
> And speaks of heaven.[1]

It is He who strengthens new Christians to fight against and overcome sin, and it is He who engenders within them a hope of fuller righteousness through faith in Christ.

> And every virtue we possess,
> And every victory won,
> And every thought of holiness,
> Are His alone.[2]

But great and gracious as this work is, it is not the fiery baptism with the Spirit that is promised. It is not the fullness of the Holy Spirit to which we are exhorted. This is only the initial work of the Spirit.

It is only the clear dawn of the day, and not the rising of the daystar. It is perfect of its kind, but it is preparatory to another and fuller work. Jesus said to His earliest disciples, concerning the Holy Spirit, that "the world [those who have not yet experienced new life in Christ] cannot receive him, because it isn't looking for him and doesn't recognize him" (John 14:17 NLT). They resist Him and will not permit Him to work in their hearts. Then Jesus added, "But you know him, because he lives with you now." He had begun His work in them, but there was more to follow, for Jesus said, "And later [He] will be in you" (John 14:17 NLT).

If you were to build yourself a house, you would be in and out of it and all around it. But we would not say you live in it until it has been completed. It is in that sense that Jesus said, "He lives with you." But when the house is finished, you sweep out all the chips and sawdust, scrub the floor, lay down the carpets, hang up your pictures, arrange the furniture, and move in with your family. Then you are in the fullest sense within it. You abide there. And it is in that sense that Jesus meant that the Holy Spirit would be in His followers. This is fitly expressed in the chorus:

Holy Spirit, come, O come!
Let Thy work in me be done!
All that hinders shall be thrown aside;
Make me fit to be Thy dwelling.[3]

Previous to the day of Pentecost, the Holy Spirit was with those first disciples, using the searching preaching of John the Baptist and the life, words, example, sufferings, death, and resurrection of Jesus as instruments with which to fashion their hearts for His indwelling. As the truth was declared to them in the words of Jesus, pictured to them in His actions, exemplified in His daily life, and fulfilled in His death and His rising from the dead, the Holy Spirit worked mightily within them. But He could not yet find perfect rest in their hearts, and so He did not yet abide within them.

They had forsaken all to follow Christ. They had been commissioned to preach the gospel, heal the sick, cleanse the lepers, raise the dead, and cast out devils. Their names were written in heaven. They were not of the world, even as Jesus was not of the world, for they belonged to Him and to the Father. They knew the Holy Spirit, for He was with them and working in them, but He was not yet living in them, for they were still carnal. That is, they were selfish, each seeking the best place for himself. They disputed among themselves as to whom should be the greatest. They were bigoted, wanting to call down fire from heaven to consume those who would not receive Jesus and forbidding those who would not follow them to cast out devils in His name. They were positive and loud in their professions of devotion and loyalty to Jesus when alone with Him—they declared they would die with Him—but they were fearful, timid, and false to Him when the testing time came. When the mocking crowd appeared, and danger was near, they all forsook Him and fled, while Peter cursed and swore and denied that he knew Him.

But the Holy Spirit did not forsake them. He still worked within them, and no doubt used their very mistakes and miserable failures to perfect within them the spirit of humility and perfect self-abasement in order that they might safely be exalted. And on the day of Pentecost His work of preparation was complete, and He moved in to abide forever.

And this experience of theirs before Pentecost is the common experience of all believers. Every child of God knows that the Holy Spirit is with him or her, and realizes that He is working within, striving to set the house in order. And with many who are properly taught and gladly obedient, this work is done quickly, and the heavenly Dove, the Blessed One, takes up His constant abode within them. The toil and strife with inbred sin is ended by its destruction, and they enter at once into the Sabbath of full salvation.

Surely this is possible. The disciples could not receive the Holy Spirit until Jesus was glorified, because the foundation for perfect, intelligent, unwavering faith was not laid until then. But since the day of Pentecost, He may be received immediately by those who have repented of all sin, believed in Jesus, and been born again. Some have assured me that they were sanctified wholly and filled with the Spirit within a few hours of their new birth in Christ. I have no doubt that this was so with many of the three thousand who experienced new life in Christ as a result of Peter's preaching on the day of Pentecost.

But often this work is slow, for He can work effectually only as we work with Him, practicing intelligent and obedient faith. Some days the work prospers and seems almost complete, and then peace and joy and comfort abound in the heart. At other times the work is hindered, and often almost undone by the strivings and stirrings of inbred sin, fits of temper, lightness and frivolity, worldliness, unholy ambitions, jealousies and envying, uncharitable suspicions and harsh judgments and selfish indulgences, slowness to believe, and neglect of watchfulness and prayer and the patient, attentive study of His Word.

"The desires of the flesh are against the Spirit" (Gal. 5:17 ESV), seeking to bring the soul back under the bondage of sin again, while the Spirit wars against the flesh, which is "the old, sinful nature." The Spirit seeks to bring every thought "into captivity to the obedience of Christ" (2 Cor. 10:5 NKJV), to lead the soul to that point of glad, wholehearted consecration to its Lord, and that simple, perfect faith in the merits of His blood which shall enable Him to cast out and destroy the old, sinful nature and, making the heart His temple, enthrone Christ within.

> Here on earth a temple stands,
> Temple never built with hands;
> There the Lord doth fill the place
> With the glory of His grace.
> Cleansed by Christ's atoning blood,
> Thou art this fair house of God.
> Thoughts, desires, that enter there,
> Should they not be pure and fair?
> Meet for holy courts and blest,
> Courts of stillness and of rest,
> Where the soul, a priest in white,
> Singeth praises day and night;
> Glory of the love divine,
> Filling all this heart of mine.[4]

What is your experience? Are you filled with the Spirit? Or is the old, sinful nature still warring against Him in your heart? Oh, that you may receive Him fully by faith right now!

NOTES

1. Harriet Auber, "Our Blest Redeemer, Ere He Breathed," 1829, public domain.

2. Ibid.

3. Richard Slater, "All the Guilty Past Is Washed Away," *The Salvation Army Songbook*, n. d., public domain.

4. Gerhard Tersteegan, "Here on Earth a Temple Stands," trans. Emma Frances Shuttleworth Bevan, 1731, public domain.

Is the Baptism with the Holy Spirit a Third Blessing? 3

There is much difference of opinion among many of God's children as to the time and order of the baptism with the Holy Spirit. And many who believe that entire cleansing is subsequent to salvation ask if the baptism with the Spirit is not subsequent to cleansing, and therefore a third blessing.

There are four types of teachers whose views appear to differ about this subject.

1. Those who emphasize cleansing, who say much of a clean heart but little, if anything, about the fullness of the Holy Spirit and power from on high.

2. Those who emphasize the baptism with the Holy Spirit and fullness of the Spirit, but say little or nothing of cleansing from inbred sin and the destruction of the carnal mind.

3. Those who say much of both but separate them into two distinct experiences, often widely separated in time.

4. Those who teach that the truth is in the union of the two and that, while we may separate them in their order (putting cleansing first), we cannot separate them in time. They cannot be separated since it is the baptism that cleanses, just as the darkness vanishes before the flash of the electric light when the right button is touched, just as the Augean stables in the fabled story of Grecian mythology were cleansed when Hercules turned in the floods of the River Arno and the refuse went out as the rushing waters poured in.

However, in John 17, Jesus prayed for His disciples, and said,

I'm not asking you to take them out of the world, but to keep them safe from the evil one. . . . Make them holy . . . that they will all be one, just as you and I are one—as you are in me, Father, and I am in you. And may they be in us. . . . I am in them and you are in me. May they experience such perfect unity. . . . Then your love for me will be in them, and I will be in them. (John 17:15, 17, 21, 23, 26 NLT)

It is first sanctification (cleansing, being made holy) then filling (divine union with the Father and the Son through the Holy Spirit). The Scriptures make plain the order of God's work, and if we looked at them alone, without diligently comparing Scripture with Scripture as God would have us do, we might conclude that the cleansing and filling were as distinct and separate in time as they are in this order of statement.

But other Scriptures give us abundant light on that side of the subject. In Acts 10:44, we read of Peter's preaching Jesus to Cornelius, the Roman centurion, and his household, and "even as Peter was saying these things, the Holy Spirit fell upon all who were listening to the message" (NLT). And in Acts 15:7–9, at the first Council of Jerusalem, we have Peter's rehearsal of the experience of Cornelius and his household: "At the meeting, after a long discussion, Peter stood and addressed them as follows: 'Brothers, you all know that God chose me from among you some time ago to preach to the Gentiles so that they could hear the Good News and believe. God knows people's hearts, and he confirmed that he accepts Gentiles by giving them the Holy Spirit, just as he did to us. He made no distinction between us and them, for he cleansed their hearts through faith.'" (Acts 15:7–9 NLT).

Here we see that their believing and the sudden descent of the Holy Spirit with cleansing power into their hearts constitute one blessed experience.

What patient, waiting, expectant faith reckons done, the baptism with the Holy Spirit actually accomplishes. There may be an interval of time between the act of faith by which a person begins to reckon him- or herself "dead indeed unto sin, but alive unto God through Jesus Christ our Lord" (Rom. 6:11 KJV) and the act of the Holy Spirit which makes the reckoning good. But the act and state of steadfastly, patiently, joyously, perfectly believing (which is our part) and the act of baptizing with the Holy Spirit, cleansing as by fire (which is God's part) bring about the one experience of entire sanctification. These must not and cannot be logically looked upon as two distinct blessings any more than the act of the husband and the act of the wife can be separated in the one experience of marriage.

There are two works and two workers—God and us—just as my right arm and my left arm work when my two hands come together but the union of the two hands constitutes one experience.

If my left arm acts quickly, my right arm will surely respond. And so, if the soul, renouncing self and sin and the world, with ardor of faith in the precious blood for cleansing and in the promise of the gift of the Holy Spirit, draws near to God, God will draw near to that soul, and the blessed union will be effected suddenly. In that instant, what faith has reckoned done will be done; the death stroke will be given to the old, sinful nature; sin will die; and the heart will be clean indeed and wholly alive toward God through our Lord Jesus Christ. It will not be a mere "make believe" experience, but a gloriously real one.

It is possible that some have been led into confusion on this subject by not considering all the Scriptures bearing on it. What is it that cleanses or sanctifies, and how? Jesus prayed, "Sanctify them by Your truth. Your word is truth" (John 17:17 NKJV). Here it is the Word, or truth, that sanctifies.

John said, "The blood of Jesus, his Son, cleanses us from all sin" (1 John 1:7 NLT). Here it is the blood.

Peter said, "[God] put no difference between us and them, purifying their hearts by faith" (Acts 15:9 KJV). And Paul said, "That they may receive forgiveness of sins, and inheritance among them which are sanctified by faith" (Acts 26:18 KJV). Here it is by faith.

Paul also wrote, "God chose you to be among the first to experience salvation—a salvation that came through the Spirit who makes you holy and through your belief in the truth" (2 Thess. 2:13 NLT). And again, "I bring you the Good News so that I might present you as an acceptable offering to God, made holy by the Holy Spirit" (Rom. 15:16 NLT). And Peter wrote, "God the Father knew you and chose you long ago, and his Spirit has made you holy" (1 Pet. 1:2 NLT). Here it is the Spirit that sanctifies or makes clean and holy.

Is there confusion then? Jesus said, "The truth." John said, "The blood." Paul and Peter said, "Faith" and "the Holy Spirit." Can these be reconciled? Let us see.

Picture a child in a burning house. A man risks his life and rushes to the spot above which the child stands in awful danger, and cries out, "Jump, and I will catch you!" The child hears, believes, leaps, and the man receives him. But just as he turns and places the boy in safety, a falling timber strikes him to the ground, wounded to death, and his flowing blood sprinkles the boy whom he has saved.

A breathless spectator says, "The child's faith saved him." Another says, "How quick the lad was! His courageous leap saved him." Another says, "Bless the child! He was in awful danger, and he just barely saved himself." Another says, "That man's word just reached the boy's ear in the nick of time, and saved him." Another says, "God bless that man! He saved that child." And yet another says, "That boy was saved by blood—by the sacrifice of that heroic man!"

What saved the child? Without the man's presence and promise there would have been no faith. And without faith there would have been no saving action and the boy would have perished. The man's word saved him by inspiring faith. Faith saved him by leading to proper action. He saved himself by leaping. The man saved him by sacrificing his own life in order to catch him when he leaped.

Not the child himself alone, nor his faith, nor his brave leap, nor his rescuer's word, nor his blood, nor the man himself saved the boy, but they all together saved him. And the boy was not saved until he was in the arms of the man.

So it is faith and works—and the Word and the blood and the Holy Spirit—that sanctify.

The blood, the sacrifice of Christ, underlies all, and is the meritorious cause of every blessing we receive, but the Holy Spirit is the active agent by whom the merits of the blood are applied to our needs.

During the American Civil War, certain men committed some shameful and unlawful deeds and were sentenced to be shot. On the day of the execution, they stood in a row confronted by soldiers with loaded muskets, waiting the command to fire. Just before the command was given, the commanding officer felt a touch on his elbow and, turning, saw a young man by his side, who said, "Sir, there in that row, waiting to be shot, is a married man. He has a wife and children. He is their breadwinner. If you shoot him, he will be sorely missed. Let me take his place."

"All right," said the officer. "Take his place, if you wish. But you will be shot."

"I quite understand that," replied the young man, "but no one will miss me." He went to the condemned man, pushed him aside, and took his place.

Soon the command to fire was given. The volley rang out, and the young hero dropped dead with a bullet through his heart while the other man went free.

His freedom came to him by blood. However, had he neglected the great salvation and—despising the blood shed for him and refusing the sacrifice of the friend and the righteous claims of the law—persisted in the same evil ways, he too would have been shot. The blood, though shed for him, would not have availed to set him free. But he accepted the sacrifice, submitted to the law, and went home to his wife and children. It was by the blood. Every breath he henceforth drew, every throb of his heart, every blessing he enjoyed or possibly could enjoy, came to him by the blood. He owed everything from that day forth to the blood, and every fleeting moment, every passing day, and every rolling year but increased his debt to the blood that had been shed for him.

And so we owe all to the blood of Christ, for we were under sentence of death—"The soul who sins shall die" (Ezek. 18:20 NKJV), and we have all sinned. And God, to be holy, must frown upon sin and utterly condemn it, and must execute His sentence against it.

But Jesus suffered for our sins. He died for us. "He was wounded for our transgressions, he was bruised for our iniquities . . . and with his stripes we are healed" (Isa. 53:5 KJV). "For you know that God paid a ransom to rescue you from the empty life you inherited from your ancestors. And it was not paid with mere gold or silver. . . . It was the precious blood of Christ," who loved you and gave Himself for you (1 Pet. 1:18–19 NLT; see also Gal. 2:20). And now every blessing we ever had, or ever shall have, comes to us by the divine sacrifice, by "the precious blood." And "how shall we escape, if we neglect so great salvation" (Heb. 2:3 KJV)? His blood is the meritorious cause not only of our pardon, but also of our cleansing, our sanctification. But the Holy Spirit is the ever-present, living, active cause.

The truth or Word that sanctifies is the record God has given us of His will and of that divine sacrifice, that "precious blood." The faith that purifies is the sure confidence in that Word which leads to renunciation of all self-righteousness, utter abandonment to God's will, full dependence on the merits of the precious blood, and "faith expressing itself in love" (Gal. 5:6 NLT), for "faith without works is dead" (James 2:20 KJV). And thus we draw near to God, God draws near to us, and the Holy Spirit falls upon us, comes into us, and cleanses our hearts by the destruction of sin and the infilling of God's love.

The advocates of entire sanctification as an experience wrought in the soul by the baptism with the Spirit subsequent to regeneration call it "the second blessing." But many good people object to the term and say that they have received the first, second, third, and fiftieth blessing. No doubt they have. But the people who speak of "the second blessing" are right in the sense in which they use the term. In that sense there are only the two blessings.

Some years ago a man heard things about a lady that filled him with admiration for her and made him feel that they were of one mind and heart. Later he met her for the first time and fell in love with her. After some months, following an enlarged acquaintance and much consideration and prayer, he told her of his love and asked her to become his wife. After due consideration and prayer on her part she consented, and they promised themselves to each other and in a sense gave themselves to each other.

That was the first blessing, and it filled him with great peace and joy, but not perfect peace and joy. And there were many blessings following that. Every letter he received, every tender look, every pressure of the hand, every tone of her voice, every fresh assurance of enduring and increasing affection was a blessing. But it was not the second blessing.

Then one day, after patient waiting and full preparation, they came together in the presence of friends and before a representative of God, and in the most solemn and irrevocable manner gave themselves to each other to become one and were pronounced husband and wife. That was the second blessing, an epochal experience, unlike anything which preceded or anything to follow. And now their peace and joy and rest were full.

There had to be the first and second blessings in this relationship of husband and wife, but there is no third. And yet in the sense of those who say they have received fifty blessings from the Lord, there have been countless blessings in their wedded life. Indeed, it has been a river of blessing, broadening and deepening in gladness, joy, sweet affections, and fellowship with the increasing years.

But let us not confuse things by disputing over terms and wrangling about words. The first blessing in Jesus Christ is salvation, with its negative side of remission of sins and forgiveness, and its positive side of renewal or regeneration—the new birth—one experience.

The second blessing is entire sanctification, with its negative side of cleansing and its positive side of filling with the Holy Spirit—one whole, rounded, glorious, epochal experience. And while there may subsequently be many refreshings, girdings, illuminations, and secret tokens and assurances of love and favor, there is no third blessing in this large sense, in this present time. But when time is no more, when the everlasting doors have lifted up and the King of Glory comes in with His bride, and He makes us, forever redeemed and crowned, to sit down with Him on His throne, then in eternity we shall have the third blessing—we shall be glorified.

The Witness of the Spirit 4

How shall I know that I am accepted by God—that I am saved or sanctified? The Bible declares God's love and pity for sinners, including me, and reveals His offer of mercy to me in Jesus Christ, on condition that I fully repent of my sins and, yielding myself to Him, believe in Jesus Christ, take up my cross, and follow Him. But how shall I know that I have met these conditions in a way to satisfy Him?

The Bible cannot tell me this. It tells me what to do, but it does not tell me when I have done it, any more than the sign at the country crossroads, pointing out the road leading to the city, tells me when I have arrived at the city.

My religious teachers and friends cannot tell me, for they cannot read my heart, nor the mind of God toward me. How can they know when I have in my heart repented and believed, and when His righteous anger is turned away? They can encourage me to repent, believe, and obey. They can assure me that if I do, He will accept me, and I shall be a new creation. But beyond that they cannot.

My own heart, owing to its darkness, deceitfulness, and liability to error, is not a safe witness previous to the assurance God Himself gives. If my neighbor is justly offended with me, it is not my own heart, but his testimony that first assures me of his favor once more.

How, then, shall I know that I am justified or wholly sanctified? There is only one way, and that is by the witness of the Holy Spirit. God must notify me and make me to know it. And this He does when, despairing of my own works of righteousness, I cast my poor soul fully and in faith upon Jesus. "For you did not receive a spirit of slavery to fall back into fear," said Paul, "but you have received the Spirit of adoption as sons, by whom we cry, 'Abba! Father!' The Spirit himself bears witness with our spirit that we are children of God" (Rom. 8:15–16 ESV). "And because we are his children, God has sent the Spirit of his Son into our hearts, prompting us to call out, 'Abba, Father'" (Gal. 4:6 NLT). Unless He Himself assures me, I shall never know that He accepts me, but must continue in uncertainty all my days.

> Come, Holy Ghost, Thyself impress
> On my expanding heart:
> And show that in the Father's grace
> I share a filial part.[1]

William Booth said, "Assurance is produced by the revelation of forgiveness and acceptance made by God Himself directly to the soul. This is the witness of the Spirit. It is God testifying in my soul that He has loved me, and given Himself for me, and washed me from my sins in His own blood. Nothing short of this actual revelation, made by God Himself, can make anyone sure of salvation."[2]

John Wesley said, "By the testimony of the Spirit, I mean an inward impression of the soul, whereby the Spirit of God immediately and directly witnesses to my spirit that I am a child of God; that 'Jesus hath loved me, and given himself for me'; that all my sins are blotted out, and I, even I, am reconciled to God."[3]

This witness of the Spirit addressed to my consciousness enables me to sing with joyful assurance,

> My God is reconciled;
> His pardoning voice I hear:
> He owns me for His child;
> I can no longer fear:
> With confidence I now draw nigh,
> And, "Father, Abba, Father," cry.[4]

When the Holy Spirit witnesses to me that I am saved and adopted into God's family as His child, then other evidences begin to abound also. For instance:

1. My own spirit witnesses that I am a new creature. I know that old things have passed away and all things have become new. My very thoughts and desires have been changed. Love and joy and peace reign within me. My heart no longer condemns me. Pride, selfishness, lust, and temper no longer control my thoughts nor lead captive my will. I infer without doubt that this is God's work in me.

2. My conscience bears witness that I am honest and true in all my purposes and intentions, that I am without guile, that my eye is focused only on the glory of God, and that with all simplicity and sincerity of heart I serve Him. And, since by nature I am only sinful, I again infer that this sincerity of heart is His blessed work in my soul and is a fruit of salvation.

3. The Bible becomes a witness to my salvation. In it are accurately portrayed the true characteristics of the children of God, and as I study it prayerfully and find these characteristics in my heart and life, I again infer that I am God's child. This is true self-examination, and is most useful.

These evidences are most important to guard us against any mistake as to the witness of the Holy Spirit.

The witness of the Spirit is not likely to be mistaken for something else, just as the sun is not likely to be mistaken for a lesser light—a glowworm or a moon. But one who has not seen the sun might mistake some lesser light for the sun. So those who have not truly experienced new life in Christ may mistake some flash of fancy or some pleasant emotion for the witness of the Spirit. But if they are honest, the absence of these secondary evidences and witnesses will correct them. They must know that so long as sin masters them and reigns within them, and they are devoid of the tempers, graces, and dispositions of God's people as portrayed in the Bible, that they are mistaken in supposing that they have the witness of the Spirit. The Holy Spirit cannot witness to what does not exist. He cannot lie. Not until sin is forgiven does He witness to the fact. Not until we are justified from our old sins and born again does He witness that we are children of

God. And when He does so witness, these secondary evidences always follow. Charles Wesley expresses this in one of his matchless hymns:

> How can a sinner know
> His sins on earth forgiven?
> How can my gracious Savior show
> My name inscribed in heaven?
>
> We who in Christ believe
> That He for us hath died,
> We all His unknown peace receive,
> And feel His blood applied.
>
> His love, surpassing far
> The love of all beneath,
> We find within our hearts, and dare
> The pointless darts of death.
>
> Stronger than death and hell
> The mystic power we prove;
> And conquerors of the world, we dwell
> In heaven, who dwell in love.[5]

The witness of the Spirit is far more comprehensive than many suppose. Multitudes do not believe there is any such thing, while others confine it to the forgiveness of sins and adoption into the family of God. But the truth is that the Holy Spirit witnesses to much more than this.

He witnesses to sinful souls that they are guilty, condemned before God, and lost. This we call conviction, but it is none other than the witness of the Spirit to our true condition. And when we realize it, nothing can convince us to the contrary. Our friends may point out our good works, our kindly disposition, and try to assure us that we are not a bad person. But so long as the Spirit continues to witness to our guilt, nothing can console us or reassure our quaking heart. This convicting witness may come at any time, but it is usually given under the searching preaching of the gospel or by the burning testimony of those who have been gloriously saved and sanctified, or in time of danger, when the soul is awed into silence so that it can hear the "still small voice" of the Holy Spirit.

The Holy Spirit also witnesses not only to the forgiveness of sins and acceptance with God, but also to sanctification. "For by a single offering," said the author of Hebrews, "he has perfected for all time those who are being sanctified. And the Holy Spirit also bears witness to us" (Heb. 10:14–15 ESV).

Indeed, one who has this witness can no more doubt it than someone with two good eyes can doubt the existence of the sun when stepping forth into the splendor of a cloudless noonday. It satisfies and prompts the exulting cry, "We know, we know!"

Paul seemed to teach that the Holy Spirit witnesses to every good thing God works in us, for he said, "We have received, not the spirit of the world, but the spirit which is of God; that we might know the things that are freely given to us of God" (1 Cor. 2:12 KJV). It is for our comfort and encouragement to know our acceptance of God and our rights, privileges, and possessions in Jesus Christ, and the Holy Spirit is given for this purpose—that we may know.

But it is important to bear in mind God's plan of work in this matter.

The witness of the Spirit is dependent upon our faith. God does not give it to those who do not believe in Jesus. And if our faith wavers, the witness will become intermittent. If faith fails, it will be withdrawn. Owing to the unsteadiness of their faith, many new Christians get into uncertainty. Happy are they at such times if someone is at hand to instruct and encourage them to look steadfastly to Jesus. Unfortunately, many Christians of longer experience, through unsteady faith, walk in gloom and uncertainty and, instead of encouraging newer believers, they discourage them. Steadfast faith will keep the inward witness bright.

We must not get our attention off Jesus, and the promises of God in Him, and fix it upon the witness of the Spirit. The witness continues only while we look to Jesus and trust and obey Him. When we take our eyes off Him, the witness is gone. Many people fail here. Instead of quietly and confidently looking to Jesus and trusting Him, they vainly look for the witness—which is like trying to realize the sweetness of honey without receiving it in your mouth, or the beauty of a picture while looking inward upon oneself instead of outward upon the picture. Jesus saves. Look to Him, and He will send the Spirit to witness to His work.

The witness may be brightened by diligence in the discharge of duty, frequent seasons of glad prayer, definite testimony to salvation and sanctification, and by stirring up our faith.

The witness may be dulled by neglect of duty, sloth in prayer, inattention to the Bible, indefinite and hesitating testimony, and by carelessness, when we should be careful to walk soberly and steadfastly with the Lord.

I dare not say that the witness of the Spirit is dependent upon our health, but there are some forms of nervous and organic disease that seem to so distract or becloud the mind as to interfere with the clear discernment of the witness of the Spirit. I knew a nervous little child who when being carried across the street in her father's arms would be so distracted with fear by an approaching carriage that she seemed to be incapable of hearing or heeding his reassuring voice. It may be that there are some diseases that for the time prevent the sufferer from discerning the reassuring witness of the heavenly Father. Dr. Asa Mahan told me of an experience of this kind which he had during a very dangerous sickness. And Dr. Daniel Steele had a similar experience while lying at the point of death with typhoid fever. But some of the happiest Christians the world has seen have been racked with pain and tortured with disease. And so, while there may be seasons of fierce temptation when the witness is not clearly discerned, we may rest assured that if our hearts cleave to Jesus Christ and duty, He will never leave or forsake us.

But the witness will be lost if we willfully sin or persistently neglect to follow where He leads. This witness is a pearl of great price, and Satan will try to steal it from us. Therefore, we must continually guard it with watchful prayer.

If lost, the witness may be found again by prayer and faith and a dutiful taking up of the cross that has been laid down. Thousands who have lost it have found it again, and often they have found it with increased brightness and glory. If you have lost it, look up in faith to your loving God, and He will restore it to you. It is possible to live on the right side of plain duty without the witness, but you cannot be sure of your salvation, joyful in service, or glad in God, without it. And since it is promised to all God's children, no one who professes to be His should be without it.

If you do not have it, seek it now by faith in Jesus. Go to Him, and do not let Him go till He notifies you that you are His. Listen to Charles Wesley:

> From the world of sin, and noise,
> And hurry, I withdraw;
> For the small and inward voice
> I wait with humble awe;
> Silent am I now and still,
> Dare not in Thy presence move;
> To my waiting soul reveal
> The secret of Thy love.[6]

Do you want the witness to abide? Then study the Word of God and live by it. Sing and make melody in your heart to the Lord. Praise the Lord with your first waking breath in the morning, and thank Him with your last waking breath at night. Flee from sin. Keep on believing. Look to Jesus, cleave to Him, follow Him gladly, trust the efficacy of His blood, and the witness will abide in your heart. Be patient with the Lord. Let Him mold you, and "He will take delight in you with gladness. With his love, he will calm all your fears. He will rejoice over you with joyful songs" (Zeph. 3:17 NLT), and you shall no longer doubt, but know that you are His.

There are in this loud stunning tide
Of human care and crime,
With whom the melodies abide
Of th' everlasting chime;
Who carry music in their heart
Through dusky lane and wrangling mart,
Plying their task with busier feet
Because their secret souls a holy strain repeat.[7]

And that "holy strain" is but the echo of the Lord's song in their hearts, which is the witness of the Spirit.

NOTES

1. Philip Doddridge, "Sovereign of All the Worlds on High," 1739, public domain.

2. Source unknown.

3. John Wesley, *Sermons on Several Occasions* (Hudson: William E. Norman, 1810), 311.

4. Charles Wesley, "Arise, My Soul, Arise," 1742, public domain.

5. Charles Wesley, "How Can a Sinner Know His Sins on Earth Forgiven?," 1749, public domain.

6. Charles Wesley, "Open, Lord, My Inward Ear," 1812, public domain.

7. John Keble, "There Are in This Loud Stunning Tide," *Old Favourites from the Elder Poets with a Few Newer Friends*, ed. Matilda Sharpe (London: Williams and Norgate, 1881), 338.

Purity  5

A minister of the gospel, after listening to an eminent servant of God preaching on entire sanctification through the baptism with the Spirit, wrote to him, saying, "I like your teaching on the baptism with the Holy Ghost. I need it, and am seeking it; but I do not care much for entire sanctification or heart cleansing. Pray for me that I may be filled with the Holy Ghost."

The brother knew him well, and immediately replied, "I am so glad you believe in the baptism with the Holy Ghost and are so earnestly seeking it. I join my prayer with yours that you may receive that gift. But let me say to you, that if you get the gift of the Holy Ghost, you will have to take entire sanctification with it, for the first thing the baptism with the Holy Ghost does is to cleanse the heart from all sin." Thank God, he humbled himself and permitted the Lord to sanctify him. And he was filled with the Holy Spirit and mightily empowered to work for God.

Many have looked at the promise of power when the Holy Spirit is come, the energy of Peter's preaching on the day of Pentecost, and the marvelous results which followed, and have hastily and erroneously jumped to the conclusion that the baptism with the Holy Spirit is for work and service only.

It does bring power—the power of God. And it does fit for service, probably the most important service to which any created beings are commissioned—the proclamation of salvation and the conditions of peace to a lost world. But not that alone, nor primarily. The primary, the basal work of the baptism, is that of cleansing.

You may turn a flood into your millrun, but until it sweeps away the logs and brushwood and dirt that obstruct the course, you cannot get power to turn the wheels of your mill. The flood first washes out the obstructions, and then you have power.

The great hindrance in the hearts of God's children to the Holy Spirit's power is inbred sin—that dark, defiant, evil something within that struggles for the mastery of the soul and will not submit to be meek and lowly and patient and forbearing and holy, as was Jesus. And when the Holy Spirit comes, His first work is to sweep away that something, that carnal principle, and make free and clean all the channels of the soul.

Peter was filled with power on the day of Pentecost. But evidently the baptism's purifying effect made a deeper and more lasting impression upon his mind than the empowering effect, for years after, in the Council of Jerusalem, he stood up and told about the spiritual baptism of Cornelius, the Roman centurion, and his household. He said, "God, who knows the heart, acknowledged them by giving them the Holy Spirit, just as He did to us, and made no distinction between us and them, purifying their hearts by faith" (Acts 15:8–9 NKJV). He called attention not to power, but to purity, as the baptism's effect. When the Holy Spirit comes in to abide, the old, sinful nature goes out.

This destruction of inbred sin is made perfectly plain in that wonderful Old Testament type of the baptism with the Holy Spirit and fire recorded in the sixth chapter of Isaiah. The prophet was a most earnest preacher of righteousness (see Isa. 1:10–20), yet he was not sanctified wholly. But he had a vision of the Lord upon His throne and of the seraphim crying one to another, "Holy, holy, holy is the LORD of Heaven's Armies! The whole earth is filled with his glory!" (Isa. 6:3 NLT). "Their voices shook the Temple to its foundations"—and how much more should the heart of the prophet be moved! And so it was. He cried out, "It's all over! I am doomed, for I am a sinful man. I have filthy lips, and I live among a people with filthy lips. Yet I have seen the King, the LORD of Heaven's Armies" (Isa. 6:4–5 NLT).

When unsanctified people have a vision of God, it is not their lack of power that troubles them, but their lack of purity, their unlikeness to Christ, the Holy One. And so it was with the prophet. But he added, "Then one of the seraphim flew to me with a burning coal he had taken from the altar with a pair of tongs. He touched my lips with it and said, 'See, this coal has touched your lips. Now your guilt is removed, and your sins are forgiven'" (Isa. 6:6–7 NLT). Again, it is purity rather than power to which our attention is directed.

We have another type of this spiritual baptism in the thirty-sixth chapter of Ezekiel. In Isaiah the type was that of fire, but in Ezekiel it is that of water—for water and oil, and the wind and rain and dew, are all used as types of the Holy Spirit.

The Lord said through Ezekiel, "Then I will sprinkle clean water on you, and you will be clean. Your filth will be washed away, and you will no longer worship idols. And I will give you a new heart, and I will put a new spirit in you. I will take out your stony, stubborn heart and give you a tender, responsive heart. And I will put my Spirit in you so that you will follow my decrees and be careful to obey my regulations" (Ezek. 36:25–27 NLT).

Once again, the incoming of the Holy Spirit means the outgoing of all sin, of all "your filth . . . and you will no longer worship idols." How plainly it is taught! Yet many of God's dear children do not believe it is their privilege to be free from sin and pure in heart in this life. But, may we not? Let us consider this.

It is certainly desirable. Every sincere Christian—and none can be a Christian who is not sincere—wants to be free from sin, to be pure in heart, to be like Christ. Sin is hateful to every true child of God. The Spirit within us cries out against the sin, the wrong temper, the pride, the lust, the selfishness, the evil that lurks within the heart. Surely, it is desirable to be free from sin.

> He wills that I should holy be:
> That holiness I long to feel;
> That full Divine conformity
> To all my Savior's righteous will.[1]

It is necessary, for "those who are not holy will not see the Lord" (Heb. 12:14 NLT). Sometime, somehow, somewhere, sin must go out of our hearts—all sin—or we cannot go into heaven. Sin would spoil heaven just as it spoils earth, just as it spoils the peace of hearts and homes, of families and neighborhoods and nations here. Why God in His wisdom allows sin in the world, I do not know, I cannot understand. But this I understand: that He has one world into which He will not let sin enter. He has notified us in advance that no sin—nothing that defiles—can enter heaven and mar the blessedness of that holy place. "Who may climb the mountain of the LORD? Who may stand in his holy place? Only those whose hands and hearts are pure, who do not worship idols and never tell lies" (Ps. 24:3–4 NLT). We must get rid of sin to get into heaven, to enjoy the full favor of God. It is necessary.

Choose I must, and soon must choose
Holiness, or heaven lose.
If what heaven loves I hate,
Shut for me is heaven's gate!

Endless sin means endless woe;
Into endless sin I go
If my soul, from reason rent,
Takes from sin its final bent.

As the stream its channel grooves,
And within that channel moves;
So does habit's deepest tide
Groove its bed and there abide.

> Light obeyed increaseth light;
> Light resisted bringeth night;
> Who shall give me will to choose
> If the love of light I lose?
>
> Speed, my soul, this instant yield;
> Let the light its scepter wield.
> While thy God prolongs His grace,
> Haste thee to His holy face.[2]

This purification from sin is promised. Nothing can be plainer than God's promise on this point. "Then I will sprinkle clean water on you, and you will be clean. Your filth will be washed away, and you will no longer worship idols" (Ezek. 36:25 NLT). When all is removed, nothing remains. When all filthiness and all idols are taken away, none are left.

"Where sin abounded, grace abounded much more, so that as sin reigned in death, even so grace might reign through righteousness to eternal life through Jesus Christ our Lord" (Rom. 5:20–21 NKJV). Grace reigns, not through sin, but "through righteousness" which has expelled sin. Grace brings in righteousness and sin goes out: "If we are living in the light, as God is in the light, then we have fellowship with each other, and the blood of Jesus, his Son, cleanses us from all sin" (1 John 1:7 NLT). "Having been set free from sin, you became slaves of righteousness" (Rom. 6:18 NKJV).

These are sample promises and assurances, any one of which is sufficient to encourage us to believe that our heavenly Father will save us from all sin, if we meet His conditions.

This deliverance is possible. It was for this that Jesus Christ, the Father's Son, came into the world and suffered and died, that He might "save his people from their sins" (Matt. 1:21 KJV). It was for this that He shed His precious blood—to cleanse us from all sin. It was for this that the Word of God, with its wonderful promises, was given, that we may "share his divine nature and escape the world's corruption caused by human desires" (2 Pet. 1:4 NLT), by which is meant escape from inbred sin. It was for this that ministers of the gospel are given to the church "for the perfecting of the saints" (Eph. 4:12 KJV) and for the saving and sanctifying of souls (see Acts 26:18). It is primarily for this that the Holy Spirit comes as a baptism of fire—that sin might be consumed out of us, so that we might "share in the inheritance that belongs to his people, who live in the light" (Col. 1:12 NLT), that we might be ready without a moment's warning to go into the midst of the heavenly hosts in white garments, washed in the blood of the Lamb.

And shall all these mighty agents and this heavenly provision and these gracious purposes of God fail to destroy sin out of any obedient, believing heart? Is sin omnipotent? No!

If you will look to Jesus right now, trusting the merits of His blood, and receive the Holy Spirit into your heart, you shall be "made free from sin" (Rom. 6:18 KJV). It "shall not have dominion over you" (Rom. 6:14 KJV). Under the fiery touch of His holy presence, your iniquity shall be taken away and your sin shall be purged. And you yourself shall burn like the bush Moses saw—yet, like the bush, you shall not be consumed. And by this holy fire, this flame of love that consumes sin, you shall be made proof against that unquenchable fire that consumes sinners.

Come, Holy Ghost, Thy mighty aid bestowing;

Destroy the works of sin, the self, the pride;

Burn, burn in me, my idols overthrowing:

Prepare my heart for Him, for my Lord crucified.[3]

NOTES

1. Charles Wesley, "He Wills That I Should Holy Be," 1762, public domain.

2. Joseph Cook, "God's Time Now," 1887, public domain.

3. Catherine Booth-Clibborn, "At Thy Feet I Fall," *The Salvation Army Songbook*, 1884, public domain.

Power 6

Just before His ascension, Jesus met His disciples for the last time, repeated His command, "Do not leave Jerusalem until the Father sends you the gift he promised," and reiterated His promise that they would soon be "be baptized with the Holy Spirit" (Acts 1:4–5 NLT). Then they asked Him, "Lord, has the time come for you to free Israel and restore our kingdom?" They were still eager for an earthly kingdom. But He said, "The Father alone has the authority to set those dates and times, and they are not for you to know." And then He added, "But you will receive power when the Holy Spirit comes upon you" (Acts 1:6 NLT).

They wanted power and He assured them they would have it, but said nothing of its nature or of the work and activities into which it would thrust them and for which it would equip them, beyond the fact that they would be His witnesses, "telling people about me everywhere—in

Jerusalem, throughout Judea, in Samaria, and to the ends of the earth" (Acts 1:8 NLT). After that, the Holy Spirit Himself was to be their teacher.

And then Jesus left them. Earth lost its power to hold Him, and while they beheld Him, He began to ascend—a cloud bent low from heaven, receiving Him out of sight, and they were left alone, with His promise of power ringing in their ears and His command to wait for the promise of the Father checking any impatience that might lead them to go fishing (as Peter had done some days before), or cause an undue haste to begin their life work of witnessing for Him before God's appointed time.

For ten days they waited, not listlessly, but eagerly, as a maid for her mistress or a servant for a master who is expected to come at any moment. They forgot their personal ambitions. They ceased to judge and criticize one another, and in the sweet unity of brotherly love, "with one accord" (Acts 2:1 KJV) they rejoiced, prayed, and waited. And then on the day of Pentecost, at their early morning prayer meeting, when they were all present, the windows of heaven opened, and such a blessing as they could not contain was poured out upon them: "Suddenly, there was a sound from heaven like the roaring of a mighty windstorm, and it filled the house where they were sitting. Then, what looked like flames or tongues of fire appeared and settled on each of them. And everyone present was filled with the Holy Spirit" (Acts 2:2–4 NLT). This was the inaugural day of the church of God, the dawn of the dispensation of the Holy Spirit, the beginning of the days of power.

In the morning of that day, there were only a few Christians in the world. The New Testament was not written, and it is doubtful if they had among them all a copy of the Old Testament. They had no church buildings, colleges, or religious books and papers. They were poor and despised, unlearned and ignorant. But before night they had enrolled three thousand new followers from among those who a few weeks before had crucified their Lord, and they had aroused and filled all Jerusalem with questionings and amazement. What was the secret? Power. What was the source? God the Holy Spirit. He had come, and this work was His work. And they were His instruments.

When Jesus came, a body was prepared for Him (see Heb. 10:5) and through that body He performed His wondrous works. But when the other Comforter comes, He takes possession of those bodies that are freely and fully presented to Him, and He touches their lips with grace. He shines peacefully and gloriously on their faces. He flashes beams of pity, compassion, and heavenly affection from their eyes. He kindles a fire of love in their hearts and lights the flame of truth in their minds. They become His temple, and their hearts are a Holy of Holies in which His blessed presence ever abides. And from that central citadel He works, enduing all who have received Him with power.

If you ask how the Holy Spirit can dwell within us and work through us without destroying our personality, I cannot tell. How can electricity fill and transform a dead wire into a live one, which you dare not touch? How can a magnetic current fill a piece of steel and transform it into a mighty force which by its touch can raise tons of iron as a child would lift a feather? How can fire dwell in a piece of iron until its very appearance is that of fire and it becomes a firebrand? I cannot tell.

Now, what fire and electricity and magnetism do in iron and steel, the Holy Spirit does in the spirits of those who believe in Jesus, follow

Him wholly, and trust Him intelligently. He dwells in them and inspires them, till they are all alive with the very life of God.

The transformation wrought in us by the baptism with the Holy Spirit, and the power that fills us, are amazing beyond measure. The Holy Spirit gives power.

1. Power over the world. They become "dead to the world and all its toys, its idle pomps and fading joys."[1] The world masters and enslaves people who do not have the Holy Spirit. To one it offers money, and he falls down and worships, selling his conscience and character for gold. To another it offers power, and she falls down and worships and sacrifices her principles and sears her conscience for power. To another it offers pleasure, to another learning, to another fame, and they fall down and worship and sell themselves for these things. But men and women who are filled with the Holy Spirit are free. They can turn from these things without a pang, as they would from pebbles. Or they can take them and use them as their servants for the glory of God and the good of others.

What did Peter and James and John care for the great places in the kingdoms of this world after they were filled with the Holy Spirit? They would not have exchanged places with Herod the king or with Caesar himself. For the gratification of any personal ambition these things were no more attractive to them now than the lordship over a tribe of ants on their tiny hill. They were now kings and priests unto God. Theirs was an everlasting kingdom, and its glory exceeds the glory of the kingdoms of this world as the splendor of the sun exceeds that of the glowworm.

The head of some great business enterprises was making many thousands of dollars every year, but when the Holy Spirit filled him, money lost its power over him. He still retained his position and made vast sums. But as a steward of the Lord, he poured it into God's work, and has been doing so for more than thirty years.

The disciples in Jerusalem after Pentecost held all their possessions in common, so completely were they freed from the power and love of money.

A rising young lawyer was filled with the Spirit and the next day said to his client, "I cannot plead your case. I have a retainer from the Lord Jesus." And he became one of the mightiest preachers the world has ever seen.

A popular boy got the fiery baptism and went to his baseball team and said, "Boys, you swear, and I am now a Christian and cannot play with you anymore." And God made him the wonder of all his old friends and a happy winner of souls.

A fashionable woman got the baptism, and God gave her power to break away from her worldly set and surroundings and to live wholly for Him. And He gave her an influence that circled the globe.

Paul said, "The world is crucified unto me, and I unto the world" (Gal. 6:14 KJV). Men could whip and stone and imprison his body and cut off his head, but his soul was free. It was enslaved and driven by no unholy or inordinate ambition, no lust for gold, no desire for power or fame, no fear of others, no shame of worldly censure or adverse public opinion. He had power over the world, and this same power is the birthright of every follower of Jesus, and the present possession of everyone who is wholly sanctified by the baptism with the Holy Spirit.

2. Power over the flesh. The body, which God intended for a "house beautiful" for the soul and a temple holy unto Himself, is often

reduced to a sty, where the imprisoned soul wallows in lusts and passions, and degrades itself below the level of beasts. But this baptism gives a person power over his or her body.

God has given us such desires and passions as are necessary to secure our continued existence, and not one is in itself evil, but good and only good. And these, when controlled and used—but not abused—will help to develop and maintain the purest and highest humanity. The appetites for food and drink are necessary to life. Another desire is intended to secure the continuance of the human race. And so all the desires and appetites of the body have useful ends, were given to us in love by our heavenly Father for high and essential purposes, and are necessary to us as human beings.

The soul that is cut off by sin from fellowship with God, however, seeks satisfaction in sensual excesses and in the unlawful gratification of these appetites, and so sinks to depths of degradation to which no beast ever falls. That soul then becomes a slave, as swollen and raging passion takes the place of innocent appetites and desires.

But when the Holy Spirit enters the heart and sanctifies the soul, He does not destroy these desires but purifies and regulates them. He reinforces the soul with the fear and love of God, and gives it power, complete power, over the fleshly appetites. He restores it to its full fellowship with God and its kingship over the body.

While these appetites and desires are not in themselves sinful, but are necessary for our welfare and our complete humanity, and while their diseased and abnormal power is cured when we are sanctified, they are still avenues through which we may be tempted. Therefore, they must be guarded with care and ruled in wisdom.

Many people stumble at and reject the doctrine of entire sanctification because they do not understand these things. They mistake that which is natural and essential to a human being for the diseased and abnormal propensity caused by sin, and so miss the blessed truth of full salvation.

I knew a doctor who had used tobacco for over sixty years, who was delivered from the abnormal appetite instantly through the sanctification of the Spirit. I knew an old man who had been a drunkard for over fifty years, similarly delivered. I knew a young man, the slave of a vicious habit of the flesh, who was set free at once by the fiery baptism. Electrical current cannot transform the dead wire into a live one quicker than the Holy Spirit can flood a soul with light and love, destroy the carnal mind, and fill a soul with power over all sin.

3. Power over the Devil. The indwelling presence of the Holy Spirit destroys all doubt as to the personality of the Devil. He is discerned, and his malice is felt and known as never before.

A soldier may be so skillfully attacked in the dark that the enemy is not discovered—but not in the day. Many people in these days deny that there is any Devil, only evil. But they are in the dark, so much in the dark that they not only say that there is no Devil, but that there is no personal God, only good. But the day comes with the Holy Spirit's entrance, and then God is intimately known and the Devil is discovered. And as he assailed Jesus after His baptism with the Spirit, so he does today all who receive the Holy Spirit. He comes as an angel of light to deceive, and as a roaring lion to devour and overcome with fear. But the soul filled with the Spirit outwits the Devil and, clad in the whole armor of God, overcomes the old Enemy.

"Power . . . over all the power of the enemy" (Luke 10:19 KJV) is God's purpose for all His children. Power to do the will of God patiently and effectively, with naturalness and ease, or to suffer the will of God with patience and good cheer, comes with this blessed baptism. It is power for service or sacrifice, according to God's will. Have you this power? If not, it is for you. Yield yourself fully to Christ right now, and if you ask in faith you shall receive.

NOTE

1. Charles Wesley, "Come, Jesus, Lord, with Holy Fire," 1880, public domain.

Testing the Spirits 7

Those who do not have the Holy Spirit, or who do not heed Him, fall easily and naturally into formalism, substituting lifeless ceremonies, sacraments, genuflections, and ritualistic performances for the free, glad, living worship inspired by the indwelling Spirit. They sing, but not from the heart. They say their prayers, but they do not really pray.

"I prayed last night, Mother," said a child.

"Why, my child, you pray every night!" replied the mother.

"No," said the child, "I only said prayers, but last night I really prayed." And his face shone. He had opened his heart to the Holy Spirit and had at last really talked with God and worshiped.

But those who receive the Holy Spirit may fall into fanaticism, unless they follow the command of John to "test the spirits to see whether they are from God" (1 John 4:1 NIV).

We are commanded not to "scoff at prophecies," but at the same time we are told to "test everything" (1 Thess. 5:20–21 NLT). "There are many false prophets in the world" (1 John 4:1 NLT) and they will lead us astray, if possible. So we must beware. As someone has written, we must "believe not every spirit; regard not, trust not, follow not every pretender to the Spirit of God, or every professor of vision, or inspiration, or revelation from God."[1]

The higher and more intense the life, the more carefully must it be guarded, lest it be endangered and go astray. It is so in the natural world and likewise in the spiritual world.

When Satan can no longer rock people to sleep with religious lullabies or satisfy them with the lifeless form, then he comes as an angel of light, probably in the person of some purveyor or teacher of religion, and seeks to usurp the place of the Holy Spirit. But instead of leading "into all truth," he leads the unwary soul into deadly error. Instead of directing people onto the highway of holiness and into the path of perfect peace, where no ravenous beast ever comes, he leads them into a wilderness where their souls, stripped of the beautiful garments of salvation, are robbed and wounded and left to die, unless some Good Samaritan, with patient pity and Christlike love, comes that way.

When the Holy Spirit comes in His fullness, He strips us of our self-righteousness and pride and conceit. We see ourselves as the chief of sinners and realize that only through Jesus' stripes are we healed, and ever after, as we live in the Spirit, our boast is in Him and our glory is in the cross. Remembering the hole of the pit from which we were quarried, we are filled with tender pity for all who are not in the

Way. And, while we do not excuse or belittle sin, yet we are slow to believe evil and our judgments are full of charity.

> Judge not; the workings of his brain
> And of his heart thou canst not see:
> What looks to thy dim eyes a stain,
> In God's pure light may only be
> A scar, brought from some well-won field,
> Where thou wouldst only faint and yield.[2]

But people who have been thus snared by Satan forget their own past miserable state, boast of their righteousness, thank God that they are not like others, and begin to beat their fellow servants with heavy denunciations, thrust them through with sharp criticisms, and pelt them with hard words. They cease to pity and begin to condemn. They no longer warn and entreat others in tender love but are quick to believe evil and swift to pass judgment not only upon others' actions, but upon their motives as well.

True charity does not wink at iniquity, but it is as far removed from a sharp, condemning spirit as light is from darkness and as honey is from vinegar. It is quick to condemn sin, but is full of saving, long-suffering compassion for the sinner.

A humble, teachable mind marks those in whom the Holy Spirit dwells. They esteem very highly in love those who are over them in the Lord and are glad to be admonished by them. They submit themselves one to the other, welcome instruction and correction, and esteem "open rebuke . . . better than secret love" (Prov. 27:5 KJV).

They believe that the Lord has yet many things to say to them, and they are willing and glad for Him to say them by whomever He will, but especially by their leaders and their brothers and sisters. While they do not fawn and cringe before others or believe everything that is said to them without proving it by the Word and Spirit of God, they believe that God "gave some to be apostles, some prophets, some evangelists, and some pastors and teachers, for the equipping of the saints for the work of ministry, for the edifying of the body of Christ" (Eph. 4:11–12 NKJV) and, like Cornelius, they are ready to hear these appointed ministers and receive the word of the Lord from them.

But Satan seeks to destroy all this lowliness of spirit and humbleness of mind. Those in whom his deadly work has begun are wiser in their own conceit "than seven [people] who can answer sensibly" (Prov. 26:16 ESV). They are wiser than all their teachers, and no one can instruct them. One of these deluded souls, who had previously been marked by modesty and humility, declared of certain of God's chosen leaders whose spiritual knowledge and wisdom were everywhere recognized, that "the whole of them knew no more about the Holy Ghost than an old goose." Paul, Luther, and Wesley were much troubled, and their work greatly hurt, by some of these misguided souls, and every great spiritual awakening is likely to be marred more or less by such people, so that we cannot be too much on our guard against false spirits who would counterfeit the work and leadings of the Holy Spirit.

It is this huge conceit that has led some to announce themselves as apostles and prophets to whom all must listen or fall under God's wrath, while others have declared that they were living in resurrection bodies and should not die. Still others have reached that pitch of fanaticism where they could calmly proclaim themselves to be the Messiah or the Holy Spirit in bodily form. Such people will be quick to deny the infallibility of the pope, while they assume their own infallibility and denounce all who dispute it.

The Holy Spirit may lead to a holy rivalry in love and humility, and kindness and self-denial and good works, but He never leads His servants into such swelling conceit that they can no longer be taught by others.

Those who are filled with the Spirit are tolerant of others who may differ from them in opinion or in doctrine. They are firm in their own convictions, and ready at all times with meekness and fear to explain and defend the doctrines which they hold and are convinced are according to God's Word, but they do not condemn all those who differ. They are glad to believe that people are often better than their creed and may be saved in spite of it. Like mountains whose bases are bathed with sunshine and clothed with fruitful fields and vineyards while their tops are covered with dark clouds, so human hearts are often fruitful in the graces of charity while their heads are yet darkened by doctrinal error.

Anyway, as servants of the Lord, they will "not be quarrelsome but kind to everyone, able to teach, patiently enduring evil, correcting . . . opponents with gentleness. [For] God may perhaps grant them repentance leading to a knowledge of the truth, and they may come to their senses and escape from the snare of the devil, after being captured by him to do his will" (2 Tim. 2:24–26 ESV).

But Satan, under guise of love for and loyalty to the truth, will introduce the spirit of intolerance. It was this spirit that crucified Jesus, burned John Hus at the stake, hanged Girolamo Savonarola, and inspired the massacre of St. Bartholomew and the horrors of the Inquisition. And the same spirit (in a milder but possibly more subtle form) blinds the eyes of many professing Christians to any good in those who differ from them in doctrine, forms of worship, or methods of government. They murder love to protect what they often blindly call truth. What is truth without love? A dead thing, an encumbrance, "the letter [that] kills" (2 Cor. 3:6 ESV).

The body is necessary to our life in this world, but life can exist in a deformed and even mutilated body. And such a body with life in it is better than the most perfect body that is only a corpse. So, while truth is most precious, and sound doctrine to be esteemed more than silver and gold, yet love can exist where truth is not held in its most perfect and complete forms, and love is the one thing needful.

> The love of God is broader
> Than the measure of man's mind:
> And the heart of the Eternal
> Is most wonderfully kind.[3]

The Holy Spirit produces a spirit of unity among Christians. People who have been sitting behind their sectarian fences in self-complacent ease, proselytizing zeal, or grim defiance are suddenly lifted above the fence and find sweet fellowship with each other when He comes into their hearts.

They delight in each other's company. They esteem others better than themselves, and in honor they prefer one another before themselves (see Phil. 2:3; Rom. 12:10). They fulfill the psalmist's ideal: "How good and pleasant it is when God's people live together in unity!"

(Ps. 133:1 NIV). Here is a picture of the unity of Christians in the beginning in Jerusalem: "And they were all filled with the Holy Spirit. Then they preached the word of God with boldness. All the believers were united in heart and mind. And they felt that what they owned was not their own, so they shared everything they had" (Acts 4:31–32 NLT).

What an ideal this is! And since it has been attained once, it can be attained again and retained, but only by the indwelling of the Holy Spirit. It was for this that Jesus poured out His heart in His great intercessory prayer just before His arrest in the garden of Gethsemane: "I am praying not only for these disciples but also for all who will ever believe in me through their message. I pray that they will all be one" (John 17:20–21 NLT). And what was the standard of unity to which He would have us come? Listen: "As you are in me, Father, and I am in you. And may they be in us so that the world will believe you sent me" (John 17:21 NLT). Such unity has a wondrous power to compel the belief of worldly men and women. "I have given them the glory you gave me, so they may be one as we are one. I am in them and you are in me. May they experience such perfect unity that the world will know that you sent me and that you love them as much as you love me" (John 17:22–23 NLT). Wondrous unity! Wondrous love!

It is for this His blessed heart eternally yearns, and it is for this that the Holy Spirit works in the hearts of those who receive Him. But Satan constantly seeks to destroy this holy love and divine unity. When he comes, he arouses suspicions, stirs up strife, quenches the spirit of intercessory prayer, engenders backbiting, and causes separations.

After enumerating various Christian graces, and urging the Colossians to put them on, Paul wrote, "Above all, clothe yourselves with love, which binds us all together in perfect harmony" (Col. 3:14 NLT). These graces were garments, and love was the belt that bound and held them together—and so love is the bond that holds true Christians together. Divine love is the great test by which we are to measure ourselves and all teachers and spirits.

Love is not puffed up. Love is not bigoted. Love is not intolerant. Love is not schismatic. Love is loyal to Jesus and to all His people. If we have this love shed abroad in our hearts by the Holy Spirit (see Rom. 5:5), we shall discern the voice of our Good Shepherd and shall not be deceived by the voice of the stranger. And so we shall be saved from both formalism and fanaticism.

NOTES

1. Matthew Henry, *An Exposition of All the Books of the Old and New Testaments*, vol. 5 (London: W. Baynes, 1806), 639.

2. Adelaide A. Procter, "Judge Not," n. d., public domain.

3. Frederick W. Faber, "There's a Wideness in God's Mercy," 1854, public domain.

It is the work of the Holy Spirit to guide God's people through the uncertainties and dangers and duties of this life to their home in heaven. When He led the children of Israel out of Egypt by the hand of Moses, He guided them through the mountainous wilderness in a pillar of cloud by day and of fire by night, thus assuring their comfort and safety. And this was but a type of His perpetual spiritual guidance of His people.

"But how may I know for certain what God wants of me?" is sure to be the earnest and, often, agonizing cry of every humble and devoutly zealous young Christian. "How may I know the guidance of the Holy Spirit?"

We must get it fixed in our minds that we need to be guided always by Him. A ship was wrecked on a rocky coast far off the course that the captain thought he was taking. On examination, it was found that the compass had been slightly deflected by a bit of metal that had lodged in the box.

The voyage of life on which we sail is beset by as many dangers as the ship at sea, and how shall we surely steer our course to our heavenly harbor without divine guidance? There is a nearly infinite number of influences to deflect us from the safe and certain course. We start out in the morning and we know not what person we may meet, what paragraph we may read, what word may be spoken, what letter we may receive, what subtle temptation may assail or allure us, or what immediate decisions we may have to make during the day, that may turn us almost imperceptibly but nonetheless surely from the right way. We need the guidance of the Holy Spirit.

We not only need divine guidance, but we may have it. God's Word assures us of this: "The LORD will guide you continually" (Isa. 58:11 ESV). Not occasionally, not spasmodically, but "continually." The psalmist said, "This is God, our God forever and ever. He will guide us forever" (Ps. 48:14 ESV). Jesus said of the Holy Spirit, "When the Spirit of truth comes, he will guide you into all truth" (John 16:13 NLT). And Paul wrote, "All who are led by the Spirit of God are children of God" (Rom. 8:14 NLT).

These Scriptures establish the fact that the children of God may be guided always by the Spirit of God.

> Guide me, O Thou great Jehovah,
> Pilgrim through this barren land!
> I am weak, but Thou art mighty:
> Hold me with Thy powerful hand.[1]

How does God guide us? "The LORD says, 'I will guide you along the best pathway for your life'" (Ps. 32:8 NLT). He does this in a number of ways:

- By faith. Paul said, "We walk by faith, not by sight" (2 Cor. 5:7 KJV) and, "The just shall live by faith" (Rom. 1:17 KJV). So we may conclude that God never leads us in such a way as to do away with the necessity of faith. We read that when God warned Noah, it was by faith that Noah was led to build the ark (see Heb. 11:7). When God told Abraham to go to a land which He would show him, it was by faith that Abraham went (see Heb. 11: 8). If we believe, we will surely be guided. But if we do not believe, we shall be left to ourselves. Without faith it is impossible to please God or to follow where He leads.

- By "sanctified common sense." The Spirit guides us in such manner as to demand the exercise of our best judgment. He enlightens our understanding and directs our judgment by sound reason and sense. As the psalmist said, "The meek will he guide in judgment" (Ps. 25:9 KJV).

I knew a man who was eager to obey God and be led by the Spirit but had the mistaken idea that the Holy Spirit sets aside human judgment and common sense and speaks directly upon the minutest and most commonplace matters. He wanted the Holy Spirit to direct him just how much to eat at each meal, and he has been known to take food out of his mouth at what he supposed to be the Holy Spirit's notification that he had eaten enough. He believed that if he swallowed that mouthful, it would be in violation of the leadings of the Spirit.

No doubt, the Spirit will help an honest person to arrive at a safe judgment even in matters of this kind, but it will be through the use of sanctified common sense. Otherwise, we would be reduced to a state of mental infancy and kept in intellectual swaddling clothes. He will guide us, but only as we resolutely— and in the best light we have—exercise judgment. John Wesley said that God usually guided him by presenting reasons to his mind for any given course of action.

- By enlightening our study. The psalmist received a promise: "The LORD says . . . 'I will advise you and watch over you'" (Ps. 32:8 NLT). And the psalmist affirmed this had proven true when he said, "You guide me with your counsel, leading me to a glorious destiny" (Ps. 73:24 NLT). Now, advice, counsel, instruction, and teaching not only imply effort upon the part of the teacher, but also study and close attention on the part of the one being taught. The guidance of the Holy Spirit will require us to listen attentively, study diligently, and patiently learn the lessons He would teach us. The Holy Spirit does not set aside our powers and faculties but seeks to awaken and stir them into full activity and develop them into well-rounded perfection, thus making them channels through which He can intelligently influence and direct us. He seeks to illuminate our whole spiritual being as the sun illuminates our physical being, and to bring us into such union and sympathy, such oneness of thought, desire, affection, and purpose with God, that we shall know at all times, by a kind of spiritual instinct, the mind of God concerning us, and never be in doubt about His will.

- By opening up to our minds the deep, sanctifying truths of the Bible, especially by revealing to us the character and spirit of Jesus and His apostles, and leading us to follow in their footsteps—the footsteps of their faith and love and unselfish devotion to God and others, even to the laying down of their lives.
- By the circumstances and surroundings of our daily life.
- By the counsel of others, especially of devout, wise, and experienced men and women of God.
- By deep inward conviction, which increases as we wait upon Him in prayer and readiness to obey. It is by this sovereign conviction that men and women are called to preach, to go to foreign fields as missionaries, and to devote their time, talents, money, and lives to God's work.

Why do people seek for guidance and not find it?

- Because they do not diligently study God's Word and seek to be filled with its truths and principles. They neglect the cultivation of their minds and hearts in the school of Christ, and so miss divine guidance. One of the mightiest men of God now living used to carry his Bible with him into the coal mine when he was only a boy. He spent his spare time filling his mind and heart with its heavenly truths and so prepared himself to be divinely led in mighty labors for God.
- Because they do not humbly accept the daily providences, circumstances, and conditions of their everyday life as a part of God's present plan for them, as His school in which He would

train them for greater things, as His vineyard in which He would
have them diligently labor. A young woman imagined she was
called to devote herself entirely to saving souls, but under the
searching training through which she had to pass, she saw her
selfishness and said she would have to return home, live a holy
life there, and seek to get her family members into right relationships with God—something she had utterly neglected—
before she could go into the work. If we are not faithful at home
or in the shop, mill, or place where we work, we shall miss
God's way for us.

- Because they are not teachable and are unwilling to receive
  instruction from other Christians. They are not humble.
- Because they do not wait on God and listen to and heed the inner
  leadings of the Holy Spirit. They are self-willed. They want their
  own way. Someone has said, "That which is often asked of God
  is not so much His will and way, as His approval of our way."[2]
  And another has said, "God's guidance is plain, when we are
  true."[3] If we promptly and gladly obey, we shall not miss the
  way. Paul said, "I was not disobedient unto the heavenly vision"
  (Acts 26:19 KJV). He obeyed God at all costs, and thus the Holy
  Spirit could guide him.
- Because of fear and unbelief. It was this fearfulness and unbelief that caused the Israelites to turn back and not go into Canaan
  when Caleb and Joshua assured them that God would help them
  to possess the land. They lost sight of God and feared the giants
  and walled cities, and so missed God's way for them and perished in the wilderness.

- Because they do not take everything promptly and confidently to God in prayer. Paul told us to be "instant in prayer" (Rom. 12:12 KJV), and I am persuaded that it is slowness and delay, sloth and sleepiness in prayer, that rob God's children of the glad assurance of His guidance in all things.

- Because of impatience and haste. Some of God's plans for us unfold slowly, and we must patiently and calmly wait on Him in faith and faithfulness, assured that in due time He will make plain His way for us, if our faith does not fail. It is never God's will that we should get into a headlong hurry but rather that, with patient steadfastness, we should learn to stand still when the pillar of cloud and fire does not move, and that with loving confidence and glad promptness we should strike our tents and march forward when He leads.

> When we cannot see our way,
> Let us trust and still obey;
> He who bids us forward go,
> Cannot fail the way to show.
>
> Though the sea be deep and wide,
> Though a passage seem denied;
> Fearless, let us still proceed,
> Since the Lord vouchsafes to lead.[4]

Finally, we may rest assured that the Holy Spirit never leads His people to do anything that is wrong or contrary to God's will as revealed in the Bible. He never leads anyone to be impolite and discourteous. "Be courteous" is a divine command (1 Pet. 3:8 KJV). He would have us respect the minor graces of gentle, kindly manners, as well as the great laws of holiness and righteousness.

He may sometimes lead us in ways that are hard for flesh and blood, and that bring to us sorrow and loss in this life. He led Jesus into the wilderness to be sorely tried by the Devil, to Pilate's judgment hall, and to the cross. He led Paul in ways that meant imprisonment, stonings, whippings, hunger and cold, and bitter persecution and death. But He upheld Paul until he cried out, "Most gladly therefore will I rather glory in my infirmities, that the power of Christ may rest upon me. Therefore I take pleasure in infirmities, in reproaches, in necessities, in persecutions, in distresses for Christ's sake" (2 Cor. 12:9–10 KJV). Oh, to be thus led by our heavenly Guide!

He leadeth me! Oh, blessed thought!
Oh, words with heavenly comfort fraught!
Whate'er I do, where'er I be,
Still 'tis God's hand that leadeth me.

Sometimes 'mid scenes of deepest gloom,
Sometimes where Eden's bowers bloom,
By waters still, o'er troubled sea,
Still 'tis God's hand that leadeth me.

Lord, I will clasp Thy hand in mine,

Nor ever murmur nor repine,

Content, whatever lot I see,

Since 'tis my God that leadeth me.

And when my task on earth is done,

When by Thy grace the victory's won,

E'en death's cold wave I will not flee,

Since God through Jordan leadeth me.[5]

NOTES

1. William Williams, "Guide Me, O Thou Great Jehovah," 1745, public domain.

2. Sarah F. Smiley, quoted in Mary Wilder Tileston, *Daily Strength for Daily Needs* (Boston: Roberts Brothers, 1889), 267.

3. F. W. Robertson, ibid.

4. Thomas Kelly, "When We Cannot See Our Way," 1842, public domain.

5. Joseph H. Gilmore, "He Leadeth Me," 1862, public domain.

The Meek and Lowly Heart 9

I know a man whose daily prayer for years was that he might be meek and lowly in heart as was his Master. "Take my yoke upon you, and learn of me," said Jesus, "for I am meek and lowly in heart" (Matt. 11:29 KJV).

How lowly Jesus was! He was the Lord of life and glory. He made the worlds and upholds them by His word of power. But He humbled Himself, became human, and was born of the virgin in a manger among the cattle. He lived among the common people and worked at the carpenter's bench. And then, anointed with the Holy Spirit, He went about doing good, preaching the gospel to the poor, and ministering to the manifold needs of the sick and sinful and sorrowful. He touched the lepers. He was the friend of sinners. His whole life was a ministry of mercy to those who most needed Him. He humbled Himself to our low estate. He was a King who came "humble, riding on a donkey—

riding on a donkey's colt" (Zech. 9:9 NLT). He was a King, but His crown was of thorns and a cross was His throne.

Paul gave us a picture of the mind and heart of Jesus. He exhorted the Philippians, saying, "Don't be selfish; don't try to impress others. Be humble, thinking of others as better than yourselves" (Phil. 2:3 NLT), and then he added, "You must have the same attitude that Christ Jesus had. 'Though he was God, he did not think of equality with God as something to cling to. Instead, he gave up his divine privileges; he took the humble position of a slave and was born as a human being. When he appeared in human form, he humbled himself in obedience to God and died a criminal's death on a cross'" (Phil. 2:5–8 NLT).

When the Holy Spirit finds His way into a man or woman's heart, the Spirit of Jesus has come to that person and produces the same meekness of heart and lowly service that were seen in the Master. Ambition for place and power and money and fame vanishes, and in its place is a consuming desire to be good and do good, to accomplish in full God's blessed, beneficent will.

Some time ago I met a woman who—as a trained nurse in Paris, nursing rich, English-speaking foreigners—received pay that in a few years would have made her independently wealthy. But the spirit of Jesus came into her heart, and she is now nursing the poor, giving her life to them, doing the most loathsome and exacting service for them, and doing it with a smiling face, for her food and clothes.

Some capable men in one of the largest American cities lost their spiritual balance, cut themselves loose from all other Christians, and made quite a religious stir among many good people for a while. They were very clear and powerful in their presentation of certain phases of truth, but they were also very strong, if not bitter, in their denunciations of all existing religious organizations. They attacked the churches, pointing out so skillfully and with such professions of sanctity what they considered wrong that many people were made most dissatisfied with the churches (including The Salvation Army).

A Salvation Army captain (minister) listened to them and was greatly moved by their fervor, their burning appeals, their religious ecstasy, and their denunciations of the lukewarmness of other Christians. She began to wonder if they were right after all and the Holy Spirit was not among us. Her heart was full of distress, and she cried to God. And then the vision of our slum officers rose before her eyes. She saw their devotion and sacrifice, their lowly, hidden service year after year among the poor and ignorant and vicious, and she said to herself, "Is not this the Spirit of Jesus? Would these men who denounce us so be willing to forgo their religious ecstasies and spend their lives in such lowly, unheralded service?" And the mists that had begun to blind her eyes were swept away, and she saw Jesus still among us going about doing good in the person of our slum officers—and all who for His name's sake sacrifice their time, money, and strength to bless and save others.

Another captain used to slip out of bed early in the morning to pray and then black his own and his assistant's boots, and God mightily blessed him. I saw him recently—now a commissioner with thousands under his command—at an outing in the woods by the lakeshore, looking after poor and forgotten souls and giving them food with his own hand. Like the Lord, his eyes seemed to be in every place beholding opportunities to do good, and his feet and hands always followed his eyes. That is the fruit of the indwelling Holy Spirit.

You who have visions of glory and rapturous delight, and so count yourselves filled with the Spirit, do these visions lead you to virtue and to lowly, loving service? If not, watch yourselves, lest, exalted like Capernaum to heaven, you are at last cast down to hell (see Matt. 11:23). Thank God for the mounts of transfiguration where we behold His glory! But down below in the valley are suffering children, and to them He would have us go with the glory of the mount on our faces, lowly love and vigorous faith in our hearts, and clean hands ready for any service. He would have us give ourselves to them. And if we love Him, if we follow Him, if we are truly filled with the Holy Spirit, we will.

Hope

Are you ever cast down and depressed in spirit? Listen to Paul: "I pray that God, the source of hope, will fill you completely with joy and peace because you trust in him. Then you will overflow with confident hope through the power of the Holy Spirit" (Rom. 15:13 NLT). What cheer is in those words! They ring like the shout of a triumph.

God Himself is "the source of hope." There is no gloom, no depression, no wasting sickness of deferred hope in Him. He is a brimming fountain and ocean of hope eternally, and He is our God. He is our hope.

Out of His infinite fullness He is to fill us—not half fill us, but fill us "completely with joy and peace."

And this is not by some condition or means that is so high and difficult that we cannot perform our part, but it is simply by trusting in Him—something the little child and the aged philosopher, the poor and the rich, the ignorant and the learned can do. And the result will be an overflowing "with confident hope through the power of the Holy Spirit."

And what power is that? If it is physical power, then the power of a million Niagaras and flowing oceans and rushing worlds is as nothing compared to it. If it is mental power, then the power of Plato and Bacon and Milton and Shakespeare and Newton is as the light of a firefly to the sun when compared to it. If it is spiritual power, then there is nothing with which it can be compared. But suppose it is all three in one, infinite and eternal! This is the power, throbbing with love and mercy, to which we are to bring our little hearts by living faith, and God will fill us with joy and peace and hope by the incoming of the Holy Spirit.

God's people are a hopeful people. They hope in God, with whom there is no change, no weakness, no decay. In the darkest night and the fiercest storm they still hope in Him, though it may be feebly. But He would have His people "abound in hope" (Rom. 15:13 KJV) so that they should always be buoyant, triumphant.

But how can this be in a world such as this? We are surrounded by awful, mysterious, and merciless forces that may overwhelm us at any moment. The fire may burn us, the water may drown us, the hurricane may sweep us away, friends may desert us, foes may master us. There is the depression that comes from failing health or poverty, from overwork and sleepless nights and constant care, from thwarted plans, disappointed ambitions, slighted love, and base ingratitude. Old age comes on with its gray hairs, failing strength, dimness of sight, dullness of hearing, tottering step, shortness of breath, and general weakness and decay. The friends of youth die, and a new, strange, pushing generation that knows you not comes, elbowing you aside and taking your place. Though in time past some blessed outpouring of the Spirit saw the work of God revive, suffering souls saved, Zion put on her beautiful garments, reforms of all kind advance, the desert blossom as the rose, the waste place become a fruitful field, and the millennium seemed just at hand, the woeful day arrives in which the spiritual tide recedes; the forces of evil are emboldened and they mass themselves and sweep again over the heritage of the Lord, leaving it waste and desolate. And the battle must be fought over again.

How can one be always hopeful, always abounding in hope, in such a world? It is possible only "through the power of the Holy Spirit," and this power will not fail as long as we fix our eyes on eternal things and believe.

The Holy Spirit, dwelling within, turns our eyes from that which is temporal to that which is eternal, from the trial itself to God's purpose in the trial, from the present pain to the precious promise.

I am now writing in a little city made rich by vast potteries. If the dull, heavy clay on the potter's wheel and in the fiery oven could think and speak, it would doubtless cry out against the fierce agony. But if it could foresee the potter's purpose in it, and the thing of use and beauty he meant to make it, it would nestle low under his hand and rejoice in hope.

We are clay in the hand of the divine Potter, but we can think and speak and in some measure understand His high purpose in us. It is the work of the Holy Spirit to make us understand. And if we will not be dull and senseless and unbelieving, He will illuminate us and fill us with peaceful, joyous hope.

He would reveal to us that our heavenly Potter has Himself been on the wheel and in the fiery furnace, learning obedience and being fashioned into "the captain of [our] salvation" (Heb. 2:10 KJV) by the things He suffered. When we are tempted and tried and tempest-tossed, He raises our hope by showing us Jesus suffering and sympathizing with us, tempted in all points as we are, and so able and wise and willing to help us in our struggle and conflict (see Heb. 2:9–18).

He assures us that Jesus, into whose hands is committed all power in heaven and earth, is our elder Brother, "touched with the feeling of our infirmities" (Heb. 4:15 KJV), and He encourages us to rest in Him and not be afraid. So we abound in hope through His power as we believe.

He also reveals to us God's eternal purpose in our trials and difficulties. Listen to Paul: "All things work together for good to them that love God" (Rom. 8:28 KJV). "We know this," said Paul. But how can this be? Ah, there is where faith must be exercised. It is in believing that we "overflow with confident hope through the power of the Holy Spirit" (Rom. 15:13 NLT).

God's wisdom and ability to make all things work together for our good are not to be measured by our understanding but firmly held by our faith. My child is in serious difficulty and does not know how to help himself, but I say, "Leave it to me." He may not understand how I am to help him, but he trusts me, and rejoices in hope. We are God's dear children, and He knows how to help us and make all things work together for our good, if we will only commit ourselves to Him in faith.

Thou art as much His care as if beside

Nor man nor angel lived in heaven or earth;

Thus sunbeams pour alike their glorious tide,

To light up worlds, or wake an insect's mirth.[1]

When afflictions overtake us, the Holy Spirit encourages our hope and makes it abound by many promises: "For our present troubles are small and won't last very long. Yet they produce for us a glory that vastly outweighs them and will last forever! So we don't look at the troubles we can see now; rather, we fix our gaze on things that cannot be seen. For the things we see now will soon be gone, but the things we cannot see will last forever" (2 Cor. 4:17–18 NLT).

But such a promise as that only mocks us if we do not believe. "In all their suffering he also suffered, and he personally rescued them. In his love and mercy he redeemed them. He lifted them up and carried them through all the years" (Isa. 63:9 NLT). And He is just the same today. To some He says, "I have refined you in the furnace of suffering" (Isa. 48:10 NLT), and nestling down into His will and believing, they "overflow with confident hope through the power of the Holy Spirit" (Rom. 15:13 NLT).

He turns our eyes back upon Job in his loss and pain, Joseph sold into Egyptian slavery, Daniel in the lions' den, the three Hebrews in the fiery furnace, and Paul in prison and shipwreck and manifold perils. And, showing us their steadfastness and their final triumph, He prompts us to hope in God.

When weakness of body overtakes us, He encourages us with such assurances as these: "My health may fail, and my spirit may grow weak, but God remains the strength of my heart; he is mine forever" (Ps. 73:26 NLT) and, "Though our bodies are dying, our spirits are being renewed every day" (2 Cor. 4:16 NLT).

When old age comes creeping on apace, we can rely on His promise to meet the need, that our hope fail not. The psalmist prayed, "And now, in my old age, don't set me aside. Don't abandon me when my strength is failing. . . . Now that I am old and gray, do not abandon me, O God. Let me proclaim your power to this new generation, your mighty miracles to all who come after me" (Ps. 71:9, 18 NLT).

And through Isaiah the Lord replied, "Even to your old age and gray hairs I am he, I am he who will sustain you. I have made you and I will carry you; I will sustain you and I will rescue you" (Isa. 46:4 NIV).

And David cried out, "But the godly will flourish like palm trees and grow strong like the cedars of Lebanon. For they are transplanted to the LORD's own house. They flourish in the courts of our God. Even in old age they will still produce fruit; they will remain vital and green. They will declare, 'The LORD is just! He is my rock!'" (Ps. 92:12–15 NLT).

The Bible is full of such promises. They have been given by infinite wisdom and love to meet us at every point of doubt and fear and need that, in believing them, we may have a steadfast and glad hope in God. He is pledged to help us. He says, "Don't be afraid, for I am with you. Don't be discouraged, for I am your God. I will strengthen you and help you. I will hold you up with my victorious right hand" (Isa. 41:10 NLT).

When life's waves and billows seemed to sweep over the psalmist, and his soul was bowed within him, three times he cried, "Why am I discouraged? Why is my heart so sad? I will put my hope in God! I will praise him again—my Savior and my God!" (Ps. 42:5 NLT).

And Jeremiah, remembering the wormwood and the gall, and the deep mire of the dungeon into which they had plunged him and from which he had scarcely been delivered, said, "It is good to wait quietly for salvation from the LORD" (Lam. 3:26 NLT).

When the Holy Spirit is come, He brings to remembrance these precious promises and makes them living words. And if we believe, the whole heaven of our soul shall be lit up with abounding hope. It is only through ignorance of God's promises, or through weak and wavering faith, that hope is dimmed. Oh, that we may heed the still small voice of the heavenly Comforter and steadfastly, joyously believe!

My hope is built on nothing less
Than Jesus' blood and righteousness;
When all around my soul gives way,
He then is all my hope and stay.[2]

NOTES

1. John Keble, quoted in Mary Wilder Tileston, *Daily Strength for Daily Needs* (Boston: Roberts Brothers, 1889), 56.

2. Edward Mote, "My Hope Is Built on Nothing Less," 1834, public domain.

The Holy Spirit's Substitute for Gossip and Evil-Speaking 11

The other day I heard a man of God say, "We cannot bridle the tongues of the people among whom we live; they will talk." And by "talk," he meant gossip and criticism and faultfinding.

> You never can tell when you send a word
> Like an arrow shot from a bow
> By an archer blind, be it cruel or kind,
> Just where it will chance to go.
> It may pierce the breast of your dearest friend,
> Tipped with its poison or balm,
> To a stranger's heart in life's great mart
> It may carry its pain or its calm.[1]

The wise mother, when she finds her little boy playing with a sharp knife or looking glass or some dainty dish, does not snatch it away with a slap on his cheek or harsh words, but quietly and gently substitutes a safer and more interesting toy, and so avoids a storm.

A sensible father who finds his boy reading a book of dangerous tendency will kindly point out its character and substitute a better book that is equally interesting.

When children want to spend their evenings on the street, thoughtful and intelligent parents will seek to make their evenings at home more healthfully attractive.

When we seek to rid our minds of evil and hurtful thoughts, we will find it wise to follow Paul's exhortation to the Philippians: "Fix your thoughts on what is true, and honorable, and right, and pure, and lovely, and admirable. Think about things that are excellent and worthy of praise" (Phil. 4:8 NLT). Anyone who faithfully, patiently, and persistently accepts this program of Paul's will find evil thoughts vanishing away.

This is the Holy Spirit's method. He has a pleasant and safe substitute for gossip and faultfinding and slander. Here it is: "Be filled with the Holy Spirit, singing psalms and hymns and spiritual songs among yourselves, and making music to the Lord in your hearts. And give thanks for everything to God the Father in the name of our Lord Jesus Christ" (Eph. 5:18–20 NLT). This is certainly a fruit of being filled with the Spirit.

Many years ago the Lord gave me a blessed revival in a little village in which nearly every soul in the place, as well as farmers from the surrounding country, experienced new life in Christ. One result was that they now had no time for gossip and doubtful talk about their neighbors. They were all talking about religion and rejoicing in the things of the Lord. If they met each other on the street or in some shop or store, they praised the Lord and encouraged each other to press on in the heavenly way. If they met someone who wasn't a Christian, they tenderly besought him or her to be reconciled to God, to give up his or her sins, to "flee from the wrath to come" (Luke 3:7 KJV), and to start at once for heaven. If they met in each other's houses, they gathered around the organ or piano and sang hymns and songs, and did not part until they had united in prayer.

There was no criticizing of their neighbors, no grumbling and complaining about the weather, no faultfinding with their lot in life or their daily surroundings and circumstances. Their conversation was joyous, cheerful, and helpful to one another. Nor was it forced and out of place, but rather it was the natural, spontaneous outflow of loving, humble, glad hearts filled with the Spirit, in union with Jesus, and in love and sympathy with everyone.

This is our heavenly Father's ideal of social and spiritual interaction for His children on earth. He would not have us separate ourselves from each other and shut ourselves up in convents and monasteries in austere asceticism on the one hand, nor would He have us light and foolish, or faultfinding and censorious on the other hand, but sociable, cheerful, and full of tender, considerate love.

On the day of Pentecost, when they were all filled with the Holy Spirit and a multitude came to faith in Christ, we read that they "worshiped together at the Temple each day, met in homes for the Lord's Supper, and shared their meals with great joy and generosity—all the while praising God and enjoying the goodwill of all the people" (Acts 2:46–47 NLT). This is a sample of the brotherly love and unity our heavenly Father would have throughout the whole earth. But how the breath of gossip and evil-speaking would have marred this heavenly fellowship and separated these "chief friends" (Prov. 16:28 KJV).

> Lord! subdue our selfish will;
> Each to each our tempers suit
> By Thy modulating skill,
> Heart to heart, as lute to lute.[2]

However, let no one suppose that the Holy Spirit accomplishes this heavenly work by some overwhelming baptism that does away with the need of our cooperation. He does not override us but works with us, and we must intelligently and determinedly work with Him in this matter.

People often fall into idle and hurtful gossip and evil-speaking not so much from ill-will as from old habit, as a wagon falls into a rut. Or they drift into it with the current of conversation about them. Or they are beguiled into it by a desire to say something and be pleasant and entertaining.

But when the Holy Spirit comes, He lifts us out of the old ruts, and we must follow Him with care lest we fall into them again, possibly never more to escape. He gives us life and power to stem the adverse currents about us, but we must exercise ourselves not to be swept downward by them. He does not destroy the desire to please, but He subordinates it to the desire to help and bless, and we must stir ourselves up to do this.

When Frances Ridley Havergal was asked to sing and play before a worldly company, she sang a sweet song about Jesus and, without displeasing anybody, greatly blessed the company. At a breakfast party John Fletcher told his experience so sweetly and naturally that all hearts were stirred, the Holy Spirit fell upon the company, and they ended with a glorious prayer meeting. William Bramwell used to steadily and persistently turn the conversation at meals into spiritual channels, to the blessing of all who were present, so that they had two meals—one for the body and one for the soul. To do this wisely and helpfully requires thought and prayer and a fixed purpose—and a tender, loving heart filled with the Holy Spirit. I know a mother who seeks to have a brief season of prayer and a verse of Scripture just before going to dinner to prepare her heart to guide the conversation along spiritual highways.

Are you similarly careful? Do you have victory in this matter? If not, seek it right now in simple, trustful prayer, and the Lord who loves you will surely answer and will be your helper from this time forth. He surely will. Believe right now, and henceforth "conduct yourselves in a manner worthy of the gospel of Christ" (Phil. 1:27 NIV).

I ask Thee, ever blessed Lord,

That I may never speak a word,

Of envy born, or passion stirred.

First, true to Thee in heart and mind,

Then always to my neighbor kind,

By Thy good hand to good inclined.

Oh, save from words that bear a sting,

That pain to any brother bring:
Inbreathe Thy calm in everything.
Let love within my heart prevail,
To rule my words when thoughts assail,
That, hid in Thee, I may not fail.
I know, my Lord, Thy power within
Can save from all the power of sin;
In Thee let every word begin.
Should I be silent? Keep me still,
Glad waiting on my Master's will:
Thy message through my lips fulfill.
Give me Thy words when I should speak,
For words of Thine are never weak,
But break the proud, but raise the meek.
Into Thy lips all grace is poured,
Speak Thou through me, Eternal Word,
Of thought, of heart, of lips the Lord.[3]

NOTES

1. Ella Wheeler Wilcox, "You Never Can Tell," *The Best Loved Poems of the American People*, ed. Hazel Felleman (New York: Doubleday, 1936), 144.

2. Charles Wesley, "Lord, Subdue Our Selfish Will," 1848, public domain.

3. Author unknown, "Speak Thou through Me," *The Herald of Christ's Kingdom* 29, no. 2 (February 1946), n. p.

The Sin against the Holy Spirit

God is love, and the Holy Spirit is ceaselessly striving to make this love known in our hearts, to work out God's purposes of love in our lives, and to transform and transfigure our characters by love. And so we are solemnly warned against resisting the Spirit and almost tearfully and always tenderly exhorted to "quench not the Spirit" (1 Thess. 5:19 KJV) and not to "grieve the Holy Spirit of God, by whom you were sealed for the day of redemption" (Eph. 4:30 NKJV).

There is one great sin against which Jesus warned, as a sin never to be forgiven in this world or in that which is to come. That was blasphemy against the Holy Spirit.

That there is such a sin, Jesus taught in Matthew 12:31–32; Mark 3:28–30; and Luke 12:10. And it may be that this is the sin referred to in Hebrews 6:4–6 and 10:29.

Since many of God's dear children have fallen into dreadful distress through fear that they had committed this sin, it may be helpful for us to carefully study what constitutes it.

On one occasion, Jesus was casting out devils, and Mark said that "the teachers of religious law who had arrived from Jerusalem said, 'He's possessed by Satan, the prince of demons. That's where he gets the power to cast out demons'" (Mark 3:22 NLT). To this Jesus replied with gracious kindness and searching logic: "How can Satan cast out Satan? . . . A kingdom divided by civil war will collapse. Similarly, a family splintered by feuding will fall apart. And if Satan is divided and fights against himself, how can he stand? He would never survive. Let me illustrate this further. Who is powerful enough to enter the house of a strong man like Satan and plunder his goods? Only someone even stronger—someone who could tie him up and then plunder his house" (Mark 3:23–27 NLT).

In this quiet reply, we see that Jesus did not rail against them, nor flatly deny their base assertion that He did His miracles by the Devil's power, but showed how logically false their statement was. And then, with grave authority (and I think with solemn tenderness in His voice and eyes), He added, "I tell you the truth, all sin and blasphemy can be forgiven, but anyone who blasphemes the Holy Spirit will never be forgiven. This is a sin with eternal consequences" (Mark 3:28–29 NLT). Then Mark added, "He told them this because they were saying, 'He's possessed by an evil spirit'" (Mark 3:30 NLT).

Jesus came into the world to reveal God's truth and love to people, and to save them, and we are saved by believing in Him. But how could the people of His day—who saw Him working at the carpenter's bench and living the life of an ordinary man of humble toil and daily temptation and trial—believe His stupendous claim to be the only-begotten Son of God, the Savior of the world, and the final Judge of all? Any willful and proud impostor could make such a claim. But people *could* not and *ought* not to believe such an assertion unless the claim was supported by indisputable evidence. This evidence Jesus began to give not only in the holy life He lived and the pure gospel He preached, but also in the blind eyes He opened, the sick He healed, the hungry thousands He fed, the seas He stilled, the dead He raised to life again, and the devils He cast out of bound and harassed souls.

The scribes and Pharisees witnessed these miracles and were compelled to admit these signs and wonders. Nicodemus, one of their number, said to Jesus, "Rabbi . . . we all know that God has sent you to teach us. Your miraculous signs are evidence that God is with you" (John 3:2 NLT). Would they now admit His claim to be the Son of God, their promised and long-looked-for Messiah? They were thoughtful and very religious, but not spiritual. The gospel He preached was Spirit and life; it appealed to their conscience and revealed their sin, and to acknowledge Him was to admit that they themselves were wrong. It meant submission to His authority, the surrender of their wills, and a change of front in their whole inner and outer life. This meant moral and spiritual revolution in every heart and life, and to this they would not submit. And so to avoid such plain inconsistency, they had to discredit His miracles. And since they could not deny them, they declared that He performed them by the Devil's power.

Jesus worked these signs and wonders by the Holy Spirit's power, that He might win their confidence and that they might reasonably believe and become His followers. But they refused to believe, and in their malignant obstinacy heaped scorn upon Him, accusing Him of being in league with the Devil. So how could they be saved? This was the sin against the Holy Spirit against which Jesus warned them. It was not so much one act of sin as a deep-seated, stubborn rebellion against God that led them to choose darkness rather than light, and so to blaspheme against the Spirit of truth and light. It was sin full and ripe and ready for the harvest.

Someone has said,

> This sin cannot be forgiven, not because God is unwilling to forgive . . . but because one who thus sins against the Holy Spirit has put himself where no power can soften his heart or change his nature. A man may misuse his eyes and yet see; but whosoever puts them out can never see again. One may misdirect his mariner's compass and turn it aside from the north pole by a magnet or piece of iron, and it may recover and point right again; but whosoever destroys the compass itself has lost his guide at sea.[1]

Many of God's dear children—honest souls—have been persuaded that they have committed this awful sin. Indeed, I once thought that I myself had done so, and for twenty-eight days I felt that, like Jonah, I was in "the belly of hell" (Jon. 2:2 KJV). But God, in love and tender mercy, drew me out of the horrible pit of doubt and fear, and showed me that this is a sin committed only by those who, in spite of all evidence, harden their hearts in unbelief and deny and blaspheme the Lord to shield themselves in their sins. It is a result of willful refusal and rejection of light, and in that direction lies hardness of heart beyond recovery, fullness of sin, and final impenitence, which are unpardonable.

Doubtless many through resistance to the Holy Spirit come to this awful state of heart. But those troubled, anxious souls who think they have committed this sin are not usually among the number.

One night a gentleman arose during a revival in Canada and with deep emotion urged those present to yield themselves to God, accept Jesus as their Savior, and receive the Holy Spirit. He told them that he had once been a Christian, but that he had not walked in the light and consequently had sinned against the Holy Spirit and could nevermore be pardoned. Then, with all earnest tenderness, he exhorted them to be warned by his sad state and not to harden their hearts against the gracious influences, and he entreated them to yield to the Savior. Suddenly the scales of doubt dropped from his eyes, and he saw that he had not in his inmost heart rejected Jesus, and so had not committed the unpardonable sin. He saw that,

> The love of God is broader
> Than the measure of man's mind:
> And the heart of the Eternal
> Is most wonderfully kind.[2]

In an instant his heart was filled with light and love and peace and sweet assurance that Christ Jesus was his Savior.

I have known three people—in one meeting—who thought they had committed this sin, and who, bowed with grief and fear, came to the penitent form (the kneeler in the church where forgiveness is sought) to find deliverance.

The English poet William Cowper was plunged into unutterable gloom by the conviction that he had committed this awful sin. But God tenderly brought him into the light and sweet comforts of the Holy Spirit again, and doubtless it was in the sense of such loving-kindness that he wrote:

> There is a fountain filled with blood,
> Drawn from Emanuel's veins;
> And sinners plunged beneath that flood
> Lose all their guilty stains.[3]

John Bunyan was also afflicted with horrible fears that he had committed this sin. In *Grace Abounding to the Chief of Sinners* (a book I earnestly recommend to all), he tells how he was delivered from his doubts and was filled once more with the joy of the Lord. There are portions of his book *The Pilgrim's Progress* that should be interpreted in the light of this grievous experience.

Those who think they have committed this sin may generally be assured that they have not. Their hearts are usually very tender, while this sin must harden the heart past all feeling. They are full of sorrow and shame for having neglected God's grace and trifled with the Savior's dying words, but such sorrow could not exist in a heart so fully given over to sin that pardon was impossible. God says, "Whosoever will may come" (see Rev. 22:17). So if they find it in their hearts to come, they will not be cast out but freely pardoned and received with loving-kindness through the merits of Jesus' blood. God's promise will not fail. His faithfulness is established in the heavens. Those who have committed this sin are full of evil, do not care to come, and will not, and therefore are never pardoned. Their sin is eternal.

NOTES

1. F. N. Peloubet, *The Teachers' Commentary on the Gospel According to St. Matthew* (New York: Oxford University Press, 1901), 153.

2. Frederick W. Faber, "There's a Wideness in God's Mercy," 1854, public domain

3. William Cowper, "There Is a Fountain Filled with Blood," 1772, public domain.

Offenses against the Holy Spirit 13

One day in a fit of boyish temper, I spoke hot words of anger—
somewhat unjustly—against another person, and this deeply grieved
my mother. She said little, and though her sweet face has moldered
many years beneath the Southern daisies, I can still see her look of grief
across the years of a third of a century. That is the one sad memory of
my childhood. A stranger might have been amused or incensed at my
words, but Mother was grieved—grieved to her heart by my lack of
generous, self-forgetful, thoughtful love.

We can anger a stranger or an enemy, but it is only a friend we
grieve. The Holy Spirit is such a friend, more tender and faithful than
a mother. And shall we carelessly offend Him and estrange ourselves
from Him in spite of His love?

There is a sense in which every sin is against the Holy Spirit. Of
course, not every such sin is unpardonable, but the tendency of all sin

is in that direction, and we are only safe as we avoid the very beginnings of sin. Only as we "walk in the Spirit" are we "free from the law of sin and death" (Rom. 8:2 KJV). Therefore, it is infinitely important that we be aware of offenses against the Spirit, "lest any of you be hardened through the deceitfulness of sin" (Heb. 3:13 KJV).

Grieving the Holy Spirit is a very common and sad offense of professing Christians, and it is to this that much of the weakness and ignorance and joylessness of so many followers of Christ must be attributed.

Jesus is grieved, as was my mother, by the unloving speech and spirit of God's children. Paul, in his letters to the Ephesians, said, "Don't use foul or abusive language. Let everything you say be good and helpful, so that your words will be an encouragement to those who hear them." And then he added,

> And do not bring sorrow to God's Holy Spirit by the way you live. Remember, he has identified you as his own, guaranteeing that you will be saved on the day of redemption. Get rid of all bitterness, rage, anger, harsh words, and slander, as well as all types of evil behavior. Instead, be kind to each other, tenderhearted, forgiving one another, just as God through Christ has forgiven you. Imitate God, therefore, in everything you do, because you are his dear children. Live a life filled with love, following the example of Christ. He loved us and offered himself as a sacrifice for us, a pleasing aroma to God. (Eph. 4:29—5:2 NLT)

What does Paul teach us here? That it is not by some huge wickedness, some Judas-like betrayal, some tempting and lying to the Holy Spirit as Ananias and Sapphira did (see Acts 5:1–9) that we grieve Him, but by that which most people count little and unimportant: by talk that corrupts instead of blessing and building up those that hear, by gossip, by bitterness, and by uncharitable criticisms and faultfindings. This was the sin of the elder son when the prodigal returned, and it was by this he pierced with grief the kind old father's heart (see Luke 15:11–32).

We grieve Him by getting in a rage; by loud, angry talking and evil-speaking and petty malice; by unkindness and hard-heartedness and an unforgiving spirit. We grieve Him by not walking through the world as in our Father's house and among our neighbors and friends as though among His dear children, by not loving tenderly and making kindly sacrifices for one another. And this is not a matter of little importance. It may have sadly momentous consequences.

It is a bitter, cruel, and often irreparable thing to trifle with a valuable earthly friendship. How much more when the friendship is heavenly — when the friend is our Lord and Savior, our Creator and Redeemer, our Governor and Judge, our Teacher, Guide, and God? When we trifle with a friend's wishes — especially when such wishes are all in perfect harmony with and for our highest possible good — we may not estrange the friend from us, but we estrange ourselves from our friend. Our hearts grow cold toward him or her, though his or her heart may be breaking with longing toward us. The more Saul ill-treated David, the more he hated David.

Such estrangement may lead little by little to yet greater sin, to strange hardness of heart, to doubts and unbelief and denial of the Lord.

The cure for all this is a clean heart full of sweet, gentle, self-forgetful, generous love. Then we shall be "followers of God, as dear children," then we shall "walk in love, as Christ . . . loved us, and [gave] himself for us" (Eph. 5:1–2 KJV).

But there is another offense—that of quenching the Spirit—which accounts for the comparative darkness and deadness of many of God's children.

In 1 Thessalonians 5:16–19, the apostle said, "Always be joyful. Never stop praying. Be thankful in all circumstances, for this is God's will for you who belong to Christ Jesus. Do not stifle the Holy Spirit" (NLT).

When will the Lord's dear children learn that the religion of Jesus is a lowly thing and that it is the little foxes that spoil the vines? Does not the apostle here teach that it is not by some desperate, dastardly deed that we quench the Spirit, but simply by neglecting to rejoice and pray and give thanks at all times and for all things?

It is not necessary to blot the sun out of the heavens to keep the sunlight out of your house—just close the blinds and draw the curtains. Nor do you pour barrels of water on the flames to quench the fire—just shut off the draft. Nor do you dynamite the city reservoir and destroy all the mains and pipes to cut off your supply of sparkling water, but just refrain from turning on the main.

So you do not need to do some great evil, some deadly sin, to quench the Spirit. Just cease to rejoice, through fear of human opinion and of being peculiar; be prim and proper as a white and polished gravestone; let gushing joy be curbed; neglect to pray when you feel a gentle pull in your heart to get alone with the Lord; omit giving hearty thanks for all God's tender mercies, faithful discipline, and loving chastening, and soon you will find the Spirit quenched. He will no longer spring up joyously like a well of living water within you.

But give the Spirit a vent, an opening, a chance, and He will rise within you and flood your soul with light and love and joy.

Some years ago a sanctified woman of clear experience went alone to keep her daily hour with God. But, to her surprise, it seemed that she could not find Him, either in prayer or in His Word. She searched her heart for evidence of sin, but the Spirit showed her nothing contrary to God in her mind, heart, or will. She searched her memory for any breach of covenant, any broken vows, any neglect, any omission, but could find none.

Then she asked the Lord to show her if there were any duty unfulfilled, any command unnoticed, which she might perform, and quick as thought came the often-read words, "Rejoice evermore" (1 Thess. 5:16 KJV). "Have you done that this morning?"

She had not. It had been a busy morning, and a well-spent one, but so far there had been no definite rejoicing in her heart, though the manifold riches and ground for joy of all Christians were hers.

At once she began to count her blessings and thank the Lord for each one, and to rejoice in Him for all the ways He had led her and the gifts He had bestowed, and in a very few minutes the Lord stood revealed to her spiritual consciousness.

She had not committed sin, nor resisted the Spirit, but a failure to rejoice in Him who had daily loaded her with benefits had in a measure quenched the Spirit. She had not turned on the main, and so her soul was not flooded with living waters. She had not remembered the command, "Rejoice before the LORD your God in all that you undertake" (Deut. 12:18 ESV). But that morning she learned a lifelong lesson, and she has ever since safeguarded her soul by obeying the many commands to "Rejoice in the Lord" (Phil. 4:4 KJV).

Grieving and quenching the Spirit will not only leave an individual soul barren and desolate, but it will do so for a church, community, whole nation, or continent. We see this illustrated on a large scale by the long and weary Dark Ages, when the light of the gospel was almost extinguished, and only here and there was the darkness broken by the torch of truth held aloft by some humble, suffering soul that had wept and prayed and through painful struggles had found the light.

We see it also in those churches, communities, and countries where revivals are unknown, or are a thing of the past, where souls are not born into the kingdom, and where there is no joyous shout of victory among the people of God.

Grieving and quenching the Spirit may be done unintentionally by lack of thought and prayer and hearty devotion to the Lord Jesus, but they prepare the way and lead to intentional and positive resistance to the Spirit. To resist the Spirit is to fight against Him.

The person who listens to the gospel invitation and—convicted of sin—refuses to submit to God in true repentance and faith in Jesus is resisting the Holy Spirit. We have bold and striking historical illustrations of the danger of resisting the Holy Spirit in the disasters that befell Pharaoh and the terrible calamities that came upon Jerusalem.

The ten plagues that came upon Pharaoh and his people were ten opportunities and open doors into God's favor and fellowship, which they themselves shut by their stubborn resistance, only to be overtaken by dreadful catastrophe.

To the Jewish leaders in Jerusalem, Stephen said, "You always resist the Holy Spirit!" (Acts 7:51 NIV). And the siege and fall of Jerusalem, the butchery and banishment and enslavement of its inhabitants, and all the woes that came upon that city's people, followed their rejection of Jesus and the hardness of heart and spiritual blindness which swiftly overtook them when they resisted all the loving efforts and entreaties of His disciples baptized with the Holy Spirit.

And what befalls nations and people also befalls individuals. Those who receive and obey the Lord are enlightened and blessed and saved; those who resist and reject Him are sadly left to themselves and surely swallowed up in destruction.

Likewise, professing Christians who hear of heart-holiness and cleansing from all sin as a blessing they may now have by faith and—convicted of their need of the blessing and of God's desire and willingness to bestow it upon them now—refuse to seek it in wholehearted affectionate consecration and faith, are resisting the Holy Spirit. And such resistance imperils the soul beyond all possible computation.

We see an example of this in the Israelites who were brought out of Egypt with signs and wonders and led through the Red Sea and the wilderness to the borders of Canaan but, forgetting, refused to go over into the land. In this they resisted the Holy Spirit in His leadings as surely as Pharaoh did, and with quite as disastrous results to themselves, perishing in their evil way. For their sin was much greater than his as their light exceeded his.

Hundreds of years later, a prophet, writing of this time, said, "In all their suffering he also suffered, and he personally rescued them. In his love and mercy he redeemed them. He lifted them up and carried them through all the years. But they rebelled against him and grieved his Holy Spirit. So he became their enemy and fought against them" (Isa. 63:9–10 NLT).

We see from this that Christians must beware and watch and pray and walk softly with the Lord in glad obedience and childlike faith if they would escape the darkness and dryness that result from grieving and quenching the Spirit and the dangers that surely come from resisting Him.

Arm me with jealous care,

As in Thy sight to live;

And, O, Thy servant, Lord, prepare,

A strict account to give.

Help me to watch and pray,

And on Thyself rely,

Assured if I my trust betray,

I shall forever die.[1]

NOTE

1. Charles Wesley, "A Charge to Keep I Have," 1762, public domain.

The Holy Spirit and Sound Doctrine 14

Is Jesus Christ divine? Is the Bible an inspired book? Are we fallen creatures who can be saved only through the suffering and sacrifice of the Creator? Will there be a resurrection of the dead and a day in which God will judge the world by the Man, Christ Jesus? Is Satan a personal being, and is there a hell in which the wicked will be forever punished?

These are great doctrines that have been held and taught by the followers of Christ since the days of Jesus and His apostles, and yet they are ever being attacked and denied.

Are they true? Or are they only fancies and falsehoods, or figures of speech and distortions of truth? How can we find truth and know it? Jesus said, "When he, the Spirit of truth, is come, he will guide you into all truth" (John 16:13 KJV).

What truth? Not the truth of the multiplication table, or of physical science, or art, or secular history, but spiritual truth—the truth about

God, His will and character, and our relations to Him in Christ, that truth which is necessary to salvation and holiness. Into all this truth the Holy Spirit will guide us. "He shall teach you all things," said Jesus (John 14:26 KJV).

How, then, shall we escape error and be sound in doctrine? Only by the Holy Spirit's help. How do we know Jesus Christ is divine? Because the Bible tells us so? Infinitely precious and important is this revelation in the Bible, but not by this do we know it. Because the church teaches it in its creed and we have heard it from the catechism? Nothing taught in any creed or catechism is of more vital importance, but neither by this do we know it.

How then? Listen to Paul: "No one can say Jesus is Lord, except by the Holy Spirit" (1 Cor. 12:3 NLT). "No one," said Paul. Then learning it from the Bible or catechism is not to know it except as the parrot might know it, but all are to be taught this by the Holy Spirit, if they are to really know it.

Then it is not a revelation made once for all, and only to those who walked and talked with Jesus, but it is a spiritual revelation made anew to each believing heart that in penitence seeks Him and so meets the conditions of such a revelation.

Then the poor, ignorant outcast at The Salvation Army penitent form in the slums of London or Chicago who never heard of a creed and the primitive villager who never saw the inside of a Bible may have Christ revealed in them, and know by the revelation of the Holy Spirit that Jesus is Lord.

"It pleased God . . . to reveal his Son in me," wrote Paul (Gal. 1:15–16 KJV), who also said, "Christ lives in me" (Gal. 2:20 NLT). He wrote to the Galatians, "My dear children, for whom I am again in the pains of childbirth until Christ is formed in you" (Gal. 4:19 NIV), as though Christ is to be spiritually formed in the heart of each believer by the operation of the Holy Spirit, as He was physically formed in the womb of Mary by the same Spirit (see Luke 1:35). And again: "The mystery hidden for ages and generations but now revealed to his saints . . . is Christ in you, the hope of glory" (Col. 1:26–27 ESV). "That Christ may dwell in your hearts by faith" (Eph. 3:17 KJV). "Examine yourselves to see whether you are in the faith; test yourselves. Do you not realize that Christ Jesus is in you—unless, of course, you fail the test" (2 Cor. 13:5 NIV).

"When I am raised to life again," said Jesus, when making His great promise of the Comforter to His disciples, "you will know that I am in my Father, and you are in me, and I am in you" (John 14:20 NLT). And in His Great Priestly Prayer, He said, "I have revealed you to them, and I will continue to do so. Then your love for me will be in them, and I will be in them" (John 17:26 NLT).

It is this ever-recurring revelation to penitent, believing hearts, by the agency of the ever-present Holy Spirit, that makes faith in Jesus Christ living and invincible. "I know He is Lord, for He saves my soul from sin, and He saves me now," is an argument that rationalism and unbelief cannot answer nor overthrow, and as long as there are men and women in the world who can say this, faith in the divinity of Jesus Christ is secure. And this experience and witness come by the Holy Spirit.

I worship Thee, O Holy Ghost,

I love to worship Thee;

My risen Lord for aye were lost

But for Thy company.[1]

And so it is by the guidance and teaching of the Holy Spirit that all saving truth becomes vital to us.

It is He who makes the Bible a living book, He who convinces the world of judgment (see John 16:8–11), He who makes us certain there is a heaven of surpassing and enduring glory and joy and a hell of endless sorrow and woe for those who sin away their day of grace and die in impenitence.

Who have been the mightiest and most faithful preachers of the gloom and terror and pain of a perpetual hell? Those who have been the mightiest and most effective preachers of God's compassionate love.

In all periods of great revival, when men and women seemed to live on the borderland and in the vision of eternity, hell has been preached. The leaders in these revivals have been people of prayer and faith and consuming love, but they have also been people who knew the terrors of the Lord (see Job 6:4) and therefore preached the judgments of God. And they proved that the law with its penalties is a schoolmaster to bring souls to Christ (see Gal. 3:24). Fox the Quaker, Bunyan the Baptist, Baxter the Puritan, Wesley and Fletcher and Whitefield and Caughey the Methodists, Finney the Presbyterian, Edwards and Moody the Congregationalists, and William Booth the Salvationist have preached it—not savagely, but tenderly and faithfully, as a mother might warn her child against some great danger that would surely follow careless and selfish wrongdoing.

Who have loved and labored and sacrificed as these have? Their hearts have been a flaming furnace of love and devotion to God and an overflowing fountain of love and compassion for souls. But just in proportion as they have discovered God's love and pity for humanity, so have they discovered His wrath against sin and all obstinate wrongdoing. And as they have caught glimpses of heaven and declared its joys and everlasting glories, so they have seen hell with its endless punishment, and with trembling voice and overflowing eyes have they warned people to "flee from the wrath to come" (Matt. 3:7 KJV).

Were these preachers, throbbing with spiritual life and consumed with devotion to the kingdom of God and the everlasting well-being of their fellow human beings, led to this belief by the Spirit of truth, or were they misled?

"The things of the Spirit . . . are spiritually discerned," said Paul (1 Cor. 2:14 KJV). It is not by searching and philosophizing that these things are found out, but by revelation. "Flesh and blood has not revealed this to you," said Jesus to Peter, "but my Father who is in heaven" (Matt. 16:17 ESV). The great teacher of truth is the Spirit of truth, and the only safe expounders and guardians of sound doctrine are men and women filled with the Holy Spirit.

Study and research have their place, and an important place. But in spiritual things they will be no avail unless prosecuted by spiritual men and women. As well might someone blind from birth attempt to study the starry heavens and someone born deaf undertake to expound and criticize the harmonies of Bach and Beethoven. We must see and hear if we are to speak and write intelligently on such subjects. And so we must be spiritually enlightened to understand spiritual truth.

The greatest danger to any religious organization is that people should arise in its ranks and hold its positions of trust who have learned its great fundamental doctrines by rote, but have no experiential knowledge of their truth inwrought by the mighty anointing of the Holy Spirit, and who are destitute of "an anointing from the Holy One," which, said John, "teaches you about all things" (1 John 2:20, 27 NIV). Why do people deny the divinity of Jesus Christ? Because they have never placed themselves in that relation to the Spirit and met those unchanging conditions that would enable Him to reveal Jesus to them as Savior and Lord.

Why do people dispute the inspiration of the Scriptures? Because the Holy Spirit, who inspired "holy men of God" to write the Book (2 Pet. 1:21 KJV), hides its spiritual sense from unspiritual and unholy men and women.

Why do people doubt a day of judgment and a state of everlasting doom? Because they have never been bowed and broken and crushed beneath the weight of their sin and by a sense of guilt and separation from a holy God that can only be removed by faith in His dying Son.

A horseman lost his way in a pitiless storm on a black and starless night. Suddenly his horse drew back and refused to take another step. He urged it forward, but it only threw itself back upon its haunches. Just then a vivid flash of lightning revealed a great precipice upon the brink of which he stood. It was but an instant, and then the pitchy blackness hid it again from view. But he turned his horse and anxiously rode away from the terrible danger.

A distinguished professor of religion said to me some time ago, "I dislike, I abhor, the doctrine of hell." And then after a while he added, "But three times in my life I have seen that there was eternal separation from God and an everlasting hell for me, if I walked not in the way God was calling me to go."

Into the blackness of the sinning soul's night the Holy Spirit, who is patiently and compassionately seeking the salvation of all humanity, flashes a light that gives a glimpse of eternal things which, heeded, would lead to the sweet peace and security of eternal day. For when the Holy Spirit is heeded and honored, the night passes; the shadows flee; the day dawns; the Sun of Righteousness arises with healing in His wings (see Mal. 4:2); and men and women, saved and sanctified, walk in His light in safety and joy. Doctrines which before were repellent and foolishness to the carnal mind or a stumbling block to the heart of unbelief now become precious and satisfying to the soul, and truths which before were hid in impenetrable darkness or seen only as through dense gloom and fog are now seen clearly as in the light of broad day.

Hold thou the faith that Christ is Lord,
God over all, who died and rose;
And everlasting life bestows
On all who hear the Living Word.
For thee His life blood He out-poured,
His Spirit sets thy spirit free;
Hold thou the faith—He dwells in thee,
And thou in Him, and Christ is Lord![2]

NOTES

1. William Warren, "I Worship Thee, O Holy Ghost," 1877, public domain.

2. Source unknown.

Praying in the Spirit 15

An important work of the Holy Spirit is to teach us how to pray, instruct us what to pray for, and inspire us to pray earnestly without ceasing—and in faith—for the things we desire and the things that are dear to the Lord's heart. In a familiar verse, the poet James Montgomery said:

> Prayer is the burden of a sigh,
> The falling of a tear,
> The upward glancing of the eye,
> When none but God is near.[1]

And no doubt he is right. Prayer is exceedingly simple. The faintest cry for help, a whisper for mercy, is prayer. But when the Holy Spirit comes and fills the soul with His blessed presence, prayer becomes more than a cry. It ceases to be a feeble request and often becomes a strife (see Rom. 15:30; Col. 4:12) for greater things, a conflict, an invincible argument, a wrestling with God, and through it men and women enter into the divine councils and rise into a blessed and responsible fellowship in some important sense with the Father and the Son in the moral government of the world.

It was in this spirit and fellowship that Abraham prayed for Sodom (see Gen. 18:23–32), that Moses interceded for Israel and stood between them and God's hot displeasure (see Ex. 32:7–14), and that Elijah prevailed to shut up the heavens for three years and six months, and then again prevailed in his prayer for rain (see 1 Kings 17–18).

God would have us come to Him not only as a foolish and ignorant child comes, but as an ambassador to His home government, as a full-grown son who has become of age and entered into partnership with his father, as a bride who is one in all interests and affections with the bridegroom.

He would have us "come boldly unto the throne of grace" (Heb. 4:16 KJV) with a well-reasoned and scriptural understanding of what we desire, and with a purpose to ask, seek, and knock (see Matt. 7:7) till we get the thing we wish, being assured that it is according to His will. And this boldness is not inconsistent with the profoundest humility and a sense of utter dependence. Indeed, it is always accompanied by self-distrust and humble reliance upon the merits of Jesus, or else it is merely presumption and unsanctified conceit. This union of assurance and humility, of boldness and dependence, can be secured only by the baptism with the Holy Spirit, and only so can one be prepared and fitted for such prayer.

Three great obstacles hinder mighty prayer: selfishness, unbelief, and the darkness of ignorance and foolishness. The baptism with the

Spirit sweeps away these obstacles and brings in the three great essentials to prayer: faith, love (divine love), and the light of heavenly knowledge and wisdom.

Selfishness must be cast out by the incoming of love. The ambassador must not be seeking personal ends, but the interests of the government and people he or she represents. The son must not be seeking private gain, but the common prosperity of the partnership in which he will fully and lawfully share. The bride must not forget him to whom she belongs, and seek separate ends, but in all ways identify herself with her husband and his interests. So the child of God must come in prayer, unselfishly.

It is the work of the Holy Spirit, with our cooperation and glad consent, to search and destroy selfishness out of our hearts and fill them with pure love for God and others. And when this is done we shall not then be asking selfishly, to please ourselves and gratify our appetites, pride, ambition, ease, or vanity (see James 4:3). We shall seek only our Lord's glory and the common good of our fellow human beings, in which, as coworkers and partners, we shall have a common share.

If we ask for success, it is not that we may be exalted but that God may be glorified, that Jesus may secure the purchase of His blood, that others may be saved, and that the kingdom of heaven be established upon earth. If we ask for daily bread, it is not that we may be full but that we may be fitted for daily duty. If we ask for health, it is not only that we may be free from pain and filled with physical comfort but that we may be spent "in publishing the sinner's Friend,"[2] in fulfilling the work for which God has placed us here.

Unbelief must be destroyed. Doubt paralyzes prayer. Unbelief quenches the spirit of intercession. Only as the eye of faith sees our Father God upon the throne guaranteeing to us rights and privileges by the blood of His Son—and inviting us to come without fear and make our wants known—does prayer rise from the commonplace to the sublime. Only then does it cease to be a feeble, timid cry, and become a mighty spiritual force, moving God Himself in the interests it seeks.

Those who are wise with the wisdom of this world but poor and naked and blind and foolish in matters of faith ask, "Will God change His plans at the request of mere men and women?" And we answer, "Yes," since many of God's plans are made contingent upon the prayers of His people, and He has ordered that prayer offered in faith, according to His will, revealed in His Word, shall be one of the controlling factors in His government of men and women.

Is it God's will that the tides of the Atlantic and Pacific should sweep across the Isthmus of Panama? That tunnels should run under the Alps? That thoughts and words should be winged across the ocean without any visible or tangible medium? Yes. It is His will, if people will it and work to those ends in harmony with His great physical laws. So in the spiritual world there are wonders produced by prayer, and God wills the will of His people when they come to Him in faith and love.

What else is meant by such promises and assurances as these: "I tell you, you can pray for anything, and if you believe that you've received it, it will be yours" (Mark 11:24 NLT). "The earnest prayer of a righteous person has great power and produces wonderful results. Elijah was as human as we are, and yet when he prayed earnestly that no rain would fall, none fell for three and a half years! Then, when he prayed again, the sky sent down rain and the earth began to yield its crops" (James 5:16–18 NLT).

The Holy Spirit dwelling within the heart helps us to understand the things we may pray for, and the heart that is full of love and loyalty to God wants only what is lawful. This is mystery to people who are under the dominion of selfishness and the darkness of unbelief, but it is a soul-thrilling fact to those who are filled with the Holy Spirit.

"What do you want me to do for you?" asked Jesus of the blind man (Luke 18:41 NLT). He respected the will of the blind man, and granted his request, seeing he had faith. And He still respects the vigorous, sanctified will of His people—the will that has been subdued by consecration and faith into loving union with His will.

The Lord answered Abraham on behalf of Sodom till he ceased to ask (see Gen. 18:16–33). "The Lord has had his way so long with Hudson Taylor," said a friend, "that now, Hudson Taylor can have his way with the Lord."

Adoniram Judson lay sick with a fatal illness in faraway Burma. His wife read to him an account of the conversion of a number of Jews in Constantinople through some of his writings. For a while, the sick man was silent, and then he spoke with awe, telling his wife that for years he had prayed that he might be used in some way to bless the Jews, yet had never seen any evidence that his prayers were answered. But now, after many years and from far away, the evidence of answer had come. And then, after further silence, he spoke with deep emotion, saying that he had never prayed a prayer for the glory of God and the good of others but that, sooner or later (even though for the time being he had forgotten), he found that God had not forgotten but had remembered and patiently worked to answer his prayer.

Oh, the faithfulness of God! He means it when He makes promises and exhorts and urges and commands us to pray. It is not His purpose to mock us, but to answer and "to do exceeding abundantly above all that we ask or think" (Eph. 3:20 KJV).

Knowledge and wisdom must take the place of foolish ignorance. Paul said, "We don't know what God wants us to pray for," and then added, "but the Holy Spirit prays for us with groanings that cannot be expressed in words" (Rom. 8:26 NLT). If my little child asks for a glittering razor, I refuse the request; but when my full-grown son asks for one I grant it. So God cannot wisely answer some prayers, for they are foolish or untimely. Hence, we need not only love and have faith, but also have wisdom and knowledge that we may ask according to God's will.

It is this that Paul had in mind when he said that he would not only pray with the Spirit, but "pray with the understanding also" (1 Cor. 14:15 KJV). We should think before we pray, and study that we may pray wisely.

When the Holy Spirit comes, there pours into the soul not only a tide of love and simple faith, but a flood of light as well, and prayer becomes not only earnest, but intelligent also. And this intelligence increases as, under the leadership of the Holy Spirit, the Word of God is studied and its heavenly truths and principles are grasped and assimilated.

Thus we may come to know God and become His friends, whose prayers He will assist and not deny. Then we will talk with God as friend with friend, and the Holy Spirit will help our infirmities, encourage us to urge our prayer in faith, teach us to reason with God, enable us to come boldly in the name of Jesus—even when oppressed with a sense of our own insignificance and unworthiness—and, when words fail us and we scarcely know how to voice our desires, He will intercede within us with unutterable groanings, according to the will of God (see Rom. 8:26–27; 1 Cor. 2:11).

A young man felt called to mission work in China, but his mother offered strong opposition to his going. An agent of the mission, knowing the need of the work and vexed with the mother, one day laid the case before Hudson Taylor.

He said, "Mr. Taylor listened patiently and lovingly to all I had to say, and then gently suggested our praying about it. Such a prayer I have never heard before! It seemed to me more like a conversation with a trusted friend whose advice he was seeking. He talked the matter over with the Friend from every point of view—from the side of the young man, from the side of China's needs, from the side of the mother and her natural feelings, and also from my side. It was a revelation to me. I saw that prayer did not mean merely asking for things—much less asking for things to be carried out by God according to our ideas—but that it means communion, fellowship, partnership with our heavenly Father. And when our will is really blended with His, what liberty we may have in asking for what we want!"

> My soul, ask what thou wilt,
> Thou canst not be too bold;
> Since His own blood for thee He spilt,
> What else can He withhold?[3]

NOTES

1. James Montgomery, "Prayer Is the Soul's Sincere Desire," 1818, public domain.

2. Charles Wesley, "Give Me the Faith Which Can Remove," 1749, public domain.

3. John Newton, "Behold, the Throne of Grace," 1779, public domain.

Characteristics of the Anointed Preacher 16

Since God saves men and women by "the foolishness of preaching" (1 Cor. 1:21 KJV), preachers have an infinitely important work, and they must be fitted for it. But what can fit a person for such sacred work? Not education alone, nor knowledge of books, nor gifts of speech, nor winsome manners, nor a magnetic voice, nor a commanding presence, but only God. Preachers must be more than themselves—they must be themselves plus the Holy Spirit.

Paul was such a man. He was full of the Holy Spirit, and in studying his life and ministry we get a life-sized portrait of an anointed preacher living, fighting, preaching, praying, suffering, triumphing, and dying in the power and light and glory of the indwelling Spirit.

In the second chapter of 1 Thessalonians, he gave us a picture of his character and ministry (which were formed and inspired by the

Holy Spirit), a sample of his workmanship, and an example for all gospel preachers.

At Philippi he had been terribly beaten with stripes on his bare back, he had been roughly thrust into the inner dungeon, and his feet were made fast in the stocks, but that did not break nor quench his spirit. Love burned in his heart, and his joy in the Lord brimmed full and bubbled over. And at midnight, in the damp, dark, loathsome dungeon, he and Silas, his companion in service and suffering, "prayed, and sang praises unto God" (Acts 16:25 KJV). God answered with an earthquake, and the jailer and his household entered the kingdom of God. Paul was set free and went at once to Thessalonica, where— regardless of the shameful way he had been treated at Philippi—he preached the gospel boldly, and a blessed revival followed with many people experiencing new life in Christ. But persecution arose, and Paul had to flee again. His heart, however, was continually turning back to the new Christians there, and at last he sat down and wrote them their letter. From this we learn the following.

He was a joyful preacher. He was no pessimist, croaking out doleful prophecies and lamentations and bitter criticisms. He was full of the joy of the Lord. It was not the joy that comes from good health, a pleasant home, plenty of money, wholesome food, numerous and smiling friends, and sunny, favorable skies, but a deep, springing fountain of solemn, gladdening joy that abounded and overflowed in pain and weariness, in filthy, noisome surroundings, in loneliness and poverty, and in danger and bitter persecutions. No earth-born trial could quench it, for it was heaven-born; it was "the joy of the LORD" (Neh. 8:10 KJV) poured into his heart with the Holy Spirit.

He was a bold preacher. After his experience at Philippi, worldly prudence would have constrained Paul to go softly at Thessalonica, lest he arouse opposition and meet again with personal violence. But instead he said, "Yet our God gave us the courage to declare his Good News to you boldly, in spite of great opposition" (1 Thess. 2:2 NLT). Personal considerations were all forgotten or cast to the winds in his impetuous desire to declare the gospel and save their souls. He lived in the will of God and conquered his fears. "The wicked" are fearful and "run away when no one is chasing them, but the godly are as bold as lions" (Prov. 28:1 NLT).

This boldness is a fruit of righteousness, and is always found in those who are full of the Holy Spirit. They forget themselves, and so lose all fear. This was the secret of the martyrs when burned at the stake or thrown to the wild beasts.

Fear is a fruit of selfishness. Boldness thrives when selfishness is destroyed. God esteems it, commands His people to be courageous, and makes spiritual leaders only of those who possess courage (see Josh. 1:9).

Moses did not fear the wrath of the king, refused to be called the son of Pharaoh's daughter, and boldly espoused the cause of his despised and enslaved people. Joshua was full of courage. Gideon fearlessly attacked one hundred twenty thousand Midianites with just three hundred unarmed men. Jonathan and his armor-bearer charged the Philistine garrison and routed hundreds singlehanded. David faced the lion and the bear, and inspired all Israel by battling with and killing Goliath.

The prophets were men and women of the highest courage, who fearlessly rebuked kings, and at the risk of life (and often at the cost of life) denounced popular sins and called the people back to righteousness and the faithful service of God. They feared God and so lost the fear of people. They believed God and so obeyed Him, found His favor, and were entrusted with His high missions and everlasting employments.

"Don't be afraid, for I am with you," the Lord said (Isa. 41:10 NLT). The apostle Paul believed this, and so was able to say, "We were bold in our God" (1 Thess. 2:2 NKJV). God was Paul's high tower, his strength and unfailing defense, and so he was not afraid.

His boldness toward people was a fruit of his boldness toward God. That, in turn, was a fruit of Paul's faith in Jesus as his High Priest, who understood his weaknesses, and through whom he could "come boldly unto the throne of grace . . . [to] obtain mercy, and find grace to help in time of need" (Heb. 4:16 KJV).

It is the timidity and delicacy with which people attempt God's work that often accounts for their failure. Let them speak out boldly, as ambassadors of heaven who are not afraid to represent their King, and they will command attention and respect and reach the hearts and consciences of those who hear them.

I have read that Bishop Hugh Latimer, who was later burned at the stake, having preached a sermon before King Henry VIII which greatly displeased the monarch, was ordered to preach again on the next Sunday and apologize for the offense given. The day came, and with it a crowded assembly anxious to hear the bishop's apology. Reading his text, he commenced thus:

Hugh Latimer, dost thou know to whom thou art this day to speak? To the high and mighty monarch, the king's most excellent majesty, who can take away thy life if thou offendest; therefore, take heed that thou speakest not a word that may displease. But, then, consider well, Hugh Latimer, dost thou not know from *whence* thou comest, and upon *whose* message thou art sent? Even by the GREAT GOD, who is all-present and beholdeth all thy ways, who is omnipotent and able to cast both *body* and *soul* into hell together; therefore, take heed and deliver thy message faithfully.[1]

He then repeated the sermon of the previous Sunday, word for word, but with double its former energy and emphasis. The court was full of excitement to learn what would be the fate of this plain-dealing and fearless bishop. He was ordered into the king's presence, who, with a stern voice, asked, "How dared you thus offend me?" "I merely discharged my duty," was Latimer's reply. The king arose from his seat and embraced the good man, saying, "Blessed be God I have so honest a servant."

He was a worthy successor of Nathan, who confronted King David with his sin and said, "Thou art the man" (2 Sam. 12:7 KJV). This divine courage will surely accompany the fiery baptism of the Spirit. What is it but the indwelling of the Holy Spirit that gives courage to anointed preachers, enabling them to face danger and difficulty and loneliness with joy, and attack sin in its worst forms as fearlessly as David attacked Goliath?

"'Not by might nor by power, but by My Spirit,' says the LORD of hosts" (Zech. 4:6 NKJV).

Shall I, for fear of feeble man,

The Spirit's course in me restrain? . . .

Awed by a mortal's frown, shall I

Conceal the Word of God most high? . . .

Shall I, to soothe the unholy throng,

Soften Thy truth, or smooth my tongue? . . .

How then before Thee shall I dare

To stand, or how Thine anger bear? . . .

Yea, let men rage; since Thou wilt spread

Thy shadowing wings around my head;

Since in all pain Thy tender love

Will still my sure refreshment prove.[2]

He was without guile. Paul wrote to the Thessalonians, "You can see we were not preaching with any deceit or impure motives or trickery. For we speak as messengers approved by God to be entrusted with the Good News. Our purpose is to please God, not people. He alone examines the motives of our hearts" (1 Thess. 2:3–4 NLT).

Paul was frank and open. He spoke right out of his heart. He was transparently simple and straightforward. Since God had honored him with this infinite trust of preaching the gospel, he sought to so preach it that he would please God regardless of people's opinions. And yet that is the surest way to please people. People who listen to such preachers feel their honesty and realize that they are seeking to do them good, to save them rather than to tickle their ears and win their applause, and in their hearts they are pleased.

But whether or not people are pleased, anointed preachers deliver the message as ambassadors and look to their home government for their reward. They get their commission from God, and it is God who will try their hearts and prove their ministry. Oh, to please Jesus! Oh, to stand perfect before God after preaching His gospel!

He was not a time-server, nor a covetous man. Paul said, "Never once did we try to win you with flattery, as you well know. And God is our witness that we were not pretending to be your friends just to get your money!" (1 Thess. 2:5 NLT).

There are three ways of reaching someone's purse or wallet: (1) directly; (2) by way of the head with flattering words; or (3) by way of the heart with frank, honest, saving words. The first way is robbery. The second way is also robbery, with the poison of a deadly, but pleasing, opiate added, which may damn the hearer's soul. The third reaches the purse by saving the soul and opening in the heart an unfailing fountain of benevolence to bless the hearer and the world.

It would be better for a preacher to become a criminal and rob people with a club than to rob them with flattery, with smiles and smooth words and feigned and fawning affection, while their poor souls, neglected and deceived, go down to hell. How could anyone meet them in the day of judgment and look into their horror-stricken faces, realizing that he or she toyed with their fancies and affections and pride to get money and, instead of faithfully warning them and seeking to save them, with flattering words fattened their souls for destruction!

Not so did Paul. "I don't want what you have—I want you," he wrote the Corinthians (2 Cor. 12:14 NLT). It was not their money but their souls he wanted. But such faithful love will be able to command all others have to give. Why, to some of his newly minted Christians he wrote, "I am sure you would have taken out your own eyes and given them to me if it had been possible" (Gal. 4:15 NLT). But he sought not to please them with flattering words, only to save them.

Paul was so faithful in this matter, and so conscious of his integrity, that he called God Himself into the witness stand. "God is our witness," he said (1 Thess. 2:5 NLT). Blessed is anyone who can call on God to witness for him or her. And those in whom the Holy Spirit dwells in fullness can do this.

Paul was not vain, nor dictatorial, nor oppressive. Some people care nothing for money, but they care mightily for power and place and worldly glory. But Paul was free from this spiritual itch. Listen to him: "As for human praise, we have never sought it from you or anyone else" (1 Thess. 2:6 NLT).

Solomon said, "To seek one's own glory is not glory" (Prov. 25:27 NKJV), it is only vainglory. Jesus asked, "How can you believe since you accept glory from one another but do not seek the glory that comes from the only God?" (John 5:44 NIV).

Paul was free from all this, and so is everyone who is full of the Holy Spirit. And it is only as we are thus free that with the whole heart and with a single eye we can devote ourselves to the work of saving others.

With all his boldness and faithfulness, he was gentle. "We were gentle among you," Paul said, "just as a nursing mother cherishes her own children" (1 Thess. 2:7 NKJV). The fierce hurricane that casts down the giant trees of the forest is not so mighty as the gentle sunshine, which, from tiny seeds and acorns, lifts aloft the towering spires of oak and fir on a thousand hills and mountains.

The wild storm that lashes the sea into foam and fury is feeble compared to the gentle yet immeasurably powerful influence which twice a day swings the oceans in resistless tides from shore to shore. And as in the physical world the mighty powers are gentle in their vast workings, so it is in the spiritual world. The light that falls on the eyelids of the sleeping infant and wakes it from its slumber is not more gentle than the "still small voice" (1 Kings 19:12 KJV) that brings assurance of forgiveness or cleansing to them that look to Jesus.

Oh, the gentleness of God! "Your gentleness made me great," said David (Ps. 18:35 ESV). "By the humility and gentleness of Christ, I appeal to you," wrote Paul (2 Cor. 10:1 NIV). And again, "The fruit of the Spirit is love, joy, peace, longsuffering, gentleness" (Gal. 5:22 KJV). And as the Father, Son, and Holy Spirit are gentle, so will be the servant of the Lord who is filled with the Spirit.

I shall never forget the gentleness of a mighty man of God I knew, who on the platform was clothed with zeal as with a garment and in his overwhelming earnestness was like a lion or a consuming fire, but when dealing with a wounded or broken heart or with a seeking soul, no nurse with a little babe could be more tender than he.

Finally, Paul was full of self-forgetful, self-sacrificing love. Paul told the Thessalonians, "We loved you so much that we shared with you not only God's Good News but our own lives, too" (1 Thess. 2:8 NLT).

No wonder he shook those cities, overthrew their idols, and had great revivals! No wonder his jailer became a Christian and his churches would have gladly plucked out their eyes for him! Such tender, self-sacrificing love compels attention, begets confidence, enkindles love, and surely wins its object.

This burning love led him to labor and sacrifice and so live and walk before them that he was not only a teacher, but also an example of all he taught, and he could safely say, "Follow my example" (1 Cor. 11:1 NIV). This love led him to preach the whole truth that he might by all means save them. He kept back no truth because it was unpopular, for it was their salvation and not his own reputation and popularity he sought.

He did not preach himself, but a crucified Christ, without the shedding of whose blood there is no remission of sins. And through that precious blood he preached present cleansing from all sin and the gift of the Holy Spirit for all who obediently believe. And this love kept him faithful and humble and true to the end, so that at last in sight of the martyr's death, he saw the martyr's crown and cried out: "My life has already been poured out as an offering to God. . . . I have fought the good fight, I have finished the race, and I have remained faithful. And now the prize awaits me—the crown of righteousness, which the Lord, the righteous Judge, will give me on the day of his return" (2 Tim. 4:6–8 NLT).

Paul had been faithful, and at the end was oppressed with no doubts and harassed with no bitter regrets, but looked forward with eager joy to meeting his Lord and beholding the blessed face of Him he loved.

Have you received the Holy Ghost?

'Twill fit you for the fight,

'Twill make of you a mighty host,

To put your foes to flight.

Have you received the Holy Power?

'Twill fall from heaven on you,

From Jesus' throne this very hour,

'Twill make you brave and true.

Oh, now receive the Holy Fire!

'Twill burn away all dross,

All earthly, selfish, vain desire,

'Twill make you love the Cross.[3]

NOTES

1. William Suddards, *The British Pulpit: Consisting of Discourses by the Most Eminent Living Divines in England, Scotland, and Ireland* (Philadelphia: Grigg and Elliot; Desilver, Thomas and Company, 1837), 107.

2. Johann Joseph Winckler, "Shall I for Fear of Feeble Man," trans. John Wesley, 1739, public domain.

3. Author unknown, *Salvation Army Songs*, comp. William Booth (London: The Salvation Army Book Department, 1911), 339.

Preaching 17

"Where are the wise?" asked Paul. "Where are the legal experts? Where are today's debaters? Hasn't God made the wisdom of the world foolish?" And then he declared, "In God's wisdom, he determined that the world wouldn't come to know him through its wisdom. Instead, God was pleased to save those who believe through the foolishness of preaching" (1 Cor. 1:20–21 CEB).

What kind of preaching is this? He did not say, "foolish preaching," but the foolishness of such a thing as preaching. Certainly, it is not the moral essay, or the intellectual or semi-intellectual kind of preaching most generally heard throughout the world today that will change lives, for thousands of such sermons move and change no one. Nor is it a mere noisy declamation called a sermon—noisy because empty of all earnest thought and true feeling. But it must be the kind of which Peter spoke when he wrote of "those who preached in the power of the Holy Spirit sent from heaven" (1 Pet. 1:12 NLT).

No one is equipped to rightly preach the gospel and undertake the spiritual oversight and instruction of souls until he or she has been anointed with the Holy Spirit.

The disciples had been led to Jesus by John the Baptist, whose mighty preaching laid a deep and broad foundation for their spiritual education. Then for three years they had listened to both the public and private teachings of Jesus and had been "eyewitnesses of his majesty" (2 Pet. 1:16 KJV), of His life and death and resurrection, and yet He commanded them to remain in Jerusalem and wait for the Holy Spirit, who was to fit them for their ministry. And if they—trained and taught by the Master Himself—had need of the Holy Spirit to enable them to preach and testify with wisdom and power, how much more do you and I need His presence!

Without Him they could do nothing. With Him they were invincible and could continue Jesus' work. The mighty energy of His working is seen in Peter's preaching on the day of Pentecost. The sermon itself does not seem to have been very remarkable; indeed, it is principally composed of testimony backed up and fortified by Scripture quotations, followed by exhortation, as are the sermons that are most effective today in the immediate salvation and sanctification of souls. "True preaching," said Horace Bushnell, "is a testimony."[1]

Peter's Scripture quotations were apt, fitting the occasion and the people to whom they were addressed. The testimony was bold and joyous, the rushing outflow of a warm, fresh, throbbing experience. And the exhortation was burning, uncompromising in its demands, and yet tender and full of sympathy and love. But a divine Presence was at work in that vast, mocking, wondering throng, and it was He who made Peter's simple words search like fire and carry such overwhelming conviction to the hearts of the people.

And it is still so that whenever and wherever someone preaches "in the power of the Holy Spirit sent from heaven" (1 Pet. 1:12 NLT) there will be conviction.

Under Peter's sermon, "they were cut to the heart" (Acts 2:37 ESV). The truth pierced them as a sword until they said, "What shall we do?" They had been doubting and mocking a short time before, but now they were earnestly inquiring the way to be saved.

The speech may be without polish, the manner uncouth, and the matter simple and plain, but conviction will surely follow any preaching in the burning love and power and contagious joy of the Holy Spirit.

A few years ago, a poor young man in Africa, who had been stolen for a slave and most cruelly treated, heard a missionary talking of the indwelling of the Holy Spirit, and his heart hungered and thirsted for Him. In a strange manner, he worked his way to New York to find out more about the Holy Spirit, introducing the captain of the ship and several of the crew to Jesus Christ on the way. The brother in New York to whom he came took him to a meeting the first night he was in the city and left him there, while he went to fulfill another engagement. When he returned at a late hour, he found a crowd at the penitent form, led there by the simple words of this young man. He took him to his Sunday school and put him up to speak while he attended to some other matters. When he turned from these affairs that had occupied his attention for only a little while, he found the penitent form full of teachers and scholars, weeping before the Lord. What the young man had said he did not know, but he was bowed with wonder and filled with joy, for it was the power of the Holy Spirit.

The hearers of Wesley, Whitefield, Finney, and others used to fall as though cut down in battle under their preaching. And while there may not be the same physical manifestation at all times, there will surely be the same opening of eyes to spiritual things, breaking of hearts, and piercing of consciences. The Holy Spirit will often come upon a congregation like a wind under the preaching of someone filled with the Spirit, and heads will droop, eyes will brim with tears, and hearts will break under His convicting power. I remember a proud young woman, who had been mercilessly criticizing us for several nights, smitten in this way. She was smiling when suddenly the Holy Spirit winged a word to her heart and instantly her countenance changed. Her head drooped and for an hour or more she sobbed and struggled while her proud heart broke, and she found her way with true repentance and faith to the feet of Jesus and her heavenly Father's favor. How often have we seen such sights as this under the preaching of General William Booth! And it ought to be a common sight under the preaching of all servants of God, for what are we sent for but to convict people of their sin and their need, and by the power of the Spirit to lead them to the Savior? And not only will there be conviction under such preaching, but generally, if not always, there will be salvation and sanctification.

Three thousand people accepted Christ after Peter's Pentecostal sermon. Later five thousand were added to the kingdom, and a multitude of the priests were obedient to the faith. And it was so under the preaching of Philip in Samaria, of Peter in Lydda and Saron and Caesarea, and of Paul in Ephesus and other cities.

To be sure, Stephen's preaching, in its immediate effect, only resulted in enraging his hearers until they stoned him to death. But it is highly probable that the ultimate result was the conversion of Paul, who held the clothes of those who stoned Stephen. And through Paul came the evangelization of the Gentiles.

One of the greatest of American evangelists sought the baptism with the Holy Spirit with agonizing prayers and tears, and received it. And then, he said, he preached the same sermons, but where before it had been as one beating the air, now hundreds experienced new life through faith in Jesus Christ.

It is this that has made Salvation Army officers (ministers) successful. Young, inexperienced, without special gifts and without learning, but with the baptism, they have been mighty to win souls. The hardest hearts have been broken, the darkest minds illuminated, the most stubborn wills subdued, and the wildest natures tamed by them. Their words have been "with power" (Luke 4:32 KJV) and have convicted and saved and sanctified souls, and whole communities have been transformed by their labors.

But without this Presence, great gifts and profound and accurate learning are without avail in the salvation of souls. We often see people with great natural powers, splendidly trained, and equipped with everything save this fiery baptism, and they labor and preach year after year without seeing a soul enter God's kingdom. They have spent years in study but they have not spent a day (much less ten days) fasting and praying and waiting upon God for His anointing that would fill them with heavenly wisdom and power for their work. They are like a great gun loaded and primed, but without a spark of fire to turn the powder and ball into an irresistible lightning bolt.

It is fire we need, and we get it from God in agonizing, wrestling, listening prayer that will not be denied. And when we get it, and not until then, will we preach with the Holy Spirit sent down from heaven, and surely souls will be saved. Such preaching is not foolish. On the contrary:

Preaching in the power of the Holy Spirit is reasonable. It takes account of human reason and conforms to the dictates of common sense. We read that Paul reasoned with the people in the synagogues (see Acts 17:2; 18:4, 19). His preaching was not a noisy harangue nor a rose-water essay of pretty, empty platitudes, but a life and death— eternal life and death—grapple with the intelligence of his listeners. God is the Author of our intellectual powers, and He endowed Paul with reason. The Holy Spirit respects these powers and appeals to reason when He inspires men and women to preach.

Preaching in the power of the Holy Spirit is persuasive. "Come now, let us reason together, says the LORD" (Isa. 1:18 ESV). He takes account of people's feelings, sensibilities, fears, hopes, and affections, and persuades them. Human beings are not all intellect, a mere logic machine. They are a bundle of sensibilities as well. And true preaching—the kind that is inspired by the Holy Spirit—appeals to the whole person. It appeals to the intelligence with reasons and arguments, but is also penetrated through and through with such a spirit of compassionate persuasiveness that wholesome fears are aroused, shame of sin is created, conscience is unshackled, desires for purity and goodness are resurrected, tender affections are quickened, the will is energized, and the whole person is fired and illuminated by a flame of saving emotions, kindled by the fire in the preacher's heart. And this flame enables the hearer to see and feel the realities of things eternal, of God and judgment, of heaven and hell, of the final fixedness of moral character, and of the importance of immediate repentance and acceptance of God's offer of mercy in Jesus Christ.

Preaching in the power of the Holy Spirit is scriptural. The gospel is not opposed to natural religion and reason but it has run far ahead of them. It is a revelation from God of facts, of grace and truth, of mercy and love, and of a plan of redemption that humans could not discover for themselves. And this revelation is recorded in the Scriptures. So we find that Paul "reasoned with them out of the scriptures" (Acts 17:2 KJV). The truths of the Bible cover people's moral needs as a glove covers a hand, fits their moral nature and experience as a key fits its lock, and reveals the condition of their heart as a mirror reveals the state of a face.

No one can read the Bible thoughtfully without either hating it or hating his or her own sins. But while it reveals our sin and our lost condition, it also declares God's love and His plan of redemption. It shows us Jesus Christ, the way by which we come to Him, and how through Him we get deliverance from sin and become a new creation. It is in the Bible, and only there, that this revelation can be found. And that is what the Holy Spirit inspires men and women to preach.

"We preach Christ crucified," wrote Paul (1 Cor. 1:23 KJV). And again, "We preach not ourselves, but Christ Jesus the Lord" (2 Cor. 4:5 KJV). And he exhorted Timothy to "preach the word" (2 Tim. 4:2 KJV).

It is the unsearchable but revealed "riches of Christ" that we are to preach (Eph. 3:8 KJV).

The Holy Spirit makes the Word alive. He brings it to the remembrance of the preachers in whom He abides, and He applies it to the heart of the hearers, lightening up the soul as with a sun until sin is seen in all its hideousness, or cutting as a sharp sword, piercing the heart with irresistible conviction of the guilt and shame of sin.

Peter had no time to consult the Scriptures and prepare a sermon on the morning of Pentecost. But the Holy Spirit quickened his memory and brought to his mind the Scriptures appropriate to the occasion.

Hundreds of years before, the Holy Spirit, by the mouth of the prophet Joel, had foretold that in the last days the Spirit would be poured out upon all flesh and their sons and daughters would prophesy. And the same Spirit that spoke through Joel now made Peter see and declare that this Pentecostal baptism was that of which Joel spoke.

By the mouth of David, He had said, "You will not leave my soul among the dead or allow your holy one to rot in the grave" (Ps. 16:10 NLT), and now Peter, by the inspiration of the same Spirit, applied this Scripture to the resurrection of Jesus, and so proved to his fellow Jews that the One they had condemned and killed was the Holy One foretold in prophecy and psalm.

And so today the Holy Spirit inspires those who receive Him to use the Scriptures to awaken, convict, and save souls.

When Finney was a young preacher, he was invited to a country schoolhouse to preach. On the way there, he became much distressed in soul, and his mind seemed blank and dark, when all at once this text, spoken to Lot in Sodom by the angels, came to his mind: "Up, get you out of this place; for the LORD will destroy this city" (Gen. 19:14 KJV). He explained the text, told the people about Lot and the wickedness of Sodom, and applied it to them. While he spoke, they began to look exceedingly angry, and then, as he earnestly exhorted them to give up their sins and seek the Lord, they began to fall from their seats as though stricken down in battle and cried to God for mercy. A great revival followed. Many came to faith in Christ, and a number of those became ministers of the gospel.

To Finney's amazement, he learned afterward that the place was called Sodom because of its extreme wickedness, and the old man who had invited him to preach was called Lot, because he was the only God-fearing man in the place. Evidently the Holy Spirit worked through Finney to accomplish these results. And such inspiration is not uncommon with those who are filled with the Spirit.

But this reinforcement of the mind and memory by the Holy Spirit does not do away with the need of study. The Spirit quickens that which is already in the mind and memory, as the warm sun and rains of spring quicken the sleeping seeds that are in the ground, and only those. The sun does not put the seed in the soil, nor does the Holy Spirit without our attention and study put the Word of God in our minds. For that we should prayerfully and patiently study.

The apostles of Jesus said, "We will give ourselves continually to prayer, and to the ministry of the word" (Acts 6:4 KJV). And Paul wrote to Timothy, "Be diligent to present yourself approved to God, a worker who does not need to be ashamed, rightly dividing the word of truth" (2 Tim. 2:15 NKJV).

Those who have most carefully and prayerfully studied the Word of God, and most constantly and lovingly meditated upon it, have been best able to rightly divide the Word, and have been most mightily used by the Holy Spirit.

Preaching in the power of the Holy Spirit is healing and comforting. It is indescribably searching in its effects. But it is also edifying, strengthening, and comforting to those who are wholly the Lord's. It cuts, but only to cure. It searches, but only to save. It is constructive as well as destructive. It tears down sin and pride and unbelief, but it builds up faith and righteousness and holiness and all the graces of a Christian character. It warms the heart with love, strengthens faith, and confirms the will in all holy purposes.

Every preacher baptized with the Holy Spirit can say with Jesus, "The Spirit of the Lord is upon me, for he has anointed me to bring Good News to the poor. He has sent me to proclaim that captives will be released, that the blind will see, that the oppressed will be set free, and that the time of the Lord's favor has come" (Luke 4:18–19 NLT).

Seldom is there a congregation in which there are only those who need to be convicted. There will also be meek and gentle ones to whom should be brought a message of joy and good tidings, broken-hearted ones to be bound up, wounded ones to be healed, tempted ones to be delivered, and those whom Satan has bound by some fear or habit to be set free. And the Holy Spirit who knows all hearts will inspire the word that shall bless these needy ones.

The preacher filled with the Holy Spirit, who is instant in prayer, constant in the study of God's Word, and steadfast and active in faith, will surely be so helped that he or she can say with Isaiah, "The Sovereign

Lord has given me his words of wisdom, so that I know how to comfort the weary" (Isa. 50:4 NLT). And as with little Samuel, the Lord will "let none of his words fall to the ground" (1 Sam. 3:19 KJV). Such a preacher will expect results, and God will make them follow his or her preaching as surely as corn follows the planting and cultivating of the farmer.

NOTE

1. Horace Bushnell, *Nature and the Supernatural Together Constituting the One System of God* (New York: Charles Scribner, 1858), 515.

The Holy Spirit's Call 18

The testimony of the worker God is this: "The Spirit of the Sovereign LORD is upon me, for the LORD has anointed me to bring good news to the poor" (Isa. 61:1 NLT). God chooses His own coworkers, and it is the office of the Holy Spirit to call whom He will to preach the gospel. I do not doubt that He calls people to other employments for His glory, and would still more often do so, if people would just listen and wait upon Him to know His will.

He called Bezaleel and Aholiab to build the tabernacle. He called and commissioned the Gentile king, Cyrus, to rebuild Jerusalem and restore His chastised and humbled people to their own land. And did He not call Joan of Arc to her strange and wonderful mission? And Washington and Lincoln?

And, no doubt, He leads most men and women by His providence to their lifework. But the call to preach the gospel is more than a providential leading; it is a distinct and imperative conviction. Methodist

bishop Matthew Simpson, in his *Lectures on Preaching*, said:

> Even in its faintest form there is this distinction between the
> call to the ministry and the choice of other professions: The
> young man may *wish* to be a physician; he may *desire* to enter
> the navy; he *would like* to be a farmer; but he feels he *ought* to
> be a minister; and it is this feeling of "ought" and obligation
> which in its feeblest form indicates the divine call. It is not in
> the aptitude, taste, or desire, but in the *conscience* that its root
> is found. It is God's voice to the man's conscience, saying:
> "You *ought* to preach."[1]

Sometimes the call comes as distinctly as though a voice had spoken from the skies into the depths of the heart.

A young man who was studying law experienced new life in Christ. After a while, he was convicted for sanctification and while seeking heard a voice saying, "Will you devote all your time to the Lord?" He replied, "I am to be a lawyer, not a preacher, Lord." But not until he had said, "Yes, Lord," could he find the blessing.

A thoughtless, godless young fellow was working in the cornfield when a telegram was handed to him announcing the death of his brother, a brilliant and devoted Salvation Army officer (pastor). There and then, unsaved as he was, God called him, showed him a vast Army with ranks broken, where his brother had fallen, and made him to feel that he should fill the breach in the ranks. Fourteen months later he took up the sword and entered the fight from the same platform from which his brother fell, and is today one of our most successful and promising officers.

Again, the call may come as a quiet suggestion, a gentle conviction, as though a gossamer bridle were placed upon the heart and conscience to guide that person into the work of the Lord. The suggestion gradually becomes clearer. The conviction strengthens until it masters the one who is called, and if that person seeks to escape it, he or she finds the silken bridle to be one of stoutest thongs and firmest steel.

It was so with me. When I was just a boy of eleven, I heard a man preaching, and I said to myself, "Oh, how beautiful to preach!" Two years later I became a Christian, and soon the conviction came upon me that I should preach. Later, I decided to follow another profession but the conviction to preach increased in strength, while I struggled against it and turned away my ears and went on with my studies. Yet in every crisis or hour of stillness, when my soul faced God, the conviction that I must preach burned itself deeper into my conscience. I rebelled against it. I felt I would almost rather (but not quite) go to hell than to submit. Then at last a great "Woe is me if I do not preach the gospel" (1 Cor. 9:16 NKJV) took possession of me, and I yielded, and God won.

The first year He gave me three revivals, with many souls. And now I would rather preach Jesus to skeptics and seekers and feed His lambs than be an archangel before the throne. Someday He will call me into His blessed presence and I shall stand before His face and praise Him forever for counting me worthy and calling me to preach His glad gospel and share in His joy of saving the lost. The "woe" is lost in love and delight through the baptism of the Spirit and the sweet assurance that Jesus is pleased.

When the Holy Ghost Is Come

Occasionally, the call comes to someone who is ready and responds promptly and gladly. When Isaiah received the fiery touch that purged his life and purified his heart, he "heard the voice of the Lord, saying, 'Whom shall I send, and who will go for us?'" And in the joy and power of his new experience, he cried out, "Here am I; send me." (Isa. 6:8 KJV).

When Paul received his call, he said, "I did not rush out to consult with any human being" (Gal. 1:16 NLT) but got up and went as the Lord led him.

But more often it seems the Lord finds people preoccupied with other plans and ambitions, or encompassed with obstacles and difficulties, or oppressed with a deep sense of unworthiness or unfitness. Moses argued that he could not talk. He said, "O Lord, I'm not very good with words. I never have been, and I'm not now, even though you have spoken to me. I get tongue-tied, and my words get tangled" (Ex. 4:10 NLT).

And then the Lord condescended, as He always does, to reason with the backward man: "Who makes a person's mouth? Who decides whether people speak or do not speak, hear or do not hear, see or do not see? Is it not I, the LORD? Now go! I will be with you as you speak, and I will instruct you in what to say" (Ex. 4:11–12 NLT).

When the call of God came to Jeremiah, he shrank back, and said, "O Sovereign LORD . . . I can't speak for you! I'm too young!' But the Lord said in response, "Don't say, 'I'm too young,' for you must go wherever I send you and say whatever I tell you. And don't be afraid of the people, for I will be with you and will protect you. I, the LORD, have spoken!" (Jer. 1:6–8 NLT). And so the call of God comes today to those who shrink and feel that they are the most unfit or most hedged in by insuperable difficulties.

I know a man who, when he became a Christian, could not tell A from B. He knew nothing whatever about the Bible and stammered so badly that, when asked his own name, it would usually take him a minute or so to tell it. Added to this, he lisped badly and was subject to a nervous affliction which seemed likely to unfit him for any kind of work whatever. But God poured light and love into his heart, called him to preach, and today he is one of the mightiest soul-winners in the whole round of my acquaintance. When he speaks, the house is always packed to the doors and the people hang on his words with wonder and joy.

He entered God's kingdom at a camp meeting and was sanctified wholly in a cornfield. He learned to read, but—being too poor to afford a light in the evening—he studied a large-print Bible by the light of the full moon. Today, he has the Bible almost committed to memory, and when he speaks he does not open the Book but reads his lesson from memory, quotes proof texts from Genesis to Revelation without mistake, and gives chapter and verse for every quotation. When he talks, his face shines, and his speech is like honey for sweetness and like bullets fired from a gun for power. He is one of the weak and foolish ones God has chosen to confound the wise and mighty (see 1 Cor. 1:27).

If God calls you, He will so corroborate the call in some way that others will know there is a prophet among them. It will be with you as it was with Samuel: "And Samuel grew, and the LORD was with him, and did let none of his words fall to the ground. And all Israel from Dan even to Beersheba knew that Samuel was established to be a prophet of the LORD" (1 Sam. 3:19–20 KJV).

If you are uncertain about the call, God will deal patiently with you, as He did with Gideon, to make you certain. Your fleece will be wet with dew when the earth is dry, or dry when the earth is wet. Or you will hear of some tumbling barley cake smiting the tents of Midian, that will strengthen your faith and make you know that God is with you (see Judg. 6:36–40; 7:9–15).

If the door is shut and difficulties hedge the way, God will go before the one He calls, open the door, and sweep away the difficulties (see Isa. 45:2–3).

If others think you so ignorant and unfit that they doubt your call, God will give you such grace or such power to win souls that they shall have to acknowledge that God has chosen you. It was in this way that God made a whole Salvation Army national headquarters, from the top down, to know that He had chosen the elevator operator for His work. The young man got scores of his passengers on the elevator saved, and then he was commissioned and sent into the field to devote all his time to saving souls.

The Lord will surely let your brothers and sisters know, as surely as He did the church at Antioch, when "the Holy Spirit said, 'Dedicate Barnabas and Saul for the special work to which I have called them'" (Acts 13:2 NLT).

Sometimes the one who is called will try to hide it in his or her heart, and then God stirs up someone to lay a hand on a shoulder, and ask, "Are you not called to the work?" And the called one finds it impossible to hide or escape from the call, no more than Adam could hide himself from God behind the trees of the garden or Jonah escape God's call by taking a ship for Tarshish.

Happy are they who do not try to escape but, though trembling at the mighty responsibility, assume it and with all humility and faithfulness set to work by prayer and patient, continuous study of God's Word to fit themselves for God's work. They will need to prepare themselves, for the call to the work is also a call to preparation, continuous preparation of the fullest possible kind.

Those whom God calls cannot safely neglect or despise the call. They will find their mission on earth, their happiness and peace, their power and prosperity, their reward in heaven, and probably heaven itself, bound up with that call and dependent upon it. They may run away from it, as Jonah did, and find a waiting ship to favor their flight, but they will also find fierce storms and bellowing seas overtaking them, and big-mouthed fishes of trouble and disaster ready to swallow them.

But if they heed the call and cheerfully go where God appoints, God will go with them; they shall nevermore be left alone. The Holy Spirit will surely accompany them, and they may be among the happiest souls on earth, one of the gladdest creatures in God's universe.

"Be sure of this: I am with you always, even to the end of the age" (Matt. 28:20 NLT), said Jesus as He commissioned His disciples to go to all nations and preach the gospel. "I will personally go with you" (Ex. 33:14 NLT), said Jehovah to Moses, when sending him to face Pharaoh, free Israel, and lead them to the Promised Land.

And to the boy Jeremiah, He said, "Don't be afraid of the people, for I will be with you and will protect you. . . . They will fight you, but they will fail. For I am with you" (Jer. 1:8, 19 NLT).

I used to read these words with a great and rapturous joy as I realized by faith that they were also meant for me, and for everyone sent of God, and that His blessed presence was with me every time I spoke to the people or dealt with an individual soul or knelt in prayer with a penitent seeker after God. And I still read them so.

Has He called you? Are you conscious of His helpful, sympathizing, loving presence with you? If so, let no petty offense, hardship, danger, or dread of the future, cause you to turn aside or draw back. Stick to the work till He calls you out, and when He so calls you can go with open face and a heart abounding with love, joy, and peace, and He will still go with you.

NOTE

1. Matthew Simpson, *Lectures on Preaching* (London: Richard D. Dickinson, 1879), 25.

The Sheathed Sword: A Law of the Spirit   19

Just as the moss and the oak are higher in the order of creation than the clod of clay and the rock, the bird and beast higher than the moss and the oak, the human than the bird and the beast, so the spiritual being is higher than the natural being. The sons and daughters of God are a new order of being. The Christian is a "new creation" (2 Cor. 5:17 ESV).

Just as there are laws governing the life of the plant, and other and higher laws that apply to the bird and beast, so there are higher laws for human beings, and still higher for the Christian. It was with regard to one of these higher laws that govern the heavenly life of the Christian that Jesus said to Peter, "Put away your sword" (Matt. 26:52 NLT).

Jesus said to Pilate, "My Kingdom is not an earthly kingdom. If it were, my followers would fight" (John 18:36 NLT). The unspiritual person's kingdom is of this world, and it is the law of the carnal nature to fight with fist and sword, tongue and wit. Therefore, that person will fight for it with such weapons as this world furnishes.

Christians, however, are citizens of heaven, and they are subject to its law, which is universal, wholehearted love. In this kingdom, we conquer not by fighting but by submitting. When an enemy takes my coat, I overcome him not by going to the law but by generously giving him my cloak also. When my enemy compels me to go a mile with him, I vanquish the enemy by cheerfully going two miles with him. When I am smitten on one cheek, I win my foe by meekly turning the other cheek. This is the law of the new life from heaven, and only by recognizing and obeying it can that new life be sustained and passed on to others. This is the narrow way that leads to life eternal, and few find it (see Matt. 7:14) or, finding it, are willing to walk in it.

A Russian peasant named Sutajeff could get no help from the religious teachers of his village, so he learned to read, and while studying the Bible he found this narrow way and walked gladly in it. One night neighbors of his stole some of his grain, but in their haste or carelessness they left a bag. He found it and ran after them to restore it. "For," said he, "fellows who have to steal must be hard up." And by this Christlike spirit he saved both himself and them, for he kept the spirit of love in his own heart, and they were won to the faith and became his most ardent disciples.

On another occasion, a beggar woman to whom he gave lodging stole the bedding and ran away with it. She was pursued by the neighbors and was just about to be put in prison when Sutajeff appeared, became her advocate, secured her acquittal, and gave her food and money for her journey. He recognized the law of his new life and gladly obeyed it, and so was not overcome by evil, but persistently and triumphantly overcame evil with good (see Rom. 12:21).

This is the spirit and method of Jesus. He came not to be ministered unto, but to minister and to give His life a ransom for many. And by those who are filled with this spirit and following this method He will yet win the world. His spirit is not one of self-seeking but of self-sacrifice. Some mysterious majesty of His presence or voice so awed and overcame His foes that they stepped back and fell to the ground before Him in the garden of His agony, but He meekly submitted Himself to them. And when Peter drew his sword and cut off the ear of the high priest's servant, Jesus said to him, "Put your sword back into its sheath. Shall I not drink from the cup of suffering the Father has given me?" (John 18:11 NLT).

This was the spirit of Isaac. When he dug a well, the Philistines disputed with his servants for it. So he dug another. And when they claimed that, he removed and dug yet another. "This time there was no dispute over it, so Isaac named the place Rehoboth (which means 'open space'), for he said, 'At last the LORD has created enough space for us to prosper in this land' . . . [And] the LORD appeared to him on the night of his arrival. 'I am the God of your father, Abraham,' he said. 'Do not be afraid, for I am with you and will bless you. I will multiply your descendants, and they will become a great nation'" (Gen. 26:22, 24 NLT).

This was the spirit of David when Saul was hunting for his life. Twice David could have slain him, and when urged to do so, he said, "Surely the LORD will strike Saul down someday, or he will die of old age or in battle. The LORD forbid that I should kill the one he has anointed!" (1 Sam. 26:10–11 NLT).

This was the spirit of Paul. He said, "We bless those who curse us. We are patient with those who abuse us. We appeal gently when evil things are said about us" (1 Cor. 4:12–13 NLT). "A servant of the Lord must not quarrel," wrote Paul to Timothy, "but must be kind to everyone" (2 Tim. 2:24 NLT). This is the spirit of our King. This is the law of His kingdom.

Is this your spirit? When you are reviled, demeaned, and slandered, and are tempted to retort, Jesus says to you, "Put away your sword" (Matt. 26:52 NLT). When you are wronged and ill-treated, and people ride roughshod over you, and you feel it would be simple justice to smite back, He says, "Put away your sword" and, "Live in peace with everyone" (Rom. 12:18 NLT). Your weapons are not carnal but spiritual now that you belong to Him and have your citizenship in heaven. If you fight with the sword, if you retort and strike back when you are wronged, you quench the Spirit—you get out of the narrow way, and your new life from heaven will perish.

A Salvation Army officer went to a hard corps (church) and found that his predecessor was sending back to friends, asking for money. The successor, losing sight of the spirit of Jesus, made a complaint about it, and the money was returned. But he became lean in his soul. He had quenched the spirit. He had broken the law of the kingdom. He had not only refused to give his cloak, but had also fought for and secured the return of the coat. He had lost the smile of Jesus, and his poor heart was sad and heavy within him. He came to me with anxious inquiry as to what I thought of his action. I had to admit that the other man had transgressed and that the money ought to be returned. But I felt that the officer should have been more grieved over the un-Christlike spirit of his brother than over the loss of the money, and that like Sutajeff, the Russian peasant, he should have said, "Poor fellow! He must be hard up; I will send him money myself." When I told him that story, he came to himself very quickly and was soon back in the narrow way and rejoicing in the smile of Jesus once again.

"But," you ask, "will not people walk over us if we do not stand up for our rights?" I do not argue that you are not to stand up for your rights but that you are to stand up for your higher rather than your lower rights, the rights of your heavenly life rather than your earthly life, and that you are to stand up for your rights in the way and spirit of Jesus rather than in the way and spirit of the world.

If others wrong you intentionally, they wrong themselves far worse than they wrong you. And if you have the spirit of Jesus in your heart, you will pity them more than you pity yourself. They nailed Jesus to the cross and hung Him up to die. They gave Him gall and vinegar to drink. They cast votes for His seamless robe and divided His garments between them while the crowd wagged their heads at Him and mocked Him. Great was the injustice and wrong they were inflicting upon Him, but He was not filled with anger, only pity. He thought not of the wrong done Him, but of the wrong they did themselves, and their sin against His heavenly Father. And He prayed not for judgment upon them, but that they might be forgiven, and He won them, and is winning and will win the world.

"By mercy and truth iniquity is purged," wrote Solomon (Prov. 16:6 KJV). "Put away your sword" and take mercy and truth for your weapons, and God will be with you and for you. And great shall be your victory and joy.

Victory over Suffering 20

Had there been no sin, our heavenly Father would have found other means by which to develop passive virtues in us and train us in the graces of meekness, patience, longsuffering, and forbearance, which so beautify and display the Christian character. But since sin is here—with its contradictions and falsehoods, its darkness, wars, brutalities, and injustices, producing awful harvests of pain and sorrow—God, in wonderful wisdom and loving-kindness, turns even these into instruments by which to fashion beautiful graces in us. Storm succeeds sunshine, and darkness the light. Pain follows hard on the heels of pleasure, while sorrow peers over the shoulder of joy. Gladness and grief, rest and toil, peace and war, interminably intermingled, follow each other in ceaseless succession in this world. We cannot escape suffering while in the body. But we can receive it with a faith that robs it of its terror and extracts from it richest blessing; from the flinty rock will gush forth living waters, and the carcass of the lion will furnish the sweetest honey.

This is so even when the suffering is a result of our own folly or sin. It is intended not only in some measure as a punishment, but also as a teacher, a corrective, a remedy, a warning. And it will surely work for good if, instead of repining and vainly regretting the past, we steadily look to Jesus and learn our lesson in patience and thankfulness.

> If all the skies were sunshine,
> Our faces would be fain
> To feel once more upon them
> The cooling plash of rain.
> If all the world were music,
> Our hearts would often long
> For one sweet strain of silence
> To break the endless song.
> If life were always merry,
> Our souls would seek relief
> And rest from weary laughter
> In the quiet arms of grief.[1]

Doubtless all our suffering is a result of sin, but not necessarily the sin of the sufferer. Jesus was the sinless One, but He was also the Chief of sufferers. Paul's great and lifelong sufferings came upon him not because of his sins but rather because he had forsaken sin and was following Jesus in a world of sin and seeking the salvation of others. In this path there is no escape from suffering, though there are hidden and inexpressible consolations. "In the world you will have tribulation," said Jesus (John 16:33 ESV). "Everyone who wants to live a godly life in Christ Jesus will suffer persecution," wrote Paul (2 Tim. 3:12 NLT). Sooner or later, suffering in some form comes to each of us. It may come through broken health; or through pain and weariness of body; or through mental anguish, moral distress, spiritual darkness, and uncertainty. It may come through the loss of loved ones, betrayal by trusted friends, deferred or ruined hopes, or base ingratitude. It may come in unrequited toil and sacrifice and unfulfilled ambitions. But nothing more clearly distinguishes the person filled with the Spirit from one who is not than the way each receives suffering.

One person, with triumphant faith and shining face and strong heart glories in tribulation counts it all joy. To this class belong the apostles, who, beaten and threatened, "departed from the presence of the council, rejoicing that they were counted worthy to suffer shame for his name" (Acts 5:41 KJV). The other responds with doubts and fears, murmurs and complaints, and to other miseries adds that of a rebellious heart and discontented mind.

One sees the Enemy's armed host and unmixed distress and danger; the other sees the angel of the Lord, with abundant help and safety (see 2 Kings 6:15–17). A pastor went one morning to visit two women who were greatly afflicted. They were about the same age and had long been professing Christians and members of the church. He asked the first one upon whom he called, "How is it with you this morning?"

"Oh, I have not slept all night," she replied. "I have so much pain. It is so hard to have to lie here. I cannot see why God deals so with me."

Evidently, she was not filled with the Spirit but was in a controversy with the Lord about her sufferings and would not be comforted.

Leaving her, he called immediately upon the other woman and asked, "How are you today?"

"Oh, I had such a night of suffering!" she replied. Then, there broke upon her worn face, furrowed and pale, a beautiful radiance, and she added, "but Jesus was so near and helped me so, that I could suffer this way and more, if my Father thinks best." On she went with similar words of cheer and triumph that made the sick room a vestibule of glory. No lack of comfort in her heart, for the Comforter Himself, the Holy Spirit, had been invited and had come in. One had the Comforter in fullness, the other had not.

Probably no one ever suffered more than Paul, but with soldier-like fortitude he bore his heavy burdens; faced his constant and exacting labors; and endured his sore trials, disappointments, and bitter persecutions by fierce and relentless enemies. He stood unmoved amid shipwrecks, stripes, imprisonments, cold, hunger, and homelessness without a whimper that might suggest repining or discouragement or an appeal for pity. Indeed, he went beyond simple uncomplaining fortitude, and said, "We glory in tribulations" (Rom. 5:3 KJV), "I am exceeding joyful in all our tribulation" (2 Cor. 7:4 KJV), and "I take pleasure in infirmities, in reproaches, in necessities, in persecutions, in distresses for Christ's sake" (2 Cor. 12:10 KJV). After a terrible scourging upon his bare back, he was thrust into a loathsome inner dungeon, his feet fast in the stocks, with worse things probably awaiting him on the morrow. Nevertheless, we find him and Silas, his companion in suffering, at midnight praying and singing praises to God (see Acts 16:25).

What was his secret? Listen to him: "Because God's love has been poured into our hearts through the Holy Spirit who has been given to us" (Rom. 5:5 ESV). His prayer for his Ephesian brothers and sisters had been answered in his own heart: "That from his glorious, unlimited resources he will empower you with inner strength through his Spirit. Then Christ will make his home in your hearts" (Eph. 3:16–17 NLT). And this inner strength and consciousness, through faith in an indwelling Christ, enabled Paul to receive suffering and trial, not stoically, nor hilariously, in a spirit of bravado, but cheerfully and with a thankful heart.

Dr. Thomas Arnold, headmaster of Rugby School, wrote something about a "most dear and blessed sister" that illustrates the power flowing from exhaustless fountains of inner joy and strength through the working of the Holy Spirit. He said:

I never saw a more perfect instance of the spirit and power of love and of a sound mind . . . a daily martyrdom for twenty years, during which she adhered to her early formed resolution of never talking about herself—enjoying everything lovely, graceful, beautiful, high-minded, whether in God's work or man's, with the keenest relish; inheriting the earth to the very fullness of the promise; and preserved through the very valley of the shadow of death from all fear or impatience, or from every cloud of impaired reason which might mar the beauty of Christ's glorious work.[2]

It is not by hypnotizing the soul, nor by blessing it into a state of ecstatic insensibility, that the Lord enables the person filled with the

Spirit to thus triumph over suffering. Rather it is by giving the soul a sweet, constant, and unshaken assurance through faith: First, that it is freely and fully accepted in Christ.

Second, that whatever suffering comes, it is measured, weighed, and permitted by love infinitely tender, and is guided by wisdom that cannot err.

Third, that however difficult it may be to explain suffering now, it is nevertheless one of the "all things" which "work together for good to them that love God" (Rom. 8:28 KJV) and that in a "little while" it will not only be swallowed up in ineffable blessedness and glory, but that in some way it is actually helping to work out "a far more exceeding and eternal weight of glory" (2 Cor. 4:17 KJV).

Fourth, that though the furnace has been heated seven times hotter than usual, yet "the form . . . like the Son of God" is walking with us in the fire (Dan. 3:25 KJV); though triumphant enemies have thrust us into the lions' den, yet the angel of the Lord arrived first and locked the lions' jaws; though foes may have formed sharp weapons against us, yet they cannot prosper, for His shield and buckler defend us; though all things be lost, yet "you remain forever" (Heb. 1:11 NLT); and though "my health may fail, and my spirit may grow weak . . . God remains the strength of my heart; he is mine forever" (Ps. 73:26 NLT).

Not all God's dear children thus triumph over their difficulties and sufferings, but this is God's standard, and they may attain to it if, by faith, they will open their hearts and "be filled with the Holy Spirit" (Eph. 5:18 NLT).

Here is the testimony of a Salvation Army officer:

Viewed from the outside, my life as a sinner was easy and untroubled, over which most of my friends expressed envy; while these same friends thought my life as a Christian full of care, toil, hardship, and immense loss. This, however, was only an outside view, and the real state of the case was exactly the opposite of what they supposed. For in all the pleasure-seeking, idleness, and freedom from responsibility of my life apart from God, I carried an immeasurable burden of fear, anxiety, and constantly recurring disappointment; trifles weighed upon me, and the thought of death haunted me with vague terrors.

But when I gave myself wholly to God, though my lot became at once one of toil, responsibility, comparative poverty, and sacrifice, yet I could not feel pain in any storm that broke over my head, because of the presence of God. It was not so much that I was insensible to trouble, as sensible of His presence and love; and the worst trials were as nothing in my sight, nor have been for over twenty-two years. While as for death, it appears only as a doorway into more abundant life, and I can alter an old German hymn, and sing with joy:

> Oh, how my heart with rapture dances.
> To think my dying hour advances!
> Then, Lord, with Thee!
> My Lord, with Thee!

This is faith's triumph over the worst the world can offer through the blessed fullness of the indwelling Comforter.

Here speaks the Comforter, Light of the straying,

Hope of the penitent, Advocate sure,

Joy of the desolate, tenderly saying,

Earth has no sorrow that heaven cannot cure.[3]

NOTES

1. Henry Van Dyke, "If All the Skies," *Songs Out of Doors* (New York: Charles Scribner's Sons, 1922), 39.

2. Robert Gracey Ferguson, *Baccalaureate Sermons* (Boston: Richard G. Badger, The Gorham Press, 1919), 75.

3. Thomas Moore, "Come, Ye Disconsolate," 1816, public domain.

The Overflowing Blessing

Moses instructed the children of Israel to give tithes of all they had to the Lord, and in return God promised to richly bless them, making their fields and vineyards fruitful and causing their flocks and herds to safely multiply. But they became covetous and unbelieving, and began to rob God by withholding their tithes, and then God began to withhold His blessing from them.

But still God loved and pitied them, and spoke to them again and again by His prophets. Finally, by the prophet Malachi, He said, 'Bring all the tithes into the storehouse so there will be enough food in my Temple. If you do,' says the LORD of Heaven's Armies, 'I will open the windows of heaven for you. I will pour out a blessing so great you won't have enough room to take it in! Try it! Put me to the test!' (Mal. 3:10 NLT). He promised to make their barns overflow if they would be faithful, if they would pay their tithes and discharge their obligations to Him.

Now, this overflow of barns and granaries is a picture of how our hearts and lives overflow when we give ourselves fully to God, the blessed Holy Spirit comes in, and Jesus becomes all and in all to us. The blessing is too big to contain, but just bursts out and overflows through the life, the looks, the conversation, and the very tones of the voice, and gladdens and refreshes and purifies wherever it goes. Jesus calls it "rivers of living water" (John 7:38 KJV).

There is an overflow of love. Sin brings in an overflow of hate, so that the world is filled with wars and murders, slanders, oppression, and selfishness. But this blessing causes love to overflow. Schools, colleges, and hospitals are built. Shelters, rescue homes, and orphanages are opened. Sinners love their own, but this blessing makes us to love all—strangers, the ungodly, and even our enemies.

There is an overflow of peace. It settles old quarrels and grudges. It makes a different atmosphere in the home. The children know it when father and mother get the Comforter. Kindly words and sweet goodwill take the place of bitterness and strife. I suspect that even the dumb beasts realize the overflow.

I heard a humorous story of a man whose cow would switch her tail in his face and then kick over the pail when he was milking her, after which he would always give her a beating with the stool on which he sat. But he got the blessing, and his heart was overflowing with peace. The next morning he went to milk that cow, and when the pail was nearly full, *swish* came the tail in his face, and with a vicious kick she knocked over the pail and then ran across the barnyard. The blessed man picked up the empty pail and stool and went over to the cow, which stood trembling, awaiting the usual kicks and beating. But instead he patted her gently, and said, "You may kick over that pail as often as you please but I am not going to beat you anymore." And the cow seemed to understand, for she dropped her head, quietly began to eat, and never kicked again! That story is good enough to be true, and I don't doubt that it is, for certainly when the Comforter comes a great peace fills the heart and overflows through all the life.

There is an overflow of joy. It makes the face to shine. It glances from the eye and bubbles out in thanksgiving and praise. You never can tell when one who has the blessing will shout out, "Glory to God! Praise the Lord! Hallelujah! Amen!"

I have sometimes seen a whole congregation awakened and refreshed and gladdened by the joyous overflow from one clean-hearted soul. A man or woman with an overflow of genuine joy is worth a whole company of ordinary folks, a host within him- or herself, and a living proof of the text, "The joy of the LORD is your strength" (Neh. 8:10 NLT).

There is an overflow of patience and long-suffering. A man got this blessing and his wife was so enraged that she left him, went across the way, and lived as the wife of his unmarried brother. He was terribly tempted to take his gun and go over and kill them both. But he prayed about it, and the Lord gave him the patience and long-suffering of Jesus, who bears long with the one who leaves Him and joins with the world. And the man continued to treat them with the utmost kindness, as though they had done him no wrong. Some people might say the man was weak, but I would say he was unusually "strong in the grace that is in Christ Jesus" (2 Tim. 2:1 KJV), and a neighbor of his told me that all his neighbors believed in his faith.

There is an overflow of goodness and generosity. I read the other day of a poor man who supports eight workers in the foreign mission field. When asked how he did it, he replied that he did his own washing, denied himself, and managed his affairs in order to do it.

Do you ask, "How can I get such a blessing?" You will get it by bringing in all the tithes, by giving yourself in love and obedience and wholehearted, joyous consecration to Jesus, as a true bride gives herself to her husband. Do not try to bargain with the Lord and buy it of Him, but wait on Him in never-give-in prayer and confident expectation, and He will give it to you. And then you must not hold it selfishly for your own gratification, but let it overflow to the hungry, thirsty, fainting world about you. God bless you even now and do for you exceeding abundantly above all you ask or think!

One person went from one of my meetings recently with a heart greatly burdened for the blessing, and for two or three days and nights did little else but read the Bible and pray and cry to God for a clean heart filled with the Spirit. At last the Comforter came, and with Him fullness of peace and joy and soul rest, and that day this individual led a number of others into the blessing. "If you then, though you are evil, know how to give good gifts to your children, how much more will your Father in heaven give the Holy Spirit to those who ask him!" (Luke 11:13 NIV). "Ask . . . seek . . . knock" (Matt. 7:7 KJV).

The Key to Spiritual Leadership 22

A mighty man or woman inspires and trains others to be mighty. We wonder and exclaim often at the slaughter of Goliath by David, and we forget that David was the forerunner of a race of fearless, invincible warriors and giant killers. If we would only study and remember the story of David's mighty men in this light, it would be most instructive to us.

Moses inspired a tribe of cowering, toiling, sweaty, grimy, spiritless slaves to lift up their heads, straighten their backs, and throw off the yoke, and he led them forth with songs of victory and shouts of triumph from under the iron bondage of Pharaoh. He fired them with a national spirit and welded and organized them into a distinct and compact people that could be hurled with irresistible power against the walled cities and trained warriors of Canaan.

But what was the secret of David and Moses? David was only a stripling shepherd boy when he immortalized himself. What was his secret? To be sure, Moses was "learned in all the wisdom of the Egyptians" (Acts 7:22 ESV) and doubtless had been trained in all the civil, military, and scientific learning of his day, but he was so weak in himself that he feared and fled at the first word of questioning and disparagement that he heard (see Ex. 2:14) and spent the next forty years feeding sheep for another man in the rugged wilderness of Sinai.

What, then, was their secret? Doubtless, they were cast in a finer mold than most, but their secret was not in themselves.

Joseph Parker declared that great lives are built on great promises, and so they are. These men had so far humbled themselves that they found God. They got close to Him, and He spoke to them. He gave them promises. He revealed His way and truth to them, and as they trusted Him—believing His promises and fashioning their lives according to His truth, His doctrine—everything else followed. They became workers together with God (see 2 Cor. 6:1), heroes of faith, leaders of others, builders of empire, and, in an important sense, saviors of humanity.

Their secret is an open one. It is the secret of every truly successful spiritual leader from then till now, and there is no other way to success in spiritual leadership.

- They had an experience. They knew God.
- This experience, this acquaintance with God, was maintained and deepened and broadened in obedience to God's teaching, or truth, or doctrine.

- They patiently yet urgently taught others what they themselves had learned, and declared, so far as they saw it, the whole counsel of God.

They were abreast of the deepest experiences and fullest revelations God had yet made to humanity. They were leaders, not laggards. They were not in the rear of the procession of God's warriors and saints; they were in the forefront.

Here we discover the importance of the doctrine and experience of holiness through the baptism of the Holy Spirit to leaders. We are to know God and glorify Him and reveal Him to others. We are to finish the work of Jesus, and "fill up . . . what is lacking in the afflictions of Christ" (Col. 1:24 NKJV). We are to rescue the slaves of sin, to make a people, to fashion them into a holy nation, and to inspire and lead them forth to save the world. How can we do this? Only by being in the forefront of God's spiritual hosts—not in name and in titles only, but in reality—by being in glad possession of the deepest experiences God gives, and the fullest revelations He makes to humanity.

The astonishing military and naval successes of the Japanese are said to be due to their profound study, clear understanding, and firm grasp of the theory—the principles, the doctrines—of war; their careful and minute preparation of every detail of their campaigns; the scientific accuracy and precision with which they carry out all their plans; and their utter personal devotion to their cause.

Our war is far more complex and desperate than theirs, its issues are infinitely more far-reaching, and we must equip ourselves for it. And nothing is so vital to our cause as a mastery of the *doctrine* and an assured and joyous possession of the Pentecostal *experience* of holiness through the indwelling Spirit.

THE DOCTRINE

What is the teaching of God's Word about holiness? If we carefully study God's Word, we find that He wants His people to be holy, and the making of a holy people, after the pattern of Jesus, is the Holy Spirit's crowning work. He commands us to "cleanse ourselves from all filthiness of the flesh and spirit, perfecting holiness in the fear of the Lord" (2 Cor. 7:1 KJV). It is prayed that we may "increase and abound in love to one another and to all . . . so that He may establish [our] hearts blameless in holiness before our God and Father at the coming of our Lord Jesus Christ with all His saints" (1 Thess. 3:12–13 NKJV). He says, "As he who called you is holy, you also be holy in all your conduct, since it is written, 'You shall be holy, for I am holy'" (1 Pet. 1:15–16 ESV). And in the most earnest manner we are exhorted to "pursue peace with all people, and holiness, without which no one will see the Lord" (Heb. 12:14 NKJV).

As we further study the Word, we discover that holiness is more than simple freedom from condemnation for wrongdoing. A helpless invalid lying on a bed of sickness, unable to do anything wrong, may be free from the condemnation of actual wrongdoing, and yet it may be in that person's heart to do all manner of evil. Holiness on its negative side is a state of heart purity; it is heart cleanness—cleanness of thought and temper and disposition, cleanness of intention and purpose and wish—a state of freedom from all sin, both in- and outward (see Rom. 6:18). On the positive side it is a state of union with God in Christ, in which the whole individual becomes a temple of God and filled with the fruit of the Spirit, which is "love, joy, peace, patience, kindness, goodness, faithfulness, gentleness, and self-control" (Gal. 5:22–23 NLT). It is moral and spiritual sympathy and harmony with God in the holiness of His nature.

We must not, however, confuse purity with maturity. Purity is a matter of the heart and is secured by an instantaneous act of the Holy Spirit. Maturity is largely a matter of the head and results from growth in knowledge and experience. In one, the heart is made clean and is filled with love. In the other, the head is gradually corrected and filled with light, and so the heart is enlarged and more firmly established in faith; consequently, the experience deepens and becomes stronger and more robust in every way. It is for this reason that we need teachers after we are sanctified, and to this end we are exhorted to humbleness of mind.

My little boy—with a heart full of sympathy and love for his father—may voluntarily go into the garden to weed the vegetables. But, being yet unlearned, lacking light in his head, he pulls up my sweet corn with the grass and weeds. His little heart glows with pleasure and pride in the thought that he is helping Papa, and yet he is doing the very thing I don't want him to do. But if I am a wise and patient father, I will be pleased with him, for what is the loss of a few stalks of corn compared to the expression and development of his love and loyalty? And I shall commend him for the love and faithful purpose of his little heart, while I patiently set to work to enlighten the darkness of his little head. His heart is pure toward his father, but he is not yet mature. In this matter of light and maturity, holy people often widely differ, and this causes much perplexity and needless and unwise anxiety. In the fourteenth chapter of Romans, Paul discussed and illustrated the principle underlying this distinction between purity and maturity.

As we continue to study the Word under the illumination of the Spirit, who is given to lead us into all truth, we further learn that holiness is not a state we reach in experiencing salvation. The apostles had forsaken all to follow Jesus (see Matt. 19:27–29). Their names were written in heaven (see Luke 10:20). Yet they were not holy. They doubted and feared, and were rebuked again and again for the slowness and littleness of their faith. They were bigoted and wanted to call down fire from heaven to consume those who would not receive Jesus (see Luke 9:51–56). They were frequently contending among themselves as to who should be the greatest, and when the supreme test came they all forsook Jesus and fled. Certainly, they were not only afflicted with darkness in their heads but—far worse—carnality in their hearts. They were His, and they were very dear to Him, but they were not yet holy; they were still impure of heart.

Paul made this point very clear in his epistle to the Corinthians. He told them plainly that they were yet only babes in Christ, because they were carnal and contentious (see 1 Cor. 3:1). They were followers of Jesus, they were in Christ, but they were not holy.

It is of great importance that we keep this truth well in mind that people may truly have entered into new life, may be babes in Christ, and yet not be pure in heart. We shall then sympathize more fully with them and see more clearly how to help them and guide their feet into the way of holiness and peace.

Those who hold that we are sanctified wholly when we experience salvation will meet with much to perplex them in their converts and are not intelligently equipped to bless and help God's little children.

A continued study of God's teaching on this subject will clearly reveal to us that purity of heart is obtained after we experience new life in Christ. Peter made this very plain in his address to the Council of Jerusalem, where he recounted the outpouring of the Holy Spirit upon Cornelius and his household. After mentioning the gift of the Holy Spirit, he added, "And put no difference between us and them, purifying their hearts by faith" (Acts 15:9 KJV). Among other things, then, the baptism of the Holy Spirit purifies the heart. But the disciples were converted before they received this Pentecostal experience, so we see that heart purity, or holiness, is a work performed in us after conversion.

Again, we notice that Peter said, "Purifying their hearts by faith." If it is by faith, then it is not by growth, nor by works, nor by death, nor by purgatory after death. It is God's work. He purifies the heart, and He does it for those—and only those—who, devoting all their possessions and powers to Him, seek Him by simple, prayerful, obedient, expectant, unwavering faith through His Son our Savior.

Unless we grasp these truths and hold them firmly, we shall not be able to rightly divide the Word of Truth and so shall hardly be "approved to God, a worker who does not need to be ashamed" (2 Tim. 2:15 NKJV). Someone has written that "the searcher in science knows that if he but stumble in his hypotheses—that if he but let himself be betrayed into prejudices or undue leaning toward pet theory, or anything but absolute uprightness of mind—his whole work will be stultified, and he will fail ignominiously. To get anywhere in science he must follow truth with absolute rectitude."[1]

And is there not a science of salvation, of holiness, of eternal life, that requires the same absolute loyalty to "the Spirit of truth" (John 16:13 KJV)? How infinitely important, then, that we know what that truth is, that we may understand and hold that doctrine.

A friend of mine, who some time ago finished his course with joy and was called into the presence of his Lord to receive his crown, has pointed out some mistakes we must carefully avoid:

It is a great mistake to substitute repentance for Bible consecration.

The people whom Paul exhorted to full sanctification were those who had "turned from their idols to serve the living and true God," and to wait for His Son from heaven.

Only people who are citizens of His kingdom can claim His sanctifying power. Those who still have idols to renounce may be candidates for conversion, but not for the baptism with the Holy Ghost and fire.

It is a mistake in consecration to suppose that the person making it has anything of his own to give. We are not our own, but we are bought with a price, and entire sanctification is simply taking our hands off from God's property. To willfully withhold anything from God is to be a God-robber.

It is a mistake to substitute a mere mental assent to God's proprietorship and right to all we have, while withholding complete devotion to Him.

This is theoretical consecration—a rock on which we fear multitudes are being wrecked.

Consecration which does not embrace the crucifixion of self and the funeral of all false ambitions is not the kind which will bring the holy fire.

A consecration is imperfect which does not embrace the speaking faculty [the tongue] and the believing faculty [the heart]; the imagination; and every power of mind, soul, and body, and give all absolutely and forever into the hands of Jesus, turning a deaf ear to every opposing voice.

Reader, have you made such a consecration? . . . It must embrace all of this, or it will prove a bed of quicksand to sink your soul, instead of a full salvation balloon, which will safely bear you above the fog and malaria and turmoil of the world, where you can triumphantly sing: "I rise to float in realms of light, above the world and sin, with heart made pure and garments white, and Christ enthroned within."

It is a mistake to teach seekers for entire sanctification to "only believe," without complete abandonment to God at every point; for they can no more do it than an anchored ship can sail.

It is a mistake to substitute mere verbal assent for obedient trust. "Only believe" is a fatal snare to all who fall into [these] traps.

It is a mistake to believe that the altar sanctifies the gift without the assurance that all is on the altar. If even the end of your tongue, or one cent of your money, or a straw's weight of false ambition, or spirit of dictation, or one ounce of your reputation or will or believing powers be left off the altar, you can no more believe than a bird without wings can fly.

"Only believe" is only for those seekers of holiness who are truly converted, fully consecrated, and completely crucified to everything but the whole will of God. For these, and these only.

Teachers who apply it to people who have not yet reached the stations named should be taught. All who have reached them may lift up their hands in faith, and look God in the face, and triumphantly sing: "The blood, the blood is all my plea, Hallelujah, for it cleanseth me."[2]

THE EXPERIENCE

Simply to be skilled in the doctrine is not sufficient for us as leaders. We may be as orthodox as Paul himself and yet be as "sounding brass, or a clanging cymbal" (1 Cor. 13:1 NKJV) unless we are rooted in the blessed experience of holiness. If we would save ourselves and those who follow us, if we would make havoc of the Devil's kingdom and build up God's kingdom, we must not only know and preach the truth, but we must be living examples of the saving and sanctifying power of the truth. We are to be living epistles, "known and read by all" (2 Cor. 3:2 ESV). We must be able to say with Paul, "Follow me as I follow Christ" (see 1 Cor. 11:1) and, "Whatever you have learned or received or heard from me, or seen in me—put it into practice. And the God of peace will be with you" (Phil. 4:9 NIV).

We must not forget that we are ourselves simple Christians, individual souls struggling for eternal life and liberty, and we must by all means save ourselves. To this end we must be holy, or else we shall at last experience the awful woe of those who, having preached to others, are yet castaways themselves (see 1 Cor. 9:27).

We also must not forget that we are leaders upon whom multitudes depend. It is a joy and honor to be a leader, but it is also a grave responsibility. James said we "will be judged more strictly" (James 3:1 NLT). How inexpressible shall be our blessedness and how vast our reward if, wise in the doctrine and rich and strong and clean in the experience of holiness, we lead our people into their full heritage in Jesus! But how terrible shall be our condemnation and how great our loss if, in spiritual slothfulness and unbelief, we stop short of the experience ourselves and leave them to perish for want of the gushing waters and heavenly food and divine direction we should have brought them! We need the experience for ourselves, and we need it for our work and for our people.

What the roof is to a house, the doctrine is to our system of truth. It completes it. What sound and robust health is to our bodies, the experience is to our souls. It makes us every whit whole and fits us for all duty. Sweep away the doctrine, and the experience will soon be lost. Lose the experience, and the doctrine will surely be neglected, if not attacked and denied. No one can have the heart—even if he or she has the head—to fully and faithfully and constantly preach the doctrine without the experience.

Spiritual things are spiritually discerned, and as this doctrine deals with the deepest things of the Spirit, it is clearly understood and best recommended, explained, defended, and enforced only by those who have the experience.

Without the experience, the presentation of the doctrine will be faulty and cold and lifeless, or weak and vacillating, or harsh and sharp and severe. With the experience, the preaching of the doctrine will be with great joy and assurance, and will be strong and searching, but at the same time warm and persuasive and tender.

I shall never forget the shock of mingled surprise and amusement and grief with which I heard a Salvation Army captain loudly announce in one of my meetings many years ago that he was "going to preach holiness now" and his people "have to get it" if he had to "ram it down their throats." Poor fellow! He did not possess the experience himself, and never pressed into it, and soon forsook his people.

Anyone with a clear experience of the blessing will never think of "ramming" it down people but will—with much secret prayer, constant meditation and study, patient instruction, faithful warning, loving persuasion, and burning, joyful testimony—seek to lead them into that entire and glad consecration and that fullness of faith that never fails to receive the blessing.

Again, the most accurate and complete knowledge of the doctrine, and the fullest possession of the experience, will fail us at last unless we carefully guard ourselves at several points, and unless we watch and pray.

We must not judge ourselves so much by our feelings as by our volitions. It is not my feelings, but the purpose of my heart, the attitude of my will, that God looks at, and it is to that I must look. "If our heart condemn us not, then have we confidence toward God" (1 John 3:21 KJV). A friend of mine who had firmly grasped this thought and walked continually with God used to testify, "I am just as good when I don't feel good as when I do feel good." Another mighty man of God said that all the feeling he needed to enable him to trust God was the consciousness that he was fully submitted to all the known will of God.

We must not forget that the Devil is "the accuser of our brothers and sisters" (Rev. 12:10 NLT), and that he seeks to turn our eyes away from Jesus—who is our Surety and our Advocate—to ourselves, our feelings, our infirmities, our failures. And if he succeeds in this, gloom will fill us, doubts and fears will spring up within us, and we shall soon fail and fall. We must be wise as the conies and build our nest in the cleft of the Rock of Ages.

We must not divorce conduct from character or works from faith. Our lives must square with our teaching. We must live what we preach. We must not suppose that faith in Jesus excuses us from patient, faithful, laborious service. We must live "by every word that comes from the mouth of God" (Matt. 4:4 NLT). That is, we must fashion our lives, our conduct, our conversation by the principles laid down in His Word, remembering His searching saying, "Not everyone who says to me, 'Lord, Lord,' will enter the kingdom of heaven, but only the one who does the will of my Father who is in heaven" (Matt. 7:21 NIV).

This subject of faith and works is very fully discussed by James (see James 2:14–26), and Paul was very clear in his teaching that, while God saves us not by our works but by His mercy through faith, yet we may "devote [our]selves to doing what is good" (Titus 3:14 NIV) and, "We are God's handiwork, created in Christ Jesus to do good works, which God prepared in advance for us to do" (Eph. 2:10 NIV). Faith must work through love (see Gal. 5:6), emotion must be transmitted into action; joy must lead to work; and love must be turned into faithful, self-sacrificing service, or else they become a kind of pleasant and respectable—but nonetheless deadly—debauchery, and at last ruin us.

However blessed and satisfactory our present experience may be, we must not rest in it, but remember that our Lord has yet many things to say to us, as we are able to receive them. We must stir up the gift of God that is in us, and say with Paul, "One thing I do, forgetting those things which are behind, and reaching forth [like a runner] unto those things which are before, I press toward the mark for the prize of the high calling of God in Christ Jesus" (Phil. 3:13–14 KJV). It is at this point that many fail. They seek the Lord, they weep and struggle and pray, and then they believe—but instead of pressing on, they sit down to enjoy the blessing, and then it escapes them. The children of Israel had to follow the pillar of cloud and fire. It made no difference when it moved. By day or by night, they followed. And when the Comforter comes we must follow, if we would abide in Him and be filled with all the fullness of God. And, oh, the joy of following Him!

Finally, if we have the blessing—not the harsh, narrow, unprogressive exclusiveness which often calls itself by the sweet, heavenly term of *holiness*, but the vigorous, courageous, self-sacrificing, tender, Pentecostal experience of perfect love—we shall both save ourselves and enlighten the world. Our converts will be strong, our candidates for ministry will multiply, and will be able, daredevil men and women. And our people will come to be like the brethren of Gideon, of whom it was said, "each one resembled the children of a king" (Judg. 8:18 KJV).

NOTES

1. John Brisben Walker, "What Is Education? The Studies Most Important for the Modern Man," *The Cosmopolitan Magazine*, vol. 37, August 1904.

2. M. W. Knapp, quoted in Aaron Merritt Hills, *A Hero of Faith and Prayer; Or, Life of Rev. Martin Wells Knapp* (Cincinnati: Mount of Blessings, 1902), 151–153.

Victory over Evil Temper 23

Two letters recently reached me (one from Oregon and one from Massachusetts) inquiring if I thought it possible to have temper destroyed. The person from Oregon wrote, "I have been wondering if the statement is correct when one says, 'My temper is all taken away.' Do you think the temper is destroyed or sanctified? It seems to me that if one's temper were actually gone [one] would not be good for anything."

The person from Massachusetts wrote, "Two of our young people have had the question put to them: 'Is it possible to have all temper taken out of our hearts?' One claims it is possible. The other holds that the temper is not taken out, but God gives power to overcome it." Evidently these are questions that perplex many people, and yet the answer seems simple to me.

Temper, in the sense in which the word is generally used, is not a faculty or power of the soul, but is rather an irregular, passionate, violent expression of selfishness. When selfishness is destroyed by love, by the incoming of the Holy Spirit—revealing Jesus to us as an uttermost Savior and creating within us a clean heart—of course such evil temper is gone, just as the friction and consequent wear and heat of two wheels is gone when the cogs are perfectly adjusted to each other. The wheels are far better off without friction, and just so we are far better off without such temper.

We do not destroy the wheels to get rid of the friction, but we readjust them. That is, we put them into right relations with each other, and then they do their work noiselessly and perfectly. So, strictly speaking, sanctification does not destroy self, but it destroys selfishness—the abnormal and mean and disordered manifestation and assertion of self. I myself am to be sanctified, rectified, purified, brought into harmony with God's will as revealed in His Word, and united to Him in Jesus, so that His life of holiness and love flows continually through all the avenues of my being, as the sap of the vine flows through all parts of the branch. "I am the vine; you are the branches," said Jesus (John 15:5 NLT).

When people are thus filled with the Holy Spirit, they are not turned into putty or made into jellyfish, with all powers of resistance taken out. They do not have any less force and "push" and "go" than before, but rather more, for all natural energy is now reinforced by the Holy Spirit and turned into channels of love and peace instead of hate and strife.

They may still feel indignation in the presence of wrong, but it will not be rash, violent, explosive, and selfish, as before they were sanctified, but calm, orderly, holy, and determined, like that of God. It will be the wholesome, natural antagonism of holiness and righteousness to all unrighteousness and evil.

Such people will feel it when they are wronged, but it will be much in the same way that they feel when others are wronged. The personal, selfish element will be absent. At the same time there will be pity and compassion and yearning love for the wrongdoer and a greater desire to see that person saved than to see him or her punished.

A sanctified man was walking down the street the other day with his wife when a filthy fellow on a passing wagon insulted her with foul words. Instantly the temptation came to the man to want to get hold of him and punish him, but just as quickly the indwelling Comforter whispered, "If you forgive those who sin against you" (Matt. 6:14 NLT), and instantly the clean heart of the man responded, "I will, I do forgive him, Lord." Then, instead of anger a great love filled his soul, and instead of hurling a brick or hot words at the poor Devil-deceived fellow, he sent a prayer to God in heaven for him. There was no friction in his soul. He was perfectly adjusted to his Lord. His heart was perfectly responsive to his Master's word, and he could rightly say, "My temper is gone." We must have our spiritual eyes wide open to discern the difference between sinful temper and righteous indignation.

Many people wrong and rob themselves by calling their fits of temper "righteous indignation." On the other hand, there is here and there a timid soul who is so afraid of sinning through temper as to suppress the wholesome antagonism that righteousness, to be healthy and perfect, must express toward all unrighteousness and sin.

It takes the keen-edged Word of God, applied by the Holy Spirit, to cut away unholy temper without destroying righteous antagonism, to enable us to hate and fight sin with spiritual weapons (see 2 Cor. 10:3–5) while pitying and loving the sinner, to so fill us with the mind of Jesus that we will feel as badly over a wrong done to a stranger as though it were done to us, and to help us put away the personal feeling and be as calm and unselfish and judicial in opposing wrong as is the judge upon the bench. Into this state of heart and mind we who are entirely sanctified by the indwelling Holy Spirit are brought.

Dr. Asa Mahan, Finney's friend and coworker, had a quick and violent temper in his youth and young manhood. But one day he believed, God sanctified him, and for fifty years he said he never felt but one uprising of temper, and that was but for an instant, about five years after he received the blessing. For the following forty-five years, though subjected to many trials and provocations, he felt only love and peace and patience and goodwill in his heart.

A Christian woman was confined to her bed for years with nervous and other troubles, and was very cross and touchy and petulant. At last she became convinced that the Lord had a better experience for her, and she began to pray for a clean heart full of patient, holy, humble love. She prayed so earnestly, so violently, that her family became alarmed lest she should wear out her poor, frail body in her struggle for spiritual freedom. But she told them she was determined to have the blessing, if it cost her life, and so she continued to pray, until one glad, sweet day the Comforter came. Her heart was purified, and from that day forth, in spite of the fact that she was still a nervous invalid, suffering constant pain, she never showed the least sign of temper or impatience, but was full of meekness and patient, joyous thankfulness.

Love took up the harp of Life, and smote on all the

chords with might;

Smote the chord of Self, that, trembling, pass'd

in music out of sight.[1]

Such is the experience of one in whom Jesus lives without a rival and in whom grace has done its perfect work.

"No form of vice, not worldliness, not greed of gold, not drunkenness itself, does more to unchristianize society than evil temper,"[2] says a distinguished and thoughtful writer. If this is true, it must be God's will that we be saved from it. And it is provided for in the uttermost salvation that Jesus offers.

Do you want this blessing? If so, be sure of this: God has not begotten such a desire in your heart to mock you; you may have it. God is able to do even this for you. From a human perspective, it is impossible, but not from God's perspective. Look at Him just now for it. It is His work, His gift. Look at your past failures and acknowledge them. Look at your present and future difficulties, count them up and face them every one, and admit that they are more than you can hope to conquer, but then look at the dying Son of God, your Savior—the Man with the seamless robe, the crown of thorns, and the nail-prints. Look at the fountain of His blood. Look at His Word. Look at the almighty Holy Spirit, who will dwell within you, if you trust and obey, and cry out, "It shall be done! The mountain shall become a plain; the impossible shall become possible!" Quietly, intelligently, abandon yourself to the Holy Spirit right now in simple, glad, obedient faith, and the blessing shall be yours.

NOTES

1. Alfred Lord Tennyson, "Locksley Hall," 1835, public domain.

2. Henry Drummond, *The Greatest Thing in the World*, rev. ed. (Grand Rapids, MI: Revell, 2011), 30.

Samuel L. Brengle's Holy Life Series

This series comprises the complete works of Samuel L. Brengle, combining all nine of his original books into six volumes, penned by one of the great minds on holiness. Each volume has been lovingly edited for modern readership by popular author (and long-time Brengle devotee) Bob Hostetler. Brengle's authentic voice remains strong, now able to more relevantly engage today's disciples of holiness. These books are must-haves for all who would seriously pursue and understand the depths of holiness in the tradition of John Wesley.

Helps to Holiness
ISBN: 978-1-63257-064-2
eBook: 978-1-63257-065-9

The Heart of Holiness
ISBN: 978-1-63257-066-6
eBook: 978-1-63257-067-3

The Servant's Heart
ISBN: 978-1-63257-068-0
eBook: 978-1-63257-069-7

Ancient Prophets and Modern Problems
ISBN: 978-1-63257-070-3
eBook: 978-1-63257-071-0

Come Holy Guest
ISBN: 978-1-63257-072-7
eBook: 978-1-63257-073-4

Resurrection Life and Power
ISBN: 978-1-63257-074-1
eBook: 978-1-63257-075-8

Samuel L. Brengle's
Holy Life Series Box Set
ISBN: 978-1-63257-076-5

SAMUEL L. BRENGLE'S HOLY LIFE SERIES

THE HEART OF HOLINESS

Bob Hostetler, General Editor

wesleyan
PUBLISHING HOUSE
wphstore.com

CREST BOOKS

Copyright © 2016 by The Salvation Army
Published by Wesleyan Publishing House
Indianapolis, Indiana 46250
Printed in the United States of America
ISBN: 978-1-63257-066-6
ISBN (e-book): 978-1-63257-067-3

Library of Congress Cataloging-in-Publication Data

Brengle, Samuel Logan, 1860-1936.
    The heart of holiness / Samuel L. Brengle ; Bob Hostetler, general editor.
        pages cm. -- (Samuel L. Brengle's holy life series)
    "This work is a revised combination of the following books by The Salvation
Army: Heart Talks on Holiness and The Way of Holiness."
    ISBN 978-1-63257-066-6 (pbk.)
    1. Holiness. I. Hostetler, Bob, 1958- editor. II. Brengle, Samuel Logan. 1860-1936.
Way of holiness. III. Brengle, Samuel Logan, 1860-1936. Heart talks on holiness.
IV. Title.
    BT767.B78 2016
    234'.8--dc23
                                        2015025626

This work is a revised combination of the following books from The Salvation
Army: *Heart Talks on Holiness* and *The Way of Holiness*.

Contents

Preface

Samuel Logan Brengle was an influential author, teacher, and preacher on the doctrine of holiness in the late nineteenth to early twentieth century, serving from 1887–1931 as an active officer (minister) in The Salvation Army. In 1889 while he and his wife, Elizabeth Swift Brengle, were serving as corps officers (pastors) in Boston, Massachusetts, a brick thrown by a street "tough" smashed Brengle's head against a door frame and caused an injury severe enough to require more than nineteen months of convalescence. During that treatment and recuperation period, he began writing articles on holiness for The Salvation Army's publication, *The War Cry*, which were later collected and published as a "little red book" under the title *Helps to Holiness*. That book's success led to eight others over the next forty-five years: *Heart Talks on Holiness*, *The Way of Holiness*, *The Soul-Winner's Secret*, *When the Holy Ghost Is Come*, *Love-Slaves*, *Resurrection Life and Power*,

Ancient Prophets and Modern Problems, and *The Guest of the Soul* (published in his retirement in 1934).

By the time of his death in 1936, Commissioner Brengle was an internationally renowned preacher and worldwide ambassador of holiness. His influence continues today, perhaps more than any Salvationist in history besides the founders, William and Catherine Booth.

I hope that the revised and updated editions of his books that comprise the Samuel L. Brengle's Holy Life Series will enhance and enlarge that influence, introduce these writings to new readers, and create fresh interest in those who already know the godly wisdom and life-changing power of these volumes.

While I have taken care to preserve the integrity, impact, and voice of the original writing, I have carefully and prayerfully made changes that I hope will facilitate greater understanding and appreciation of Brengle's words for modern readers. These changes include:

- Revising archaic terms (such as the use of King James English) and updating the language to reflect more contemporary usage (such as occasionally employing more inclusive gender references);
- Shortening and simplifying sentence structure and revising punctuation to conform more closely to contemporary practice;
- Explaining specific references of The Salvation Army that will not be familiar to the general population;
- Updating Scripture references (when possible retaining the King James Version—used exclusively in Brengle's writings—but frequently incorporating modern versions, especially when doing so will aid the reader's comprehension and enjoyment);

- Replacing Roman numerals with Arabic numerals and spelled out Scripture references for the sake of those who are less familiar with the Bible;
- Citing Scripture quotes not referenced in the original and noting the sources for quotes, lines from hymns, etc.;
- Aligning all quoted material to the source (Brengle, who often quoted not only Scripture, but also poetry from memory, often quoted loosely in speaking and writing);
- Adding occasional explanatory phrases or endnotes to identify people or events that might not be familiar to modern readers;
- Revising or replacing some chapter titles, and (in *Ancient Prophets and Modern Problems*) moving one chapter to later in the book; and
- Deleting the prefaces that introduced each book and epigraphs that preceded some chapters.

In the preface to Brengle's first book, Commissioner (later General) Bramwell Booth wrote, "This book is intended to help every reader of its pages into the immediate enjoyment of Bible holiness. Its writer is an officer of The Salvation Army who, having a gracious experience of the things whereof he writes, has been signally used of God, both in life and testimony, to the sanctifying of the Lord's people, as well as in the salvation of sinners. I commend him and what he has here written down to every lover of God and His kingdom here on earth."

In the preface to Brengle's last book, *The Guest of the Soul*, The Salvation Army's third general (and successor to Bramwell Booth) wrote: "These choice contributions . . . will, I am sure, serve to

strengthen the faith of the readers of this book and impress upon them the joyousness of life when the heart has been opened to the Holy Guest of the Soul."

I hope and pray that this updated version of Brengle's writings will further those aims.

—Bob Hostetler

general editor

PART ONE

Heart Talks on Holiness

The Death of the Old Nature 1

The Son of God came into this world—and lived, toiled, taught, suffered, died, and rose again—in order to accomplish a twofold purpose. The apostle John explained that twofold work. First, speaking of Jesus, John said, "He appeared in order to take away sins" (1 John 3:5 ESV). This is justification and regeneration, which are done for us and in us. Second, John added, "The reason the Son of God appeared was to destroy the works of the devil" (1 John 3:8 ESV). That is entire sanctification, which is a work done in us. Now upon an examination of experience and Scripture, we find this is exactly what each of us needs.

First, we need to get rid of our own sins and have a new principle of life planted in us. "For all have sinned, and come short of the glory of God" (Rom. 3:23 KJV), and when we come to God, we come burdened with a sense of our own wrongdoings and tempers. Our sins condemn us but, thank God, Jesus came to take away our sins. When you come with a penitent heart, acknowledging your sins, and put your trust in Jesus, you will find yourself suddenly freed from your sins. The sense of guilt will vanish. The power of evil will be broken. The burden will roll away. Peace will fill your heart. You will see that your sins were laid on another, even on Jesus, and you will realize that "with his wounds we are healed" (Isa. 53:5 ESV).

This is a result of that free pardon, that free justification for all past offenses that God gives to all who surrender themselves heartily to Jesus and trust in Him. At the same time, God plants in your heart a new life. You are born of God and receive what Paul called the washing of regeneration, which washes away all your guilt and all the sin for which you were responsible.

At this time, too, love, joy, peace, and the various fruit of the Spirit will be planted in your heart, and if your experience is very marked, as such experiences frequently are, you will probably think there is nothing more to be done. But if you walk in humility (which, by the way, is a much-neglected fruit of the Spirit), speak often and freely with those who love the Lord, and carefully search the Word of God and meditate on it day and night, you will soon find that sin's disease is deeper and more deadly than you thought. You will discover that behind and below your own sins are the "works of the devil" (1 John 3:8 KJV) that must also be destroyed before the work of grace in your soul can be complete.

You will find a big, dark something in you that wants to get mad when things are against you, something which will not be patient, something that is touchy and sensitive, something that wants to grumble and find fault, something that is proud and shuns the shame of the cross, something that sometimes suggests hard thoughts against God, something that is self-willed and ugly and sinful. You hate this "something" in you and want to get rid of it. You probably condemn yourself for it and may feel that you are a greater sinner now than ever before. But you are not. In fact, you are not a sinner at all so long as you resist this something in yourself.

Now, what is the problem? What is the name of this troublesome "something"? Paul called it by several names. In Romans 8:7, he called it "the sinful nature" and said it "is always hostile to God. It never did obey God's laws, and it never will" (NLT). You cannot fix it up. You cannot whitewash it over. You cannot make it better by culture or growth, or by any effort whatever. It is an enemy of God and cannot be anything else.

In another place Paul called it the "life that is dominated by sin and death" and wondered how he could get deliverance from it (Rom. 7:24 NLT). In Ephesians and Colossians he called it the "old sinful nature" (Eph. 4:22; Col. 3:9 NLT). In Galatians he called it "the sinful nature" (Gal. 5:17 NLT). James called it "rampant wickedness" (James 1:21 ESV), which is also well rendered, "all that remains of wickedness" (James 1:21 NASB).

John called it "sin" (as distinct from "sins") and the "works of the devil" (1 John 3:8 KJV). In Ezekiel it is called a "stony heart" (Ezek. 36:26 KJV). Theologians call it "inbred sin," "original sin," and "depravity." Whatever you wish to call it, it is something evil and awful that remains in the heart after a person has experienced new life in Christ.

Some say it is dealt with at the moment of salvation, but I never saw any people who found it so. And John Wesley, who was a much wiser man than I am (and who had a far wider range of observation), examined thousands of people on this very point, and he said he never knew of one who got rid of this troublesome thing at the moment they experienced new life in Christ.

Some people say that growing in grace is the remedy. Others say you never get rid of it while you live—that it will remain in you and war against you till you die. They are not altogether prophets of despair, for they say the new life in you will overcome it and keep it down, but that you will have to stand on guard and watch it and club and repress it as you would a maniac, until death relieves you.

Personally, this subject once gave me great concern. These warring opinions perplexed me, while the "old sinful nature" made increasing war against all my holy desires and purposes. But while I found human teachings and theories perplexing, God's teachings were plain and light as day.

God does not admit that we get rid of this at the moment in which we experience salvation, for all His teachings and exhortations concerning it are addressed to Christians. And those who hold this doctrine will have to admit one of two things: either that it is not removed by the experience of salvation or that a great number of earnest people who claim to be Christians have never experienced salvation at all. Personally, I cannot admit the latter for an instant.

God does, by the mouth of Peter, exhort us to grow in grace, but that simply means to grow in favor with God by obedience and faith and does not touch the subject in hand. Corn may grow beautifully and delight the farmer, but all its growth will not rid the field of weeds, and the farmer will have to look to some other method to get rid of those troublesome things.

Neither does God anywhere teach that this thing has to bother us till death or that death will destroy it. Nor do I find any warrant in the whole Bible for purgatorial fires being the deliverer from this evil.

But I do find that God teaches very plainly how we are to get rid of it. Paul said, "Throw off your old sinful nature" (Eph. 4:22 NLT). James said, "[Put] aside all filthiness and all that remains of wickedness" (James 1:21 NASB). John said, "The blood of Jesus, his Son, cleanses us from all sin" (1 John 1:7 NLT)—not part or some, but *all* sin. Again, John said Jesus "came to destroy the works of the devil" (1 John 3:8 NLT), and God said through Ezekiel, "I will take out your stony, stubborn heart" (Ezek. 36:26 NLT).

All these passages teach that we are to get rid of something that bothers us and hinders our spiritual life. They show plainly that this work is not to be a slow, evolutionary process, but an instantaneous work, accomplished in the heart of the humble believer by the Holy Spirit. And the Bible further teaches that the one necessary thing on our part to secure this operation of the Holy Spirit is an obedient faith that laughs at impossibilities and cries, "It shall be done!"[1]

If this teaching of the Bible is true, then it can be proven by experience. If one person proves it to be so, that establishes the Bible testimony against all the doubters in the world. Everyone used to believe the world was flat; Columbus rose up and said it was round and proved it to them all. There may be some ignorant old fogies yet who believe the world is flat, but they can prove it to be round if they will take the trouble, and whether they prove it or not, their purblind unbelief does not change the fact.

Just so, the greater part of humankind believes that the old sinful nature is destined to live to the end. But as Paul asked, "Will their unbelief make the faithfulness of God without effect?" (Rom. 3:3 NKJV). Humble men and women are rising up every day to declare it is possible, and they can prove that the old sinful nature can be destroyed, if they will meet the conditions.

Oh, that we could get people to understand this! Oh, that we could get them to take counsel with faith and not with unbelief! Oh, that we could get them to see what Jesus really came to do!

I proved this in my life fifteen years ago, and ever since I have been walking in a day that has no setting sun, and everlasting joy and gladness have been on my head and in my heart.

It is no little salvation that Jesus Christ came to work out for us. It is a "great salvation" (Heb. 2:3 NLT), and it saves. It is not a pretense or make believe. It is a real salvation from all sin and uncleanness, all doubt and fear, all guile and hypocrisy, all malice and wrath.

When I begin to consider it and write about it, I want to fill the page with praises to God. The hallelujahs of heaven begin to ring all through my soul, and my heart cries out with those four mystical beasts before the throne, "Holy, holy, holy, Lord God Almighty" (Rev. 4:8 KJV). And in spirit I fall down with the twenty-four elders and worship "the one who lives forever and ever" (Rev. 4:9 NLT), who has taken away my sins, destroyed the works of the Devil out of my heart, and come to dwell in me.

"Be careful then, dear brothers and sisters. Make sure that your own hearts are not evil and unbelieving. . . . For only we who believe can enter his rest" (Heb. 3:12; 4:3 NLT).

NOTE

1. Charles Wesley, "Father of Jesus Christ, My Lord," 1742, public domain.

Holiness—What It Is Not and What It Is

Holiness is not necessarily a state in which there is perpetual rapturous joy. The prophet Isaiah told us that Jesus was "a man of sorrows, acquainted with deepest grief" (Isa. 53:3 NLT). Paul told us that he himself had continual sorrow and great heaviness because of the rejection of Jesus by His fellow Jews (see Rom. 9:2–3). Joy is the normal state of a holy heart, but it may be mingled with sorrow and grief and perplexities and heaviness as a result of various temptations. The low water mark, however, in the experience of a holy person is one of perfect peace. The high water mark is up in the third heaven somewhere, although this third-heaven experience is not likely to be constantly maintained. Jesus and the disciples had to come down off the Mount of Transfiguration and go to casting out devils, and Paul returned from the third-heaven to be attacked by Satan, and stoned and whipped and imprisoned.

Holiness is not a state of freedom from temptation. This is a world of trial and of conflict with principalities, powers, darknesses, and terrible evils, and the holy soul who is in the forefront of the conflict may expect the fiercest assaults of the Devil and the heaviest and most perplexing and prolonged temptations. Our Lord was tried and tempted for forty days and forty nights by the Devil, and the servant must not be surprised if he or she is like the Master in this.

The author of Hebrews told us that Jesus was tempted in all points as we are (see Heb. 4:15) and that He is able to help us when we are tempted (see Heb. 2:18). It is no sin to be tempted. In fact, the apostle James told us to rejoice when we are subjected to all manner of temptations, because the resulting trial of our faith will produce in us strength and force of holy character, so that we shall be lacking in nothing (see James 1:2–4).

Holiness is not a state of freedom from infirmities. It does not produce a perfect head, but rather a perfect heart! The saints have always been compassed about with infirmities that have proved a source of great trial but, when patiently endured for His dear sake, have also proved a source of great blessing. Paul had a thorn in the flesh, an infirmity, a messenger of Satan to buffet him. Possibly it was weak eyes, for he was once stoned and dragged out of the city and left for dead, and in writing to the Galatians, he told them they would have plucked out their eyes and given them to him had it been possible (see Gal. 4:15). Or it may have been a stammering tongue, for he told us he was a clumsy speaker (see 2 Cor. 11:6). Anyway, it was an infirmity he longed to be rid of, doubtless feeling that it interfered with his usefulness. Three times he prayed to the Lord for deliverance, but instead of getting the prayed-for deliverance, the Lord said to him, "My grace is all you need. My power works best in weakness" (2 Cor. 12:9 NLT).

Then Paul cried out, "So now I am glad to boast about my weaknesses, so that the power of Christ can work through me. That's why I take pleasure in my weaknesses, and in the insults, hardships, persecutions, and troubles that I suffer for Christ. For when I am weak, then I am strong" (2 Cor. 12:9–10 NLT).

In the letter to the Hebrews we are told that Jesus "understands our weaknesses" (Heb. 4:15 NLT). We may be faulty in memory, judgment, or understanding. We may have many infirmities of body and mind. But God looks upon the purity of the heart, the singleness of the eye, and the loyalty of our affection; and if He does not find us faulty there, He counts us perfect. It is not in the mere natural perfection that the power and glory of God are shown, but rather in goodness and purity and patience and love and meekness and longsuffering, shining through infirmities of flesh and imperfections of mind.

Holiness is not a state of freedom from affliction. The saints of all ages have been chosen "in the furnace of suffering" (Isa. 48:10 NLT). Job and Jeremiah and Daniel and Paul and the mighty army of martyrs have, and shall always, come up through great tribulations. It is not God's purpose to take us to heaven on flowery beds of ease, clothe us in purple and fine linen, and keep a sugarplum in our mouths all the time. That would not develop strength of character nor cultivate simplicity and purity of heart—nor in that case could we really know Jesus and the fellowship of His sufferings. It is in the furnace of fire, the lion's den, and the dungeon cell that God most freely reveals Himself to His people.

Other things being equal, the holy man or woman is less liable to afflictions than the soul that is not holy. He does not run into the same excesses as others. She is free from the pride, the temper, the jealousies, the vaulting ambitions, and the selfishness that plunge so many into terrible affliction and ruin. Yet we must not presume that we will get through the world without heavy trials, sore temptations, and afflictions. Job was a perfect man, but he lost all his property, his children, and in a day was made a childless pauper. But he proved his perfection by giving God glory. Then when his wife bade him curse God and die, he said to her, "You talk like a foolish woman. Should we accept only good things from the hand of God and never anything bad?" (Job 2:10 NLT). And when his three friends tried to undermine his faith, he looked up from his ash heap and out of his awful sorrow, desolation, and fierce pain cried out, "Though he slay me, yet will I trust in him" (Job 13:15 KJV).

Joseph is one of the few men in the Bible about whom nothing negative is recorded but, like Daniel, his very holiness and righteousness led to the terrible trials he endured in Egypt. And so it may be, and is, with us today. But while we may be afflicted, yet we can comfort ourselves with David's assurance, "Many are the afflictions of the righteous, but the LORD delivers him out of them all" (Ps. 34:19 NKJV). A friend of mine said he would rather have a thousand afflictions and be delivered out of them all than to have half a dozen and get stuck in the midst of them.

Holiness is not a state in which there is no further development. When the heart is purified it develops more rapidly than ever before. Spiritual development comes through the revelation of Jesus Christ in the heart, and the holy soul is in a condition to receive such revelations constantly. And since the finite can never exhaust the infinite, these revelations will continue forever and prove an increasing and never-ending source of development. It would be as wise to say that a child afflicted with rickets would grow no more after receiving treatment or that corn would grow no more when the weeds were destroyed, as to say that a soul will cease to grow in grace when it is made holy.

Holiness is not a state from which we cannot fall. Paul told us that we stand by faith (see Rom. 6:16–22), and he said, "If you think you are standing strong, be careful not to fall" (1 Cor. 10:12 NLT). It is an unscriptural and dangerous doctrine that there is any state of grace in this world from which we cannot fall. Probation does not end the moment we believe in Jesus, but rather the moment we leave the body. It is only those who endure to the end who shall be saved (see Matt. 10:22). While here, we are in the Enemy's country and must watch, pray, examine ourselves daily, and keep ourselves in the love of God, lest we fall from His grace and shipwreck our faith. But while we may fall, thank God holiness is a state from which we need not fall. In fact, it is a state that Paul called, "this place of undeserved privilege where we now stand" (see Rom. 5:2 NLT).

Some have asked the question, "How can a holy soul be tempted or how can it fall?" I will ask the question, how could the angels fall? And how could Adam, just fresh from the hands of his Maker—in whose image he was made—fall? And I will ask the more startling question still: How could Jesus, the blessed incarnate God Himself, be tempted? We have our five senses and various bodily appetites, none of which are sinful in themselves, but each of which may become an avenue by which the holy soul may be tempted to sin. Each of these senses and appetites must be regulated by the Word of God and dominated by the love of Jesus if we wish to keep a holy heart and "stand firm in all the will of God, mature and fully assured" (Col. 4:12 NIV).

Finally, holiness is a state of conformity to the divine nature. God is love, and there is a sense in which a holy man or woman can be said to be love. That is, like God, not in God's natural perfection of power, wisdom, knowledge, and omnipresence, but in patience, humility, self-control, purity of heart, and love. As the drop out of the ocean is like the ocean not in its bigness but in its essence, so is the holy soul like God. As the branch is like the vine, not in its self-sufficiency but in its nature, its sap, its fruitfulness, and its beauty, so is the one who is holy like God.

This inexpressible blessing is provided for us by our compassionate heavenly Father through the shed blood of our Lord Jesus Christ and is received through a complete renunciation of all sin, an uttermost consecration to all the known will of God, importunate prayer, and childlike faith. Fifteen years ago I obtained this crowning blessing of the gospel through the conscious incoming of the Holy Spirit when I believed after weeks of earnest seeking. He still abides with me, and my peace and joy increase and abound. Many have been my afflictions, and fierce and perplexing and prolonged have been my temptations, but with a daredevil faith I have pressed on, claiming victory through the blood, testifying to what I claimed by faith, and proving day by day this grace to be sufficient while the path shines "ever brighter until the full light of day" (Prov. 4:18 NLT).

Holiness—How to Get It 3

Holiness is that state of our moral and spiritual nature which makes us like Jesus in His moral and spiritual nature. It does not consist in perfection of intellect, though the experience will give much greater clearness to our intellect and simplify and energize our mental operations. Nor does it necessarily consist in perfection of conduct, though a holy person will seek wholeheartedly to make the outward conduct correspond to the inward light and love. But holiness does consist in complete deliverance from the sinful nature and in the perfection of the spiritual graces of love, joy, peace, longsuffering, gentleness, goodness, truth, meekness, and self-control.

Righteousness is conformity to the divine law, but holiness is conformity to the divine nature. That there is such an experience is revealed to us in three ways.

The reality of this experience is revealed to us by the Scriptures. The Bible tells us that God chastens us "for our good, that we may share his holiness" (Heb. 12:10 ESV). And He has "given us great and precious promises . . . that enable you to share his divine nature and escape the world's corruption caused by human desires" (2 Pet. 1:4 NLT). In the Bible, God makes us very precious promises of holiness. He gives us very solemn and imperative commands to be holy. He earnestly exhorts us and graciously encourages us to be holy, and teaches us to pray for holiness.

That there is such an experience is revealed to us by the testimony of holy men and women who declare that God has brought them into this glorious experience. It is also revealed by the hunger and thirst of our own regenerate hearts. If these desires—to be like God and to have His love and holiness so fill our hearts as to cast out every sinful thought and desire—are begotten in us by the Spirit of God, then they may be considered as proof that holiness is possible. The Spirit of God will not plant desires in the hearts of His trusting children only to mock them.

Nearly all Christians expect to be made holy either before they die or at the moment of death. And everybody agrees that we must be holy before we can enter heaven. Some other Christians maintain that we are sanctified at the moment of death by some mysterious operation of the Spirit of God. Others insist that we grow into the experience. But I believe it is the gift of God and the heritage of every soul that is born again, an inheritance into which we can enter at once by hearty consecration and childlike faith.

How then is holiness obtained? Not by purgatorial fires but by Holy Spirit fire. Not by works; that would make you your own savior and sanctifier. A great trick of the Devil is to lead people to think they will get it by doing something, but we might as well try to lift ourselves over the fence by our own bootstraps as to transform ourselves into the divine nature by works. We can get it no more by works than we can change the color of our eyes by works. We can no more rid ourselves of an inherited temper or banish lust from our hearts—or hatred or pride—by getting baptized, going to church, reading the Bible, or doing any other religious act, than we can get bacteria out of our blood or add an inch to our height with such measures. "Not a result of works, so that no one may boast" (Eph. 2:9 ESV). However, a holy person is abundant in good works, and so is one who is truly seeking the blessing. But more about this further on.

Not by growth. Growth adds to us, but takes nothing from us. Neither does it change the nature and disposition. Holiness consists in having something taken from us and in having our spiritual nature made over into Jesus' image. In order to be holy we must have every unclean desire and temper and passion of the soul removed. We must "throw off" the "old sinful nature . . . which is corrupted by lust and deception" (Eph. 4:22 NLT), just as we take off an old coat. And we must put on the "new nature, created to be like God—truly righteous and holy" (Eph. 4:24 NLT), just as we put on a new coat. This is the way God told Paul to tell us to do it. It would be nonsense to talk of growing out of an old coat into a new one. Put off the old coat; put on a new one! Put off the old Adam; put on the new Adam!

It is not by death. I used to think it was, because I was taught so. But I dreaded the thought of being killed by lightning or shot by a stray bullet. I did not want to die suddenly; I wanted time to get ready.

But I learned that holiness is not obtained by death, and now I am ready to meet that old enemy.

Well, then, how can you get it? From Jesus, the very same Jesus who delivered you and spoke peace to your troubled conscience when you feared you were going to sink into hell—the very same Jesus who died for you. But how? By asking. By giving yourself freely and forever to Him, to be not only your Savior, but also your Lord and Master, to do and suffer all His blessed, wise, and tender will. By believing and receiving.

If you knew you had to die at sunset tonight, what would you do? You would give yourself to God. If you had any grudges against your neighbors, you would give them up, and if you had the opportunity, you would ask them to forgive you for hating them, even though they had wronged you or some of your friends. You would not stop to think how they would treat you. You would not care. You would consider it your business to get right, and you would leave them with God. If you had robbed anyone, you would try to restore to that person what was stolen. If you had any selfish plans or ambitions, they would sink into molehills before the mighty mountains of eternity, and you would give them up quickly. If you had been unfaithful in the discharge of any duty, you would confess it, mourn over it, and do all in the limited time left to make the matter right. You would prepare the way of the Lord and make His paths straight. You would throw up your hands in helplessness and ask God to forgive you for Jesus' sake, and not because there was any merit in yourself. And if you really trusted, you would receive forgiveness and be at peace. You would feel Jesus to be your Savior, and you would rejoice in Him.

Now you would be a candidate for holiness. If the Holy Spirit should now reveal to you the hidden corruption of the human heart, and show you that it was out of this bad soil that grew the bad weeds of hatred and pride, selfish ambitions and envy, lies, adulteries, murders, drunkenness, thefts, and such like, you would cry to God to rid you not only of the weeds, but to entirely change the condition of your heart out of which such unholy things grew. And there would be only one way to get this done: You would ask God to do it for Jesus' sake, trust Him to do it, and wait with full expectation until He did it.

And He would do it. He would purge your heart of all unholy conditions by the baptism of the Holy Spirit and fire, as surely as fire purges gold of dross. This is just what He wants to do. He wants all His children to be like His well-beloved Son, Jesus. It was for this that He sent Jesus into the world, and it is for this that He baptizes with the Holy Spirit and fire.

Some time ago a lady came to the penitent form (a special place at the altar for asking for forgiveness) in one of my meetings, seeking sanctification. After I had questioned her and explained the subject as fully as I could and we had prayed, she claimed the blessing. She did not get any special witness that the work was done, but soon she came again to one of my meetings and testified. And her testimony threw light on the difficulty for many people.

She said that for several days after she left that first meeting she did not feel any different, but as she went about her housework a thought came to her mind—no doubt the Holy Spirit, the Sanctifier Himself, suggested it to her—that her sanctification was a part of her Father's will for her and that He offered it to her on the simple conditions of full consecration and childlike faith in Him. Then it dawned upon her that she had met these conditions and that now instead of waiting for any unusual feelings she must just act as though it were done.

She then added that when she began to count it done and to act as though it *were* done, she began to realize that God *was* doing His part. She began to feel the mighty workings of the Spirit in her heart.

It is just at this point that many people fail. They wait for feeling and hesitate and doubt and wonder and go with their heads down and repine and maybe throw away their confidence. Instead, they should recklessly but intelligently give themselves over to Jesus to be His forever, to do His will unto death. They should step out on the promise with humility and adoring faith toward God and, with a shout of defiance to the Devil and all their fears, count the work done.

One day ten lepers met Jesus. "And they lifted up their voices and said, 'Jesus, Master, have mercy on us!' So when He saw them, He said to them, 'Go, show yourselves to the priests'" (Luke 17:13–14 NKJV). Oh, how He loved them and yearned over them in their misery! But His yearnings over their sick bodies were feeble compared to His mighty yearnings over your diseased soul, my friend.

It was a law among the Jews that when a leper was healed, he must go to the priest and show that he could be safely among other people. But these poor fellows might have objected and said to Jesus, "But look at us! We are not healed. We are not different since you spoke to us. We shall be fools to go in this plight, and we shall not be received if we do go. Heal us and make us feel different, that we may know we are healed; then we will go."

But they did not talk that way. They did not stop to reason with their doubts and fears. They did not stop to examine their feelings or compare themselves with the healthy folks around them. Jesus had spoken the word and it was theirs to trust and obey. So they hobbled off, I imagine, as fast as they could go. "And it came to pass, that, as they went, they were cleansed" (Luke 17:14 KJV). That was cleansing through "the obedience of faith" (Rom. 16:26 KJV), and it is written for our encouragement and instruction.

Do you want this experience? If you have it, rejoice and praise God for it. Don't merely keep on seeking it or you will get into darkness, but go to thanking God for it and testifying of it to others. But if you do not have it, give yourself up fully to God right now, ask for it, believe for it, and if it does not come at once, patiently and expectantly wait for it. Expect it, expect it, expect it! He gives His people "an expected end" (Jer. 29:11 KJV). Remind God of His promises. Don't give Him any rest till He comes and sanctifies you. Tell Him you have come to stay and that you will not let Him go till He blesses you. Nestle down on His promises close to the loving heart of Jesus and stay there, expecting till you know the work is done.

If the Devil and an evil heart of unbelief say, "It is for others, but not for you," answer, "I am all the Lord's; get behind me, Satan," and tell Jesus about it.

If the Devil says, "You don't feel any different," answer, "I am all the Lord's; get behind me, Satan," and tell Jesus about this also. If the Devil says, "You can't keep it if you do get it," answer, "I am all the Lord's; get behind me, Satan," and don't forget to tell this to Jesus.

Act out your faith, regardless of your feelings. A heaven of love, joy, peace, and patience will soon fill your poor heart, and you will get "lost in wonder, love, and praise."[1] Don't bother yourself about your feelings. Your business is to wait on God for orders and inspiration, and then to trust and obey. It is His part of the business to shine upon you and cleanse you, fill you with the Holy Spirit, and make your heart bubble over with joy.

Claim the promise. Feed on the Word of God. Feast yourself on His love and faithfulness in Jesus. Wait on Him in believing, expectant prayer and you will be satisfied "more than the richest feast" (Ps. 63:5 NLT). You will become strong to work for God and win souls. You will rise above discouragements and difficulties. You will chase a thousand of your enemies, and if you can find someone with a kindred spirit, the two of you will put ten thousand to flight (see Deut. 32:30).

Go to believing just now and you will have peace. Continue to believe and your peace will flow like a river. Hold on this way, resisting the Devil, firm in your faith, reminding Jesus of His promises and encouraging your own heart with them, and it will not be long before your patient, expectant faith receives a great reward. God will say, "It is enough; this one has come to stay. So be it done." And, calling to mind His ancient promise, He will open the windows of heaven and "pour out a blessing so great you won't have enough room to take it in" (Mal. 3:10 NLT). Then down into your waiting, trusting, expecting heart will come the Comforter, the blessed Holy Spirit, and up from the deepest center of your soul will spring the artesian well of living waters of holy love and praise. Then the meek and lowly Jesus will come and dwell in your clean heart, and you will love Him more than a mother loves her firstborn babe, more than the bridegroom loves his bride. You will adore Him, worship Him, pour out your heart's treasures upon Him, and loathe yourself for all your sins that crowned Him with thorns and nailed Him to the cross and for your unbelief and hardness of heart that kept Him from you so long.

Have the blessing now. Let God search you and show you all your heart. Don't be afraid. Heartily give yourself to Him and trust, expect, ask, wait, receive.

NOTE

1. Charles Wesley, "Love Divine, All Loves Excelling," 1747, public domain.

Hindrances to Holiness 4

God has provided a salvation for us that is perfect in every particular, one that satisfies both the heart and the mind. It makes its possessor more than a conqueror over the world, the flesh, and the Devil, and enables him or her to do God's will on earth as it is done in heaven. It is altogether worthy of its Author. It is a "great salvation" (Heb. 2:3 KJV). It is not a mere set of beliefs, nor a poor pitiful little profession, but a full, joyous, all-conquering life. This is the more-abundant life. Jesus said, "I am come that they might have life, and that they might have it more abundantly" (John 10:10 KJV). Praise the Lord, this life is mine and has been for fifteen years.

But, for the sake of those who have not obtained this crowning blessing, I wish to point out some of the hindrances to its reception and the reason why so few (comparatively) have it.

Many are ignorant of it. Vast multitudes of professing Christians have never heard of a second work of the Holy Spirit that purifies the heart and perfects it in love. It is, strange to say, an unpopular theme and is not much spoken of outside of The Salvation Army holiness meetings, and so God could say today, as He did long ago, "My people are destroyed for lack of knowledge" (Hos. 4:6 KJV). This ignorance is not altogether due to the fact that it is a subject little spoken about, but also because so few people go to God's Word for their standard of life and experience. It is all written out there so plain that a fool need not err (see Isa. 35:8). Most religious folk, however, prefer to take their standard from the people around about them rather than from God's Book. Paul said of such folks, "But they measuring themselves by themselves, and comparing themselves among themselves, are not wise" (2 Cor. 10:12 KJV). And they never will be wise, unless they cease looking at poor, perishing people and look to Jesus only. Wisdom is from above (see James 3:17) and must be sought from God Himself and from the study of His Word, not from the conduct of the people about us.

Others are unbelieving. Many people who are familiar with the Word of God lack an appropriating faith. They read the "exceeding great and precious promises" (2 Pet. 1:4 KJV), but it never occurs to them that on the fulfillment of the conditions they can and will have the things promised. It is said of these people that they failed to believe what they heard, and the message did not do them any good (see Heb. 4:2). Instead of crying to God to bring their experience up to the standard of the Bible, they explain the Bible down to the level of their experience, and so never receive the glorious revelation of Jesus to their hearts and the fullness of grace He promises.

Some seek the wrong thing. They expect the blessing of full salvation to bring deliverance from temptations, infirmities, natural consequences of broken laws, and the like. I once heard an educated minister pray, "Lord save us from our impurities and infirmities." My heart said amen to the first part, but not to the latter. Full salvation always delivers from impurity, but not always from infirmities in this world. God uses our infirmities to bless us. Paul gloried in his infirmities because through them the power of Christ rested upon him (see 2 Cor. 12:9–10). We read also that Jesus was "touched with the feeling of our infirmities" (Heb. 4:15 KJV).

Infirmities and temptations are incorporated by our heavenly Father into His educational and disciplinary plans for us. They are for our highest good, and we need not expect to be entirely free from them while we are in the body. If we were free from them, we could not enter into the fellowship of the sufferings of Jesus nor sympathize with our brothers and sisters, and that would be an immeasurable loss to us. It is because Jesus was tempted in all points as we are and was touched with the feeling of our infirmities that He is able to sympathize with and help us when we are tempted (see Heb. 2:18). And it is only as we enter into the common temptations and trials and are afflicted with the common infirmities of humanity that we can be touched with tender sympathy for others and be used to bless them. Thus, we should not seek for an experience that will save us from these things, but rather should do as we are told and "count it all joy" when we meet "trials of various kinds" (James 1:2 ESV).

Nor does this experience of full salvation save us from the natural consequences of broken laws. We may be enjoying the fullness of

God's salvation but if we ignorantly break the laws of finance or health we may expect to go into bankruptcy or lose our health as surely as anyone else. And this does not at all suggest that our heavenly Father is displeased with us morally or that we have lost any measure of our salvation.

Nor does this experience enable us to please everybody and appear perfect to everyone. Our hearts may be as pure as the heart of an archangel and we may love with a perfect love, yet our conduct may be misjudged and we may be accounted by others as anything but fully saved. The brother of Jesus did not believe in Him (see John 7:5), and His critics called Him a glutton and a winebibber or heavy drinker (see Matt. 11:19). His servants will hardly be above their Master, but should rejoice to be like Him.

There are two reasons for this. One is that we "have this treasure in jars of clay" (2 Cor. 4:7 NIV). That is, the love of God in our hearts may be perfect and His salvation complete, but because of our natural infirmities we may not be able to fully express in our conduct the holy affections and tender sympathies of our hearts. Just as clear water will look blue in a blue bottle or yellow in a yellow bottle, so the pure, crystal-like salvation of God in our hearts takes on the color of our clay jars.

The other reason is that, just as when you look at a landscape through fogged glasses everything looks foggy, so the eyesight of many people is so distorted and blurred by sin, prejudice, and unbelief, that even if our conduct is perfect, they—looking at us through the medium of their own sinfulness—will criticize us as they criticized our Lord before us. This being so, we need not expect the experience of full salvation to make us appear perfect in the eyes of other people, but must content ourselves with having "a clear conscience before God and all people" (Acts 24:16 NLT), and in having His assurance that our ways please Him.

Others expect a sort of "third heaven" experience, similar to what Paul had, in which they will see visions, hear voices, be visited by angels, and constantly have tumultuous and rapturous joy. Like Peter on the Mount of Transfiguration, they say, "Master, it is good for us to be here" (Luke 9:33 KJV), not knowing that Jesus wants to lead them down into the valley to cast out devils. Far be it from me to discourage any soul from seeking any godly experience mentioned in the Bible! Has not my own heart almost burst with fullness of joy and love? Cannot I, in the Spirit, say with Paul, "Have I not seen Jesus Christ our Lord" (1 Cor. 9:1 KJV)? Truly, the revelation Jesus gave me of Himself is unutterable, but I got this revelation not by seeking some marvelous experience, but by humbling myself to walk with Him, wait for His counsel, do His will, and believe what He said. Then He came to me and took up His abode in my heart. He has shown me, however, that although I am to have His joy, holiness does not consist so much in rapturous, sublimated experiences, as in lowly, humble, patient, trustful love.

But while some people fail to get the experience because they put it up among the clouds, others make the mistake of leaving it down among the fogs. They think the blessing of holiness consists in simply being free from condemnation, forgetting that a justified soul is not condemned. For instance, a man has been condemned about the use of tobacco, or a woman about the styles she wears. Each feels that such things are not consistent with a Christian life, and, after a struggle with pride and habit, yields and casts away the offending thing. Of course there is now no longer any condemnation, and that soul feels justified. But it may not yet be sanctified, and it is not, unless, when the offending thing was cast off, the Holy Spirit came in, destroying every root of bitterness and sin out of the heart. Holiness is a thing of the heart. It is the purging away of the dross of the soul. It is the renewing of our whole nature so that we are made "partakers of the divine nature" (2 Pet. 1:4 KJV). It makes "the tree good" (Matt. 12:33 KJV).

My little eight-year-old boy had the nature of holiness revealed to him by the Holy Spirit. Some time ago he said he experienced new life in Christ, and I think he did, though he is not so saintly as I feel confident he yet will be. However, one evening, not long afterward, he said to his mother, "Mama, I'm tired of living this way." His mother responded, "Why, darling, what's the matter now?"

"I want to be good all the time," said George. "You tell me to go and do things, and I go and do them, but I feel angry inside. I want to be good all the time." The next morning, as soon as he woke up, he said, "Mama, I want you to put that verse, 'Create in me a clean heart, O God,' in my textbook" (Ps. 51:10 KJV). And then when he prayed he pleaded the prayer of the royal psalmist, "Search me, O God, and know my heart: try me, and know my thoughts: and see if there be any wicked way in me" (Ps. 139:23–24 KJV).

Holiness makes one good all the time—not only in conduct, but also in character; not only in outward act, but also in inward thought and wish and feeling. Those who are content with anything less than this will miss the blessing.

Another hindrance is the failure to rightly consider "this Jesus whom we declare to be God's messenger and High Priest" (Heb. 3:1 NLT) and to appropriate the grace He offers us. The other day an earnest Christian woman was complaining to me at her breakfast table about her pride and her temper, which she had found unconquerable. I suggested that she should consider Jesus and asked her how she could be proud in the presence of His deep humility. I asked her to imagine Him, the King of Kings, the Lord of life and glory, humbling Himself and meekly carrying His cross up Calvary, amid the mocking crowd, while she walked by His side or followed His train in pride, with high and haughty head. She saw the point, and while we were at family prayers, she said she could never forget that lesson in humility. If people would simply study the life and spirit of Jesus, and gladly let His mind be in them, the subject of holiness would be greatly simplified. Paul said, "Let this mind be in you, which was also in Christ Jesus" (Phil. 2:5 KJV), and then he went on to show us that this mind is one of deepest humility, which led Jesus to empty Himself of His glory and humble Himself to die on the cross as the vilest of men. It is this humble, self-forgetful, loving mind Paul pleaded with us to have.

Holiness is not some lofty experience, unattainable except to those who can leap to the stars. It is a lowly experience, which lowly men and women in the lowly walks of life can share with Jesus by letting His mind be in them.

The Outcome of a Clean Heart 5

David prayed, "Create in me a clean heart, O God. . . . Then I will teach transgressors your ways, and sinners will return to you" (Ps. 51:10, 13 ESV). He recognized that the blessing of a clean heart would give him wisdom, power, and the spirit to teach wayward souls, and to teach them in such a way that they would submit to God. It is the same truth Jesus expressed when He said, "First get rid of the log in your own eye; then you will see well enough to deal with the speck in your friend's eye" (Matt. 7:5 NLT). The log is inbred sin; the speck is the transgressions that result from inbred sin.

The following are some of the results of a clean heart.

A clean heart filled with the Spirit makes a soul-winner out of the person who receives the blessing. It was so on the day of Pentecost, when the disciples, having their hearts purified by fire and filled with the Holy Spirit, won three thousand souls to the Lord in one day. With the blessing of a clean heart comes a passion of love for Jesus, and with it a passionate desire for the salvation and sanctification of men and women. It makes apostles, prophets, martyrs, missionaries, and fiery-hearted soul-winners. It opens the channel of communion between God and the soul wide and clear, so that His power, the power of the Holy Spirit, works through the person who has a clean heart, surely convicting and graciously transforming and sanctifying souls.

The blessing results in a constancy of spirit. The soul finds its perfect balance in God. Fickleness of feeling, uncertainty of temper, and waywardness of desire are gone, and the soul is buoyed up by steadiness and certainty. It no longer has to be braced up by vows and pledges and resolutions, but moves forward naturally, with quietness and assurance.

The blessing brings perfect peace. The warring element within is cast out. The fear of falling from faith is gone. Self no longer struggles for supremacy, for Jesus has become all and in all, and that word in Isaiah is fulfilled: "You will keep in perfect peace all who trust in you, all whose thoughts are fixed on you" (Isa. 26:3 NLT). The soul is made possessor of "the peace of God, which transcends all understanding" (Phil. 4:7 NIV).

The saved soul already had peace *with* God—that is, a cessation of rebellion and strife—but now it has the peace *of* God, as the bay has the fullness of the sea. Anxiety about the future and worry about the present and past go. It took perfect faith to get a clean heart, and perfect faith destroys fret and worry. They cannot abide in the same heart. A saint is noted as having said, "I cannot trust and worry at the same time." John Wesley replied, "I would as soon swear as fret."

With the blessing, joy is perfected. There may be sorrow and heaviness on account of manifold temptations, there may be great trials and perplexities, but the joy of the Lord flows and throbs through the heart of one who is sanctified like a great Gulf Stream in an unbroken current. God becomes that person's joy. David knew this when he said, "I will go . . . to God—the source of all my joy" (Ps. 43:4 NLT).

Do all who have the blessing of a clean heart realize this full joy? Probably not. But they may, if they will take time to commune with God and appropriate the promises to themselves. Jesus said, "Ask, using my name, and you will receive, and you will have abundant joy" (John 16:24 NLT). And John said, "We are writing these things so that you may fully share our joy" (1 John 1:4 NLT). And again Jesus said, "I will see you again; then you will rejoice, and no one can rob you of that joy" (John 16:22 NLT).

This joy could not be beaten out of Paul and Silas with many stripes, but bubbled up and overflowed at the midnight hour in the dark dungeon, when their feet were in the stocks and their backs were bruised and torn. It turned Madame Guyon's[1] cell into a palace and Bedford Jail into an anteroom of heaven, from which the saintly tinker, John Bunyan, saw the Delectable Mountains and the Citizens of the Celestial City. It makes a deathbed as "soft as downy pillows."[2]

When the blessing comes, love is made perfect. To be born of God is to have divine love planted in the heart. "Like begets like," and when we are born of God we are made partakers of His nature. And "God is love" (1 John 4:8 KJV). But this love is comparatively feeble in the new Christian, and there is much remaining corruption in the heart to check and hinder it, if not to destroy it. But when the heart is cleansed, all conflicting elements are destroyed and cast out, and the heart is filled with patient, humble, holy, flaming love. Love is made perfect. It flames upward toward God and spreads abroad toward all. It abides in the heart, not necessarily as a constantly overflowing emotion, but always as an unfailing principle of action, which may burst into emotion at any time. It may suffer, being abused and ill-treated, but it "is kind" (1 Cor. 13:4 KJV). Others may be promoted and advanced beyond it, but it is not jealous. It may be subjected to pressure of all kinds, but it is not boastful. It is not rash. It may prosper, but it is not proud (see 1 Cor. 13:4 NLT). Love "does not act unbecomingly" (1 Cor. 13:5 NASB) or, as John Wesley said, "It is not ill-bred."

Love "does not demand its own way. It is not irritable, and it keeps no record of being wronged" (1 Cor. 13:5 NLT). It is not suspicious. Love "does not rejoice about injustice but rejoices whenever the truth wins out" (1 Cor. 13:6 NLT). An evangelist had been abused by people who were professing Christians. When his attackers fell from faith, the evangelist's friends rejoiced, but he grieved. His heart was full of love, and he could not rejoice in the triumph of iniquity even over his enemies. Love "never gives up, never loses faith, is always hopeful, and endures through every circumstance" (1 Cor. 13:7 NLT).

A clean heart makes the Bible a new book. It becomes self-interpreting. God is in it speaking to the soul. I do not mean by this that all the types and prophecies are made plain to the unlearned mind, but all that is necessary to salvation will be found and fed upon in the Bible. The person with a clean heart understands the word of Jesus: "People do not live by bread alone, but by every word that comes from the mouth of God" (Matt. 4:4 NLT). That person can say, like

Job, "I . . . have treasured his words more than daily food" (Job 23:12 NLT) and like David, "I rejoice in your word like one who discovers a great treasure" (Ps. 119:162 NLT). Like the blessed soul of Psalm 1, people with clean hearts meditate on God's Word day and night in order to be sure to obey everything written in it and prosper in all they do (see Ps. 1:2–3; Josh. 1:8).

The blessing of a clean heart begets the shepherd spirit and destroys the spirit of lordship over God's people. Peter was not like many who have followed him, for instead of lording it over the flock, he wrote, "To the elders among you, I appeal as a fellow elder and a witness of Christ's sufferings who also will share in the glory to be revealed: Be shepherds of God's flock that is under your care, watching over them—not because you must, but because you are willing, as God wants you to be; not pursuing dishonest gain, but eager to serve; not lording it over those entrusted to you, but being examples to the flock" (1 Pet. 5:1–3 NIV).

If the cleansed person is a leader, the blessing will make him or her patient and considerate. If that person is a subordinate, he or she will be made willing and obedient. It is the fruitful root of courtesy, pity, compassion, and utterly unselfish devotion. "The good shepherd sacrifices his life for the sheep" (John 10:11 NLT).

A clean heart quickly recognizes temptation, and easily overcomes it through steadfast faith in Jesus. The holy man or woman takes the shield of faith, and with it quenches all the fiery arrows of the Enemy (see Eph. 6:16).

When the blessing comes in, divine courage possesses the heart. The sanctified soul sings with David, "I will have no fear. What can mere people do to me?" (Ps. 118:6 NLT) and, "Though a mighty army surrounds me, my heart will not be afraid" (Ps. 27:3 NLT). The clean heart says with Paul, "I can do everything through Christ, who gives me strength" (Phil. 4:13 NLT), for "we are more than conquerors through him who loved us" (Rom. 8:37 NIV).

In the clean heart, there is a keener sense than ever before of the weakness of the flesh, of the absolute inability of any man or woman to help us, and of our own utter dependence on God for all things. The pure heart sings evermore, "The blood, the blood, is all my plea."[3]

When we experience a clean heart, we make a covenant with our eyes and become careful which way and how we look. We also remember the words of Jesus, "Pay attention to how you hear" (Luke 8:18 NLT), and again, "Pay close attention to what you hear" (Mark 4:24 NLT). Likewise, we bridle our tongues and season our words with salt, not with sugar; salt is better than sugar for seasoning, but it is only for seasoning. We remember "that everyone will have to give account on the day of judgment for every empty word they have spoken" (Matt. 12:36 NIV). We do not "despise the day of small things" (Zech. 4:10 NIV) and can content ourselves with humble things. Finally, we realize "that the common deeds of the common day are ringing bells in the far-away."[4]

We live "as seeing him who is invisible" (Heb. 11:27 KJV) and with glad humility and wholehearted faithfulness discharge our duty with an eye focused on the glory of God, without any itching desire for the honor this world can give or other reward than the "well done" of the Lord.

NOTES

1. Madame Guyon (1648–1714) was a wealthy French woman whose brave advocating of prayer and personal and intimate relationship with Jesus was opposed by the Catholic Church and led to her imprisonment.

2. Isaac Watts, "Why Should We Start and Fear to Die," 1707, public domain.

3. John Parker, "I'm Kneeling at the Cross," 1873, public domain.

4. Henry Burton, "Beyond," in *At the Evening-Time, and Other Poems* by W. M. L. Jay and Anne E. Hamilton (New York: E. P. Dutton and Co., 1892), 93–94.

How to Keep a Clean Heart 6

It is possible to lose the blessing of a clean heart but, thank God, it is also gloriously possible to keep it. How to do this is a vital question. Two or three years ago, a brother going to the foreign field arose in one of my meetings and said, "I got the blessing three times but lost it twice. The third time I got it, the Lord taught me how to keep it through this text: 'As you received Christ Jesus the Lord, so walk in him'" (Col. 2:6 ESV).

That is one of the simplest and most complete statements of how to keep the blessing that can be given. The conditions of getting it are the conditions of keeping it.

To keep the blessing of holiness, there must be continued joyful and perfect consecration. We put all on the altar to get it. We must leave all on the altar to keep it. "All the tithes" must be brought into God's house (Mal. 3:10 NLT). We must present our bodies to Him as "a living sacrifice"

(Rom. 12:1 KJV), recognizing ourselves as no longer our own, but His, by the purchase of His blood, and ourselves as stewards only of all that is ours. Our health and strength; time and talent; money and influence; body, mind, and spirit—all, all are His, to be used for His glory as fully as the fondest bride would use her all in the interest of her husband. And this consecration must keep pace with increasing light. The journey of life is not always through grassy lawns and flowery gardens, but often over burning, shifting, sandy deserts, rocky steeps, fetid swamps, and dark and tangled jungles, as the Lord leads the soul in ways it has not known. And at such times, self-interest may cry out against the sacrifice. But if the consecration is perfect and grounded in love, there will be no turning back, no plunging into seductive and easy bypaths, but a steady marching forward, if necessary, to Gethsemane's lonely agony, Pilate's judgment hall of shame, and Golgotha's dark and awful hour. But, thank God, it will not be alone for He says, "My Presence will go with you" (Ex. 33:14 NIV).

To keep the blessing, there must be steadfast, childlike faith. It took faith unmixed with doubt to grasp the blessing. Unbelief was banished. Doubts were put away. The assurance of God's love in Jesus was heartily believed. His ability and willingness to save to the uttermost was fully accepted, and His word simply trusted when the blessing was received. And, of course, this same faith must be maintained in order to keep it. God cannot require less of the sanctified man or woman to keep the blessing than He did of that person to get it. Peter wrote of being "kept by the power of God through faith" (1 Pet. 1:5 KJV). It is the power of God that keeps us, but it is faith that links us to the power as the coupling links the railway car to the locomotive. Faith is the coupling. Paul said of himself, "The life I now live in the flesh I live by faith in the Son of God" (Gal. 2:20 ESV). And again he told us that the Jews were cut off through unbelief and that we stand by faith.

We may suffer prolonged trials, great perplexities, and fierce temptations—they are a part of the discipline of life—but we must:

> Keep on believing, Jesus is near;
> Keep on believing, there's nothing to fear;
> Keep on believing, this is the way;
> Faith in the night as well as the day.[1]

To keep the blessing, we must pray to and commune much with the Lord. We pray when we talk to God and ask Him for things. We commune with Him when we are still and listen and let God talk to us, mold us, show us His love and His will, and teach us in the way He would have us go. We should pray often and not be in too great a hurry, but "take time to be holy,"[2] take time to "taste and see that the LORD is good" (Ps. 34:8 KJV) and to hear what He will say. And this we should do in the morning, if possible, that we may be strengthened and nourished and gladdened for the day. Falling from faith usually begins through neglected, or hurried, secret prayer.

Someone has said, "Stay with God in prayer, stay till He melts you, and then stay when you are melted and plead with God, and He will answer, and you will get changed and transformed and renewed, and you will do execution."[3]

To keep the blessing, we must give diligent attention to the Bible. The soul needs the food of truth, and Jesus said, "People do not live by bread alone, but by every word that comes from the mouth of God" (Matt. 4:4 NLT). God commanded Joshua, "Keep this Book of the Law always on your lips; meditate on it day and night." What for? "So that you may be careful to do everything written in it." And what shall follow? "Then you will be prosperous and successful" (Josh. 1:8 NIV). Then you will keep the blessing.

David said that truly blessed people "delight in the law of the LORD, meditating on it day and night" (Ps. 1:2 NLT). And Paul wrote that the Scriptures are "useful for teaching, rebuking, correcting and training in righteousness, so that the servant of God may be thoroughly equipped for every good work" (2 Tim. 3:16–17 NIV). And Peter said, "Like newborn babies, crave pure spiritual milk, so that by it you may grow up in your salvation" (1 Pet. 2:2 NIV). Some professed Christians are smaller ten years after birth than when they were born because they have not fed on God's Word. Catherine Booth, the cofounder of The Salvation Army, read the Bible through several times before she was twelve years old, and so grew until it is not to be wondered at that she became a "mother of nations" (Gen. 17:16 KJV). I once gave a talk on the use of the Bible to my soldiers (church members), and some of them caught the inspiration and carried their Bibles in their pockets after that and spent all the spare time they had in reading and praying. And we could fairly see them grow, until they became powers for God. Some of them are spiritual giants to this day.

To keep the blessing of holiness, we must confess it. We must be aggressive and seek to get others into it. "For with the heart one believes and is justified, and with the mouth one confesses and is saved" (Rom. 10:10 ESV). Those who withhold their testimony to this grace will lose it. This light, hid under a bushel, will go out. God gives it to us that we may put it on a candlestick and give light to all who are in the house and in our church, community, and nation. Don't limit the power of testimony by unbelief. A torch loses no light and heat by lighting a thousand other torches.

Touch a piece of steel with a magnet and it in turn becomes a magnet. It can then be used to turn ten thousand other pieces into magnets with no loss, but rather with increase of power to itself. But hang it up in idleness and it gradually loses its power. So it is with us. Let the Holy Spirit touch us with cleansing power, and we become divine magnets. And in touching other souls we will quicken them and get added power and clarity of experience ourselves. But let us withhold our testimony and we lose our power and, like Samson, soon find ourselves "as weak as anyone else" (Judg. 16:7 NLT).

Testify, testify, testify—clearly, definitely, constantly, courageously, humbly—if you would keep the blessing. When faith is weak and devils all around, definite testimony scatters the devils, strengthens faith, and stirs up and brightens the inward witness. Testify to the Lord, tell Him you have the blessing, and thank Him for it. Testify to your companions. Testify to your own heart and to the Devil. John said that the white-robed multitude in heaven overcame by the blood of the Lamb and the word of their testimony (see Rev. 12:11). So testify, if you would overcome and keep the blessing.

To keep the blessing, we must constantly live in the spirit of self-denial. By yielding to fleshly desires, selfish ambitions, and the spirit of the world, we may lose the labor of years in an instant. The hard hand of the old Enemy is always stretched forth to snatch our treasure from us. We must watch and pray, and keep low at Jesus' feet in profoundest humility, if we would keep it. It is all summed up in the words, "walk in the Spirit" and "walk in love" (Gal. 5:25; Eph. 5:2 KJV).

Finally, there must be no resting in present attainments. The Lord has clearer revelations of Himself for us. We may be filled to the limit of our capacity today, but we should always pray, "Oh, Lord, enlarge the vessel," and expect Him to do it. Like Paul, "forgetting the past and looking forward to what lies ahead, I press on to reach the end of the race and receive the heavenly prize for which God, through Christ Jesus, is calling us" (Phil. 3:13–14 NLT), always remembering that He is able "to accomplish infinitely more than we might ask or think" (Eph. 3:20 NLT). Not according to some mysterious power to which we are strangers, but "through his mighty power at work within us" (Eph. 3:20 NLT), the power of the Holy Spirit that saved us and made us His dear children.

NOTES

1. Lucy Booth-Hellberg, "Keep on Believing," *The Salvation Army Songbook*, public domain.

2. William D. Longstaff, "Take Time to Be Holy," 1882, public domain.

3. Rev. J. H. James, "How the Blessing May Be Retained," in *The Guide to Holiness*, eds. W. C. Palmer and Phoebe Palmer (New York: Walter C. Palmer, Jr., 1871), 29.

Holiness before the Flood 7

What a remarkable biography Enoch has! The Bible says, "Enoch lived 365 years, walking in close fellowship with God. Then one day he disappeared, because God took him" (Gen. 5:23–24 NLT). Nowadays people write hundreds of pages about their heroes and do not say as much as that. But there is a good reason. There is not so much as that to say.

Enoch was a mighty man with a wonderful life who lived under very unfavorable circumstances. And I have profited much by meditating upon his life and what I think must have been his secret.

We are prone to look upon past ages and distant places as peculiarly favorable to godliness. I remember that years ago I thought if I could go to London and listen to Charles Spurgeon each week, I could be a Christian. In my boyhood I wished that I had lived in the days of Jesus, had heard His wondrous words, and had questioned Him about the mysteries of godliness, for then I could certainly have been His true follower. Usually the further back we go, the more godly seems the age, and the more blessed seem the men and women of that day.

But really this is not so, and especially is it not so of Enoch's age and place. The age was most ungodly, and people had very little religious light. The world was hastening to that dreadfulness of sin and unbelief that would cause God to sweep away its people by the deluge and leave but eight persons in it. They had no Bible. They had no law. They did not yet have a divine revelation from heaven telling them they must worship God; keep the Sabbath day; honor their parents; and not kill, commit adultery, steal, lie, or covet. Try to imagine an age and place with no such teaching as that! Everyone a law unto him- or herself, all their evil passions and lusts and tempers having no restraint put upon them, thus plunging them continually deeper and deeper into sin and corruption.

They also had no gospel, with Jesus revealed as a loving Savior. They had only one promise of hope and mercy, and that rather vague— the one given to the woman after that awful fall in Eden, the promise of the Seed that someday would come to bruise the Serpent's head. It was a black night, with only one lone dim star shining in the darkness. But Enoch held on to that promise, and in its light and hope he walked with God for three hundred years.

We have a whole Bible, a finished revelation. We have the holy, just, good law of God, showing us what we ought to do and what we ought not to do. We have the gospel, with its full noonday light, showing us how to keep the law and how to get life and power to fulfill the will of God on earth as the angels do in heaven. We have Jesus, crucified before our eyes for our sins; dead, buried, and raised to glorious life

again for our justification; and ascended on high to the right hand of
God, far above all created things and all opposing powers of evil, to
intercede for us, pour out the Holy Spirit upon us in rich measure, and
live in us through the Spirit. We have commandments, precepts, and
thousands of promises. Instead of a midnight, with one lone, dim star
shining fitfully in the darkness, we have a midday, with all the splendor
of the sun in its strength, together with ten thousand reflected lights,
shining upon us. Yet we, in our trembling, pitiful, shameful unbelief,
wonder how Enoch could ever walk with God!

I imagine that Enoch made up his mind that it was possible to walk
with God—that is, to be agreed with God, to be of the same mind and
heart and purpose as God. Of course, there were stupendous difficulties in the way. There were no churches or Sunday schools. There
were no holiness conventions, no days with God and nights of prayer,
no Bible, no Christian books or magazines, and no libraries. In fact,
instead of these helps to walk with God, he found the whole community against him—in fact, the whole world, for in Jude we read that
Enoch had to prophesy against the ungodliness he found around him.

Then, not only did Enoch have these extraordinary difficulties to
face, but he had all the ordinary difficulties as well. He got married
and had a large family of boys and girls to care for; he had all the anxiety of a father to provide for his family and protect them from the
influences all about them. Then, I cannot imagine that he did not have
the ordinary infirmities and the sinful nature of other human beings.
No doubt he might have said, as you and I have said, that his temperament was peculiar. And he might have said that while others with
a happier temperament might be able to walk with God, yet with his

peculiarly crooked and difficult make-up it was quite out of the question for him to hope to be holy and walk with God. And, of course, he had the Devil to fight.

I think that Enoch not only believed in the possibility of walking with God, but he made up his mind that he would walk with God. He put his will into this matter.

Not only did Enoch believe in the possibility of walking with God and determine that as for him he would walk with God, but he took such steps as were necessary to do so. He separated himself in spirit from the ungodly people around him, raised his voice against their evil ways, and became not only a negatively righteous man, but also a positively holy man.

Enoch had his reward. It paid him to walk with God. He loved God, and God loved him. And their affection became so intense that one day God's love overcame the power of death and drew Enoch from earth to heaven.

I suppose that most people, in reading the story, think that Enoch's reward consisted in getting to heaven without dying. This was certainly a most unusual and blessed experience, and one I suppose that people have wished for all through the ages. There is something about death that is awful, and from which we shrink. And yet, since Jesus has died and gone down into the grave and risen again, the terror is lost to the Christian. Still, it is probable that if allowed to choose, most people would say, "Let us go to heaven like Enoch did." But I cannot consider this Enoch's chief reward.

For three hundred years God was his friend, his counselor, his comforter, his constant companion. Oh, what fellowship was that!

What an opportunity to gain wisdom, to build up and round out and ennoble a person's character! How easy to be good and do good! How life must have almost burst with fullness of gladness! Walking with God! Talking with God! Communing with God! Having mutual sympathy with God and entering into a union with God as intimate as the union of the bay with the sea—and all this by faith, by simple trust, by childlike confidence. This was Enoch's reward, and it may be yours, if you will meet the conditions as Enoch did.

Paul—A Pattern 8

Paul told us that the Lord Jesus made him "a pattern to them which should hereafter believe" (1 Tim. 1:16 KJV). This fact makes his life and experience exceptionally interesting and valuable to us. And it is a special mark of our heavenly Father's wisdom and love that He has given us in Paul such a striking example in every particular of the saving power of Jesus. People say Jesus was divine, and so excuse themselves for their unlikeness to Him. But Paul was human, and if he was like Jesus, so may we be.

Let us study his experience.

HIS SUFFERINGS

It is difficult to conceive any form of suffering to which Paul was not subjected, yet in every instance the grace of Christ was all-sufficient.

Here is a catalogue of Paul's sufferings he recorded in 2 Corinthians
11:23–28 (NLT):

- "I have worked harder." If anyone exceeds him in their labors,
  it is only because of the improved facilities of later ages for
  doing more in the same space of time.
- "Whipped times without number"—so many and so often
  inflicted as to be beyond his computation.
- "In prisons more often . . . faced death again and again. . . . Once
  I was stoned." I was stoned once with one brick, and nearly
  killed, but Paul received many stones and was dragged out of the
  city like a beast and left for dead.
- "Three times I was shipwrecked." There have been Salvationist
  leaders who suffered shipwreck, but it was one time and they
  escaped immediately. But Paul "spent a whole day and night
  adrift at sea."
- "I have traveled on many long journeys," under such disagreeable circumstances as we who live in the days of modern travel
  can scarcely imagine.
- "I have faced danger from rivers and from robbers . . . [and]
  from my own people, the Jews"—who hated him bitterly and
  sought his life in every city—"as well as from the Gentiles,"
  whom he sought to save through the knowledge of Jesus, but
  who clung to their idols.
- "I have faced danger in the cities"—by wild, mad mobs.
- "I have faced danger . . . in the deserts"—from ferocious beasts
  and yet more ferocious men.

- "I have faced danger . . . on the sea"—from drowning and from monsters of the deep.

- "I have faced danger from men who claim to be believers but are not"—to whom he would naturally look for help and sympathy.

- "I have worked hard and long, enduring many sleepless nights. I have been hungry and thirsty and have often gone without food. I have shivered in the cold, without enough clothing to keep me warm. Then, besides all this, I have the daily burden of my concern for all the churches." Those churches were organized from Jewish and Gentile converts, were bitterly opposed by the idolatrous pagans on one side and religious Jews on the other, and must have been far more difficult to properly organize, train, and manage than any church or Salvation Army corps. Nor could Paul look forward to brighter days, when circumstances would be more favorable and life more free from pain and care, for he said, "The Holy Spirit tells me in city after city that jail and suffering lie ahead" (Acts 20:23 NLT).

HIS FAITH IN GOD AND LOVE FOR HUMANITY

In spite of all these afflictions, physical sufferings, and bitter persecutions, Paul maintained a joyful faith in God and a tender, self-sacrificing love for everyone. And when God the Holy Spirit testified there would be no "let up" to Paul's stupendous trials, he cried out, "But none of these things move me; nor do I count my life dear to myself" (Acts 20:24 NKJV). "I take pleasure in my weaknesses, and in the insults, hardships, persecutions, and troubles that I suffer for Christ" (2 Cor. 12:10 NLT). And in face of all these things he asked,

"Who shall separate us from the love of Christ? Shall tribulation, or distress, or persecution, or famine, or nakedness, or peril, or sword?" And though he added, "We are accounted as sheep for the slaughter," yet "in all these things we are more than conquerors through him that loved us. For I am persuaded, that neither death, nor life, nor angels, nor principalities, nor powers, nor things present, nor things to come, nor height, nor depth, nor any other creature, shall be able to separate us from the love of God, which is in Christ Jesus our Lord" (Rom. 8:35–39 KJV).

And at the last, almost in sight of the block and ax, where Paul's multitudinous sufferings were to be crowned by a martyr's death, he exclaimed, "I have fought a good fight, I have finished my course, I have kept the faith" (2 Tim. 4:7 KJV).

Just as his faith in his Lord was not in the least hindered or destroyed by his sufferings, so also did his love for his fellow human beings remain untouched by them. He said of the Jews of that day, who were his perpetual and bitter enemies: "With Christ as my witness, I speak with utter truthfulness. My conscience and the Holy Spirit confirm it. My heart is filled with bitter sorrow and unending grief for my people, my Jewish brothers and sisters. I would be willing to be forever cursed—cut off from Christ!—if that would save . . . the people of Israel" (Rom. 9:1–4 NLT).

This is perfect love. It is love that "is patient and kind" (1 Cor. 13:4 NLT). It is love like that of the Lord Jesus Himself.

Then again, in writing to the church in Corinth, in which many seemed to have gone wrong and to have made many unjust and contemptuous criticisms of Paul himself, he said, "I don't want what you have—I want you. . . . I will gladly spend myself and all I have for you, even though it seems that the more I love you, the less you love me" (2 Cor. 12:14–15 NLT). Many floods could not quench his love nor drown his faith.

THE SECRET

The secret of Paul's marvelous endurance, his quenchless faith and burning love is found in his testimony, "I was not disobedient to the vision from heaven" (Acts 26:19 NIV).

Way back in the days when he was a persecutor and was scattering the little flock of Christ and driving them to death, Jesus met him—met him just as He meets men and women today—showed him the narrow way and hard road that lead to life (see Matt. 7:14). And Paul was not disobedient to the vision from heaven. Obedience meant social ostracism, banishment from home and friends, the overturning of all his plans and ambitions, a life of toil and shame and suffering, the loss of all things, and the sacrifice of his life, yet he was not disobedient to the heavenly vision. And, maintaining this obedient spirit to the end, everything else followed. The reason so few have an experience like Paul's is because so few count the cost as he did and obey the heavenly vision Jesus gives them.

Several years ago a girl of eighteen, full of fun and love of society, was induced by a friend to enter a Salvation Army meeting for the first time. No sooner had she entered than the people's faces enchained her eyes and their testimonies went to her heart. She sat for a while, and Jesus came to her, not in visible presence, but in a spiritual vision. She left the meeting convicted of sin. On her way home, the vision spoke with her: "You ought to have gotten saved tonight."

"But I am engaged for that dance next Wednesday night."

"You should give up the dance."

"But there are my lovely white dress and slippers. I will get saved after the dance."

"But you may die before Wednesday night, and lose your lovely dress and the dance—and your soul."

That was sufficient for this young girl. She tore the feathers from her hat and threw them into the fire. She rushed upstairs, got her lovely white dress, cut it up, and cast it into the fire.

The next evening she went to the meeting. At last a woman, probably discerning in her face the hunger of her heart, went to her and asked, "Don't you want to get saved tonight?"

"Of course I do," replied the girl. "Why did you not come to me before?" Immediately she rushed to the penitent form (the special place for prayer before the altar) where, in obedience to the heavenly vision, she found Jesus almighty to save. And after four years her face shines with the glory of her Lord, and her voice rings with triumph as she testifies to the cleansing power of His blood and the sanctifying power and presence of His Spirit. She was not disobedient to the heavenly vision.

A man, a millionaire, came into a meeting and listened to an Army captain (minister), and the heavenly vision came to him. He saw the cross, the narrow way, and the hard road, and like the rich young man who came to Jesus (see Mark 10:17–22), he went away saying, "If it were not for the red stripes round that fellow's collar (on his Salvation

Army uniform), I would have gone forward." He was disobedient to the heavenly vision.

Sooner or later the heavenly vision comes to everyone. It comes in the whisperings of conscience, in the strivings of the Spirit, in the calls of duty, in the moments of regret for an evil past, in moments of tenderness and sorrow, in the crises of life, and in the entreaties of God's people. It comes in afflictions and losses; in the thunders of the law; in fearful, ominous threats of eternal judgment; in the death of loved ones; and in crushed hopes, disappointed plans, and thwarted ambitions. In all these things, Jesus hides Himself as He hid Himself in the burning bush, which Moses saw on Horeb. If people would but turn aside and heed the vision as Moses did, a voice would speak and cause them to know the Lord, and if they would not be disobedient to the heavenly vision, Jesus would turn them back from the pit and satisfy every questioning of their minds and every longing of their hearts. God so satisfied the heart and mind of Paul.

Some people imagine that Paul was describing the state he was in during his best religious experience when he cried out, "Oh, what a miserable person I am! Who will free me from this life that is dominated by sin and death?" (Rom. 7:24 NLT). But the fact is, he was describing his condition under the law, when, as a convicted sinner, the law showed him what he ought to do but brought no power to deliver him from his guilty past and the corruptions of his own heart. However, in the eighth chapter of Romans he found the secret of deliverance from the condemnation of the past and the carnal mind, which prevented him from doing the will of God on earth as the angels do in heaven.

From that point he rose to such marvelous testimonies as, "I have been crucified with Christ and I no longer live, but Christ lives in me. The life I now live in the body, I live by faith in the Son of God, who loved me and gave himself for me" (Gal. 2:20 NIV). And through a consecration in which he counted all things loss for Christ and a faith by which he reckoned himself to be "dead to the power of sin and alive to God through Christ Jesus" (Rom. 6:11 NLT), he entered into an experience in which, as one has well said, he was:

Free from a repining temper, for he had learned in every state therewith to be content. He was free from vanity, pride, and unsanctified ambitions, for he gloried only in the cross of Christ. He was free from every feeling of resentment, for he was ready to die accursed [by] his enemies. He was free from selfishness, for he was ready to spend and be spent for those whose love diminished for him in proportion as his love abounded for them. He was free from covetousness, for he counted all things but dung and dross for Christ. He was free from unbelief, for he knew in whom he had trusted and was persuaded that nothing could separate him from the love of Christ. He was free from the fear of man, for stripes, imprisonments, and martyrdom had no terrors—being ready to be offered up. He was free from love of the world, having a desire to depart and to be with Christ. The absence of these corruptions implied the maturity of the graces of the Holy Spirit—the fullness of love. Indeed it was that love which constrained him, which cast out fear and counteracted every tendency opposed to its hallowing influence.[1]

What a great salvation was this that Paul found through obeying the heavenly vision! It is ten million leagues beyond the poor little salvation from wrongdoing which most people seek in order to escape hell. It is a salvation not only from sin, but also from self; a divine union with God in Christ so intimate and so sacred that father and mother and husband and wife and brother and sister and child and even one's own life are all shut outside. And yet it does not make one nerveless and lead one to "sing self away to everlasting bliss,"[2] but rather to lavish love upon all, regardless of their hatred or affection, and to pour out life, a sacrifice for the world. Well might one say like Paul, "Be imitators of me, as I am of Christ" (1 Cor. 11:1 ESV).

And by the grace of God, I will follow.

Will you?

NOTES

1. Dr. Cooke (full name not known), quoted in John S. Stanwell, "Christian Holiness: Its Nature and Limits," *The Primitive Methodist Magazine*, 66 (n.d.): 230.

2. Isaac Watts, "Welcome, Sweet Day of Rest," 1707, public domain.

Testify to the Blessing 9

A lieutenant got the blessing of a clean heart in one of my meetings the other day, and then told us that he had the blessing once before but lost it because he failed to testify to it. The Devil suggested that it was a great thing to testify to cleansing from all sin and that people would not understand it, that they would criticize him, that he would do better to live it and say nothing about it, and so on. He heeded these suggestions, kept quiet, and so lost the blessing.

That is an old trick of the Devil's by which he has cheated many a soul out of this pearl of greatest price.

Paul said, "For with the heart one believes and is justified, and with the mouth one confesses and is saved" (Rom. 10:10 ESV). The confession is as necessary as the believing. We insist upon this in the matter of justification, and it is equally important in the matter of sanctification. If we do not testify definitely, humbly, and constantly to the blessed experience, we put our light under a bushel and it goes out.

The late Miss Frances E. Willard received the blessing of holiness under the ministry of Phoebe Palmer. Miss Willard was filled with joy and peace and gave a burning testimony of the fullness of the Spirit. Soon afterward she became a teacher in a section of the country where there was much controversy over the doctrine of holiness. She was advised by her mistaken friends to keep still about sanctification, which she did. Years afterward she sorrowfully wrote, "I kept still until I soon found I had nothing in particular to keep still about. The experience left me. That sweet persuasiveness, that heaven in the soul of which I came to know in Mrs. Palmer's meeting, I do not now feel."

Fletcher of Madeley, whom John Wesley believed to be the holiest man since the days of the apostle John, made this confession to his people:

My dear brethren and sisters, God is here. I feel Him in this place; but I would hide my face in the dust because I have been ashamed to declare what He has done for me. For many years I have grieved His Spirit, but I am deeply humbled and He has again restored my soul. Last Wednesday evening He spoke to me by these words: "Reckon ye also yourselves to be dead indeed unto sin, but alive unto God through Jesus Christ our Lord" [Rom. 6:11 KJV]. I obeyed the voice of God; I now obey it, and tell you all to the praise of His love, I am freed from sin, dead unto sin, and alive unto God. I received this blessing four or five times before, but I lost it by not obeying the order of God, who has told us, "with the heart man believeth unto righteousness and with the mouth confession is made unto salvation" [Rom. 10:10 KJV]. But the Enemy offered his bait under various colors to keep me from a public declaration of what God had wrought.

When I first received the grace, Satan made me wait awhile till I saw more of the fruits. I resolved to do so, but I soon began to doubt the witness which before I had felt in my heart, and I was in a little while sensible that I had lost both. A second time after receiving this salvation [with shame I confess it] I was kept from being a witness for my Lord by the suggestion, "Thou art a public character: the eyes of all are upon thee: and if, as before, by any means thou lose the blessing, it will be a dishonor to the doctrine of heart-holiness." I held my peace and again forfeited the gift of God. At another time I was prevailed upon to hide it by reasoning: How few even of the children of God will receive this testimony! Many of them suppose that every transgression of the Adamic law is sin: and therefore, if I profess myself to be free from sin, all these will give my profession the lie; because I am not free in their sense I am not free from ignorance, mistakes, and infirmities: I will therefore enjoy what God hath wrought in me, but I will not say, I am perfect in love. Alas! I soon found again: "He that hideth his Lord's talent, and improveth it not, from that unprofitable servant shall be taken away even that which he seemeth to have."

Now, my brethren, you see my folly; I have confessed it in your presence, and now I resolve, before you all, to confess my Master; I will confess Him to all the world; and I declare unto you, in the presence of God the *holy Trinity*, I am now "dead indeed unto sin . . . and alive unto God! And remember all this is "through Jesus Christ our Lord". . . . He is my indwelling holiness.[1]

This confession put Mr. Fletcher on record and was the beginning of a life of holiness that has but few parallels for beauty and power. It is only at this point of glad, definite testimony that Christian life and experience become irresistibly catching, like fire when it bursts into flame.

Those who profess this blessing are often accused of boasting. But this is not true. They are simply declaring that Jesus has done for them what He died to do—that is, to save them from sin. They do it in the spirit of those who, healed of a deadly disease, declare what the doctor has done for them. It is done to bring honor to the doctor and to encourage other poor sufferers to seek healing. To withhold such testimony in the presence of multitudes of needy ones would be a crime.

David said, "My soul shall make its boast in the LORD; the humble shall hear of it and be glad" (Ps. 34:2 NKJV). As for me, I feel I am under a solemn obligation to let everybody know that Jesus is alive and that He can save to the uttermost.

NOTE

1. A. M. French, "Confession of Perfect Love," *Beauty of Holiness in Heart and Life*, vol. 12 (New York: Rev. M. French, 1861), 109–110.

Knowing Jesus 10

What an astonishing thing that we can know Jesus! And yet nothing is more clearly taught in Scripture or more joyously testified to in experience by godly people than this fact.

This is an age of specialists, when men and women devote their lives to the pursuit of special departments of knowledge. One learned scholar will give fourteen hours a day for forty years to the study of fish, another to the study of birds, another to that of bugs, and yet another to that of old bones. Another devotes his or her entire life to the study of history, the rise and fall of nations, and yet another to astronomy, the origin and history of worlds. But to know Jesus Christ is infinitely better than to know all that has been learned or dreamed of by those great minds, for He it was who "created everything," and "nothing was created except through him" (John 1:3 NLT).

Personally, I am inclined to think that to know Edison would be worth more than knowing one or all of his works, and so to know Jesus Christ is the first and best of all knowledge.

The knowledge of the naturalist, astronomer, and historian may be of passing value, but in due time it will be outdated and fail. But the knowledge of Jesus Christ is of infinite value and will never pass away. It is profitable for this world and for that which is to come; and only by it can we come to the knowledge of ourselves, without which it would be better never to have been born.

In this knowledge of Jesus is hidden the germ of all knowledge, for Paul told us that in Him "lie hidden all the treasures of wisdom and knowledge" (Col. 2:3 NLT). Am I eager for learning and knowledge? Then let me constantly seek to know Him, and in due time, in this world or in the next, I shall know all that is of value for me to know.

In this knowledge lies true culture of both head and heart—especially of the heart. In the words of one of the greatest Christian philosophers, such knowledge will "enlarge the individual life with universal ideals . . . lift time into the stream of an eternal purpose and fill it with eternal issues, and . . . make the simplest moral act great as a real factor in the evolution of a higher order and immortal character."[1] It will make you patient with the ignorant and erring and wayward, courteous to your equals and superiors, kindly and generous to your subordinates, and gentle and considerate in your own home and to your husband or wife (as you were when you were new sweethearts). It will make you loving and forbearing with children and thoughtful and tender with the aged. In short, the knowledge of Jesus (not simply scraps of knowledge about Jesus) will make its possessor like Jesus.

The essence of this knowledge is love. John said, "Anyone who loves is a child of God and knows God. But anyone who does not love does not know God, for God is love" (1 John 4:7–8 NLT). This love is a heavenly thing. Even those who are farthest away from God love their own, love those who love them and do them good. But this love is that which pours itself out upon strangers, enemies, and those who spitefully use us and say all manner of evil against us. Thus we come to see that to know Jesus, we must be like Jesus, must have an affinity with Him, must be transformed into His image. In other words, we must be born again and sanctified by His indwelling Spirit.

Judas lived with Jesus in the intimacy of a disciple for three years, but if he ever knew Jesus he must have lost that knowledge or he could not have gone out to betray Him with a kiss. So we may profess the knowledge of Jesus, but when by wicked tempers and unholy conduct and deceitful and sinful character we manifest a spirit contrary to His, we give the lie to our profession. Insofar as we are unlike Him, to that extent we are ignorant of Him.

How then shall we come to the knowledge of Jesus?

We must utterly and forever renounce sin and seek forgiveness for past bad conduct, trusting in the merits of His atonement for acceptance with God, singing from our hearts, "The Blood, the Blood, is all my plea."[2] When we do this, we shall come into an initial knowledge of our Lord Jesus Christ.

But we must not only renounce our sins; we must also renounce self. In an all-night of prayer several years ago, I looked at the great audience and queried of the Lord in my heart, "How can all these people get to heaven?" And in the depths of my soul sounded back the words, "He bowed his head and gave up his spirit" (John 19:30 NIV).

And I saw how people get to heaven, and how they gain the knowledge of Jesus. He gave Himself for us, and we must give ourselves for Him. We must trust and obey, and wait expectantly until He comes to our hearts and reveals Himself to our wondering souls, for we only know Him as He reveals Himself to us. And He will do this when we seek Him with all our heart. He surely will.

Paul said, "But whatever were gains to me I now consider loss for the sake of Christ" (Phil. 3:7 NIV), by which he referred to his lineage from Abraham, his exact fulfillment of the law, and his zeal for his church. Then he added, "What is more, I consider everything a loss because of the surpassing worth of knowing Christ Jesus my Lord, for whose sake I have lost all things. I consider them garbage, that I may gain Christ and be found in him . . . to know Christ" (Phil. 3:8–10 NIV).

People who seek this knowledge without this sacrifice of self may flatter themselves that they know Him, but when the testing time comes—the hours of loneliness and loss, sickness and pain, disappointment and perplexity, and thwarted hopes and desolation—they will find their sad mistake. The fire will reveal their dross and sin. But to those who make and abide in this sacrifice and, fighting the good fight of faith, steadfastly and joyously believe, furnace fires and lions' dens and dungeon cells will only disclose more fully the loveliness of His face, the certainty of His presence, and the unfailing strength and comforts of His love.

This knowledge, to be maintained, must be cultivated, which is done by communion with Him. It is possible for a husband and wife to live together for many years and, instead of increasing in the knowledge of each other (except in the most superficial way) to grow apart, until after many years they are heart strangers to each other, with separate interests, conflicting desires and tempers, and alien affinities. To really know each other they must be bound together by stronger ties than mere legal forms. They must commune with each other, live in each other's hearts, enter into each other's joys, share each other's sorrows, counsel each other in perplexity, seek the same ends, and cultivate the same spirit.

And so to know Jesus, sympathy, fellowship, and friendship must be constantly cultivated. The heart must turn to Him, pour itself out before Him, and share its hopes, joys, and fears with Him. It must draw its consolations, strength, courage, sufficiency—its life—from Him. It must trust and obey Him and delight itself in Him as its everlasting portion.

Secret prayer must often bring the soul face to face with Him. The Bible, God's record of Himself, must be daily, diligently, and lovingly searched, and faithfully applied to the daily life. Thus shall we know Him, and become "more and more like him as we are changed into his glorious image" (2 Cor. 3:18 NLT), and people shall see and feel Christ in us, "the hope of glory" (Col. 1:27 KJV).

O Jesus, Savior, how I bless You that You sought me when I was lost and far from You and altogether unlike You, that You wooed me and won me and led me to Yourself and revealed Yourself to me, and that You made me to know You, ravished my heart, humbled my pride with the joy and love and glory that that best of all knowledge brings! Still reveal Yourself, O Lord, to Your people, that they may know You and glorify You and be satisfied with Your loving-kindness and fill the earth with Your fame!

NOTES

1. A. M. Fairbairn, "The Churches and the Ideal of Religion," *The Contemporary Review*, vol. 45 (London: Isbister and Company, Ltd., 1884), 377.

2. F. C. Baker, "I Knew That God in His Word Had Spoken," 1883, public domain.

Freedom from Sin 11

The most startling thing about sin is its power to enslave. Jesus said, "Everyone who commits sin is the slave of sin" (John 8:34 NASB), and everyday life and experience prove the saying to be true. Let a young woman tell a lie and she is henceforth the servant of falsehood unless freed by a higher power. Let the bank clerk misappropriate funds, let the businessman yield to a trick in trade, let the young man surrender to lust, let the youth take an intoxicating glass, and henceforth he is a slave. The cords that hold them may be light and silken, and they may say they are free, but they deceive themselves; they are no longer free, but are slaves.

We may choose the path in life we will take—the course of conduct, the friends with whom we will associate, the habits we will form, whether good or bad. But, having chosen the ways of sin, we are then swept on without further choice with a swiftness and certainty down to hell, just as those who choose to board a ship are surely taken to the destined harbor, however much they may wish to go elsewhere. We choose and then we are chosen. We grasp and then we are grasped by a power stronger than ourselves—like the man who takes hold of the poles of an electric battery; he grasps, but he cannot let go at his will.

Just so, sinners are in the grasp of a higher power than their own. They choose drink, dancing, gambling, worldly pleasure, or human wisdom and fame and power, but soon find themselves captive, only to be surely crushed and ruined forever, unless delivered by some power outside themselves. What shall they do? Is there hope? Is there a deliverer? Yes, thank God, there is. Jesus said, "If the Son sets you free, you will be free indeed" (John 8:36 ESV).

Some years ago near Boston, a young artist stopped me and said, "Brother Brengle, do you mean to say that Jesus can save a man from all sin?"

"Yes, sir," I replied, "that is exactly what I mean to say."

"Well, if He can," said he, "I want Him to save me, for I am the victim of a habit that masters me. I struggle and vow and make good resolutions, but fall again, and I want deliverance."

I pointed him to Jesus. We prayed, and the work was done. He remained in and around Boston for six months, shining and shouting for Jesus, and then went to California. Eleven years later I went to San Francisco. One day, I heard a knock on my door. A young man entered, looked at me and inquired, "Do you know me?"

I replied, "Yes, sir. You are the young man that Jesus saved from a bad habit about twelve years ago, near Boston."

"Yes," said he, "and He saves me still."

The one whom the Son makes free is free indeed.

He breaks the power of canceled sin,
He sets the prisoner free.[1]

This freedom is altogether complete. Jesus told the disciples to "loose" a colt that was tied and bring it to Him. Mark told us that He "loosed" the tongue of a dumb man and he spoke plainly. John told us that when Lazarus came forth from the grave he was "bound hand and foot with graveclothes: and his face was bound about with a napkin." Jesus said, "Loose him, and let him go" (John 11:44 KJV).

John used exactly the same Greek word when he said of Jesus, "The reason the Son of God appeared was to destroy [loose] the works of the devil" (1 John 3:8 ESV).

In other words, the one whom Jesus makes free is loosed from the works of the Devil—unhitched from them—as fully as was the colt from the post to which it was tied or as was Lazarus from his grave clothes. Our souls are bound to our guilty past until Jesus forgives and forgets it, and then we are no longer subject to the penalty of the broken law. Our souls that are risen to new life through faith in Christ are bound to our inbred sin, but Jesus looses us and we are free indeed.

It is a complete deliverance, a perfect liberty, a heavenly freedom that Jesus gives, by bringing the soul under the law of liberty, which is the law of love.

NOTE

1. Charles Wesley, "O, For a Thousand Tongues to Sing," 1739, public domain.

Wrestlers with God 12

The evangelist William Bramwell wrote in one of his letters, "Almost every night there has been a shaking among the people, and I have seen nearly twenty set at liberty." Then he added these heart-rending words: "I believe I should have seen many more, but I cannot yet find one pleading man. There are many good people, but I have found no wrestlers with God."

O, my Lord, that is what we want! In these days of organizations, societies, leagues, committees, multiplied and diversified soul-saving and ecclesiastical machinery together with worldwide opportunity, above all other things we want wrestlers with God—men and women who know how to pray and who do pray. Not men and women who *say* prayers, but who pour out their hearts to Him and "keep not silence, and give him no rest, till he establish, and till he make Jerusalem a praise in the earth" (Isa. 62:6–7 KJV).

Some weeks ago I went to a Salvation Army corps (church) for the Sunday morning meeting—just the one meeting. Not many people knew I was coming. No special preparation was made. Snow was on the ground, and less than one hundred people were present. But a wrestler with God was there, and oh, how he prayed! My heart melts within me yet as I think of it. He pleaded with God. He poured out his heart before Him. In his manner and words he was wondrously familiar with God, but it was that sweet familiarity that comes from utter self-abasement and deepest humility, and which enables its possessor to come, with unabashed faith, face-to-face with God and ask great things of Him, because it is asking only for His honor and the glory of His Son. That morning twenty-four people knelt at the penitent form seeking the Lord!

Several years ago I wrote an article on the prayers of soul-winners. It fell into the hands of two young officers (ministers), one of whom is now in India, and they began to pray. One of them, it was reported, prayed all Saturday night. The next day they went to a Salvation Army corps where it had almost been impossible to get anyone to make a start for heaven, and that day they saw sixty-two people seeking God.

The same article was read by a Salvation Army captain in another corps. She read it to her soldiers (church members), urging them to greater diligence in prayer. The spirit of prayer fell on them, and some of them used to ask the captain for the key to the chapel and spend half the night wrestling with God until His power fell on the people. Scores of people were drawn to the Savior, the largest corps in that state was built up, and the whole city was stirred.

The other day, a staff officer in charge of a band of boys told me that, a short time before, he went with his boys into a town, and after two hours' wrestling with God, he got the assurance of a revival. In eighteen days, they saw one hundred and fifty people seeking salvation, and fifty more seeking the blessing of a clean heart.

More than all else the Lord wants these wrestling, pleading souls.

Indeed, there are many good men and women, but few wrestlers with God. There are many who are interested in the cause of Christ, and who are pleased to see it prosper in their corps, their church, their city, their country. But there are few who bear the burden of the world upon their souls day and night, who make His cause in every climate their very own, and who, like Eli, would die if the ark of God were taken—who feel it an awful shame and a consuming sorrow if victory is not continually won in His name.

This spirit of prayer is fed on the Word of God. Those who neglect diligent, daily study of and meditation on the Word of God will soon neglect secret prayer, while those who feed upon it will be constantly pouring out their hearts in prayer and praise. And in this as in all things, regular practice will cultivate, increase, and perfect the spirit of prayer.

This spirit of prayer will thrive only where faith is active. Lazy, slow faith quenches prayer. Prayer must be followed by watchfulness and dead-in-earnest, patient work, or it will soon grow sickly and die.

Light and foolish talking and jesting will surely quench the spirit of prayer, as will pride, over-sensitiveness that leads to suspicion, jealousy, envy, selfish ambition (even in Christian work), indulgence of appetite, love of the applause of others and desire for the honor this world can give, an uncharitable spirit, criticism, and the like.

Jesus said we "should always pray and never give up" (Luke 18:1 NLT), while Paul said, "Pray without ceasing" (1 Thess. 5:17 KJV).

Union with Jesus 13

Jesus said, "I and my Father are one" (John 10:30 KJV), and it is His loving purpose that you and I shall be able to say that too. He wants us to be able say it now in this present time, in the face of the Devil, and in holy, triumphant defiance of a frowning world and of shrinking, trembling flesh.

There is a union with Jesus as intimate as that of the branch and the vine, or as that of the various members of the body with the head, or as that between Jesus and the Father. This is shown by such Scriptures as that in which Jesus said, "I am the vine; you are the branches" (John 15:5 NLT), and in His great intercessory prayer, where He prayed "that they will all be one, just as you and I are one—as you are in me, Father, and I am in you" (John 17:21 NLT).

It is also shown in such passages as that in which Paul, speaking of Jesus, said that God "has put all things under the authority of Christ and has made him head over all things for the benefit of the church. And the church is his body" (Eph. 1:22–23 NLT), and that we "may grow up in all things into Him who is the head—Christ" (Eph. 4:15 NKJV). And again, "For both He who sanctifies and those who are being sanctified are all of one" (Heb. 2:11 NKJV). It is also shown clearly in Paul's testimony: "My old self has been crucified with Christ. It is no longer I who live, but Christ lives in me" (Gal. 2:20 NLT).

This union is not physical, of course, but spiritual, and can be known to the one who has entered into it by the direct witness of the Spirit. But it can be known to others only by its effects and fruits in the life.

This spiritual union is mysterious and yet simple, and many of our everyday relationships partially illustrate it. Where two people have the same interests or purposes, they are to that extent one. A Republican or Democrat is one with everyone else of his or her party throughout the whole country insofar as they hold similar principles. This is an imperfect sort of union, but it is union. The general, the worldwide leader of The Salvation Army, may be in any part of the world, pushing forward his mighty schemes of conquest for Jesus, and every other Salvationist, however humble, insofar as he or she has the same spirit and ideals as the general, is one with him. A husband and wife, or a parent and child, may be separated by continents and seas, and yet be one. For six months, three thousand miles of wild waves rolled between me and a woman I rejoiced to call my wife, but my heart was as absolutely true to her and my confidence in her fidelity was as supreme as now when we sit side by side—and we were one.

But more perfect, more tender, more holy, and infinitely more self-consuming and ennobling and enduring is the union of the soul with

Jesus than is any other possible relationship. It is like the union of the bay with the sea. It is a union of nature, a commingling of spirit, an eternal marriage of heart, soul, and mind.

It is a union of will. Jesus said, "I came down from heaven, not to do mine own will, but the will of him that sent me" (John 6:38 KJV), and, "My nourishment comes from doing the will of God, who sent me" (John 4:34 NLT). And so it is with those who are one with Jesus. The psalmist said, "I delight to do your will, O my God" (Ps. 40:8 ESV), and that is the testimony of everyone who has entered into this divine union. There may, and doubtless will, be times when this will is hard for flesh and blood, but even then the soul says with its Lord, "Not my will, but yours, be done" (Luke 22:42 ESV), and prays always, "May your will be done on earth, as it is in heaven" (Matt. 6:10 NLT).

There can be no union with Jesus without this union of will, for there is really very little of a man or woman but the will. That is really all we can call our own. The mind, with all its splendid powers and possibilities, may be reduced to idiocy. We may be robbed of our property. Health and even life itself may be taken away from us, but who can enter into the domain of our wills and rob us of that?

I say it reverently: So far as we know, not even God Himself can compel one's will. God wants to enter into a partnership, an infinitely tender and exalting fellowship, a spiritual marriage with our will. He approaches us with tremendous inducements and motives of infinite profit and loss, and yet we may resist and utterly thwart the loving thought and purpose of God. We can refuse to surrender. But surrender we must, if there is to be a union between us and God, for God's will, based as it is on eternal righteousness, founded in infinite knowledge and wisdom and love, is unchangeable, and our highest good is in a hearty and affectionate surrender to it and a union with it.

Union with Jesus is a union of faith—of mutual confidence and esteem. It is a state in which God trusts a man or woman. God can entrust faithful people with the honor of His name and His holy character in the midst of a world of rebels. God can empower them and beautify them with His Spirit and adorn them with all heavenly graces, without any fear that they will take the glory of these things to themselves. God can heap upon them riches and treasures and honors without any fear that they will use them for selfish ends or prostitute them to unholy purposes.

It is also a state in which we trust God—even when we cannot trace Him. We have confidence in the faithfulness and love of God in adversity as well as in prosperity. We do not have to be fed on sweets and live in sunshine and sleep on roses in order to believe that God is for us. God can mingle bitter with all His sweets and allow the thorns to prick and the storm clouds to roll all around, and yet we will stubbornly trust on. Like Job, our property may be swept away in a day and our children taken from us, and yet with Job we will say, "The Lord gave, and the Lord has taken away; blessed be the name of the Lord" (Job 1:21 esv) and still trust on.

Our own life may be menaced and filled with weariness and pain, and our closest companion may tell us to curse God and die, and yet we will say, "Should we accept only good things from the hand of God and never anything bad?" (Job 2:10 nlt) and still trust on.

Our friends may gather around, attack our Christian integrity and character, and foolishly assault the foundations of our faith by assuring us that if we were right with God these calamities could never befall us. Yet we will look up from the ash heap and out of our utter wreck and ruin and desolation, cry, "Though he slay me, yet will I trust in him" (Job 13:15 KJV). And though communities or nations conspire against us, we will say with David, "The LORD is my light and my salvation; whom shall I fear? The LORD is the strength of my life; of whom shall I be afraid? . . . .Though an host should encamp against me, my heart shall not fear: though war should rise against me, in this will I be confident" (Ps. 27:1, 3 KJV).

A woman said to me the other day, "I dread to think of the end of the world. It makes me afraid." But though worlds, like drunken men, tumble from their orbits, and though the universe crash into ruin, the childlike confidence of those who trust God will enable them to sing with the psalmist: "God is our refuge and strength, always ready to help in times of trouble. So we will not fear when earthquakes come and the mountains crumble into the sea. Let the oceans roar and foam. Let the mountains tremble as the waters surge!" (Ps. 46:1–3 NLT).

God can be familiar with us when we are faithful. He can take all sorts of liberties with our property, reputation, position, friends, health, and life, and allow devils to test and taunt. But the soul that is unchangeably fixed in its estimate of God's holy character and everlasting love will still triumphantly trust on.

It is a union of suffering, of sympathy. Once when I was passing through what seemed to me a perfect hell of spiritual temptation and sufferings, the Lord supported me with this text: "In all their affliction he was afflicted" (Isa. 63:9 KJV). The prophet refers in these words to the afflictions of the children of Israel in Egypt and in the wilderness after their escape from the hard bondage of Pharaoh, and he said in all their sufferings Jesus suffered with them.

Let her child be racked with pain and scorched with fever and struggling to breathe, and the mother suffers more than the child; so let the people of God be sore tempted and tried, and Jesus agonizes with them. He is the world's great sufferer. His passion is forever. He once tasted death for everyone; He suffers still with everyone. There is no cry of anguish or heartache or pang of spiritual pain in all the world that does not reach His ear and stir all His mighty sympathies. But especially does He suffer and sympathize with His own believing children. And in turn those who are one with Jesus suffer and sympathize with Him.

Any injury to the cause of Christ causes them more pain than any personal loss. They mourn over the desolations of Zion more than over the loss of their own property. The luke-warmness of Christians cuts them to the heart. The cry of sinful souls for the gospel of salvation is the cry of the travail, the agony of Jesus Himself, to them. They gladly say, with David, "The insults of those who insult you have fallen on me" (Ps. 69:9 NLT). They esteem the reproach of Christ greater treasure than all the pleasure and power and profits of this world combined. As the true wife gladly suffers privation and shame and reproach with her husband whom she knows to be righteous and honorable, so those who are one with Jesus rejoice that they are "counted worthy to suffer shame for his name" (Acts 5:41 KJV). They suffer and sympathize with Jesus.

It is a union of purpose. Most Christians serve God for reward; they do not want to go to hell, but to heaven. And that is right. But it is not the highest motive. There is a union with Jesus in which the soul is not so anxious to escape hell as it is to be free from sin, and in which heaven is not so desirable as holiness. The soul in this state thinks very little about its reward. His smile of approval is its heaven. The housekeeper wants wages, but the husband or wife never thinks of such a thing. They serve out of love. They are one in purpose with each other. His triumphs are hers. Her losses are his. All he has is hers, and all she has is his. And, as the apostle said, "Everything belongs to you, and you belong to Christ, and Christ belongs to God" (1 Cor. 3:22–23 NLT). The will of God is the supreme good of such a person. Someone has said that if two angels were sent into this world, one of whom was to rule it and the other was to sweep street crossings, that the sweeper would be so satisfied with his heavenly Father's will that he would not exchange places with the ruler.

The purpose of Jesus is to save the world and uphold the honor of God, and to establish truth in the lives, hearts, laws, and customs of men and women. And this is the purpose of every soul that is in union with Christ. To do this, Jesus sacrificed every earthly prospect and laid down His life. Those who live in union with Christ do the same. They do not stand in the presence of the world's great crying need and hesitate and wonder if the Lord really wants them to give a few cents or dollars for the salvation of others. They do not quibble as to whether God really requires the sacrifice of leaving their dog kennel and chicken coop and barn and house furnished a little below the neighbors' standard of beauty and luxury. They do not struggle and kick against the pricks when they feel God would have them forsake business and preach the gospel. They would loathe themselves to have such mean thoughts.

They do not say, "If I were rich," but out of the abundance of their poverty they pour into the lap of the world's need, and like the widow they gladly give their all to save the world. When God looks about for someone to stand up for His honor and warn a wicked world and offer terms of peace to sinners, souls in union with Christ do not say, "If only I were educated or gifted I would go," but with hearts flaming with love for Jesus and the world He has bought with His blood, they cry out, "Here am I, send me" (Isa. 6:8 KJV). It can be said of such a person as it was of the Lord, "Passion for your house consumes me" (John 2:17 CEB).

A young carpenter in New England, whose name was unknown, came every few months to The Salvation Army's divisional head-quarters and gave a hundred or more dollars for the work of God in India or some other portion of the world. He was one with Jesus in His purpose to save the world.

On a bitter wintry day, a poor woman came to John Wesley's apart-ment in Oxford University. She was shivering with cold. Wesley asked her why she did not dress more warmly. She replied that she had no warmer garments. When she was gone, Wesley looked at the pictures on his walls and said to himself, in substance, "If my Lord should come, would He be pleased to see these on my walls when His poor are suffering with cold?" Then he sold the pictures and gave to the poor. And in this way began that mighty and lifelong beneficence and almost matchless self-sacrifice that has led to the blessing of millions upon millions of people.

O, my God, that Your people might see what union with You really means.

Do you ask, "How can I enter into this union?" Read God's promises until you see that it is possible. Especially read and ponder over John 15 and 17. Read and ponder over the Commandments until you see that it is necessary. Without this union here there will be no union in eternity. Make the sacrifice that is necessary in order to become one with Jesus.

The woman who will be the true wife of a man must be prepared to give up all other lovers; leave her home; forsake father, mother, brothers, and sisters; change her name; and utterly identify herself, her prospects for life, and her all, with the man she loves. And so must you be prepared to identify yourself utterly with Christ, to be hated, despised, rejected, and crucified, but also armed, baptized with the Holy Spirit, and crowned by God.

Does your heart consent to this? If so, make a perpetual covenant with your Lord right now. Do it intelligently. Do it with a true heart, in full assurance of faith, and God will seal you for His own. Do not waver. Do not doubt. Do not cast away your confidence because of your feelings or lack of feelings, but stand on the facts. Walk by faith, and God will soon prove His ownership in you in a way that will be altogether satisfactory to both your head and your heart, and convincing to men, women, angels, and devils.

In God's School 14

Human beings are the supreme product in this world, and the struggle with adversity and evil forces is a part of God's plan of developing us for mansions and thrones and crowns and kingdoms in the world to come. Therefore we must believe and hope and love and struggle on. "At just the right time we will reap a harvest of blessing if we don't give up" (Gal. 6:9 NLT). We must beware of discouragement and keep from running away from the conflict. If we flee, we shall perish forever. If we fight to the finish, we shall conquer though we die.

Nothing can come to us that God does not permit and which by His grace cannot be made to work out our higher good. God wants to build us up in holy character, but holy character is for eternity; it is many sided and therefore must be subjected to manifold testings. We must be taught by both pain and pleasure. We must learn how to abound and to suffer need (see Phil. 4:12). And to this end we shall often be plunged from the heights to the depths, and hurled from the depths to the heights again.

Today the sun shines and the world is full of beauty, but tomorrow the storm clouds lower, the beauty is hidden, and we are prone to fear that the sun will shine no more. Today people look upon us and smile and shout, "Hosanna!" but tomorrow they frown and gnash their teeth and cry out, "Crucify!" Today we have plenty and can feed the multitudes of the hungry with what we have to spare; tomorrow we ourselves are hungry and know not where to turn for bread. Today our pulse is full, and we feel strong enough to chase a thousand; tomorrow we are feeble, and life is a burden. Today we pray and God answers while we are yet speaking; tomorrow we plead and weep and moan, the heavens seem shut, and the mocking Tempter whispers, "Where is your God now?"

Today Job is the richest man in all the East, and his sons are the strongest and his daughters the fairest in the land; tomorrow he is a pauper and childless. Today Joseph is the pet of his father's heart and home; tomorrow he is under the lash and is toiling and galled with the slave gang's chain. Today David weds the king's daughter; tomorrow the king, with murderous hate, hurls his javelin at him and chases him over and around the mountains as he would a partridge or a wolf. Today Daniel sits next to the king in the midst of the hundred and twenty princes and counselors; tomorrow he is in the lions' den.

What does all this uncertainty and mystery of pleasure and pain, hope and despair, favor and disfavor mean? Ah, it means that God wants us for Himself. "Whom the LORD loves He [disciplines]" (Heb. 12:6 NKJV). It means that He sees in us something worth His while to educate, and He is educating us.

A friend of mine owned a gold mine. He promised the Lord every penny of profit from it. He made nothing, but lost twenty thousand pounds in that mine. He went to the Lord about it. The Lord said, "I am educating you, and I can afford to spend millions to do so." My friend cried out, "O Lord, if Thou canst afford it, I can, for Thou knowest I want to be educated in Thy school!"

God would make us strong in faith, mighty in prayer, unfailing in hope, content whatever our lot, perfect in love, fearless in our devotion to truth, lovers of all, and more than conquerors.

He would wean us from reliance on ourselves or others—in whom there is no help—to dependence on Him. He would detach us from the world and fasten us by every tie to heaven. When Job shall have learned his lesson, which is not for himself alone, but for ten thousand times ten thousand other perplexed sufferers as well, he shall have his riches doubled and restored to him again with stronger sons and fairer daughters.

Joseph shall leave the prison cell and slave gang's chain and sit as favorite in Pharaoh's palace and rule his empire. The king shall die by his own hand, and David shall sit upon his throne. Daniel shall escape from the lions' den and rise to higher honor and esteem than he knew before. Thus shall it be with the man or woman who does not kick against the pricks, but nestles low under God's hand and rejoices and obeys and trusts and doubts not while God educates.

Flowers need night's cool darkness, the moonlight and the dew;
So Christ from one who loved it, His shining oft withdrew.
And then for cause of absence my troubled soul I scanned,
But glory shadeless shineth in Emmanuel's land.[1]

The secret of peace and victory under all these circumstances is "a little more faith in Jesus."[2] In God's school, we learn through the heart rather than through the head, and by faith rather than logic. "Lord, I believe!" (see Mark 9:24; John 9:38).

NOTES

1. Anne Cousin, "The Sands of Time Are Sinking," 1857, public domain.

2. From an American spiritual; direct source information is unknown.

Holiness and Self-Denial 15

One day John Wesley was to dine with a rich man. One of his preachers who was present said, "Oh, sir, what a sumptuous dinner! Things are very different to what they were formerly. There is but little self-denial now among the Methodists." Wesley pointed to the table and quietly remarked, "My brother, there is a fine opportunity for self-denial."

Denial that is not self-imposed is not self-denial. It might have been self-denial on the part of the host to present a less sumptuous table, but there would then have been no self-denial on the part of the guest. Adverse circumstances or selfish people may deprive us of the luxuries and even of the necessities of life. But our deprivation would not be self-denial. We deny ourselves only when we voluntarily give up that which we like and might lawfully keep. And I have no doubt that God often allows us luxuries and abundance, not that we may consume them upon ourselves, but rather that we may deny ourselves joyfully for His dear sake, and the sake of the needy ones around us.

Often when urging upon well-to-do people the importance of denying themselves in dress and furniture and equipage and the luxuries of life, I have had them turn to me and say, "If God did not mean for me to have these things and enjoy them, then why did He give me the means to get them?" And they thought they had crushed me with their logic.

But the answer is simple. God meant them to be stewards, but they considered themselves owners. God meant them to have the greater blessedness of giving, for "it is more blessed to give than to receive" (Acts 20:35 KJV), but they contented themselves with receiving. God meant them to pass on His bounty to the needy multitudes around them, but they dammed up and diverted the streams of God's mercy and reveled in what they considered God's special favor and license to unlimited self-indulgence, while the multitudes for whom God really intended those blessings perished of want. They show unmistakably by their conduct that they have not the Spirit of Jesus, who, "though he was rich, yet for your sake he became poor, so that you by his poverty might become rich" (2 Cor. 8:9 ESV), and on the judgment day they will surely be found wanting, and woeful will be their condemnation.

Why does God give a woman wealth? That she may spend it on feathers and flowers, silks and satins, and luxurious apartments? No, but that she may spend it upon those who are hungry and cold and dying of bitter want.

Why does God give a mother strapping sons and lovely daughters? That she may enjoy their presence and train them for society and a career before the world? No, but that she may train them to be martyrs, slum angels, missionaries to the nations and to the barefooted, debauched, neglected, devil-ridden children of the saloons and brothels. Oh, as I have looked at my sweet baby boy and girl and realized the almost infinite difference between their training and that of millions of little ones who have the same rights in Jesus Christ that my children have—as I have realized the tender care with which they are unceasingly watched and sheltered and trained for God and righteousness— my heart has poured itself out to God in unutterable longings. Not that they might be great, but that they might be good; not that they might fill the earth with their fame, but that they might utterly sacrifice themselves for those who have never known the love and instruction of a sainted mother and a Christian home.

Why does God give any of us power and influence and fame? That we may be great in the eyes of others and lord it over our fellows and clothe ourselves in purple and fine linen and live luxuriously? No, but that we may throw every bit of our power and influence into the scale for righteousness of conduct and holiness of character and hasten the utter establishment of the kingdom of God upon earth.

Self-denial almost ceases to be self-denial when practiced from such a high and holy motive. It is the denial of the lower, base, earthly self, and the gratification of the higher and heavenly self. It is a turning from earth to heaven, from that which is fleeting and temporal to that which is eternal. It enlightens the mind, ennobles the character, perfects the heart, and brings us into fellowship with Jesus.

"If anyone wishes to come after Me, he must deny himself, and take up his cross daily and follow Me" (Luke 9:23 NASB).

I once read an illustration of Charles Finney's that has had a marked influence on my life. In substance, it was this:

Suppose a man were traveling in a foreign land, and, being waylaid and captured by brigands, he were sold into slavery, and a great ransom demanded for his release. At last, word reaches his anxious wife, informing her of his sad state, and the only condition upon which he could possibly be restored to her. His bondage is cruel and is fast wearing his life away, but there is no way of escape except for the ransom to be paid.

All the love, affection, pity, and sympathy of the wife's heart are aroused to the uttermost. She fears for her loved one's life. She can feel the galling chain. She can see the cruel lash of the slave driver. She can realize the heart-loneliness and bitter bondage of her darling, and she wishes she could fly to his side and share his burden and his sorrow, and no sacrifice seems too great to gain his liberty. She sells all her property, and lays her case before her friends and neighbors and they assist her, yet she falls far below the amount of the ransom demanded. She labors and toils early and late, and hastens to earn what money she can to add to what she already has. She denies herself every luxury and almost begrudges every necessity of life. She thinks of the hard fare of her husband; the coarse, scanty food; the miserable hovel; the hard, filthy bed; the heavy, unremitting labor; and the thought of selfish gratification is painful to her.

At last, a stranger hears her sad story, visits her, and gives her twenty pounds. She does not for an instant think, "Now I shall be able to get me a new dress and hat in the latest fashion, or get a nice piece of furniture for my rooms, or furnish my table better than in the past." No, no. She bursts into tears. She thanks the giver, and she cries, "Now I shall be able to ransom my love, and soon I shall have him in my arms again."[1]

Now, when Christians whose hearts throb with love for the Savior realize that Jesus puts Himself in the place of the prisoner in a lonely, dark cell; the slave toiling without recompense under the lash with the galling, clanking chain; the sick one on the bed of sleeplessness and pain; the helpless orphan and the poor widow and the outcast, and says, "When you did it to one of the least of these my brothers and sisters, you were doing it to me!" (Matt. 25:40 NLT), they must deny themselves.

When we see Jesus, lonely and full of toil and sorrow, again, in the person of these suffering ones, we find it easier to deny rather than to indulge ourselves. Self-sacrifice becomes a joy, while self-indulgence becomes a grief and a moral impossibility.

It is for this reason that I deny myself. It is for Jesus and the souls for whom He died. For years I lived for myself. All my hopes and ambitions centered on myself. Even my desire to go to heaven was more a desire to escape the pains of hell than to enjoy the society of Jesus and redeemed souls, and to do good and be holy. But at last all this was changed! My sins became a burden. I loathed myself. The righteous indignation and wrath of God against evildoers took hold upon me, and I feared I would be lost forever. But I found deliverance through Jesus. Through Him I found forgiveness of sins and freedom from the bondage of selfishness. He did not upbraid me, but loved me freely, won my heart, and filled me with a confidence and love toward Him that were unutterable.

With that love for Him came a love for the whole world of saints and sinners. At first I groped about somewhat blindly to know how to express that love, but true love will always finally express itself in uttermost self-sacrifice for its object, and in so doing adds fuel to its flame. Since then, I have found it easier to give than to withhold. I began by giving one-tenth of my income, but I could not stop there. Any case of need, any appeal for help, wrung my heart with an anguish of desire to give, until if it were not for the foresight of a prudent wife, who gets me to lay up money with her for a needed suit, I should frequently be without suitable clothes to wear.

This is not natural. It is spiritual—supernatural. In the old days when I had plenty of money, I can remember that it was rather grudgingly that I subscribed two dollars a year to the support of the gospel! I should be decidedly ashamed to tell this, but for the fact that I am now "a new creature" (2 Cor. 5:17 KJV) and an honest confession is good for the soul.

How can I indulge myself while others suffer? How can I hoard up wealth and this world's goods while others perish of want? Why can I not trust Him to supply my wants, He who feeds the sparrows with unfailing supply? Why did He speak so, if it was not to encourage one to cast abroad with an open, liberal hand and trust Him for daily bread?

I want the "full strength of trust to prove,"[2] and how can I have such trust if I never once in my life give away all I have and boldly trust Him to supply my need and confound a taunting devil? I have done it, and He has not failed me. Instead of finding my feet on quicksand, I found them on granite. Instead of starvation, I found plenty. Oh, there is a divine philosophy in self-denial that the wise folks of this world never dream of!

NOTES

1. Charles Finney; original source information unknown.

2. Charles Wesley, "Come, Jesus, Lord, with Holy Fire," n. d., public domain.

Spiritual Power 16

God is the source of all spiritual power and should be sought for constantly in two ways if we would have and retain power—by meditation on His Word and by secret prayer.

Several years ago I was preaching at a New England corps (church) commanded by a rather gifted officer. He appeared to be much impressed by my familiarity with and use of the Bible, and one day he remarked that he would be willing to give a fortune, if he had it, for an equal knowledge of the Scriptures. He was much taken back when I assured him that he was quite mistaken as to the strength of his desire, for if he really wanted to get acquainted with his Bible, he could easily do so by spending the hour and more that he gave to the newspapers each day in prayerful study of God's Word.

Men and women everywhere are crying and sighing for power and the fullness of the Spirit but neglect the means by which this power and fullness are secured.

The saintly John Fletcher said, "An over-eager attention to the doctrines of the Holy Spirit made me in some degree overlook the medium by which the Spirit works; I mean the Word of truth, by which that heavenly fire warms us. I rather expected lightning, than a steady fire by means of fuel."[1]

Glad, believing, secret prayer and patient, constant meditation on the Word of God will keep the sanctified man or woman full of power, full of love and faith, full of God.

But neglect of these results in spiritual weakness and dryness, joyless labor, and fruitless toil. If you have lost the power and sweetness of your experience through neglect of these simple means, you will not receive the blessing back again by working yourself up into a frenzy of agony in prayer, but rather by quieting yourself, talking plainly to God about it, and then hearkening diligently to what God says in His Word and by His Spirit. Then peace and power will soon return and need never be lost any more.

Most people give about ten hours a day to their bodies for eating, drinking, dressing, and sleeping, and maybe a few minutes to their souls. We ought to give at least one solid hour every day to restful, loving devotion with Jesus over our open Bible, for the refreshing, developing, and strengthening of our spiritual lives. If we would do this, God would have an opportunity to teach, correct, inspire, and comfort us, reveal His secrets to us, and make spiritual giants of us. If we will not do this, we shall surely be spiritual weaklings all our days, however we may wish to be strong.

The Devil will rob us of this hour if we do not steadfastly fight for it. He will say "Go and work" before we have gained the spiritual food that strengthens us for work. The Devil's piety and eager interest in God's work is amazing when he sees us on our knees! It is then that he transforms himself into an angel of light, and woe be to the soul that is deceived by him at this point!

I do thank God that, for many years, in various ministry roles, He has helped me to resist the Devil at this point and to take time with Him until my soul has been filled with His glory and strength, and has been made triumphant over all the power of the Enemy.

NOTE

1. John Fletcher, *The Works of the Reverend John Fletcher* (London: John Mason, 1859), 166.

Jesus—The Workingman

Peter the Great, czar of all Russia, and in some respects the mightiest monarch of his day, used to make shoes like a common cobbler, so that he might sympathize with his people and help them realize that labor is not menial, but honorable and full of dignity. It was a great stoop from the throne of Russia to a cobbler's bench, but I will tell you of a greater stoop.

We are told that God made the worlds by His Son, and that the Son upholds "all things by the word of his power" (Heb. 1:3 KJV).

John tells us that "in the beginning was the Word, and the Word was with God, and the Word was God. . . . All things were made by him; and without him was not anything made that was made" (John 1:1, 3 KJV). He is the master workman whom the heaven of heavens cannot contain; inhabiting eternity (see Isa. 57:15); stretching forth the heavens as a curtain; making mighty systems of sun, moon, and stars; creating worlds and hurling them into the awful abyss of space; and causing them to move, not in chaotic confusion, but in more than clocklike harmony by the silent, resistless energy of all-embracing laws.

He scoops out the bed of mighty oceans. He tosses aloft hoary mountains and stretches forth vast prairies and sandy deserts. He peoples the worlds with living creatures, until the imagination is almost paralyzed by the contemplation of the wonders of His handiwork. He is maker of the infinitely great and the infinitely small. He made the fixed star billions of miles away and millions of times bigger than the earth on which we live, and He made the tiny insect so small that it can be seen only by the aid of the microscope. And He fitted that little mite with its perfect organs of digestion, respiration, and reproduction.

He garnished the heavens and stretches forth the rainbow, and He painted the insect's wings and polished the lens of its little eye. Oh, He is a wondrous workman!

But John told us, "The Word became flesh and dwelt among us, and we beheld His glory, the glory as of the only begotten of the Father, full of grace and truth" (John 1:14 NKJV). And another writer said, "Because God's children are human beings—made of flesh and blood—the Son also became flesh and blood. For . . . the Son did not come to help angels; he came to help the descendants of Abraham. Therefore, it was necessary for him to be made in every respect like us, his brothers and sisters" (Heb. 2:14, 16–17 NLT).

And when He clothed Himself with our flesh, when He hid His dignity under the humble garb of our humanity, He did not come as an aristocrat, but He took a lowly place in a peasant's home.

He alone of the whole human race chose His own mother, and He chose one who was poor and humble and unknown. In His mighty descent from the bosom of the Father to the womb of the virgin, He might have stopped at the throne of some mighty earthly empire or among the rich and lordly. But instead of that He went down past thrones and palaces and was born in a stable in a manger among the cattle so that He might not be other than the lowliest of His brothers and sisters. He came to a life of obscurity, poverty, and toil, and He who made the worlds and upheld them by the word of His power learned to be a carpenter.

Artists, when they paint a picture of Jesus, paint a face of almost feminine softness. They would picture Him to us as a delicate man, with hair parted in the middle and with patrician hands and tapering fingers. But the Bible rather pictures Him as a callus-handed man of toil, whose back was bent to labor and who earned His bread by the sweat of His brow. Indeed, He was "made in every respect like us, his brothers and sisters" (Heb. 2:17 NLT). He became brother to the humblest son of toil, and since He has been a workingman, He has put a dignity on labor that exceeds the dignity of kings and queens.

Jesus was a workingman, and as such understands working men and women. He knows their weakness; He has been pinched with their poverty; He can sympathize with them in their long hours of toil that bars them from that culture of mind which, no doubt, many crave. He understands. But while He suffered and toiled and was tempted and tried as we are, and was excluded from the luxuries of wealth and the culture of schools, yet He was not excluded from culture of the heart and fellowship with His Father. He was nonetheless pure, holy, loving, patient, kind, and true, even to the point of dying for us to escape from our sins and become like Him.

We may not be great, but we may be good. We may not erect a Brooklyn Bridge or build a St. Peter's Basilica, but we can do our little task well and in the spirit of Jesus. We can be kind and patient, faithful and true. We can become partakers of His Spirit and do our work as unto Him, and when we enter into His glory we shall not be rewarded for the greatness of the work we have done, but rather for the faithfulness with which we have done it. The carpenter who has built houses, the blacksmith who has shod horses, the worker who has carried a hood, the boy who has blacked boots, the clerk who has toiled over the ledger, the farmer who has plowed the fields and fed cattle, if they have done it faithfully—with hearts washed in the blood and full of love for the Master and their fellow human beings, in the spirit of prayer and thanksgiving—will have as abundant an entrance into the everlasting kingdom of Jesus the carpenter and will have a place as near the throne as anyone who preached the gospel to thousands of governed states and ruled kingdoms.

The Legacy of Holiness 18

We must die! We feel that we must live, must live for the sake of our children, for the people of God whom we love as our own souls, and for those who are perishing all around us. We are prone to magnify our own importance, to think no one's faith is so mighty, no one's industry is quite so fruitful, no one's love is quite so unfailing, and no one's presence is quite so necessary as ours. But the Bible says, "After Abraham's death, God blessed his son Isaac" (Gen. 25:11 NLT). After we die, the blessed God will still live—His years fail not—and He will bless our sons and daughters and carry on His work.

Have faith in God. He will bless your children after you are dead.

Be sure you have given your children to God, not in order that they may be saved from hell, but that they may be saved from sin, from enmity with God, from pride and worldliness and selfishness and unbelief—saved that they may be saviors of others, and God will bless them when you are dead.

Do not choose ease and wealth and worldly power and fame for your children, but rather choose the lowly way of the cross. Jesus was a Man of Sorrows and acquainted with grief. He was despised and rejected. Ask the Lord with all your heart to make your children like their Master and to lead them in the paths He trod, and when you are dead God will remember your prayers and bless them.

Some years ago I was talking with a young lady whom God marvelously blessed and used in His work. Each of us had lost both of our parents when we were quite young. They were godly parents, who had given us to the Lord, and then, when it seemed we most needed their counsel and discipline, they died. But God took us up and blessed us. As we talked about the past, we could see the hand of God, through corrections and faithful fatherly chastenings, shaping our whole lives and bringing blessings out of what seemed the greatest calamities, until we were lost in wonder at His wisdom and goodness, and our mouths were filled with praise.

If our parents could have foreseen how God would tenderly care for us and bless us, how it would have softened their dying pillows!

Ah, there is the secret cause of our trouble, one that we cannot foresee! The more reason then why we should trust. "We walk by faith, not by sight" (2 Cor. 5:7 KJV), therefore we should trust. "God is love" (1 John 4:8 KJV), therefore we should trust. "You will keep in perfect peace all who trust in you, all whose thoughts are fixed on you! Trust in the LORD always, for the LORD GOD is the eternal Rock" (Isa. 26:3–4 NLT).

God may have blessed Isaac before Abraham's death, but I am glad we are told that He blessed him after Abraham's death. God has a memory; He does not forget. God is faithful; He breaks no promises. God is good; He delights to show mercy and bestow blessings.

Be faithful yourself. God said of Abraham, "For I have chosen him, that he may command his children and his household after him to keep the way of the LORD by doing righteousness and justice, so that the LORD may bring to Abraham what he has promised him" (Gen. 18:19 ESV).

Do your part as well as you know how. Search the Bible to know what God will have you do, and do it.

Pray for wisdom. "If you need wisdom, ask our generous God, and he will give it to you" (James 1:5 NLT). God will not upbraid you for your ignorance, if you want to be wise; therefore pray for wisdom.

Pray for patience. If you plant corn, it does not spring up the next morning. It lies in the ground for many days and dies. But God's eye is upon it, and He will bless it and cause it to bring forth fruit. And so will it be with your seed sowing in the hearts of your children—but you must have patience. Pray for patience. If you are patient and have faith in God, and are not walking by sight, you will continue to pray in hope and to sow the seed which is the Word of God (see Luke 8:11), though it seems to be utterly useless. It is not useless. Though you may die, yet after you are dead, God will bless your Isaacs. He surely will!

Thanksgiving 19

As lilies of the valley pour forth perfume, so good hearts pour forth thanksgiving. No mercy is too small to provoke it, no trial too severe to restrain it. As Samson got honey from the carcass of the lion he slew, and as Moses got water from the flinty rock, so the pure in heart are possessed of a sort of heavenly alchemy, a divine secret by which they get blessings out of all things, and for which there is giving of thanks.

A jubilant, saintly woman in Boston reached old age in deepest poverty and had to live on the charity of such friends as God raised up—and He raised them up. He who fed Elijah in the wilderness by the brook and in the poverty-stricken home of the desolate widow found a way to feed His child in Boston. God is not blind nor deaf. He is neither indifferent nor indigent. He is not "the silent God" that some people in their self-conceit and wayward unbelief suppose. He knows how to be silent and how to hide Himself from the proud in heart. But

He cannot hide Himself anywhere in His big universe from childlike faith and pure, obedient, longsuffering, patient love.

This old saint believed, obeyed, and rejoiced in God, and He raised up friends to supply her needs. One day one of them went upstairs with a dinner for the old lady, and as she came to the door, she heard a voice within. Thinking there was a visitor present, and delicately wishing that her charity should not be a cause of embarrassment, she stopped and listened. It was the voice of the old Christian at her table, and she was saying, "O Father, I do thank Thee with all my heart for Jesus and this crust."

To her thankful heart that crust was more than a feast and a well-filled cupboard and a fat bank account to one who has not a trustful, thankful spirit.

I heard of a rich man the other day who killed himself because he feared he might become poor. He *was* poor. Jesus said, "Life is not measured by how much you own" (Luke 12:15 NLT). Nor do your real riches depend upon your possessions, but rather the spirit with which you possess them.

Heaven is not parceled off into lots and estates. The angels own nothing and yet they possess all things and are eternally rich. And so with the true saint who trusts God and loves and obeys and is thankful.

The stars in their courses fight for such people. They are in harmony with the elemental and heavenly forces and eternal laws of the universe of God, and all things work together for their good. Not a hair of their head falls without God's notice. Not a desire rises in their heart but God's great heart throbs responsive to fulfill it, for does not the psalmist say, "He grants the desires of those who fear him" (Ps. 145:19 NLT)? Not only the fervent prayer shall be fulfilled, but also the timid, secret desire that has not been voiced in prayer. And how dare God do that? Because holy fear will not allow a desire that is not in harmony with God's character and the interests of His kingdom.

Napoleon gave blank checks on his bank to one of his marshals. One complained to the emperor that the drafts made were enormous and should not be allowed. "Let him alone; he trusts and honors me, and I will trust him," said Napoleon. God puts all things at the command of His saints, and trusts them while He asks them to trust Him. Why, then, should we not be thankful?

Nothing will keep the heart so young, banish care so quickly, smooth the wrinkles from the brow so certainly, fill the life with such beauty, make one's influence so fragrant and gracious, and shed abroad such peace and gladness as this sweet spirit of thankfulness.

This spirit can and should be cultivated. There is much for each of us to be thankful. We should thank Him for personal liberty and for the measure of health we have. I know a good old soul up the Hudson River who for thirty years or so has been lying in bed, while her bones have softened and she is utterly helpless and always in pain, but she praises and praises and praises God.

We should thank Him that we are not insane, that our poor minds are not unbalanced and rent and torn by horrid nightmares and dread and nameless terrors and deep despair and wild, restless ravings. We should thank Him for the light and blessings of civilization, past mercies, present comforts, and future prospects. We should thank Him for food, the appetite to eat it, and the power to digest it. We should thank Him for clothes to wear and books to read. We should thank Him for the church; The Salvation Army; the open Bible; the revelation of

Jesus Christ; and the Fountain opened for sin, uncleanness, and the glorious possibility of escape from the penalty, power, consequences, and character of sin. We should thank Him for home and friends and heaven bending over all, with God's sweet invitation, "Come!"

Truly, we have much to thank God for. But if we would be thankful, we must set our hearts to do it with a will. We grumble and complain without thought, but we must think to give thanks. To murmur and repine is natural; to give thanks—to really give thanks—is supernatural, gracious, and a spirit not earth-born, but which comes down from God out of heaven. And yet, like all things from God, it can be cultivated.

David said, "I will praise you, LORD" (Ps. 9:1 NLT). He put his will into it. Daniel "prayed, and gave thanks" (Dan. 6:10 KJV) three times a day. David outdid Daniel, for he said, "Seven times a day I praise you" (Ps. 119:164 ESV).

If you are not thankful, your heart is still bad and your soul unclean, for good hearts and pure souls are thankful. So go to the root of the matter and get rid of sin and get filled with the Holy Spirit. Flee to Jesus for riddance from the unholy spirit and the subtle selfishness that possesses you.

People who live in the midst of foul odors and harsh sounds cease to smell and hear them, but if for a while they could slip away to the sweet air and holy quiet of the woods and fields and then return to their noxious and noisy homes, their quickened senses would be shocked by their noisome surroundings. And so selfish people often live in themselves so long that they do not realize their selfishness and sin, except as light from heaven falls upon them. But when God's sweet breath blows over them and His light shines into them, then they are amazed at themselves. When some humble saint, full of faith and joy and the Holy Spirit, crosses their path, if they will but look, they may see themselves as in a glass.

But especially is this so when we look at Jesus. And if we continue, the look will transform us. It is of this that the apostle spoke when he said, "And we all, with unveiled face, beholding the glory of the Lord, are being transformed into the same image from one degree of glory to another. For this comes from the Lord who is the Spirit" (2 Cor. 3:18 ESV). And when this change has taken place, the joy of Jesus will be poured into the heart and praise will well up and bubble forth in thanksgiving as an unfailing fountain of sweet waters, filling it with joy, and filling earth—your little corner of earth—with peace, gladdening all who see and hear. But if that change has not fully taken place in you, do not withhold the praise that is God's due, but think of his loving-kindness and tender and multiplied mercies, and begin to thank Him now. Your very giving of thanks will help to hasten the change. Begin now!

Don't Flinch 20

The other evening I asked a Salvation Army captain (minister) for the story of her coming to faith in Jesus Christ. She told me that a few lines in a little book showed her the way to Jesus. She saw through these lines that if she would ask God to save her and would "not flinch" in her faith, He would do it. So she prayed and then waited for Jesus to come. She lived in a country that was full of spiritual darkness, and there was no one to teach her. And in her ignorance she thought Jesus would come in bodily presence, so she put her room in order and earnestly waited and watched for Him to open the door and come in. But He did not come.

Then she remembered that God had promised to answer the prayers of two or three, so she wrote a note to a minister to come and pray with her. But something seemed to whisper to her that this was trusting the minister's prayer and not the Lord, and this was doubting God. So she tore up the note and, looking to God without flinching, she trusted.

Then suddenly Jesus came, not in bodily presence, but in Spirit, and her whole soul was flooded with light and love and the glory of God.

I fully believe it is just at this point that many souls draw back and fail. They flinch at the final test of faith. Just when all is on the altar and there is not one thing more to do but to stand still and see God come, they give in to "an evil heart of unbelief" (Heb. 3:12 KJV), or Satan comes suggesting something more to do. And the soul, dropping its eyes from the bending heavens, gets into the endless treadmill of endeavor to either help itself or to get somebody to help it, and so misses the prize and never finds God, or rather never gives God a chance to show forth His saving power and make His presence known.

While faith stands waiting and trembling, taunted by mocking devils and all manner of suggestions to doubt, it is hard not to flinch. But flinching will prove as fatal to the revelation of Jesus to your soul as a movement will prove to your picture when you sit before the photographer's camera. Be still in your heart and trust, look and wait, and Jesus will surely come. There may be ceaseless outward activity, but this inward soul-quiet and watchfulness and faith are absolutely necessary to the revelation of the Lord.

Abraham slew his birds and beasts and laid them on the altar and waited expectantly for God to come. And God came.

Solomon built his temple, placed everything in order, then prayed and waited. And the glory of God filled the temple till the priests could not stand in His presence.

Elijah slew his bullock, placed it on the altar, poured water over it as a final work of faith, then prayed and waited till the heavens opened and fire fell and consumed his sacrifice.

The disciples prayed and waited on God for ten days; then suddenly the Holy Spirit fell on them in tongues of fire that filled the world with light.

If they had flinched when the time came to steadfastly look to God and believe, the world would never have heard of them.

A minister friend of mine lost the blessing of full salvation. I found him in this state and dealt faithfully with him. He went to his church that night, told his people his condition, and called them around the altar with him, but he failed to get the blessing. A wise friend of mine, who happened to be present, explained his failure by saying, "He didn't stay on his knees long enough. He was in too big a hurry. He didn't give God time to deal with him." He flinched when the time came to steadily watch and wait and trust.

The Lord God declared by the mouth of Isaiah, "Whoever believes will not be in haste" (Isa. 28:16 ESV). It is in this attitude of unflinching watching and waiting that faith and patience are made perfect. And when this perfection is attained, the Lord will come suddenly to the heart that has waited for Him.

Myriad are the souls who can say with the psalmist, "I waited patiently for the LORD to help me, and he turned to me and heard my cry. He lifted me out of the pit of despair, out of the mud and the mire. He set my feet on solid ground and steadied me as I walked along. He has given me a new song to sing, a hymn of praise to our God" (Ps. 40:1–3 NLT).

Faith Is What You Want 21

I met a sister in one of our holiness meetings who was evidently in great spiritual distress with intense hunger for full salvation. After a few moments of conversation, I felt assured that she was ready to accept the blessing of holiness, and so we knelt in prayer. But for some reason our prayers did not prevail. I asked if she was sure her consecration was complete. She declared it was; she was willing to die for it.

"Then," said I, "sister, there are three things you must believe. First, do you believe God is able to sanctify you wholly?"

"Yes."

"Second, do you believe He is willing?"

"Yes."

"Then, with your perfect consecration, there is but one other step to take and the wonder work of grace will be done. Will you believe that He does it? For the promise is, 'Whatever you ask in prayer, believe that you have received it, and it will be yours' (Mark 11:24 ESV). Will you believe this?"

"But I don't feel that He does."

"That makes no difference, sister; your faith must precede all feeling."

"But I can't believe that He has done it."

"I don't ask you to believe that He has done it, but that He is doing it in answer to your present faith. You must believe that He does it if ever you are to get the witness of the Spirit. Say, 'I will believe God.'"

"Well, I will try."

"No, that won't do; you must believe, not try to believe."

"Well, I am determined to struggle on till the blessing comes."

"No, sister, your struggles will do no good unless you believe; and, until you do this, you are making God a liar."

"But won't I be lying to say I will believe, when I don't feel like it?"

"No, for 'faith comes by hearing, and hearing by the word of God' [Rom. 10:17 NKJV], and the Word of God to you is, 'You are already clean because of the word I have spoken to you' [John 15:3 NIV], and 'Ask and you will receive' [John 16:24 NIV]."

That evening I saw her again. She said, "I have committed myself to God and shall trust Him, till the witness of my acceptance comes."

The next day she was in the meeting and related her experience, telling us that in the night God awoke her with an assurance of His love and gave her the clear witness of the Spirit that she was entirely sanctified, putting glory in her heart and hallelujahs on her tongue.

Entire consecration is not entire sanctification. You are commanded to "present your bodies a living sacrifice, holy, acceptable unto God"

(Rom. 12:1 KJV). This is entire consecration. But it is also said, "For it is by believing in your heart that you are made right with God, and it is by openly declaring your faith that you are saved" (Rom. 10:10 NLT). So then, there must be entire consecration, unwavering faith, and a frank, artless confession of both to Jesus. This is your part, and, when these simple conditions are met and steadfastly maintained, against all contrary feelings, God will suddenly come into His holy temple, filling the soul with His presence, purity, and power. This twofold work by you and God constitutes the one experience of entire sanctification. When this experience is yours, confess it before others at your very earliest opportunity.

Practical Lessons of the Resurrection 22

Paul told us that the same power which raised Christ from the dead is in us who believe (see Eph. 1:17–20). He said of Jesus, "When he ascended to the heights, he led a crowd of captives and gave gifts to his people" (Eph. 4:8 NLT). He said of himself, "Whatever gain I had, I counted as loss for the sake of Christ. Indeed, I count everything as loss because of the surpassing worth of knowing Christ Jesus my Lord. For his sake I have suffered the loss of all things and count them as rubbish, in order that I may gain Christ . . . that I may know him and the power of his resurrection" (Phil. 3:7–8, 10 ESV).

The practical, everyday teaching of these Scriptures to me is this: Since Jesus rose from the dead and ascended on high, He puts at my disposal the same power to do and suffer His will that His heavenly Father gave to Him. Jesus "was crucified in weakness, [but] now lives by the power of God" (2 Cor. 13:4 NLT). And when He rose from the dead He broke every fetter forged by Satan, sin, and hell. He carried them captive and opened a way by which every human soul may go free, enter into union with God through the indwelling Holy Spirit, and have the power of God working mightily and triumphantly in him or her.

In ancient times, victorious generals carried captive the captains and kings they conquered, with all the wealth they could lay their hands upon, and when they returned to their own people, they distributed gifts from the spoils of the enemy. So Jesus, having triumphed over all the power of the Enemy, distributes gifts of love, joy, faith, patience, and wisdom to His people that shall enable them also to have power over all the power of the Enemy.

He came as a lowly stranger into the iron furnace of this sin-cursed, devil-enslaved world. He toiled with its toiling millions, suffered their sorrows and sicknesses, their poverty and temptations, and when He had impressed upon a few of them a faint sense of His divinity, which He hid under the humble garb of His humanity, He suffered their death and dashed their hopes (as they supposed) forever. But He rose again and ascended "far above all principality, and power, and might, and dominion" (Eph. 1:21 KJV) and is seated at the right hand of the Father as our intercessor and our advocate. From that place of power He pleads our cause, watches our interests, guides our steps, strengthens our hearts, and illuminates our minds. He secures for us boundless gifts and graces and immunities, which we are at liberty to take by faith and use for the advancement of His kingdom of holiness, and to foster humility, righteousness, and joy, in our hearts and the hearts of others.

It is His purpose that we should, in a most important sense, sustain the same relation to Him now that He sustained to His heavenly Father in the days of His humanity—that we should be baptized with the same Spirit, preach with the same authority, secure the same results, gain the same final and eternal victory, and at last sit down with Him on His throne forevermore.

This being so, I am under as much obligation now to be holy, to be empowered by the Spirit, and to be about my Lord's business, as I shall be in heaven. And this is not only an obligation, but also an inspiration!

Who, having caught a glimpse of this high and holy purpose of our resurrected Lord, can be content ever again to grope in the malarial fogs of unbelief and grovel on the dung hill of this world's poor little pleasures and riches and honors? Who would not forsake father and mother, wife and children, houses and lands; pluck out a right eye; cut off a right hand or foot; cast off every weight and easily besetting sin; deny him- or herself; take up his or her cross; esteem all this world's gain as loss; and even sacrifice his or her life in order to "know . . . the power of his resurrection" (Phil. 3:10 KJV), enter into this life "hid with Christ in God" (Col. 3:3 KJV), and not disappoint our Lord? It was for this we were born, and to fall short of this will be infinite, eternal loss and doom us to an everlasting night of shame and contempt.

Evil Speaking 23

"Speak evil of no one," the Bible says (Titus 3:2 ESV). This is a command of God. It should be meditated upon and obeyed. A failure to do this leads to innumerable evils. Because of it, myriads of souls have fallen into sin and multitudes, almost persuaded, have turned back into darkness. Many revivals have been quenched and many houses of God have become spiritual sepulchers, all because of evil speaking.

What is evil speaking? It is evil to tell lies about anyone or slander others in any way. "You shall not bear false witness against your neighbor," God says (Ex. 20:16 NASB). A person's reputation and character are sacred in God's sight, and just as He forbids us to rob others of their property or take their lives, so He forbids us to lie about them or rob them of their good names. This is a holy commandment and commends itself to everyone's conscience.

It is evil to retell the faults and infirmities of others. This is a very common form of evil speaking, but love will cover up such faults and infirmities. Just as it is beautiful in children to never speak about or appear to notice the club feet or hunchback or crossed eyes of a little playmate, so it is lovely and Christlike in us to pass by faults and infirmities, and evil not to do so. It is evil to tell of someone else's sins and actual wrongdoing where and when it will do no good.

Why should we speak evil of no one? It is a grievous wrong to speak evil of anyone because in doing so we wrong that person. You do not like anyone to speak evil of you, and you consider it wrong for anyone to do so. Why? When you have answered, you have given yourself a reason not to speak evil of others.

Because in speaking evil of anyone we wrong those to whom we thus speak. It fills their minds with unholy, unjust prejudice. It excludes good thoughts and tempts them to think and speak evil.

Because we wrong our own souls by evil speaking. It destroys all generous and kindly thoughts in us and quenches love. It opens our hearts for the Devil to enter, and he will make haste to come in. It prevents us from praying in faith and love for the person, which would be infinitely better than speaking evil of him or her, and which he or she especially needs, if he or she is in any way wrong.

Because in speaking evil of anyone we grieve the Holy Spirit and break the commandment of God. The Holy Spirit leads us to love everyone—including our enemies—even as Jesus loved them. But evil speaking destroys love. The Holy Spirit leads us to pray for others, especially for those who are faulty and sinful, but evil speaking quenches the spirit of prayer as water quenches fire.

Because in speaking evil of anyone we wrong Jesus. He died for that person. He bought that soul with His blood, and even though he or she may be a skeptic, hypocrite, or rebel who refuses to obey God and love and trust Jesus, yet Jesus loves and spares that soul and is wronged when the object of His love is slandered. Jesus identifies Himself with those to whom we give a cup of cold water in His name and says the good we do that person is done to Him. And so He will identify Himself with those we wrong by evil speaking and in the judgment will face us with the wrong as done to Himself unless we hastily and heartily repent.

What is the remedy? If someone is bad or faulty in any way, consider the fact that he or she may have secret trials and temptations that you know nothing about. He may have business troubles and cares that lead him to wrong, or family trials to which you are a stranger, or she may have had very faulty early training which has marred her for life. Not that these things will excuse anyone in the day of judgment, but they should lead you and me to pity rather than to abuse by speaking evil of another person.

Think about your own evils. This will be far more profitable to you than to think about anyone else's, and will be infinitely more likely to make a better man or woman of you.

> I often see in my own thoughts,
> When they lie nearest Thee,
> That the worst men I ever knew
> Were better men than me.[1]

One of the chief dangers to ourselves in evil speaking is that we come to underestimate everybody else and to esteem ourselves more highly than we ought. We come to look at our own virtues and other people's faults, when we ought to look long at their virtues and at our own faults.

> Yes, they have caught the way of God,
> To whom self lies displayed
> In such clear vision as to cast
> O'er others' faults a shade.[2]

If we want to be like Jesus, we must obey the command, "Be humble, thinking of others as better than yourselves" (Phil. 2:3 NLT), but this will be impossible where evil speaking is indulged in.

Consider how Jesus loves others. If Jesus loved them enough to die for them, and still loves them enough to spare them, in spite of all their faults and sins, and to accept them the moment they repent, trust, and obey, how dare we speak evil of them! And if they are followers of Jesus and children of God, even though they may be very imperfect, how dare we speak evil of them! Would we dare speak evil of an angel by the throne of God and expect God to be deaf and allow our sin to go unpunished? Would we not rather expect His holiness to flame out in terrible wrath and consume us? And is any poor sinful soul who has looked to Jesus for salvation any less dear to the heart of God than the shining angels around His throne?

"Hypocrite! First get rid of the log in your own eye; then you will see well enough to deal with the speck in your friend's eye" (Matt. 7:5

NLT). Get a clean heart, full of the Holy Spirit, full of love, and you cannot speak evil of anyone. With a heart flaming with love, you will pray for the wrongdoer, and if you see evil in anyone, you will go to that person in love and try to correct him or her, just as you would go to a blind person walking toward a precipice and try to turn him or her from certain death.

I need Thy mercy for my sin;
But more than this I need
Thy mercy's likeness, in my soul, for others' sin to bleed.
All bitterness is from ourselves,
All sweetness is from Thee;
Sweet God, for evermore be Thou
Fountain and fire in me.[3]

NOTES

1. Frederick William Faber, "Harsh Judgments," n. d., public domain.

2. Ibid.

3. Ibid.

How to Study the Bible 24

The other day a young Salvation Army officer asked for a few suggestions as to how to read and study the Bible. Here they are.

1. Read and study it as two young lovers read and study each other's letters. As soon as the mail brings a letter from his sweetheart, the young man grabs it and, without waiting to see if there is not another letter for him, runs off to a corner and reads and laughs and rejoices over it and almost devours it. If he is a particularly desperate and demonstrative lover—Lord, make us desperate and demonstrative lovers of our Lord Jesus Christ!—he will probably kiss it and carry it next to his heart till the next one comes.

He meditates on it day and night and reads it again and again. He carries it with him, and appears very quiet and thoughtful, till all at once a twinkle comes into his eye, out comes the letter, and choice portions are read over again. He delights in that letter. If any part is hard to understand, a letter is sent off post haste for explanations, and the explanation and letter will be most carefully compared, and possibly also previous letters will be studiously compared with this one. I knew a young man whose fate was hanging in the balance. He wanted assurance, but the young woman was coy, and she veiled her true feelings and left him in uncertainty. He studied her letters and weighed every word and phrase, brought them to me, and had me compare letter with letter, as we should compare Scripture with Scripture, in order, if possible, to discover the state of her mind and heart and his prospects. In due time he was abundantly rewarded.

That is the way to read the Bible. It is God's will and testament. It is His own carefully written instructions as to what manner of people He wants us to be, how we shall behave ourselves, what we shall do and not do, what our rights and privileges in Jesus are, what our peculiar dangers are, how we shall know our enemies and conquer them, and how we shall enter into and constantly enjoy His favor and escape hell and get safely home to heaven.

2. Receive it like the disciples in Berea did. "They received the word with all readiness of mind" (Acts 17:11 KJV). A frank and noble mind is open to the truth and wants it more than gold or pleasure or fame or power.

"[They] searched the scriptures" (Acts 17:11 KJV). They wanted to know for themselves, and not by mere hearsay. They searched. Precious things are deeply hidden. Pebbles and stones and autumn leaves abound everywhere, but gold and silver and precious stones are hidden deep in the bowels and rocky ribs of the earth. Shells cover the seashore, but pearls are hidden in its depths. And so it is with truth. Some truth may lie on the surface of the Bible, but truth that will altogether satisfy and distinguish us and make us wise unto salvation is found only after diligent search, even as for hidden treasure. Search the Scriptures, for as Jesus said, "The Scriptures point to me!" (John 5:39 NLT). If you would know Jesus, search the Scriptures, and you will come to know Him and see His face and be like Him.

"[They] searched . . . daily" (Acts 17:11 KJV). They dug into the Word of God daily, not spasmodically, by fits and starts, but habitually, to find out if the things Paul preached were so. And just so must you do. "Meditate on it day and night" (Josh. 1:8 NLT), was God's instruction to Joshua. And once this habit is formed, the delight in God's Word will become unspeakable.

"When I discovered your words, I devoured them," said Jeremiah. "They are my joy and my heart's delight" (Jer. 15:16 NLT). "Oh, how I love your instructions!" cried the psalmist. "I think about them all day long" (Ps. 119:97 NLT).

In forming the habit of Bible study, we may have to begin and follow it up for a time from a sense of duty. But once the habit is formed, if we are not only hearers but doers of the Word, we shall follow through for very joy, until we can say with Job, "I . . . have treasured his words more than daily food" (Job 23:12 NLT).

3. Read and study the Word not to get a mass of knowledge in the head but a flame of love in the heart. "Knowledge puffs up while love builds up" (1 Cor. 8:1 NIV). Read it to fuel affection and to find food for reflection, direction for judgment, and guidance for conscience. Read it not that you may know but that you may do.

4. Follow carefully the line of thought from verse to verse and chapter to chapter. Often the first part of one chapter belongs to the last part of the preceding chapter. For instance, in the last verse of the fourth chapter of Ephesians, we read, "Be kind to each other, tenderhearted, forgiving one another, just as God through Christ has forgiven you" (Eph. 4:32 NLT), and in the first verse of the fifth chapter we read, "Imitate God, therefore, in everything you do, because you are his dear children" (Eph. 5:1 NLT). Those two verses belong together. We are to follow God in what? Why, in the spirit of kindness and tenderheartedness and forgiveness.

Again, in John 7:53, we read, "They went each to his own house" (ESV), and in John 8:1, "But Jesus went to the Mount of Olives" (ESV). Those two verses belong together. Jesus had no house, so when each of them went to his own house for the night, Jesus went to the cold, dark mount!

5. Finally, do not be discouraged if progress in the knowledge of the Word seems slow at first. It is like learning to play an instrument or master a trade—for the first few days or weeks it appears impossible, but it is not so. Some glad day a brain cell will expand or a veil drop from your face and scales from your eyes and you will find yourself doing the impossible with ease.

So it will be in acquainting yourself with the Word of God. Keep at it, keep at it, keep at it! Cry to God with David, "Open my eyes to see the wonderful truths in your instructions" (Ps. 119:18 NLT).

Pray for an understanding heart. You will only love and understand the Word as Jesus reveals it to you. So walk with Him, take up your cross, and follow Him through evil as well as good. Luke's gospel tells us that Jesus came to two of His trembling, heartbroken, disappointed disciples after His resurrection and "took them through the writings of Moses and all the prophets, explaining from all the Scriptures the things concerning himself" (Luke 24:27 NLT). Later Luke said, "Then he opened their minds to understand the Scriptures" (Luke 24:45 NLT).

There are things in the Bible hard to be understood, and we may not know them till we stand by the crystal sea. But we can learn those things that will make us meek and lowly in heart as was Jesus— watchful, patient, loving, kind, forgiving, and utterly zealous and self-sacrificing for the salvation of souls. Happy shall we be if, like David, we can say, "I have hidden your word in my heart, that I might not sin against you" (Ps. 119:11 NLT).

How to Prepare for the Meeting **25**

Luke told us in his gospel that when Jesus was a boy of twelve, He went with His parents and neighbors up to Jerusalem to the Feast of the Passover. On the return of the company, the child Jesus tarried behind in Jerusalem. "His parents didn't miss him at first, because they assumed he was among the other travelers. But when he didn't show up that evening, they started looking for him among their relatives and friends. When they couldn't find him, they went back to Jerusalem to search for him there" (Luke 2:43–45 NLT).

Their mistake was in taking it for granted that Jesus was in the company. Joseph knew He was not with him, Mary knew He was not with her, the kinsfolk and acquaintances knew He was not with them, and each took it for granted that He was in the company with someone else. But when they sought Him, they found Him not; He was not there.

Just so, frequently in meetings and conventions the people all suppose Jesus is in the company, and yet there may not be one that is personally conscious of His presence. They take it for granted that He is with someone else, yet He may not be in their midst at all. He has not been perseveringly, importunately, humbly, and believingly sought and invited to come, and so He has stayed behind.

I remember going to a camp meeting (outdoor revival meeting) a number of years ago, hoping to find Jesus there in power. I got there two or three days after the opening, and I found, if I now remember rightly, that no one had come to faith in Jesus. There was no grip and power in the meetings. At the appointed hour, the bell would ring, and the people in attendance, who had been laughing and joking and singing songs and visiting with each other and generally making merry, would come strolling into the meetings with smiles on their faces and "God bless you" on their tongues, but with apparently no solemn consciousness of the holy presence of the Crucified One in their midst. Then the meeting would begin with a rush and a bang, songs and prayers and jokes and laughter and collection and smart testimonies and a Bible reading would follow, and the meeting would end again without souls. They would all go out good-naturedly, make a rush for the best seats at the dinner table, and enjoy themselves beautifully until the next meeting. Everyone seemed to take it for granted that Jesus was in the company, yet no one seemed especially conscious of His presence.

At last it was pointed out that the meetings were galloped through but no souls were saved, and it was suggested that perhaps Jesus was missing. A prayer meeting was called, and some of the people present had to allow that Jesus was not with them. Then some of them went to their tents to look for Jesus, some others went to the woods and got down on their knees to look for Him, and they would not give up the search until at last He was found. And when He was told that He was expected, that He must come, and that we would not let Him go unless He blessed us, then He came. Then there was a shout of a King in the camp (see Num. 23:21), and He gave us a touch of His baptism, which is with the Holy Spirit and with fire.

The saints became earnest, and skeptics and seekers grew alarmed and convicted so that they were no longer concerned about what they should have for dinner. And some seemed so anxious to talk with Jesus and get filled with His Spirit and His great thoughts, and to get Him to put the dynamite of the Holy Spirit into their testimonies and songs and prayers, that they lost their appetites and did not care whether they had any dinner at all, if only they could be fed with bread from heaven.

Oh, I tell you, the transformation that came over that campground when Jesus got there was wonderful! The shallow joy that caused them to smile and make an empty racket gave way before that deep joy of the Lord which makes men and women weep and be serious, fills their faces with the solar light of heaven, and makes their shout almost as terrible to the wicked as will be the trumpet peals and awful thunders of the judgment day.

The presence of Jesus in the power of the Holy Spirit on that campground made the remaining days of the camp meeting into veritable judgment days for some folks. Then the news went abroad that Jesus was in the camp, and the people poured in from the country all around, and mighty things were done in His name. Weak folks were made strong. Timid folks became bold as lions. Broken hearts were healed.

Sad folks were made into glad folks. The lame leaped. The blind saw. The deaf heard. The dumb spoke. The hungry multitudes were fed. Spirits that were full of passion and like a storm-tossed sea became peaceful and calm. And dead souls were raised to life!

I tell you it was the presence of Jesus that saved that camp meeting from being recorded as a dismal failure, and instead caused it to be remembered as a time of wondrous refreshing from the presence of the Lord.

Now Jesus is ready and willing to go up to every camp meeting and convention and council and indoor and outdoor meeting all over the world and make His personal presence felt by everyone, but each one must seek Him as Moses did. God had given Moses the tremendous task of ruling a mob of ignorant Israelites just rescued from centuries of hard bondage and leading them through a barren, mountainous wilderness to the Promised Land, where they would meet armed hosts, strongly entrenched in fortified cities. The burden was too heavy for Moses, and he cried out to God: "'If you don't personally go with us, don't make us leave this place. How will anyone know that you look favorably on me—on me and on your people—if you don't go with us?' . . . The LORD replied to Moses, 'I will indeed do what you have asked, for I look favorably on you, and I know you by name. . . . I will personally go with you, Moses, and I will give you rest'" (Ex. 33:15–17, 14 NLT).

I do not wonder any longer at the mighty things Moses did. If God goes with you and tells you what to do and how to do it, and gives you the wisdom and strength with which to do it, then there is nothing too hard for you. God becomes a servant of such a person as much as that person is the servant of God. They are coworkers. Someone like that can chase a thousand, and if he or she finds another, the two shall put ten thousand to flight (see Deut. 32:30).

But Jesus is holy and humble and cannot walk with any but those who are humble and holy, so if you want Him to go with you, you must humble yourself and be holy. Moses was the meekest of men, we read (see Num. 12:3).

Then, too, if we want Jesus to go with us to the meeting, we must invite Him home with us after the meeting. He will not come to the meeting and walk back with us to our door, if when we get there we find it in our hearts to bid Him goodnight, close the door in His face, and go in, scold the children, talk about our neighbors, and forget to whom we belong. Our walk with Him must be constant, not fitful, or we will seek for Him someday and not find Him.

Oh, that we may always make sure that He is with us, and not take it for granted, else we find we have been going on a fool's errand without Him! Poor Joseph and Mary lost five days and had no one knows how much anxiety and heartache, all because they supposed Jesus was in the company, but did not make sure. But they found Him after searching diligently! Is He with you now? If He is not, then get your Bible and go off alone and seek Him, and if you wake up and seek Him with all your heart, He will be found.

A Word to You Who Would Be Useful

Does the Devil ever tempt you to feel that you are of no use and can do nothing? Every genuine Christian wants to be useful, fruit bearing, and a soul-winner. This desire is characteristic of the new nature, received along with the new birth. When Paul met Jesus, he wanted to go back to Jerusalem and tell all his old friends about it, that they, too, might experience new life in Christ. When you came to faith, your heart went out to God for the salvation of your friends, and you tried to so live your life before them that they would be brought to Jesus. But now that you are further along, do you ever feel that you are useless, that you can do nothing, that your words are powerless to lead people to Jesus?

I find a great many such people, and maybe you are one. If so, it is for you I write. I have often felt as you do, and therefore can sympathize with you, and maybe can write something to encourage you.

First I would say, do what you can. Angels can do no more. Your talents may not be great, but use what talents you have and God will surely increase them. It is a law of God that what is used shall be increased. Everything that has life begins small. The largest oak was once enfolded in an acorn. The most skillful musician in the world at one time did not know one note from another. The most learned scholar now living once did not know A from Z. Moses was once a helpless babe in a floating ark of bulrushes. But these people grew and increased. If there is spiritual life in you, you will grow, if you will do with your might what your hands find to do.

Cultivate your talents. There are many thousands of musicians in The Salvation Army today who at one time could not play an instrument and who did not know a cornet from a concertina. But they began to practice. It was slow work at first. But they kept at it. Probably, the first day they could not see that they had made any progress at all, nor the second day, but in a week or a month they could see. They began, kept patiently at it, and at last succeeded. That is the way to cultivate any talent. That is the way to become mighty in prayer, to become acquainted with the Bible, to learn to speak or sing or fish for souls. Begin and keep at it.

Do not get discouraged because you cannot do as well as someone else. God has a work for you to do, and no one else can do it. God meant that work for you and you for that work, and if you do not do it, it will never be done. The thing then for you to do is to go to God and thank Him for what gifts you have and for giving you some work to do, and then ask Him for wisdom to do it bravely, faithfully, and wisely, and He will surely be with you.

Do not sit down in the discouragement of unbelief and think that because you do not have the talents of some gifted person you know that therefore you can do nothing. That is wicked. It is dishonoring to God, pleasing to the Devil, and will surely result in a great loss to your soul, if not in the final loss of your soul. Jesus tells us that the man with five talents put his money to use and gained five talents more, and likewise the man with two talents. But He says the man with one talent went and wrapped it in a cloth and hid it, and so lost it, and was cast out as a slothful and wicked servant into outer darkness, where there is weeping and gnashing of teeth (see Matt. 25:14–30).

Second, encourage your poor, trembling heart with the promises and examples in the Bible. Here is a promise for you: "So, my dear brothers and sisters, be strong and immovable. Always work enthusiastically for the Lord, for you know that nothing you do for the Lord is ever useless" (1 Cor. 15:58 NLT). The Devil tells you that your labor is useless, but God says it is not. Believe God, and go on with your work. The Lord says, "You will always harvest what you plant" (Gal. 6:7 NLT). David tried on Saul's armor, but he could not fight in it, so he laid it aside, went out in the name of the Lord, with his sling and a smooth stone out of the brook, and killed the giant.

Saul's armor, wrought at the forge, may be like the education and culture gained in the theological schools and universities, while the sling and the stone are like the wisdom given by the Holy Spirit to simple, humble, faithful hearts in mills and shops and kitchens and the lowly places of secret prayer and daily toil. Go in the name of the Lord with the wisdom He gives you, and you shall slay giants.

Paul told us, "Few of you were wise in the world's eyes or powerful or wealthy when God called you. Instead, God chose things the world considers foolish in order to shame those who think they are wise. And he chose things that are powerless to shame those who are powerful. God chose things despised by the world, things counted as nothing at all, and used them to bring to nothing what the world considers important. As a result, no one can ever boast in the presence of God" (1 Cor. 1:26–29, NLT).

If you were learned and wise and mighty and did great things, people would give all the glory to your learning and wisdom. But if you are little and foolish, then they have to give the glory to God. Go on, then, and do what you can.

When the Spirit of God came on Shamgar he struck down six hundred Philistines with an oxgoad. Samson killed one thousand with the jawbone of an ass. And Gideon, with three hundred men armed only with earthen pitchers and torches, routed the hosts of Midian.

When Jesus blessed a boy's five little loaves and two small fishes, they fed a crowd of five thousand. And so if you will pray and believe, He will bless your words and works to multitudes. Remember, it is not what you say or do alone, but it is His blessing added to what you say and do that accomplishes the work, and He will surely add His blessing if you will trust and obey.

I read of an educated minister who had a skeptical lawyer in his congregation, whom he wanted very much to see come to faith and be united with the church, and for whose benefit he prepared some very learned and labored sermons. One day, to the minister's delight, the lawyer came to his study with the glad news that he had experienced new life in Christ and wished to join the church. After some conversation, the pastor rather blushingly inquired, "May I ask you which one of my sermons it was that led you to Christ?"

Then the lawyer, with some little confusion, replied, "Well, to tell you the truth, Pastor, it was not one of your sermons that led me to Christ at all. It was this way: A few Sundays ago, as we were leaving the church, the steps were very slippery, and old Auntie Blank was trying to descend them. She was crippled and feeble and in danger of falling, when I took hold of her arm and assisted her to the sidewalk. She looked up into my eyes and thanked me, and with a bright smile on her face, asked, 'Do you love my Jesus?' That led me to Christ." It was like the smooth stone that killed the giant when Saul's armor and sword had failed!

Be a man or woman of much secret prayer. Acquaint yourself with God. Take time to listen to His voice. Read your Bible; love it, pray over it. Read good books. Get your mind stored with truths that will be to you as David's smooth stones, and God will surely use you and make you a blessing.

I remember well the first time I attempted to speak from a text. I utterly failed and was filled with confusion. But by seeking His face the Lord has long since given me victory, and I rejoice unutterably at the privilege of speaking for Him. And, by living a life of constant prayer down at Jesus' feet and by a determined exercise of faith, I seldom open my mouth to speak for Him without feeling a deep conviction in my soul that my words are accompanied by the Holy Spirit and are hitting the mark and reaching hearts. And this may be your experience, too, if you utterly forsake sin, consecrate yourself fully to the interests of Jesus, steadfastly believe, and continue in prayer. God said to Moses, "I will be with you as you speak" (Ex. 4:12 NLT), and He is no respecter of persons; He will say the same to you if you wait on Him.

Fools for Christ's Sake

To the natural heart and the unsanctified mind the commands of God are foolishness. "The LORD had said to Abram, 'Leave your native country, your relatives, and your father's family, and go to the land that I will show you'" (Gen. 12:1 NLT). How foolish to leave home and wealth and greatness to go to a land that he knew not! But Abraham believed and obeyed and became heir of the world.

God's word to Moses was, "Now go, for I am sending you to Pharaoh. You must lead my people Israel out of Egypt" (Ex. 3:10 NLT). What folly for this poor shepherd—who forty years before had fled from the face of Pharaoh as a hunted murderer and vagabond— to seek to deliver a nation of slaves from the iron hand of the haughtiest, mightiest monarch on earth! But he believed and obeyed, and the proud king was humbled to the dust and the nation of slaves was freed.

The Lord said to Paul, "I have appeared to you to appoint you as my servant and witness. Tell people that you have seen me, and tell them what I will show you in the future. And I will rescue you from both your own people and the Gentiles. Yes, I am sending you to the Gentiles to open their eyes, so they may turn from darkness to light and from the power of Satan to God. Then they will receive forgiveness for their sins and be given a place among God's people, who are set apart by faith in me" (Acts 26:16–18 NLT).

Think of it! One lone man belonging to a conquered, despised, hated people, sent to the proud, idolatrous, utterly godless nations with the message that a crucified Jew is the Son of God, the Savior of the world, and that there was no salvation except in His name.

What foolhardiness for this man without wealth, national prestige, political power, or social favor to start out in the face of bitter religious hatred and contempt, and national and political antagonism, to convert a lost world to this new faith! But he was "not disobedient unto the heavenly vision" (Acts 26:19 KJV). He went, and the Holy Spirit went with him. He went to unparalleled toils and sufferings, but he won unparalleled victories and heavenly joys and consolations.

He was whipped time and again. He was stoned. He was thrust into dark, loathsome dungeons, reeking with slime and filth. Three times he suffered shipwreck. He made many long and tedious journeys when there were no express trains with Pullman coaches and dining cars. He was in perils from the water, from robbers, in the city, in the wilderness, in the sea, and, worst of all, among false brothers. He suffered from weariness and pain, from wakeful nights when it would have been death to him to go to sleep, from hunger and thirst, from cold and nakedness, and from fasts, often when his spirit was so engaged with his tremendous labors and difficulties that his body refused food. Added to all of that was his burden for all the churches with their new Christians just delivered from their former way of life and continually beset by false teachers within as well as suffering the most dreadful persecutions from without.

But none of these things moved him, and God helped him to do more to bring the world to God than anyone else who ever lived.

Does your call to work for God seem foolish, unreasonable, and impossible? "Have faith in God" (Mark 11:22 KJV). Obey like Abraham and Moses and Paul, and you will yet praise Him for all the way He led you and for the part He gave you in winning the world from Satan back to God.

A Salvation Army officer who is now by my side had been a soldier for some years. At last a call to go into full-time ministry came while his hammer was lifted to strike a blow. He was not disobedient to the call of God. The blow was not struck, and before noon he had sold his kit of tools. And for years now he has been a successful officer and is daily increasing in the gifts and graces of those God calls to be leaders.

Does God call you? Do not disobey the heavenly vision. Let nothing hinder you. Go and God will be with you as He was with Moses and Paul. And, as the years speed by, you will increasingly thank God that no business prospects, no fond friendships, no lust of power or love of secluded ease kept you from the battle's front with its burdens and bitter conflicts and fierce sorrows and soul-satisfying triumphs. One soul joining in the anthem of the redeemed ones around the throne, saved from hell through your labors, will pay you for all your toils. One look at the face of Jesus will reward you for all your privations. What do Peter and John and Paul care now if they did lose all to follow Jesus and did suffer and die for those they sought to save? And what will you care?

PART TWO

The Way of Holiness

What Is Holiness? 1

Many years ago, a young woman asked me, "What is this sanctification, or holiness, that people are talking so much about?"

She had heard the experience testified to, and talked and preached about, for nearly a year, until I thought that, of course, she understood it. Her question surprised and almost discouraged me, but I rallied, and asked, "Do you have a bad temper?"

"Oh, yes," she said. "I have a temper like a volcano."

"Sanctification," I replied, "is to have that bad temper taken out." That definition set her thinking, and did her good, but it was too narrow. If I had said, "Sanctification is to have temper and all sin taken away, and the heart filled with love for God and others," that would have done, for that is sanctification. That is holiness. It is, in our measure, to be made like God. It is to be made a "[partaker] of the divine nature" (2 Pet. 1:4 KJV).

A spark from the fire is like the fire. The tiniest twig on the giant oak or the smallest branch of the vine has the nature of the oak or the vine and is in that respect like the oak or the vine. A drop of water on the end of your finger from the ocean is like the ocean—not in its size, of course, for the big ships cannot float upon it, nor the big fish swim in it—but it is like the ocean in its essence, its character, its nature. Just so, a holy person is like God. Not that he or she is infinite as God is or knows everything or has all power and wisdom as God has, but is like God in his or her nature. Such a person is good and pure, and loving and just, in the same way that God is.

Holiness, then, is conformity to the nature of God. It is likeness to God, as He is revealed in Jesus.

But someone will cry out, "Impossible! We are poor sinful creatures. We cannot be like Jesus. He was divine. Show me someone who is like Jesus Christ."

Well, now, let us be patient and keep quiet and go to the Bible and see what that says about the matter before we further define holiness. What did Jesus Himself say?

We are to be like Jesus in separation from the world. In speaking of the separation of His disciples from the world, Jesus said, "They do not belong to the world, just as I do not belong to the world" (John 17:14 NLT). And again, "Just as you sent me into the world, I am sending them into the world" (John 17:18 NLT). He was in the world, but He was not of the world. He took no pleasure in its wicked ways. He was not spoiled at all by its proud, sinful, selfish spirit. While He worked and associated with bad people to do them good, He was always separate from them in spirit.

One of our dear, pure Salvation Army rescue officers went to a house of prostitution to see a sick girl. While she was there, the health authorities declared the girl's sickness to be smallpox, and they sealed up the place. The officer was shut in for weeks among those poor lost women. She was in an evil place, but she was not of it. Her pure spirit was utterly opposed to the spirit of sin that ruled there. Similarly, Jesus was in the world but not of it. And in the same way, holy people are so changed that, while they are in the world, they are not of it. They belong to heaven and are but strangers and pilgrims doing all the good they can while passing through this world to their Father's house, their heavenly home. They are separate from the world.

We are to be pure like Jesus. The apostle John, speaking of those who expect to see Jesus and be like Him in heaven, said, "All who have this hope in him purify themselves, just as he is pure" (1 John 3:3 NIV). That is a lofty standard of purity, for there was no impurity in Jesus. He allowed no unclean habits. He indulged in no impure thoughts or desires. He used no unkind words. He kept Himself pure in all things. So we are to be pure in heart and in life as He was.

We are to be like Jesus in love to God and to others. Jesus said, in speaking of God's kindness and love for unjust and evil people, "Be perfect, as your heavenly Father is perfect" (Matt. 5:48 ESV). He said, "A new commandment I give to you, that you love one another." How? According to what standard? "Just as I have loved you, you also are to love one another" (John 13:34 ESV). We are, then, to be like Jesus in love to God and others, especially to our brothers and sisters in the Lord.

We are to be like Jesus by having God dwelling in us. In speaking of Himself, Jesus said, "Believe that I am in the Father and the

Father is in me" (John 14:11 NLT). And then He said of His disciples, "In that day"—the day of Pentecost, when the Comforter comes—"you will know that I am in my Father, and you in me, and I in you" (John 14:20 ESV).

So we see that the Bible teaches that we can be like Jesus. We are to be like Him in our separation from the world, in purity, in love, and in the fullness of the Spirit. This is holiness.

This work was begun when you first experienced new life. You gave up your sins. You were in some measure separated from the world. The love of God was shed abroad in your heart, and you felt that God was with you. But unless you have been sanctified wholly, you also feel that there are yet roots of bitterness within: quickness of temper, stirrings of pride, too great a sensitivity to praise or blame, shame of the cross, love of ease, worldly mindedness, and the like. These must be taken away before your heart can be made clean, your love to God and others be made perfect, and the Holy Spirit have all His way in you. When this is done, you will have the experience the Bible calls holiness, which is the birthright of all God's dear children.

Holiness, then, for you and for me, is not maturity, but purity—a clean heart in which the Holy Spirit dwells, filling it with pure, tender, and constant love to God and others.

There is a plant in South America, called the "pitcher plant," on the stalk of which is a little cuplike formation that is always full of water. When it is very small it is full. As it grows larger it is still full. And when it reaches its maturity it is full. That illustrates holiness. All that God asks is that the heart should be cleansed from sin and full of love, whether it be the tender heart of the little child with feeble powers of loving, of the full grown adult, or of the flaming archangel before the throne. This is holiness, and this only. It is nothing less than this, and it can be nothing more.

Jesus, Thine all victorious love
Shed in my heart abroad;
Then shall my feet no longer rove,
Rooted and fixed in God.[1]

NOTE

1. Charles Wesley, "My God, I Know, I Feel Thee Mine," 1740, public domain.

Why Should We Be Holy? 2

We should be holy because God wants us to be holy. He commands it. He says, "You must be holy in everything you do, just as God who chose you is holy. For the Scriptures say, 'You must be holy because I am holy'" (1 Pet. 1:15–16 NLT). God is in earnest about this. It is God's will, and it cannot be evaded. Just as you or I want our watches to keep perfect time, our friends to be steadfast, our children to be obedient, our husband or wife to be faithful, so God wants us to be holy.

To many, however, the command seems harsh. They have been accustomed to commands accompanied by curses or kicks or blows. But we must not forget that "God is love" (1 John 4:8 NLT), and His commands are not harsh, but kind. They come from the fullness of an infinitely loving and all-wise heart. They are meant for our good. If a railway train could think or talk, it might argue that running on two rails over the same road year after year was very commonplace. But if it insisted on larger liberty, and so jumped the track, it would certainly ruin itself. So anyone who wants freedom and refuses to obey God's commands to be holy, destroys him- or herself. The train was made to run on the tracks, and we were made to live according to God's commandment to be holy, and only in that way can we gain everlasting good.

Oh, how tender are His words! Listen: "And now . . . what does the LORD your God require of you? He requires only that you fear the LORD your God, and live in a way that pleases him, and love him and serve him with all your heart and soul. And you must always obey the LORD's commands and decrees that I am giving you today for your own good" (Deut. 10:12–13 NLT).

For your good! Do you not see it? It is "for your good." There is nothing harsh, nothing selfish in our dear Lord's command. It is your good He is seeking, for "God is love" (1 John 4:8 NLT).

We should be holy, because Jesus died to make us holy. He gave Himself to stripes, spitting, cruel mockings, the crown of thorns, and death on the cross for this purpose. He wants a holy people. For this He prayed: "Make them holy by your truth; teach them your word, which is truth" (John 17:17 NLT). For this He died: "He gave his life to free us from every kind of sin, to cleanse us, and to make us his very own people, totally committed to doing good deeds" (Titus 2:14 NLT). "Christ loved the church. He gave up his life for her to make her holy and clean. . . . He did this to present her to himself as a glorious church without a spot or wrinkle or any other blemish. Instead, she will be holy and without fault" (Eph. 5:25–27 NLT). Let us not disappoint Him. Let not His precious blood be spent in vain.

We should be holy in order that we may be useful. Who have been the mightiest men and women of God through the ages? They have been holy people, with clean hearts on fire with love for God and others—unselfish, humble, and faithful souls who forgot themselves in their love and toil for others, whose lives were "hidden with Christ in God" (Col. 3:3 NLT). Moses, the meekest of men; Paul, who would gladly pour out his life as a sacrifice for others; Luther and Fox, St. Francis and Wesley, William and Catherine Booth, and ten thousand times ten thousand other men and women who were "great in the sight of the Lord" (Luke 1:15 KJV). These are the ones whom God has used.

So long as there are any roots of sin in the heart, the Holy Spirit cannot have all His way in us, and so our usefulness is hindered. But when our hearts are clean, the Holy Spirit dwells within, and then we have power for service. Then we can work for God and do good, in spite of all our ignorance and weakness.

A plain, humble young Irishman heard about the blessing of a clean heart and got alone and fell on his knees before the Lord and cried to him for it. A man happened to overhear him and wrote about it, saying,

I shall never forget his petition. "O God, I plead with Thee for this blessing!" Then, as if God was showing him what was in the way, he said, "My Father, I will give up every known sin, only I plead with Thee for power." And then, as if his individual sins were passing before him, he said again and again, "I will give them up; I will give them up."

Then without any emotion he rose from his knees, turned his face heavenward, and simply said, "And now, I claim the blessing." For the first time he now became aware of my presence, and with a shining face reached out his hand to clasp mine. You could feel the presence of the Spirit as he said, "I have received Him; I have received Him!"

And I believe he had, for in the next few months he led more than sixty men into the kingdom of God. His whole life was transformed.[1]

To be holy and useful is possible for each one of us, and it is far better than to be great and famous. To save a soul is better than to command an army, win a battle, rule an empire, or sit on a throne.

We should be holy that we may be safe. Sin in the heart is more dangerous than gunpowder in the cellar. Before Peter got the blessing of a clean heart and the baptism of the Holy Spirit, he yielded to the sinful nature within and cursed and swore and denied Jesus. Before David got this experience, he too fell into awful sin and nearly lost his soul.

Remember that holiness is nothing more nor less than perfect love, for God and humanity, in a clean heart. If we love God with all our hearts, we shall gladly keep all His commandments and do all His will as He makes it known to us. And if we love our fellow human beings as we love ourselves, we shall not knowingly do any wrong to them. So we see that this holy love is the surest possible safeguard against all kinds of sin, either against God or humanity, and we cannot count ourselves safe unless we have it. Without it, Peter and David fell. But with it, Joseph and Daniel resisted the temptations of kings' courts, and the three Hebrew children and the fire-baptized Stephen and Paul gladly faced death rather than deny their Lord.

Finally, we should be holy, because we are most solemnly assured that "those who are not holy will not see the Lord" (Heb. 12:14 NLT), and God has made all things ready so that we may have the blessing if we will, thus leaving those who refuse or trifle and fail without excuse.

I bless Him that years ago He awakened me to the infinite importance of this matter, sent holy people to testify to and explain the experience, enabled me to consecrate my whole being to Him and seek Him with all my heart, and gave me the blessing,

Will you have it, too? If so, receive Jesus as your Sanctifier right now.

> My idols I cast at Thy feet,
> My all I return Thee, who gave;
> This moment the work is complete,
> For Thou art almighty to save.

> O Savior, I dare to believe,
> Thy blood for my cleansing I see;
> And, asking in faith, I receive
> Salvation, full, present, and free.[2]

NOTES

1. Attributed to J. Wilbur Chapman, quoted in J. W. Mahood, *The Art of Soul-Winning* (Cincinnati: Jennings and Pye, 1901).

2. Bramwell Booth, "O When Shall My Soul Find Her Rest," 1880, public domain.

How to Get Holiness **3**

God never raises a crop of potatoes or a field of wheat or a bushel of oats without human help. He takes us into partnership with Him in such matters. He furnishes the sunshine and the air; the rain and dew; the day and night; the fruitful seasons; and the busy, burrowing little earthworms and insects which keep the lungs of the earth open so that it can breathe, and He gives life to the seed so that it may grow. We must prepare the ground, plant the seed, keep down the weeds, and gather in the harvest. People sometimes think they are doing it all, but they are quite mistaken in this. Our loving heavenly Father has been preparing the earth for thousands of years for every potato that grows, and He works ceaselessly, by day and by night, to help us raise our crops.

And so it is in matters that concern our souls. God and we must work together, both to save and to sanctify. God never saves a sinner without that person's help, and usually the help of some other folks as well, who preach or pray or write and sing—or suffer—that he or she may be saved. Ages before we were born, God provided the means of salvation for all. Angels and prophets spoke God's truth. Jesus came and showed us God's love and died for our sins. The Holy Spirit was given, the blessed Bible was written, and all things were made ready.

But now, the sinner must hear the truth, repent, confess, ask God for pardon, and believe, before he or she can experience new life in Christ. And for anyone to expect salvation without doing this would be as big a piece of folly as for a farmer to expect a crop of potatoes without having planted them.

And so, to get the priceless gift of the Holy Spirit—a clean heart— we must work together with God. On God's side, all things are ready and He waits and longs to give the blessing. But before He can do so, we must, with His help, get ourselves ready. We must do our part, which is very simple and easily within our power to do.

We must see our need of the blessing, and to see this need, we must be clearly justified. No sinner has the spiritual eyes to see the need of a clean heart. He or she is blind to these things. She may have dreadful hatred in her heart, but so long as she restrains herself and does the hated person no harm, she thinks she is a very good sort of person. She cannot see that in the eyes of God she is a murderer, for did not God say, "Anyone who hates another brother or sister is really a murderer at heart" (1 John 3:15 NLT)? He may have lust in his heart, but so long as he does not commit adultery, he flatters himself that he is quite respectable in God's sight, in spite of the fact that Jesus said that the look of lust is adultery (see Matt. 5:28).

The first thing, then, is to be well-saved and to live so fully in the light of God's smile that we can see our need of cleansing.

We must not try to hide the need, but frankly confess it. Let me ask, do you know that you are saved? You say, "Oh, yes, I know that I have given my heart to God, I feel that my sins have been forgiven and my life has been changed, and I feel that I am saved." Good, but do you know that your heart is clean? Are all the roots of bitterness gone? Do you bear patiently the faults of others? Do you bear meekly, and with a forgiving spirit, the unkindness of others? Do you love God with all your heart and soul and mind, and your neighbor as yourself? Do you feel that all malice and pride, jealousy and envy, evil and filthy desire, unholy ambition and unbelief, and all foolish things have been taken out of your heart, and that the Holy Spirit has His own way in you all the time? Remember that holiness has to do with the heart, and, as Solomon said, "Your heart . . . determines the course of your life" (Prov. 4:23 NLT). It is at the heart that Jesus looks, and He says, "Blessed are the pure in heart" (Matt. 5:8 KJV). If your heart is not clean, do not be afraid or ashamed to say so, but frankly tell your heavenly Father the whole truth about the matter.

The next thing is to believe that the blessing is for you. Of course, if you do not believe that you can be cleansed from envy and jealousy and quick temper and all sin, and be kept pure and good all the time, you will not seek it.

Satan will surely do all he can to discourage you and make you doubt the possibility of holiness for yourself. He will tell you that it is for other people, but not for you. But he might as well tell you that the sun shines for other people, but not for you! Our heavenly Father "gives his sunlight to both the evil and the good, and he sends rain on the just and the unjust alike" (Matt. 5:45 NLT). He is no respecter of persons (see Acts 10:34), and He offers His full salvation to all who will take it.

Satan will tell you that your disposition is so peculiar, or your circumstances at home, at school, or in the shop, mine, or mill are so disagreeable that you cannot hope to be holy. Your disposition may be peculiar, but God will take all the sin out of it, so that where it is now peculiarly impatient, jealous, envious, lustful, and bad, it will be peculiarly good, patient, loving, generous, humble, and chaste. A highly strung, quick-tempered girl got sanctified, and it made her gentle like Jesus. A proud, ambitious young man I know got a clean heart, and he was made humble and self-sacrificing until his friends hardly knew him.

As for your circumstances, holiness will make you their master instead of their servant. The other day, I wanted a hole in the hard rubber cap of the fountain pen with which I am writing these words, so I heated a pin and burned the hole right through. If the pin had been cold, I should probably have broken either the pin or the cap, and would certainly have failed to make that hole. Holiness will make you hot enough to burn your way through your circumstances. "Our God is a consuming fire" (Heb. 12:29 KJV), and holiness is God in you.

Satan may tell you that you have failed so often that God will not now give you the blessing. That is a lie of the Devil. Don't believe it. Your mother might treat you that way, but God won't, for "God is love" (1 John 4:8 KJV). He knows all about your failures, and pities you, and loves you still, and wants to give you the blessing far more than you want to receive it. Peter failed again and again during the three years he was with Jesus, and finally there was an awful failure during that sad hour when he cursed and swore that he did not know Him. But in spite of it all, Jesus loved him, and within a few weeks of that time, Peter got the blessing, and we find him winning three thousand souls in a single day.

Satan may tell you that if you do get the blessing, people will not believe that you have it. Well, suppose they do not, what then? Will you refuse to believe God because people will not believe you? If you get the blessing, and live in the joy and sweetness and power and glory of it, they will have to believe you sooner or later, just as people have to believe there is fire in the stove when they feel it.

To get the blessing, you must resist the Devil and believe that it is for you. You must believe that it is for you now. It is astonishing how sinners wish to put off the time of salvation, and it is even more astonishing how saved people put off seeking a clean heart until some other time. The Devil and their evil hearts of unbelief keep saying, "Some time, but not right now." But the dear Lord in mercy keeps whispering, "Behold, now is the accepted time; behold, now is the day of salvation" (2 Cor. 6:2 KJV). "Today when you hear his voice, don't harden your hearts" (Heb. 3:15 NLT). Nothing grieves the Holy Spirit and hardens the heart like this delay of unbelief.

The next thing to do is to come to Jesus for the blessing, with a true heart, holding back nothing, but giving your all to Him for time and eternity that He may give His all to you. At this point there must be no hypocrisy, no double dealing, no halfheartedness, no holding back part of the price. The Lord offers us the biggest blessing this side of heaven. He offers us perfect cleansing from sin, perfect victory over the Devil, and the Holy Spirit to dwell in our clean hearts to teach and guide and comfort us. But in exchange He asks us to give Him our all.

How infinitely and hopelessly foolish shall we be if we are so selfish or tearful or unbelieving as to refuse! It is as though a king should offer a poor beggar garments of velvet and gold in exchange for rags, diamonds in exchange for dirt, and a glorious palace in place of a cellar or attic. How foolish would the beggar be who insisted on keeping a few of his rags, a little handful of dirt, and the privilege of going back to his cellar now and then until the king finally withdrew all the splendid things he had offered! And yet so foolish, and more so, are they who try to get this blessing from God while refusing to consecrate their all and obey Him fully.

The Lord's Word to us on this point is, "'Bring all the tithes into the storehouse so there will be enough food in my Temple. If you do,' says the LORD of Heaven's Armies, 'I will open the windows of heaven for you. I will pour out a blessing so great you won't have enough room to take it in!'" (Mal. 3:10 NLT). It is no little blessing, but an overflowing one that the Lord means to give you.

When Jonathan Edwards, one of God's mighty men of the past, was but a boy student, he wrote as follows in his diary:

I have this day solemnly renewed my . . . covenant and self-dedication. . . . I have been before God and given myself, all that I am and have, to God; so that I am not, in any respect, my own. I can [claim] no right in this understanding, this will, these affections, which are in me. Neither have I any right to this body, or any of its members—no right to this tongue, these hands, these feet; no right to these senses, these eyes, these ears, this smell, or this taste. I have given myself clear away and have not retained anything as my own. . . . I have given every power to Him; so that, for the future, I'll [claim] no right in myself.[1]

Does such a life seem unattractive to you? Someone has written, "A cathedral window seen from without is dull and meaningless; but enter, and the light of heaven streaming through it glorifies it with every beauty of form and color. Consecration to God for service may seem dull enough when seen from without, but enter into that experience, and the light of the Divine Love streaming through it shall glorify your life with a beauty and blessedness which are heaven's own."[2]

To make such a consecration we may have to go over it several times and assure ourselves that we have given all, and that we mean it with all our heart. But, having done this, until we can look up into the face of Jesus without a doubt and sing "My all is on the altar, I'm waiting for the fire,"[3] we may be sure we are near the blessing.

If we thus give ourselves to God, there is but one thing more to do—that is, to take it by faith and wait patiently on Him for the witness of the Spirit that it is done.

A nobleman whose son was sick came to Jesus: "When he heard that Jesus had come from Judea to Galilee, he went and begged Jesus to come to Capernaum to heal his son, who was about to die. Jesus asked, 'Will you never believe in me unless you see miraculous signs and wonders?' The official pleaded, 'Lord, please come now before my little boy dies.' Then Jesus told him, 'Go back home. Your son will live!' And the man believed what Jesus said and started home" (John 4:47–50 NLT).

The next day when he got home, he found his boy well. That is the kind of faith that walks off with the blessing.

Jesus will not fail you at this point if you patiently look to Him and hold fast your faith.

Again and again I have seen people burst into the light when they have consecrated their all and believed in this way. Some time ago in a holiness meeting, the penitent form was full of seekers, among whom were several earnest young men. I asked one of them who seemed to be the most deeply in earnest, "Do you now give yourself and your all to God?"

"Yes, I do," said he.

"Well, whose man are you, then?" I inquired.

"I am the Lord's."

"Can you trust the Lord to sanctify His own man?"

"Yes, I can."

"When?"

"Now!" And he burst into the holy joy of faith and began to praise the Lord at once. And several others got the blessing that morning in the same way.

You, too, can have the blessing just now, if you thus meet the conditions.

Faith, mighty faith, the promise sees,

And looks to that alone;

Laughs at impossibilities,

And cries, it shall be done.[4]

NOTES

1. Jonathan Edwards, *The Works of Jonathan Edwards*, vol. 1, chapter 4, January 12, http://www.ccel.org/ccel/edwards/works1.i.iv.html.

2. Josiah Strong, *The Times and Young Men* (New York: Baker and Taylor Company, 1901), 191.

3. Mary Dagworthy James, "My Body, Soul, and Spirit," 1869, public domain.

4. Charles Wesley, "Father of Jesus Christ, My Lord," 1742, public domain.

When Can We Be Made Holy? 4

A bright young man got up in one of my meetings several years ago and said, "Since the Lord converted me, I never wanted any bad thing, but there was something in me that did."

I think again of the little boy of my acquaintance who got blessedly saved, and was very happy and good for some time until that one day he came to his mother and said, "Mama, I'm tired of living this way."

"Why, what is the matter now?" asked the mother.

"I want to be good all the time," said the little fellow. "You tell me to go and do things, and I go and do them; but I feel angry inside, and I want to be good all the time."

Both the young man and the boy had experienced new life in Christ. Each wanted to be good, but each found in himself something wrong and knew that while that something remained, he was not holy. However correct the outward life might be, the heart was not clean.

This is the experience of every true follower of Jesus who has not pressed on into holiness, and it corresponds to the Scripture in which Paul said, "When I would do good, evil is present with me" (Rom. 7:21 KJV).

When we experience new life in Christ, our sins are forgiven, we feel a sweet peace within, we love God and others, and we want to do good and be good all the time. And we have power to do good and overcome bad habits and temptation. But there is still something in our hearts that needs to be removed before we are holy. That something within, the Bible calls the "old self" (Eph. 4:22; Col. 3:9 ESV). It is the old nature that gets angry when people or things do not suit us, and that is deceitful, proud, unclean, disobedient, silly, and selfish. Of course, the experience of salvation gives a great blow to this "old self," subdues it, and makes it behave itself, so that it no longer acts so badly as it once did. But it is still alive and watching for a chance to get the victory again. And, sad to say, it often does get the victory, causing followers of Jesus to do and say things that are wrong and that grieve and quench the Holy Spirit. The "old self" causes quarrels and jealousies and envying and evil speaking, in all kinds of churches, leads to failures of all kinds, and causes the ruin of many Christian lives. Paul had a church that was greatly troubled in this way (see 1 Cor. 3).

Before we can be holy, this "old self" must be put off. This evil within must die. This seed of all sin must be destroyed, and this is something that can and does take place just as soon after the new birth as we see the need and possibility of its being done and we come to Jesus with all our heart and with perfect faith to have it done.

Some people say we cannot get rid of this evil nature until we die. But we must stick to the Bible and believe what that Book says. And the Bible certainly teaches that we can be made holy in this life. The Bible says, "Be holy" (1 Pet. 1:16 NLT), and that means now, not after death. If a father says to his son, "Be honest, be truthful," he means, be honest and truthful *now*, for this world, not in heaven only. So God means that we must be holy here and now.

The Bible says, "Throw off your old sinful nature and your former way of life, which is corrupted . . . [and] put on your new nature, created to be like God—truly righteous and holy" (Eph. 4:22–24 NLT). We are told to "put off all these; anger, wrath, malice, blasphemy, filthy communication out of your mouth" (Col. 3:8 KJV). And we are told to "be filled with the Spirit" (Eph. 5:18 KJV). All this is to take place now.

We read of the disciples who "were all filled with the Holy Spirit" (Acts 2:4 ESV) and of believers whose hearts were purified by faith (see Acts 15:9) long before they got to heaven. God is no respecter of persons (see Acts 10:34), and just as He gave this great blessing to the early Christians, He will surely give it to us when we give ourselves fully to Him.

I shall never forget how a beautiful girl of sixteen, after hearing of the possibility and blessedness of a pure heart one Sunday afternoon, walked straight up to the penitent form, fell on her knees, and lifting her face to heaven with tears, told the Lord how she wanted a clean heart filled with the Holy Spirit just then. She saw that she need not wait, but that now was the accepted time. And oh, how God blessed her! Soon the smiles were chasing away the tears, and the joy of heaven was shining on her face. Years after, I found her on the platform, a Salvation Army lieutenant, with her face still shining and her heart still cleansed.

And so may this priceless blessing be yours. Jesus has died to purchase this uttermost salvation, and it is your heavenly Father's will for you, right now. Have faith in God, give yourself utterly to Him, and begin to seek the blessing with a determination never to stop seeking until it is yours, and you shall not be long without it.

> Savior, to Thee my soul looks up,
> My present Savior Thou;
> In all the confidence of hope
> I claim the blessing now.
>
> 'Tis done! Thou dost this moment save,
> With full salvation bless;
> Salvation through Thy blood I have,
> And spotless love and peace.[1]

NOTE

1. Charles Wesley, "Come, O My God, the Promise Seal," 1838, public domain.

Holiness—A Love Service 5

"I wish I knew the secret of Paul's piety," said that good man, Asa Mahan, to Charles Finney one day.

Finney replied, "Paul said, 'The love of Christ constraineth us'" (2 Cor. 5:14 KJV). Just then the glorious truth burst upon Mahan's mind that we are sanctified not by works, but by faith which works by love, and that the religion of Jesus is not one of vows and resolutions and terrible struggle and effort, but of life and power and joyous love. He went out of Finney's room, saying, "I see it; I see it!" and from that hour his life was one of triumphant holiness.

Oh, that everyone would see this—that the way of holiness is a "new and living way" (Heb. 10:20 KJV), not an old, dead, tiresome, heart-aching, heartbreaking way of forms and ceremonies that leaves the soul still baffled and unsatisfied and with a sense of failure and defeat! It is a way of victory and joy.

The simple secret of this new and living way is the constraining love of Christ. When we realize that He loves us and died for us and that He wants a service of love, and then give ourselves up heartily, in faith, to such a love service, the secret becomes ours.

"Will I have to go and tell Mother and my brothers and my church how inconsistent I have been?" asked a young woman with whom I was talking about the blessing. "I don't feel that I can ever do that."

She had been defeated again and again by fits of temper, and I felt she ought to confess to those whom she had probably hindered by her inconsistency. But I saw that she would not get the blessing by doing it because she must, but because she wanted to, out of very love for Jesus and others. So I replied that the Lord did not want a slavish service from her, but a love service, and that if she felt it would really do any good to make such a confession, and loved Jesus enough to do it to please Him and to help those whom she had wronged by an inconsistent life, God would be pleased with it, but otherwise not. I assured her that if she did it in that spirit, she would find it a joy.

After some further conversation we knelt to pray. She told the Lord all about herself, asked Him to cleanse her heart and fill it with His Spirit and love, and then she claimed the blessing. Here is a note I received from her several weeks later:

I am very happy in the possession of a clean heart. Through God I have been able to gain victories that before I thought were absolutely impossible. The confessions that I told you I could not make, I only waited until the next day to make, and for the very love of it too, as you said I would. It has not been easy—anything but that; but such a burden has gone from my heart that I am happy even in the hardness. I fell one night through my old temper, and felt as though my heart would break; but God forgave me and showed me through that how weak I was; for I had almost thought that we could not fall after receiving the blessing. I suppose God took that way to show me that unless I trusted in Him I should fall. However, at the present time there is nothing between the Lord and me, and I am happy.

Have you been serving the Lord blindly and slavishly, simply because it is your duty, and yet with a constant feeling of unrest and unfitness? Oh, how He loves you and wants to catch your ear, win your heart, and draw you into a glad love service!

"But I am so weak and faulty," you say. "I have failed so often. Surely, the Lord must be discouraged with me." No, no, not if you are in earnest, any more than your mother was discouraged with you when as a little toddler just learning to walk you fell again and again. She did not cast you off, but picked you up, kissed the knees and nose that were bumped, and loved you more than you dreamed. And in all your other failures she still bore with you and hoped for you. So it is with Jesus.

Let this love constrain you. "We love him, because he first loved us" (1 John 4:19 KJV). Trust Him. Give yourself wholly and heartily to Him, be sure you serve Him for love, and you will have learned the secret of a holy, happy life.

Oh, let Thy love my heart constrain,

Thy love for every sinner free:

That every fallen soul of man

May taste the grace that found out me;

That all mankind with me may prove

Thy sovereign, everlasting love.[1]

NOTE

1. Charles Wesley, "Would Jesus Have the Sinner Die?" 1741, public domain.

Holiness and the Sanctification of the Body 6

The prophet Isaiah said that God inhabits eternity (see Isa. 57:15) and Solomon said, "The heavens, even the highest heaven, cannot contain you" (1 Kings 8:27 NIV). But—wonder of wonders—Paul said that we are a habitation of God. He wrote, "Do you not know that your body is a temple of the Holy Spirit within you, whom you have from God?" (1 Cor. 6:19 ESV) and, "Do you not know that you are God's temple and that God's Spirit dwells in you?" (1 Cor. 3:16 ESV).

This is a very solemn truth. But it also ought to be a joy-giving one. It certainly adds dignity and honor to us beyond anything that earthly rulers could possibly bestow, and it lifts our bodies from their kinship to the beasts into a sacred fellowship with the Lord. This fact makes the sanctification of the body both a glorious privilege and an important duty.

Many people think that sanctification, or holiness, has to do only with the soul. But the truth is that it has to do with every part of our nature and every article of our possession. The body is to be sanctified as well as the soul. Paul wrote to the Thessalonians, "Now may the God of peace himself sanctify you completely, and may your whole spirit and soul and body be kept blameless at the coming of our Lord Jesus Christ" (1 Thess. 5:23 ESV). By this He meant that the body is to be set apart and kept as a holy thing for the Lord.

We are to make a present of our bodies to the Lord. Paul said, "I plead with you to give your bodies to God because of all he has done for you. Let them be a living and holy sacrifice—the kind he will find acceptable. This is truly the way to worship him" (Rom. 12:1 NLT). Just as the soldier surrenders his or her personal liberty and gives his or her body to his or her country for hard campaigns, toilsome marches, weary sieges, and, if need be, death, so we are to present our bodies to the Lord. Jesus gave His body for us, and we are to give our bodies to Him.

Not only are we to present our bodies as a whole to the Lord, but each part as well—the eyes, ears, hands, feet, tongue—each and all are to be given to Him (see Rom. 6:13).

Our eyes are to be turned away from things that would wean the soul from God. General William Booth told of a holy man he knew, who, when he walked the streets, kept his eyes straight before him, not looking into the shop windows lest his communion with God be hindered and his mind be filled with worldly, foolish, and covetous thoughts.

Some years ago, silver bracelets were very fashionable, and a girl who had plenty of money went to buy a pair. But before she found any pretty and dainty enough to suit her she experienced salvation in Christ, and then she knew she had no right to spend her money foolishly or to wear such things even if she had them. But her eyes had gotten into the habit of searching shop windows for those bracelets in every city where she went, and she found that the habit was very bad for her soul. It made her care less to pray, hindered her thinking about Jesus when she was out walking, and actually lessened her desire to get souls saved. So she had to give her eyes to God, to be kept from leading her away from Jesus, and for years afterward, she said she never went through a shopping street without praying David's prayer, "Turn my eyes from worthless things" (Ps. 119:37 NLT).

It was a longing look toward the fertile plains of Sodom and Gomorrah that led to all of Lot's sorrows and losses. It was a covetous look at the Babylonian garment and wedge of gold that led to Achan's utter ruin. It was a lustful look that led to David's sad downfall and shame.

There are some things that a Christian should not look at, and if by chance our eyes should fall upon them, we should be turned away quickly lest sin get into our heart through eye-gate. Everyone who wishes to be holy will say with Job, "I made a covenant with my eyes" (Job 31:1 NLT).

The ears also are to be sanctified. Holy men and women will guard themselves lest sin enter into their hearts through ear-gate. Jesus said, "Take heed what you hear" (Mark 4:24 NKJV) and, "Take heed how you hear" (Luke 8:18 NKJV). As surely as the body can be poisoned or flourished and strengthened by the things we eat, according to whether they are good or bad, so can the soul be poisoned or nourished by the things we hear. No pure-minded man or woman, boy or girl, will listen to an impure story, an obscene song, or unclean talk.

Some time ago, two Salvation Army officers (ministers) were traveling by train. The railway carriage was crowded, and they were separated. One of them sat down by an elderly man, and in a short time, they were in conversation with a gentleman in front of them. Soon the elderly man looked about and said, "There are no women near, who can hear, are there? I want to tell a story." The officer was at once on guard, and said, "I am a Salvationist, sir. I do not wish to hear a story that would be unfit for ladies to hear." The old man looked ashamed and the gentleman in front looked a look of wonder. The nasty story was not told and the Salvationist, no doubt, escaped a great temptation.

But while we should not listen to evil, neither should we speak it. Sometimes it is impossible to avoid hearing wicked and filthy things, however much we may wish to do so, for we cannot control the tongues of others. That was one of the sorrows of Lot in Sodom. His soul was "vexed with the filthy conversation of the wicked" (2 Pet. 2:7 KJV). While we cannot control the tongues of others, we must control our own, and while we may not always be able to avoid hearing wicked and evil and unclean things, we can avoid saying them.

If we would be holy and enjoy God's smile, we must sanctify our tongues and keep our lips pure. "Don't use foul or abusive language. Let everything you say be good and helpful, so that your words will be an encouragement to those who hear them" (Eph. 4:29 NLT). We must not forget, however, that the heart is the fountain from which flows all our talk, and if that is clean the conversation will be pure. Jesus said, "Out of the abundance of the heart the mouth speaks" (Matt. 12:34 NKJV). Therefore, "Guard your heart above all else, for it determines the course of your life" (Prov. 4:23 NLT).

Take my voice, and let me sing

Always, only for my King;

Take my lips, and let them be

Filled with messages from Thee.[1]

Let the feet also be given to the Lord, no longer to walk in the ways of sin, but to walk patiently and gladly in the path of duty and to run on errands of mercy.

Take my feet, and let them be

Swift and beautiful for Thee.[2]

The hands are to be used for holy service and no longer to smite and pilfer.

Take my hands and let them move

At the impulse of Thy love.[3]

Thus the whole body is to be given to the Lord and kept and used for Him. Since Jesus ascended to heaven, He has no body upon earth. Will you prove your love to Him by letting Him have yours? If so, no sexual impurity is to be allowed, no unclean habit is to be indulged, and no appetite is to be permitted to gain the mastery, but the whole body is to be kept under control and made the servant of the soul.

Athletes—football and cricket players and prizefighters—when in training are exceedingly careful about their health. They select their food with care and eat nothing that would disagree with them, omitting heavy suppers. They abstain from strong drink and tobacco. They bathe their bodies daily. They go to bed and get up at regular hours. They sleep with open windows, and, of course, have plenty of fresh air and systematic exercise. They do this for months, and sometimes for years, simply that they may beat some other fellows in contests of strength and skill. Now they do it, said Paul, "to receive a perishable wreath, but we an imperishable." And then he added, "I discipline my body and keep it under control, lest after preaching to others I myself should be disqualified" (1 Cor. 9:25, 27 ESV).

I know a man who noticed that when he ate too much he became irritable and was subject to various temptations from which a careful diet freed him. He had to control his appetite in order to keep a clean heart.

Young people are likely to squander their health in all sorts of useless and careless ways, and are tempted to laugh and sneer at their elders when they lift a warning voice. But they will someday find that advance in holiness, progress toward heaven, and happiness and usefulness are more dependent on the right care of the body than they supposed.

"Dear friend, I pray that you may enjoy good health and that all may go well with you, even as your soul is getting along well" (3 John 2 NIV).

> Let my hands perform His bidding,
> Let my feet run in His ways,
> Let mine eyes see Jesus only,
> Let my lips speak forth His praise.
> All for Jesus! All for Jesus!
> Let my lips speak forth His praise.[4]

NOTES

1. Frances Ridley Havergal, "Take My Life and Let It Be," 1874, public domain.

2. Ibid.

3. Ibid.

4. Mary D. James, "All for Jesus," 1873, public domain.

Holiness and Unconscious Influence 7

Some people sing, "Oh, to be nothing, nothing." But in reality, to be something—to be useful—is one of the first and strongest desires that spring up in the heart of a true follower of Jesus Christ. And one of the blessed things about a holy life is its supernatural, constant, and often unconscious influence for good. A holy person does not have to resolve and struggle to be a blessing. Without conscious effort, such a person's life and talk and looks inspire the fainthearted, encourage the timid, instruct the ignorant, feed the hungry, and rebuke the proud, selfish, and wayward. He or she blesses people in all sorts of ways, without at the time knowing it, and is often surprised to learn how the Lord has been blessing.

Luke wrote of Jesus, "Everyone tried to touch him, because healing power went out from him, and he healed everyone" (Luke 6:19 NLT). And, just so, virtue goes out from holy people as perfume floats from a rose or warmth from fire or light from a flame.

A sanctified Salvation Army officer said to a colleague who was resigning, "I feel that woe is me, if I preach not the gospel." Some weeks later another officer said to him, "I overheard you that day when you said, 'Woe is me, if I preach not the gospel,' and it stirred my soul and made me feel that way too." Those words had been said quietly, but God was in them, and they surged with power. This fits Solomon's saying, "The words of the wise heard in quietness are better than the shouting of a ruler among fools" (Eccl. 9:17 NASB).

A number of years ago in America, two sanctified Salvationists — a man and his wife — were followed home from their meetings several nights by a nurse from the hospital nearby. She could not get away from her duties long enough to attend the meetings, but she said to herself, "I will walk home behind them, and maybe I shall get something for my soul."

And she did. All unconscious that a hungry heart was feeding upon their words, the Salvationists talked out of their clean hearts about Jesus, His love, His Word, and His uttermost salvation, and as a result, the nurse was so filled with desire to glorify God and save souls that she left her work for people's bodies, became a missionary, and is now in the Far East. This strange story came back to the two Salvationists from Korea, after many days, to surprise and gladden them and fill them with wonder at the unconscious power of holy conversation.

The very silence of a holy life is powerful. I have known such silence to still the voice of slander and foolishness and to hush the laugh of silliness and folly. An officer with a clean heart aflame with love met a girl who had offered herself for The Salvation Army's slum work. She was giggling and chattering in a way that convinced him that instead of being filled with the Holy Spirit, she was empty. He wanted to speak to her about her soul, but hardly knew how to begin, so he was silent and prayed in his heart for her. Afterward she said, "I looked at his face and said to myself, 'There is a holy man, a man dead to sin. But I am alive yet.'" And that sight of his face led her to seek and find the blessing, and now for years she has been a devoted officer. The very presence of such a person is a rebuke to sin and half-heartedness and folly, and a mighty inspiration to goodness.

After the overthrow of Sisera and all his host, Deborah and Barak sang a song of triumph and thanksgiving and closed it with these words: "Let those who love Him be like the rising of the sun in its might" (Judg. 5:31 NASB). Think of it! How mighty the sun is! How it floods the world with light! How it melts the snow, thaws the iceberg, warms the whole earth, and quickens and gladdens every living thing! None can stop the sun in its course, and so God means that it shall be with holy men and women. They comfort those who are right and convict those who are wrong, just as the sun energizes everything that has life and hastens the dissolution of everything that is dead.

But while holy people have power to bless and do good, they also have a strange influence often to arouse persecution. They prove the saying of Jesus, "I came not to send peace, but a sword" (Matt. 10:34 KJV).

But even this will turn into a blessing. God makes it work for good to them who love Him, and it often leads to the salvation of the persecutors. The godly life and testimony of Joseph rebuked his unclean brothers, and they sold him into slavery. But years after, when he ruled over all Egypt and his brothers were seeking his forgiveness and mercy, he said, "Don't be afraid. . . . You intended to harm me, but God intended it all for good. He brought me to this position so I could save the lives of many people" (Gen. 50:19–20 NLT). Thus persecution often leads to the salvation of many people.

This very power of a holy life to arouse hatred and persecution and opposition is a part of the unconscious influence of holiness. It is mightily used by God for the advancement of His kingdom on earth, so that many have been able to say with Paul when he was put into jail, that locking them up only made the gospel spread more and made others bolder to preach it (see Phil. 1:12–20).

"Come," said a distinguished Scottish professor to a German skeptic, "and I will show you a student who will make you think of Jesus."

A Chinese Christian's fellow townspeople described him with the words, "There is no difference between him and the Book."

"You are the light of the world," said Jesus; "You are the salt of the earth" (Matt. 5:14, 13 NLT).

Such lives are full of healing, cleansing, helping, comforting power. And such may be your life, too, no matter how dark your surroundings, if you will consecrate yourself entirely to God, take up your cross and follow Jesus, and seek, ask for, and receive the Holy Spirit as your Sanctifier.

Oh, that He may come into your heart right now and nevermore be grieved or allowed to depart!

Oh, make my life one blazing fire

Of pure and fervent heart desire,

The lost to find, the low to raise,

And give them cause Thy name to praise,

Because, wherever I may go,

I show Thy power to every foe![1]

NOTE

1. T. C. Marshall, "O Jesus, Saviour, Hear My Cry," *The Salvation Army Songbook*, 1900, public domain.

Holiness and Humility **8**

Those who oppose holiness often say that we who profess it are proud and that the doctrine tends to spiritual pride. But the truth is, holiness goes down to the root of all pride and digs it up utterly. Holy people are those who have found themselves out, pronounced judgment against themselves, and come to Jesus to be made every whit whole. And so long as they keep the blessing, they are deeply humble.

God said to Israel by the prophet Ezekiel, "Then you will remember your past sins and despise yourselves for all the detestable things you did" (Ezek. 36:31 NLT).

This is a certain effect of entire sanctification. The sinful heart apologizes for itself, excuses inbred sin, favors it, argues for it. Those who still have the carnal mind say, "I think one ought to have a little pride. I would not give a snap of my finger for those who had not some temper. Anyone who will not stand up for his rights is weak." And so they excuse and argue in favor of the sin in their own heart.

Not so those who are holy. They remember their former pride and loathe themselves for it. They long and pray to sink deeper and deeper into the infinite ocean of the Savior's humility until every trace and stain of pride is forever washed away. They remember their hasty temper, and hate it, and cry day and night for the perfect meekness of the Lamb of God, who, like a sheep dumb before its shearers, "opened not his mouth" (Isa. 53:7 KJV) while His enemies worked their fiendish will and—so far from smiting back—would not even talk back, but prayed, "Father, forgive them" (Luke 23:34 KJV).

They see the beauty of God's holiness and love it. They see the full extent of their former corruption and acknowledge and loathe it. Before, they thought we all had some natural goodness, but now they know and confess that "the whole head is sick, and the whole heart faint. From the sole of the foot even unto the head there is no soundness in it; but wounds, and bruises, and putrifying sores" (Isa. 1:5–6 KJV).

They see their own evil ways. At one time they thought there was not one holy person on earth, for they could see a mote in everyone's eye. But now they discover that there are many holy men and women, and the mote they were sure they saw in their neighbor's eye, they now find to have been the shadow of the beam that was in their own eye.

An earnest, sanctified man once said to me, "There are certain sins I once thought it was morally impossible for me to commit, but the Holy Spirit has shown me the awful deceitfulness of my heart. I now see that before He cleansed me the seeds of all iniquity were in me, and there is no sin I might not have committed and no depth of moral degradation to which I might not have sunk, but for the restraining grace of God."

One who has thus seen the plague of his or her own heart may be cleansed in the precious blood and may have a holy heart, but will never say to another, "Stand thou there, for I am holier than thou." Rather, remembering their own former condition, they will point others to the Lamb of God who takes away the sins of the world.

True humility makes a person particularly attractive to God. Listen to what Isaiah said, "The high and lofty one who lives in eternity, the Holy One, says this: 'I live in the high and holy place with those whose spirits are contrite and humble. I restore the crushed spirit of the humble and revive the courage of those with repentant hearts'" (Isa. 57:15 NLT).

Jesus said, "Those who exalt themselves will be humbled, and those who humble themselves will be exalted" (Matt. 23:12 NLT). And James said, "God opposes the proud but gives grace to the humble" (James 4:6 NLT).

"Do you wish to be great?" asked St. Augustine. "Then begin by being little."[1]

"Anyone who becomes as humble as this little child," said Jesus, "is the greatest"—not shall be, but *is* greatest—"in the Kingdom of Heaven" (Matt. 18:4 NLT).

Here are some of the marks of a truly humble person.

Truly humble souls do not take offense easily, but are "pure, then peaceable, gentle, open to reason, full of mercy" (James 3:17 ESV).

Holy people are not jealous of their position and dignity, or quick to resent what seems to touch them. Before the disciples were sanctified, they found a man who was casting out devils in the name of Jesus. They took offense because he did not follow them, and they tried to stop him. Self is very sensitive. But Jesus said, "Don't stop him" (Mark 9:39 NLT).

One day the Spirit of the Lord rested on two men in the camp of Israel in the wilderness, and they prophesied. "A young man ran and reported to Moses. . . . Joshua son of Nun, who had been Moses' assistant since his youth, protested, 'Moses, my master, make them stop!' But Moses [the meekest of men, according to Num. 12:3] replied, 'Are you jealous for my sake? I wish that all the Lord's people were prophets and that the LORD would put his Spirit upon them all!'" (Num. 11:27–29 NLT).

Truly humble people do not seek great things for themselves, but agree with Solomon when he said, "Better to live humbly with the poor than to share plunder with the proud" (Prov. 16:19 NLT). They rejoice in lowly service and are more anxious to be faithful to duty and loyal to principle than to be renowned among other men and women.

The disciples often disputed among themselves about who was the greatest, but Jesus washed their feet as an object lesson and commanded them to become servants of one another, if they would be great.

Humble people are modest in dress. They think more of "the ornament of a meek and quiet spirit" (1 Pet. 3:4 KJV) than of the clothes they wear. They will endeavor always to be clean and neat, but never fine and showy.

They are also plain and simple in speech. They seek to speak the truth with clearness and accuracy and in the power of the Holy Spirit, but never with "great swelling words" (2 Pet. 2:18 KJV) and bombast, or with forced tears and pathos that will arouse admiration for themselves. They never try to show off. To them it is painful to have people say, "You are clever" or "That was a fine speech." But they are full of humble, thankful joy when they learn that through their word a sinful soul was saved, an erring one corrected, or a tempted one delivered. They speak not to please others, but to please their heavenly Master; not to be applauded, but to feed hungry hearts; not to be admired by others, but to be approved by God.

On the other hand, their humility keeps them from criticizing and judging those who have not these marks of humility. They pray for such people and leave all judgment to God, who in His own time will try everyone's work by fire (see 1 Cor. 3:13).

"Be clothed with humility, for 'God resists the proud, but gives grace to the humble'" (1 Pet. 5:5 NKJV).

> Anger and sloth, desire and pride,
> This moment be subdued!
> Be cast into the crimson tide
> Of my Redeemer's blood![2]

NOTES

1. St. Augustine, quoted in Jacque Marsollier, *The Life of St. Francis of Sales*, trans. W. H. Coombes (London: Shepton-Mallet, 1812), 501.

2. Charles Wesley, "Come, O My God, the Promise Seal," 1810, public domain.

How to Keep Holiness 9

Do you ask, "How can I keep the blessing?"

Do not let your poor heart be burdened with the thought that you have to do it all yourself. In this, as in all else, you are only a worker together with God. He loves you more than a mother loves her little child, and He is going to help you to keep the blessing. Remember that the blessing is simply the result of His indwelling in your heart, and you are not to think so much about keeping the blessing as about keeping Him.

It will not be a hard matter to keep Him in your heart if you are in earnest, for He wanted to get there when you were lost in sin, and He certainly desires to stay there as long as you will let Him. And if you will let Him, He will keep you.

One of our leading officers, who is a personal friend of mine, once told me that when he first heard the doctrine of holiness, he felt that he could not be holy while engaged in worldly business. But one day he read the prayer of Jesus: "I'm not asking you to take them out of the world, but to keep them safe from the evil one" (John 17:15 NLT). He saw at that moment that God could keep him, and he sought and found the blessing, and has been rejoicing ever since.

Oh, how it rested me and comforted my heart one day, when, sore tempted by the Devil, I read these words: "Now unto him that is able to keep you from falling, and to present you faultless before the presence of his glory with exceeding joy" (Jude 24 KJV). I saw that He was able to keep me, I knew that He was willing, and my heart rested on the promise. And, bless Him, He does keep me.

He says, "Don't be afraid, for I am with you. Don't be discouraged, for I am your God. I will strengthen you and help you. I will hold you up with my victorious right hand" (Isa. 41:10 NLT).

Paul got fairly jubilant over the keeping power of God. It was his boast when he wrote, "Who shall separate us from the love of Christ? Shall tribulation, or distress, or persecution, or famine, or nakedness, or peril or sword? . . . Nay, in all these things we are more than conquerors through him that loved us. For I am persuaded, that neither death, nor life, nor angels [fallen angels, or demons], nor principalities, nor powers [no combination of devils or mortals], nor things present, nor things to come, nor height [of prosperity], nor depth [of adversity], nor any other creature, shall be able to separate us from the love of God, which is in Christ Jesus our Lord" (Rom. 8:35, 37–39 KJV). Paul trusted God to keep him, and so must we. We would surely fall if God withheld His help for a moment.

But James tells us that "faith without works is dead" (James 2:20 KJV), so we must not only trust God, but also work together with God if we would keep the blessing. To keep the blessing, you must keep all upon the altar. What you have given to the Lord you must not take back. You gave all to get the blessing, and you must continue to give all to keep it.

"My all is on the altar, I'll take it back no more"[1] must be your motto and your song. The Devil will try to get you to come down from the cross. The world will allure you, the flesh will cry out against you, your friends may weep over you or frown upon you, or tease and torment or threaten you. Some will criticize you and doubt you, but you must stick to Jesus and take back nothing you have given to Him. There is usefulness and peace and God's smile and a crown and a kingdom before you, but only condemnation, ruin, and hell behind.

A little boy in Africa heard a sermon about Jesus and His tender dying love and saving power. He gave himself fully to the Lord, and Jesus came into his heart. This so enraged his father that he said, "I'll get this Jesus out of him; I'll beat him out." And he beat the little fellow most cruelly. But the boy was still true. Then the father said, "I'll smoke this Jesus out of him." So he put the boy into a hut, shut up the opening in the roof, and nearly smothered him with smoke. That failed also. Then he tried starvation, and he gave the boy nothing to eat for several days. All persecution failed, however, and the little fellow remained true. He had given all to Jesus, and he would have nothing back. When asked how he had endured all the terrible trials he had passed through, he quietly said, "I just stuck to Jesus."

If you would keep the blessing of holiness, you must be quick to obey God. I do not mean by this that you are to get into such haste that you will not take time to think and pray about all you do. God wants you to use your head and heart and all the good sense He has given you. He wants you to take time to speak to Him, consider, and find out His will. But once you have found it out, if you would have His smile and favor, and keep the blessing, you must not delay, but obey at once.

Oh, the losses of peace and power and joy and sweet communion with God that people suffer through hesitation at this point! Like the Roman governor Felix, they wait for "a convenient season" (Acts 24:25 KJV), which never comes! And, like Felix, they lose all. "Strike while the iron is hot." "Make hay while the sun shines." "Put out to sea while the tide is in."

A Salvation Army soldier (church member) who was greatly used of God told me that he was one day reading a half-religious novel. He had reached a most thrilling point in the story when the Holy Spirit seemed to say to him, "Stop reading this at once, and you shall never regret it." He closed the book at once, put it down, and never opened it again—and such a blessing came into his soul as he was hardly able to contain. Years after, when he told me this, he was still rejoicing that he had promptly obeyed the voice of the Lord and left that sort of thing forever.

If you have lost the blessing through a failure to promptly obey, do not be utterly discouraged, but begin over again, and the Lord will restore you. But do not trifle with God again. Pray and believe for His help to obey, lest a worse thing come upon you.

If you would keep the blessing, you must not depend upon your feelings but, as a friend of mine used to say, "Stand by your facts." Young Christians are very likely to be betrayed into mistakes by their feelings—by their happy feelings as well as their unhappy ones. When they are happy, they are in danger of thinking themselves better than they are, and of not watching and praying as they should. And when they are not happy, they are likely to get discouraged, cast away their confidence in the Lord, and conclude that it is useless for them to try to be holy. The safest way is to pay attention to your facts and let your feelings take care of themselves.

If people are kind to you, your digestion is good, and your sleep sound, you will probably feel well. But if people are unkind, the east wind blows, you eat something that lies heavy in your stomach, and your sleep is broken by horrid dreams, you will probably not feel well. But in neither case is your relation to God changed. Your facts are just the same. If you have given yourself to God and have taken nothing back, but can look up into His dear face and say, "My all is on the altar, and I trust in You," then you are His, and your business is to stand by that fact and trust that the blood of Jesus keeps you clean (see 1 John 1:7).

When you are happy, sing songs, and when you are heavyhearted, pray—and try to sing a little too—and never cast away your confidence, for there is a great reward before you, if you hold fast.

One of the greatest helps to keeping the blessing is for two or three people who have it to meet together as often as possible to read the Bible and pray with and encourage each other. This can usually be done just before or between times of worship on Sunday. This practice helped me more than anything else, I think, when I first got the blessing. Put a burning coal or stick by itself, the fire will go out, and it will be cold and black. But put several sticks or coals together and they will burn brightly. So it is with hearts full of holy fire.

At such little meetings, it is well to unite in prayer for others whom you are eager to see come to faith or enter into the blessing, and as you see them getting saved and sanctified, this will add mightily to your own faith and love.

Finally, wholehearted and continued consecration and self-denial, earnest prayer, joyful and diligent study of God's Word, deep humility before the Lord, aggressive work for others, and humble, definite testimony to the blessing, will surely establish us in holiness and keep us from falling.

How blest are they who still abide
Close sheltered in Thy bleeding side:
Who life and strength from Thee derive,
And for Thee fight, and in Thee live.[2]

NOTES

1. A variant chorus to Mary James, "My Body, Soul, and Spirit," 1869, public domain.

2. Nicholas von Zinzendorf, trans. John Wesley, "I Thirst, Thou Wounded Lamb of God," 1740, public domain.

Holiness and Zeal for Souls 10

"Follow me, and I will make you fishers of men" (Matt. 4:19 KJV), said Jesus to Peter and Andrew. And now as then, when Jesus saves a soul, that soul wants to "catch" other souls and see them experience new life in Christ. Holiness increases this desire and makes it burn with a quenchless flame.

The zeal of other people blazes up, burns low, and often dies out, but the zeal of someone with a clean heart, full of the Holy Spirit, increases year by year. Others run away from the prayer meeting, but the holy man or woman holds on. Others do not grieve if souls are not brought into God's kingdom, but holy hearts feel that they must see souls saved, or they must die. Others are zealous for flashy events, tea parties, ice cream socials, and musical festivals, but nothing pleases the sanctified soul as much as a prayer meeting where souls are crying to God for pardon and cleansing, and others are shouting for joy.

And this zeal for the salvation and sanctification of others leads such men and women to do something to reach them. He lets his light shine; she speaks to people not only from the platform and the pulpit at long range, but also "buttonholes" them and speaks to them wherever she finds them. Holiness makes it easy for them to do this. They love to do it. They find that, as they follow the Spirit, the Lord fills their mouths with truth and gives them something to say.

A number of years ago a young man full of the Holy Spirit stopped for a few minutes at a watering trough to give his horse a drink. At the same time a stranger rode up to water his horse. For about five minutes the young man—with a heart overflowing with love—told the stranger about Jesus. Then they separated to meet no more in this world. But the stranger followed Jesus Christ as a result of that five minutes of faithful, personal dealing and became a soul-winner in Africa. He often wondered who that heaven-sent young man was who pointed him to Jesus. One day in Africa he received a box of books from America, and on opening a small volume of memoirs, there he saw the face and the name of the man to whom he owed his soul's salvation, and whose cry to God was, "Give me souls, give me souls, O Lord, or I cannot live."[1]

There are two things for us to remember. First, most people who are far from God hope that someone will speak to them about their soul.

"Why did you not speak to me about my soul?" asked a student of his roommate.

"I thought you would not like it," was the reply.

"Why, that was the reason I roomed with you," said he.

A father prayed earnestly in the meeting for the salvation of souls. After the meeting, he and his boy walked home a mile away. The boy hoped his father would speak to him about Jesus and salvation, for he was under deep conviction, but the father never said a word. Then the boy said within himself, "After all, there is nothing in religion," and became a reckless unbeliever—all because his father did not speak to him about his soul.

Poor souls! People who have not experienced new life in Christ often laugh and make merry when their hearts are well nigh breaking with sorrow or conviction, and they are only waiting for someone to point them to Jesus.

Second, when God moves us to speak to people, we may be sure that He has been dealing with their hearts and preparing the way for us. When the Lord sent Philip to speak to the Ethiopian, He had the Ethiopian all ready for Philip's message.

A friend of mine in Cleveland used to meet a certain railroad conductor almost every day. One day my friend felt he ought to speak to that conductor about his soul. The conductor was a big, splendid fellow, but my friend was a small man and trembled and ran away like Jonah, disobedient and in great misery. After three weeks of agony he went out of his office and saw that conductor again. He could stand it no longer. He braced himself and said, "Lord, help me! I will speak to him, if he knocks me down." Then he spoke, and to his surprise, the big man burst into tears and said, "I have really been wanting someone to speak to me about my soul for three weeks."

God is faithful; He had been to that man before He sent my friend to him. And there are hungry souls all around us like that one. Holiness not only makes us eager for the salvation of souls, but also fills us with unutterable longings for the perfecting of the saints. "We want to present them to God, perfect in their relationship to Christ" (Col. 1:28 NLT). I have never known anyone to get the blessing without this desire following.

Oh, how God longs to have a holy people on earth! Will you give yourself to Him to help Him to get such a people? You can be a yoke-fellow with Jesus, a worker with God. Will you? If so, begin right now to pray for the one you feel God would have you help to find salvation or sanctification, and you will be working with Jesus. And if you continue, great shall be your reward.

> Not my own! My time, my talents,
> Freely all to Christ I bring,
> To be used in joyful service,
> For the glory of my King.[2]

NOTES

1. This man is identified as James Brainerd Taylor in S. L. Brengle, *The Soul-Winner's Secret* (New York: The Salvation Army, 1900).

2. Daniel Webster Whittle, "Not My Own, but Saved by Jesus," 1878, public domain.

Holiness and Worry 11

Worry is a great foe to holiness, and perfect trust puts an end to worry. "I would as soon swear as fret," said John Wesley. The murmuring and complaining of His children has always been a great sin in the sight of God and has led to untold suffering on their part.

Most people do not see this to be a sin, but it is. It dishonors God, blinds the eyes to His will, and deafens the ears to His voice. It is the ditch on one side of the pathway of trust. Lazy or heartless indifference is the ditch on the other side. Happy is the Christian who keeps out of either ditch and walks securely on the pathway. Though it may often be narrow and difficult, it is safe.

Worrying prevents quiet thought and earnest believing prayer and is therefore always bad. If circumstances are against us, we need quietness of mind, clearness of thought, decision of will, and strength of purpose with which to face these circumstances and overcome them. But all this is prevented or hindered by fret or worry.

First, we should not worry over things that we can help, but set to work to put them right. Sir Isaac Newton, one of the greatest of men, labored for eight years preparing the manuscript of one of his great works when one day he came into his study and found that his little dog, Diamond, had knocked over a candle and burned all his papers. Without a sign of anger or impatience, the great, good man quietly remarked, "Ah, Diamond, little do you know the labor and trouble to which you have put your master!" and without worrying sat down to do that vast work over again.

Second, we should not worry over the things we cannot help, but quietly and confidently look to the Lord for such help as He sees best to give. There is no possible evil that may befall us from which God cannot deliver us, if He sees that it is best for us, or give us grace to bear it, if that is best. Holiness of heart enables us to see this. An accident befell a little child I heard of, which for twenty-four hours endangered the child's life. The sanctified mother did all she could, then committed her darling to the Lord and peacefully awaited the issue. Within twenty-four hours the danger was passed and the child was safe. An old woman who had witnessed the calm trust of the mother expressed amazement.

"Well," said the mother, "I couldn't trust the Lord and worry too. So I did what I could, and trusted, and you see that all is well. And I have had the peace of God in my heart for twenty-four hours."

Paul wrote, "Don't worry about anything; instead, pray about everything. Tell God what you need, and thank him for all he has done. Then you will experience God's peace, which exceeds anything we can understand. His peace will guard your hearts and minds as you live in Christ Jesus" (Phil. 4:6–7 NLT).

And Isaiah said, "You will keep in perfect peace all who trust in you, all whose thoughts are fixed on you!" (Isa. 26:3 NLT).

Our business is, then, always to pray, give thanks for such blessings as we have, keep our minds stayed on God, and worry about nothing.

Holiness makes us so sure of the presence and love and care of God that, while doing with our might what our hands find to do, we refuse to worry, and sing from our heart:

> I will trust Thee, I will trust Thee,
> All my life Thou shalt control.[1]

And we are certain that while we trust and obey, neither devils nor people can do us real harm, nor defeat God's purpose for us.

The heart realization of heavenly help, of God's presence in time of trouble, of angels encamping round about them that fear Him, is the secret of a life of perfect peace in which anxious care is not shunned, but joyously and constantly rolled on the Lord who cares for us and bids us cast our care on Him (see 1 Pet. 5:7). Are you poor and tempted to worry about your daily bread? God sent the ravens to feed Elijah and later made him dependent upon a poor widow woman who had only enough flour and oil to make one meal for herself and her child. But through long months of famine God did not allow that flour to waste nor that oil to fail.

The God of Elijah is the God of those who trust in Him forevermore. Such trust is not a state of lazy indifference, but of the highest activity of heart and will, and it is both a privilege and a duty. Of course, only such a perfect trust can save from undue anxiety, but this trust is an unfailing fruit of the Holy Spirit dwelling in a clean heart. And we can only keep this trust by constant obedience to the Holy Spirit; strict attention to daily duty; watchfulness against temptation; much believing, persevering, unhurried prayer; and by nourishing our faith on God's Word daily. The promises are given to us to believe, and so we may rest in God's love and care and not worry and fret ourselves with useless anxiety.

Has someone talked unkindly or falsely about you? Don't worry, but pray, and go on loving that person and doing your duty, and someday God will "bring forth your righteousness as the light, and your justice as the noonday" (Ps. 37:6 ESV).

Are you sick? Don't worry, but pray. The Lord can raise you up (see James 5:15) or make the sickness work for good (see Rom. 8:28), as He did for a sister I knew in Chicago, who for five years was helpless in bed with rheumatism, but had five sons come to faith in Jesus during that time and would not have had those five years spent in any other way.

Have your own wrongdoings brought you into trouble? Don't worry, but repent, trust in Jesus, and walk in your present light, and the blood will cleanse you and God will surely help you.

Are you troubled about the future? Don't worry. Walk with God today in obedient trust, and tomorrow He will be with you. He will never fail you nor forsake you.

If our trust were but more simple,

We should take Him at His word;

And our lives would be all sunshine

In the sweetness of our Lord.[2]

NOTES

1. Herbert Booth, "Blessed Lord, in Thee Is Refuge," *The Salvation Army Songbook*, 1886, public domain.

2. Frederick William Faber, "There's a Wideness in God's Mercy," 1862, public domain.

Holiness and Duty **12**

If holiness delivers us from worry, it increases the sense of duty and of personal responsibility. It was the holiness of His heart that led the twelve-year-old boy Jesus to say to His mother, "Did you not know that I must be about My Father's business?" (Luke 2:49 NKJV). To Him the world was not a playground only, but a field of labor. His Father had given Him work to do, and He must do it before the night came in which no one can work.

By this I do not understand that He was continually engaged in ceaseless, grinding toil, with no hours of recreation and rest. We know that in after years He went away with His disciples to rest awhile. He took time to enjoy the flowers, to consider the lilies, to watch the sparrows, to view the grass of the field. But He neglected no duty. He did not slight or shirk His work. He was no trifler. He was honest. What He did, He did well and with His might. And this spirit always accompanies true holiness of heart.

Most people divide the work of the world into what they call sacred and secular work. Preaching, praying, reading the Bible, conducting meetings, and the like, they consider to be sacred work, but washing and ironing and learning, building houses and making shoes, practicing law or medicine, working in mines and mills and shops and stores and on shipboard—that, they call secular work.

But why make such a distinction? It is not the work but the heart and purpose behind the work that God looks at. The Salvation Army officer or minister or missionary who works for the salary, or for social position, or for an opportunity for study and travel and personal culture has a secular heart and makes the work secular. But the farmer, lawyer, cook, shoemaker, miner, or secretary who has a holy heart and does good work as unto the Lord makes his or her work sacred.

The time was when people built their own houses, made their own shoes, sheared their sheep, dyed the wool, spun and wove it, and made it into clothes for their household. They raised corn and meat and prepared it for food, and so they lived independent of the world on the fruits of their own toil. But times have changed. Society is now a great organism in which there are a thousand different occupations, and people must divide the work between them. And God wants each of us to be faithful and holy and happy where we are, doing our own work faithfully as Jesus would do it.

A poor German woman in Massachusetts used to say, "I am a scrubbing woman and a missionary by the grace of God." She went to the homes of the rich to scrub and clean, and she testified of Jesus everywhere she went. She scrubbed to pay expenses and preached the gospel. And she scrubbed well that the gospel might not be despised.

They tried to arrest Paul in Damascus after his conversion, but he was let down through a window by the wall in a basket and so escaped. Someone has said that possibly one of the early Christians made the rope that held the basket, and that by making a good rope, he saved Paul's life. And so in his humble way, without knowing it, he helped in all the mighty missionary labors and salvation warfare of Paul. But what if he had carelessly made a poor rope that had broken with Paul!

We know not what part of our work God is going to use in His plans for saving the world. Therefore, let it all be good and true.

We are God's tools. He is the workman. I took an axe to cut down a tree, but I took a tiny gimlet to bore a hole in a piece of furniture I wished to mend. I could not cut down the tree with the gimlet nor bore the hole with the axe, and yet both pieces of work were important. So the Lord has different kinds of work for which he must have different kinds of workers.

General William Booth stirs the world and lifts it toward God. You, perhaps, teach a few ragged boys. Do not despise your work or be discouraged. You are as important to God as the gimlet was to me. Do your duty. Do it as though Jesus were in the class you teach; by the bench where you work; in your kitchen, office, store, or mill. Do it without murmuring. Do it gladly, and He may take it up and make it a part of His great plan long after you have laid it down, as He did the rope which saved Paul. Never mind what your work is. Moses tended sheep. Jesus was a carpenter. Paul was a tentmaker. Gideon was a farmer's man. Dorcas was a dressmaker, Martha a housekeeper, Luke a doctor, and Joseph and Daniel governors and statesmen. In every relation of life and in all duty, they were faithful, or we would not have heard of them.

If you are true, you will "adorn the doctrine of God our Saviour in all things" (Titus 2:10 KJV). You will have the sweet approval of your own conscience, the smile of God, and however humble your work may have been, if you are steadfast unto the end, you will someday hear Him say, "Well done, good and faithful servant. You have been faithful over a little; I will set you over much. Enter into the joy of your master" (Matt. 25:21 ESV).

True promotion which is from God, both in this world and that which is to come, is the reward of faithfulness over little things and few, as well as over great and many, and if you have the experience of holiness you will be faithful.

You must not, however, be anxious about the reward. This is largely deferred into the next world. It is your duty and mine to be faithful, to be faithful unto death. If reward is delayed, it will be all the greater when it comes, be assured of that. God will see to it that your treasure which you lay up with Him bears compound interest. What a surprise to the man who made that rope, if he finds at the judgment day that he had a share in the wealth piled up by Paul's labors!

There is one part of the reward, however, that is never delayed, and that is happiness and contentment and God's favor.

In service which Thy love appoints,

There are no bonds for me:

My happy heart has learned the truth

That makes Thy children free;

A life of self-renouncing love

Is a life of liberty.[1]

NOTE

1. Anna L. Waring, "Father, I Know That All My Life," 1850, public domain.

Holiness and Prayer 13

Prayer is a puzzle to unbelievers, but a sweet privilege to us. A stranger will hesitate to approach a king, but the king's child will climb on the king's knee, whisper in the king's ear, and ask all sorts of favors of the king—and get them, too, because he or she is the king's child. That is the secret of prayer.

When we have repented of sin, given ourselves to God, and been born again, we are His dear children, and we have a right to come to Him in prayer. The Devil will try to hinder us, and if our faith is weak, we may doubt and hesitate. But God invites; He wants us to come—with all our wishes, cares, burdens, sorrows, perplexities, everything. Nothing that is of interest to us is too small to interest Him. Many people do not believe this, but it is true. They think God is interested only in big things. But the same God who made the flaming suns and mighty worlds made the tiny insect and fashioned the lenses of its little eye and painted with brightest colors its dainty wing. He is interested in the little quite as much as in the great. Therefore we may bring everything to Him in prayer.

I once heard a very intelligent old saint, past fourscore years of age, say, "I moved into a flat by myself so that I could be alone with Jesus. He and I keep house together, and when I lose anything, I ask Him to help me to find it, and He does." She was right, and people who think God does not want His children to be so familiar as that are wrong and have much yet to learn.

We should be definite and pray for what we want. A Christian told me the other day that she could come to God for a clean heart but not for a new dress. She was wrong. If she seeks "first the kingdom of God, and his righteousness" (Matt. 6:33 KJV), she has just as much right to lay before the Lord her need of a new dress as of a spiritual blessing. Of course, spiritual blessings are by far the most important and should be sought first. But Jesus wants us to talk to Him about everything and bring to Him all our wants. Let this sink deep into your heart if you would be holy, happy, and useful.

For many days there had been no rain in Ohio. The fields were parched and brown, and everything cried out for water. The people were anxious and knew not what to do. One Sunday, before his sermon, evangelist Charles Finney prayed for rain. One who heard that prayer reported it after twenty-three years, and said it was as fresh in his mind as though he had heard it but yesterday. Mr. Finney told the Lord all about their great need, and among other things said:

We do not presume to dictate to Thee what is best for us, yet Thou dost invite us to come to Thee as children to a father and tell Thee what we want. We want rain. Our pastures are dry. The cattle are lowing and wandering about in search of water. Even the little squirrels in the woods are suffering for the want of it. Unless Thou dost give us rain our cattle must die, for we shall have no hay for them for winter; and our harvests will come to nought. O Lord, send us rain, and send it now! Although to us there is no sign of it, it is an easy thing for Thee to do. Send it now, Lord, for Christ's sake![1]

And the Lord sent it. Before the service was half over the rain came in such torrents that the preacher's voice could not be heard. So, with tears of wonder and joy and thanksgiving, they sang:

> When all Thy mercies, O my God,
> My rising soul surveys,
> Transported with the view, I'm lost
> In wonder, love and praise.[2]

Finney took God at His word and dared to ask for what he wanted. He used to say, "Lord, I hope Thou dost not see that I can be denied."

Many people pray for things they want, but James tells us that they do not get them because they ask amiss, to consume them upon their lusts. They want things for worldly pleasure or profit, or for sinful, selfish purposes (see James 4:3).

The secret of prevailing prayer is this: that we are so in love with Jesus, so at one with Him, that we do not want anything to use or spend in any way that would grieve Him. I want a new suit of clothes.

What for? That I may strut around in pride or to show myself off to the people I know? No, no, but that I may be suitably clothed for my work for God. I want food. What for? To strengthen me for sinful, selfish pleasures and labors? No, no, but to glorify God. I want a clean heart. What for? That I may be happy and get to heaven? No, no, not that alone, but that I may honor God and help Him to win others to love and trust and obey Him. When I want things in that spirit, then the Lord can trust me with anything for which I ask Him, for I will not ask Him for anything that is not for His glory. If I am in doubt about anything being for His glory, then I will ask Him to give it to me only if He sees it is best to do so.

And we must pray in faith. It is sad the way people doubt God, and the cold, lifeless prayers they utter before Him are heartbreaking! You would not want a friend to come to you for anything you had promised to give, with such faithless asking, would you? God is much more willing to give good things to us than we are to give good gifts to our children. And we should come with lively faith that will not be denied. The only reason some prayers accomplish so little is because they ask so little and with such feeble faith. The promise is, "Whatever you ask for in prayer, believe that you have received it, and it will be yours" (Mark 11:24 NIV).

You ask, "How can I get faith?" I answer, through God's Word. Hunt up His promises, and go to God with them. Say with David, "Remember your word to your servant, in which you have made me hope" (Ps. 119:49 ESV). That is what Finney did. He wanted rain, and he went to God with the promise: "When the poor and needy search for water and there is none, and their tongues are parched from thirst, then I, the LORD, will answer them. I, the God of Israel, will never abandon them" (Isa. 41:17 NLT).

But again, we must persevere in prayer. We must hold on to God and not let go till the answer comes or until God shows us why it does not come. Sometimes the answer to prayer comes at once. The first person I remember praying with after God sanctified me got the blessing at once.

One morning I prayed for a suit of clothes which I very much needed. A great peace came into my heart, and I got off my knees laughing, knowing that God had heard and answered my little request. How and when the suit was to come I did not know. After breakfast I went out, and when I returned a man was waiting for me to go to the tailor's and be measured for the best suit in his shop. I knew absolutely nothing about this when I prayed, but God did.

But sometimes the answer is delayed. At such times we must not fold our hands and idly conclude that it is not God's will. Instead, we must search our hearts to make sure the hindrance is not in us and still continue to plead with God, and in due time the answer will come.

Hold on to God for the salvation and sanctification of your loved ones, and God will hear and answer you. "[We] always ought to pray and not lose heart," said Jesus (Luke 18:1 NKJV). Wrestle with Him, give Him no rest, remind Him every day of His promise and your burning desire, and He must hear and answer you.

A young man prayed for his friend for thirteen months and finally died without seeing the friend surrender his life to Christ. But God was faithful and remembered the prayers of His child, and in due time that friend entered into new life and became a martyr for Christ in Africa.

Finally, we should mingle thanks with our prayers, even before we see the answer. "In everything by prayer and supplication, with thanksgiving, let your requests be made known to God," wrote Paul (Phil. 4:6 NKJV). A mother got gloriously sanctified at a Salvation Army penitent form, and then she began to pray in faith for the salvation of her daughter. For some time she prayed, but one day she said, "Lord, I am not going to pray for this any longer, but I am going to thank Thee for the salvation of my child." Within a week, the girl gave her life to Jesus Christ and is now a Salvation Army officer.

Holy people are in vital union and partnership with God, and their prayers inspired by the Holy Spirit move all heaven on their behalf. Will you give yourself to a life of glad, persevering, believing prayer? If so, you shall be one of God's princes and princesses on earth.

Behold the throne of grace!

The promise calls me near;

There Jesus shows a smiling face,

And waits to answer prayer.

My soul! Ask what thou wilt,

Thou canst not be too bold:

Since His own blood for thee He spilt,

What else can He withhold?[3]

NOTES

1. Joseph Adams, *Reminiscences of Rev. Charles G. Finney* (New York: E. J. Goodrich, Edward O. Jenkins, 1876), http://www.gospel truth.net/Reminiscenses/remin02.htm.

2. Joseph Addison, "When All Thy Mercies, O My God," 1712, public domain.

3. John Newton, "Behold the Throne of Grace," 1779, public domain.

Samuel L. Brengle's Holy Life Series

This series comprises the complete works of Samuel L. Brengle, combining all nine of his original books into six volumes, penned by one of the great minds on holiness. Each volume has been lovingly edited for modern readership by popular author (and long-time Brengle devotee) Bob Hostetler. Brengle's authentic voice remains strong, now able to more relevantly engage today's disciples of holiness. These books are must-haves for all who would seriously pursue and understand the depths of holiness in the tradition of John Wesley.

Helps to Holiness
ISBN: 978-1-63257-064-2
eBook: 978-1-63257-065-9

The Heart of Holiness
ISBN: 978-1-63257-066-6
eBook: 978-1-63257-067-3

The Servant's Heart
ISBN: 978-1-63257-068-0
eBook: 978-1-63257-069-7

Ancient Prophets and Modern Problems
ISBN: 978-1-63257-070-3
eBook: 978-1-63257-071-0

Come Holy Guest
ISBN: 978-1-63257-072-7
eBook: 978-1-63257-073-4

Resurrection Life and Power
ISBN: 978-1-63257-074-1
eBook: 978-1-63257-075-8

Samuel L. Brengle's Holy Life Series Box Set
ISBN: 978-1-63257-076-5

SAMUEL L. BRENGLE'S HOLY LIFE SERIES

HELPS TO HOLINESS

Bob Hostetler, General Editor

wesleyan
PUBLISHING HOUSE
wphstore.com

CREST BOOKS

Copyright © 2016 by The Salvation Army
Published by Wesleyan Publishing House
Indianapolis, Indiana 46250
Printed in the United States of America
ISBN: 978-1-63257-064-2
ISBN (e-book): 978-1-63257-065-9

Library of Congress Cataloging-in-Publication Data

Brengle, Samuel Logan, 1860-1936.
  Helps to holiness / Samuel L. Brengle ; Bob Hostetler, general editor.
    pages cm. -- (Samuel L. Brengle's holy life series)
  Originally published: London : Simpkin, Marshall, Hamilton, Kent & co., ltd.,
  1896.
  ISBN 978-1-63257-064-2 (pbk.)
  1. Holiness. I. Hostetler, Bob, 1958- editor. II. Title.
  BT767.B8 2016
  234'.8--dc23
                                    2015025625

Scripture quotations marked (NLT) are taken from the Holy Bible, New Living Translation, copyright © 1996, 2004, 2007, 2013 by Tyndale House Foundation. Used by permission of Tyndale House Publishers, Inc., Carol Stream, Illinois 60188. All rights reserved.

Scripture quotations marked (KJV) are taken from the HOLY BIBLE, KING JAMES VERSION.

Scripture quotations marked (ESV) are from The Holy Bible, English Standard Version® (ESV®), copyright © 2001 by Crossway, a publishing ministry of Good News Publishers. Used by permission. All rights reserved.

Scripture quotations marked (NIV) are taken from the Holy Bible, New International Version®, NIV ®. Copyright © 1973, 1978, 1984, 2011 by Biblica, Inc. Used by permission of Zondervan. All rights reserved worldwide. www.zondervan.com. The "NIV" and "New International Version" are trademarks registered in the United States Patent and Trademark Office by Biblica, Inc.

Scripture quotations marked (CEV) are taken from the *Contemporary English Version* © 1991, 1992, 1995 by American Bible Society. Used by Permission.

Scripture quotations marked (CEB) are taken from the *Common English Bible.* Copyright © 2011 by the *Common English Bible.* All rights reserved. Used by Permission.

Scripture quotations marked (NASB) are taken from the *New American Standard Bible®,* Copyright © 1960, 1962, 1963, 1968, 1971, 1972, 1973, 1975, 1977, 1995 by The Lockman Foundation. Used by permission.

Scripture quotations marked (NKJV) are taken from the New King James Version. Copyright © 1982 by Thomas Nelson, Inc. Used by permission. All rights reserved.

Scripture quotations marked (NRSV) are from the *New Revised Standard Version Bible,* copyright © 1989 by the National Council of the Churches of Christ in the United States of America. Used by permission. All rights reserved.

Contents

Preface

Samuel Logan Brengle was an influential author, teacher, and preacher on the doctrine of holiness in the late nineteenth to early twentieth century, serving from 1887–1931 as an active officer (minister) in The Salvation Army. In 1889 while he and his wife, Elizabeth Swift Brengle, were serving as corps officers (pastors) in Boston, Massachusetts, a brick thrown by a street "tough" smashed Brengle's head against a door frame and caused an injury severe enough to require more than nineteen months of convalescence. During that treatment and recuperation period, he began writing articles on holiness for The Salvation Army's publication, *The War Cry*, which were later collected and published as a "little red book" under the title *Helps to Holiness*. That book's success led to eight others over the next forty-five years: *Heart Talks on Holiness*, *The Way of Holiness*, *The Soul-Winner's Secret*, *When the Holy Ghost Is Come*, *Love-Slaves*, *Resurrection Life and Power*,

Ancient Prophets and Modern Problems, and *The Guest of the Soul* (published in his retirement in 1934).

By the time of his death in 1936, Commissioner Brengle was an internationally renowned preacher and worldwide ambassador of holiness. His influence continues today, perhaps more than any Salvationist in history besides the founders, William and Catherine Booth. I hope that the revised and updated editions of his books that comprise the Samuel L. Brengle's Holy Life Series will enhance and enlarge that influence, introduce these writings to new readers, and create fresh interest in those who already know the godly wisdom and life-changing power of these volumes.

While I have taken care to preserve the integrity, impact, and voice of the original writing, I have carefully and prayerfully made changes that I hope will facilitate greater understanding and appreciation of Brengle's words for modern readers. These changes include:

- Revising archaic terms (such as the use of King James English) and updating the language to reflect more contemporary usage (such as occasionally employing more inclusive gender references);
- Shortening and simplifying sentence structure and revising punctuation to conform more closely to contemporary practice;
- Explaining specific references of The Salvation Army that will not be familiar to the general population;
- Updating Scripture references (when possible retaining the King James Version—used exclusively in Brengle's writings—but frequently incorporating modern versions, especially when doing so will aid the reader's comprehension and enjoyment);

- Replacing Roman numerals with Arabic numerals and spelled out Scripture references for the sake of those who are less familiar with the Bible;

- Citing Scripture quotes not referenced in the original and noting the sources for quotes, lines from hymns, etc.;

- Aligning all quoted material to the source (Brengle, who often quoted not only Scripture, but also poetry from memory, often quoted loosely in speaking and writing);

- Adding occasional explanatory phrases or endnotes to identify people or events that might not be familiar to modern readers;

- Revising or replacing some chapter titles, and (in *Ancient Prophets and Modern Problems*) moving one chapter to later in the book; and

- Deleting the prefaces that introduced each book and epigraphs that preceded some chapters.

In the preface to Brengle's first book, Commissioner (later General) Bramwell Booth wrote, "This book is intended to help every reader of its pages into the immediate enjoyment of Bible holiness. Its writer is an officer of The Salvation Army who, having a gracious experience of the things whereof he writes, has been signally used of God, both in life and testimony, to the sanctifying of the Lord's people, as well as in the salvation of sinners. I commend him and what he has here written down to every lover of God and His kingdom here on earth."

In the preface to Brengle's last book, *The Guest of the Soul*, The Salvation Army's third general (and successor to Bramwell Booth) wrote: "These choice contributions . . . will, I am sure, serve to

strengthen the faith of the readers of this book and impress upon them the joyousness of life when the heart has been opened to the Holy Guest of the Soul."

I hope and pray that this updated version of Brengle's writings will further those aims.

—Bob Hostetler

general editor

Introduction

On January 9, 1885, at about nine o'clock in the morning, God sanctified my soul. I was in my own room at the time, but in a few minutes I went out and met a man and told him what God had done for me. The next morning, I met another friend on the street and told him the story. He shouted and praised God and urged me to preach full salvation and confess it everywhere. God used him to encourage and help me. So the following day I preached on the subject as clearly and forcibly as I could, and ended with my testimony.

God mightily blessed the Word to others, but I think He blessed it most to me. That confession put me on record. It cut down the bridges behind me. Three worlds were now looking at me as one who professed that God had given him a clean heart. I could not go back now. I had to go forward. God saw that I meant to be true till death. So two mornings after that, just as I got out of bed and was reading some of Jesus' words,

He gave me such a blessing as I never had dreamed a man could have this side of heaven: a heaven of love came into my heart. I walked out over Boston Common before breakfast weeping for joy and praising God. Oh, how I loved! In that hour I knew Jesus, and I loved Him till it seemed my heart would break with love. I loved the sparrows; I loved the dogs; I loved the horses; I loved the little urchins on the streets; I loved the strangers who hurried past me; I loved the whole world.

Do you want to know what holiness is? It is pure love. Do you want to know what the baptism of the Holy Spirit is? It is not a mere sentiment. It is not a happy sensation that passes away in a night. It is a baptism of love that brings every thought into captivity to the Lord Jesus (see 2 Cor. 10:5); casts out all fear (see 1 John 4:18); burns up doubt and unbelief as fire burns flax; makes you "meek and lowly in heart" (Matt. 11:29 KJV); makes you hate uncleanness, lying and deceit, a flattering tongue, and every evil way with a perfect hatred; makes heaven and hell eternal realities; makes you patient and gentle with the disobedient and sinful; makes you "pure . . . peaceable . . . open to reason, full of mercy and good fruits, impartial and sincere" (James 3:17 ESV), and brings you into perfect and unbroken sympathy with the Lord Jesus Christ in His toil and travail to bring a lost and rebellious world back to God.

Oh, how I had longed to be pure! Oh, how I had hungered and thirsted for God—the living God! And He did all that for me. He gave me the desire of my heart. He satisfied me—I weigh my words—He satisfied me!

All the years since then have been wonderful. God has become my teacher, my guide, my counselor, and my all in all.

He has allowed me to be perplexed and tempted, but it has been for my good. I have no complaint to make against Him. Sometimes it has seemed that He left me alone, but it has been as the mother who stands away from her little child to teach him to use his own legs that he may walk. He has not suffered me to fall.

He has helped me to speak of Jesus and His great salvation in such a way so as to instruct, comfort, and save other souls. He has been light to my darkness, strength to my weakness, wisdom in my foolishness, and knowledge in my ignorance.

When my way has been hedged up and it seemed that no way could be found out of my temptations and difficulties, He has cut a way through for me, just as He opened the Red Sea for Israel.

When my heart has ached, He has comforted me. When my feet have nearly slipped, He has held me up. When my faith has trembled, He has encouraged me. When I have been in desperate need, He has supplied every necessity. When I have been hungry, He has fed me. When I have thirsted, He has given me living water.

What has He not done for me? What has He not been to me? I recommend Him to the world. He has taught me that sin is the only thing that can harm me, and that the only thing that can profit me is "faith working through love" (Gal. 5:6 ESV). He has taught me to hang upon Jesus by faith for my salvation from all sin and fear and shame, and to show my love by obeying Him in all things and by seeking in all ways to lead others to obey Him.

I praise Him! I adore Him! I love Him! My whole being is His for time and eternity. I am not my own. He can do with me as He pleases, for I am His. I know that what He chooses must work out for my eternal good.

He is too wise to make mistakes and too good to do me evil. I trust Him, I trust Him, I trust Him! "My hope is from him" (Ps. 62:5 ESV), not from others, not from myself, but from Him. I know He will never fail me.

Since that long-past January day, God has enabled me to keep a perfect, unbroken purpose to serve Him with my whole heart. No temptation has caused me to swerve from that steadfast purpose. No worldly or ecclesiastical ambition has had an atom of weight to allure me. My whole heart has cried within me, as Ephraim's did, "What have I to do any more with idols? I have heard him, and observed him" (Hos. 14:8 KJV).

"Holiness to the LORD" (Ex. 28:36 KJV) has been my motto. In fact, it has been the only motto that could express the deep desire and aspiration of my soul.

For a year and a half at a stretch, I have been laid aside from work by physical weakness. At one time, I would have thought this to be a cross too heavy to bear. But in this, as in all things, God's grace was sufficient.

Lately, God has been blessing me even more. My heart pants after Him and, as I seek Him in fervent, patient, believing prayer and in diligent searching of His Word, He is deepening the work of grace in my soul.

—Samuel L. Brengle

Holiness—What Is It? 1

God's Word commands His people: "Be holy!" (1 Pet. 1:16 NIV).
It says, "It is God's will that you should be sanctified. . . . For God did
not call us to be impure, but to live a holy life" (1 Thess. 4:3, 7 NIV).
It goes so far as to say, "Without holiness no one will see the Lord"
(Heb. 12:14 NIV).

Anyone who reads the Bible in sincerity, not "handling the word
of God deceitfully" (2 Cor. 4:2 KJV), will see that it plainly teaches that
God expects His people to be holy, and that we must be holy to be
happy and useful here and to enter the kingdom of heaven hereafter.
Once a Christian is convinced that the Bible teaches these facts and that
this is God's will, he or she will next inquire, "What is this holiness?
When can I get it, and how?"

There is much difference of opinion on all these points, although the
Bible is simple and plain on each one to every honest seeker of truth.

The Bible tells us that holiness is perfect deliverance from sin. "The blood of Jesus . . . cleanses us from *all* sin" (1 John 1:7 NLT, emphasis added). Not one bit of sin is left, for your old self is crucified with Him, "that the body of sin might be brought to nothing, so that we would no longer be enslaved to sin" (Rom. 6:6 ESV), for we have "been set free from sin" (Rom. 6:18 ESV). And we are henceforth to count ourselves "dead to sin and alive to God in Christ Jesus" (Rom. 6:11 ESV).

The Bible also tells us that holiness is "perfect love," a love which must expel from the heart all hatred and every evil disposition contrary to love, just as you must first empty a cup of all oil that may be in it before you can fill it with water.

Thus, holiness is a state in which there is no anger, malice, blasphemy, hypocrisy, envy, love of ease, selfish desire for good opinion of others, shame of the cross, worldliness, deceit, debate, contention, covetousness, nor any evil desire or tendency in the heart.

It is a state in which there is no longer any doubt or fear.

It is a state in which God is loved and trusted with a perfect heart.

But though the heart may be perfect, the head may be very imperfect, and through such imperfections of memory, judgment, or reason, the holy man or woman may make many mistakes. But God looks at the sincerity of that person's purpose, at the love and faith of the heart rather than the imperfections of the head, and calls him or her holy.

Holiness is not absolute perfection, which belongs to God only. Nor is it angelic perfection. Nor is it Adamic perfection for, no doubt, Adam had a perfect head as well as a perfect heart before he sinned against God. But it is Christian perfection—such perfection and obedience of the heart as a poor fallen creature, aided by almighty power and boundless grace, can give.

It is that state of heart and life which consists of being and doing all the time—not by fits and starts, but steadily—just what God wants us to be and do.

Jesus said, "Make the tree good and its fruit good" (Matt. 12:33 ESV). Now, an apple tree is an apple tree all the time and can bring forth nothing but apples. So holiness is that perfect renewal of our nature that makes us essentially good, so that we continually bring forth fruit unto God—"the fruit of the Spirit [which] is love, joy, peace, patience, kindness, goodness, faithfulness, gentleness, [and] self-control" (Gal. 5:22–23 ESV)—with never a single work of the flesh grafted in among this heavenly fruit.

It is possible, right down here, where sin and Satan have once ruined us, for the Son of God thus to transform us, by enabling us to "put off the old self" with its deceitful desires and to "put on the new self, created after the likeness of God in true righteousness and holiness" (Eph. 4:22, 24 ESV), being "renewed in knowledge after the image of its creator" (Col. 3:10 ESV).

But someone may object: "Yes, all you say is true, but I don't believe we can be holy until the hour of death. The Christian life is a war, and we must fight the good fight of faith until we die. And *then* I believe God will give us dying grace."

Many honest Christians hold exactly this view and put forth no real effort to "stand firm in all the will of God, mature and fully assured" (Col. 4:12 NIV). And though they pray daily for God's kingdom to come and His will to be done on earth as it is in heaven (see Matt. 6:10), they do not believe it is possible for them to do the will of God, and so they make Jesus the author of a vain prayer, which is idle mockery to repeat.

But it is as easy for me to be and to do what God wants in this life every day as it is for the archangel Gabriel to be and do what God wants of him. If this is not the case, then God is neither good nor just in His requirements of me. God requires me to love and serve Him with all my heart, and Gabriel can do no more than that. And by God's grace, it is as easy for me as for the archangel.

Besides, God promises that if we return to the Lord and obey His commands with all our heart and soul, that He will circumcise our hearts that we may love Him with heart and soul (see Deut. 30:2, 6). And He promises "to rescue us from the hand of our enemies, and to enable us to serve him without fear in holiness and righteousness before him all our days" (Luke 1:74–75 NIV). This promise in itself ought to convince any honest soul that God means for us to be holy in this life.

The good fight of faith is a fight to retain this blessing against the assaults of Satan, the fogs of doubt, and the attacks of an ignorant and unbelieving church and world.

It is not a fight against ourselves after we are sanctified, for Paul expressly declared that "our struggle is not against flesh and blood, but against the rulers, against the authorities, against the powers of this dark world and against the spiritual forces of evil in the heavenly realms" (Eph. 6:12 NIV).

In the whole Word of God, there is not one sentence to prove that this blessing is not received before death. And surely it is only by accepting from God's hands His offered living grace that we can hope to be granted dying grace.

But the Bible declares that "God is able to make all grace abound to you, so that having all sufficiency in all things at all times, you may abound in every good work" (2 Cor. 9:8 ESV)—not at death, but in this life, when grace is needed and where our good works are to be done.

Holiness—How to Get It 2

A man more than eighty years old once said, "I believe in holiness, but I don't think it is all got at once, as you people say. I believe we grow into it."

This is a common mistake, second only to that which makes death the savior from sin and the giver of holiness, and it is a mistake which has kept tens of thousands out of the blessed experience. It does not recognize the exceeding sinfulness of sin (see Rom. 7:13), nor does it know the simple way of faith by which alone sin can be destroyed.

Entire sanctification is at once a process of subtraction and addition.

First, there are laid aside "all malice and all deceit and hypocrisy and envy and all slander" (1 Pet. 2:1 ESV)—in fact, every evil inclination and selfish desire that is unlike Christ—and the soul is cleansed. This cannot be by growth, for this cleansing takes something from the soul, while growth always adds something to it. The Bible says, "Put off all these: anger, wrath, malice, blasphemy, filthy language out of your mouth" (Col. 3:8 NKJV). The apostle Paul, who penned those words, talked as though we were to put these off in much the same way as we would a coat. It is not by growth that a person puts off a coat, but by an active, voluntary, and immediate effort of the whole body. This is subtraction.

But the apostle added: "Clothe yourselves with compassion, kindness, humility, gentleness and patience" (Col. 3:12 NIV). Neither does a person put on clothing by growth, but by a similar effort of the whole body.

You may grow *in* your coat, but not *into* your coat; you must first get it on. Just so, we may grow in grace, but not into grace. We may swim in water, but not into water.

It is not by growth that you get the weeds out of your garden, but by pulling them up and vigorously using your hoe and rake. It is not by growth that you expect that dirty little boy, who has been tumbling around with the dog and cat in the backyard, to get clean. He might grow to manhood and get dirtier every day. It is by washing with much pure water that you expect to make him at all presentable. So the Bible speaks of "him that loved us, and washed us from our sins in his own blood" (Rev. 1:5 KJV), saying, "the blood of Jesus, his Son, cleanses us from all sin" (1 John 1:7 NLT).

And it is just this we sing about:

> To get this blest washing I all things forgo;
> Now wash me, and I shall be whiter than snow.[1]

There is a fountain filled with blood

Drawn from Immanuel's veins,

And sinners plunged beneath its flood

Lose all their guilty stains.²

These facts were told to the old brother mentioned above, and he was asked if, after sixty years of Christian experience, he felt any nearer to the priceless gift of a clean heart than when he first began to serve Christ. He honestly confessed that he did not. He was asked next if he thought sixty years was long enough to prove the growth theory, if it were true. He thought it was, and so was asked to come forward and seek the blessing at once.

He did so, but did not win through that night. But the next night he came forward again and had scarcely knelt five minutes before he stood up and, stretching out his arms, while tears ran down his cheeks and his face glowed with heaven's light, he cried out, "As far as the east is from the west, so far has He removed [my] transgressions from [me]" (Ps. 103:12 NKJV). For some time after, he lived to witness to this wondrous grace of God in Christ.

"But," a man said to me, as I urged him to seek holiness at once, "I got this when I was converted. God didn't do a half work with me when He saved me. He did a thorough job."

I answered, "True, God did a thorough work, brother. When He gave you new life in Jesus Christ, He forgave all your sins, every one of them. He did not leave half of them unforgiven, but blotted out all of them, to be forgotten forever. He also adopted you into His family and sent His Holy Spirit into your heart to tell you that blessed bit of heavenly news. And that information made you feel happier than to have been told that you had fallen heir to a million dollars or been elected governor of a state, for this made you an heir of God and a joint heir of all things with our Lord and Savior Jesus Christ. It is a great thing. But, brother, are you saved from all impatience, anger, and like sins of the heart? Do you live a holy life?"

"Well, you see," the man said, "I don't look at this matter exactly as you do. I do not believe we can be saved from all impatience and anger in this life." And so, when pressed to the point, he begged the question and contradicted his own assertion that he had received holiness when he experienced new life in Christ. As a friend wrote, he "would rather deny the sickness than take the medicine."[3]

The fact is, neither the Bible nor experience proves that we get a clean heart when we enter the kingdom, but just the opposite. Our sins are forgiven. We receive the witness of adoption into God's own family. Our affections are changed. But before we go very far we find our patience mixed up with some degree of impatience, our kindness with wrath, our meekness with anger, our humility with pride, our loyalty to Jesus mixed with a shame of the cross, and, in fact, the fruit of the Spirit all mixed up together with the works of the flesh, in greater or lesser degree.

But this will be done away with when we get a clean heart, and it will take a second work of grace, preceded by a wholehearted consecration and as definite an act of faith to get it as that which preceded conversion.

After conversion, we find our old sinful nature much like a tree that has been cut down, but the stump still left. The tree causes no more bother, but the stump will still bring forth little shoots if it is not watched. The quickest and most effective way is to put some dynamite under the stump and blow it up.

Just so, God wants to put the dynamite of the Holy Spirit (the word *dynamite* comes from the Greek word for power, in Acts 1:8) into every follower of Jesus and forever do away with that old troublesome, sinful nature, so that he or she can truly say, "Old things are passed away; behold, all things are become new" (2 Cor. 5:17 KJV).

This is just what God did with the apostles on the day of Pentecost. Nobody will deny that they were followers of Jesus before Pentecost, for Jesus Himself had told them to "rejoice, because your names are written in heaven" (Luke 10:20 KJV), and a person must be a true follower of Jesus before his or her name is written in heaven.

And again Jesus said of His earliest followers, "They are not of the world, even as I am not of the world" (John 17:16 KJV), and this could not be said of the unregenerate. So we may conclude that they had entered the kingdom of God, yet did not have the blessing of a clean heart until the day of Pentecost.

That they did receive it there, Peter declared about as plainly as possible when he said, later, "God, who knows the heart, showed that he accepted them by giving the Holy Spirit to them, just as he did to us. He did not discriminate between us and them, for he purified their hearts by faith" (Acts 15:8–9 NIV).

Before Peter got this great blessing he was filled with presumption one day and fear the next. One day he told Jesus, "Even if all fall away on account of you, I never will. . . . Even if I have to die with you, I will never disown you" (Matt. 26:33, 35 NIV). And shortly after,

when the mob came to arrest his Master, he boldly attacked them with
a sword; but a few hours later, when his blood had cooled and the
excitement was over, he was so frightened by a maid that he cursed
and swore and denied his Master three times.

He was like a good many folks, who are tremendously brave when
trumpets blow and the winds are favorable—and who can even stand
an attack from persecutors, where muscle and physical courage can
come to the front—but who have no moral courage when they have
to face the scorn of their colleagues and the jeers of strangers. These
are soldiers who love dress parade, but do not want hard fighting at
the front of the battle.

But Peter got over that on the day of Pentecost. He received the
power of the Holy Spirit coming into him. He obtained a clean heart,
from which perfect love had cast out all fear. And then, when shut in
prison for preaching on the street and commanded by the supreme
court of the land not to do so any more, he answered, "Whether it's
right in God's sight to listen to you rather than to God, you must judge;
for we cannot keep from speaking about what we have seen and heard"
(Acts 4:19–20 NRSV). And then, just as soon as he was released, into
the street he went again to preach the good news of salvation "to the
uttermost" (Heb. 7:25 KJV).

You could not scare Peter after that, nor could he be lifted up with
spiritual pride. For one day, after God used him to heal a lame man
and "all the people were astonished and came running," Peter saw it
and said, "Fellow Israelites, why does this surprise you? Why do you
stare at us as if by our own power or godliness we had made this man
walk? The God . . . of our fathers, has glorified his servant Jesus. . . .

By faith in the name of Jesus, this man whom you see and know was made strong. It is Jesus' name and the faith that comes through him that has completely healed him" (Acts 3:12–13, 16 NIV).

Nor did Peter have any of that ugly temper he showed when he cut off that poor fellow's ear the night Jesus was arrested, but armed himself with the mind that was in Christ (see 1 Pet. 4:1) and followed Him who left us an example that we should follow His steps.

"But we cannot have what Peter obtained on the day of Pentecost," wrote someone to me recently. However, Peter himself, in that great sermon which he preached that day, declared that we can, for he said, "You will receive the gift of the Holy Spirit. The promise is for you and your children and for all who are far off"—nineteen hundred years from now—"for all whom the Lord our God will call" (Acts 2:38–39 NIV).

Any child of God can have this. You must give yourself wholly to God and ask for it in faith. "Ask, and it will be given to you; seek, and you will find. . . . If you then, who are evil, know how to give good gifts to your children, how much more will the heavenly Father give the Holy Spirit to those who ask him!" (Luke 11:9, 13 ESV).

Seek Him with all your heart, and you shall find Him. You shall indeed, for God says so, and He is waiting to give Himself to you.

A dear young fellow, a candidate for Salvation Army ministry, felt his need of a clean heart. He went home from the holiness meeting,[4] took his Bible, knelt down by his bed, read the second chapter of Acts, and then told the Lord that he would not get up from his knees till he got a clean heart, full of the Holy Spirit. He had not prayed long before the Lord came suddenly to him and filled him with the glory of God. And his face did shine, and his testimony did burn in people's hearts after that!

You can have it, if you will go to the Lord in the Spirit and with the faith of that brother. And the Lord will do for you "immeasurably more than all [you] ask or imagine, according to the power that is at work within [you]" (Eph. 3:20 NIV).

NOTES

1. James L. Nicholson, "Whiter Than Snow," 1872, public domain.

2. William Cowper, "There Is a Fountain Filled with Blood," 1772, public domain.

3. The source for this quote is unknown.

4. *Holiness meeting* in The Salvation Army has been the name for the Sunday morning or sometimes Friday night worship service when traditionally the doctrine of holiness and exhortation to holy living has taken place.

Hindrances to Obtaining the Blessing 3

Holiness does not have legs and does not walk around, visiting idle people, as one Christian seemed to think who told me that he thought the experience would come to him someday. A Christian sister aptly remarked, "He might as well expect the church building to come to him."

The fact is, there are hindrances in the way of holiness with most people. But you who seek the experience must put from you forever the thought that any of these hindrances are in God, or in your circumstances, for they are not, but are altogether in yourselves. This being true, it is extreme folly to sit down with indifference and quietly wait with folded hands for the blessed experience to come to you. Be sure of this: it will not come, any more than a crop of potatoes will come to the lazy fellow who sits in the shade and never lifts his hoe, nor does a stroke of labor through all the spring and summer

months. The rule in the spiritual world is this: "If you don't work, you
don't eat" (2 Thess. 3:10 CEV) and "You will harvest what you plant"
(Gal. 6:7 CEV).

Therefore, the way of wisdom is to begin at once—by a diligent
study of God's Word, much secret prayer, unflinching self-examination,
rigid self-denial, hearty obedience to all present light, and a faithful
attendance at the meetings of God's people—to find out what these
hindrances are, and by the grace of God to put them away, though it
cost as much pain as to cut off a right hand or to pluck out a right
eye.

The Bible tells us—and the testimony and experience of all holy
people agree—that one great practical hindrance to holiness is
imperfect consecration.

Before a watchmaker can clean and regulate my watch, I must give
it unreservedly into his hands. Before a doctor can cure me, I must
take her medicine in the manner and at the time she requires. Before
a captain can navigate me across the trackless ocean, I must get on
board his ship and stay there. Just so, if I would have God cleanse and
regulate my heart with all its affections, if I would have Him cure my
sin-sick soul, if I would have Him take me safely across the ocean of
time into that greater ocean of eternity, I must put myself fully into His
hands and stay there. I must be perfectly consecrated to Him.

A Salvation Army captain knelt with her soldiers, and sang: "Anywhere with Jesus I will go," adding: "Anywhere but to h____, Lord."
Her consecration was imperfect, and today she is out of Salvation
Army work. There were some things she would not do for Jesus, and
therefore Jesus would not cleanse or keep her.

The other day, a poor man who had strayed from God told me that he knew, at one time, that he ought to give up tobacco. God wanted him to do so, but he held on to it and used it secretly. His imperfect consecration kept him from holiness and led to his downfall, and today he walks the streets as a common drunkard, on the open road to hell.

In his heart was secret disloyalty, and God could not cleanse or keep him. God wants perfect loyalty in the secret of your own heart, and He demands it, not only for His glory, but also for your good—for, if you can understand it, God's highest glory and your highest good are one and the same thing.

This consecration consists in a perfect putting off of your own will, disposition, temper, desires, likes, dislikes, and a perfect putting on of Christ's will, disposition, temper, desires, likes, and dislikes. In short, perfect consecration is giving up your own will in all things and receiving Jesus' will instead. This may seem impossible and disagreeable to your unsanctified heart. But if you mean business for eternity, and will intelligently and unflinchingly look at this strict gate through which so few enter, and tell the Lord that you want to go through that way though it cost you your life, the Holy Spirit will soon show you that it is not only possible but easy and delightful thus to yield yourself to God.

The second hindrance in the way of the person who would be holy is imperfect faith. When Paul wrote to the church in Thessalonica, he praised them for being "an example to all the believers in Macedonia and in Achaia," and added, "your faith in God has gone forth everywhere" (1 Thess. 1:7–8 ESV). That was the best believing church in all Europe, and so real and sturdy was their faith that they could endure much persecution. But their faith was not perfect, for Paul added, "We pray most earnestly night and day that we may see you face to face and supply what is lacking in your faith" (1 Thess. 3:10 ESV). And because of their imperfect faith they were not sanctified; so we find the apostle prayed, "May the God of peace himself sanctify you completely" (1 Thess. 5:23 ESV).

All who are born of God and have the witness of His Spirit to their justification know full well that it was not through any good works of their own, nor by growing into it, that they were saved, but it was "by grace . . . through faith" (Eph. 2:8 KJV). But very many of these dear people seem to think that we are to grow into sanctification, or are to get it by our own works. But the Lord settled that question, and made it as plain as words can make it, when He told Paul that He sent him to the Gentiles to "open their eyes, so that they may turn from darkness to light and from the power of Satan to God, that they may receive forgiveness of sins and a place among those who are sanctified by faith in me" (Acts 26:18 ESV). Not by works, nor by growth, but by faith were they to be made holy.

If you will be holy you must come to God "with a true heart in full assurance of faith" (Heb. 10:22 ESV), and then, if you will wait patiently before Him, the wonderwork shall be done.

Consecration and faith are matters of the heart, and the trouble with most people is there. But some people's trouble is with the head. They fail to get the blessing because they seek something altogether too small.

Holiness is a great blessing. It is the renewal of the whole heart and life in the image of Jesus. It is the utter destruction of all hatred, envy, malice, impatience, covetousness, pride, lust, love of ease, love of human admiration and applause, love of splendor, shame of the cross, self-will, and the like. It makes its possessors "gentle and lowly in heart" (Matt. 11:29 ESV), as Jesus was, as well as patient, kind, full of compassion and love, full of faith, benevolent, and zealous in every good word and work.

I have heard some people claim the blessing of holiness because they had given up tobacco or something of that sort while they were still impatient, unkind, or absorbed with the cares of this life. Thus, they soon got discouraged, concluded there was no such blessing, and became bitter opponents of the doctrine of holiness. Their trouble was in seeking too small a blessing. They gave up certain outward things, but the inward self-life was still uncrucified. The gold miner washes the dirt off his ore, but he cannot wash the dross out of it. The fire must do that, and then the gold will be pure. So the laying aside of outward things is necessary, but only the baptism of the Holy Spirit and of fire can purify the secret desires and affections of the heart and make it holy. And this you must earnestly seek by perfect consecration and perfect faith.

Other people fail to obtain the blessing because they seek something altogether distinct from holiness. They want a vision of heaven, of balls of fire, of some angel. Or they want an experience that will save them from all trials and temptations and from all possible mistakes and infirmities. Or they want a power that will make sinners fall as if dead when they speak.

They overlook the verse that declares, "The purpose of the commandment is love from a pure heart, from a good conscience, and from sincere faith" (1 Tim. 1:5 NKJV). That verse teaches us that holiness is nothing more than a pure heart filled with perfect love, a clear conscience toward God and others, which comes from a faithful discharge of duty and simple faith without any hypocrisy. They overlook the fact that purity and perfect love are so Christlike and so rare in this world, that they are in themselves a great, great blessing.

They overlook the fact that while Jesus was a great man, King of Kings and Lord of Lords, He was also a lowly carpenter and "emptied himself by taking the form of a slave and . . . humbled himself" (Phil. 2:7–8 CEB). They overlook the fact that they are to be—as Jesus was— "in this present world," and that "this present world" is the place of His humiliation, where He is "despised and rejected," a "man of sorrows, acquainted with deepest grief," with "nothing beautiful or majestic about his appearance, nothing to attract us to him" (Isa. 53:2–3 NLT). His only beauty in "this present world" is that inward "beauty of holiness" (1 Chron. 16:29 KJV), that humble spirit of gentleness and love, "the unfading beauty of a gentle and quiet spirit, which is so precious to God" (1 Pet. 3:4 NLT).

Is your soul hungering and thirsting for the righteousness of perfect love? Do you want to be like Jesus? Are you prepared to suffer with Him and to be hated by all for His name's sake? Then, "lay aside every weight, and the sin which so easily ensnares" you (Heb. 12:1 NKJV), present your body "a living sacrifice, holy, acceptable unto God, which is your reasonable service" (Rom. 12:1 KJV), and "run with patience the race that is set before [you], looking unto Jesus the author and finisher of [your] faith" (Heb. 12:1–2 KJV). If you will then resist all Satan's temptations to doubt, you will soon find all your hindrances gone, and yourself rejoicing "with joy inexpressible and full of glory" (1 Pet. 1:8 NKJV).

"Now may the God of peace make you holy in every way, and may your whole spirit and soul and body be kept blameless until our Lord Jesus Christ comes again. God will make this happen, for he who calls you is faithful" (1 Thess. 5:23–24 NLT).

The Temptations of the Sanctified

"How can someone who is dead to sin be tempted?" an earnest but unsanctified Christian asked me some time ago. If the very tendencies and inclinations to sin are destroyed, what is there in the person to respond to a solicitation to evil?

Everyone asks this question sooner or later, and when God showed me the answer, it threw great light on my pathway and helped me to defeat Satan in many a pitched battle.

The truly sanctified believer who is dead to sin does not have any inclinations remaining that respond to ordinary temptations. As Paul declared, "We wrestle not against flesh and blood"—against the sensual, fleshly, and worldly temptations which used to have such power over us—"but against principalities, against powers, against the rulers of the darkness of this world, against spiritual wickedness in high places" (Eph. 6:12 KJV).

If he were once a drinking man, he is no longer tempted in the least to get drunk, for he has "died" and his life "is hidden with Christ in God" (Col. 3:3 NLT). If she were ever proud and vain, delighting in dress and jewels, she is no longer allured by the cheap glitter and the vain pomp and glory of this world, for she has set her affection on things above, not on things on the earth (see Col. 3:2). If they once coveted the honor and praise of others, they now count such as dung and dross, that they may win Christ and have the honor that comes from God only. If they once desired riches and ease, they now gladly give up all earthly possessions and comforts that they may have treasure in heaven; they do not get "tied up with civilian matters, so that they can please the one who recruited them" (2 Tim. 2:4 CEB). Such things now have no more attraction for the sanctified heart than the baubles and trinkets of childhood.

I do not mean to say that Satan will never hold up any of these worldly and fleshly pleasures and honors to induce the soul to leave Christ, for he will. But I do mean to say that the soul being now dead to sin—having the very roots of sin destroyed—does not respond to the suggestion of Satan, but instantly rejects it. Satan may send along a beautiful adulteress, as he did to Joseph in Egypt, but the sanctified person will flee away and cry out, as Joseph did, "How could I do this terrible thing and sin against God?" (Gen. 39:9 CEB).

Or Satan may offer great power and honor and riches, as he did to Moses in Egypt, but comparing these with the infinite fullness of glory and power that are found in Christ, the sanctified heart will instantly reject the Devil's offer, "choosing rather to endure ill treatment with the people of God than to enjoy the passing pleasures of sin, considering the reproach of Christ greater riches than the treasures of Egypt" (Heb. 11:25–26 NASB).

Or again, Satan may tempt the sanctified person's palate with the dainty wines and rich delicacies of a king's palace, as he did Daniel in Babylon. But like Daniel, he or she will choose discipline and obedience over indulgence (see Dan. 1:8).

All these worldly baits were held out to Jesus (see Matt. 4:1–11; Luke 4:2–13), but we see in the biblical account how gloriously He triumphed over every suggestion of the Tempter. And just as He rejected Satan's temptations and gained the victory, so will sanctified men and women, for they have Christ Himself dwelling in their hearts and fighting their battles, and they can now say with the Master, "the ruler of the world is coming, and he has nothing in Me" (John 14:30 NASB).

Those who have died to sin have found such satisfaction, peace, joy, comfort, purity, and power in Christ that the power of temptation along any of the old lines is completely broken, and they now enjoy the liberty of the sons and daughters of God. They are as free as any archangel, for "if the Son sets you free, you are truly free" (John 8:36 NLT), even with "the liberty by which Christ has made us free" (Gal. 5:1 NKJV).

But while Christ has set the sanctified man or woman at liberty, and the fight against the old worldly passions and fleshly appetites is a thing of the past, a continual warfare with Satan to keep this liberty remains. This warfare is what Paul called "the good fight of faith" (1 Tim. 6:12 KJV).

The sanctified believer must fight to hold fast his or her faith in the Savior's blood, in the Spirit's sanctifying power. Although not seen by the world, this fight is as real as that of Waterloo or Gettysburg, and its far-reaching consequences for good or evil are infinitely greater.

By faith, we who are sanctified become heirs of God with Jesus Christ (see Rom. 8:17), and our faith makes this heavenly inheritance so real to us that the influence of unseen things far surpasses the influence of the things we see, hear, and handle. We say with Paul, and fully realize it in our hearts as we say it, that "the things that are seen are transient, but the things that are unseen are eternal" (2 Cor. 4:18 ESV) and will remain when "the elements shall melt with fervent heat" (2 Pet. 3:10 KJV), and "the skies roll up like a scroll" (Isa. 34:4 ESV).

These things can only be held by faith. But so long as we thus hold them, Satan's power over us is utterly broken. This the Devil knows quite well, so he begins systematic warfare against the faith of such a person.

He will accuse us of sin, when our conscience is as clear of willfully breaking God's law as is the conscience of an angel. But Satan knows that if he can get us to listen to his accusations and lose faith in the cleansing blood of Jesus, he has us at his mercy. Satan, "the accuser of our brothers and sisters" (Rev. 12:10 NLT), will then turn right around and declare that it is the Holy Spirit, instead of himself, condemning us! Here is the difference we want to notice: the Devil accuses us of sin; the Holy Spirit convicts us of sin. If I break any of God's commandments, the Holy Spirit will convict me at once. Satan will accuse me of having sinned when I have not, and he cannot prove it.

For instance, a sanctified person talks to others about their souls and urges them to give their hearts to God, but they do not. Then Satan begins to accuse the Christian: "You did not say the right things; if you had, they would have given in to God."

It is no use arguing with the Devil. The Christian can only look to the Savior and say, "Dear Lord, you know I have done the best I could. If I have done anything wrong or left anything undone, I trust Your blood to cleanse me."

If we meet Satan this way at the beginning of his accusation, our faith will gain a victory and we will rejoice in the Savior's cleansing blood and the Spirit's keeping power. But if we listen to the Devil until our conscience and faith are both wounded, it may take a long time for our faith to regain the strength that will enable us to shout and triumph over all the power of the Enemy.

When Satan has injured the faith of the sanctified individual, he will begin to blacken God's character. He will suggest to that person that the Father no longer loves him or her with that mighty love He had for His Son, Jesus; yet Jesus declares that He does. Then Satan will suggest that, maybe, the blood does not cleanse from all sin and that the Holy Spirit cannot—or at least, does not—keep anybody spotless and blameless, and that, after all, there is no such thing as a holy life down here in this world.

As a further result of this wounded faith, that person's secret prayer loses much of its blessedness; a formerly intense desire to speak to others about spiritual things will grow dull; the joy of witnessing for Christ will grow less, and dry talk will take the place of burning testimony; and the Bible will cease to be a constant source of blessing and strength. Then the Devil will tempt that soul to actual sin, through the neglect of some of these duties.

Now if that person listens to Satan and begins to doubt, does not cry mightily to God, does not search the Bible to know God's will and find His promises and plead them day and night, as Jesus did, "who in the days of his flesh . . . offered up prayers and supplications with strong crying and tears unto him that was able to save him from death" (Heb. 5:7 KJV), woe be to his or her faith! If that sanctified soul does not hurl these promises at Satan and resolutely shut his or her ears to every suggestion to doubt God, it is only a question of time until that person is numbered among those who have a reputation of life yet are dead (see Rev. 3:1), whose prayers and testimonies are lifeless, whose Bible study and exhortations and works are dead because there is no living faith in them, "having a form of godliness but denying its power" (2 Tim. 3:5 NIV), and perhaps in time even turning from the faith altogether.

What shall the sanctified person do to overcome the Devil? Listen to what Peter said: "Be sober-minded; be watchful. Your adversary the devil prowls around like a roaring lion, seeking someone to devour. Resist him, firm in your faith" (1 Pet. 5:8–9 ESV).

Hear James: "Resist the devil, and he will flee from you" (James 4:7 NLT).

Listen to Paul: "Fight the good fight of faith" (1 Tim. 6:12 KJV). "The righteous shall live by faith" (Rom. 1:17 ESV). Take "the shield of faith with which you will be able to quench all the fiery darts of the wicked one" (Eph. 6:16 NKJV).

And John: "This is the victory that has overcome the world—our faith" (1 John 5:4 ESV). "And they overcame him," (the Devil, the accuser), "by the blood of the Lamb, and by the word of their testimony; and they loved not their lives unto the death" (Rev. 12:11 KJV). They obeyed God at all costs and denied themselves to the uttermost.

And the author of Hebrews attached the same importance to testimony when saying: "Let us hold fast the confession of our hope without wavering" (Heb. 10:23 ESV).

"Take care, brothers and sisters, that none of you may have an evil, unbelieving heart that turns away from the living God" (Heb. 3:12 NRSV) and "do not throw away this confident trust in the LORD. Remember the great reward it brings you!" (Heb. 10:35 NLT).

After the Holiness Meeting 5

Did you come forward to the penitent form[1] at the holiness meeting? Did Jesus make your heart clean? Did you receive the Holy Spirit?

If you gave yourself to God in the very best way you knew but did not receive the Holy Spirit, I beg you not to be discouraged. Do not take a backward step. Stand where you are, and hold fast to your faith. The Lord means to bless you. Keep looking to Jesus, and fully expect Him to satisfy your heart's desire. Tell Him you expect it, and plead His promises. He said, "For I know the plans I have for you. . . . They are plans for good and not for disaster, to give you a future and a hope. In those days when you pray, I will listen. If you look for me wholeheartedly, you will find me. I will be found by you" (Jer. 29:11–14 NLT). This is a wonderful promise, and it is for you.

Has the Devil tempted you, more than ever, since then? Well, here is another promise for you: "Suffering one, storm-tossed, uncomforted, look, I am setting your gemstones in silvery metal and your foundations with sapphires. I will make your towers of rubies, and your gates of beryl, and all your walls of precious jewels. . . . You will be firmly founded in righteousness" (Isa. 54:11–12, 14 CEB).

God is going to do wonderful things for you, if you will not cast away your faith and your boldness.

Remember, you not only gave yourself to God, but God gave Himself to you. You did receive the Holy Spirit. When He came in, self went out. You abhorred—loathed—yourself, and sank into nothingness, while Jesus became all and in all. That is the first thing the Holy Spirit does when He comes into the heart in all His fullness—He glorifies Jesus. We see Jesus as we never saw Him before. We love Him. We adore Him. We ascribe all honor and glory and power to Him, and we realize, as we never did before, that through His precious blood we are saved and sanctified.

The Holy Spirit will not call attention to Himself, but will point to Jesus (see John 15:26; 16:13–14). Nor does He come to reveal any new truth, but rather to make us understand the old. "He will teach you all things and bring to your remembrance all that I have said to you" (John 14:26 ESV). He will make your Bible a new book to you. He will teach you how to apply it to everyday life, so that you will be safely guided by it.

The reason people get mixed up over the Bible is because they do not have the Holy Spirit. A young Christian full of the Holy Spirit can tell more about the Bible than all the doctors of divinity and theological professors in the world who are not filled with the Holy Spirit. The Holy Spirit will make you love your Bible, and you will say with Job, "I have treasured the words of His mouth more than my necessary food" (Job 23:12 NASB), and with the psalmist you will declare His judgments to be "sweeter also than honey and the honeycomb" (Ps. 19:10 KJV). No book or paper can take its place; but, like the blessed person of Psalm 1, you will "meditate [therein] day and night" (Ps. 1:2 KJV; see also Josh. 1:8). The Holy Spirit will make you tremble at the warnings of God's Word (see Isa. 66:2), exult in God's promises, and take delight in the commandments. You will say with Jesus, "No one can live only on food. People need every word that God has spoken" (Matt. 4:4 CEV). You will understand what Jesus meant when He said, "The words that I have spoken to you are spirit and life" (John 6:63 ESV).

While you walk in humble obedience and childlike faith, trusting in the blood of Jesus to cleanse you from all sin, the Comforter will abide with you, and the "low water mark" of your experience will be perfect peace. I will not dare to say what the high water mark may be! Like Paul, you may get "caught up to the third [heaven]" at times and hear "things so astounding that they cannot be expressed in words, things no human is allowed to tell" (2 Cor. 12:4 NLT). Oh, there are unspeakable breadths, lengths, depths, and heights of the love of God for you to revel in and discover by the telescope and microscope of faith! You need not fear that the experience will wear out or grow tame. God is infinite, and your little mind and heart cannot exhaust the wonders of His wisdom and goodness and grace and glory in one short lifetime.

Do not think, however, when the tide flows out to the low water mark that the Comforter has left you. I remember well how, after I had received the Holy Spirit, I walked for weeks under a weight of divine joy and glory that was almost too much for my body to bear. Then the joy began to subside, and there would be alternate days of joy and peace. And on the days when there was no special experience, the Devil would tempt me with the thought that I had in some way grieved the Holy Spirit and that He was leaving me. But God taught me that it was the Devil's lie, and I must "hold fast the profession of [my] faith without wavering" (Heb. 10:23 KJV). So I say to you, do not think that just because you are not overflowing with emotion it means He has left you. Hold fast to your faith. He is with you. After the great trouble He went through to get into your heart, He will not leave you without first letting you know just why He goes. The Holy Spirit is not capricious and fickle. He has to strive long to get into your heart, and He will strive long before He will leave it, unless you willfully harden your heart and drive Him from you.

I am not writing this, however, for those who are careless and would as soon grieve Him as not, but for you whose heart is tender, who love Him and would rather die than lose Him out of your heart. I say to you, trust Him! When I had almost yielded to Satan's lie that the Lord had left me, God gave me this text: "The people of Israel argued with Moses and tested the LORD by saying, 'Is the LORD here with us or not?'" (Ex. 17:7 NLT).

I saw that to doubt God's presence with me, even though I felt no special sign of His presence, was to tempt Him. So I promised the Lord then that I would not doubt, but would be strong in faith. He has not left me yet, and I am persuaded He never will. I can trust my wife when I cannot see her, and so I have learned to trust my Lord, even if I do not always feel the same mighty stirrings of His power in me. I tell Him that I trust Him, I believe He is with me, and I will not please the Devil by doubting.

Just at this stage, after having received the Holy Spirit, many people get confused. In time of temptation they think the Spirit has left them, and instead of trusting and acknowledging His presence and thanking Him for stooping so low as to dwell in their poor hearts, they begin to seek Him as though He had not already come, or as if He had gone away. They should stop seeking at once and start fighting the Devil by faith, telling him to get behind them, and go on praising the Lord for His presence with them. If you will seek light when you have light, you will find darkness and confusion. If you begin to seek the Holy Spirit when you already have Him, you will grieve Him. What He wants is that you have faith. Therefore, having received Him into your hearts, continually acknowledge His presence, obey Him, glory in Him, and He will abide with you forever, and His presence will be powerful in you.

Do not keep seeking and crying for more power. Rather, seek by prayer and watchfulness, the study of your Bible, and the honest improvement of every opportunity to be a perfectly free channel for the power of the Holy Spirit, who is now in you. Believe God and do not obstruct the way of the Holy Spirit, that He may work through you. Ask Him to teach and guide you, that you may not hinder Him in His work. Seek to think His thoughts, speak His words, feel His love, and exercise His faith. Seek to be so guided by Him that you will pray when He wants you to pray, sing when He wants you to sing, and last but not least be silent when He wants you to be silent. "Live in the Spirit . . . walk in the Spirit" (Gal. 5:25 KJV) and "be filled with the Spirit" (Eph. 5:18 KJV).

Finally, do not be surprised if you have very unusual temptations. Remember that it was after Jesus was baptized with the Holy Spirit that he was led into the wilderness to be tempted by the Devil for forty

days and forty nights (see Matt. 3:16–17; 4:1–3). "Disciples are not
better than their teacher" (Matt. 10:24 CEV). But when you are tempted,
"count it all joy" (James 1:2 KJV). Your very trials and temptations will
lead you into a deeper acquaintance with Jesus, for as He was, so are
you to be in this present world. Remember He said, "My grace is sufficient for you" (2 Cor. 12:9 NIV), and it is written of Him: "Since he
himself has gone through suffering and testing, he is able to help us
when we are being tested" (Heb. 2:18 NLT). "For we do not have a high
priest who is unable to empathize with our weaknesses, but we have
one who has been tempted in every way, just as we are—yet he did
not sin" (Heb. 4:15 NIV). So then, "What shall we then say to these
things? If God be for us, who can be against us?" (Rom. 8:31 KJV).

Be true. Be full of faith, and you will be able to say with Paul,
"In all these things we are more than conquerors through him that
loved us. For I am persuaded, that neither death, nor life, nor angels,
nor principalities, nor powers, nor things present, nor things to come,
nor height, nor depth, nor any other creature, shall be able to separate us from the love of God, which is in Christ Jesus our Lord"
(Rom. 8:37–39 KJV).

NOTE

1. The penitent form, also called the mercy seat, is a bench-like
furnishing at the front of Salvation Army chapels. People are invited,
usually at the conclusion of the meeting, to come, kneel, and pray
about their spiritual needs.

Fight the Good Fight of Faith 6

A friend with whom I once billeted claimed the blessing of a clean heart and testified to it at the breakfast table the next morning. He said he had doubted whether there was such an experience, but since going to The Salvation Army he had been led to study the Bible and observe the lives of those who professed the blessing, and he had come to the conclusion that he could not serve God acceptably without holiness of heart. The difficulty was to reach the point where he would take it by faith. He said he had expected to get it sometime, had hoped for it, and had looked forward to the time when he should be pure, but finally he saw that it must be claimed. And right there began his fight of faith. He took hold of one end of the promise, and the Devil got hold of the other end, and they pulled and fought for the victory.

The Devil had often gotten the victory before. This time the man would not cast away his confidence, but came "boldly unto the throne of grace" (Heb. 4:16 KJV). The Devil was conquered by faith, and the brother walked off with the blessing of a clean heart. That morning he said, "God filled me with the Spirit last night," while the glad tones of his voice and the bright light of his face backed up his words.

The last thing a soul has to give up, when seeking salvation or sanctification, is "an evil heart of unbelief" (Heb. 3:12 KJV). This is Satan's stronghold. You may drive him from all his outposts and he does not care much, but when you assail this citadel he will resist with all the lies and cunning he can command. He does not care much if people give up outward sin. A respectable sinner will suit his purpose quite as well as the most disreputable. In fact, I am not sure that some people are worse than the Devil wants them to be, for they are a bad advertisement for him. Nor does he care very much if people indulge a hope of salvation or of purity. Indeed, I suspect he likes them to do so, if he can get them to stop there. But let a poor soul say, "I want to know I am saved now. I must have the blessing now. I can't live any longer without the witness of the Spirit that Jesus saves me now, and cleanses me now," and the Devil will begin to roar and lie and use all his wits to deceive that soul and switch it onto some side track or rock it to sleep with a promise of victory at some future time.

This is where the Devil really begins. Many people who say they are fighting the Devil do not know what fighting the Devil means. It is a fight of faith in which the soul takes hold of the promise of God and holds on to it and believes it and declares it to be true in spite of all the Devil's lies—in spite of all circumstances and feelings to the contrary—and obeys God, whether God seems to be fulfilling the promise or not. When a soul gets to the point where he or she will do this, and will hold fast to the profession of faith without wavering, he or she will soon get out of the fogs and mists and twilight of doubt and uncertainty into the broad day of perfect assurance. Such a soul shall know that Jesus saves and sanctifies, and shall be filled with a humbling, yet unutterably joyful sense of God's everlasting love and favor.

A friend whom I love as my own soul sought the blessing of a clean heart and gave up everything but his "evil heart of unbelief"— but did not understand that he was still holding on to that. He waited for God to give him the blessing. The Devil whispered to him, "You say you are on the altar for God, but you don't feel any different." The "evil heart of unbelief" in the poor fellow's heart took the Devil's part and said, "That is so." So my friend felt all discouraged, and the Devil got the victory.

Again he gave himself up, after a hard struggle—all but the "evil heart of unbelief." Again the Devil whispered, "You say you are all the Lord's, but you do not feel as other folks say they felt when they yielded all to God." The "evil heart of unbelief" again said, "That's so," and again the man fell, through unbelief.

A third time, after much effort, he sought the blessing and gave God all but the "evil heart of unbelief." The third time the Devil whispered, "You say you are all the Lord's, but you know what a quick temper you have. Now, how do you know but what next week an unlooked-for temptation may come that will overthrow you?" Again the "evil heart of unbelief" said, "That's so," and for the third time my friend was beaten back from the prize.

But at last he became so desperate in his hunt for God and in his desire for holiness and the Spirit's witness that there and then he was willing for God to show him all the depravity of his soul. And God showed him that his "evil heart of unbelief" had been listening to the Devil's voice and taking the Devil's part all the time. Good people, professing Christians, do not like to admit that they have any unbelief remaining in them, but until they acknowledge all the evil that is in them and take God's part against themselves, He cannot sanctify them.

Again he came and put his all on the altar, and told God he would trust Him. Again the Devil whispered, "You don't feel any different," but this time the man hushed the evil spirit of unbelief and answered, "I do not care if I do not feel any different. I am all the Lord's."

"But you do not feel as other folks say they feel," whispered the Devil.

"I do not care if I do not. I am all the Lord's, and He can bless me or not, just as He pleases."

"But there is your quick temper."

"I do not care. I am the Lord's, and I will trust Him to manage my temper. I am the Lord's! I am the Lord's!"

And there he stood, resisting the Devil, "steadfast in the faith" (1 Pet. 5:9 NKJV), and refusing to listen to the suggestions of "an evil heart of unbelief" all that day and night and the following day. There was a stillness in his soul and a fixed determination to stand on the promises of God forever, whether God blessed him or not. About ten o'clock the second night, as he was getting ready to go to bed, without any unusual expectation or premonition, God fulfilled His ancient promise: "The Lord, whom you seek, will suddenly come to His temple" (Mal. 3:1 NKJV). Jesus, the Son of God, was revealed in him, and made known to his spiritual consciousness, until he was "lost in wonder, love and praise."[1] Oh, how he exulted and triumphed in God his Savior and rejoiced that he had held fast his faith and resisted the Devil!

Now, every soul that gets into the kingdom of God must come to this point. The soul must die to sin, renounce all unbelief, and give up all doubts. He or she must consent to be "crucified with Christ" (Gal. 2:20 KJV) now. When this is done, that soul will touch God, feel the fire of His love, and be filled with His power, as surely as an electric streetcar receives power when proper connection is made with the wire above.

May God help you to see that now is "just the right time" (2 Cor. 6:2 NLT). Remember, if you are all given up to God, everything that makes you doubt is from Satan and not from God, and God commands you to "resist the devil and stay strong in your faith" (1 Pet. 5:9 CEV); "do not cast away your confidence, which has great reward" (Heb. 10:35 NKJV).

NOTE

1. Charles Wesley, "Love Divine, All Loves Excelling," 1747, public domain.

The Heart of Jesus 7

We sang the following verse with all our might one morning when I was a cadet (student) in The Salvation Army training school:

> Give me a heart like Thine;
> By Thy wonderful power,
> By Thy grace every hour,
> Give me a heart like Thine.[1]

In one of those hours of heart humbling and heart searching, at least one of the cadets looked through the words and caught the spirit of the song. He came to me at the close of the meeting with a serious look and a tone of earnest inquiry and asked, "Do we really mean it, that we can have a heart like His?" I told him that I was certain we could and that the dear Lord wanted to give us hearts just like His own—

A humble, lowly, contrite heart,

Believing, true, and clean.

A heart in every thought renewed,

And full of love Divine;

Perfect and right and pure and good,

A copy, Lord, of Thine.[2]

Indeed, Jesus was "the firstborn among many brothers and sisters" (Rom. 8:29 NLT). He is our "elder brother" (see Heb. 2:10–11) and we are to be like Him. "As he is, so are we in this world" (1 John 4:17 KJV), and "Those who say they live in God should live their lives as Jesus did" (1 John 2:6 NLT). Now, it is impossible for us to walk like Him, to live like Him, unless we have a heart like His.

We cannot bear the same kind of fruit unless we are the same kind of tree. So Jesus wants to make us like Himself. We judge trees by their fruit, and so we judge Jesus, and then we can find out what kind of a heart He had. Let us judge and consider what His heart was.

We find love in Him; therefore Jesus had a loving heart. He bore the luscious fruit of perfect love. There was no hatred with His love, no venom, no spite, no selfishness. He loved His enemies and prayed for His murderers. It was not a fickle love, but a changeless, eternal love. "I have loved you with an everlasting love" (Jer. 31:3 ESV), God says. How marvelous that is!

It is just this kind of love He wants us to have. He said, "A new commandment I give to you, that you love one another: just as I have loved you" (John 13:34 ESV). That is tremendous, to command me to love my brothers and sisters even as Jesus loves me. But that is what He says, and to do that I must have a heart like Jesus.

I know if we examine love we find that it includes all the other graces; but we will look into the heart of Jesus for some of them.

Jesus had a humble heart. He said of Himself, "I am humble and gentle at heart" (Matt. 11:29 NLT). Paul told us that He "made himself nothing by taking the very nature of a servant" (Phil. 2:7 NIV).

He did humble Himself, for, though He is the Lord of life and glory, He stooped to be born of a lowly virgin in a manger, worked as an unknown carpenter for thirty years, and chose to live with the poor, ignorant, and vile instead of the rich, noble, and learned. While Jesus never seemed ill at ease or constrained in the presence of those who were mighty with this world's greatness or wise with its learning, His simple, humble heart found its mates among the lowly, hardworking, common people. He cleaved to them. He would not be lifted up. They wanted to do it for Him, but He slipped away for prayer among the mountains and then returned and preached such a straight sermon that nearly all His disciples left Him.

Just before His death, He took the menial place of a slave, washed His disciples' feet, and then said, "I have given you an example, that you also should do just as I have done to you" (John 13:15 ESV).

How that helped me in The Salvation Army training school! My second day there they sent me into a dark little cellar to blacken half a cartload of dirty boots for the other cadets. The Devil came at me and reminded me that a few years before I had graduated from a university, had attended a leading theological school, had been pastor of a metropolitan church, had just left evangelistic work in which I saw hundreds seeking the Savior, and that now I was only blacking boots for a lot of ignorant lads. But I reminded my old Enemy of my Lord's example, and the Devil left me. Jesus said, "Now that you know these things, you will be blessed if you do them" (John 13:17 NIV). I was doing them; the Devil knew it and left me alone, and I was happy. That little cellar was changed into one of heaven's anterooms, and my Lord visited me there.

"God opposes the proud but shows favor to the humble" (James 4:6 NIV). If you would have a heart like that of Jesus, it will be one filled with humility. It will be a heart that "is not puffed up," that "does not seek its own" (1 Cor. 13:4–5 NKJV). So as Peter said, "Be clothed with humility" (1 Pet. 5:5 KJV).

Jesus had a meek and gentle heart. Paul spoke of "the meekness and gentleness of Christ" (2 Cor. 10:1 KJV). Peter told us that "when he was reviled, he did not revile in return; when he suffered, he did not threaten" (1 Pet. 2:23 ESV). He did not strike back when He was injured. He did not try to justify Himself, but committed His cause to His heavenly Father.

That was the very perfection of meekness, that not only would He not strike back when He was lied about, but suffered the most cruel and shameful wrongs. "Out of the abundance of the heart the mouth speaks" (Matt. 12:34 NKJV), and because meekness filled His blessed heart He did not thunder back at His enemies.

It is just this kind of heart He wants us to have: "Do not resist an evildoer. But if anyone strikes you on the right cheek, turn the other also . . . and if anyone forces you to go one mile, go also the second mile" (Matt. 5:39, 41 NRSV).

I know a brother of African descent, over six feet tall with a full chest and brawny arms, who was recently put off a streetcar in the most indecent and brutal manner, where he had as much right to be as the conductor. Someone asked, "Why don't you fight him, George?" "I couldn't fight him," replied George. "For God has taken all the fight out of me. When you put your knife in the fire and draw the temper out of it, it won't cut," he added, and he fairly shouted for joy.

"Blessed are the meek" (Matt. 5:5 KJV), for "he crowns the humble with victory" (Ps. 149:4 NLT).

NOTES

1. Homer A. Rodeheaver, "Give Me a Heart Like Thine," 1922, public domain.

2. Charles Wesley, "O for a Heart to Praise My God," 1742, public domain.

The Secret of Power 8

If I were dying and had the privilege of delivering a last exhortation to all the Christians of the world, and that message had to be condensed into three words, I would say, "Wait on God!"

Wherever I go, I find people—from various church backgrounds— falling away from faith by the thousands, until my heart aches as I think of the great army of discouraged souls, of the way in which the Holy Spirit has been grieved, and of the way in which Jesus has been treated.

If these wayward ones were asked the cause of their present condition, ten thousand different reasons would be given. But, after all, there is only one, and that is this: they did not wait on God. If they had waited on Him when the fierce assault was made that overthrew their faith and robbed them of their courage and bankrupted their love, they would have renewed their strength and mounted over all obstacles as though on eagles' wings. They would have run through their enemies and not been weary. They would have walked in the midst of trouble and not fainted.

Waiting on God means more than a prayer of thirty seconds on getting up in the morning and going to bed at night. It may mean one prayer that gets hold of God and comes away with the blessing, or it may mean a dozen prayers that knock and persist and will not be put off until God arises and bares His arm on behalf of the pleading soul.

There is a drawing near to God—a knocking at heaven's doors, a pleading of the promises, a reasoning with Jesus, a forgetting of self, a turning from all earthly concerns, a holding on with determination to never let go—that puts all the wealth of heaven's wisdom and power and love at our disposal, little though we may be, so that we shout and triumph when all others tremble and fail and fly, and become more than conquerors in the very face of death and hell.

It is in the heat of just such seasons of waiting on God that every great soul gets the wisdom and strength that make it an astonishment to others. They, too, might be "great in the sight of the Lord" (Luke 1:15 KJV), if they would wait on God and be true instead of getting excited and running here and there for help when the testing times come.

The psalmist had been in great trouble, and this is what he said of his deliverance: "I waited patiently for the LORD to help me, and he turned to me and heard my cry. He lifted me out of the pit of despair, out of the mud and the mire. He set my feet on solid ground and steadied me as I walked along. He has given me a new song to sing, a hymn of praise to our God. Many will see what he has done and be amazed. They will put their trust in the LORD" (Ps. 40:1–3 NLT).

I went to a poor little corps (The Salvation Army church) where nearly everything had been going wrong. Many were cold and discouraged, but I found one sister with a wondrous glory in her face, and glad, sweet praises in her mouth. She told me how she had looked at others falling around her, had seen the carelessness of many, and had noted the decline of vital piety in the corps, until her heart ached and she felt disheartened and her feet almost slipped. But she went to God and got down low before Him. She prayed and waited until He drew near to her and showed her the awful precipice on which she herself was standing. He showed her that her one business was to follow Jesus, to walk before Him with a perfect heart, and to cleave to Him, though the whole corps lost faith. Then she renewed her covenant until an unutterable joy came to her heart and God put His fear in her soul and filled her with the glory of His presence.

She told me that the next day she fairly trembled to think of the awful danger she had been in and declared that that time of waiting on God in the silence of the night saved her, and now her heart was filled with the full assurance of hope for herself, and not only for herself, but also for the corps. Oh, for ten thousand more like her!

David said, "My soul, wait silently for God alone, for my expectation is from Him" (Ps. 62:5 NKJV). Again he declared: "I wait for the LORD, my whole being waits, and in his word I put my hope. I wait for the LORD more than watchmen wait for the morning" (Ps. 130:5–6 NIV). And David sent out this ringing exhortation and note of encouragement to you and me: "Wait patiently for the LORD. Be brave and courageous. Yes, wait patiently for the LORD" (Ps. 27:14 NLT).

The secret of all failures—and all true success—is hidden in the attitude of the soul in its private walk with God. We who courageously wait on God are bound to succeed. We cannot fail. To others we may appear for the present to fail, but in the end they will see what we knew all the time: that God was with us, making us successful, in spite of all appearances (see Gen. 39:2).

Jesus put the secret into these words: "When you pray, go into your room and shut the door and pray to your Father who is in secret. And your Father who sees in secret will reward you" (Matt. 6:6 ESV).

Know, then, that all failure has its beginning in the closet, in neglecting to wait on God until filled with wisdom, clothed with power, and all on fire with love.

The Leakage of Spiritual Power

9

James Caughey, a man of God and lover of souls, told in one of his books how he was invited out to tea one evening and, though there was nothing harmful in the talk of the hour, when he went into the revival meeting at night his soul was like a loosely strung bow. He couldn't shoot the King's arrows into the hearts of the King's enemies, for he had no power. It had been lost at the tea table.[1]

I knew an officer (The Salvation Army minister) once who let all his spiritual power leak out until he was as dry as an old bone when he got into the meeting. It was in this way. We had to ride three miles in a street car to get to the hall, and all the way there he was talking about things that had no bearing upon the coming meeting. Nothing wrong or trifling was said, but it was not to the point; it turned his mind from God and the souls he was so soon to face and plead with to be reconciled to God. The result was that instead of going before the people clothed with power, he went stripped of power. I remember the meeting well. His prayer was good, but there was no power in it. It was words, words, words! The Bible reading and talk were good. He said many true and excellent things, but there was no power in them. The soldiers (church members) looked indifferent, the others in attendance looked careless and sleepy, and altogether the meeting was a dull affair.

That officer had not faltered in his faith; he had a good experience. Nor was he unintelligent; on the contrary, he was one of the brightest, keenest officers I know. The trouble was that, instead of keeping quiet and communing with God in his own heart on that car, until his soul was ablaze with faith and hope and love and holy expectation, he had wasted his power in useless talk.

God says, "If you speak good words rather than worthless ones, you will be my spokesman" (Jer. 15:19 NLT). Think of it! That officer might have gone into that meeting filled with power. His mouth should have been to those people as the mouth of God, and his words would have been "living and powerful, and sharper than any two-edged sword, piercing even to the division of soul and spirit, and of joints and marrow," and proving to be "a discerner of the thoughts and intents of the heart" (Heb. 4:12 NKJV). But instead of that, he was like Samson after his locks were shorn by Delilah—as powerless as anyone else.

There are many ways of letting spiritual power leak away. I knew a soldier who came to The Salvation Army meeting hall very early every evening, and instead of getting his soul keyed up to a high pitch of faith and love, spent the time playing soft, dreamy music on his

violin, and though faithfully, lovingly warned, continued that practice till he lost his faith.

I have also known people whose power leaked out through a joke.
They believed in making things lively, so they told funny stories and
played the clown. And things were lively, but it was not with divine
life. It was the liveliness of mere animal spirits, and not of the Holy
Spirit. I do not mean by this that someone who is filled with the power
of the Spirit will never make others laugh. He or she will and may
say tremendously funny things. But this person will not be doing it
just to have a good time. It will come naturally, and it will be done in
the fear of God and not in a spirit of lightness and jesting.

There is no substitute for the Holy Spirit. He is life. He is power.
And if He is sought in earnest, faithful prayer, He will come, and when
He comes the little meeting will be mighty in its results.

The Holy Spirit should be sought in earnest, secret prayer. Jesus
said, "When you pray, go away by yourself, shut the door behind you,
and pray to your Father in private. Then your Father, who sees everything, will reward you" (Matt. 6:6 NLT). He will do it.

I know of a man who, if possible, gets alone with God for an hour
before every meeting, and when he speaks it is with the power and
demonstration of the Spirit.

People who want power when it is most needed must walk with
God. They must be friends of God. They must keep the way always
open between their hearts and God. God will be the friend of such
souls and will bless and honor them. God will tell them His secrets.
He will show them how to appeal to the hearts of others. God will
make dark things light, crooked places straight, and rough places

smooth for such men and women. God will be on their side and help them.

Such a man or woman must keep a constant watch over the mouth and the heart. David prayed, "Set a watch, O LORD, before my mouth; keep the door of my lips" (Ps. 141:3 KJV). And Solomon said, "Guard your heart above all else, for it determines the course of your life" (Prov. 4:23 NLT). We must walk in unbroken communion with God. We must cultivate a spirit of joyful recollection by which we will be always conscious that we are in God's presence.

"Take delight in the LORD," said the psalmist, "and he will give you your heart's desires" (Ps. 37:4 NLT). Oh, how happy are they who find God to be their delight, who are never lonely, because they know God, talk with God, and delight in God. Happy are they who feel how lovable God is and give themselves up to loving, serving, and trusting God with all their hearts!

Brothers and sisters, "Do not stifle the Holy Spirit" (1 Thess. 5:19 NLT), and He will lead you thus to know and love God, and God will make you the instrument of His own power.

NOTE

1. This is most likely in reference to chapter 44 in James Caughey, *Showers of Blessing from Clouds of Mercy* (Boston: J. P. Magee, 1857), 325–327.

The Person God Uses

10

A while ago I was talking with a Christian merchant who expressed a great and important truth. He said, "People are crying to God to use them, but He cannot. They are not given up to Him. They are not humble and teachable and holy. There are plenty of people who come to me and want work in my store, but I cannot use them; they are not fit for my work. When I must have someone, I have to go and advertise, and sometimes spend days in trying to find a man who will fit into the place I want him for, and then I have to try him and prove him to know whether he will suit me or not."

The fact is, God is using everyone He can and using them to the full extent of their fitness for His service. So instead of praying so much to be used, people should search themselves to know whether they are usable.

God cannot use anybody and everybody who comes along any more than the merchant could. Only those who are "holy, useful to the Master and prepared to do any good work" (2 Tim. 2:21 NIV) can He bless with great usefulness.

God wants men and women, and He is hunting for them everywhere. But like the merchant, He has to pass by hundreds before He finds the right individuals. The Bible says, "For the eyes of the LORD run to and fro throughout the whole earth, to shew himself strong in the behalf of them whose heart is perfect toward him" (2 Chron. 16:9 KJV).

Oh, how God wants to use you! But before you ask Him again to do so, see to it that your heart is perfect toward Him. Then you may depend upon it that God will show Himself strong on your behalf.

When God searches for a man or woman to work in His vineyard, He does not ask, "Has he great natural abilities? Is she thoroughly educated? Is he a fine singer? Is she eloquent in prayer?"

Rather, He asks, "Is his heart perfect toward Me? Is she holy? Does he love much? Is she willing to walk by faith and not by sight? Does he love Me so much and has he such childlike confidence in My love for him that he can trust Me to use him when he doesn't see any sign that I am using him? Will she be weary and faint when I correct her and try to fit her for greater usefulness? Or will she, like Job, cry out, 'Though he slay me, yet will I trust in him' (Job 13:15 KJV)? Does he search My Word, and 'meditate on it day and night' in order to 'be sure to obey everything written in it' (Josh. 1:8 NLT)? Does he wait on Me for My counsel and seek in everything to be led by My Spirit? Or is he stubborn and self-willed, like the horse and the mule, which have to be held in with bit and bridle, so that I cannot 'guide him with mine eye' (Ps. 32:8 KJV)? Is she a people-pleaser and a time-server, or is she willing to wait for her reward, seeking solely for 'the honor that comes from the only God' (John 5:44 NKJV)? Does he 'preach the word' and is he 'ready in season and out of season' (2 Tim. 4:2 NASB)? Is she meek and lowly in heart and humble?"

When God finds someone like that, He will use him or her. God and that person will have such a friendly understanding with each other and such mutual sympathy and love and confidence that they will at once become partners (see 2 Cor. 6:1).

Paul was a man God used, and the more his persecutors whipped and stoned him and tried to rid the earth of him, the more God used him. At last they shut him up in prison, but Paul declared with unshaken faith, "I am suffering, bound with chains as a criminal. But the word of God is not bound!" (2 Tim. 2:9 ESV). And so he spoke God's Word, and neither devils nor mortals could shackle it, but it pierced right through the prison walls and flew across oceans and continents and down through the long centuries, bearing the glorious tidings of the blessed gospel, overthrowing thrones and kingdoms and powers of evil, and everywhere bringing light and comfort and salvation to dark, troubled, sinful hearts. Though more than eighteen hundred years have passed since they cut off Paul's head and thought they were done with him forever, yet his usefulness increases and his mighty words and works are today bearing such fruit to the good of humanity and the glory of God as passes the comprehension of an archangel.

Oh, how surprised Paul will be when he receives his final reward at the general judgment day and enters into possession of all the treasures he has laid up in heaven and the everlasting inheritance prepared for him!

Poor, troubled soul, cheer up! You think you are useless, but be of good courage! Trust God!

Paul saw dark days. He wrote to Timothy and said, "As you know, everyone from the province of Asia has deserted me" (2 Tim. 1:15 NLT). Study Paul's life in the Acts and the Epistles and see what conflicts and discouragements he had, and take courage!

Jesus said, "Anyone who believes in me may come and drink! For the Scriptures declare, 'Rivers of living water will flow from his heart.' (When he said 'living water,' he was speaking of the Spirit, who would be given to everyone believing in him)" (John 7:38–39 NLT).

See to it that you are a believer. See to it that you are "filled with the Holy Spirit" (Eph. 5:18 NLT), and Jesus will see to it that out of your life shall flow rivers of holy influence and power to bless the world. And you, too, will be surprised, at the reckoning day, to behold the vastness of your reward as compared with the littleness of your sacrifices and your work.

Your Own Soul 11

I was once asked, "Cannot one take too much care of one's own soul? I see all about me, everywhere, so much sorrow and suffering and injustice that I am perplexed at God's way of ruling the world, and it seems to me as though every Christian ought to be trying to help others instead of looking out for one's own soul."

This is a common perplexity. We see all around us sorrow and suffering which we cannot help, and our perplexity at the sight is the Lord's prompting for us to take the very uttermost care of our own souls, lest we stumble and fall through doubt and discouragement.

By the care of your soul I do not mean that you should coddle and pet and pity yourself, nor work yourself up into some pleasant feeling. I mean that you should pray and pray and pray and seek the presence and teaching of the Holy Spirit, until light and strength fill your soul such that you may have unquestioning faith in the wisdom and love of God, you may have unwearied patience in learning His will (see Heb. 6:12), and your love may be equal to the great need you see all about you.

Maybe you are troubled by the sight of unhelped wretchedness near you. No living soul can answer to your satisfaction the questions that will rise up within you nor counter the suggestions of Satan as you look on the world's misery. But the blessed Comforter will satisfy your heart and your head if you have the faith and patience to wait while He teaches you "all things" and leads you "into all truth" (John 16:13 KJV).

"They who wait for the LORD shall renew their strength" (Isa. 40:31 ESV). You cannot help people if you go to them robbed of your strength because of doubts, fears, and perplexities. So, wait on God till He strengthens your heart.

Do not become impatient. Do not try beforehand to find out what God will say or just how He will say it. He will surely teach you, but you must let Him do it in His own way, and then you will be able to help people with all the might and wisdom of Jehovah.

You must trust His love and abide His time, but you also must wait on Him and expect Him to teach you. If the king or queen of England is coming to Windsor Castle, the servants do not lie around listlessly nor hunt up a lot of work to do; everyone stands in his or her own place and waits with eager expectancy. This is what I mean by waiting upon God. You cannot do too much of this kind of taking care of your own soul, and do not let anyone drive you from it by ridicule or entreaty.

The woodsman would be very foolish who thought he had so much wood to cut that he could not take time to grind his ax. The servant who went to the city to buy things for her master would be useless if she was in such a hurry that she did not come to her master for orders and the needed money. How much worse are those who attempt to do God's work without God's direction and God's strength!

One morning, after a half-night of prayer which I led, and in which I had worked very hard, I got up early to ensure an hour with God and my Bible, and God blessed me till I wept. An officer (minister) who was with me was much moved and then confessed, "I do not often find God in prayer—I have not time." People who do not find God in prayer must hinder His cause instead of helping it.

Take time. Miss breakfast if necessary, but take time to wait on God, and when God has come and blessed you, then go to the miserable ones around you and pour upon them the wealth of joy, love, and peace God has given you. But do not go until you know you are going in His power.

I once heard William Booth say in a gathering of officers, "Take time to pray God's blessing down on your own soul every day. If you do not, you will lose God. God is leaving men every day. They once had power. They walked in the glory and strength of God but they ceased to wait on Him and earnestly seek His face, and He left them. I am a very busy man, but I take time to get alone with God every day and commune with Him."

Paul said, "Keep watch over yourselves and over all the flock, of which the Holy Spirit has made you overseers" (Acts 20:28 NRSV). And again, "Pay close attention to yourself and to your teaching; persevere in these things, for as you do this you will ensure salvation both for yourself and for those who hear you" (1 Tim. 4:16 NASB).

Paul did not mean to promote selfishness by telling us to first take heed to ourselves. But he did mean to teach that, unless we do take heed to ourselves and are full of faith, hope, and love in our own souls, we shall be unable to help others.

Gideon's Band 12

One hundred and twenty thousand Midianites had come up to fight against Israel, and thirty-two thousand Israelites rose up to fight for their wives, children, homes, liberty, and lives. But God saw that if one Israelite whipped nearly four Midianites, he would be so puffed up with pride and conceit that he would forget God, and say, "My own hand has saved me" (Judg. 7:2 ESV).

The Lord also knew that there were a lot of weak-kneed followers with cowardly hearts among them, who would like an excuse to run away. So He told Gideon to say, "Whoever is fearful and trembling, let him return home and hurry away" (Judg. 7:3 ESV). The sooner fearful folks leave us the better. "Then 22,000 of the people returned, and 10,000 remained" (Judg. 7:3 ESV). They were afraid to show the enemy their faces, but they were not ashamed to show them their backs.

But the Lord saw that if one Israelite whipped twelve Midianites he would be even more puffed up, so he made a further test.

He said to Gideon, "The people are still too many. Take them down to the water, and I will test them for you there" (Judg. 7:4 ESV). God often tries people at the table and the teapot.

So he brought the people down to the water. And the LORD said to Gideon, "Every one who laps the water with his tongue, as a dog laps, you shall set by himself. Likewise, every one who kneels down to drink." And the number of those who lapped, putting their hands to their mouths, was 300 men, but all the rest of the people knelt down to drink water. And the LORD said to Gideon, "With the 300 men who lapped I will save you and give the Midianites into your hand, and let all the others go every man to his home." (Judg. 7:5–7 ESV)

These three hundred men meant business. They were not only unafraid, but they were also not self-indulgent. They knew how to fight, but they knew something even more important—how to deny themselves. They knew how to deny themselves, not only when there was very little water, but when a river rolled at their feet. They were no doubt quite as thirsty as the others, but they did not throw down their arms and fall down on their faces to drink while in the presence of the enemy. They stood up, kept their eyes open, watched the enemy, and kept one hand on shield and bow, while with the other they brought water to their thirsty lips. The other fellows were not afraid to fight, but they would drink first, even if the enemy did steal a march on them while they were prostrate on the ground satisfying their thirst. Number one must be cared for, even if the army was crushed. They were self-indulgent and never dreamed of denying themselves for the common good, so God sent them home along with those who were afraid, and with the three hundred He routed the Midianites. That was one to four hundred. No chance of self-conceit there! They won the victory and became immortal, but God got the glory.

There are fearful people who cannot face a laugh or a sneer, much less a determined foe. If they cannot be led to lay hold of the strength and boldness of the Lord, the sooner they quit the field, the better. Let them go back to their spouses, children, and parents.

But there are many who are not afraid. They rather enjoy a fight. They would just as soon march in the streets, face a mob, and sing and pray and testify in the presence of enemies as they would stay at home—perhaps more so. But they are self-indulgent. If they like a thing they must have it, however much it may hurt them and make them unfit for the fight.

I am acquainted with some people who know that tea, cake, and candy injure them, but they like these things, and so they indulge themselves at the risk of grieving the Spirit of God and destroying their health, which is the capital God has given them to do His work with.

I know some people who ought to know that a big supper before a worship service or evangelistic meeting taxes the digestive organs, draws the blood from the head to the stomach, and makes one drowsy, dull, and heavy. Thus it unfits the soul to feel spiritual realities keenly and to stand between God and the people, pleading with God in mighty, believing, Elijah-like prayer, and prevailing with the people

in clear testimony and burning exhortation. But they are hungry. They
like such things, and so they tickle their palate with the things they like,
punish their stomachs, spoil their meetings, disappoint the starving,
hungry souls of the people, and grieve the Holy Spirit—all to gratify
their appetites.

I know people who cannot watch with Jesus through a half-night
of prayer without buns and coffee. Imagine Jacob in that desperate
all-night of prayer wrestling with the angel for the blessing before
meeting his injured brother Esau in the morning, stopping to have
buns and coffee! If his soul had been no more desperate than that, he
could have had his buns, but on his return to wrestle he would have
found the angel gone. And the next morning, instead of learning that
the angel who had disjointed his thigh (but left his blessing) had also
melted Esau's hard heart, he would have found an angry brother, who
would have been ready to carry out his threat of twenty years before
and take his life. But Jacob was desperate. He wanted God's blessing
so much that he forgot all about his body. In fact, he prayed so earnestly
that his thigh was put out of joint, and he did not complain. He had
gained the blessing.

When Jesus prayed, agonized, and sweated great drops of blood in
the garden, His disciples slept, and He was grieved that they could not
watch with Him one hour. And He must be grieved today that so many
cannot, or will not, watch with Him and so deny their inmost self to win
victory over the powers of hell and snatch souls from the bottomless pit.

We read of Daniel, that for three long weeks he ate no pleasant
food, but gave himself to prayer during all the time he possibly could,
so eager was he to know the will of God and get the blessing. And he

got it. One day God sent an angel who said to him, "O man greatly beloved" (Dan. 10:19 KJV) and then told him all he wanted to know.

In Acts 14:23, we read that Paul and Barnabas prayed and fasted—not feasted—that the people might be blessed before they left the churches of Asia Minor. They were greatly interested in the souls they left behind them.

We know that Moses, Elijah, and Jesus fasted and prayed for forty days and, immediately after, mighty works were done.

And so, all mighty men and women of God have learned to deny themselves and keep their bodies under discipline, and God has set their souls on fire, helped them to win victory against all odds, and blessed the whole world.

We should not deny ourselves food and drink to the injury of our bodies. But one night of watching and fasting and praying can starve no one. And those who are willing to forget their bodies occasionally for a short time, in the interest of their own souls and the souls of others, will reap blessings which will amaze them and all who know them.

But this self-restraint must be constant. It will not do to fast all night and feast all the next day. The apostle Paul wrote of being "temperate in all things" (1 Cor. 9:25 KJV)—and he might have added, "at all times."

Again, Gideon's band did some night work, or early morning work. They got ahead of their enemies by getting up early (see Judg. 7:19).

People who indulge their bodies in food and drink also usually indulge them in sleep. They eat late at night and sleep heavily and lazily the next morning, and usually need a cup of strong coffee or tea to clear their heads. By getting up late, the work of the day crowds upon them and they have almost no time to praise the Lord, pray, and read the Bible. Then the day's cares press upon them and their hearts get full of things other than the joy of the Lord. Jesus must wait till they have done everything else before He can catch their ear, and so their day is spoiled.

Oh, that they knew the advantage, the luxury, the hilarious joy of early rising to fight the Midianites! It seems that Gideon, the captain, was up and about all night. He roused his people early, and they had the Midianites all whipped and scattered before dawn.

Four hundred devils cannot stand before the man or woman who makes it a rule of life to get up early to praise the Lord and plead for God's blessing on his or her own soul and on the world. They will flee away.

John Fletcher used to mourn if he knew of a laborer getting out to his daily toil before he himself was up praising God and fighting the Devil. He said, "What! Does that man's earthly master deserve more ready service than my heavenly Master?" Another old saint lamented greatly if he heard the birds singing before he got up to praise God.

We read that Jesus arose early and went out alone to pray. Joshua, we learn, got up early in the morning to set battle in array against Jericho and Ai.

John Wesley went to bed at ten o'clock sharp—unless he had an all-night prayer—and woke promptly at four. Six hours of sleep was all he wanted. And when he was eighty-two years old, he said he was a wonder to himself, for during the twelve years previous he had not been sick a day, nor felt weary, nor lost an hour's sleep, although he traveled thousands of miles each year, in winter and summer, on horseback and in carriages, as he preached hundreds of sermons, and did work that not one in a thousand could do. All of this he attributed to the blessing of God on his simple, plain way of living and to a clear conscience. He was a very wise and useful man, and he considered the matter of such grave importance that he wrote and published a sermon on "Redeeming the Time" from sleep.

A captain (experienced officer) in The Salvation Army wrote me the other day that he had begun to do his praying in the morning when his mind was fresh and before the cares of the day had begun to rush in on him.

It means more to belong to Gideon's band than most people ever dreamed of, but I have joined it, and my soul is on fire. It is a joy to live and belong to such a company.

The Chained Ambassador 13

My soul was stirred the other morning by Paul's appeal for the prayers of the church, in which he declared himself to be "an ambassador in chains" (Eph. 6:20 ESV).

You know what an ambassador is—a person who represents one government to another. The person of such a man or woman is considered sacred. Their words are powerful. The dignity and authority of their country and government stands behind them. Any injury or indignity to them is an injury and indignity to the country they represent.

Now Paul was an ambassador of heaven, representing the Lord Jesus Christ to the people of this world. But instead of being respected and honored, he was thrust into prison and chained between two ignorant, and probably brutal, Roman soldiers.

What stirred me was the quenchless zeal of the man and the work he did in the circumstances. Most Christians would have considered their

work done or, at least, broken off till they were free again. But not so
with Paul. From his prison and chains, he sent forth a few letters that
have blessed the world and will bless it to the end of time. He also taught
us that there is a ministry of prayer, as well as of more active work. We
live in an age of restless work and rush and excitement, and we need to
learn this lesson.

Paul was the most active of all the apostles—"in labours more
abundant" (2 Cor. 11:23 KJV)—and it seemed as if he could hardly be
spared from the oversight of the new Christians and the new churches
he had so recently opened, which were in such desperate circumstances and surrounded by implacable enemies. But as he was set to
be the chief exponent of the doctrines of the gospel of Christ, so he
was set to be the chief exponent of its saving and sanctifying power
under the most trying conditions.

It is difficult—if not impossible—to conceive of a trial to which
Paul was not subjected, from being worshiped as a god to being
whipped and stoned as the vilest slave. But he declared that none of
these things moved him. He had learned in whatsoever state he was
to be content (see Phil. 4:11), and he triumphantly wrote at the end of
his life, "I have fought the good fight, I have finished the race, and I
have remained faithful" (2 Tim. 4:7 NLT). He did not lose faith. He
did not even murmur, but kept on his way, trusting in the love of Jesus,
and, through faith in Him, coming off more than a conqueror.

Many have fairly well learned the lessons of activity Paul taught
us, but it will be well for us all to learn the lessons his imprisonment
teaches us. Doubly important is it for those who are sick or recover-
ing to learn these lessons. We get impatient of waiting, are tempted to

murmur and repine, and imagine that we can do nothing. But the fact is, God may possibly use us more widely in prayer and praise, if we will believe and rejoice and watch and pray in the Holy Spirit, than if He used us at the head of a battalion of soldiers. We should watch over in prayer those who are at work and for those in need of the salvation of God.

I write from experience. For eighteen months, I was laid aside with a broken head. God put His chain on me, and I had to learn the lessons of a passive ministry of prayer, praise, and patience, or lose faith altogether. It seemed as if I should never be able to work any more. But I did not lose faith. God helped me to nestle down into His will, and, like David, to behave and quiet myself, as a child weaned of his mother, until my soul was even as a weaned child (see Ps. 131:2). Yet my heart longed for the glory of God and the salvation of nations, and I prayed, watched reports of the salvation war, studied the needs of some parts of the world, and prayed on until I knew God heard and answered me. And my heart was made as glad as though I had been in the thick of the fight.

During that time I read of a great country, and my heart ached, burned, and longed for God to send salvation there. In secret and in family prayer, I poured out my heart to God, and I knew He heard and would yet do great things for that dark, sad country. Shortly after this, I learned of dreadful persecutions and the banishment of many simple, earnest Christians to this country, and while I was greatly grieved at their sufferings, yet I thanked God that He was taking this way to get the light of His glorious salvation into that loveless, needy land.

The fact is, sick and resting saints of God can move Him to bless the world if they have faith and will storm heaven with continuous prayers.

There are more ways to chain God's ambassadors than between Roman soldiers in Roman dungeons. If you are hopelessly sick, you are chained. If you are shut in by family cares and claims, you are chained. But remember Paul's chain, and take courage.

I sometimes hear those who have deserted their posts and lost their ministry lamenting their sad fate and declaring they can do nothing. Let them bow beneath God's judgment, kiss the hand that smites them, and no longer chafe under the chain that binds them, but cheerfully and patiently begin to exercise themselves in the ministry of prayer. If they are faithful, God may yet unloose their chain and let them out into the happier ministry of work. Esau sold his birthright for a mess of pottage and missed the mighty blessing he should have had—but he still received a blessing (see Gen. 27:38–40).

If we really long to see God's glory and souls saved rather than just to have a good time, why should we not be content to lie on a sickbed or stand by a loom and pray, as well as to stand on a platform and preach, if God will bless one as much as the other?

The man or woman on the platform can *see* much of the work and its fruit; the prayer warrior can only feel it. But the certainty of being in touch with God and being used by Him may be as great as or greater than that of one who sees with the eye. Many a revival has had its secret source in the closet of some poor washerwoman or blacksmith who prayed in the Holy Spirit but was chained to a life of desperate daily toil. The person on the platform gets glory on earth, but the neglected, unknown, or despised chained ambassador who prayed will share largely in the general triumph, and, it may be, will march by the King's side while the preacher comes on behind.

God sees not as we see. He looks at the heart, regards His children's cry, and marks for future glory and renown and boundless reward all those who cry and sigh for His honor and the salvation of souls.

God could have loosed Paul, but He did not choose to do so. But Paul did not grumble, sulk, fall into despair, or lose his joy and peace and faith and power. He prayed and rejoiced and believed. He thought about the poor little struggling churches and the weak souls he had left behind. He wrote to them, bore them on his heart, wept over them, and prayed for them night and day, and in so doing moved God to bless ten thousand times ten thousand folks whom he never saw and of whom he never even dreamed.

But let no one called of God imagine that this lesson of the chained ambassador is for those who are free to go. It is not. It is only for those who are in chains.

Faith: The Grace and the Gift

There is an important difference between the grace of faith and the gift of faith, and I fear that a failure to note this difference and to act accordingly has led many people into darkness, and possibly some have even been led to cast away all faith and to plunge into the black night of skepticism.

The grace of faith is that which is given to everyone to work with, and by which he or she can come to God. The gift of faith is that which is bestowed upon us by the Holy Spirit at the point where we have made free use of the grace of faith.

Those who are exercising the grace of faith say, "I believe God will bless me" and seek God wholeheartedly. They pray secretly and publicly. They search the Bible to know God's will. They talk with Christians about the way God deals with the soul. They take up every cross, and at last, when they have reached the limits of the grace of faith, God suddenly, by some word of Scripture, testimony, or inward reasoning, bestows upon them the gift of faith by which they are enabled to grasp the blessings they have been seeking. Then they no longer say, "I believe God will bless me," but they joyfully exclaim, "I believe God does bless me!" Then the Holy Spirit witnesses that it is done, and they shout for joy and declare, "I know God blesses me!" And they would not thank an angel to tell them that it is done, for they know it is done, and neither mortals nor devils can rob them of this assurance. Indeed, what I have here called the gift of faith might be called (and probably is by some) the assurance of faith. However, it is not the name but the fact that is important.

Now the danger lies in claiming the gift of faith before having fully exercised the grace of faith. For instance, a person is seeking the blessing of a clean heart. She says, "I believe there is such a blessing, and I believe God will give it to me." Now, believing this, she should at once seek it from God, and if she perseveres in seeking, she will surely find. But if someone comes up and gets her to claim it before she has by the grace of faith fought her way through the doubts and difficulties she has to meet, and before God has bestowed upon her the gift of faith, she will probably drift along for a few days or weeks and then fall back and probably conclude that there is no such blessing as a clean heart. She should be warned, instructed, exhorted, and encouraged to seek till she gets the assurance.

Or suppose someone is sick, and says, "There are some people who have been sick, and God has healed them, and I believe He will heal me." Having this faith, he should seek this healing from God. But if someone persuades him to claim healing before he has, by the grace of faith, worked his way through the difficulties that oppose him, and before God has bestowed upon him the gift of faith by which he receives the healing, he will probably crawl out of bed for a short time, find out he is not healed, get discouraged, and maybe call God a liar, or possibly declare that there is no God and cast away all confidence forever.

Or, again, suppose an officer or other minister has her heart set on seeing souls saved and reasons with herself that it is God's will to save souls. Then she declares, "I am going to believe for twenty souls to experience new life tonight"—but night comes and twenty souls are not saved. Then she wonders what was the matter. The Devil tempts her. She doubts and, probably, falls into skepticism.

What was the trouble? Why, she said she was going to believe before she had earnestly and intelligently wrestled and pleaded with God in prayer and listened for God's voice till God wrought in her the assurance that twenty souls should be saved. "God . . . rewards those who sincerely seek him" (Heb. 11:6 NLT).

"But," says someone, "should we not urge seekers to believe that God does the work?"

Yes, if you are certain that they have sought Him with all their hearts. If you feel sure they have exercised the grace of faith fully and yielded all, then urge them tenderly and earnestly to trust Jesus. But if you are not sure of this, beware of urging them to claim a blessing God has not given them. Only the Holy Spirit knows when a soul is ready to receive God's gift, and He will notify that person when he or she is to be blessed. So beware not to attempt to do the Holy Spirit's work yourself. If you help seekers too much, they may die on your hands. But if you walk closely with God in a spirit of humility and prayer, He will reveal to you the right word to say that will help them through.

Again, let no one suppose that the grace of faith will necessarily have to be exercised a long time before God gives the assurance. You may get the blessing almost at once, if you urge your claim with a perfect heart, fervently, without any doubt and without any impatience toward God. But, as the prophet said, "If [the vision] seems to tarry, wait for it; it will surely come, it will not delay" (Hab. 2:3 NRSV). "In just a little while, he who is coming will come and will not delay" (Heb. 10:37 NIV). If the blessing should tarry, do not think because it is delayed that it is therefore denied. But, like the woman who came to Jesus in Mark 7:26, press your claim in all meekness and lowliness of heart, with undaunted faith. He will in love soon say to you, "Your faith is great. Your request is granted" (Matt. 15:28 NLT).

Don't Argue 15

In seeking to lead a holy, blameless life, I have been helped at one point by the advice of two men and the example of two others.

Some years ago in Boston, I attended an all-night of prayer. It was a blessed time, and scores of people sought the blessing of a clean heart that night. The Scriptures were read, many prayers were offered, many songs were sung, and many testimonies and exhortations were given. But of all the many excellent things said that night, only one burned itself into my memory, never to be forgotten. Just before the meeting closed, Commissioner James Dowdle, speaking to those who had been to the penitent form, said, "Remember, if you want to retain a clean heart, don't argue!" There were twenty years of practical holiness behind that advice, and it fell on my ears like the voice of God.

In writing to young Timothy, the aged apostle Paul poured out his heart to one he loved as a son of the gospel. He sought to fully instruct

him in the truth, so that on the one hand Timothy might escape all the
snares of the Devil, walk in holy triumph and fellowship with God,
and thus save himself, and on the other hand be "thoroughly equipped"
to instruct and train others (2 Tim. 3:17 NIV). Among other earnest
words, these have deeply impressed me: "Remind everyone about
these things, and command them in God's presence to stop fighting
over words. Such arguments are useless, and they can ruin those who
hear them" (2 Tim. 2:14 NLT).

I take it that Paul meant by this, that instead of arguing with people and so losing time, and maybe temper, we are to go right for their
hearts and do our best to win them for Christ and get them saved and
sanctified.

He continued: "Again I say, don't get involved in foolish, ignorant arguments that only start fights. A servant of the Lord must not
quarrel but must be kind to everyone, be able to teach, and be patient
with difficult people. Gently instruct those who oppose the truth. Perhaps God will change those people's hearts, and they will learn the
truth" (2 Tim. 2:23–25 NLT).

Clearly the apostle thought this advice was important, for he
repeated it in writing to Titus: "Avoid foolish controversies and
genealogies and arguments and quarrels about the law, because these
are unprofitable and useless" (Titus 3:9 NIV).

I am certain that Paul was right in this. It takes fire to kindle fire, and
it takes love to kindle love. Cold logic will not make anyone love Jesus,
and it is only the one who loves who "is born of God" (1 John 4:7 KJV).

We who have had the gospel taught to us in such simplicity and
purity can scarcely realize the awful darkness through which some

have had to struggle, even in so-called Christian countries, to find the true light.

Years ago, among the luxurious and licentious nobility of France, the Marquis de Renty attained a purity of faith, simplicity of life and character, and cloudless communion with God that greatly adorned the gospel and proved a blessing, not only to the people of his own community and age, but also to many people of succeeding generations. His social position, wealth, and business ability led to him being associated with others in various enterprises of a secular and religious character, in all of which his faith and godly sincerity shone with remarkable luster.

In reading the story of his life a few years ago, I was struck by his great humility, his sympathy for the poor and uneducated (and his zealous, self-denying efforts to instruct and save them), his diligence and fervor in prayer and praise, and his constant hungering and thirsting after all the fullness of God. But what impressed me as much as, or more than, all the rest was the way he avoided all argument of any nature, for fear he might grieve the Holy Spirit and quench the light in his soul. Whenever matters of a business or religious nature were discussed, he carefully thought the subject over and then clearly, fully, and quietly expressed his views and the reasons upon which he based them. Then, however heated the discussion might become, he declined to be drawn into any further debate. His quiet, peaceful manner, added to his clear statements, gave great force to his counsels. But whether his views were accepted or rejected, he always went to his opponents afterward and told them that, in expressing sentiments contrary to their own, he acted with no intention of opposing them personally, but simply that of declaring what seemed to him to be the truth.

In this he seems to me to have been closely patterned after "the meekness and gentleness of Christ" (2 Cor. 10:1 KJV), and his example has encouraged me to follow a like course, and so "keep the unity of the Spirit in the bond of peace" (Eph. 4:3 KJV), when otherwise I should have been led into wranglings and disputes which would have clouded my soul and destroyed my peace, even if the Holy Spirit were not utterly driven from my heart.

The enemies of Jesus were constantly trying to entangle Him in His words and involve Him in arguments, but He always turned the subject in such a way as to confound His foes and take every argument out of their mouths.

They came to Him one day and asked whether it was lawful to pay tribute to Caesar or not. Without any discussion, He asked for a coin. He then asked whose image was on the coin.

"Caesar's," they replied.

"Well, then," He said, "give to Caesar what belongs to Caesar, and give to God what belongs to God" (Matt. 22:21 NLT).

On another occasion, they brought to Him a woman who had been caught in the act of adultery. His loving heart was touched with compassion for her, but instead of arguing with her captors as to whether she should be stoned or not, He simply said, "Let the one who has never sinned throw the first stone!" (John 8:7 NLT). And the whole crowd of hypocrites was so convicted and baffled by His simplicity, that they sneaked out one by one until the woman was left alone with her Savior.

And so, all through the Gospels, I fail to find Jesus engaged in argument, and His example is of infinite importance to us.

It is natural to the "carnal mind" to resent opposition. But we are to be "spiritually minded" (Rom. 8:6 KJV). By nature we are proud of our persons and protective of our opinions, and we are ready to stoutly resist those who oppose either us or our principles. Our object at once is to subdue others, whether by force of argument or force of arms. We are impatient of contradiction and are hasty in judging others' motives and condemning all who do not agree with us. And then we are apt to call our haste and impatience "zeal for the truth," when, in fact, it is often a hotheaded, unkind, and unreasoning zeal for our own way of thinking. I am strongly inclined to believe that this is one of the last fruits of the carnal mind which grace ever subdues.

But let us who have become "partakers of the divine nature" (2 Pet. 1:4 KJV) see to it that this root of the carnal nature is utterly destroyed. When others oppose us, let us not argue, revile, or condemn, but lovingly instruct them—not with an air of superior wisdom and holiness, but with meekness, solemnly remembering that "the LORD's servant must not be quarrelsome but kindly to everyone, an apt teacher, patient, correcting opponents with gentleness" (2 Tim. 2:24–25 NRSV).

I find that often, after having plainly, fully, and calmly stated my views to one who is opposing the truth as I see it, I am strongly tempted to strive for the last word. But I also find that God blesses me most when I then commit the matter into His hands, and by so doing I most often win my adversary. I believe this is the way of faith and the way of meekness. While it may seemingly leave us defeated, we generally win our foe in the end. And if we have true meekness, we shall rejoice more over having won him or her to "a knowledge of the truth" (2 Tim. 2:25 NIV) than in having won an argument.

Letting the Truth Slip 16

The truth that saves the soul is not picked up as we would pick up the pebbles along the beach. Rather, it is obtained as gold and silver, after diligent searching and much digging. Solomon said, "If you call out for insight and raise your voice for understanding, if you seek it like silver and search for it as for hidden treasures, then you will understand the fear of the LORD and find the knowledge of God" (Prov. 2:3–5 ESV). Those who seek to obtain the truth will have to use their wits. They will need much prayer, self-examination, and self-denial. They must listen diligently in their own soul for God's voice. They must watch lest they fall into sin and forgetfulness, and must meditate in the truth of God day and night.

Men and women who are full of the truth—who are walking embodiments of the truth—have not become so without effort. They have dug for truth. They have loved it. They have longed for it more than for their necessary food. They have sacrificed all for it. When they have fallen, they have risen again, and when defeated they have not yielded to discouragement, but with more care and watchfulness and greater earnestness, they have renewed their efforts to attain the truth. They have not counted their lives dear unto themselves so they might know the truth. Wealth, ease, fame, reputation, pleasure, and everything the world holds has been counted as dung and dross in their pursuit of truth. And just at that point where truth took precedence over all creation, they found it—the truth that saves the soul, satisfies the heart, answers the questions of life, and brings fellowship with God and joy unutterable and perfect peace.

Just as it costs effort to find the truth, so it requires watching to keep it. "Riches have wings"[1] and, if unguarded, fly away. So with truth. It will slip away if not earnestly heeded. "Buy the truth and do not sell it" (Prov. 23:23 NIV). It usually slips away little by little. It is lost as leaking water is lost—not all at once, but by degrees.

Here is a man who was once full of the truth. He loved his enemies and prayed for them. But, little by little, he neglected that truth that we should love our enemies, and it slipped away, and instead of love and prayer for his enemies has come bitterness and sharpness.

Another once poured out his money upon the poor and for the spread of the gospel. He was not afraid to trust God to supply all his wants. He was so full of truth that all fear was gone, and he was certain that if he sought "first the kingdom of God, and his righteousness," all other things would be added to him (Matt. 6:33 KJV). He did not fear that God would forget him and forsake him and leave his children to beg for bread. He served God gladly and with all his heart.

He was satisfied with a crust and was as happy and careless as the sparrow that tucks its tiny head under its little wing and goes to sleep, not knowing from where its breakfast is to come, but trusts to the great God who opens His hand and satisfies the desire of every living thing and gives them their food as they need it (see Ps. 145:15–16). But, little by little, the Devil's prudence got into his heart, and he let the truth of God's faithfulness and fatherly, provident care slip, and now he is stingy, grasping, and anxious about tomorrow and altogether unlike his liberal, loving Lord.

Here is another who was once praying all the time. She loved to pray. Prayer was the very breath of her life. But, little by little, she lost her grip on the truth that we "should always pray and never give up" (Luke 18:1 NLT), and now prayer is a cold, dead form with her.

Another once seized every opportunity for corporate worship. But he began to neglect the truth that we should not "stop meeting together with other believers, which some people have gotten into the habit of doing" (Heb. 10:25 CEB), and now he prefers going to the park, lake, or gym to attending public worship services.

Another once sprang to his feet the moment an opportunity to testify was given, and whenever he met someone on the street he would speak of the good things of God. But, little by little, he gave way to "obscenity, foolish talk or coarse joking, which are out of place" (Eph. 5:4 NIV), and neglected the truth "that everyone will have to give account on the day of judgment for every empty word they have spoken" (Matt. 12:36 NIV). He no longer remembers that the Bible says, "Death and life are in the power of the tongue" (Prov. 18:21 KJV) and that we must always "let [our] conversation be gracious and attractive" (Col. 4:6 NLT). As a result, he can now talk glibly on every subject but that of personal faith and holiness. The old, thoughtful, fiery testimony that stirred the hearts of others, warned scoffers, encouraged fainting, timid hearts, and brought cheer and strength to his brothers and sisters has given place to a few set phrases which have lost their meaning to his own heart and have about the same effect on others that big icicles would have on a fire, and which are altogether as fruitless as broken shells in last year's bird's nest.

Another once believed with all her heart that "women who profess godliness" should "adorn themselves in respectable apparel, with modesty and self-control, not with braided hair and gold or pearls or costly attire, but with . . . good works" (1 Tim. 2:9–10 ESV). But, little by little, she let the truth of God slip. She listened to the Tempter's smooth whisperings, and she fell as surely as Eve fell when she listened to the Devil and ate the forbidden fruit. Now, instead of neat, respectable apparel, she is decked out in gaudy and "costly attire," but she has lost "the beauty that comes from within, the unfading beauty of a gentle and quiet spirit, which is so precious to God" (1 Pet. 3:4 NLT).

But what shall these people do?

Let them remember the heights from which they have fallen, repent, and do their first works over again (see Rev. 2:5). Let them dig for truth again as miners dig for gold, and search for it as for hidden treasures, and they will find it again, for God "rewards those who sincerely seek him" (Heb. 11:6 NLT).

This may be hard work; it is hard to dig for gold. It may be slow work; so it is to search for hidden treasure. But it is sure work: "Keep on seeking, and you will find" (Luke 11:9 NLT). And it is necessary work. Your soul's eternal destiny depends upon it.

What shall those who have the truth do to prevent its slipping? First, heed the word of David to his son Solomon: "Observe and seek out all the commandments of the LORD your God" (1 Chron. 28:8 ESV). Second, do what God commanded Joshua: "Meditate on it day and night." For what? So you will be sure to obey some of the things written in it? No! "Everything written in it" (Josh. 1:8 NLT).

A young rabbi asked his old uncle if he might not study Greek philosophy. The old rabbi quoted the text, "This Book of the Law shall not depart from your mouth, but you shall meditate on it day and night" (Josh. 1:8 ESV), and then replied, "Find an hour that is neither day nor night; in that hour you may study Greek philosophy."

The blessed person of David's psalm is not only one who "who does not walk in step with the wicked or stand in the way that sinners take or sit in the company of mockers, but"—notice—"whose delight is in the law of the LORD, and who meditates on his law day and night" (Ps. 1:1–2 NIV).

If you want to hold the truth fast and not let it slip, you must read and reread the Bible. You must constantly refresh your mind with its truths, just as the diligent student constantly refreshes his mind by reviewing his textbooks and as the lawyer who wishes to succeed constantly studies his law books or the doctor her medical works.

John Wesley, in his old age, after having read and reread the Bible all his life, said of himself, "I am *homo unius libri*"—a man of one book.

The truth will surely slip if you do not refresh your mind by constantly reading and meditating on the Bible. The Bible is God's recipe book for making holy people. You must follow the recipe exactly if you want to be a holy, Christlike person. The Bible is God's guidebook to show men and women the way to heaven. You must pay strict attention to its directions and follow them accurately if you are ever to get there. The Bible is God's doctor's book to show people how to get rid of soul-sickness. You must diligently consider its diagnosis of soul-diseases and its methods of cure if you want soul-health.

Jesus said, "People won't live only by bread, but by every word spoken by God" (Matt. 4:4 CEB). And again He said, "The very words I have spoken to you are spirit and life" (John 6:63 NLT).

Third, "Do not quench the Spirit" (1 Thess. 5:19 NIV). Jesus calls the Holy Spirit "the Spirit of truth" (John 14:17; 15:26; 16:13 NIV). Therefore, if you do not wish the truth to slip, welcome the Spirit of truth into your heart and ask Him to abide with you. Cherish Him in your soul. Delight yourself in Him. Live in Him. Yield yourself to Him. Trust Him. Commune with Him. Consider Him your friend, your guide, your teacher, your comforter. Do not look upon Him as some school children look upon their teacher—as an enemy, as one to be outwitted, as one who is constantly watching for a chance to punish and reprove and discipline. Of course, the Holy Spirit will do this when necessary, but such a necessity grieves Him. His delight is to comfort and cheer the children of God. He is love! "Do not grieve the Holy Spirit of God, by whom you were sealed for the day of redemption" (Eph. 4:30 ESV).

NOTE

1. Francis Bacon, *Essays, Civil and Moral*, The Harvard Classics, vol. 3, part 1 (New York: P. F. Collier & Son, 1909–1914), n.p.

If You Have Lost the Blessing 17

When a person falls into sin, the difficulty in the way of restoration is in him- or herself, not in the Lord. It is difficult for us to trust one whom we have wronged, and the difficulty is doubled when that one has been a tender, loving friend. See the case of Joseph's brothers. They grievously wronged him by selling him into Egypt, and at last, when they discovered that he was alive and they were in his power, they were filled with fear.

But Joseph assured them of his goodwill and finally won their confidence by his kindness. This confidence was apparently perfect until the death of their father, Jacob, and then all their old fears revived.

Now that their father was dead, Joseph's brothers became fearful. "Now Joseph will show his anger and pay us back for all the wrong we did to him," they said.

So they sent this message to Joseph: "Before your father died, he instructed us to say to you: 'Please forgive your brothers for the great wrong they did to you—for their sin in treating you so cruelly.' So we, the servants of the God of your father, beg you to forgive our sin." When Joseph received the message, he broke down and wept. . . .

But Joseph replied, "Don't be afraid of me. Am I God, that I can punish you? . . . No, don't be afraid. I will continue to take care of you and your children." So he reassured them by speaking kindly to them. (Gen. 50:15–17, 19, 21 NLT)

If you have fallen into sin, see your situation in this simple story. By your sin you have done violence to your own sense of justice, and now it is next to impossible for you to trust your grievously wronged brother, Jesus. And yet His tender heart is close to breaking over your distrust: "Joseph wept when they spoke to him" (Gen. 50:17 ESV). If you have not committed the unpardonable sin—and you have not, if you have any desire whatsoever to be the Lord's—your first step is to renew your consecration to the Lord, confessing your sins. Then your second and only step is to cry out with Job, "Though he slay me, yet will I trust in him" (Job 13:15 KJV), and this ground you must steadfastly hold, till the witness comes of your acceptance.

Many people fail at this point by constantly looking for the same emotions and joy they had when they were first saved, and they refuse to believe because they do not have that same old experience. Do you remember that the children of Israel went into captivity several times after they had entered Canaan, but never did God divide Jordan for them again? God never took them in again in the same manner as at first. God says, "I will lead the blind in a way that they do not know, in paths that they have not known I will guide them" (Isa. 42:16 ESV). But if you are seeking the old experience, you are refusing to acknowledge that you are blind and are insisting upon going in the paths you have known. In other words, you want to walk by sight and not by faith. You must yield yourself to the Holy Spirit, and He will surely lead you into the Promised Land. Seek simply to be right with God. Do whatever He tells you to do. Trust Him, love Him, and He will come to you, for He (Jesus) "became for us . . . sanctification" (1 Cor. 1:30 NKJV). It is not a blessing you want, but the Blesser, whom you have shut out by your unbelief.

A recently sanctified man at the School of Theology in Boston said, "I have been here studying theology for three years, but now I have the *Theos* [God] in me." Be satisfied with Him by whatever way He may come, whether as King of Kings and Lord of Lords or as a humble, simple, peasant carpenter. Be satisfied with Him, and He will more and more fully reveal Himself to your childlike faith.

Do not be frightened by roaring lions; they are chained. Steadfastly refuse to wonder about the future, but trustfully rest in Him for the present moment. "Don't worry about tomorrow, for tomorrow will bring its own worries. Today's trouble is enough for today" (Matt. 6:34 NLT).

Satan wants to create great concern in your mind about your ability to persevere. Especially if you lost your experience through disobedience, Satan will flaunt that fact in your face. Remember, "My grace is sufficient for thee" (2 Cor. 12:9 KJV). Be sure not to worry about tomorrow.

I heard a friend pray, "Father, you know what intolerable anguish I have suffered by looking ahead and wondering if I could do so-and-so at such-and-such a time and place." Of course he would suffer. The simple remedy was not to look into the future but to "hold up the shield of faith to stop the fiery arrows of the devil" (Eph. 6:16 NLT). He was suffering from fiery arrows. Be sure of this: It is not Jesus who is torturing you with thoughts of the future, for He has commanded you, "Don't worry about tomorrow" (Matt. 6:34 NLT). "Resist the devil, and he will flee from you" (James 4:7 NLT). But when you come up to the point of obedience, be true, even if it takes your life. "If you remain faithful even when facing death, I will give you the crown of life" (Rev. 2:10 NLT). Be among those who win heaven's commendation: "They did not love their lives so much that they were afraid to die" (Rev. 12:11 NLT).

One woman who had lost the experience said, "I gave myself back to Jesus and trusted for some time without any feeling. A young lady came to the house, and I felt I ought to speak to her about her soul. It seemed very hard, but I told the Lord I would be true. I spoke to her. Tears filled her eyes, and joy filled my heart. The Blesser had come, and now she is sweetly trusting in Jesus." Give yourself back to God, and let your very life enter into the consecration.

A woman who had wandered for ten years, but had just been reclaimed and filled with the Holy Spirit, said the other night, "Put your all on the altar, and leave it there; do not take it back, and God's fire will surely come and consume the offering."

Do it. Do it! God will surely come if you can wait; and you can wait, if you mean business for eternity. "That is why the LORD says, 'Turn to me now, while there is time. Give me your hearts. Come with fasting, weeping, and mourning. Don't tear your clothing in your grief, but tear your hearts instead.' Return to the LORD your God, for he is merciful and compassionate, slow to get angry and filled with unfailing love. He is eager to relent and not punish" (Joel 2:12–13 NLT).

Soul-Winners and Their Prayers

All great soul-winners have been people of much and mighty prayer, and all great revivals have been preceded and carried out by persevering, prevailing knee-work in the closet. Before Jesus began His ministry, when great multitudes followed Him, He spent forty days and nights in secret prayer and fasting (see Matt. 4:1–11).

Paul prayed without ceasing. Day and night his prayers and pleadings and intercessions went up to God (see Acts 16:25; Phil. 1:3–11; Col. 1:3, 9–11). The Pentecostal baptism of the Spirit and the three thousand who experienced new life in one day were preceded by ten days of prayer and praise and heart-searching and Scripture-searching (see Acts 2:4–6). And they continued in prayer until, on another day, five thousand were added to the church (see Acts 4:4), and "many of the Jewish priests were converted, too" (Acts 6:7 NLT).

Luther used to pray three hours a day, and he broke the spell of ages and set captive nations free. John Knox used to spend nights in prayer, crying to God, "Give me Scotland, or I die!" And God gave him Scotland. Richard Baxter stained the walls of his study with praying breath and sent a tide of salvation through all the land.

Over and over again, John Wesley in his journals—which, for lively interest, are next to the Acts of the Apostles—tells of half and whole nights of prayer in which God drew near and blessed people beyond expectation, and then he and his helpers were empowered to rescue England from paganism and send a revival of pure, aggressive religion throughout the whole earth.

David Brainerd used to lie on the frozen ground at night, wrapped in a bear's skin and spitting blood, and cry to God to save the native tribes of North America. And God heard him, and redeemed and sanctified men and women by the hundreds.

The night before Jonathan Edwards preached the wonderful sermon that started the revival which convulsed New England, he and some others spent the night in prayer.

A young man named David Livingstone, in Scotland, was appointed to preach at one of the great assemblies. Feeling his utter weakness, he spent the night in prayer, and the next day preached a sermon, and five hundred people entered into the kingdom of God. Oh, my Lord, raise up some praying people!

Charles Finney used to pray until whole communities were brought under the influence of the Spirit of God and no one could resist the mighty influence. At one time, he was so prostrated by his labors that his friends sent him on a voyage of rest to the Mediterranean Sea. But he was so intent upon the salvation of others that he could not rest, and on his return he got into an agony of soul for the evangelization of the world. At last, the earnestness and agony of his soul became so great that he prayed all day, till in the evening he got a restful assurance that God would carry on the work. On reaching New York, he delivered his "Revival Lectures," which were published at home and abroad and resulted in revivals all over the world. Then his writings fell into the hands of Catherine Booth and mightily influenced her, so that The Salvation Army is in part God's answer to that man's agonizing, pleading, prevailing prayer that God would glorify His own name and save the world.

A young American evangelist seems to unleash a "revival tornado" everywhere he goes, bringing hundreds of people to faith in Christ Jesus. I wondered what the secret of his power might be until a lady at whose house he stopped said he prayed all the time—so much so, she could hardly get him to his meals from his mighty wrestlings with God.

Before joining The Salvation Army, I was one day talking with Dr. Charles Cullis of Boston, that man of simple, wonder-working faith. He was showing me some photographs, and among them was one of Bramwell Booth, our Chief of the Staff (territorial leader), who later became the second General (worldwide leader) of The Salvation Army.

"There," said the doctor, "that man leads the mightiest holiness meetings in all England."

He then told me about those famous Whitechapel meetings. When I went to England, I determined, if possible, to find out the secret of them.

"For one thing," said an officer, "Mr. Bramwell used to conduct young men's meetings at headquarters at that time, and he used to ask each saved young fellow to spend five minutes alone with God every day, wherever they could get it, praying for those Friday night meetings. One, who is a brigadier[1] now and was then employed in a large warehouse, had to squeeze himself into a great wicker packing case to get a chance to pray for five minutes."

God has not changed. He waits to do the will of praying men and women.

Mr. Finney tells of a church in which there was a continuous revival for thirteen years. At last the revival stopped, and everybody feared and questioned why, till one day a tearful man arose and told how for thirteen years he had prayed every Saturday night till after midnight for God to glorify himself and save the people. But two weeks before, he had stopped this praying, and then the revival had stopped. If God will answer prayer like that, what a tremendous responsibility rests on us all to pray!

Oh, for a holy soldier in every corps and a believing member in every church, who would spend half of every Saturday night in prayer! Here is work for those who are convalescing and for people who cannot go into ministry because of insurmountable difficulties. You can do some needed knee-work.

But let no one imagine that prayer is easy work. It is difficult and amounts sometimes to an agony, but it will turn into an agony of joy in union and fellowship with Jesus.

The other day a Salvation Army captain, who prays an hour or more each morning and half an hour before his evening meeting, and who is very successful in getting souls saved, was lamenting to me that he often has to force himself to secret prayer. But all men and women of much prayer have suffered the same. The Reverend William Bramwell, who used to see hundreds of people saved and sanctified everywhere he went, prayed six hours a day, and yet he said he always went to secret prayer reluctantly. He had to pull himself up to it. And after he began to pray, he would often have dry seasons. But he persevered in faith, and the heavens would open, and he would wrestle with God until the victory came. Then when he preached, the clouds would break and rain down blessings on the people.

One man asked another the reason why Reverend Bramwell was able to say such new and wonderful things that brought blessings to so many people. "Because," said the other, "he lives so near the Throne that God tells him His secrets, and then he tells them to us."

The Reverend John Smith—whose life, William Booth once told me, had been a marvelous inspiration to him—always spent much time in prayer. He always found it hard to begin and then got so blessed that it was hard to stop. Everywhere he went, mighty revival waves also went with him.

This reluctance to secret prayer may arise from one or more of several causes. First, from wicked spirits. I imagine the Devil does not care much when he sees the majority of cold-hearted people on their knees in public, for he knows they do it simply because it is proper and fashionable. But he hates to see anyone on his or her knees in secret, for that one means business and, persevering in faith, is bound to move God and all heaven. So the devils oppose that person's efforts. Second, from the sluggishness of the body and mind, caused by sickness, loss of sleep, too much sleep, or overeating, which unduly taxes the digestive organs, clogs the blood, and dulls all the higher and nobler powers of the soul. Third, from a failure to respond quickly when we feel led by the Spirit to go to secret prayer. If, when we feel we should pray, we hesitate longer than is necessary and continue reading or talking when we could just as well be praying, the spirit of prayer will be quenched.

We should cultivate gladness at the thought of getting alone with Jesus in secret communion and prayer, as much as lovers expect pleasure and joy in each other's company. We should promptly respond to the inward call to prayer. "Resist the devil, and he will flee from you" (James 4:7 KJV). We must discipline our bodies and our wills, lest we become disqualified (see 1 Cor. 9:27). Jesus made it clear that we "should always pray and never give up" (Luke 18:1 NLT), and Paul enjoined us to "pray without ceasing" (1 Thess. 5:17 KJV).

One daredevil, praying, believing man or woman can get the victory for a whole city or nation sometimes. Elijah did on Mount Carmel. Moses did for backsliding Israel. Daniel did in Babylon. But if a number of people can be led to pray in this way, the victory will be all the more sweeping. Let no one imagine, in a wicked heart of unbelief, that God is grudging and unwilling to answer prayer. He is more willing to answer those whose hearts are right with Him than parents are to give bread to their children. When Abraham prayed for Sodom, God answered till Abraham stopped asking (see Gen. 18:22–33). And is He not often angry with us because we ask so timidly and for such small blessings, just as the prophet Elisha was angry with the king who struck the ground but three times when he should have done so five or six times (see 2 Kings 13:18–19)?

Let us come boldly to the throne of grace and ask largely, that our joy may be full (see Heb. 4:16)!

NOTE

1. Brigadier is a former rank between major and lieutenant-colonel of a commissioned (ordained) Salvation Army officer. It was usually given after thirty years of service.

Present-Day Witnesses to the Resurrection 19

I once knelt in prayer with a young woman who wanted to be holy. I asked if she would give up everything for Jesus. She answered that she would. I then thought I would put a hard test to her and asked if she would be willing to go to Africa as a missionary. She said, "Yes." Then we prayed, and while we were praying, she burst into tears and cried out, "O Jesus!"

She had never seen Jesus. She had never heard His voice, and before this hour she had no more idea of such a revelation of Jesus to her soul than someone who was born blind has of a rainbow. But she knew Him! She had no more need that someone should tell her this was Jesus than you have need of the light of a tallow candle to see the sun come up. The sun brings its own light, and so does Jesus.

She knew Him; she loved Him; she rejoiced in Him with "joy unspeakable and full of glory" (1 Pet. 1:8 KJV). And from that hour she testified of Him and followed Him—even to Africa—till one day He said to her, "Well done, good and faithful servant . . . enter thou into the joy of thy lord" (Matt. 25:23 KJV), and then she went to heaven, to behold with open vision His unveiled glory.

That young woman was a witness for Jesus—a witness that He is not dead but living, and as such was a witness to His resurrection. Such witnesses are needed in every age. They are needed today as much as in the days of the apostles. People's hearts are just as wicked, their pride just as stubborn, their selfishness just as universal, and their unbelief just as obstinate as at any time in the world's history, and it takes just as powerful evidence to subdue their hearts and beget living faith in them as it ever did.

There are two kinds of evidence, each of which seems to be necessary to get people to accept the truth and come to faith in Jesus Christ. They are: the evidence we get from history and the evidence we get from living men and women who speak of their experience.

In the Bible and in the writings of early Christians, we have the historical evidences of God's plans for us and His dealings with us, of the life and death and resurrection of the Lord Jesus, and of the coming of the Holy Spirit. But these records alone do not seem sufficient to destroy people's unbelief and bring them into humble, glad submission to God, and into childlike faith in His dear love. They may produce historical faith. That is, people may believe what these writings say about God, humankind, sin, life, death, judgment, heaven and hell, just as they believe what history says about Julius Caesar, Napoleon Bonaparte, or George Washington. And this faith may lead them to be very religious, build temples, deny themselves, and go through many forms of worship. It may prompt them to forsake gross outward sin and live lives of decorum and morality, and yet leave them dead to God. It does not lead them into that living union with the Lord Jesus which slays inward and outward sin, takes away the fear of death, and fills the heart with joyful hope of immortality.

The faith that saves is the faith that brings the life and power of God into the soul—a faith that makes the proud heart humble, the impatient heart patient, the stingy heart generous, the lustful heart clean and chaste, the liar truthful, and the thief honest. It transforms a flippant and foolish person into someone who is thoughtful and prudent. It changes a fighting, quarrelsome spirit into someone who is meek and gentle. It is a faith that purifies the heart, sets the Lord always before the eyes, and fills the soul with humble, holy, patient love toward God and others.

To beget this faith, what is needed is not only the Bible with its historical evidences, but also a living witness, one who has "tasted the good word of God, and the powers of the world to come" (Heb. 6:5 KJV), who knows that Jesus is not dead, but alive, and can witness to the resurrection, because he or she knows the Lord, who is "the resurrection, and the life" (John 11:25 KJV).

I remember a young girl in Boston, whose quiet, earnest testimony for Jesus drew people to our meetings just to hear her speak. One day, as we were walking along the street, she said to me, "The other evening, as I was in my room getting ready for the meeting, Jesus was with me. I felt He was there, and I knew Him."

I replied, "We may be more aware of His presence than of any earthly friend."

Then, to my surprise and joy, she said, "Yes, for He is in our hearts."

Paul had to be such a witness in order to bring salvation to the Gentiles. He was not a witness of the resurrection in the sense that he saw Jesus in the body with his natural eyes but in the higher, spiritual sense that "God . . . was pleased to reveal his Son" to Paul (Gal. 1:15–16 NIV)—and his testimony was just as mighty in convincing people of the truth and slaying their unbelief as was that of Peter or John.

And this power to witness was not confined to the apostles who had been with Jesus, and to Paul who was specially chosen to be an apostle; it is the common heritage of believers. Many years after Pentecost, Paul wrote to the Corinthians, far away in Europe, "Surely you know that Jesus Christ is among you" (2 Cor. 13:5 NLT). And, in writing to the Colossians, he said the mystery of the gospel is "Christ in you, the hope of glory" (Col. 1:27 KJV). In fact, this is the very highest purpose for which Jesus promised to send the Holy Spirit. He said, "When the Spirit of truth comes . . . he will not speak on his own. . . . He will bring me glory by telling you whatever he receives from me" (John 16:13–14 NLT).

This is the Holy Spirit's chief work—to reveal Jesus to the spiritual consciousness of each individual believer, and by so doing purify the heart, destroy all evil dispositions, and implant in the soul of the believer the very tempers and dispositions of Jesus Himself.

Indeed, the inward revelation of the mind and heart of Jesus through the baptism of the Holy Spirit was necessary in order to make fit witnesses out of the very men who had been with Him for three years and who were eyewitnesses of His death and resurrection.

Jesus did not rise from the dead and send His disciplies out at once to tell the fact to everyone they met. He remained with them a few days, teaching them certain things, and then just before He ascended to heaven, instead of saying to them, "You have been with Me for three years, you know My life, you have heard My teachings, you saw Me die, you witnessed My resurrection—now go into all the world and tell them about these things," He commanded them, "Do not leave Jerusalem until the Father sends you the gift he promised, as I told you before. John baptized with water, but in just a few days you will be baptized with the Holy Spirit. . . . You will receive power when the Holy Spirit comes upon you. And you will be my witnesses" (Acts 1:4–5, 8 NLT).

The disciples had been with Jesus for three years, but they did not understand Him. He had been revealed to them in flesh and blood, but now He was to be revealed in them by the Spirit. And in that hour they knew His divinity and understood His character, His mission, His holiness, His everlasting love, and His saving power as they otherwise could not had He lived with them in the flesh to all eternity. This was what led Jesus to say to them, just before His death, "It is [better] for you that I go away: for if I go not away, the Comforter will not come unto you" (John 16:7 KJV). And if the Comforter had not come, they could not possibly have known Jesus except in the flesh.

Oh, how tenderly Jesus loved them, and with what unutterable longings did He wish to make Himself fully known to them! Just so today, does He want to make Himself fully known to His people and reveal Himself in their hearts. It is this knowledge of Jesus that skeptics and seekers want to see in Christians before they believe.

Now, if it is true that the children of God can so know Christ, that the Holy Spirit does so reveal Him, that Jesus does so earnestly wish to be known by His people, and that skeptics and seekers long to see evidence of in Christians before they will believe, is it not the duty of all followers of Jesus to seek Him wholeheartedly until they are filled with this knowledge and this power to witness? Further, this knowledge should be sought, not simply for usefulness, but for personal comfort and safety, because it is salvation—it is eternal life. Jesus said, "This is the way to have eternal life—to know you, the only true God, and Jesus Christ, the one you sent to earth" (John 17:3 NLT).

One may know ten thousand things about the Lord, may be very eloquent in speaking about His character and His works, and yet be utterly destitute of any heart acquaintance with Him. A peasant may know many things about an earthly ruler—may believe in his justice and be ready to trust his clemency, though he has never seen him—but it is his son and daughter and the members of his household who really know him. This universal revelation of the Lord Jesus is more than salvation—it is the positive side of that experience which we call a clean heart or "holiness." Do you want to know Him in this way? If your whole soul desires it, you may.

First, be sure your sins are forgiven. If you have wronged anybody, undo the wrong so far as you can. Zacchaeus said to Jesus, "I will give half my wealth to the poor, Lord, and if I have cheated people on their taxes, I will give them back four times as much!" (Luke 19:8 NLT), and Jesus saved him right on the spot. Submit to God, confess your sins, then trust Jesus, and as sure as you live all your sins shall be forgiven, and He will blot out all your transgressions as a thick cloud and remember them no more (see Jer. 31:34).

Second, now that you are forgiven, come to Him with your will, your affection, your very self, and ask Him to cleanse you from every evil temper, every selfish wish, every secret doubt; to come and dwell in your heart and keep you pure; and to use you for His own glory. Then struggle no more, but walk in the light He gives you and patiently, expectantly trust Him to answer your prayer. And as sure as you live you shall soon "be filled with all the fullness of God" (Eph. 3:19 KJV).

At this point, do not become impatient and yield to secret doubts and fears, but "hold fast the profession of [your] faith" (Heb. 10:23 KJV) for, as the writer of Hebrews said, "Patient endurance is what you need now, so that you will continue to do God's will. Then you will receive all that he has promised" (Heb. 10:36–37 NLT). God will come to you! He will! And when He comes, He will satisfy the uttermost longings of your heart.

The Radicalism of Holiness 20

Do not think you can make holiness popular. It cannot be done. There is no such thing as holiness separate from "Christ in you" (Col. 1:27 KJV), and it is an impossibility to make Christ Jesus popular in this world. To the sinful and insincere, the real Christ Jesus has always been and always will be "like a root in dry ground . . . despised and rejected" (Isa. 53:2–3 NLT). "Christ in you" is "the same yesterday, today, and forever" (Heb. 13:8 NLT)—hated, reviled, persecuted, crucified.

"Christ in you" came not to send peace on earth, but a sword. He came "to set a man against his father, and a daughter against her mother, and a daughter-in-law against her mother-in-law" (Matt. 10:35–36 NLT).

"Christ in you" will not quench the smoking flax, nor break the bruised reed of penitence and humility (see Isa. 42:3), but He will pronounce the most terrible, yet tearful, maledictions against hypocritical formalists and lukewarm churchgoers who are the friends of the world and, consequently, the enemies of God. "Don't you realize that friendship with the world makes you an enemy of God? I say it again: If you want to be a friend of the world, you make yourself an enemy of God" (James 4:4 NLT). "When you love the world, you do not have the love of the Father in you" (1 John 2:15 NLT).

In the homes of the poor and the haunts of the outcast, "Christ in you" will seek and save the lost, and will sweetly, tenderly whisper, "Come to me . . . I will give you rest" (Matt. 11:28 NLT). But in stately church and cathedral, where pomp and pride and conformity to the world mock God, He will cry out with weeping and holy indignation, "I tell you the truth, corrupt tax collectors and prostitutes will get into the Kingdom of God before you do" (Matt. 21:31 NLT).

"Christ in you" is not a gorgeously robed aristocrat, arrayed in purple and fine linen and gold and pearls, but a lowly, peasant carpenter—a calloused, truth-telling, servant of servants, seeking always the lowest seat in the synagogues and at feasts, condescending to wash the feet of others. He "does not respect the proud" (Ps. 40:4 NKJV), nor is He like those who "flatter with their tongue" (Ps. 5:9 NKJV), but His words are "pure words, like silver refined in a furnace on the ground, purified seven times" (Ps. 12:6 ESV), words that are "living and powerful, and sharper than any two-edged sword . . . [discerning] the thoughts and intents of the heart" (Heb. 4:12 NKJV).

Seek to know and follow in the footsteps of the true, real Jesus, the humble, holy peasant of Galilee. For truly, many "false christs" as well as "false prophets" have gone out into the world.

There are dreamy, poetical christs, whose words are "soothing as lotion, but underneath are daggers" (Ps. 55:21 NLT). There are fashionable christs, "lovers of pleasure rather than lovers of God, having the appearance of godliness, but denying its power [holiness of heart]" (2 Tim. 3:4–5 ESV), who "work their way into people's homes and win the confidence of vulnerable women who are burdened with the guilt of sin and controlled by various desires . . . forever following new teachings, but . . . never able to understand the truth" (2 Tim. 3:6–7 NLT).

There are mercantile christs, who make God's house a den of thieves (see Matt. 21:13). There are feeding christs, who would catch people by feeding the stomach rather than the heart and head (see Rom. 16:18). There are learned, philosophical christs, who deceive people with "empty philosophies and high-sounding nonsense that come from human thinking" (Col. 2:8 NLT). There are political reform christs, who forget their Father's business in an all-absorbing effort to obtain power. They travel halfway across the continent to deliver a speech while a hundred thousand souls are going to hell at home and vainly endeavor to club the fruit off the branches rather than to lay the axe at the root of the tree, that the tree may be good (see Matt. 3:10).

They wanted to make Christ a king one day, but He wouldn't be a king, except of people's hearts. They wanted to make Him a judge one day for about five minutes, but He wouldn't be a judge. He made Himself of no reputation (see Phil. 2:7). He might have stopped on the throne of imperial Rome, or among the upper classes of society, or in the middle classes, but He went from His Father's bosom, down past the thrones and the upper, middle, and lower classes of society to the lowest place on earth and became a Servant of all, that He might lift us to the bosom of the Father and make us partakers of the divine nature and of His holiness (see 2 Pet. 1:4; Heb. 12:10).

"Christ in you" gets under men and women and lifts them up. If He had stopped on the throne, He never would have reached the poor fishermen of Galilee. But, going down among the fishermen, He soon shook earthly thrones.

It will not be popular, but "Christ in you" will go down. He will not seek the honor that comes from mere humans, but "the honor that comes from the only God" (John 5:44 NKJV; see also John 12:42–43).

One day a rich and influential young man came to Jesus and said, "Good Teacher, what must I do to inherit eternal life?" (Mark 10:17 NLT). This young man may have reasoned within himself, "The Master is poor, and I am rich. He will welcome me, for I can give Him financial prestige. The Master is without influence in the state, whereas I can give Him political power. The Master is under a social ban, associating with those poor, ignorant fishermen; I can give Him social influence."

But the Master struck at the heart of the man's worldly wisdom and self-conceit, and said, "Go and sell all your possessions and give the money to the poor. . . . Then come, follow me" (Mark 10:21 NLT). In other words, "Come, but you can serve Me only in poverty, in reproach, in humility, in social obscurity. For My kingdom is not of this world, and the weapons of this warfare are not carnal, but mighty through God to the pulling down of strongholds. You must deny yourself, for if you do not have My Spirit you do not belong to Me" (see John 18:36; 2 Cor. 10:4; Matt. 16:24; Rom. 8:9). He said, in effect,

"My spirit is one of self-sacrifice. You must give up your elegant Jerusalem home and come with Me. But remember, 'the Son of Man has no place even to lay his head' (Matt. 8:20 NLT). You will be considered little better than a common tramp. You must sacrifice your ease. You must give up your riches, for 'hasn't God chosen the poor in this world to be rich in faith? Aren't they the ones who will inherit the Kingdom?' (James 2:5 NLT). And it is easier for a camel to go through the eye of a needle than for a rich man to enter that kingdom (see Matt. 19:24). Remember, when you do this, you will lose your reputation. The bankers and belles of Jerusalem will say you are beside yourself, and your old friends will not acknowledge you when they meet you on the street. My heart is drawn to you; I love you (see Mark 10:21). But I tell you plainly that if you will not take up the cross and follow Me, you cannot be My disciple (see Luke 14:27). Indeed, 'if you want to be my disciple, you must hate everyone else by comparison—your father and mother, wife and children, brothers and sisters—yes, even your own life. Otherwise, you cannot be my disciple' (Luke 14:26 NLT). If you will do this, you shall have treasure in heaven (see Matt. 19:21)."

Do you not see the impossibility of making such a radical gospel as this popular? This Spirit and the spirit of the world are as fully opposed to each other as two locomotives on the same track running toward each other at the rate of sixty miles an hour. Fire and water will consort together as quickly as the "Christ in you" and the spirit of the world.

Do not waste your time trying to fix up a popular holiness. Just be holy because the Lord God is holy. Seek to please Him without regard to the likes or dislikes of others, and those who are disposed to be saved will soon see "Christ in you," and will cry out with Isaiah, "Woe is me! For I am lost; for I am a [person] of unclean lips, and I dwell in the midst of a people of unclean lips; for my eyes have seen the King, the LORD of hosts!" (Isa. 6:5 ESV). And, falling at His feet, they will say with the leper, "Lord, if you are willing, you can make me clean." And Jesus, having compassion on them, will say, "I am willing. . . . Be clean!" (Matt. 8:2–3 NIV).

Perfect Peace

21

"You will keep [us] in perfect peace" (Isa. 26:3 NLT). A wonderful promise is that, and it ought to be the aim of every one of us to make it our experience. The way to do this is simple: keep our minds fixed on our Lord. But while it is simple, I confess it is no easy matter for most people to do it. They would rather think about business, pleasure, politics, education, music, the news of the day, or even the work of the Lord than about the Lord Himself.

Now, business and other things must take some of our thought, and we must pay attention to the work of the Lord, if we love Him and the souls for whom He died. But just as the young bride filled with new cares is in her heart communing with her husband though he may be far from her, so we should in everything think of and commune with Jesus, and let our hearts fully trust His wisdom, love, and power. Then we shall be kept in perfect peace.

Just think of it! "All the treasures of wisdom and knowledge" are hid in Him, and we, in our ignorance and foolishness, are "complete in Him" (Col. 2:3, 10 KJV). We may not understand, but He understands. We may not know, but He knows. We may be perplexed, but He is not perplexed. Then we ought to trust Him if we are His, and we shall be kept in perfect peace.

Ten thousand times I have been at my wits' end, but oh, how it comforted me to know that Jesus saw the end from the beginning and was making all things work together for my good because I loved and trusted Him! Jesus is never at His wits' end. And when we are most puzzled and confounded by our foolishness and shortsightedness, Jesus is working out the desires of our hearts if they are holy desires— for does He not say, "He will fulfill the desire of them that fear him" (Ps. 145:19 KJV)?

Jesus not only has wisdom and love, but He assured us that "all power . . . in heaven and in earth" is His (Matt. 28:18 KJV), so that the counsels of His wisdom and the tender desire of His love cannot fail for lack of power to fulfill them. He can turn the hearts of kings and make them do His will, and His faithful love will lead Him to do it, if we will trust Him. Nothing is more surprising to the children of God who trust Him and watch His ways than the marvelous and unex- pected deliverances He works out for them, and the kind of people He uses to fulfill His will.

Our hearts long to see the glory of the Lord and the prosperity of Zion, and we pray to God and wonder how the desire of our hearts is to be obtained. But we trust and look to God, and He sets to work, with the most unlikely people and in the most unheard of way, to answer our prayers and reward our patient faith. And so, in all the little vexatious trials and delays of our everyday, plodding life, if we trust and keep on rejoicing right through all that bothers us, we will find God at work for us, for He says He is a "present help in trouble" (Ps. 46:1 KJV)—all trouble—and so He is to all who keep their minds stayed on Him.

Only a short period has elapsed since the Lord has been allowing me to pass through a series of the most troublesome times, just calculated to annoy me to the uttermost. But while waiting on Him in prayer, He showed me that if I had more confidence in Him in my difficulties, I would keep on rejoicing and so get blessings out of my trials as Samson got honey out of the carcass of the lion he slew. And so I proved it to be. I did rejoice, and one trial after the other vanished away. Only the sweetness of my Lord's presence and blessing remained, and my heart has been kept in perfect peace since.

Does not God do all this to remove pride from us, to humble us and make us see that our character before Him is of more consequence than our service to Him? Does He not do it to teach us to walk by faith and not by sight and to encourage us to trust and be at peace?

Now, let no honest soul whose faith is small—nor busybodies who seem to think that if they did not worry and fret and rush about and make a great noise the universe would come to a standstill and go to ruin—suppose for an instant that there is any likeness whatever between perfect peace and perfect indifference. Indifference is a child of sloth. Peace is the offspring of a faith that is ceaseless in its activity— an activity that is the most perfect and the mightiest of which human beings are capable, for through it poor, unarmed people have "subdued kingdoms, wrought righteousness, obtained promises, stopped the mouths of lions, quenched the violence of fire, escaped the edge of the sword, out of weakness were made strong, waxed valiant in fight, turned to flight the armies of the aliens, [and] women received their dead raised to life again" (Heb. 11:33–35 KJV).

To exercise this mighty faith which brings perfect peace, we must receive the Holy Spirit into our hearts and recognize Him not as an influence or an attribute of God, but as God Himself. He is a person, and He will make us know Jesus, understand His mind and will, and realize His constant presence, if we trust Him. Jesus is ever present with us, and if we long for Him, it will so please Him that He will always help us to fix our minds on Him.

It will require some effort on our part, however, for the world, our business, the weakness of the flesh, the infirmities of our minds, the careless example of the people about us, and the Devil with all his wiles will so seek to turn our thoughts from our Lord and make us forget Him that maybe not more than once or twice in twenty-four hours shall our thoughts and affections turn to Him. And it will happen only by a strong and prolonged effort, so that even in times of prayer we may not really find God.

Let us then cultivate the habit of communing with Jesus. When our thoughts wander from Him, let us turn them back again. But let us do this quietly and patiently, for any impatience—even with ourselves— is dangerous, disturbing our inward peace, drowning the still, small voice of the Spirit and hindering the grace of God from mastering us and subduing our hearts.

But if, in all meekness and lowliness of heart, we allow the Holy Spirit to dwell in us and are obedient to His voice, He will keep our hearts in a holy calm in the midst of ten thousand cares and weaknesses and troubles.

"Don't worry about anything; instead, pray about everything. Tell God what you need, and thank him for all he has done. Then you will experience God's peace, which exceeds anything we can understand. His peace will guard your hearts and minds as you live in Christ Jesus" (Phil. 4:6–7 NLT).

Some of My Experiences in Teaching Holiness

22

I once received a letter from one of the most devoted young Salvation Army officers I know, in which he said, "I love holiness more and more, but I am just about discouraged. It seems to me that I shall never be able to teach holiness, for it seems that I get things too straight, or not straight enough." I think I know just how he feels. One day, a few months after I received the blessing of holiness, I felt most gloomy about my inability to get people sanctified. I knew, beyond the possibility of a doubt, that I had a clean heart, but somehow I felt I couldn't properly teach others how to get it.

That morning I met a certain brother who gets more people sanctified than anyone I know, and I asked him, "How shall I teach holiness so that my people will get it?" His reply was, "Load and fire, load and fire."

Light broke in on me at once. I saw that it was my business to pray and study my Bible and talk with those who had the blessing until I got myself so loaded that it would almost talk itself, and then fire away as best I could. And I saw that it was God's business to make the people receive the truth and become holy.

That was on a Saturday. The next day, I went to my people loaded with truth, backed by love and faith, and I fired as hard and straight as I knew how, and twenty people came to the penitent form seeking holiness. I had never seen anything like that before in my life, but I have seen it many times since.

From then till now I have attended strictly to my part of the business and trusted God to do His part, and I have had some success everywhere I have gone. But everywhere, also, Satan has sorely tempted me at times, especially when people hardened their hearts and would not believe and obey. Then I have often felt that the trouble must be in my way of preaching the truth. At one time the Devil would say, "You are too straight; you will drive all the people away." Then again he would remark, "You are not straight enough, and that is the reason the people don't get holy." In this way, I have suffered very much at times. But I have always gone to the Lord with my trouble and told Him that He knew my earnest desire was to preach the truth just right, so that the people would love and trust Him with perfect hearts.

Then the Lord has comforted me and shown me that the Devil was tempting me in order to get me to stop preaching holiness. A few times, so-called Christians have come to me and told me I was doing more harm than good. But they were the kind Paul described, who "act religious, but . . . reject the power that could make them godly" and I have followed his command, "Stay away from people like that" (2 Tim. 3:5 NLT). I have not dared to listen to them any more than to the Devil himself. So I have kept at it, through evil report and through good report, and the dear Lord has never left me alone but has stood by me and given me the victory, and I have repeatedly seen someone led into the glorious light of liberty and perfect love. Satan has tried in many ways to get me to stop preaching holiness, for he knew that if he could get me to stop, he would soon get me to sin and so overthrow me altogether. But the Lord put a godly fear in me from the beginning by calling my attention to the words of Jeremiah: "'O Sovereign LORD,' I said, 'I can't speak for you!'" The Lord replied, "Do not be afraid of the people, for I will be with you and will protect you. I, the LORD, have spoken!" (Jer. 1:6, 8 NLT).

"Get up and prepare for action. Go out and tell them everything I tell you to say. Do not be afraid of them, or I will make you look foolish in front of them" (Jer. 1:17 NLT). That last verse made me very careful to speak just what the Lord said. Then the words of Ezekiel impressed me very much:

> They are a stubborn and hard-hearted people. But I am sending you to say to them, "This is what the Sovereign LORD says!" And whether they listen or refuse to listen—for remember, they are rebels—at least they will know they have had a prophet among them. "Son of man, do not fear them or their words. Don't be afraid even though their threats surround you like nettles and briers and stinging scorpions. Do not be dismayed by their dark scowls, even though they are rebels. You must give them my messages whether they listen or not. But they won't listen, for they are completely rebellious! Son of man,

listen to what I say to you. Do not join them in their rebellion. Open your mouth, and eat what I give you." . . . But look, I have made you as obstinate and hard-hearted as they are. I have made your forehead as hard as the hardest rock! So don't be afraid of them or fear their angry looks, even though they are rebels." Then he added, "Son of man, let all my words sink deep into your own heart first. Listen to them carefully for yourself. Then go to your people in exile and say to them, 'This is what the Sovereign LORD says!' Do this whether they listen to you or not." (Ezek. 2:4–8; 3:8–11 NLT)

In these Scriptures, the Lord commanded me to speak His truth as He gave it to me, whether the people would hear or not. And in Ephesians 4:15, He told me how I was to preach it—in love. I then saw that I must preach the truth just as straight as I possibly could, but that I must be careful always to keep my heart full of love for the people to whom I was talking.

I read in 2 Corinthians how Paul loved the people. He said, "I don't want what you have—I want you. . . . I will gladly spend myself and all I have for you, even though it seems that the more I love you, the less you love me" (2 Cor. 12:14–15 NLT). Then in Acts, he said, "I never shrank back from telling you what you needed to hear. . . . I didn't shrink from declaring all that God wants you to know" (Acts 20:20, 27 NLT). This made me feel that to withhold the truth of holiness from the people—which is necessary to their eternal salvation—was worse than keeping back bread from starving children, as the murder of souls is even worse than the murder of bodies. So I earnestly prayed to the Lord to help me love the people and preach the whole truth to them, though they hate me for it—and He answered my prayer.

There are three points in teaching holiness that the Lord has led me to emphasize continually. First, that men and women cannot make themselves holy, any more than the leopard can change its spots. No amount of good works can cleanse the heart and take out the roots of pride, vanity, temper, impatience, lust, hatred, strife, self-indulgence, and the like, and in their stead put perfect love, peace, longsuffering, gentleness, goodness, faith, meekness, and temperance. Truly, millions who have labored to purify the secret springs of their hearts, only to fail, can testify, "It is 'not a result of works, so that no one may boast'" (Eph. 2:9 ESV).

Second, I keep prominent the fact that the blessing is received by faith. A poor woman wanted some grapes from the king's garden for her sick boy. She offered the gardener money, but he would not sell the grapes. She came again, met the king's daughter, and offered her money for the grapes. The daughter said, "My father is a king; he does not sell his grapes." Then she led the poor woman into the king's presence and told him her story, and he gave her as many as she wanted.

Our God, your Father, is King of Kings. He will not sell His holiness and the graces of His Spirit, but He will give them to all who will ask in simple, childlike faith. "Ask and it will be given to you" (Matt. 7:7 NIV). "Can we boast, then, that we have done anything to be accepted by God? No, because our acquittal is not based on obeying the law. It is based on faith" (Rom. 3:27 NLT). The apostle Paul said, "It is by believing in your heart that you are made right with God" (Rom. 10:10 NLT), and that statement is true to our experience, for where real heart faith is, it makes the impatient person patient, the proud humble, the lustful chaste, the covetous generous, the quarrelsome meek, the liar truthful, the hateful loving, and turns misery into joy and gives peace and constant comfort.

Third, I emphasize the truth that the blessing is to be received by faith *now*. The person who expects to get it by works will always have something more to do before claiming the blessing, and so never comes to the point where he or she can say, "The blessing is now mine." But the humble soul, who expects to get it by faith, sees that it is a gift and, believing that God is as willing to give it now as at some future time, trusts and receives it at once.

By thus urging the people to expect the blessing right now, I have sometimes had them get it even as I was talking. People who had often been to the penitent form and had wrestled and prayed for the blessing have received it while sitting in their seats listening to the simple "word of faith, which we preach" (Rom. 10:8 KJV).

Another Chance for You! 23

Peter vowed before his comrades that he would die with Jesus rather than deny Him. A few hours later the opportunity to do so presented itself, but Peter's heart failed him. He forgot his vow and threw away forever this unparalleled chance of proving his love for the Savior.

When the cock crowed and Jesus turned and looked at him, Peter remembered his broken vow and went out and wept bitterly. The tenderest sorrow for the way he had treated Jesus must have mingled with the fiercest regret for the lost chance for those bitter tears to appear. Oh, how his love must have reproached him, his conscience stung him, and the Devil taunted him! I doubt not he was tempted to give up all hope and said to himself, "It is of no use for me to try to be a Christian; I have made a miserable failure, and I will not try any longer." And over and over again, by day and by night, in the company of others and when by himself, Peter must have been reminded by the Devil of his lost chance and told it was no use for him to try any longer to be a Christian. And I imagine Peter sighed within himself and would have given the world to have that chance come back once more. But it was gone, and gone forever!

Peter did love Jesus, however, and while he had lost that chance to demonstrate his love, Jesus gave him another. A very simple, every-day, matter-of-fact chance it was, nothing like the startling, splendid one of dying with the Son of God on the cross, but probably of far more value to the world and the cause of Christ. All over the country where Jesus had been, there were, doubtless, many who believed with a trembling faith in Him. They needed to be faithfully fed with the truths about Jesus, and with those truths He had taught. So Jesus called Peter to Him and asked him three times the searching question: "Do you love me?" (John 21:15–17 NIV). It must have most painfully recalled to Peter's mind the three times he had denied Jesus. And in reply to Peter's positive assertion that he did love Him, Jesus three times commanded him to feed His lambs and sheep. And then Jesus assured Peter that at last he should die on a cross—as he probably would have died had he not denied his Lord.

I suspect there are many Peters among the disciples of Jesus today—many in our own ranks, who, somewhere in the past, since they began to follow Jesus, vowed they would do the thing He by His Spirit through their conscience asked them to do, vowed they would die for Him (and meant it, too); who, when the testing time came, forgot their vows, denied Jesus by word or act, and practically left Him to be crucified afresh and alone.

I remember a time when I failed my Lord, years ago, before I joined The Salvation Army but after I was sanctified. It was not a sin of commission, but one of omission—a failure to do what I felt the Lord would have me do. It was an unusual thing, but not an unreasonable one. The suggestion to act came suddenly, and it seemed to me that all heaven bent over me to bless me if I obeyed and hell yawned to swallow me if I did not. I did not say I would not, but it seemed to me I simply could not—and I did not. Oh, how I was humbled! I wept bitter tears, begged forgiveness, and promised God I would be true! I felt God had given me a chance that I had let slip by and that would never come again, and that I could never be the mighty man of faith and obedience I might have been had I been true. Then I promised God that I would do that very same thing, and I did it again and again, but no real blessing came to me, and so Satan took advantage of me and taunted me and accused me through my conscience till life became an intolerable burden to me. At last I felt I had grieved the Holy Spirit forever and that I was lost, and so I threw away my shield of faith, cast away my confidence in the love of Jesus for me, and for twenty-eight days suffered, it seemed to me, the pains of hell. I still prayed, but the heavens were like brass to me. I read my Bible, but the promises fled away from me, while the commandments and warnings were like flames of fire and two-edged swords to my quivering conscience. When it was night I longed for day; when it was day I longed for night.

I went to worship meetings, but no blessing came to me. The curse of God seemed to follow me, and yet through it all I saw that God is love. Satan tempted me to commit sin, to curse God and die, as Job's wife urged him. But God's mercy and grace followed me and enabled me to say no, and to tell the Devil that I would not sin and that though I went to hell, I would go there loving Jesus and seeking to get others to trust and obey Him, and that in hell I would declare that the blood of Jesus could cleanse from all sin. I thought I was doomed. Those terrible passages of Scripture in Hebrews 6 and 10 seemed just to fit my case, and I said, "I have lost my chance forever." But God's love is "higher than the highest heaven, deeper than the deepest sea."[1]

In twenty-eight days, He drew me up out of that horrible pit and that miry clay with these words: "Hold it for certain that all such thoughts as create disquiet proceed not from God, who is the Prince of Peace, but proceed either from the Devil, or from self-love, or from the good opinion we hold of ourselves."[2]

Quick as thought I saw it: God is the Prince of Peace. His thoughts are "thoughts of peace, and not of evil" (Jer. 29:11 KJV). I saw I had no self-love, nor good opinion of myself, and longed to be forever rid of self. Then I saw that the Devil was deceiving me, and instantly it was as though a devil loosened his long arms from about my spirit and fled away, leaving me free.

The next Saturday and Sunday I saw about fifty souls at the penitent form seeking salvation and holiness, and from that hour God has blessed me and given me souls everywhere. He has asked me, through those words He spoke to Peter, "Do you love Me?" And when, out of the fullness of my clean heart—emptied of self and made clean through His precious blood—I have said, "Lord, You know everything; You know that I love You," He has tenderly bidden me to feed His lambs and sheep—that is, to live the gospel so fully in my life and preach it so fully in my words that His people will be blessed, comforted, and encouraged to love and serve and trust Him with all their hearts.

This is my "second chance," and it can be yours, even if you have denied Him in the past.

Do not seek to do some great thing, but feed the lambs and sheep of God, and pray and work for the salvation of others. Study your Bible, pray, talk often and much with God, and ask Him to teach you so that, whenever you open your mouth, you may say something that will bless somebody, something that will encourage a discouraged brother or sister, strengthen a weak one, instruct an ignorant one, comfort a feeble-minded one, warn an erring one, enlighten a darkened one, and rebuke a sinning one.

Notice that Peter was to feed not only the lambs, but also the sheep. We must help others experience new life in Christ and, after they are "born again," we must feed them. We must feed the new Christians on those promises and instructions in God's Word that will lead them into entire sanctification. We must show them that this is God's will for them and that Jesus has opened a way for them "to enter into the holiest" (Heb. 10:19 KJV). We must warn them not to turn back into Egypt, not to be afraid of the giants in the Promised Land, nor to make any unholy alliance with the Ammonites in the wilderness. They are to come out and be separate. They are to be holy. This is their high and happy privilege and their solemn duty, since they have been redeemed, not with corruptible things such as silver and gold, but with the precious blood of Christ (see 1 Pet. 1:18–19). They are not to faint when chastened and corrected by the Lord, nor grow weary in doing good (see Gal. 6:9).

They are to watch and pray and give thanks and rejoice always. And they are not to get the blessing of a clean heart by hard work, nor only in the hour of death, but by simple faith in Jesus right now.

We must feed the sheep, the sanctified ones, on the strong meat of the gospel. Feed a strong man on white bread and tea, and he will soon be unfit for work. But give him good brown bread, butter and milk, and suitable fruits and vegetables, and the harder he works, other things being equal, the better he is in health and strength. So it is with Christians. Feed them on the chaff of stale jokes and last year's Bible readings that have lost their power on your own heart, and you will starve the sheep. But feed them on the deep things of God's Word, which reveal His everlasting love, His faithfulness, His saving power, His tender and attentive care, His shining holiness, His exact justice, His hatred of sin, His pity for the sinner, His sympathy for the weak and erring, His eternal judgments upon the finally impenitent and ungodly, and His never-ending glory and blessedness bestowed upon the righteous, and you will make them so strong that "one [shall] chase a thousand, and two put ten thousand to flight" (Deut. 32:30 KJV).

Know Jesus, and you will be able to feed His lambs and sheep. You feed them by revealing Him to them as He is revealed by the Father through the Spirit in the Bible.

Walk with Him. Talk with Him. Search the Bible on your knees, asking Him to open your understanding as He did that of the disciples on the way to Emmaus, teaching you what the Scriptures say of Him, and you will have another chance of showing your love for Him and of blessing others that the angels might well covet.

NOTES

1. Theodore Monod, "O, the Bitter Shame and Sorrow," 1874, public domain.

2. *St. Francis de Sales, Jane de Chantal, Letters of Spiritual Direction*, The Classics of Western Spirituality (Mahway, NJ: Paulist Press, 1988), 51.

Birds of Prey 24

Satan brings to bear all his devices—his sophisticated arguments and the full force of his powerful will—against the entire sanctification of believers. But the resolute soul, determined to be all the Lord's, will find him a conquered foe with no power except to deceive. The way to overcome him is to decide to steadfastly believe and agree with God, in spite of all Satan's suggested doubts.

In the fifteenth chapter of Genesis, we have an account of Abraham's sacrifice, which is very suggestive to the seeker after full salvation. Abraham took certain beasts and birds and offered them to God. But after he had made the offering and while he was waiting for the witness of God's acceptance, birds of prey came to snatch away the sacrifice. Abraham drove them away. This continued until the evening, and then the fire of God consumed the offering.

Just so, the person who would be entirely sanctified must make an unreserved offering of him- or herself to God. This act must be real, not imaginary—a real transfer of self, with all hopes, plans, prospects, property, cares, burdens, joys, sorrows, reputation, and friends to God in a "perpetual covenant that shall not be forgotten" (Jer. 50:5 KJV). When we have thus given ourselves to God, we must, like Abraham, patiently, trustingly, expectantly wait for God to witness that we are accepted. "If it seems slow in coming, wait patiently, for it will surely take place. It will not be delayed" (Hab. 2:3 NLT).

Now, during this period of waiting, the Devil will surely send his birds of prey to snatch away the offering. He will say, "You ought to feel different if you have given yourself wholly to God." Remember, that is the Devil's bird of prey—drive it away. Feelings are an effect, not a cause. To have the feeling of love, I must think of some loved one. But the very moment I get my thought off the object of my love and examine my feelings, they begin to subside. Look to Jesus and pay no attention to your emotions. They are involuntary, but will soon adjust themselves to the fixed habit of your faith and will.

"But," something suggests, "maybe your consecration is not complete; go over it again and be sure." Another bird of prey—drive it away.

Satan becomes extremely pious at this point and wants to keep you eternally on the treadmill of consecration, knowing that as long as he can keep you examining your consecration, you will not get your eyes on the promise of God and, consequently, will not believe. Thus, without faith that your offering is accepted, it is only so much dead works.

"But you do not have the joy, the deep and powerful emotions that others say they have." That is another bird of prey—drive it away.

A woman recently said to me, "I have given up all, but I have not the happiness I expected."

"Ah, sister," I said, "the promise is not unto them who seek happiness, but to them 'which hunger and thirst after righteousness, they shall be filled.' Seek righteousness, not happiness."

She did so, and in a few moments she was satisfied, for with righteousness came fullness of joy.

"But faith is such an incomprehensible something, you cannot exercise it. Pray to God to help your unbelief." The Devil's bird of prey—drive it away.

Faith is almost too simple to be defined. It is trust in the word of Jesus, simple confidence that He means just what He says in all the promises and that He means all the promises for you. Beware of being "corrupted from the simplicity that is in Christ" (2 Cor. 11:3 KJV).

I tell you, dear friend, everything contrary to present faith in the promise of God for full salvation is one of the Devil's birds of prey, and you must resolutely drive it away.

Quit reasoning with the Devil! "Demolish arguments and every pretension that sets itself up against the knowledge of God" (2 Cor. 10:5 NIV) and trust. Reason with God. "'Come now, and let us reason together,' says the LORD" (Isa. 1:18 NKJV).

At one of our watchnight services, a man knelt with quite a number of others, seeking a clean heart. He was told to give himself wholly to God and trust. Finally, he began to pray, and then he said, "I do give myself to God, and now I am going to live and work for

Him with what power I have and let Him give me the fullness of the blessing and power just when He chooses. He has promised to give it to me, and He will do it, will He not?"

"Yes, my brother," I replied. "He has promised, and He will surely perform."

"Yes, yes; He had promised it," said the man. Just then light shot through his soul, and his next words were, "Praise the Lord! Glory to God!" He reasoned together with God and, looking to the promise, was delivered. Others around him reasoned with the Devil, looked to their feelings, and were not sanctified.

But after you have taken the step of faith, God's plan is for you to talk your faith. The men and women of character, of force and influence, are those who put themselves on record. The one who has convictions, and who is not afraid to announce them to the world and defend them, is the one who has true stability. It is so in politics, in business, in all moral reforms, and in salvation. There is a universal law underlying the declaration: "With the mouth confession is made unto salvation" (Rom. 10:10 KJV). If you are sanctified and would remain sanctified, you must at the earliest opportunity put yourself on record before all the devils in hell, all your acquaintances on earth, and all the angels in heaven. You must stand before the world as a professor and possessor of heart purity. Only in this way can you burn all the bridges behind you. Until they are destroyed, you are not safe.

A woman said to me, "I have always hesitated to say, 'The Lord sanctifies me wholly,' but not until recently did I see the reason. I now see that I secretly desired a bridge behind me, so that I might escape back from my position without injury to myself. If I profess sanctification, I must be careful lest I bring myself into disrepute. But if I do not profess it, I can do questionable things and then shield myself by saying, 'I do not profess to be perfect.'"

Ah, that is the secret! Be careful not to become a religious fence rider, for all who are astride the fence are really on the Devil's side. "Whoever that is not with me is against me" (Matt. 12:30 NIV). Get onto God's side by a definite profession of your faith.

But the Devil will say, "You had better not say anything about this till you find out whether you will be able to keep it. Be careful, lest you do more harm than good." Drive that bird of prey away quickly or all you have done thus far will be of no avail. That bird has devoured tens of thousands of offerings just as honestly made as yours. You are not to "keep the blessing" at all; you are to boldly assert your faith in the Blesser, and He will keep you.

A brother said to me, "When I sought this experience, I gave myself definitely and fully to God and told Him I would trust Him; but I felt as dry as that post. Shortly after this, a friend asked me if I were sanctified, and before I had time to examine my feelings, I said 'Yes.' And God that minute blessed me and filled me full of His Spirit, and since then He has sweetly kept me."

He talked his faith and agreed with God.

"But you want to be honest and not claim more than you possess," says Satan. A bird of prey!

You must assert that you believe God to be honest and that He has promised that "whatever you ask in prayer, believe that you have received it, and it will be yours" (Mark 11:24 ESV). Count God faithful.

An acquaintance of mine gave herself to God, but did not feel any difference, and so hesitated to say that God had sanctified her wholly. "But," she said, "I began to reason over the matter thus: I know I have given myself wholly to God. I am willing to be anything, do anything, suffer anything for Jesus. I am willing to forego all pleasure, honor, and all my cherished hopes and plans for His sake, but I do not feel that God sanctifies me. And yet He promises to do so on the simple condition that I give myself to Him and believe His Word. Knowing that I have given myself to Him, I must believe or make Him a liar; so I will believe that He does now sanctify me. But," she continued, "I did not get any witness that the work was done just then. However, I rested in God, and some days after this I went to one of the holiness conventions, and there, while a number were testifying, I thought I would rise and tell them God sanctified me. I did so, and between rising up and sitting down, God came and witnessed that it was done. Now I know I am sanctified."

And her shining face was a sufficient evidence that the work was indeed done.

"Resist the devil, and he will flee from you" (James 4:7 KJV). Give yourself wholly to God, trust Him, and then confess your faith. "'Then the LORD you are seeking will suddenly come to His temple. The messenger of the covenant, whom you look for so eagerly, is surely coming,' says the LORD of Heaven's Armies" (Mal. 3:1 NLT).

With Peace Unbroken

The Reverend John Fletcher, whom Wesley thought was the holiest man who had lived since the days of the apostle John, lost the blessing five times before he was finally established in the grace of holiness, and Wesley declared that he was persuaded, from his observations, that people usually lose the blessing several times before they learn the secret of keeping it. So, if you have lost the blessing and are tormented by the old Enemy of souls—the Devil—with the thought that you can never get and keep it, let me urge you to try again and again.

You prove your real desire and purpose to be holy, not by giving up in the presence of defeat, but by rising from ten thousand falls and going at it again with renewed faith and consecration. If you do this, you shall surely win the prize and be able to keep it in the end.

The promise is: "Seek and you will find" (Matt. 7:7 NIV).

"But how long shall I seek?"

Seek till you find!

"But suppose I lose it?"

God will surprise you someday by pouring out such a full baptism of His Spirit upon you, that all your darkness and doubts and uncertainty will vanish forever, you will never fall again, God's smile will no more be withdrawn, and your sun will nevermore go down.

Oh, let me urge you to look up and trust Jesus, and keep on seeking, remembering that God's delays are not denial—Jesus is your Joshua to lead you into the Promised Land, and He can cast down all your foes before you. People who give up in the midst of defeat have much to learn of the deceitfulness and hardness of their own hearts, and of the tender forbearance, longsuffering, and mighty saving power of God. But it is not God's will that any who receive the blessing should ever lose it, and it is possible to keep it forever.

But how?

One day, as an old divinity school chum of mine, who had finished his course of study, was going to his field of labor, I followed him to the train to have a hearty handshake and to say good-bye, perhaps forever. He looked up and said, "Sam, give me a text that will do for a life motto."

Instantly I lifted my heart to God for light. Now, if you want to keep the blessing, that is one of the things you must constantly do— lift your heart to God and look to Him for light, not only in the crises and great events of life, but in all its little and seemingly trifling details. By practice, you can get into such a habit of doing this that it will become as natural for you as breathing, and it will prove quite as important to your spiritual life as breathing is to your natural life. Keep within whispering distance of God always, if you would keep the blessing. Well, I proved to be in whisper touch with Jesus that morning on the train. Immediately the first eleven verses of the first chapter of 2 Peter were suggested to my mind—not simply as a motto, but as a plain rule laid down by the Holy Spirit which, by following we may not only keep the blessing and never fall, but also prove fruitful in the knowledge of God and gain an abundant entrance into the kingdom of our Lord and Savior Jesus Christ.

Notice it, if you wish to keep the blessing of holiness. The apostle spoke of being made "partakers of the divine nature, having escaped from the corruption that is in the world because of sinful desire" (2 Pet. 1:4 ESV). That is holiness: to escape from the corruption of our evil hearts and receive the divine nature. And in verse 5 the apostle urged these holy people to diligence, and not only diligence, but "all diligence" (KJV). To keep the blessing you must use all diligence.

A lazy, sleepy man or woman cannot keep the blessing; in fact, such a person cannot get it in the first place. To get it you must seek it with all your heart. You must dig as for hidden treasure, and to keep it you must use diligence. Some people say, "Once saved, always saved," but God does not say anything of the kind. He urges us to watch and be sober and diligent, for we are in the Enemy's country. This world is not a friend to grace. If you had one hundred thousand dollars' worth of diamonds in a land of robbers, you would watch and keep your treasure with all diligence. Well, you are in the Enemy's country, with a holy heart and "the Spirit as a deposit" (2 Cor. 1:22; 5:5 NIV), your passport to heaven, your pledge of eternal life. Be diligent to keep it.

The apostle Peter said, "Beside this, giving all diligence, add to your faith virtue" (2 Pet. 1:5 KJV). You had to have faith in "the exceeding great and precious promises" (2 Pet. 1:4 KJV) to get this blessing, but you will have to add something more to your faith to keep it. This word *virtue* comes from the old Latin word which means "courage," and that is probably its meaning here. You must have courage to keep this blessing.

The Devil will roar like a lion at you at times. The world will frown upon you, and maybe beat you up and possibly kill you. Your friends will pity you, or curse you, and predict all sorts of calamities as sure to befall you. At times, even your own flesh may cry out against you. Then you will need courage.

They told me I would go crazy, and it almost seemed that I would, so earnest was I to know all the mind of God for me. They said I would land in a bog of fanaticism. They said I would end in the poorhouse. They said I would utterly ruin my health and become a lifelong, useless invalid, a torment to myself and a burden to my friends. The very bishop whose book on holiness had stirred my soul to its depths urged me after I got the blessing to say very little about it, as it caused much division and trouble. (I afterward learned that he had lost the blessing.) The Devil followed me day and night with a thousand spiritual temptations I had never dreamed of, and then at last stirred up a thug to nearly knock my brains out. For many months I was prostrated with bodily weakness until the writing of a postcard plunged me into distress and robbed me of a night's rest. So I found it took courage to keep this pearl of great price. But the Lion of the tribe of Judah, who is my Lord and Savior, is as full of courage as He is of strength and love and pity, and He has said in the Book of instruction and encouragement He has left us, "Be strong and courageous" (Josh. 1:6 NLT). He put it even stronger and said, "This is my *command*—be strong and courageous!" (Josh. 1:9 NLT, emphasis added). It is a positive command, which we are under obligation to obey. Over and over again He said this, and seventy-two times He said, "Don't be afraid." And He added, as a sufficient reason why we should not fear, "For I am with you" (Isa. 41:10 NLT). If He is with me, why should I be afraid? And why should you?

My little boy is very much afraid of dogs, as if this fear was born in him. But when he gets hold of my hand he will march boldly past the biggest dog in the country. God says, "For I, the LORD your God, hold your right hand; it is I who say to you, 'Fear not, I am the one who helps you. . . . Fear not, for I am with you; be not dismayed, for I am your God; I will strengthen you, I will help you, I will uphold you with my righteous right hand'" (Isa. 41:13, 10 ESV).

"Never will I leave you," He says. "Never will I forsake you" (Heb. 13:5 NIV). Never! Jesus, the very same Jesus who died for us, says, "I have been given all authority in heaven and on earth. . . . And be sure of this: I am with you always, even to the end of the age" (Matt. 28:18, 20 NLT). Why fear?

The Devil is an old hand at deceiving and overthrowing souls, but remember that Jesus is the Ancient of Days. From everlasting to everlasting, He is God, and He has put all the wisdom and power and courage of His Godhead at the disposal of our faith for our salvation. Certainly that ought to fill us with courage. Are you downhearted and afraid? Cheer up! Pluck up courage, and let us boldly say with King

David, who had a good deal more trouble and cause for fear than we do: "God is our refuge and strength, always ready to help in times of trouble. So we will not fear when earthquakes come and the mountains crumble into the sea" (Ps. 46:1–2 NLT).

I have been helped very much by one experience of David's. On one occasion he had to flee from Saul, who hunted for his life as men hunt for partridges on the mountains. So David went down into Philistia and dwelt in a village that the king gave him. Then the Philistines went to war against Saul, and David went too. But they were afraid David might turn against them in the hour of battle, so they sent him home. When David and his men returned to their homes, they found some enemies had been there, had burned their village to the ground, and had carried off their goods, cattle, wives, and children. The men were mad with grief and determined to stone David. Certainly there was reason for fear. But the Bible says, "David encouraged himself in the LORD" (1 Sam. 30:6 KJV). Read the story for yourself, and see how wonderfully God helped him to get everything back again (see 1 Sam. 30).

As for me, I am determined to be of good courage. God has been better to me than all my fears and the fears of all my friends. He has outwitted all my enemies and proved stronger than all my foes. And He has enabled me, by His power and infinite love and goodness, to walk in holiness before Him for many years.

Sanctification versus Consecration 26

A state senator's wife regularly attended a series of our holiness meetings. One day she came to me and said, "Brother Brengle, I wish you would call it 'consecration' instead of 'sanctification.' We could all agree on that."

I replied, "But I don't mean consecration, sister. I mean sanctification, and there is as big a difference between the two as there is between earth and heaven, between our work and God's work."

Her mistake is a common one. She wanted to rob holiness of its supernatural element and rest in her own works. It is more fashionable to be consecrated and to talk much about consecration. Lovely ladies, robed in silk and bedecked with jewels, feathers, and flowers, and gentlemen with soft hands and suits and odorous with perfume, talk with honeyed words and sweet, low voices about being consecrated to the Lord.

And I would not discourage them, but I do want to lift up my voice with a loud warning that consecration, as such people ordinarily think of it, is simply our work, and is not enough to save the soul.

Elijah piled his altar on Mount Carmel, slew his bullock and placed it on the altar, and then poured water over the whole. That was consecration.

But Baal's priests had done that, with the exception of putting on the water. They had built their altar and slain their bullocks. They had spent the day in the most earnest religious devotions and, so far as everyone could see, their zeal far exceeded that of Elijah.

What did Elijah do more than they? Nothing, except to pour water on his sacrifice—a big venture of faith. If he had stopped there, the world would never have heard of him. But he believed for *God* to do something. He expected it, he prayed for it, and God split the heavens and poured down fire to consume his sacrifice, the stones of his altar, and the very water that lay in the trenches. That was sanctification!

What power had cold stones and water and a dead bullock to glorify God and convert an apostate nation? But when they were flaming, and being consumed with the fire from heaven, then "they fell face down on the ground and cried out, 'The LORD—he is God! Yes, the LORD is God!'" (1 Kings 18:39 NLT).

What do great gifts and talk and so-called consecration amount to in saving the world and glorifying God? "If I give all my possessions to feed the poor, and if I surrender my body to be burned, but do not have love, it profits me nothing" (1 Cor. 13:3 NASB). It is God in us that enables us to glorify Him and work together with Him for the salvation of the world.

God wants sanctified men and women. Of course, we must be consecrated—that is, given up to God—in order to be sanctified. But once we have yielded ourselves to Him—yielded our very inmost selves, our memories, our minds and wills, our tongues, our hands and feet, our reputations, our doubts and fears, our likes and dislikes, and our disposition to talk back at God and pity ourselves and murmur and repine when He puts our consecration to the test—when we have really done this and taken our hands off, as Elijah placed his bullock on the altar and took his hands off, then we must wait on God and cry to Him with a humble, yet bold, persistent faith until He baptizes us with the Holy Spirit and fire. He promised to do it, and He will do it, but we must expect it, pray for it, and if it delays, wait for it.

A soldier (church member) went home from one of our meetings, fell on his knees, and said, "Lord, I will not get up from here till you baptize me with the Holy Ghost!" God saw He had a man on his hands who meant business, who wanted God more than all creation, and so He there and then baptized the man with the Holy Spirit.

But a captain and lieutenant (ministers) whom I know found that "the vision tarried," so they waited for it and spent all the spare time they had for three weeks, crying to God to fill them with the Spirit. They did not get discouraged; they held on to God with a desperate faith. They would not let Him go, and they got their heart's desire. I saw that lieutenant some time afterward, and I was amazed at the wonders of God's grace in him. The spirit of the prophets was upon him.

"All heaven is free plunder to faith," says a friend of mine.

Oh, this waiting on God! It is far easier to plunge madly at this thing and that, and do, do, do, until life and heart are exhausted in joyless and comparatively fruitless toil, than it is to wait on God in patient faith until He comes and fills you with the power of the Holy Spirit. It is the Spirit that gives you supernatural endurance and wisdom and might, enables you to do in a day what otherwise you could not do in a thousand years (yet strips you of all pride), and leads you to give all the glory to your Lord.

Waiting on God empties us that we may be filled. Few wait until they are emptied, and hence few are filled. Few will bear the heart searchings, the humiliations, the suspense, the taunt of Satan as he inquires, "Where is your God now?" Oh, the questionings and whisperings of unbelief that are involved in waiting upon God, hence the few who, in understanding, are men and women in Christ Jesus and pillars in the temple of God.

Jesus commanded the disciples, and said: "Tarry in the city of Jerusalem until you are endued with power from on high" (Luke 24:49 NKJV). That must have been quite a restraint put on restless, impulsive Peter; but he waited with his brothers and sisters, and they cried to God, searched their hearts, and forgot their fears and the angry rulers who had murdered their Lord. They forgot their jealousies and selfish ambitions and childish differences, until they were exhausted of all self-love and self-goodness and self-trust, their hearts were as the heart of one man, and they had but one desire—a mighty, consuming hunger for God. Then suddenly God came—in power, with fire, to purge, cleanse, and sanctify them through and through, and to dwell in their hearts and make them bold in the presence of their enemies, humble in the midst of success, patient in fiery conflicts and persecutions, steadfast and unswerving in spite of threats and whippings and imprisonment, joyful in loneliness and misrepresentations, and fearless and triumphant in the face of death. God made them wise to win souls and filled them with the very spirit of their Master, till they turned the world upside down and took none of the glory to themselves, either.

So, sanctification is the result of not only giving, but also receiving. And we are under as solemn an obligation to receive the Holy Spirit and "be filled with the Spirit" (Eph. 5:18 KJV) as we are to give ourselves to God. If we are not filled at once, we are not to suppose that the blessing is not for us and, in the subtle, mock humility of unbelief, fold our hands and stop our crying to God. But we should cry all the more, and search the Scriptures, and search and humble ourselves, and take God's part against unbelief, and never faint until we have taken the kingdom of heaven by storm and He says to us, "Your faith is great. Your request is granted" (Matt. 15:28 NLT).

God *loves* to be compelled. God *wants* to be compelled. God *will* be compelled by the persistent prayer and faith of His children. I imagine God is often grieved and disappointed and angry with us, as the prophet was with the king who shot only three arrows when he should have shot half a dozen or more (see 2 Kings 13), because we ask so little, are so easily turned away without the blessing we profess to want, and are so quickly satisfied with a little comfort when it is the Comforter Himself we need.

The woman who came to Jesus to have the Devil cast out of her daughter is a sample believer and puts most Christians to shame by the boldness and persistence of her faith. She would not be turned away without the blessing she sought. At first, Jesus answered her not a word, and so He often treats us today. We pray and get no answer. God is silent. Then He rebuffed her by saying that He had not come to such as she, but to the lost sheep of the house of Israel. That was enough to make blaspheming skeptics of most modern folks. But not so with her. Her desperate faith grew awfully sublime. At last, Jesus seemed to add insult to injury by declaring, "It isn't right to take food from the children and throw it to the dogs" (Matt. 15:26 NLT).

Then the woman's faith conquered and compelled Him, for she said, "That's true, Lord, but even dogs are allowed to eat the scraps that fall beneath their masters' table" (Matt. 15:27 NLT). She was willing to take the dogs' place and receive the dogs' portion. Oh, how her faith triumphed, and Jesus, amazed, said, "O woman, great is your faith! Be it done for you as you desire" (Matt. 15:28 ESV). Jesus meant to bless her all the time, if her faith would hold out. And so He means to bless you.

There are two classes of people who progress to consecrate themselves to God, but upon inquiry it will usually appear that they are consecrated to something other than God Himself. They are God's housekeepers, rather than the bride of His Son—very busy people, with little or no time nor inclination for real heart fellowship with Jesus.

The first class might be termed pleasure seekers. They see that sanctified people are happy, and, thinking it is due to what they have given and done, they begin to give and to do, never dreaming of the infinite Treasure these sanctified ones have received. The secret of him who said, "The Lord is the portion of my soul," is hidden from them. So they never find God. They are seeking happiness, not holiness. They are usually good livers, hearty eaters, very sociable, always dressed in the latest fashion—religious epicures. They will hardly admit their need of holiness—they were always good—and God is found only by those who, feeling the deep depravity and need of their hearts, want to be holy. "Blessed are those who hunger and thirst for righteousness, for they will be filled" (Matt. 5:6 NIV).

The other class may be rightly called misery hunters. They are always seeking something hard to do. They believe in being on the rack perpetually. Like Baal's priests, they cut themselves—not their bodies, but their minds and souls. They give their goods to feed the poor, they give their bodies to be burned, and yet it profits them nothing (see 1 Cor. 13:3). They wear themselves out in a hard bond service. It is not joy they want, but misery. They judge their acceptance with God, not by the joy-producing presence of the indwelling Comforter that makes the yoke easy and the burden light, but rather by the amount of misery they are ready to endure or have endured. They are not happy, and they fear they are not saved, unless there is some sacrifice for them to make that will produce in them the most exquisite torment. They have died a thousand deaths, and yet are not dead. Their religion does not consist in "righteousness and peace and joy in the Holy Spirit" (Rom. 14:17 ESV) but rather in grit and resolution and misery.

These people do not really make greater sacrifices than sanctified people; they merely make more ado over them. Not being dead, it hurts them to submit to God, and yet they feel compelled to do so. Nor are their sorrows greater than those of sanctified people; they are merely of a different kind and spring from a different root. They have misery and sorrow because of the sacrifices they have to make, while the sanctified soul counts these things all joy for Jesus' sake (while feeling continual sorrow for woes of the world which, but for the comfort and sympathy Jesus gives, would break his or her heart).

Still, these people are good and do good, God bless them! But what they need is a faith that sanctifies (see Acts 26:18), a faith that through the operation of the Spirit will kill them, put them out of their misery forever, and bring joy and peace into their tired hearts, so that in newness of life they can drink from the river of God's pleasures, never thirst anymore, and make all manner of sacrifices for Jesus' sake with utter gladness.

It is sanctification, then, that we need, that God wants us to have, and that the Holy Spirit is urging upon every one of us. It is a way of childlike faith that receives all God has to give, and of perfect love that joyfully gives all back to God. It is a way that keeps the soul from sloth and ease on the one hand, and from hard, cold bondage on the other. It is a way of inward peace and pleasantness and abounding spiritual life, in which the soul, always wary of its enemies, is not unduly elated by success nor cast down by disappointment. It is a way that does not measure itself by others, nor compare itself with others, but, looking to Jesus, attends strictly to its own business, walking by faith, and trusting Him in due time and order to fulfill all the exceeding great and precious promises of His love.

Shouting  27

Nothing is more completely hidden from wise and prudent folk than the blessed fact that there is a secret spring of power and victory in shouting and praising God. The Devil often throws a spell over people that can be broken in no other way. Many honest, seeking souls, who might step forth into perfect and perpetual liberty if they would only dare to look the Devil in the eye and shout, "Glory to God!" go mourning all their days under this spell. Frequently whole congregations will be under it. There will be a vacant or a listless or a restless look in their eyes. There is no attention, no expectation. A stifling stillness and "the serenity of death" settles upon them. But let a Spirit-baptized person with a weight of glory in the soul bless the Lord, and the spell will be broken. Everyone there will come to their senses, wake up, remember where they are, and begin to expect something to happen.

Shouting and praising God is to salvation what flame is to fire. You may have a very hot and useful fire without a blaze, but not until it bursts forth into flame does it become irresistible and sweep everything before it. So people may be very good and have an experience of salvation, but it is not until they become so full of the Holy Spirit that they are likely to burst forth in praises to their glorious God at any hour of the day or night, both in private and public, that their salvation becomes irresistibly contagious.

The shouting of some people is as terrible as the noise of an empty wagon rolling over cobblestones. It is like the firing of blank cartridges. It is all noise. Their religion consists in making a racket. But there are others who wait on God in secret places, who seek His face with their whole hearts, who groan in prayer with unutterable longing to know God in all His fullness and to see His kingdom come with power, who plead the promises, who search the Word of God and meditate on it day and night until they are full of the great thoughts and truths of God and faith is made perfect. Then the Holy Spirit comes pressing down on them with an eternal weight of glory that compels praise, and when they shout it takes effect. Every cartridge is loaded, and at times their shouting will be like the boom of a big gun and will have the speed and power of a cannonball.

An old friend of mine in Vermont once remarked that when he went into a store or railway station, he found the place full of devils, and the atmosphere choked his soul till he shouted. Then every devil sped away, the atmosphere was purified, and he had possession of the place and could say and do what he pleased.

Catherine Booth-Clibborn, who pioneered The Salvation Army in France, once wrote, "Nothing fills all hell with dismay like a reckless, daredevil shouting faith." Nothing can stand before someone with a genuine shout in his or her soul. Earth and hell flee before such a person, and all heaven throngs around to help fight that person's battles.

When Joshua's armies shouted, the walls of Jericho fell down flat before them. When Jehoshaphat's people "began to sing and to praise, the LORD set ambushes against the people of Ammon, Moab, and Mount Seir" (2 Chron. 20:22 NKJV), and God's enemies were routed.

When Paul and Silas, with bruised and bleeding backs, in the inner dungeon of that horrible Philippian jail at midnight, "prayed, and sang praises unto God" (Acts 16:25 KJV), the Lord sent an earthquake, shook the foundations of the prison, loosed the prisoners, and redeemed the jailer and all his family. And there is no conceivable difficulty that will not vanish before the person who prays and praises God.

When the Cornish evangelist Billy Bray wanted bread, he prayed and shouted to get the Devil to understand that he felt under no obligation to him but had perfect confidence in his heavenly Father. When Dr. Charles Cullis had not a penny in his treasury and heavy obligations for his home for consumptives rested upon him, and he knew not how he could buy food for the patients, he would go into his office and read the Bible and pray and walk the floor, praising God and telling Him he would trust. And money would roll in from the ends of the earth. Victory always comes where someone, having poured out his or her heart in prayer, dares to trust God and express his or her faith in praise.

Shouting is the final and highest expression of faith made perfect in its various stages. When a soul comes to God in hearty repentance and surrender, and, throwing him- or herself fully on the mercy of God, looks to Jesus only for salvation, and by faith fully and fearlessly grasps the blessing of justification, the first expression of that faith will be one of confidence and praise. No doubt there are many who claim justification who never praise God. But either they are deceived or their faith is weak and mixed with doubt and fear. When it is perfect, praise will be spontaneous.

And when regenerate souls come to see the holiness of God, the exceeding breadth of His commandment, and His absolute claim upon every power of their being, and realize the remaining selfishness and earthiness of their hearts—and when they, after many failures to purify themselves and inward questionings of soul and debatings of conscience and haltings of faith, come to God to be made holy through the precious blood and the baptism of the Holy Spirit and of fire—the final expression of the faith that resolutely and perfectly grasps the blessing will not be prayer, but praise and hallelujahs.

And when such saved and sanctified men and women, seeing the woes of a lost world and feeling the holy passion of Jesus working mightily in them, go forth to war "against evil rulers and authorities of the unseen world, against mighty powers in this dark world, and against evil spirits in the heavenly places" (Eph. 6:12 NLT), in order to rescue the slaves of sin and hell, after weeping and agonizing in prayer to God for an outpouring of the Spirit, preaching to and teaching others, pleading with them to yield utterly to God, and after many fastings and trials and conflicts in which faith and patience for others are made perfect and victorious, prayer will be transformed into praise, weeping into shouting, and apparent defeat into overwhelming victory!

Where there is victory, there is shouting. And where there is no shouting, faith and patience are either in retreat or are engaged in conflict, the conclusion of which for the time being seems uncertain.

Oh, for a faith that will not shrink
Though pressed by every foe,
That will not tremble on the brink
Of any earthly woe.
Faith, mighty faith, the promise sees,
And looks to that alone,
Laughs at impossibilities,
And cries, "It shall be done!"[1]

And what is true in individual experience is revealed to be true of the church in its final triumph. For after the long ages of stress and conflict and patient waiting and fiery trial, after the ceaseless intercessions of Jesus and the unutterable groaning of the Spirit in the hearts of believers, the church shall finally come to perfect faith and patience and unity of love, according to the prayer of Jesus in John 17. Then "the Lord himself will come down from heaven with a commanding shout, with the voice of the archangel, and with the trumpet call of God" (1 Thess. 4:16 NLT), and seeming defeat shall be turned into eternal victory.

But let no one hastily conclude that we should not shout and praise God unless we feel a mighty wave of triumph rushing through our soul. Paul said, "We don't know what God wants us to pray for. But the Holy Spirit prays for us with groanings that cannot be expressed in words" (Rom. 8:26 NLT). But if we refused to pray till we felt this tremendous pleading of the Spirit in our hearts (which John Fletcher said is "like a God wrestling with a God"²), we would never pray at all. We must stir up the gift of prayer that is within us, we must exercise ourselves in prayer until our souls sweat, and then we shall realize the mighty energy of the Holy Spirit interceding within us. We must never forget that "the spirits of prophets are subject to the prophets" (1 Cor. 14:32 NRSV). Just so we must stir up and exercise the gift of praise within us.

We must put our will into it. When Habakkuk the prophet had lost everything and was surrounded with utter desolation, he shouted, "Yet I will rejoice in the LORD, I will joy in the God of my salvation!" (Hab. 3:18 KJV). We are workers together with God, and if we will praise Him, He will see to it that we have something for which to praise Him. We often hear of Daniel praying three times a day, but we pass over the fact that at the same time he "gave thanks before his God" (Dan. 6:10 KJV), which is a kind of praise. David said, "I will praise you seven times a day" (Ps. 119:164 NLT). Over and over, again and again, we are exhorted and commanded to praise God and shout aloud and rejoice evermore. But if through fear or shame we will not rejoice, we need not be surprised that we have no joy and no sweeping victories.

But if we will get alone with God in our own hearts (note: alone with God in our own hearts; there is the place to get alone with God, and a shout is nothing more or less than an expression of joy at finding God in our hearts) and will praise Him for His wonderful works, praise Him because He is worthy of praise, praise Him whether we feel like it or not, praise Him in the darkness as well as the light, praise Him in seasons of fierce conflict as well as in moments of victory, we will soon be able to shout aloud for joy. And our joy no one will be able to take from us, but God will cause us to drink of the river of His pleasures, and He himself will be our "exceeding joy" (Ps. 43:4 KJV).

Many a soul in fierce temptation and hellish darkness has poured out his or her heart in prayer and then sunk back in despair, who, if he or she had only closed the prayer with thanks and dared in the name of God to shout, would have filled hell with confusion and won a victory that would have struck all the harps of heaven and made the angels shout with glee. Many a prayer meeting has failed at the shouting point. Songs were sung, testimonies given, the Bible read and explained, wayward souls warned and entreated, and prayers poured forth to God, but no one wrestled through to the point where he or she could and would intelligently praise God for victory, and, so far as could be seen, the battle was lost for want of a shout.

From the moment we are born of God, straight through our pilgrim journey, up to the moment of open vision where we are forever glorified and see Jesus as He is, we have a right to rejoice, and we ought to do it. It is our highest privilege and our most solemn duty. And if we do it not, I think it must fill the angels with confusion and the fiends of the bottomless pit with a kind of hideous joy. We ought to do it, for this is almost the only thing we do on earth that we shall not cease to do in heaven. Weeping, fasting, watching, praying, self-denying, cross-bearing, and being in conflict with hell will cease; but praise to God and hallelujahs "to him who loves us and has freed us from our sins by his blood, and has made us to be a kingdom and priests to serve his God and Father" (Rev. 1:5–6 NIV) shall ring through heaven eternally.

NOTES

1. Charles Wesley, "Father of Jesus Christ, My Lord," 1742, public domain.

2. John Fletcher, *The Works of the Rev. John Fletcher, Late Vicar of Madeley*, vol. 1 (London: John Mason, 1859), 195.

God did not cease speaking to humankind when the canon of Scripture was complete. Though the manner of communication may have changed somewhat, the communication itself is something to which every Spirit-born soul can joyfully testify. Everyone who is sorry for sin, sighing and crying for deliverance, and hungering and thirsting for righteousness, will soon find out, as did the Israelites, that "God can speak to us humans" (Deut. 5:24 NLT).

God has most commonly and most powerfully spoken to me through the words of Scripture. Some of them stand out to my mental and spiritual vision like mighty mountain peaks, rising from a vast, extended plain. The Spirit that moved "holy men of God" (2 Pet. 1:21 KJV) to write the words of the Bible has moved me to understand them by leading me along the lines of spiritual experience first trodden by these men, and has taken the things of Christ and revealed them to me, until I have been filled with a divine certainty as altogether satisfactory and absolute as the certainty produced in my intellect by a mathematical demonstration.

The first words I remember coming to me with this irresistible divine force came when I was seeking the blessing of a clean heart. Although I was hungering and thirsting for the blessing, yet at times a feeling of utter indifference—a kind of spiritual stupor—would come over me and threaten to devour all my holy longings, as the lean cows in Pharaoh's dream devoured the fat ones (see Gen. 41). I was in great distress and did not know what to do. I saw that to stop seeking meant infinite, eternal loss. Yet to continue seeking seemed quite out of the question with such a paralysis of desire and feeling. But one day I read, "There is no one who calls on Your name, who stirs himself up to take hold of You" (Isa. 64:7 NKJV).

God spoke to me in these words as unmistakably as He spoke to Moses from the burning bush or the children of Israel from the cloudy mount. It was an altogether new experience to me. The word came as a rebuke to my unbelief and lazy indifference, and yet it put hope into me, and I said to myself, "By the grace of God, if nobody else does I will stir myself up to seek Him, feeling or no feelings."

That was ten years ago, but from then till now, regardless of my feeling, I have sought God. I have not waited to be stirred up, but when necessary I have fasted and prayed and stirred myself up. I have often prayed, as did the royal psalmist, "Make me live again, LORD, according to your faithful love" (Ps. 119:159 CEB). But whether I have felt any immediate results or not, I have laid hold of Him, sought Him, and found Him. "Seek, and you will find" (Matt. 7:7 ESV).

Because hindrances must be removed before we can ever find God in the fullness of His love and favor, weights and easily-besetting sins must be laid aside (see Heb. 12:1), and self must be smitten in the citadel of its ambitions and hopes.

Young men and women today are ambitious. They want to be prime minister if they go into politics. They must be multimillionaires if they go into business. They aim to become a bishop if they pursue ministry in the church.

The ruling passion of my soul (and that which for years I longed after more than for holiness or heaven) was to do something and be somebody who should win the esteem and compel the applause of thoughtful, educated people. And just as the angel smote Jacob's thigh and put it out of joint, causing him forever after to limp on it, the strongest part of his body, so God, in order to sanctify me wholly and bring "into captivity every thought to the obedience of Christ" (2 Cor. 10:5 KJV), smote and humbled me in this ruling propensity and strongest passion of my nature.

For several years before God sanctified me wholly, I knew there was such an experience, and I prayed by fits and starts for it, and all the time I hungered and thirsted for—I hardly knew what! Holiness in itself seemed desirable, but I saw as clearly then as I have since I obtained the blessing that with it came the cross and an irrepressible conflict with the carnal mind in each human being I met, whether that person was a professed Christian or an avowed sinner, whether cultured and thoughtful or a raw and ignorant pagan. And this I knew instinctively would as surely bar my way to the esteem and applause of the people whose goodwill and admiration I valued, as it did that of Jesus and Paul. And yet, so subtle is the deceitfulness of the unsanctified heart, that I would not then have acknowledged it to myself, although I am now persuaded that unwillingness to take up this cross was for years the lurking foe that barred the gates against the willing, waiting Sanctifier.

However, at last I heard a distinguished evangelist and soul-winner preach a sermon on the baptism of the Holy Spirit, and I said to myself, "That is what I need and want; I must have it!" And I began to seek and pray for this, all the time with a secret thought in my heart that I, too, should become a great soul-winner and live in the eye of the world. I sought with considerable earnestness, but God was very merciful and hid Himself from me, thus arousing the wholesome fear of the Lord in my heart and at the same time intensifying my spiritual hunger. I wept and prayed and begged the Lord to baptize me with the Spirit, and wondered why He did not, until one day I read those words of Paul: "That no flesh should glory in his presence" (1 Cor. 1:29 KJV).

Here I saw the enemy of the Lord: self. There stood the idol of my soul—the passionate, consuming desire for glory—no longer hidden and nourished in the secret chambers of my heart, but discovered before the Lord as the Amalekite king Agag was before Samuel (see 1 Sam. 15). And those words, "No flesh should glory in his presence," constituted "the sword of the Spirit" (Eph. 6:17 KJV) which pierced self through and through, and showed me I never could be holy and receive the baptism of the Spirit while I secretly cherished a desire for the honor that comes from others and sought not "the honor that comes from the one who alone is God" (John 5:44 NLT). That word came to me with power, and from then till now I have not sought the glory of this world. But while I no longer sought the glory of the world, yet this same powerful principle in me still had to be further uncovered and smitten, in order to make me willing to lose what little glory I already had (or imagined I had) and be content to be accounted a fool for Christ.

The ruling propensity of the carnal nature seeks gratification. If it can secure this lawfully, it will. But gratification it will have, even if it has to gain it unlawfully. Every way is unlawful for me which would be unlawful for Jesus. Christians who are not entirely sanctified do not deliberately plan to do what they know to be wrong, but are rather betrayed by the deceitful heart within. If they are overcome (which, thank God, they need not be), they are overcome secretly or suddenly, in a way that makes them abhor themselves, but which, it seems, is the only way by which God can convince them of their depravity and need of a clean heart.

I was so betrayed on two occasions—once to cheat on an examination, and once to use the outline of another man's sermon. The first deed I bitterly repented of and confessed but the second was not so clearly wrong, since I had used materials of my own to fill in an outline, and especially since the outline was probably much better than any I could prepare (it was one of Charles Finney's outlines). In fact, if I had used the outline in the right spirit, I do not know that it would have been wrong at all. But God's Word, which is a "discerner of the thoughts and intents of the heart" (Heb. 4:12 KJV), searched me out and revealed to my astonished, humbled soul not merely the bearing and character of my act, but also of my spirit. He smote and humbled me again with these words: "If anyone speaks, they should do so as one who speaks the very words of God. If anyone serves, they should do so with the strength God provides" (1 Pet. 4:11 NIV).

When I read those words, I felt as low and guilty as though I had stolen ten thousand dollars. I began to see then the true character and mission of preachers and prophets, who are men and women sent from God and who must, if they would please God and seek the glory He alone gives, wait upon God in prayer and diligent searching of His Word till they get the message direct from the throne. Then only can they speak "as one who speaks the very words of God" and serve "with the strength God provides." I was not led to despise human teachers and human learning where God is in them, but I was led to exalt direct inspiration and to see the absolute necessity of it for everyone who sets him- or herself to turn people's hearts to righteousness and tell them how to find God and get to heaven. I saw that instead of always sitting at the feet of human teachers, poring over commentaries, studying someone else's sermons, diving into others' volumes of anecdotes, and then tickling the ears of people with pretty speeches and winning their fleeting, empty applause by elaborately finished sermons, logically and rhetorically "faultily faultless, icily regular, splendidly null,"[1] God meant me to speak His words, to sit at the feet of Jesus and learn of Him, to get alone in some secret place on my knees and study the Word of God under the direct illumination of the Holy Spirit, to study the holiness and righteous judgments of God until I got some red hot thunderbolts that would burn the itching ears of the people, arouse their slumbering consciences, prick their hard hearts, and make them cry, "What shall we do?" (Acts 2:37 KJV).

I saw that I must study and meditate on the tender, boundless compassion and love of God in Christ, the perfect atonement for sin in its
root and trunk and branch, and the simple way to appropriate it in
penitence and self-surrender by faith, until I was fully possessed of it
myself and knew how to lead every broken heart directly to Jesus for
perfect healing, to comfort mourners, to loose prisoners, to set captives free, and to proclaim the acceptable year of the Lord and the day
of vengeance of our God.

This view greatly humbled me, and I did not know what to do. At
last it was suggested to my mind that, as I had confessed the false
examination, so now I ought to stand before the people and confess
the stolen sermon outline. This fairly peeled my conscience, and it
quivered with an indescribable agony. For about three weeks I struggled with this problem. I argued the matter with myself. I pleaded
with God to show me if it was His will, and over and over again I
promised Him I would do it, only to draw back in my heart. At last I
told an intimate friend. He assured me it was not of God and said he
was going to preach in a revival meeting that night and use materials
he had gathered from another man's sermon. I coveted his freedom,
but this brought no relief to me. I could not get away from my sin.
Like David's, it was "ever before me" (Ps. 51:3 KJV).

One morning, while in this frame of mind, I picked up a little book
on experimental religion, hoping to get light. On opening it, the very
first subject my eyes fell on was confession. I was cornered. My soul
was brought to a full halt. I could seek no further light. I wanted to die,
and that moment my heart broke within me: "The sacrifices of God
are a broken spirit: a broken and a contrite heart" (Ps. 51:17 KJV).

From the depths of my broken heart, my conquered spirit said to God, "I will." I had said it before with my lips, but now I said it with my heart. Then God spoke directly to my soul, not by printed words through my eyes but by His Spirit in my heart: "If we confess our sins, he is faithful and just to forgive us our sins, and to cleanse us from all unrighteousness" (1 John 1:9 KJV). The first part about forgiveness I knew, but the last clause about cleansing was a revelation to me. I did not remember ever having seen or heard it before. The word came with power, and I bowed my head in my hands and said, "Father, I believe that." Then a great rest came into my soul, and I knew I was clean. In that instant, "the blood of Christ, who through the eternal Spirit offered himself without spot to God, [purged my] conscience from dead works to serve the living God" (Heb. 9:14 KJV).

God did not require Abraham to slay Isaac. All He wanted was a willing heart. So He did not require me to confess to the people. When my heart was willing, He swept the whole subject out of my mind and freed me utterly from slavish fear. My idol—self—was gone. God knew I withheld nothing from Him, so He filled my soul with peace and showed me that "Christ is the end of the law for righteousness to everyone who believes" (Rom. 10:4 NASB) and that the whole will of God was summed up in five words: "Faith expressing itself in love" (Gal. 5:6 NLT).

Shortly after this, I ran into my friend's room with a borrowed book. The moment his eyes fell upon me, he said, "What is the matter? Something has happened to you." My face was witnessing to a pure heart before my lips did. But my lips soon followed and have continued to this day.

The psalmist said, "I have told the glad news of deliverance in the great congregation; behold, I have not restrained my lips, as you know, O LORD. I have not hidden your deliverance within my heart; I have spoken of your faithfulness and your salvation; I have not concealed your steadfast love and your faithfulness from the great congregation" (Ps. 40:9–10 ESV).

Satan hates holy testimony, and he nearly entrapped me after I received the blessing of holiness. I felt I ought to preach it, but I shrank from the podium and the conflict I saw it would surely bring, and I hesitated to declare publicly that I was sanctified, for fear of doing more harm than good. I saw only reproach. The glory that was to follow was hidden from my eyes. Beautiful, flowery sermons that appealed to the imagination and aroused the emotions, with just enough thought to properly balance them, were my ideal. I shrank from coming down to plain, heart-searching talks that laid hold of the consciences of men and women and made saints of them, or turned them into foes as implacable as the Pharisees were to Jesus or the Jews to Paul. But before I got the blessing, God held me to it, and I had promised God I would preach it if He would give me the experience. It was Friday that He cleansed me, and I determined to preach about it on the following Sunday. But I felt weak and faint.

On Saturday morning, however, I met a noisy, shouting coachman on the street, who had the blessing, and I told him what God had done for me. He shouted and praised God, and said, "Now, Brother Brengle, you preach it. The church is dying for this."

We walked across Boston Common and Garden and talked about the matter, and my heart burned within me as did the hearts of the two disciples with whom Jesus talked on the road to Emmaus. In my inmost soul I recounted the cost, threw in my lot with Jesus crucified, and determined I would teach holiness even if it banished me forever from the pulpit and made me a byword to all my acquaintances. Then I felt strong. The way to get strength is to throw yourself away for Jesus.

The next day I went to my church and preached as best I could out of a two-days-old experience, from "Let us go on unto perfection" (Heb. 6:1 KJV). I closed with my experience, and the people broke down and wept, and some came to me afterward and said they wanted that same experience, and some of them got it! I did not know what I was doing that morning, but I knew afterward. I was burning up my ships and casting down my bridges behind me. I was now in the Enemy's land, fully committed to a warfare of utter extermination to all sin. I was on record now before heaven, earth, and hell. Angels, mortals, and devils had heard my testimony, and I must go forward or openly and ignominiously retreat in the face of a jeering foe. I see now that there is a divine philosophy in requiring us not only to believe with our hearts unto righteousness, but to confess with the mouth unto salvation (see Rom. 10:10). God led me along these lines. No one taught me.

After I had put myself on record, I walked softly with God, desiring nothing but His will and looking to Him to keep me every instant. I did not know there was anything more for me, but I meant, by God's grace, to hold what I had by doing His will as He had made it known to me and by trusting Him with all my heart.

But God meant greater things for me. On the following Tuesday morning, just after rising, with a heart full of eager desire for God, I

read these words of Jesus at the grave of Lazarus: "I am the resurrection and the life. Anyone who believes in me will live, even after
dying. Everyone who lives in me and believes in me will never ever
die. Do you believe this?" (John 11:25–26 NLT). The Holy Spirit, the
other "Comforter," was in those words, and in an instant my soul
melted before the Lord like wax before fire, and I knew Jesus. He was
revealed in me as He had promised, and I loved Him with an unutterable love. I wept and adored and loved and loved and loved. I walked
out over Boston Common before breakfast, and still wept and adored
and loved. Talk about the occupation of heaven! I do not know what
it will be—though, of course, it will be suited to, and commensurate
with, our redeemed capacities and powers—but I knew this then, that
if I could lie prostrate at the feet of Jesus for all eternity and love and
adore Him, I would be satisfied. My soul was satisfied, satisfied,
satisfied!

That experience fixed my theology. From then till now, mortals and
devils might as well try to get me to question the presence of the sun
in the heavens as to question the existence of God, the divinity of Jesus
Christ, and the sanctifying power of an ever present, almighty Holy
Spirit. I am as sure the Bible is the Word of God as I am of my own
existence, while heaven and hell are as much realities to me as day and
night, winter and summer, or good and evil. I feel the powers of the
world to come and the pull of heaven in my own soul.

It is some years now since the Comforter came, and He abides in
me still. He has not stopped speaking to me yet. He has set my soul
on fire, but, like the burning bush Moses saw in the Mount, it is not
consumed.

To all who want such an experience I would say, "Ask, and it shall be given you" (Matt. 7:7 KJV). If it does not come for the asking, "keep on seeking, and you will find" (Matt. 7:7 NLT). If it is still delayed, "keep on knocking, and the door will be opened to you" (Matt. 7:7 NLT). In other words, seek until you have sought with your whole heart, and there and then you will find Him. "Stop doubting and believe" (John 20:27 NIV). "If you will not believe, surely you shall not be established" (Isa. 7:9 NKJV).

I do not consider myself beyond the possibility of falling. I know I stand by faith and must watch and pray lest I enter into temptation, and take heed lest I fall. Yet, in view of all God's marvelous loving kindnesses and tender mercies to me, I constantly sing, with the apostle Jude: "Now unto him that is able to keep you from falling, and to present you faultless before the presence of his glory with exceeding joy, to the only wise God our Saviour, be glory and majesty, dominion and power, both now and ever. Amen" (Jude 24–25 KJV).

NOTE

1. Alfred Lord Tennyson, "Maud," *English Poetry III: From Tennyson to Whitman*, The Harvard Classics, vol. 42 (New York: P. F. Collier & Son, 1909–1914), n.p.

Samuel L. Brengle's Holy Life Series

This series comprises the complete works of Samuel L. Brengle, combining all nine of his original books into six volumes, penned by one of the great minds on holiness. Each volume has been lovingly edited for modern readership by popular author (and long-time Brengle devotee) Bob Hostetler. Brengle's authentic voice remains strong, now able to more relevantly engage today's disciples of holiness. These books are must-haves for all who would seriously pursue and understand the depths of holiness in the tradition of John Wesley.

Helps to Holiness
ISBN: 978-1-63257-064-2
eBook: 978-1-63257-065-9

The Heart of Holiness
ISBN: 978-1-63257-066-6
eBook: 978-1-63257-067-3

The Servant's Heart
ISBN: 978-1-63257-068-0
eBook: 978-1-63257-069-7

Ancient Prophets and Modern Problems
ISBN: 978-1-63257-070-3
eBook: 978-1-63257-071-0

Come Holy Guest
ISBN: 978-1-63257-072-7
eBook: 978-1-63257-073-4

Resurrection Life and Power
ISBN: 978-1-63257-074-1
eBook: 978-1-63257-075-8

**Samuel L. Brengle's
Holy Life Series Box Set**
ISBN: 978-1-63257-076-5